Maria-Theresia-Gymnasium
Regerplatz 1    81541 München

| Schul-jahr | Name | Kl. | Z |
|---|---|---|---|
| 20/21 |  |  | 1 |
|  |  |  |  |
|  |  |  |  |
|  |  |  |  |
|  |  |  |  |
|  |  |  |  |
|  |  |  |  |
|  |  |  |  |
|  |  |  |  |
|  |  |  |  |

| Gymnasium Bayern |

# access 8

Cornelsen

# Access Bayern 8

*Im Auftrag des Verlages herausgegeben von*
Prof. Dr. Engelbert Thaler, Augsburg
Prof. Jörg Rademacher, Mannheim

*Erarbeitet von*
Laurence Harger, Nürnberg
Cecile Niemitz-Rossant, Berlin

*unter Mitarbeit von*
Dr. Annette Leithner-Brauns, Dresden
Birgit Ohmsieder, Berlin
Mervyn Whittaker, Bad Dürkheim

*in Zusammenarbeit mit der Englischredaktion*
Filiz Bahşi (Projektkoordination, verantwortliche Redakteurin), Dr. Philip Devlin, Ursula Fleischhauer, Bonnie Glänzer, Stefan Höhne (Redaktionsleitung), Ingrid Raspe (Vocabulary, Dictionaries), Sophia Schneider

*Beratende Mitwirkung*
Thomas Bohlen, Traunstein
Gerhard Finster, Dillingen
Ingola Seger, Augsburg
Claudia Vetter, München
Jörg Wunderlich, München

*Illustrationen*
Christian Barz, Berlin; Tobias Dahmen, Utrecht/NL; Gregor Mecklenburg, Pinneberg; Burkhard Schulz, Düsseldorf

*Fotos*
Nigel Wilson Photography, Bristol

*Umschlaggestaltung*
hawemannundmosch, Berlin

*Layout und technische Umsetzung*
Eric Gira, Ungermeyer, Berlin

www.cornelsen.de

In diesem Werk wird in Form von Symbolen auf Audio-Material verwiesen; dieses enthält – bis auf die Hörverstehensübungen – ausschließlich optionale Unterrichtsmaterialien. Die Audio-Materialien unterliegen nicht dem staatlichen Zulassungsverfahren.

Die Mediencodes enthalten zusätzliche Unterrichtsmaterialien, die der Verlag in eigener Verantwortung zur Verfügung stellt.

Dieses Werk berücksichtigt die Regeln der reformierten Rechtschreibung und Zeichensetzung.

1. Auflage, 1. Druck 2020

Alle Drucke dieser Auflage sind inhaltlich unverändert und können im Unterricht nebeneinander verwendet werden.

© 2020 Cornelsen Verlag GmbH, Berlin

Das Werk und seine Teile sind urheberrechtlich geschützt. Jede Nutzung in anderen als den gesetzlich zugelassenen Fällen bedarf der vorherigen schriftlichen Einwilligung des Verlages.

Hinweis zu §§ 60 a, 60 b UrhG: Weder das Werk noch seine Teile dürfen ohne eine solche Einwilligung an Schulen oder in Unterrichts- und Lehrmedien (§ 60 b Abs. 3 UrhG) vervielfältigt, insbesondere kopiert oder eingescannt, verbreitet oder in ein Netzwerk eingestellt oder sonst öffentlich zugänglich gemacht oder wiedergegeben werden. Dies gilt auch für Intranets von Schulen.

Soweit in diesem Lehrwerk Personen fotografisch abgebildet sind und ihnen von der Redaktion fiktive Namen, Berufe, Dialoge und Ähnliches zugeordnet oder diese Personen in bestimmte Kontexte gesetzt werden, dienen diese Zuordnungen und Darstellungen ausschließlich der Veranschaulichung und dem besseren Verständnis des Inhalts.

Druck: Mohn Media Mohndruck, Gütersloh

ISBN 978-3-06-033492-6

ISBN 978-3-06-034318-8 (E-Book)

PEFC zertifiziert
Dieses Produkt stammt aus nachhaltig bewirtschafteten Wäldern und kontrollierten Quellen.
www.pefc.de

## Access Bayern 8 enthält folgende Teile:

| | |
|---|---|
| **Units** | die drei Kapitel des Buches |
| **Access to cultures** | landeskundliche Informationen |
| **Text File** | eine Sammlung englischer und amerikanischer Geschichten und Sachtexte |
| **Skills File** | eine Beschreibung wichtiger Lern- und Arbeitstechniken |
| **Grammar File** | eine Zusammenfassung der Grammatik jeder Unit |
| **Vocabulary** | das Wörterverzeichnis zum Lernen der neuen Wörter jeder Unit |
| **Dictionary** | alphabetisches Wörterverzeichnis zum Nachschlagen (Englisch-Deutsch / Deutsch-Englisch) |

### In den Units findest du diese Überschriften:

| | |
|---|---|
| **Background file** | Informationen über Land und Leute |
| **Everyday English** | Englisch in Alltagssituationen |
| **Looking at language** | Beispiele sammeln und sprachliche Regeln entdecken |
| **Language help** | Hilfe in Form von sprachlichen Regeln |
| **Practice** | Aufgaben und Übungen |
| **Mediation course** | zwischen Englisch und Deutsch besser vermitteln |
| **The world behind the picture** | vom Bild in den Film – Videoclips mit Aufgaben |
| **Thinking about language** | Aufgaben zur Sprachreflexion |
| **The digital compass** | Methoden/Hilfe für den Umgang mit digitalen Medien |
| **Text** | eine spannende oder lustige Geschichte |
| **Your task** | In der Lernaufgabe kannst du in jeder Unit zeigen, was du gelernt hast und dich selbst einschätzen. |
| **Checkpoint** | Auf diesen Seiten kannst du den Wortschatz und die Grammatik einer Unit wiederholen und dich auf Schulaufgaben vorbereiten. |

### Du findest auch diese Symbole:

| | |
|---|---|
| 🔊 | Texte, die du dir anhören kannst: *www.cornelsen.de/webcodes* (Webcode: *waxugu*) |
| www | zusätzliche Materialien, die du unter *www.cornelsen.de/webcodes* (Webcode: *minoso*; Kaleidoscope-Film: *dahaga*) finden kannst |
| ■■■■■ | Übungssequenz: neue Grammatik intensiv üben und dann anwenden |
| Early finisher | zusätzliche Aktivitäten und Übungen für Schüler/innen, die früher fertig sind |
| More help | zusätzliche Hilfen für eine Aufgabe |
| You choose | eine Aufgabe auswählen |
| EXTRA | zusätzliche Aktivitäten und Übungen für alle |
| My Book | schöne und wichtige Arbeiten sammeln |
| Study skills | Einführung in Lern- und Arbeitstechniken |
| 🎧 💬 📖 ✏️ | Hören   Sprechen   Lesen   Schreiben |
| | Mediation (zwischen zwei Sprachen vermitteln), Thinking about language (Sprachreflexion) |
| 👥 👥✓ 👥👥 🧩 | Partnerarbeit   Partnercheck   Gruppenarbeit   Kooperative Lernform |

# Inhaltsverzeichnis

|  | Lerninhalte | Texte |
|---|---|---|
| **Unit 1**<br>London changing | • History of London<br>• London and Canada<br>• The Commonwealth<br>• London sights<br>• The Great Fire of 1666 | A Where to now?<br>B Alyssa's photos<br>C At the top of the monument<br><br>**Text**<br>Escape from Uncle Jack (p. 26) |

**Access to cultures: Guy Fawkes: Man and mask**

 **EXTRA · Kaleidoscope · Canada**

|  | Lerninhalte | Texte |
|---|---|---|
| **Unit 2**<br>Canada | • Ice hockey<br>• Popular sports in Canada<br>• The Inuit<br>• Geography, people and wildlife of Canada<br>• Indigenous peoples of Canada<br>• Languages of Canada | A Lauren's blog: The eager beaver<br>B The eager beaver: day 2 – too many rules<br>B The final game<br><br>**Background file**<br>Geography, people and wildlife (p. 50)<br><br>Indigenous peoples (p. 51)<br><br>**Text**<br>Flash fiction: From an animal's perspective (p. 58) |

**Access to cultures: Canada: A quiz**

# Inhaltsverzeichnis

| Kompetenzen | Sprache | |
|---|---|---|
| **Viewing** <br> Bike and animal (p. 15) <br><br> **Study skills** <br> Reading for detail (p. 20) <br><br> **Mediation course** <br> Key information (p. 23) <br><br> **Thinking about language** <br> Idioms (p. 25) <br><br> **Checkpoint** <br> (p. 31) | **Vocabulary** <br> staying in touch <br><br> **Grammar** <br> simple present/simple past (Revision); <br> the passive: simple present; <br> the passive: simple past; <br> the passive with *by*; <br> verbs with two objects; <br> personal passive <br><br> **Pronunciation** <br> connected speech (p. 25) | 8 <br><br> *Skill in focus: Listening* <br><br> 34 <br><br> 36 |
| **Study skills** <br> Internet research (p. 44) <br> Writing a comment (p. 45) <br><br> **Mediation course** <br> Paraphrasing (p. 55) <br><br> **Thinking about language** <br> Multilingualism (p. 56) <br><br> **Viewing** <br> A simple life (p. 57) <br><br> **Checkpoint** <br> (p. 61) | **Vocabulary** <br> opposites <br><br> **Grammar** <br> *will*-future (Revision); conditional sentences (Revision); modal verbs (Revision); <br> present perfect with *since/for* (Revision); <br> subject-verb agreement; <br> the present perfect passive; <br> the passive with *may/can/should/must*; <br> the passive with *will*; <br> the definite article <br><br> **Pronunciation** <br> word flow (p. 54); <br> phonetic script and pronunciation (p. 54) | 38 <br><br> *Skill in focus: Writing* <br><br> 64 |

# Inhaltsverzeichnis

| | Lerninhalte | Texte |
|---|---|---|
| **Unit 3**<br>Faces of the Midwest | • High school<br>• Native American societies and cultures<br>• The Seven Years War<br>• Life on a reservation<br>• The western expansion of the United States<br>• Mount Rushmore<br>• The Boston Tea Party<br>• The Iroquois Confederacy<br>• Native American legends | A  A perfect morning<br>B  A day at the ranch<br>C  Bad news for Drew<br>D  The Boston Tea Party: Looking at history through a different lens<br><br>**Background file**<br>Native American societies (p. 78)<br>Outcomes of western expansion (p. 79)<br>The Iroquois Confederacy (p. 89)<br><br>**Text**<br>The Legend of the Great Peacemaker (p. 90) |

**Access to cultures:** Foundation of a New Nation

**Access to cultures:** Elections in the US and the UK

| **Text File** | **Text 1**<br>A guided tour to Harry Potter places in London<br><br>Travel guide |
|---|---|

| 106 | More help | 116 | Skills File | 194 | Dictionary English – German |
|---|---|---|---|---|---|
| 111 | Early finisher | 136 | Grammar File | 229 | Dictionary German – English |
| 114 | Partner pages | 154 | Vocabulary | 262 | English sounds |

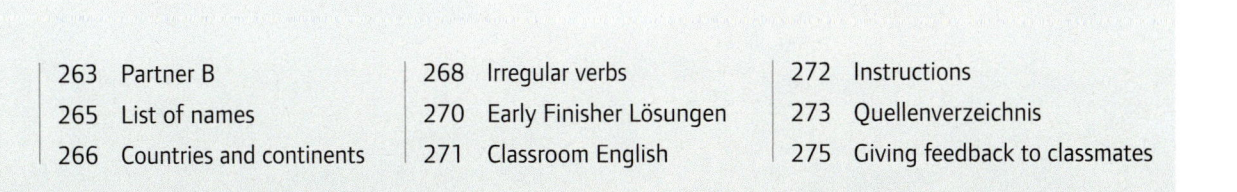

| Kompetenzen | Sprache | |
|---|---|---|
| **Thinking about language** <br> Varieties of English (p. 70) <br><br> **Mediation course** <br> Cultural differences (p. 72) <br><br> **Study skills** <br> Making a slide for a presentation (p. 84) <br><br> **Viewing** <br> Bloodlines (p. 85) <br><br> **Checkpoint** <br> (p. 93) | **Vocabulary** <br> adjectives with *-ful* and *-less* <br><br> **Grammar** <br> simple past or past progressive (Revision); <br> adjectives used as nouns; <br> gerunds; gerunds as objects; <br> gerunds after prepositions; <br> adjectives after verbs of perception; <br> adverb: word order; adverbs of degree; <br> collocations with adverbs of degree; <br> verb + infinitive / verb + gerund or infinitive | 66 |

*Skill in focus: Speaking*

| | 96 |
|---|---|
| | 98 |

| **Text 2** | | 100 |
|---|---|---|
| The Amazing Adventures of Jack London | | |
| Novel | | |

| 263 | Partner B | 268 | Irregular verbs | 272 | Instructions |
|---|---|---|---|---|---|
| 265 | List of names | 270 | Early Finisher Lösungen | 273 | Quellenverzeichnis |
| 266 | Countries and continents | 271 | Classroom English | 275 | Giving feedback to classmates |

# Unit 1
# London changing

**LONDON**

**Modern**
population 8.9 million

**Victorian**
c. 1881
pop 3.9 million

**Restoration**
c. 1666
pop 300,000

**Roman**
c. 120
pop 50,000

# Unit 1

## 1 👥 London map and pictures

a) Take two minutes to tell each other what you already know about London.

b) Look at the map and the map key on p. 8.
   Explain to each other what it tells you about London.

c) Partner A: Describe pictures A and B carefully.
   Partner B: Suggest how your partner can improve his or her description.
   Take turns for pictures C and D.
   ➜ SF 19: Describing pictures (p. 130)

d) Match the pictures to the London eras on the map key.
   Make notes on the reasons for your decision.
   Then discuss your ideas with another pair.

## 2 👥 London eras 🎧

a) Work in groups of four.
   Listen to the audio extracts 1–4 and match each one to a London era. Give reasons for your answers and check them in class.

b) Listen again and, in a table, take notes on:
   • sounds (what they are, what they tell you)
   • the situation (where, time of day, who, …)
   • events (what happens?)
   • background information (what you find out about the era, the city, the weather, people and places, …)
   Each group member should concentrate on one of the table's headings.

c) Agree on what should go in each section of the table and compare your notes with another group.

## 3 Time traveller ✎

Imagine you travel back in time to one of these London eras. Why are you there and what do you experience during your visit? Write a post for social media (about 200 words).

**More help** ➜ (p. 106)   ➜ **Workbook** 1 (p. 2)

> **Your task**
>
> **Your task for this unit:** You will plan a class trip to London with your group.

nine 9

# 1 Part A

## 1 Where to now?

*Alyssa Robertson, from Ottawa, Canada, has arrived in London to spend six months as an exchange student at a London school. Her parents have travelled with her to introduce their daughter to the city. They have been checking out websites to decide where to go and what to do before Alyssa starts school next week.*

**Whispering in the City**
Start your day at Sir Christopher Wren's magnificent St Paul's Cathedral, built after the Great Fire of London in 1666 destroyed the old one. Don't miss the coolest part, the Whispering Gallery, up inside the famous dome. Go with a friend and stand at opposite ends of the gallery. Whisper something and your friend will hear you loud and clear, although you're over 30 metres apart! How's that for acoustics?

**Experiencing Black Britain**
Head south of the river to Brixton, which has been a centre of Afro-Caribbean culture for over 60 years. Walk through the colourful indoor and outdoor markets and visit the Black Cultural Archives on Windrush Square. The Windrush was the ship that brought some of the first Caribbean workers to Britain in the 1940s. The archive tells their stories and shows how people of African and Caribbean origin have changed the UK.

**Listening to history**
Back in Central London from Brixton, your next destination is the Houses of Parliament and Big Ben clock tower, known together as the Palace of Westminster. Take an audio tour which brings a thousand years of history and modern British politics to life. Follow the route the Queen takes when she opens Parliament and find out how the place works. The tour ends with afternoon tea in a room overlooking the Thames.

**Dancing on top of the world**
When the sun goes down, finish your day with a silent disco at the top of Western Europe's tallest building, the Shard. Put on your headphones and dance to the best pop, rock and party tunes on three wireless channels. You'll be in heaven while you enjoy the most magnificent view in the city.
Teenagers can go there with their parents.

## 2 What about you?

a) Find the places Alyssa is interested in on a map of London.

b) Imagine you're in London. Rank the four sights/activities from 1 (most) to 4 (least) interesting. Note down your reasons.

c) Exchange your ranking ideas in a double circle activity.

d) Write a social media post (about 150 words). Explain which two places you are going to visit and why.

➜ Workbook 2 (p. 3)

## 3 At Trafalgar Square

Read Alyssa's chat.

Hey Lauren! Here I am in London! How are things back in Ottawa? 3:27 pm

**Lauren** It's getting cold here. Raining a lot. Hey, your new classmates look pretty old … and a bit like your mom and dad! 😜 3:30 pm

Lol! School doesn't start till next week. We're wandering round the West End of London. Almost at Trafalgar Square. 3:35 pm

**Lauren** Trafalgar Square! Send me pics! 3:37 pm

**Lauren** 😲 I didn't mean a picture of Canada, girl. I'm the one in Canada! 3:41 pm

No, it's Canada House, right on Trafalgar Square. 3:42 pm

**Lauren** ??? Canadian tourist bureau, or what? 3:44 pm

No idea 3:45 pm

**Lauren** Ask your new classmates. They're old. They'll know. LOL 3:47 pm

Dad says it's the Canadian High Commission. Like an embassy, only they don't call it an embassy, because of the Commonwealth. 3:50 pm

**Lauren** Now explain that in English. 😉 3:52 pm

Hi Lauren, how are you? Alyssa gave me her phone so I could explain. Canada is a member of the Commonwealth, an organization of countries that were British colonies once. Countries like Canada, Australia, India, South Africa. Or Jamaica where Alyssa's mom's parents were from. And lots of other countries. These countries have a special relationship with each other so they don't call their diplomatic places embassies like everyone else. They call them High Commissions. All clear? Andrew Robertson 3:50 pm

**Lauren** Thanks, Mr Robertson. Clear as mud! 😖 4:02 pm

OK, Lauren, I want to stay here with the lions but Dad says we have to go into this huge old gallery now. Catch you later. 4:05 pm

## 4 Visitors from the Commonwealth

a) Explain how the photo of the flags leads to the topic of the Commonwealth. Then say what you learn about the Commonwealth.

Find out more about the Commonwealth.

Early finisher ➜ (p. 111)

b) Compare a) *It's raining a lot.* and b) *Raining a lot.* Say which is used in the text messages and why.

Find similar examples above.

➜ Workbook 3 (p. 4)

# 1 The digital compass

## 1 WORDS Staying in touch

a) In a copy of the table, put the words/phrases from the box under the correct heading. Some may fit more than one heading. Check the meaning of any you don't know.

b) Add other words or phrases you know under the correct headings.

| Greetings | Opening phrases | Communication channels | Communication acts | Goodbyes |
|---|---|---|---|---|
| … | … | … | … | … |
| … | … | … | … | … |

> blog • chat • contact+ • dear • follow sb on … • goodnight+ • hi+ • introduce sb/sth to sb • like • phone sb • share sth+ • text sb • unsubscribe+ • block • email+ • how's things?+ • social media post • catch you later • messenger service+ • friend • letter • tweet+ • feed+ • hey • post sth • what's up? • consult with sb • follower+ • trend on+ • message+ • how are you? • later • call • send a text/email/… • good morning/… • app+ • subscribe • check out sth • hello

## 2 How do you stay in touch?

a) Think about the most common ways people communicate with each other, for example:
- with parents
- with brothers/sisters
- other family members
- with friends
- with teachers
- other adults
- …

b) Make appointments for three times with three other students. Go to your appointments and exchange your information. Discuss what the advantages and disadvantages of the communication channels for the different people are.

c) In class, share what most surprised you from your discussions.

➜ Workbook 4–5 (p. 5)

## 3 EXTRA Panel discussion

a) Have a panel discussion on the topic: **A week of digital detox would be good for us.**

b) Choose three panellists and one moderator for your discussion. Everyone else will be the audience. Then prepare for your discussion:
- Panellists: make notes on your ideas about a week with no digital communication.
- Moderator: think of questions to ask the panellists.
- Audience: note down your own ideas.

c) Have your panel discussion.
- Moderator: make sure all the panellists can say what they think. Ask for questions at the end.
- Panellists: tell each other your ideas and react to the other panellists' ideas.
- Audience: note down questions or comments/ideas you have for the end of the discussion.

More help ➜ (p. 106)

# Part A  Practice    1

## 4 REVISION  London and Ottawa (Simple present)

a) **Partner B:** Go to p. 114.
   **Partner A:** Imagine you're Lauren. Use the ideas on the right to write down questions for Alyssa about her life in London.
   Add two or three more questions of your own.
   Use the simple present.
   Example: *Do you go out much in the evenings?*
   *Is your host family's place far from the city centre? ...*

- where: live
- host family: nice? how big?
- how: get around the city
- school: what like? where?
- how: go to school
- …

b) Give your questions to your partner.
   Take the questions they give you and write down answers to them (use your imagination).

c) Return your partner's questions and your answers. Look at them together.
   Exchange your opinions on the questions and answers.
   ➡ *GF 1.1: The simple present (p. 137)*

## 5 REVISION  At the gallery (Simple past)

At the National Gallery in Trafalgar Square, Alyssa and her parents listened to a guide talk about this painting. Use the notes the guide made and the verbs in the simple past to write down what she said.

> JMW Turner – The Fighting Temeraire – 1839
> Ship: important role, Battle of Trafalgar, 1805
> In the picture – end of its life
> 1838, new steam ship along River Thames – to Rotherhithe
> How – Turner – feeling of sadness?
> Beautiful, old ship – pale, colours of ghost
> New steam ship, – dark, awful
> Sun going down – end of an age

paint · play · be · pull · express · paint · make · show

➡ *GF 1.2: The simple past (p. 137)* ➡ **Workbook** *6 (p. 6)*

## 6 REVISION  The West End (Simple present and simple past)

Complete Alyssa's email to friends back in Canada about her day with her parents in the West End of London. Decide which tense to use: simple present or simple past.

> Hey guys!
> What's up back in Ottawa? It …¹ our first day in London yesterday. We …² round the West End. That …³ the fun area of the city with all the night life and it …⁴ lots of the most famous sights, like Buckingham Palace and Trafalgar Square. Trafalgar Square …⁵ just like the photos you all …⁶. The weather …⁷ nice so we …⁸ by the big lions. Canada …⁹ its embassy right on the square – well, they …¹⁰ it an embassy because Canada …¹¹ in the Commonwealth, but I …¹² what they …¹³ it.
> We …¹⁴ into the National Gallery, which …¹⁵ also at Trafalgar Square. It …¹⁶ full of old paintings. A tour …¹⁷ just as we …¹⁸ so at least we …¹⁹ walk around on our own to find any interesting paintings.
> After the gallery, we …²⁰ up to Leicester Square (London …²¹ full of squares!) and mom and dad …²² cheap tickets for a musical (Les Mis), which we …²³ in the evening. That …²⁴ really cool!

➡ *GF 1: The simple present / simple past (p. 137)* ➡ **Workbook** *7 (p. 6)*

thirteen  13

# 1 Part A Practice

## 7 Sounds different (Pronunciation and intonation) 🎧

a) 👥 Alyssa and her parents are at a tourist information office. Read through the phrases below. Then practise saying them aloud to each other.
1  A good view <u>of</u> life in the city.
2  <u>But</u> my advice to <u>you would</u> be …
3  <u>Have</u> you <u>been</u> on a London bus yet?
4  <u>Shall</u> I show <u>you</u>?
5  Show <u>your</u> ticket.
6  Some <u>of</u> the fun <u>of</u> London …

b) 👥 Look at the underlined words in the phrases. Listen to how these words are pronounced.
Compare that with how you pronounce them. What do you notice?

c) Listen and practise the phrases aloud again. Try to imitate what you hear as well as you can.

## 8 At the tourist office 🎧

a) 👥 Alyssa and her parents are still at a tourist information office. Think of questions they might ask there.

b) 👥 Look at the phrases below. Five of them are in the conversation Alyssa and her parents have at the tourist office.
Consider your ideas for a) and say which phrases you think they are? Explain why.
1  Could you help us with …?
2  Excuse me, please.
3  Hello.
4  How can I help you?
5  How can we get to …?
6  I have this brochure here.
7  On the Tube.
8  Tower of London.
9  We'd like some information on …
10 You'll love it!

c) 👥 Listen and find out whether your ideas in a) and b) were correct. Write down the phrases that are in the conversation.

d) Complete the sentences.
1  Anyway, we … … … … … … city … school … .
2  Who … … tour … , Dad, … … Mom, … …?

e) Listen again. Take notes on:
1  what the woman in the information office finds out about Alyssa.
2  what Alyssa wants to see/do.
3  what most of the conversation is about at the end. What details do you remember?

➔ **Workbook** 8 (p. 7)

## 9 Role play 💬

a) 👥 Work in groups of three. Two of you play Tourists A and B, two English-speaking tourists to your area.
The third plays a tourist information worker (TIW) at your local visitor centre.

**Tourist A:** go to p. 114.
**Tourist B:** go to p. 263.
**TIW:** go to p. 264.

b) 👥 Study your role cards carefully.
Make notes on language you might need and information about your area.

c) 👥 Use your notes to act out a conversation at the tourist information office.

# The world behind the picture  1

## 1 Bike and animal

a) Look at the three film stills above. Imagine what the film might be about.

👥 Compare your ideas with a partner.

👥 Share your ideas with another pair.

b) Now watch the first part of the film. Describe what happens:
  - Where does the action take place?
  - Who are the boys?
  - What are they talking about?
  - Why?
  - What stops their conversation?

c) Say what you think will happen next. Collect ideas in class.

d) Watch the rest of the film. How close were your ideas from c) to what actually happens? Explain why the boy no longer wants the bike. How does the boy with the bike react?

e) Choose three adjectives from the box below (or other adjectives you know) that you think describe the film well. Explain your decision.

> absurd⁺ · boring · cool · excellent · funny · humorous⁺ · incredible · mad · magical · realistic⁺ · short · silly · slow · unusual · weird

f) Watch the whole film again. Take notes on the features of the bike and the animal that their owners describe.

| Bike | Animal |
|---|---|
| titanium frame | can fire rainbows from its horn |
| … | … |

g) 👥 In your group, talk about one of these aspects of the film and consider what it tells you about London as a diverse city:
  1 Describe the three boys (what they look like, what they want, feelings and reactions, …).
  2 Consider the unicorn. What powers does it have? What do they stand for?
  3 Think about the last scene (between the credits). What could its meaning be?

Present your ideas to the class. Why do you think the film-maker made the film?

h) The three boys have London accents and use slang words and phrases. Listen for these and say what you notice:

> you can't even get 'em 'ere · Niiiice! · What you got there? · Just a unicorn, init? · on the hill it is well fast · fank you · All right · Safe

## 2 Making the film: Long shots and close-ups

a) The film uses **long shots** and **close-ups**. Look at the three film stills again and say what they are, long shots or close-ups. Which show the setting of the film? Which show the feelings and reactions of the characters?

b) 👥 Watch the film again and choose a long shot and a close-up. Describe them to your partner and explain what they tell you.

**EXTRA** Read a short story about another 'mythical beast'. Explain how it is similar and different to the film.

# 1 Part B

## 1 Alyssa's photos

a) Look at the six photos below. Choose the one that interests you most.

b) 👥 Find a partner who has chosen a different photo.
Describe your pictures to each other. Talk about what the photos tell you about Alyssa, Brixton, etc. Then tell the class.
➡ SF 19: Describing pictures (p. 130)

**Check out my photos of our trip to Brixton.**
1. This photo was taken at the outdoor market.
2. The snacks at this trendy cafe in the indoor market are made fresh every day. Delish!
3. At the Black Cultural Archives we saw an exhibition about black music in Britain with GREAT SOUNDS!
4. This David Bowie mural is opposite the Tube station. Bowie was born and grew up in Brixton. Every year on the anniversary of his death (10 Jan), lots of flowers are laid on the ground here by his fans. The mural is protected by a cover because too many visitors write messages on it.
5. This is the Ritzy. It's one of the oldest cinemas in England! What a nice building! It has 750 seats. Mom liked it a lot.
6. Dad is a windmill freak. He told us, "There are only 9 windmills left in London. This one was built in 1816. Wheat is still ground blah blah …" (on and on for 10 minutes!). But it was kind of cool.

c) Read what Alyssa has written about her photos. Then find out more online about your favourite picture. Prepare and give a one-minute talk about it.
➡ SF 18: Internet research (p. 130)  ➡ SF 1: Skimming and scanning (p.116)

**EXTRA** Take a picture of a place from a walk around your own area.
Write a post about your photo (about 150 words).

16  sixteen

## 2 Opinion piece

a) Read the text.

### We have always come from everywhere
*by Laurence Harger, 12 September*

An exhibition at the *Black Cultural Archives* recently took me back to my childhood in Brixton. As I wandered the colourful South London streets where I grew up, my senses were treated to the sounds of many different languages and dialects, the aromas of food from all over the world. I realized how much the place had changed but also how much was still the same.

#### Always multicultural
When I was a child, Brixton already had an Afro-Caribbean vibe. Those white English nationalists who claim that multiculturalism has been a failure are clearly not Londoners like me. My London was always multicultural. In fact, the city's inhabitants have always come from everywhere.

#### 2000 years of immigrants
London – or Londinium as they called it – was founded in 43 CE by 'immigrants', the Romans who invaded Britain and made it a province of their empire. Other immigrants have been coming to the city ever since.

For centuries, foreigners have arrived here through the Port of London. Some came from not so far away: Irish, Welsh, Scots. At the time of the Great Fire in 1666 a majority of Londoners had been born abroad, like Protestant Huguenots. They were driven here by persecution in Catholic France. There were Jews who had fled pogroms in Spain or Eastern Europe. By 1800, the East End already had a Chinatown. The more the British Empire grew over the centuries, the more the Empire's peoples were attracted to its centre, London.

After the Second World War, Commonwealth people from places like India and the Caribbean islands were invited to help rebuild Britain. Many settled in London, in places like Brixton.

The free-movement policy of the European Union brought hundreds of thousands more immigrants.

#### Mixture makes London unique
This mixture, this diversity of peoples, races, colours, religions, cultures and habits is nothing new. Those who would like a return to a mythical, nostalgic one-culture Britain of old, want something that has never existed. What makes London so wonderful is its tolerance of people from all over the world and the way it learns from their traditions and cultures and transforms them into its own, unique London brand.

b) Look at the article and find the following features:
- a byline • a headline • illustrations • sub-headings

c) Then label the features on a copy of the drawing on the right.

d) Skim the article and decide which parts are the introduction, the body, the conclusion.

## 3 Facts and opinions

a) Read the article carefully. Take notes on the author's main points under the headings:
- facts about the writer
- facts about immigration and London
- opinions on London
- opinions on people who are against immigration

Check and agree on your results.

b) Exchange what you have found out in class.

## 4 Have a go

The windmill in Brixton was built in 1816. Find out and say when other buildings were built: your house/flat, your school, other buildings in your area, famous buildings in Germany or other countries.

> Our flat was built in 1982. There's a sign on the front.

> St Paul's Cathedral was built from 1675 to 1710.

➜ Workbook 9 (p. 8)

# 1 Part B Practice

## Looking at language

a) Look at these sentences:
1 The photo was taken at the outdoor market.
2 Alyssa took the photo in Brixton market.

Which sentence tells us *who* took the photo?
That sentence is *active*.
The other sentence is *passive*.

How many of these sentences have a *passive* verb form?
The windmill was built in 1816.
The mural is protected now.
Immigrants founded London.

b) Complete these sentences from pp. 16/17.
It … covered up in the 19th century.
Lots of flowers … laid on the ground here.
They … driven here by persecution …
Say what tenses the sentences are in.

c) Explain how you form the passive.

d) It is often not clear from a passive sentence who carried out the action. But how can you show this in a passive sentence?
Find two examples on p. 17.

➜ GF 2: The passive (p. 138)

## 1 Mural and windmill (Passive: simple present)

Complete the sentences about the places in Brixton with a verb in the passive.
1 Sometimes messages … on the Bowie mural and pictures … even on it. (write • paint)
2 Flowers … often … on the ground in front of the mural. (lay)
3 The Brixton Windmill … black. (paint)
4 It … every winter and … again for tours at Easter. (close • open)
5 Regular events … in the Windmill Gardens. (hold)
6 Places on the tours … very quickly because only three or four people can go together. (fill)
7 Walks with a guide … also … on Brixton Hill on Sundays when the mill is open. (offer)
8 Workshops on how the windmill works … for school groups. (give)
9 Wheat … in the Windmill Gardens and it … still … in the mill today. (grow • grind)

## 2 It wasn't founded by Britons (Passive: simple present and simple past)

Correct the wrong information about London in each sentence.
You can check the facts on pp. 16/17.
1 London was founded by Britons.
   – No, it wasn't founded by Britons. It was founded by …
2 The city was first named London.   – No, it …
3 The food in the Brixton café is cooked the night before.   – No, it …
4 The Huguenots were driven to London from Spain.
5 London was burned by a Great Fire in 1665.
6 After World War II, Europeans were brought to London. to help rebuild the country.

More help ➜ (p. 106)

**Early finisher** Look at exercise 1 again. Make three wrong sentences about the mural and/or the windmill. Find a partner to correct your sentences.   ➜ Workbook 10–12 (pp. 9–10)

**Part B** Practice    **1**

## 3 Which is the oldest? (Passive: simple past)

a) Look at the pictures of sights in London and Berlin and read the dialogue.
   A: Which one was built first?
   B: I think the Chinatown Gate was built first.
   A: Sorry, that's wrong. The Chinatown Gate was built in 2016. The Brandenburg Gate was built in the 18th century. OK, it's your turn.

b) Partner A: Continue on p. 115. • Partner B: Continue on p. 263.

Brandenburg Gate Berlin | Chinatown Gate London

## 4 *Romeo and Juliet* was written by Shakespeare (Passive with *by*)

Complete the text about Shakespeare's Globe Theatre using the passive form of the verbs in the box and *by*.

*Shakespeare's Globe:* England's most famous plays ¹… (William Shakespeare). Many of his plays ²… (the actors of the Globe Theatre) in London. The Globe ³… (a group of actors called *The Lord Chamberlain's Men*) in 1599. All actors were men in those days. Women's roles ⁴… (boys). The Globe ⁵… (a fire) in 1613 but was rebuilt. In the year 1642 all theatres ⁶… (the British government), which was very strict at that time. The theatre was built again in the late 20th Century and ⁷… (the Queen in 1997). This event ⁸… (Shakespeare fans everywhere).

build • celebrate • close • destroy • open • perform • play • write

**TIP** With the passive, we use *by* … if we want to say who did something.

**More help** ➔ *(p. 107)*    ➔ **Workbook** 13 (p. 11)

## 5 London Quiz 💬

**London Buildings**
- The White Tower is the most famous part of the Tower of London. It was built by William I in 1078. The Crown Jewels are kept in the Tower.
- 20 Fenchurch Street is called the Walkie-Talkie. It is 160m tall and was designed by Rafael Viñoly.

**London Culture**
- Most of London's most famous museums are free.
- Many famous Turner paintings are kept at the National Gallery in Room 34.
- At the British Museum, special events like sleepovers are often held for families to enjoy.

**London History**
- The city was founded by the Romans who invaded Britain in 43 CE.
- Londinium was burnt by Boudicca, queen of the Iceni, when she attacked the Roman city in 60 CE.
- In 120 CE the city was destroyed by fire again.

**London Film Stars**
- Some famous "American" film stars are actually Londoners.
- Rosamund Pike was born in London and became famous as a Bond girl.
- Idris Elba, aka Heimdall in the Marvel films, speaks with a strong East London accent.
- Emily Blunt: the new Mary Poppins was played by this South London girl.

a) Work in groups of four. Each student reads *one* fact box about London and makes questions.
   • When was … built/…? • Where is/was … ? • What/Who is/was … in … ?

b) Read the other three fact boxes.

c) Ask your questions to the group.    ➔ **Workbook** 14 (p. 11)

# 1 Part B Practice

## 6 STUDY SKILLS  Reading for detail

This page will show you how to find detail information in a text.

a) 👥 Say what you remember about scanning a text.
   Then compare your ideas with the points in the tip box.

b) 👥 Look at the text below.
   Before you read, discuss these questions.
   1  What kind of text do you think it is?
   2  Will the style be formal or informal?
   3  How will the structure of the text help you find information?

c) Kiran is an English boy with an Indian background.
   Scan his blog post to find the answers to these questions.
   1  Where did Kiran spend one month this summer?
   2  What kind of Asian statue can you see in Chinatown?
   3  Why is one area sometimes called 'Banglatown'?
   4  What kind of barbecue is very popular in New Malden?
   5  Where does Kiran say you can find the best curries in London?
   6  What carnival did Kiran enjoy very recently?

> **TIP**
> When you scan a text to find information:
> - think of keywords which will help you find the information you want.
> - if you have to answer questions, underline keywords in the questions.
> - look through the text very quickly and try to find your keywords.
> - read the parts of the text around the keywords to find the information you need.

---

**WELCOME TO MY BLOG**    **MY SUMMER TRAVELLING AROUND THE WORLD – IN LONDON**    **GALLERY** | **CONTACT ME**
— 31 AUGUST —

Hi all. I hope you've had a fabulous summer. I certainly have. I travelled around the world … without leaving London! London? Yes. My cousins Manish and Ana live there and I spent a whole month with them. I saw the famous sites, but you can read about them anywhere, so I'm going to tell you about some discoveries I made: London's most exciting multicultural districts. Read on to find out about the whole world in one city!

### OLD FAVOURITES

**Chinatown** OK, maybe Chinatown is one of London's most touristy places but it's still very, very cool. It really makes you feel like you are in China, with its beautiful gates and lion statues, and all the Chinese restaurants, shops and bakeries. Yum!

**Brick Lane** The street signs are in English and Bengali because so many people here come from Bangladesh. Brick Lane is also known a 'Banglatown' and it's a really fun place to visit. There are markets and street art and loads of bakeries and restaurants. There is food from all over South Asia but I've got an even better tip for you if you want a great curry – keep reading!

### NEW FAVOURITES

**Barbecue in 'Little Korea'** I bet you've never heard of a neighbourhood called New Malden, right? Around 20,000 Koreans live in and around this district so if you like Korean food, it's the place to go. I love a Korean barbecue. It's a great way to eat together with friends (or cousins) so we visited often.

**Indian … and everything else too** I love Tooting! It's a super-multicultural neighbourhood in South London, with the very best Indian curries outside of India! The area is lively but not touristy and you can walk around for hours discovering little shops, bakeries and restaurants from all over the world.

### NOT JUST FOOD

In case you think I'm only interested in food, let me tell you about my absolute favourite London event: the Notting Hill Carnival. It brings together music, dance, costumes, theatre, art and (yes!) food from everywhere, but especially from Africa and the Caribbean. I was there just two days ago and I can't stop thinking about how much I love London, and the cultures of the world!

➡ **Workbook** 15 (p. 12)    ➡ SF 1: Skimming and scanning (p. 116)

# Part B  Practice    1

## 7  A formal email

a) Finn Lorenz from Munich is doing a project on famous people from Brixton. He wants to write an email to the *Black Cultural Archives* to ask for information that might help him. Look at the email layout (1-9) and choose the best answers for each point.

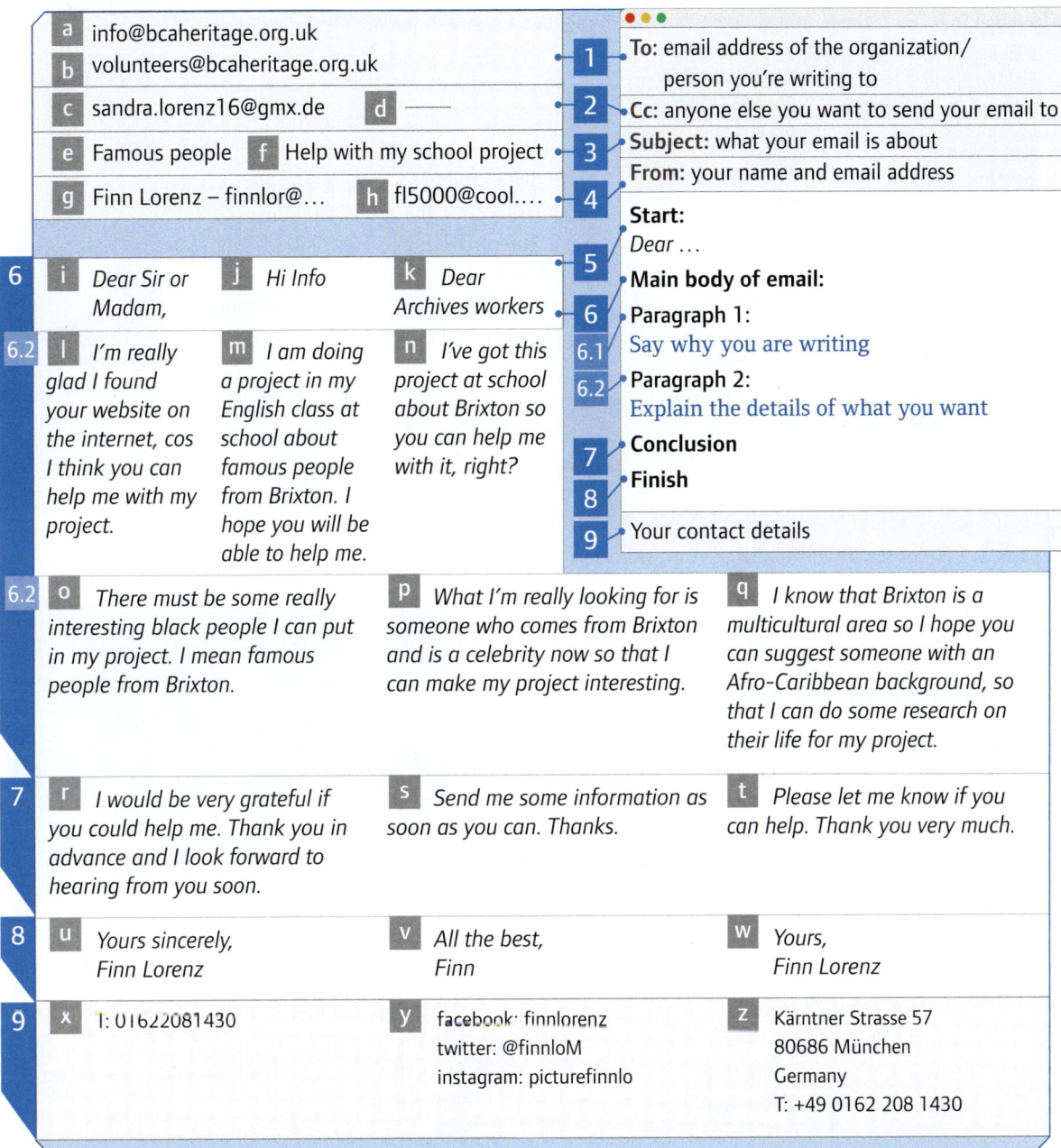

b) Compare and explain your answers in a group. Use a placemat to make a list of tips for writing a formal email.
   **More help** ➜ (p. 107)

c) Imagine you want to do a presentation on black music in Britain.
Write an email to the Black Cultural Archives or *BritishBlackMusic.com* asking for help.

➜ SF 6: Writing a formal letter or email (p. 121)   ➜ **Workbook** 16 (p. 13)

twenty-one  21

# 1 Part C

## 1 🖐 At the top of the Monument

Alyssa counted the steps under her breath: "278, 279, … How many steps did the guide say? Three hundred?"
She was walking up a spiral stone staircase that seemed to go on forever.

She looked up at her parents in front of her. "How did they get so fit?" she wondered, a frown on her face. When they had suggested this London walking tour to her the evening before, she had quickly agreed. Now, she was regretting it.
She emerged into the daylight at the top of the stairs. The tour guide smiled. "That wasn't too bad, was it? Come on. I'll show you the view and tell you some great stories. Then you'll see it was worth it."
Alyssa looked round for somewhere to sit as the guide went on talking to the group. They were shown the view. They were given all the facts and figures about this Monument to the Great Fire of London in 1666. Alyssa's mother was all ears.
"She loves this history stuff," Alyssa thought, while she herself was only half listening.

a) Look at the photos, read the text and explain:
- what the pictures show.
- who the people are.
- where they are and what they're doing.
- why they are there.

b) Look at the last sentence of the text. Explain what Alyssa thinks and how she feels.

c) 📷 Take notes on all the facts you find out about the Monument. Check with a partner.

## 2 Phoenix from the ashes 🎧

a) Before you listen, consider what you have learned about the Monument and say what you think "phoenix from the ashes" could mean?

b) Now listen to the audio. Describe the situation and say whose voices you hear.

c) 📷 Read the questions and look at the unfinished sentences. Listen again and take notes so that you can answer the questions/complete the sentences. Check the answers in your group.

1. How many steps are there to the top of the Monument?
2. The Monument commemorates …
3. Why is it exactly 202 feet high?
4. The Great Fire of London started in …
5. It lasted …
6. Why was the fire so bad?
7. What is the "phoenix from the ashes"?
8. After the fire, new buildings and streets were made of …
9. The most famous new building was …

d) 📷 Try to remember some of Alyssa's reactions to what the tour guide says and describe them to a partner.

🌐 Can you remember the nicknames of the three London skyscrapers in the photo above? Follow the link and find out more fun facts about them.

➡ **Workbook** 17 (p. 13)

twenty-two

Key information | Mediation course 1

You're a German exchange student in London. You read about 20 Fenchurch Street in your London guidebook and decide to go there at the weekend. Your host parents and their children have never been there but they might be interested in a visit and ask you about it.

1 **What your host parents want to know**
   1 Is 20 Fenchurch Street worth a visit?
   2 If so, what can you do there?
   3 What else should you know before visiting?

2 **Scan for answers.**
   Scan the extract and find the information you need to answer their questions.

3 **Take notes**
   Take notes in English or German on the information that answers their questions. Make sure your notes are only on the information you need.

   *Sa./So. 11-21 Uhr*

   Compare your notes with a partner.

4 **Say it in English**
   Discuss how to pass on the information in your notes. Don't translate from the brochure. Just put your notes into your own words.

   *Yes, I'll tell you why I think it's worth a visit. …*

5 **Role-play**
   Join another pair and act out the conversation. One pair plays the parents, the other the kids.

   **Mediation skills**
   This is what you need to do to find and work with the information you need:
   - *scan the text for the information you need.*
   - *take notes.*
   - *put your notes into your own words.*
   ➔ SF 11: Finding key information (p. 125)

➔ Workbook 18 (p. 14)

## 20 Fenchurch Street

### Das Gebäude

Seit seiner Eröffnung im Jahr 2014 ist dies eins der kontroversesten Gebäude der Stadt. Der 37 Stockwerke umfassende, 160 m hohe Wolkenkratzer erinnert an ein altmodisches Handfunkgerät und wird deswegen im Allgemeinen *Walkie-Talkie* genannt. Viele Londoner finden das Bauwerk aufdringlich, weil es die Skyline der Stadt beherrscht.

### Der Sky Garden

Der Walkie-Talkie wird aber bei London-Besuchern immer beliebter. Grund dafür ist vor allem der Sky Garden, eine außergewöhnliche Neuheit in den Wolken Londons, nämlich ein dreistöckiger Garten mit Restaurant und Café/Bar an der Spitze des Walkie-Talkie. Ein Fahrstuhl bringt Gäste in Sekundenschnelle nach oben, wo man sich inmitten exotischer Pflanzen entspannen und den 360° Panoramablick auf die Stadt genießen kann. Es sind ausreichend Sitzgelegenheiten vorhanden.

Und das Beste daran? Der Eintritt ist kostenlos. Allerdings muss man seinen Besuch vorher buchen und kann den Sky Garden dann zu dieser Zeit besuchen.

### Öffnungszeiten und Anfahrt

Montag – Freitag        Samstag/Sonntag
10:00 – 18:00           11:00 – 21:00
Gut erreichbar mit öffentlichen Verkehrsmitteln
U-Bahn: Monument
Zug: Fenchurch St., Cannon St., London Bridge
Bus: Linie 40

# 1 Part C Practice

## 1 London visitors (Verbs with two objects)

Use the information and the verbs to write about Alyssa in London. Be careful with tenses.
1. our host family – me – a great tour of the city yesterday (give)
2. I – my parents – why I love London (explain)
3. I – them – my host family – when they visit me (introduce)
4. I – them – a list of things to bring me (send)
5. First, the guide – us – the view from the Monument (show)
6. Then he – us – the nicknames of the skyscrapers (tell)
7. He also – the city before the Great Fire – the tour group (describe)

➜ Workbook 19 (p. 15)

> **Language help**
>
> a) When a verb has two objects, the normal word order is the same as in German:
> indirect object – direct object
> I'll show you the view and tell you some great stories.
>
> b) If you put the indirect object at the end of the sentence, it comes after *to*:
> They had suggested this London walking tour to her.
> With some verbs the indirect object always comes after *to*:
> describe/explain/introduce/present/report/say/suggest something to somebody
>
> ➜ GF 3: Verbs with two objects (p. 139)

## 2 Unhappy in London (Personal passive)

a) Some tourists in London weren't very happy with their holiday in the city.
Finish their sentences.
1. We … (promise) a quiet room.
2. Then we … (give) a room above the hotel disco.
3. We … (not tell) that breakfast was not included..
4. We … (not show) how the shower worked.
5. We … (offer) a bus tour of the city but … (not tell) how much it would cost.
6. When we got back home, we … (send) a bill for a tour we did not take.

b) 👥 Complete the dialogue and act it out. Use ideas from a).
Hotel staff: Oh, I'm sorry. What was the problem?
Guest: …

➜ Workbook 20 (p. 15)

> **Language help**
>
> The sentences below begin with *They* ….
> Complete the translations. Then say what is different about how the German sentences begin.
> They were shown the view.
> … wurde die Aussicht gezeigt.
> They were given all the facts and figures.
> … wurden alle Daten gegeben.
>
> ➜ GF 4: The passive: Different kinds of verbs (p. 140)

I hope you enjoyed your time in London.

Well, actually I wasn't so happy.

## 3 Likes and dislikes (Personal passive)

Some tourists gave feedback on their trip to London.
Complete the feedback with verbs in the passive form.
1. I … a trip to London by my rich uncle. Best thing I ever did!
2. We … best holiday of our lives. We love London.
3. At the top of the Monument, we … a view of all the modern skyscrapers. Ugh!
4. I … the summers in London are warmer now. I didn't believe it but it's true!
5. We reserved our Sky Garden visit online and … our ticket in seconds.

> offer •
> promise •
> send •
> show •
> tell

**Early finisher** Use verbs from the box in the passive to write a comment about a place you have visited.

**Part C** Practice  **1**

## 4 Pronunciation (Connected speech)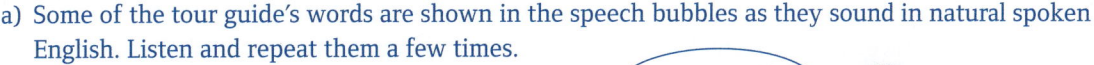

a) Some of the tour guide's words are shown in the speech bubbles as they sound in natural spoken English. Listen and repeat them a few times.

b) Write his words in normal spelling. Listen again and repeat them in spoken English.

c) In these sentences the underlined words are spoken slowly and clearly first, then in natural spoken English. Listen and compare. Then listen to the sentences in natural speech again and repeat them.
1  So London is a <u>brick and stone</u> city today.
2  <u>Lots of</u> wonderful new buildings were built.
3  <u>I am sure many of you have</u> already been to see it.
4  <u>London has been</u> getting larger and growing upwards ever since.
5  <u>See if you can guess</u> which ones I mean.

➜ **Workbook** 21–22 (p. 16)

## 5 THINKING ABOUT LANGUAGE  Idioms

a) Look at these two sentences from p. 22 and translate them word for word into German. The drawings will help.
   • Alyssa counted the steps under her breath.
   • Alyssa's mother was all ears.
   Now translate the sentences into *good* German. What do you notice?

b) In idioms and other common expressions in English, the *literal* meaning of the words is not the same as the *actual* meaning of the expression.

👥 Here are some idioms that the tour guide at the Monument uses. Match them to the right meaning from the list on the right. Then check with a partner and in class.

| 1  Give yourselves **a pat on the back**. | a) … began to burn. | d) Congratulations! |
|---|---|---|
| 2  The baker's shop **caught fire**. | b) Mind your backs. | e) I'm not helping you here. |
| 3  I'm not **pulling your leg** here. | c) I'm not joking. | |

c) Other languages have idioms too. For example, German. Can you match these German idioms to any of the English idioms you have learned about here?

   auf die Schippe nehmen • Feuer fangen • ganz Ohr sein • sich auf die Schulter klopfen

Do you know any idioms in other languages that are similar to the idioms on this page?

d) 🏴 Partner A: go to p. 115.    Partner B: go to p. 264.
   Explain to your partner in English what the German idioms mean.

e) Think of a German idiom you use yourself. Make notes so that you can explain it in English.
   👥 Then explain your idiom in English to a partner. Can they guess the German idiom?

# 1 Text

## 🔊 Escape from Uncle Jack (abridged[1] from *The Thieves of Pudding Lane* by Jonathan Eyers)

a) These terms are in the story you are going to read: London – 1666 – Pudding Lane.
   From what you have already learned in this unit, what do you think the story could be about?

b) Now read the introduction and the story. Only look up words if you really have to.
   Remember: you can often guess[2] what a new word means because it looks or sounds like a German word or a French or Latin word you know.
   Or you know part of it already, e.g. if it has a prefix[3]/suffix[4] like *un-, in-, re-, -er*, that will help you understand it. Sometimes you can make an intelligent guess and understand a word from the context.

---

*It's the year 1666. The year before, London was struck by the plague[5] and Sam's parents and his brother, Thomas, died.*
*Sam lives alone on the streets until Uncle Jack, a*
5 *man with a wooden leg, takes him in. Sam has to work as a thief during the day and bring what he steals back to Uncle Jack. In return he and the other child thieves, like Sam's new best friend Catherine, are given a place to sleep below Uncle*
10 *Jack's pub in Pudding Lane.*
*When a great fire starts in Pudding Lane, a fire that will destroy 80% of the city of London, Uncle Jack makes Catherine and Sam steal from the houses that rich people have abandoned. In one of*
15 *the houses, Sam and Catherine find Gideon, a young boy, who has become separated from his parents. The three of them decide to run away from Uncle Jack to find Gideon's parents. But things don't go quite as they planned ...*

20 'Samuel!' [...] 'Stop! It's a trap![6]'
Samuel, Gideon and Uncle Jack all froze when they heard the voice. Uncle Jack spun as fast as his leg would let him, searching for Catherine. Samuel spotted her first, clambering[7] over the rooftops
25 above them.
Uncle Jack snapped a look at Samuel, then followed his gaze up to Catherine. [...]
Uncle Jack lunged for Gideon, ready to grab him by the neck. But Samuel was too fast for him. He
30 yanked Gideon out of Uncle Jack's reach and stuck out his foot. Uncle Jack lurched[8] forwards, wooden leg first, right into Samuel's foot. The pain of the hard wood striking Samuel's shin felt like a red hot poker[9]. Samuel stumbled backwards, but didn't fall.
Uncle Jack, on the other hand, lost his balance 35
completely. He fell hard onto the cobbles[10] with a furious[11] cry. His hat and stick went flying. The lantern smashed on the ground.
'Run!' Samuel shouted to Gideon.
Gideon didn't need telling twice. 40
'Not that way!' Catherine shouted down.
Samuel grabbed Gideon by the tunic[12] and spun him around. He gave him a push in the other direction, then shot a look at [...] Uncle Jack. [...]
Samuel kicked Uncle Jack's stick further out of 45
reach then he ran too, leaving Uncle Jack to pull himself over the cobbles.
Samuel and Gideon ran parallel to the terrace[13] of houses that Catherine was scrambling across. Samuel glanced[14] at her frequently to make sure she 50
could keep up.
They soon reached the end of the terrace. Catherine had nowhere left to go but down or back the way she had come. Her dark shape appeared against the moonlit cloud as she peered[15] over the 55
eaves[16].
'There's no way down,' she cried.
'Jump!' Samuel called to her.
'I can't! It's too far.'
'We'll catch you,' Gideon shouted, lifting his arms 60
up as if to prove it.
'Yes, we'll catch you!' Samuel echoed, reaching for her too.
Catherine disappeared for a moment, and when she reappeared she came feet first, lowering[17] 65
herself as quickly as she could. Quicker than was safe, thought Samuel.

---

1 **abridged** [ə'brɪdʒd] gekürzt · 2 **guess** [ɡes] vermuten · 3 **prefix** ['priːfɪks] Präfix, Vorsilbe · 4 **suffix** ['sʌfɪks] Suffix, Nachsilbe ·
5 **plague** [pleɪɡ] Pest *(Krankheit)* · 6 **trap** [træp] Falle · 7 **(to) clamber** ['klæmbə] klettern · 8 **(to) lurch** [lɜːtʃ] schwanken, taumeln ·
9 **poker** ['pəʊkə] Schürhaken · 10 **cobble** ['kɒbl] Pflasterstein · 11 **furious** ['fjʊərɪəs] wütend · 12 **tunic** ['tjuːnɪk] Tunika ·
13 **terrace (of houses)** ['terəs] Häuserreihe · 14 **(to) glance (at)** [ɡlɑːns] kurz blicken (auf) · 15 **(to) peer** [pɪə] angestrengt schauen ·
16 **eaves** *(pl)* [iːvz] Dachgesims, Dachvorsprung · 17 **(to) lower** ['ləʊə] sinken lassen, hinunter lassen

'Get ready! Quick! […] she said. […]

'We're ready!' he told her, stretching out[18] his arms and bending his knees, ready to take the impact.[19] 'Come on!'

Catherine slipped her other leg over the side and then, without its support, […] fell with a sharp cry.

Samuel braced[20] in the fraction of a second it took for Catherine to land on top of[21] them. She knocked[22] Gideon sideways and tumbled[23] Samuel onto his back. All the breath blasted out of him as he hit the cobbles. His vision went momentarily black with the pain. It felt like the cobbles had slammed into him, not the other way around.

When he opened his eyes again Catherine was climbing off him, helped by Gideon. Samuel picked himself up and Catherine threw her arms around him. The pain vanished[24]. He hugged her back.

Not to be left out, Gideon wrapped his arms around both of them.   […]

For a moment they just looked at each other.

Then Gideon suddenly drew back. 'Oh no! Look!'

'No!' Samuel said under his breath.

Coming along the street towards them was Uncle Jack, his stick arcing[25] in quick strides[26] ahead of[27] him. His hat was gone, and his lank hair flew in the wind like dancing fire itself.

'Run!' Samuel cried. He clapped a hand on Gideon's back and grabbed Catherine's hand.

They ran around the corner and onto the next street.

'We can't go this way,' Catherine said as they ran.

'We have to,' said Samuel. 'It's the only way.'

'He's herding[28] us towards the fire. We'll be trapped.'

Samuel feared she was right. 'We'll find a way around. We have to.'

They followed the street around a bend[29], and all of them scuffed[30] to a stop. Samuel could feel the heat of the houses burning at the other end of the lane[31] from here. Red-hot embers[32] churned out of the smoke like a blizzard[33] of burning snow.

'We have to go back!' cried Gideon.

They got back to the corner in time to see Uncle Jack come around the last one.

'We're only one street away from the river,' Samuel said quickly. 'It's right on the other side of these warehouses[34]. Can you see that alley[35]?' He pointed towards the other end of the lane, towards the fire. 'That will lead us down to the water's edge. Catherine, am I wrong?'

She shook her head. 'You're not.'

'We've got to cover our heads. Come on.'

'Sam, I'm scared,' said Gideon.

Samuel loosened his tunic and pulled it up over his ears like a hood[36]. He gave the younger boy a smile. 'You do trust me, don't you?'

Gideon began to undo his top buttons.

Uncle Jack was gaining[37] on them. Not even on Pudding Lane had Samuel and Catherine got this close to the flames. The heat seemed to steal the breath from Samuel's lungs. It was so hot he was sure his clothes must actually be on fire. […]

But when they reached the turning into the alley that led down to the riverbank, things got much, much worse.

Gideon started saying 'No. No!' repeatedly.

Even Catherine was looking at Samuel and shaking her head.

Buildings on both side of the alley were on fire. Flames lapped up the walls. Tongues[38] of fire licked at the air between the buildings, flicking in the wind like whips[39] being cracked. The building at the far end had a jettied upper storey[40]. This too was burning.

Their escape route looked like a tunnel of fire.

'I can see the river,' Samuel croaked[41], as smoke churned around them. 'Look! It's only a short run. We can make it.' […]

'Don't do it!' a voice called from behind them.

They turned to see Uncle Jack. He stopped, an arm up to his face. Whether it was the heat keeping him back or he was trying not to scare them by keeping his distance, Samuel wasn't sure. […]

'That way lies only certain death,' Uncle Jack went on, creeping forward ever so slowly.

Gideon didn't back away from Uncle Jack. Now the old crook[42] wasn't the thing that terrified[43] him most. Samuel stepped in front of Gideon protectively.

---

18 **(to) stretch out (your arm)** [ˌstretʃ ˈaʊt] (den Arm) ausstrecken · 19 **impact** [ˈɪmpækt] Aufprall, (Zusammen-)Stoß · 20 **(to) brace** [breɪs] (sich) anspannen · 21 **on top of sth.** [ɒn ˈtɒp əv] auf etwas (oben) drauf · 22 **(to) knock** [nɒk] stoßen; schlagen · 23 **(to) tumble** [ˈtʌmbl] stoßen; fallen · 24 **(to) vanish** [ˈvænɪʃ] verschwinden · 25 **(to) arc** [ɑːk] kurven · 26 **stride** [straɪd] Schritt · 27 **ahead of** [əˈhed] vor · 28 **(to) herd** [hɜːd] (sich) drängen, zusammentreiben *(Tiere)* · 29 **bend** [bend] Kurve · 30 **(to) scuff** [skʌf] schlurfen · 31 **lane** [leɪn] Gasse, Straßchen · 32 **ember** [ˈembə] glühendes Stück Holz/Kohle; Glut · 33 **blizzard** [ˈblɪzəd] Schneesturm · 34 **warehouse** [ˈweəhaʊs] Lager(haus) · 35 **alley** (auch: **alleyway**) [ˈæli], [ˈæliweɪ] Gasse · 36 **hood** [hʊd] Kapuze · 37 **(to) gain on sb./sth.** [ˈɡeɪn ɒn] jn./etwas einholen · 38 **tongue** [tʌŋ] Zunge · 39 **whip** [wɪp] Peitsche · 40 **jettied storey** [ˌdʒetid ˈstɔːri] Stockwerkvorsprung · 41 **(to) croak** [krəʊk] krächzen · 42 **crook** [krʊk] Gauner/in, Kriminelle/r · 43 **(to) terrify sb.** [ˈterɪfaɪ] jm. schreckliche Angst einjagen

# 1 Text

'Come back here,' Uncle Jack implored them, reaching out a hand. 'You'll be safe.'

Even Catherine looked like she was considering it.

'You'll be safe,' Uncle Jack repeated. 'With me.'

And that was when everything changed.

'Samuel, how far is it?' Gideon asked, not taking his eyes off Uncle Jack.

'We can run it in five seconds.'

'Are you both ready to do this?' asked Catherine.

'Yes,' said Gideon.

'Yes,' said Samuel. 'Now!'

Uncle Jack roared. […].

Catherine was already running full pelt[44] into the alley, and Samuel shoved[45] Gideon after her, so hard he almost knocked the boy off his feet.

Samuel ran after them both, almost bent over, not looking where he was going, arms cradled[46] over his head. He heard Uncle Jack behind him. Over the roaring flames, the howling[47] gale[48], the creak and crack of burning timber[49], he could hear Uncle Jack's cries of fury.

Then Samuel entered the tunnel of fire. He batted away bits of burning wood falling from the jettied upper storey. He could see only his clogs kicking through ashes and embers, sending pieces of black, smoking rubble[50] flying. […]

He didn't stop, kept running, but threw his tunic back from his head. Catherine and Gideon had stopped, faces black and streaming with sweat, mouths gasping for air.

Samuel finally looked back, just in time to see Uncle Jack attempt[51] to run through the tunnel of fire. He made it halfway through before there was an almighty[52] crash. Samuel saw the look on his face. He had never seen Uncle Jack look frightened before.

Uncle Jack was still running when the jettied upper storey collapsed.

Samuel staggered[53] back as a billowing[54] cloud of thick smoke swallowed everything, […].

Catherine and Gideon were now standing on a narrow wooden wharf[55] that jutted[56] out into the River Thames. Catherine tried to drag Samuel after them.

'Come on, Sam,' she urged.

As the smoke cleared from the alleyway Samuel saw Uncle Jack writhing[57] on the ground. Daring to get closer, Samuel saw why. Uncle Jack's wooden leg was on fire. First he tried slapping at the flames, crying out as the fire seared[58] his palms[59]. Then he gave up, and tore at his breeches[60] until the stump of his knee was exposed[61]. He grabbed the cushioned[62] top of the false limb[63] and pulled it off. He threw the burning leg out of his way, but he was still surrounded by flaming rubble.

'Come on, Sam,' Catherine urged again. 'The rest of the building will collapse any moment.'

'We can't leave him like that,' said Samuel.

As if to emphasise Catherine's point, the roof of the next building suddenly burst[64] inwards, raining burning debris[65] down onto the next wharf. Some fell into the water with a loud hiss.

'We have to go,' said Gideon.

Samuel ignored them and approached Uncle Jack. He couldn't get close enough to help him. Samuel had to shout to him through the flames: 'Where's your stick?'

Uncle Jack finally stopped flailing about and locked eyes with Samuel. Yellow flames reflected in his black pupils. For a moment they just stared at each other.

'Get out of here, you stupid boy,' Uncle Jack said eventually, his voice gruff[66] and weak.

Samuel spotted Uncle Jack's stick then. It was behind him in the alley, broken in two, both parts burning.

He felt Gideon tug[67] at his arm. 'Come on, Sam. We've got to go now.'

Samuel nodded. But as he hurried after Gideon he saw a length of unburned wood lying by the side of the wharf. He grabbed it and tossed[68] it back towards Uncle Jack. He never saw whether Uncle Jack picked it up and used it as a walking stick, or whether Uncle Jack even noticed it at all.

'I can't swim,' Gideon said as they edged[69] further along the wharf, further away from the flames.

'Neither can I,' said Catherine.

---

44 **full pelt** [ˈfʊl pelt] mit Karacho *(so schnell es geht)* · 45 **(to) shove** [ʃʌv] schieben, stoßen; drängeln · 46 **(to) cradle** [ˈkreɪdl] halten *(schützend)*; wiegen · 47 **howling** [ˈhaʊlɪŋ] tosend · 48 **gale** [ɡeɪl] Sturm · 49 **timber** [ˈtɪmbə] Holz(balken), Bauholz · 50 **rubble** [ˈrʌbl] Schutt · 51 **(to) attempt** [əˈtempt] versuchen · 52 **almighty** [ɔːlˈmaɪti] riesig, allmächtig · 53 **(to) stagger** [ˈstæɡə] taumeln, torkeln, schwanken · 54 **(to) billow** [ˈbɪləʊ] aufsteigen *(z.B. Rauch)* · 55 **wharf** [wɔːf], *pl* **wharfs** *or* **wharves** Kai · 56 **(to) jut (out)** [dʒʌt] ragen · 57 **(to) writhe** [raɪð] sich winden · 58 **(to) sear** [sɪə] verbrennen *(z.B. Haut)* · 59 **palm** [pɑːm] Hand(fläche) · 60 **breeches** *(pl)* [ˈbrɪtʃɪz] Kniehose · 61 **(to) expose** [ɪkˈspəʊz] freilegen, entblößen · 62 **(to) cushion** [ˈkʊʃn] (aus)polstern · 63 **false limb** [lɪm] Prothese *(z.B. Bein)* · 64 **(to) burst** [bɜːst], **burst, burst** brechen, bersten, platzen · 65 **debris** [ˈdebriː] Schutt, Trümmer · 66 **gruff** [ɡrʌf] rau *(Stimme)* · 67 **(to) tug** [tʌɡ] ziehen *(z.B. am Ärmel)* · 68 **(to) toss** [tɒs] werfen · 69 **(to) edge** [edʒ] *(sich) (langsam)* schieben ·

# Text 1

260 'None of us can,' said Samuel. 'I thought there might be a little dinghy[70] we could take.'
'All the boats went hours ago.'
'Then we're trapped!' cried Gideon.
265 The windswept waters of the river reflected the orange firelight. It looked like the Thames was on fire too.
As he stood watching the water eddy[71] past, Samuel saw a large charred[72] piece of wood float by, just out of reach.
'We're not trapped,' he said.
270 Catherine must have realised what he was thinking a second later. 'It's the only way.'
'What is?' said Gideon.
Samuel and Catherine ran back along the wharf. Without discussion they both went for the same
275 piece of broken wood, a large unburnt beam[73] […].
'Heave!' Samuel shouted.
They both pulled at the same time. It was so heavy it didn't shift at first. Even when it did start
280 to scrape along the deck, Samuel worried it was so heavy it would not float […].
Gideon joined[74] them, grabbing the beam near the middle, but Samuel's back still sang with pain[75] by the time they reached the end of the wharf.
285 'We need to jump in after it right away, before it floats off without us,' he said.
'How deep is it?' Gideon said.
'One way to find out.'
Samuel pushed the end of the beam over the
290 edge. Its weight pulled the rest of the beam after it. As it plunged[76] into the river it shot an almighty splash into the air. Filthy, stinking water drenched[77] the three of them.
Samuel didn't hesitate. As soon as he saw the
295 beam bob to the surface, as if it was as light as a twig[78], he leapt[79] in. Catherine and Gideon jumped in after him.
After flailing for a moment, each of them hugged their arms around the beam, and then it started
310 carrying them down the river, away from the wharf, away from the fire.

---

70 **dinghy** [ˈdɪŋi] kleines Boot · 71 **(to) eddy** [ˈedi] wirbeln, strudeln · 72 **charred** [ˈtʃɑːd] verkohlt · 73 **beam** [biːm] Balken *(aus Holz)* · 74 **(to) join sb.** sich jm. anschließen · 75 **(to) sing with pain** [sɪŋ] *(jm.)* starke Schmerzen bereiten · 76 **(to) plunge** [plʌndʒ] hineinspringen · 77 **(to) drench** [drent ] durchnässen · 78 **twig** [twɪg] Zweig · 79 **(to) leap** [liːp], **leapt, leap**t [lept] springen

## 1 👥 What's it all about?

a) After you have all read the story alone, work in groups of four. Each group member sums up one part of the story:
A: lines 1–67        B: lines 68–135
C: lines 136–223     D: lines 224–311
Read your part again carefully. Look back at p. 20 for help on how to sum up a text.
➜ *SF 8: Summing up a text (p. 123)*

b) Swap what you have written with another member of your group. Read through your partner's work and give them feedback. Make corrections or changes to your own work.

**EXTRA** Join your work together and display it in class. Read some of the other groups' work.

## 2 👥 The characters

a) Work in your group of four again. Each choose one of the four characters in the story: Sam, Catherine, Gideon, Uncle Jack. Make notes on your character so that you can:
- describe them (what they look like, how they feel, what kind of person they are, how old, …)
- say what their relationship to the other characters is.

Choose one or two short quotes from the story that support your ideas about them. Write down the lines of your quotes.

b) Use your notes to tell the others in your group about your character.

## 3 Before and after ✏️

**You choose** a) or b). Write about 160 words.

a) Write what you think happened in the story before Catherine shouted "It's a trap!" (l. 20)

b) Write what you think will happen next in the story as they float down the River Thames.

➜ **Workbook** 23 (p. 17)

# 1 Your task

## Planning a class trip to London

Work in a team to plan and put together a programme for a five-day class trip to London.

### STEP 1
Discuss and agree on what needs to go into your programme. Here are some ideas:
- travel (how to get to and from London, how to travel around London, …)
- where to stay in London (where, what type, …)
- itinerary (where to go, what to see & do – mornings, afternoons, evenings)
- educational activities, entertainment
- …

### STEP 2
Decide what format your programme will take:
- poster
- digital presentation
- brochure
- …

### STEP 3
Agree on who is doing what (your roles) and set a realistic timetable before you begin.
- research
- graphics/layout
- …
- language
- coordinator

➡ SF 17: Teamwork (p. 129)

### STEP 4
Do some research and find all the information you will need to put your programme together.

➡ SF 18: Finding information online (Internet research) (p. 130)

### STEP 5
Organize all your information and ideas and put together your programme.

➡ SF 20: Putting a page together (p. 130)
➡ SF 22: Giving a good presentation (p. 132)

### STEP 6
Display or present your programme to your class.

### STEP 7
Go to pp. 275 – 276 and look at some tips on how to do better. Give feedback:
a) in your group about how your teamwork went.
b) to other groups about their programmes.

➡ SF 23: Giving feedback (p. 133)

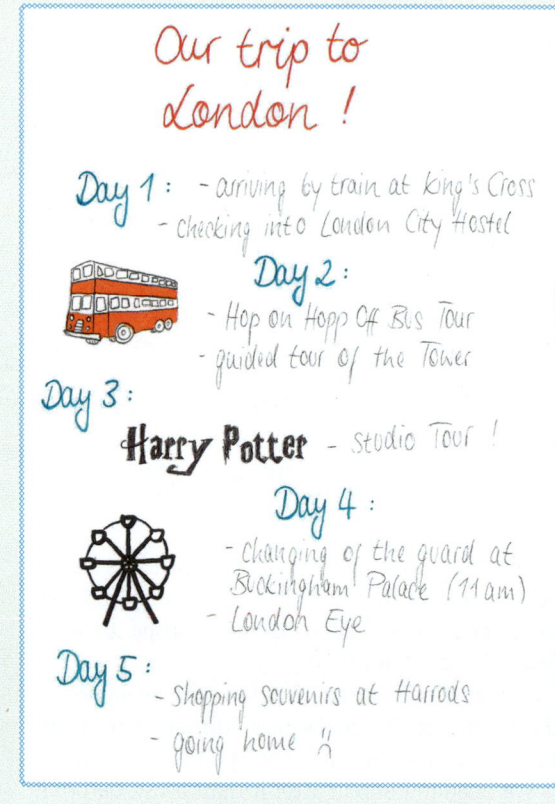

**Thursday, 11 am**

Watching the changing of the guard at Buckingham Palace

# Checkpoint 1

## 1 London quiz

Do the London quiz and see how well you know this great city.

a) Complete the missing information.
1 Do you have a T-shirt ... isn't too expensive?
2 London's tallest building is called ...
3 London was destroyed by a Great Fire in ...
4 The fire started in a street called ...
5 In Victorian London the sun was often hidden by ...
6 The financial centre of London is known as ...
7 The bridge over the Thames that opens for ships is ...
8 The church you visit to whisper to your friends is called ...

b) Name the places in pictures A–D.

c) Answer the questions.
1 Where should you sit on a London bus for the best view of the city?
2 What's the address of the Walkie-Talkie building?
3 Name a famous singer who grew up in Brixton.
4 What was built in Brixton in 1816?
5 When did lots of people from the Caribbean start coming to London?

## 2 Paraphrases

a) Sometimes you have to describe words: match the right words to these paraphrases and write them down.
1 It's the place where laws are made.
2 Someone who considers their country the best and better than all others.
3 A country that is owned and ruled by another country.
4 The idea that people from different cultures can live happily together.
5 A person who has come from somewhere else to live in a country.

b) Write English paraphrases for these words.
1 religion   2 foreigner   3 diversity   4 dialect   5 inhabitant   6 population

c) Use six words from a) and b) and write about your own town/area.

## 3 Word families

Complete the text about Westminster with a form of the words in the box. You can use a noun, a verb or an adjective.

> action • attraction • finance • government • invitation • organization • politics (x2) • possibility • tradition

The City is London's [1]... centre but another part of London is the centre of British [2]... : Westminster. The Houses of Parliament, which [3]... many tourists, are next to Westminster Bridge. All the important [4]... buildings, like 10 Downing Street, are close by too. It is not [5]... to visit Downing Street but you can take an [6]... tour of the Houses of Parliament. Visitors are even [7]... to watch the Members of Parliament in [8]... from the Commons public gallery. The British find it important to have a [9]... system that involves everyone. However, they also have a House of Lords and a monarch, which some people say are old-fashioned [10]... .

# 1 Checkpoint

## 4 Heathrow (Simple present passive)

Use the information and the simple present passive to write about Heathrow Airport, the biggest of London's five airports.

1. London · visit · over 19 million international tourists · a year
   *London is visited by …*
2. Millions of them · welcome to London · at Heathrow Airport
3. 1400 flights · manage · there every day
4. Over 60,000 cups of tea and coffee · sell · a day
5. 76,000 people · employ · at the airport
6. 53 million bags · check · a year
7. The airport · close to flights · from 11:30pm to 04:30am

## 5 London buildings (Simple past passive)

Use the information and the simple past passive to write about famous London buildings.

1. The old St Paul's Cathedral · burn · Great Fire of London · 1666
2. The new St Paul's · design · Christopher Wren
3. It · finish · 1710
4. Big Ben clock tower · open · 1859
5. Its biggest bell, Big Ben · make · in Whitechapel · and pull up tower · 1858
6. Some newer London buildings · give nicknames · after · build
7. The Shard · design · Renzo Piano · start · 2009 · and complete · 2012
8. 20 Fenchurch St · give · the nickname the Walkie-Talkie · finish · 2014 · and its Sky Garden · open to public · January 2015

## 6 MIXED BAG Fire, fire!

Complete the text about an important event in London with the right words or phrases.

London …¹ always been cool. After it … …² by the Romans and a bridge … …³ across the Thames, it …⁴ a hub for people …⁵ all over Britannia and …⁶ bigger and …⁷. Change was usually quite …⁸ but sometimes it came …⁹ London … …¹⁰ several times …¹¹ great fires. Everyone has heard of the … … …¹² London of 1666 but …¹³ parts of the city … …¹⁴ by fire much …¹⁵. In 60 CE the Roman city …¹⁶ b…¹⁷ to the ground …¹⁸ the Iceni, a tribe … …¹⁹ by Queen Boudicca. Roman Londinium b …²⁰ again in 122 CE. …²¹ 675 the cathedral … …²² by fire and f …²³ d …²⁴ large parts of London again in 1087, 1185 and 1212.
London …²⁵ to grow steadily …²⁶ all this time. After every fire, the city … …²⁷ r…²⁸ again, until a small Roman fort that w …²⁹ b…³⁰ on the mud next to a r…³¹ r…³² became one of the l…³³ and … …³⁴ cities …³⁵ earth.

## B

## 7 Then and now

I walk down those two connected London streets where I grew up and wonder, "Where have the children gone?"

Of course, there are not so many children now and there are none out on these streets where our lives took place. The whole area was somewhere to play for us. We played football in winter right across the street, with the gate to our back garden as one goal and the neighbours' wall opposite the other.
Summer was time for cricket and we painted a wicket on the wall and played with a tennis ball.
A hide-and-seek game called *Rescue* with lots of shouting was another favourite for our gang.
Our games were only seldom interrupted by a car moving slowly down the street, with just single cars parked here and there. Today, long lines of cars are parked along both sides. No chance to play football or cricket here.

On my walk up and down on a warm, sunny day, I do not meet a single kid or hear a child's voice.
The only sounds are the birds in the trees and the cars that pass by every twenty seconds or so.
It isn't a school day, so where are they all? In the parks? Hanging out in the high street up the road?
Or are they all at home, and if so, why?

# Checkpoint 1

a) Read the text and choose the right answers.
1. The writer is   **a)** a child.   **b)** an older person.   **c)** answer not in text.
2. The streets the writer describes are now   **a)** full of children.   **b)** full of cars.   **c)** somewhere to play.
3. The writer mostly played in the   **a)** back garden.   **b)** streets.   **c)** summer.
4. In the streets today, the writer hears   **a)** a child's voice.   **b)** birds and cars.   **c)** shouts.
5. It is hard to play sports in these streets now because of
   **a)** the birds.   **b)** the neighbours.   **c)** the parked cars.

b) In the text, find 3 or 4 reasons why the writer thinks there are no children on the streets.

c) Complete the sentences with the correct information: **1** We played … **2** *Rescue* … **3** The games …

d) Think of a good title for the text. Also think of two sub-headings for the text and write where they should go (before paragraph number …, etc.)

## 8 Famous diaries

Du bist ein/e Austauschschüler/in in London. Deine Klasse fängt gerade mit einem Projekt an: ‚Famous diaries'. Ihr werdet einige historisch wichtigen Tagebücher zusammen recherchieren und vorstellen. Zuerst hat jede/r die Aufgabe, ein spannendes Tagebuch zu finden und kurz der Klasse vorzustellen.

Die Lehrerin hat folgende Anweisungen gegeben:
- Say who wrote the diary and when.
- Tell us what interesting things happened at that time in history.
- Explain why the writer himself/herself was interesting.

Du hast diesen Text in einem Reiseführer gesehen und findest ihn spannend.
Mache dir Notizen und schreibe dann einen kurzen Text auf Englisch, den du der Klasse präsentieren kannst. Dein Ziel ist es, dass das Tagebuch von Samuel Pepys Teil des Klassenprojektes wird.

**Seething Lane**

*Diese enge Gasse kann man übersehen und sehr schön ist sie nicht, doch der Mann, der da 1666 nachts von seinem Dienstmädchen geweckt wurde,* 5 *hinterließ uns eins der wichtigsten Zeitdokumente der britischen Geschichte. Das Dienstmädchen weckte ihn, um zu erzählen, dass ein riesiges Feuer in der Nähe brannte. Der Mann war Samuel Pepys, der das vielleicht berühmteste Tagebuch in der* 10 *englischen Sprache geschrieben hat.*
*Geboren am 23 Februar 1633, war Pepys 1665 Zeuge der Großen Pest von London sowie des großen Brandes im darauffolgenden Jahr. Seine Aufzeichnungen sind eine unersetzliche Quelle für* 15 *die Zeitgeschichte sowie für das Alltagsleben in London. Das Tagebuch führte er von 1660 bis 1669. Eine Berühmtheit oder ein großer Machthaber war er nicht, hatte aber als Staatsekretär im Marineamt und Abgeordneter des* 20 *englischen Unterhauses einen Einblick in die politischen Entwicklungen seiner Zeit. In den Tagebüchern ging es ihm vor allem um seine individuelle Geschichte. Deswegen schildert er nicht nur z.B. große politische Ereignisse, sondern auch* 25 *ehrlich und unverfälscht seine Liebschaften und die Streitereien mit seiner Ehefrau Elizabeth.*
*Pepys Haus existiert nicht mehr, aber an der Ecke Seething Lane und Pepys Street steht seine Hauskirche Saint Olave, eines der wenigen noch* 30 *stehenden mittelalterlichen Gebäude Londons. Dort ist er begraben. Ein anderer literarischer Riese, Charles Dickens, nannte die Kirche Saint Ghastly Grim (etwa ‚Sankt Grausig Grimmig') wegen der Totenköpfe und Knochen am Tor zum Kirchhof, die* 35 *heute noch gut erhalten sind. Einige Schritte südlich der Kirche in Seething Lane Garden steht ein Denkmal für Samuel Pepys.*

# Access to cultures

# Guy Fawkes: Man and mask

## Jigsaw

a) Work in groups of four. The parts of this text (A–D) are not in the right order. Each student reads one part (A–D) of the text and takes notes on the important information.

b) Together find the links between the texts and decide on the best order for them.

c) Write a text (about 150–200 words) in English and explain how the image of someone who planned to blow up Parliament has become a symbol of resistance around the world.

### A  Guy Fawkes Night

Guy Fawkes wasn't the leader of the Gunpowder Plot, but he was its most famous conspirator. After all, he was caught under the Houses of Parliament with the gunpowder. That is why the November 5th tradition is named after him, although it has other names too: *Bonfire Night* or *Fireworks Night*. The tradition started with a 1606 law. Ever since, on Guy Fawkes Night, people have commemorated the discovery of the Catholic plot. Fireworks are let off and "guys" are burnt on bonfires.
In the weeks before November 5th children make these guys from newspaper, old clothes and a mask. They sit on the streets with their guy and ask for money to buy fireworks. "Penny for the guy" or "Please to remember/ The fifth of November" are the magic words which make people part with their money.
The idea is that when people burn the guy on the bonfire, they are celebrating the fact that the Gunpowder Plot was stopped. If that is true, then why has Guy Fawkes become such a popular figure of protest today?

*A 'guy' waiting on a bonfire*

### B  V for Vendetta

You've probably seen this mask before. It's like the Guy Fawkes mask that first appeared in a graphic novel called *V for Vendetta*. The story goes like this: after a nuclear war, the UK has become a fascist state under the government of Adam Susan. V, a rebel in a Guy Fawkes mask, and a young woman, Evey, use computer hacking and explosives in a plot to destroy the government. Like Guy Fawkes, V plots against the government, but it is clearly a terrible government that he wants to destroy.
The graphic novel was a great success and it became even more famous when a film of it, with Hugo Weaving and Natalie Portman as V and Evey, was made in 2005.

## C Protest!

Now the V for Vendetta Guy Fawkes mask has become the symbol of protesters all over the world. The trend was started by *Anonymous*, the hacktivist (if you admire them) or hacker group (if you don't). When they first came out into the real world to protest, they needed something that would protect their identities. They chose the V for Vendetta Guy Fawkes mask.

Since then, the mask has become a symbol of resistance all over the world and is worn by people in protest movements like Occupy, Wikileaks or the Arab Spring.

Alan Moore, the author of V for Vendetta, told the Guardian newspaper that he finds it very strange that his character V has somehow escaped from his book and entered the real world.

*Million Mask March, London 2015*

## D The Gunpowder Plot

On the night of November 4 to November 5, 1605, Guy Fawkes was discovered in a cellar under the Houses of Parliament. He gave his name as John Johnson.

Why would he do that? Well, he wasn't alone in the cellar. Below piles of wood, 36 barrels of gunpowder were hidden, enough to completely destroy the Houses of Parliament.

The attack was planned for the State Opening of Parliament on November 5. If Fawkes could blow up Parliament, he could kill King James I and many of the most important and powerful people in the country.

But – why would he do that? Well, religion was very important in Europe at that time. Protestants and Catholics had been fighting wars ever since protestants left the Catholic church during the Reformation in the 16th Century. Under King James, Great Britain was a protestant country, but Guy Fawkes was a Catholic.

Fawkes hadn't planned this alone. After he was arrested, he was taken to the Tower of London and tortured till he gave the names of the other conspirators.

Their plan was: kill the King and all the important protestants, start a rebellion and make the King's 9-year-old daughter Queen of a new Catholic Britain.

Of course, their plan did not work and things ended badly for the plotters. Some were killed when they were being arrested. The others, like Guy Fawkes, were dragged through the streets and executed. Then their heads were put on pikes for all to see.

*The Gunpowder plot conspirators*

➡ **Workbook** 1–4 (pp. 60-61)

# Kaleidoscope  Canada                                    EXTRA

## 1 A first look

Study the map. Use also the key and the small maps below.

Point out states, cities, mountains, water, etc. and talk about Canada.

You can watch a film about Canada.

## 2 Land and people

a) Look at the five pictures.
Say what you already know about the topics.

1 Cities
2 Geography
3 Indigenous people
4 Sports
5 Animals

b) Write down one topic that interests you most.
What would you like to find out about your topic?

Compare your ideas.

## 3 A Canada album

Each student will make one page for the album.

a) Choose your topic, e.g.:
*a Canadian city, a region of Canada, big rivers, the climate, sports …*

You can watch the film again to get ideas.

b) Now follow these steps:
- Agree with your teacher when your page should be finished.
- Collect information and pictures.
- Write your text(s).
- Make your page for the class album.

➡ SF 4, 5, 18–20 (pp. 119–120, 130–131)

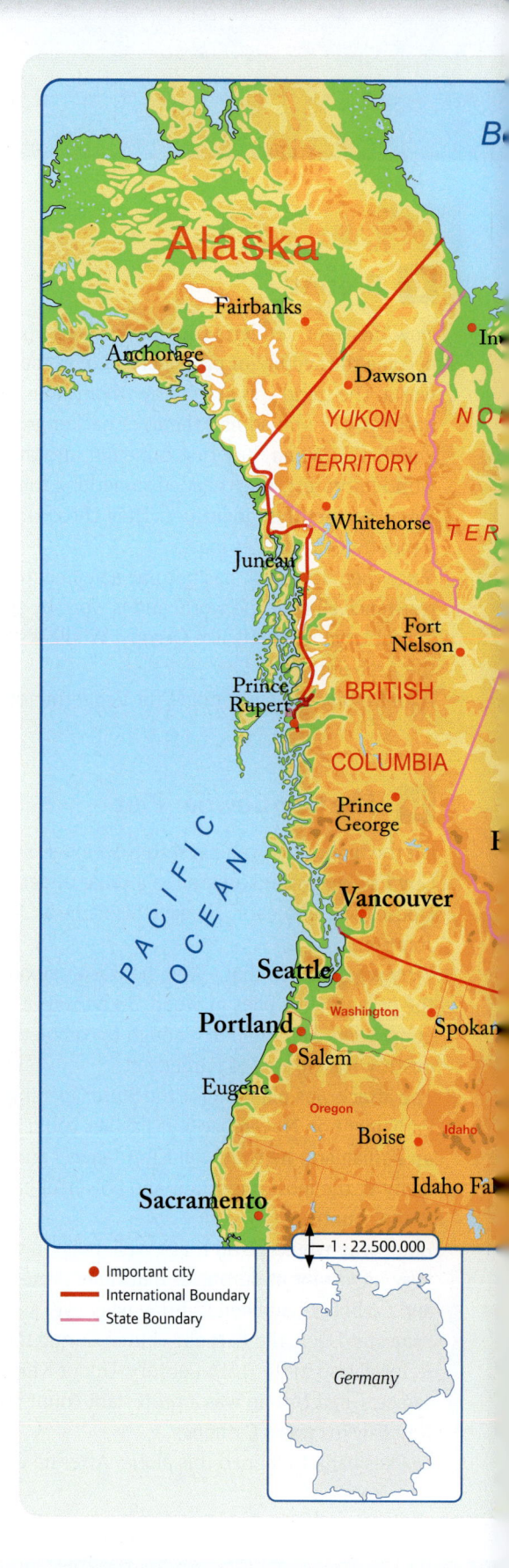

# Kaleidoscope

EXTRA

**Climate Zones**
- Polar and Subpolar Zone
- Temperate Zone
- Subtropical Zone
- Tropical Zone

**Languages**
- English
- French
- Native languages
- Spanish

thirty-seven 37

# 2 Unit

# Canada

YUKON
NORTHWEST TERRITORIES
NUNAVUT
BRITISH COLUMBIA
ALBERTA
SASKATCHEWAN
MANITOBA
ONTARIO
QUEBEC
NEWFOUNDLAND AND LABRADOR
PRINCE EDWARD ISLAND
NOVA SCOTIA
NEW BRUNSWICK

# Unit 2

## 1 Images of Canada

👥 Work in groups. Look closely at each of the photos and the map of Canada.

Discuss your ideas about what the pictures show about Canada and where they were taken.

| ice skating rink · parka · polar bears · lumberjack competition |
| --- |
| I think this photo was taken … · The people in this photo are … |

## 2 Voices of Canada 🎧

a) Listen and match what you hear to the pictures. Take notes as you listen.

b) 👥 Using your notes, agree on what you have learned.

c) 👥 Write a list of questions that you have about what you see in the pictures or about Canada in general.

## 3 Collecting information: A KWL chart

a) 👥 With your group, create a big chart with these headings:

| K: What we know now | W: What we want to know | L: What we have learned |
| --- | --- | --- |
| … | … | … |

b) 👥 Use your results from 2b) and 2c) and enter them in the first and second columns of the chart under "What we know now" and "What we want to know".

c) 👥 Join another group. Compare the information you've added to your charts. Add information you have learned from the other group.

d) Hang the KWL chart on the classroom wall. Use it throughout the unit to collect and organize information about Canada. ➡ **Workbook** *1 (p. 22)*

> **Your task**
>
> **At the end of this unit:** You will put together and film a sportscast with your class about a Canadian youth hockey tournament.

## 2  Part A

### 1 Lauren's blog: The eager beaver

Alyssa's friend Lauren plays hockey for her high school team. Both the boys' and girls' teams will travel to Quebec City to compete in the All-Canada Ice Hockey tournament.

Look at the photos and say which ones you think Lauren took during her trip. Then read the text.

November 23
Hey Riverside high schoolers, friends and parents, Lauren here! I can't believe that we will be on the bus in 10 hours. We'll finally be on our way to
5 Quebec City! Yep! It's really happening! And it's all because of your support. You've bought cake at our bake sales and cheered for us at our games. You've celebrated us when we won and lifted our spirits when we lost. You've made this trip
10 possible … I don't know how to thank you – Oh, wait, yes I do! I've decided to write this blog so you can follow us on our trip. Go Ottawa Beavers! Time to go to bed – more tomorrow! If I don't get some sleep, I'll be a very tired beaver tomorrow.

15 November 24
Hey! We've been on the bus for two hours … five and a half hours to go. We're having a great time! We've been singing that Joni Mitchell song: I drew a map of Canada with your face drawn on it twice
20 … Oh Ottawa! I could drink a case of you, and still be on my feet – I would still be on my feet.
The bus has Internet, so I'm posting this from my bus seat. I'm sitting next to Christopher. He's using FaceApp and drawing weird pictures of
25 everybody: turning the kids into old people and Coach into a baby! Hahaha! We also got into a big argument about whether hockey teams should be coed. Justin said that the girls wouldn't be able to keep up with the boys on the team. Really????
30 I've played with my brothers for as long as I can remember – sometimes I'm faster than them! Maddie thinks the main problem is that all the Bantam teams would need to go coed at the same time to make the matches fair. What do you
35 think? Write your comments below!

This is the entrance to Quebec City – St. Louis Gate. The old city Vieux-Québec has a wall around it … welcome to the 17th century! At the hostel, we're sharing a floor with two other teams – a local team from Granby, Quebec, and a team from 40 Nunavik. Maddie and I were in the game room. Two boys were playing foosball … They looked like they were having a lot of fun, so of course we joined them. Antoine is from the nearby town of Granby. He speaks English with a French accent. 45 I didn't know this: kids in primary and middle school in Quebec are taught in French. English is Antoine's second language. The other boy, Nukilik, comes from Kuujjuaq, which is about 1300 km north of Quebec City. Nukilik's team came by 50 plane because there are no main roads from there to here.
He showed us the coolest photos of the Aurora Borealis on his phone. He says he sees them every year! 55

Nukilik is Inuit and his native language is Inuktitut. He taught us how to say "How are you, my name is …" and "Thank you."

I asked Nukilik about igloos. I know that's a stereotype, but I was curious. He hasn't ever slept in one, but last year he helped an elder in his community to build one.

Nukilik was mostly interested in looking at the photos we had on our phones and listening to our playlists. We got him to laugh when we sang along with some of the songs he has on his phone. Nukilik (his name means 'the strong one') suddenly asked me a funny question. He said, "What's the strangest thing you've ever eaten?" I thought about it and said, "Hmm … A birthday cake with blue and green marshmallow frosting?" Then he told us his favorite food is Maktak, which is frozen whale skin and blubber. (Mmmm!). In his region, people eat lots of fish, seal and caribou.

All this talk about food made us really hungry, so we shared a big plate of poutine with Antoine and Nukilik. I guess you don't know what poutine is? It's French fries – or frites, as the Québecois say – served with fried cheese curds and gravy. It was delicious, but ugh! I'm soooo full!

## 2 Jigsaw reading

a) Work in groups of three. Each student reads one of these parts of Lauren's blog again.
ll. 36–47 · ll. 47–62 · ll. 63–81
Identify new information about Canada and its people. Explain to your group what you have found out.

b) Add the new information about Canada to the third column of your KWL chart.
If any of the information you've collected answers a question from the 2nd column of the KWL chart, make a visible link from the question to the information.

## 3 Alyssa's friend Lauren

a) Write a profile of Lauren (about 100 words).
**More help** ➔ *(p. 108)*

b) Read your profile to your group.

c) Talk about the style of Lauren's blog. What words would you use to describe it? For example, is her blog formal or informal? Find sentences in the text for your answers.
**More help** ➔ *(p. 108)*

*I think Lauren uses a personal style …*

*Yeah, it's like she's talking to you directly … it's also funny, …*

➔ **Workbook** *2 (p. 23)*

## 4 Write a blog post

Are you a member of a school club? Have you recently been on a class trip?
Write a blog post (about 100 words) about a recent event, game or trip you've taken part in.

**Early finisher** ➔ *(p. 112)*

# 2 Part A Practice

## 1 WORDS Strong or weak? (Opposites)

a) Find the opposites in the boxes. Make a list.
strong – weak
hungry –

b) 👥 Partner A: Cover your list from a).
Partner B: Say a word from the list.
Partner A: Say the opposite.
Swap after eight words.

c) Choose six pairs from a) and write sentences about Lauren, Nukilik or Antoine.
Nukilik's legs are strong from playing hockey every day.

> entrance · above · nearby · native · same ·
> curious · (strong) · argument · delicious · possible ·
> weird · fair · hungry · fast · funny ·
> lie down · rude
>
> polite · get up · full · unfair ·
> below · normal · foreign · agreement · bad ·
> sad · exit · far · slow · not interested · (weak)
> different · impossible

➜ Workbook 3 (p. 24)

## 2 REVISION We will be on the bus in ten hours … (*will*-future)

a) Write down where you think your partner will be in thirty minutes, two hours and ten hours and the jobs and hobbies they will do in ten and thirty years.

b) 👥 Read your partner's sentences about you, correct them and read the corrected version back to your partner.

➜ GF 5: The will-future (p. 141)

*In ten years you will be a doctor and in your free time you'll go mountain climbing.*

## 3 REVISION Consequences (Conditional sentences type I, II and III)

Complete the conditional sentences in the text about Lauren.

It is the night before Lauren's trip to Quebec City and she is excited but she has to go to bed. If she doesn't get some sleep, she ¹… very tired tomorrow. It would be a pity if her team ²… (lose) games just because players were tired. Lauren has trained hard for the ice hockey tournament. If she ³… (not) so hard, she wouldn't have got a place on the team. Now she has to play very well. The team's fans would be sad if they ⁴… badly. The fans cheered at games and bought cakes to support the team and they ⁵… (give) even more support if there had been a chance to. Lauren knows that the trip will be a lot of fun even if she ⁶… (not win) games but that is not what she wants. It ⁷… best if her team won all their matches but that probably won't happen. They just have to do their best, and that will only work if Lauren soon ⁸… asleep!

➜ GF 6: Conditional sentences (pp. 141 – 142)

➜ Workbook 4 (p. 25)

## Part A Practice 2

### 4 REVISION What should I take? (Modal verbs)

The Riverdale High School hockey coach sent a packing list home with each student on the team.

a) Read the list and write sentences which say what you *mustn't or needn't* bring.

b) 👥 Compare your sentences and make corrections if necessary.

c) Now write what you think might happen if they pack something they mustn't or needn't bring.

d) 👥 Compare your sentences with your partner.

➡ Workbook 5 (p. 25) ➡ GF 7: Modal verbs (p. 143)

**Packing list**
- warm jacket
- gloves and hat
- clothes for four days
- snacks / card games for the trip (optional)
- no unhealthy sweets
- teddy bear (optional)
- no video games, DVDs, etc.
- hockey kit
- money to spend: no more than $10/day
- drink and lunch for 7-hour bus trip (please pack enough – kids get hungry!)

### 5 REVISION Did you know? (Present perfect simple with *since/for*)

a) Use the table and write sentences about Lauren, Nukilik, Antoine and Quebec City.
   Be careful: sometimes you need *for* or *since*.
   1 Antoine has lived in Granby all his life.
   2 Lauren has been in Quebec City for a couple of days.

b) 👥 Form questions about the three friends from the table and let your partner find the right answers.

c) 👥 Read the questions. Write down how you think your partner will answer them. Then ask the questions. Were you right?
   1 How long have you known how to swim?
   2 How long have you lived in this town?

| Who/where | What | How long? |
|---|---|---|
| Lauren | play hockey | a few years |
| Antoine | eat poutine | many times |
| Nukilik | study in English | all his life |
| The Canadian kids | be in Quebec City | a long time |
| | be on the bus | the 2nd grade |
| | stay in the hostel | 2010 |
| | play cards | yesterday |
| | know each other | a couple of days |

➡ GF 8: The present perfect (p. 143) ➡ Workbook 6 (p. 26)

### 6 Education for Inuit (Subject-verb agreement)

Nukilik tells Lauren about education for people from his home. Complete the sentences with the correct form of the verbs. In some sentences, there are two possible answers.

Nukilik's family ¹… (want) to stay in Nunavik but he doesn't know how to plan a future there. Economics ²… (be) his favourite subject and he wants to study it later on. His team ³… (be) having a lot of fun in Quebec City and he thinks it might be a good place to go to university. Nukilik says that in the past, Canadian politics ⁴… (be) not on the side of Inuit students but the news ⁵… (have) been better in the last years. Time and money have been given to get good education for Inuit students. The government ⁶… (be) working to include Canadians of all backgrounds in high-quality education but that is not a simple project.

➡ Workbook 7 (p. 26)

> **Language help**
>
> - **Group nouns:** *the government / the family / a band* can be followed by a singular or plural verb depending on whether we are thinking of <u>one unit</u> (*the government **has** been successful …*) or <u>a group of individuals</u> (*the government **are** arguing about …*).
> There is an important exception: the word *Police* is always plural: *The police **are** looking for …*
> - **Singular nouns** ending in **-s**: *physics / economics / the news / politic* take singular verbs: *Maths **is** an interesting subject.*
>
> ➡ GF 9: Subject-verb agreement (p. 144)

forty-three 43

# 2 The digital compass — Internet research

You need to find out about 'coed high school sports'.
On this page you can find three internet skills that will help you to get information you need.

## 1 SEARCHING FOR A TOPIC

- An internet search can bring thousands of results.

a) Explain in what way the search engine settings in A will affect your results.

**A**

| Sprache: | Englisch |
| --- | --- |
| Land: | Kanada |

b) Look at the three searches in B. Which keywords will give you the most useful results?

**B**
- 🔍 girls boys sports →
- 🔍 coed high school →
- 🔍 coed sports high school →

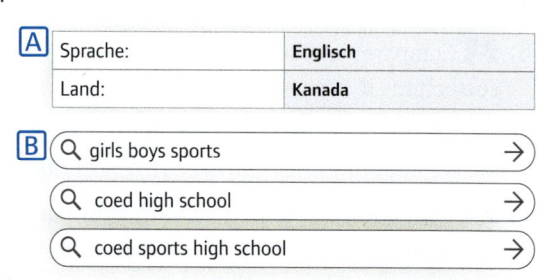

c) Write down three tips for effective searches.

## 2 CHOOSING THE BEST SEARCH RESULTS

- When you search, you get a list of site descriptions. <u>Read site descriptions carefully</u> before opening a site.

a) Compare the top two site descriptions from your search. Say which site you would click first and why.

> ### Pros of Coed Sports Teams
> https://teamsports.org/7209/sports/pros-of-coed-sports-teams.html
> Mai 23, 2018 - This is often the case for high school sports. A very important argument for **coed school sports** is that …
>
> ### Should Sports be coed?
> https://sportstimes.com/1464/sports/learning/should-sports-be-coed.html
> Oct 20, 2016 - Is it OK that women and girls compete against men and boys in **high school**?

- When you open a website, <u>skim the first page</u> to check that it has the information you need.
- <u>Check where information comes from</u> before you decide to use it.

b) Say where you would click to check who is responsible for the website you are using.

| NEWS | OPINIONS | FEATURES | **SPORTS** | QUIZZES | CLUBS | ARCHIVES | ABOUT US |

c) Suggest other ways to check if a website is reliable.
➡ *SF 18: Internet research (p. 130)*

## 3 SAVING INFORMATION YOU FIND

- Finding information can take time. So <u>add websites to your bookmarks</u> if you wish to use them.

On p. 45 you will be writing a comment on the theme of coed high school sports. Find two websites that have useful information by following the guidelines on this page.

➡ *Workbook 8 (p. 26)*

## 8 STUDY SKILLS  Writing a comment

In a comment you express your opinion about a topic you feel is important.
- Before you write, it is important to collect ideas, form your opinion and organize your content.
- There are many expressions and phrases that can help you to organize and present the ideas.
- You should support your point of view with a clear argument, facts and statistics.

Write a comment on this issue:
*Should high school sports be coed?*

a) Brainstorm ideas to find out how you feel about the issue. Make two lists:

| My own experience | Questions |
|---|---|
| - I've seen girls who can run as fast as boys | - Are boys more competitive than girls? |

b) Do research on the internet: Use what you have learned on p. 44 and try to find the answers to your questions.
Has the information you've found changed your opinion?
Write down your opinion in one or two sentences.

c) Look at the argumentative text structure and the expressions that start each paragraph.

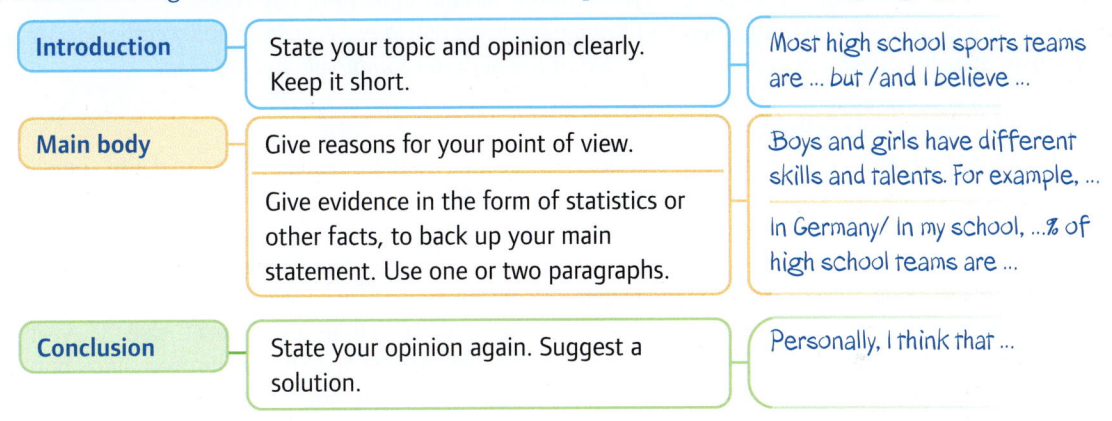

| Introduction | State your topic and opinion clearly. Keep it short. | Most high school sports teams are … but / and I believe … |
|---|---|---|
| Main body | Give reasons for your point of view. | Boys and girls have different skills and talents. For example, … |
| | Give evidence in the form of statistics or other facts, to back up your main statement. Use one or two paragraphs. | In Germany / In my school, …% of high school teams are … |
| Conclusion | State your opinion again. Suggest a solution. | Personally, I think that … |

How else could you start each paragraph? Choose an alternative.

After thinking carefully about the issue, …, • Although many people believe …, in reality, … • In my opinion … • It is often said that …, but … • There is really no evidence to support the idea that … • Some people think that … • I'd like to see … change. • It's my hope that in the future … • I think that it would be a good thing if … • I think all schools should …

d) Now write your text. You may need language to:
- talk about advantages or disadvantages:
  - A big advantage/disadvantage of … is …
  - Another/The biggest advantage/disadvantage is …
- make comparisons:
  - … is more important than …
- give examples:
  - For example, … • This is clear because …
- order arguments or examples:
  - In the first place, … • Firstly,/Secondly,/Thirdly, … • Finally, …
- make a conclusion:
  - I believe that …, • I think … should / shouldn't … • I'd like to see … I hope that in the future …, • We need to change …

e) Read your partner's text and give feedback.

→ SF 23: Giving feedback (p. 133)  → SF 7: Writing a comment (p. 122)  → Workbook 9–10 (p. 27)

## 2 Part B

### 1 The eager beaver: DAY 2 – too many rules

November 23 – Everything has been great – we won our first game! Go Beavers!!!! Nukilik showed me this newspaper article. He knows some of the kids who did this trek. He wants to go on it next year.

## Nunavik teens on 90-km trek across frozen tundra

'Dream coming true,' says 1 teen skier inspired by 4 Quebecers' 2014 trek from Mont-Tremblant to Kuujjuaq
by Catou MacKinnon · CBC News ·

Thirty-four teenagers from four villages in Quebec's Inuit territory of Nunavik set out on cross-country skis late last week across the frozen tundra, pulling their gear behind them in sleds – plastic versions of the traditional komatik.
One group, made up of high school students from Tasiujaq and Kuujjuarapik, left Thursday. A second group, students from Kuujjuaq and Kangirsuk, left a day later because of bad weather. They plan to meet Monday in Aupaluk, a village that lies between Kangirsuk and Tasiujaq.

### Inspired by Karibu expedition

The Inuit teens call themselves the Young Karibus. The organizer of the expedition, French teacher Valérie Raymond, said students were inspired after witnessing four Quebecers complete a 2,000-kilometre trek from Mont-Tremblant to Kuujjuaq two years ago.

That expedition — called Karibu — recreated for the first time a 1980 trip from the south to Fort Chimo, since renamed Kuujjuaq.

"I really wanted to be a part of this, it looked like a great experience," said Karina Gordon-Dorais, a 14-year-old from Kuujjuaq who said she's looking forward to meeting teenagers from other villages. "I've always wanted to go on an expedition, so this is like something of my dream coming true."

Gordon-Dorais and her fellow Young Karibus spent months training, in the dark after school, for the longest cross-country ski trip of their lives, over challenging terrain.

### New to skis

On a recent Saturday morning in March, a half dozen of the students met in the main hall of Kuujjuaq's Jaanimmarik High School to pack their gear, getting ready to head out for a one-night practice camping trip.

Joshua Nathan Willie Kettler told CBC he signed up after friends took part in the first such trip last year.

At the time, he'd only ever been on cross-country skis once.

"I kind of fell a few times," said 15-year-old Kettler, adding that he'd improved since but was still expecting a tough haul.

"It's probably going to be hard and cold, and we'll miss the internet there," Willie Kettler said. "But it's going to be fun."

### No looking back

Raymond said for this second expedition, a 90-kilometre trek over four days, five times more students signed up than last year.

"It's a big challenge," said Raymond. There is no protection from the wind because of the lack of trees and hilly terrain.

"Last year, the first day was by far the hardest day," she said. "You're not too far from the village, and they can just look back … and go home." She said she sat the students down and encouraged them to take the trip one day at a time — even half a day at a time.

## 'This is school, too'

65 "My goal is to show them education and school under a new lens," said Raymond. "I keep telling them, this is school too."

The teenagers have to learn how to interact with each other in less than ideal situations.

70 "We're tired, frustrated, it's not easy to be polite with each other," she said.

Raymond said the trip helps teach perseverance. She recalled one student last year who developed blisters on the first day, yet she made it through 75 the whole trip.

When the student was having trouble with mathematics, Raymond suggested thinking about it as a blister: something she could suffer and work through.

---

80 A 90-km ski trip instead of school sounds great! I'd join the group immediately.

Antoine, Nukilik, Maddie and I are having a second foosball tournament in the game room. We are leading 2 games to 0! Nukilik wants me to visit him next winter. I'll have to ask my 85 parents … I've also been invited to Granby! It's time to start those donut bake sales again!!

The only bad part are all the rules at the hostel. There is one sign in the room and one in the bathroom:

Looks like the showers haven't been cleaned for years, so 90 I don't want to spend much time there anyway!

Maddie has put up another rule: "Smelly socks should not be left on the floor, or they will be thrown away!" That's the only rule I agree with!

**HOUSE RULES**
1. All rooms must be vacated by 8 am.
2. No more than 5 guests can be in a room at one time.
3. Music can be played only until 7 pm.
4. Groups should not meet in the corridors or fire stairs.
5. Guests not respecting these rules will be fined!

**Showers should not be no longer than five minutes!**

---

## 2 A 90-km trek

a) Complete the sentences in your own words.
   1. 34 teenagers from four …
   2. … their gear …
   3. The Young Karibus …
   4. … a 2,000-kilometre trek …

b) Describe how the students cross the tundra.

c) Give the reasons why Valérie Raymond has organized the trip.

## 3 This is school too

a) In your own words, explain how taking part in the expedition is like school. Write your ideas in a short paragraph.

b) 👥 Exchange your texts with a partner. Find the similarities and differences.

## 4 Your opinion and experience

a) Say what you think about the hostel's rules.

b) Describe your experiences during a school trip. Explain what you liked and didn't like.

## 5 Have a go

Look at this hostel rule: *Smelly socks should not be left on the floor or they will be thrown away.* Now say what happens if you break these school rules:
1. Library books must be brought back on time or you will be … (fine 10 cents a day).
2. Students must arrive at class on time or they … (send to the principal).
3. Students must pass all courses or it … (note in their study book).

➜ **Workbook** 11–12 (p. 28)

## 2  Part B  Practice

### Looking at language

a) Find the sentences on p. 47 that have the same meaning as these:
   1 Antoine <u>has invited</u> me to Granby.
   2 No one <u>has cleaned</u> the shower in years.

b) Name the tense of the sentences above. How are the sentences from Lauren's blog similar/different? Explain how you form the tense in Lauren's sentences.

c) Now find the sentences on p. 47 that have the same meaning as these:
   1 Students must vacate rooms by 8 am.
   2 The hostel will fine students who do not respect these rules.

d) *May, can, should and must* are modal verbs. Find two more sentences with these verbs on p. 47. Explain how you form the passive with modal verbs.
➡ *GF 10: The passive (p. 145)*

### 1  A flag has been found (The present perfect passive)

Look at the following situations and complete the captions with the present perfect passive form of the verbs in brackets.

1. A flag from an expedition <u>has been found</u> (find) near Kuujjuaq.
2. Antoine … (give) a pair of skis for Christmas.
3. These windows … (not clean) for years.
4. Maddie … (not invite) to Justin's party.
5. The girl … (choose) for the school team.
6. Lauren's smelly socks … (throw away).

**Early finisher** Write a short dialogue for the situation in one of the pictures 4–6.

➡ **Workbook** 13–15 (pp. 28–29)

### 2  What is and isn't possible in Canada? (The passive with *may* and *can*)

Use the words in the brackets and complete the information about Canada.
1 French food … all over Quebec province.
2 Some towns in Nunavik … only by plane.
3 Inuit artworks … at the National Gallery of Canada in Ottawa.
4 Tickets for the hockey match … online.
5 The Arctic tundra … by car.
6 Poutine … with cheese curds, gravy and other toppings.

buy ·
enjoy (x2) ·
not cross ·
reach ·
see

forty-eight

## 3 Banff National Park's campfire rules (The passive with *may, can, should, must/mustn't*)

Banff National Park is in Alberta province. Like most National Parks, it has strict rules about lighting campfires.

a) Use the passive form of one of the verbs in the box with the correct modal to complete the rules below.

> light · buy · start · build · leave ·
> put out · prevent · enjoy

1 Campfires ... without a licence.
2 Licences ... for $8.80 per night, including campfire wood.
3 Even with a licence, campfires ... in windy weather.
4 Campfires ... during quiet hours (11pm to 7am).
5 Children ... alone at a campfire.
6 Campfires ... completely after they have been used.
7 Remember! Campfires ... if everyone follows these rules.

b) Read through the rules again.
Say which of these rules express possibility.
Which modals can express possibility?

➔ Workbook *16 (p. 30)*

## 4 After the final (The passive with *will*)

Read the note from the tournament organizers that describes what will happen after the final. Complete the text with the *will*-future passive. You can use these verbs:

> hold · ask · offer · serve · give · show · present

The award ceremony will be held¹ tomorrow night after the tournament final in the Quebec City Youth Centre. First, second and third-place trophies ...² to the winning teams. Official "All-Canada Ice Hockey" T-shirts ...³ to every player. Following a two-hour break, a special three-course dinner ...⁴ in the restaurant. Transport ...⁵ for $2.50. Speeches ...⁶ by the Minister of Education and Sports of Quebec City and hockey star Patrick Roy. Players ...⁷ to share their stories and impressions of the tournament. To end the evening, a short film of the best moments of the tournament ...⁸ on a large screen. We're looking forward to seeing all of you!

**More help** ➔ *(p. 108)*   ➔ Workbook *17 (pp. 30–31)*

## 5 Rules and consequences on your trip (The passive with *may, can, must, should* and *will*)

Imagine your class is going on a class trip.

a) Use what you have practised in exercises 1–4 above and discuss good, sensible and necessary rules for a class trip. Then write a list of rules (about eight) that everyone must follow and the consequences if they don't follow the rules.

b) Write six sentences that explain what should/must or can be done to prepare for the trip.

c) Share your lists of rules and consequences or preparations with your class.

## 2 Background file  Geography, people and wildlife

EXTRA

### Geography, people and wildlife of Canada

#### CANADA'S POPULATION
- one of the least populated countries in the world
  – Germany: 232 people/km²
  – Canada: 4.1 people/km²
- most people live along southern border with the U.S.
- largest cities: Ottawa, Toronto, Calgary, Montreal and Quebec City

#### CANADA'S TERRAIN
**1 Arctic tundra**
- extremely cold climate
  – ground is frozen all year
  – very short growing season
  – 11° C : average temperature in warmest summer months
- few plants and trees can grow here

**Wildlife:**
- polar bear
- grizzly and brown bear
- herds of caribou and musk ox
- Arctic fox and Arctic wolf
- wolverine
- seal, narwhal, walrus

**2 Boreal forest**
- 1,000-km wide area of land
  – treeless **tundra**: to the North
  – temperate **forest**: to the South and West
- covers 60% of Canada's land area
- largest intact forest in the world
  – evergreen trees (conifers)
- 1.5 million lakes and many of Canada's major river systems
- important breeding ground for migratory birds

**Wildlife:**
- 5 billion land and migratory birds
- beavers
- herds of caribou

#### CANADA'S GEOGRAPHY
- second-largest country in the world
  – larger than the U.S. or China
- Canada has three oceans as its borders
  – Atlantic Ocean: east
  – Pacific Ocean: west
  – Arctic Ocean: north

**3 Prairie grasslands**
- covers provinces of Saskatchewan, Manitoba and Alberta
- mostly flat grasslands
- Canada's agricultural heartland; most of the country's grain is grown here

**Wildlife**
- prairie dog
- black bear, moose
- western rattlesnake

**4 Temperate coniferous forest**
- warm summers, cool winters

**5 Deciduous forest**
- four seasons with lots of sunlight and rain throughout the year

---

**You choose** Do exercise a) or b).

a) Choose one Canadian habitat or one animal species on p. 50.

b) Choose one group of indigenous people on p. 51 and read the section again carefully.

**EXTRA**     Indigenous peoples     **Background file 2**

## Indigenous peoples of Canada

*The indigenous peoples of Canada are the original inhabitants of the land that is now known as Canada. Today 1.6 million people in Canada or 4.9% of the total population see themselves as indigenous. There are three groups: The First Nations, the Inuit and the Métis.*

### First Nations

In 2011, 1.3 million people in Canada saw themselves as coming from the First Nations. This means that they belong to one of 634
5 different Nations, e.g. the Cree and the Chiniki, and speak one of 50 distinct languages. Today, about half of the First Nations people live on reserves. A reserve is land owned by the government
10 that is reserved for indigenous people. Many communities have their own government.
In Canada during the late 19th century, indigenous children were
15 separated from their families and forced to go to 'residential schools', where they were taught to act like Europeans. In 1996 the last residential school was closed. This practice has been called a
20 'cultural genocide', with a terrible impact on indigenous peoples.

### Inuit: Life in the Arctic Tundra

There are about 60,000 Inuit living in Canada today – 73% live in the Arctic Tundra region (see map, p. 50.) The Inuit Nation were once a 25 nomadic people, hunting seals in winter and caribou in summer and fall. Today, many Inuit families still hunt for traditional foods.
Social relationships in the 30 community have always been important in Inuit culture. Children are often given the names of an elder in the community as a way to be 35 connected to their ancestors. School programs in Inuit communities play a key role in keeping Inuit culture alive. Students learn the Inuit language and about inuit inventions like the igloo and kayak, and survival 30 skills for the Arctic. About 90% of Inuit people living in Nunavut and Nunavik speak Inuktitut as their mother tongue.

### Métis: Fighting for their land and rights

35 The Métis have both European and indigenous ancestry. Their homeland is in the three prairie provinces of Alberta, Saskatchewan and Manitoba, and parts of British
40 Columbia and the Northwest Territories. They share a common language (Michif) which is a mix of both indigenous languages and French. Although they live in different regions across Southern Canada, the Métis have 45 fought since the early 19th century for the right to live on traditional lands and to be self-governing.
With European and indigenous traditions, the Métis have 50 developed a unique style of music and dance. The Métis are also known for their beadwork. Today, many Métis live in urban centres across Canada.

c) Write down what you have learned and four questions you have about your topic.

d) Research your topic. Try to find the answers to your questions.

e) 👥 Compare your questions and research notes with other students with the same topic.

f) 👥 Agree what to add to the KWL chart from p. 39

➔ **Workbook** *18 (p. 31)*

# 2  Part C

## 1 🔊 The final game

*Beep-beep, beep-beep.* 6 am. Antoine stumbled to the bathroom and splashed his face. He got dressed, wolfed down his breakfast, and went to the stadium with the other players on his team.

5 Today was the last game in the tournament. Antoine's team, the Granby Tigres, were playing the Ottawa Beavers. Tension was high. Winning this game meant going home with a big, shiny trophy. The trophy would 10 be kept in the main entrance at school, next to a photo of the whole team, for everyone to see.

A whistle blew and that familiar sound of hockey sticks hitting the ice filled Antoine's 15 ears.

Both teams were quick on the ice. By the middle of the game, the score was 3:3.

"Just one more and we'll win." Antoine thought. "One more goal, one more goal …"

20 The puck slid in his direction. The goal was open. Antoine lifted his stick and was going to strike when he felt something hit his leg. Bam! He fell flat on the ice and watched the puck slide away. He looked up and saw a Beaver jersey with the 25 number 11. Number 11 was laughing.

That boy had made him fall. Antoine was sure. He got up and pushed Number 11 in the chest. Other players skated over and began to fight. Hockey sticks slid across the ice. Antoine heard a 30 loud whistle. The referee shouted, "Get off the ice! Five minutes in the penalty box!"

The five most important minutes of the game! The whistle blew again and it was all over. The Ottawa Beavers won 4 to 3.

❖

35 Lauren entered the game room and saw Nukilik. As always, he was playing foosball. "Hey! Have you seen Antoine?" she asked.

Nukilik shot the little white ball into the goal. "Yes, he went up to his room and isn't speaking 40 to anyone. He didn't even come down for lunch."

Lauren touched his arm. "Come on, let's go up there," she said. "Maybe he'll speak to us."

Lauren opened the door to room 45. Antoine was lying on the bed, listening to music on his phone.

50 When he saw the plate of poutine they had brought for him, his eyes brightened and he began to relax. After eating most of the frites, Antoine told Lauren and 55 Nukilik his side of the story.

"Number 11?" asked Lauren.

Antoine nodded. "Yes, I'm sure. It was Number 11." Lauren shook her head. "I can't believe it. That's Justin. He jokes around a lot but it's always just 60 for fun," she said.

"I know I shouldn't have hit him," said Antoine as he sat back on the bed, "But he was laughing at me!"

Nukilik and Lauren stared at the floor. "What 65 makes me really angry is that everybody on the team thinks we lost because of me! And this guy Justin is a hero!" said Antoine.

Nukilik suddenly lifted his head, "Wait a second! I made a video of the whole game! And I was 70 sitting right behind the goal. Maybe the video will prove what really happened."

They watched the video, eating the last few frites.

"Watch this!" said Antoine, pointing to the screen 75 with a frite. "It's about to happen." They watched

the player hit Antoine behind the legs.
"It wasn't number 11!," shouted Nukilik.
"No! It was number 17."
"Number 17 – that's Warren," said Lauren shaking her head. "He's a jerk."
"What do we do now?" asked Antoine.
Lauren headed for the door. "I say we show this to your coach tout de suite!"

❖

"Well, this probably won't change the results of the game, but I'd like to show this video to the rest of the team," said Antoine's coach. "What that player did goes against the true spirit of hockey. That's not winning, and it's not hockey."

❖

The three friends went outside. Snow lay on the ground. Lauren lingered behind the two boys and formed a nice round snowball.
Pow! The snowball hit Antoine in the back.
"Hey! Who … ?" he turned around and saw Lauren laughing.
Nukilik already had snowballs at his feet.

❖

Pow! Pow! Two hit a car Lauren was hiding behind. But the moment she moved away to get more snow: Pow! One hit her in the shoulder and another got her in the leg.
Some team members must have seen them from the hostel room windows. Many came running out to join them. A few minutes later there were fourteen kids outside and a huge snowball battle had begun. Everyone was laughing. There were no fouls, no penalties, no trophies. This was a fight to have fun.

## 2 What happened?

a) Think: Make an outline about the most important events in order to retell the story.

b) 👥 Pair: Compare your outline with a partner.

c) 👥 Share: Form a group with another pair and together sum up the story.

## 3 He wolfed down his breakfast

a) 👥 Work in pairs. Find the verbs in the story. Work out their meaning in the context of the sentences.

> stumble · wolf down · strike · linger · brighten

b) Then check the meaning in a dictionary.

## 4 What could have happened?

a) Re-read lines 20–34. Consider how Antoine could have reacted differently to the situation.

b) Write a short paragraph that explains your ideas. Your text should answer these questions:
– What was the outcome of Antoine's actions?
– What could he have done differently?
– What could have happened if he had acted differently?

c) 👥 Share and defend your ideas with your group. Agree on the best solution.

## 5 The message of the story

a) In one or two sentences, write down the message of the story.

b) Compare and discuss your ideas in class.

## 6 Fight for fun 💬 ✏️

a) 👥 Work in groups. Discuss the differences between the fight on the ice and the snowball fight at the end of the story.
**More help** ➡ (p. 108)

b) Write a paragraph (about 100 words) that describes what you have done to have fun on school trips.

c) 👥 Read your story to your group and listen to their feedback.

➡ **Workbook** 19 (p. 32)

# 2 Part C Practice

## 1 People eat lots of fish (The definite article)

a) Read through the Grammar File on the definite article.
→ GF 11: The definite article (p. 146)

b) Compare these two sentences. Say what you notice about the word 'people'.
- In Nukilik's region, people eat lots of fish.
- About 4.9% of the people living in Canada have indigenous ancestry.

c) Add *the* where you need it.
1. Social relationships are important in ... life of the Inuit.
2. ... people say ... life is full of surprises.
3. Riverdale is the name of ... school Lauren goes to.
4. It's difficult for Nukilik to go to ... school in winter.
5. We know that ... pollution is a big problem.
6. We have to stop ... pollution of our oceans.
7. By morning, ... snow covered the ground.
8. All of ... snow melted the next day.
9. Lauren doesn't like ... rules at the hostel.
10. ... rules are important in competitive sports.

d) Write sentence pairs with the words in the box.
Write one sentence with *the* and one without *the*.
Write sentences that are true for you.

> music · clothes · winter · sports · summer · school · hobby

→ GF 11: The definite article (p. 146) → Workbook 20 (p. 33)

## 2 Wotcha mean? (Pronunciation: word flow)

a) Listen to a conversation that Lauren and Maddie have.
Find out who else is talking and what the situation is.

> **LISTENING TIP**
> When we speak, we do not say each word separately, pause and then say the next word. One word flows naturally into the next. This is especially true for common phrases like *What do you mean?*, which often sounds like *Wotcha mean?*

b) Listen again. Write down the number of each phrase in the order you hear it.
1. What do you mean?
2. How are you?
3. Have a good day.
4. Let me ask ...
5. Thanks so much.
6. I don't know.
7. Glad to hear it.
8. You can't miss it.

c) Listen to the phrases in b). Try to say them like the speaker.
→ Workbook 21 (p. 33)

## 3 Sounds and symbols (Phonetic script and pronunciation)

a) Let's have a look at some ice hockey words. Pronounce each word aloud and then write it down.
Compare your lists. Say what you notice about the pairs.
How do you pronounce them and how do you write them?

1. ['dʒɜːzi] – ['ʃaɪni]
2. [kaʊtʃ] – ['traʊfi]
3. [snəʊ] – [kaʊtʃ]
4. ['penəlti] – ['hɒki]
5. [braɪt] – [aɪs]
6. [kəm'piːt] – ['triːt]
7. ['iːgə] – ['biːvə]
8. ['ʃəʊldə] – [tʌf]

b) Now listen to the dialogues. Which words from a) do you hear?
Write them down.

Check with a partner.

## Paraphrasing — Mediation course 2

You have a friend in Quebec who wants to visit Germany with her parents and two younger brothers. The family loves winter sports. Your friend has asked you if you know a friendly hotel or resort where her parents can go cross-country skiing, where she can go downhill skiing or ice skating and where her brothers can learn to ski. Lessons would have to be in French or English.

You wrote to a friend who lives in the mountains and got this email from him.

a) Read the email. Note the points that are interesting for your Canadian friend.

*Hey, schön, dass du dich meldest! Ja, ich habe eine Empfehlung für deine Freunde: das ‚Chalet Welcome' bei uns am Stadtrand. Das ist ein kleines Hotel mit Skischule. Freunde meiner Familie haben es erst dieses Jahr aufgemacht. Da kann man alles machen: Skifahren, Snowboarding, Langlauf … naja, die Gegend ist mehr für Langlauf bekannt, aber der kleine Berg bei der Stadt reicht durchaus für eine gute Abfahrt, eine Rodelbahn*
5 *gibt es auch, und die Lernpiste ist super. Kinder sind da genau richtig. Die Eltern können Langlauf machen, während die kleinen Brüder Skifahren lernen. Die Kinderbetreuung ist super. Unsere Freunde sind echt tolle und nette Skilehrer, und sie sprechen Englisch (nur ihre Webseite gibt es noch nicht auf Englisch, aber das kommt noch). Ich weiß, in Quebec spricht man Französisch, aber deine Freunde werden doch auch Englisch können, oder ist das da nicht so? Ich kenne mich nicht aus.*
10 *Also, das Hotel hat keinen großen Wellnessbereich oder so, aber das ist ja auch nicht das, was deine Freunde suchen, oder? Falls doch, würden sie alles in der Therme in der Stadt finden. Das einzige, das ich für euch nicht finden kann, ist eine Eisbahn, die mit denen in Kanada mithalten kann. Es gibt ja die Eissporthalle, aber ich befürchte, deine Freundin wird eher enttäuscht sein. Eissport kann sie besser in Kanada machen. Bei uns geht es um Schnee und Berge. Da kann man nicht enttäuscht sein. Sie werden eine tolle Zeit haben!*
15 *Sag mir Bescheid, wenn das gut klingt und ich frage unsere Freunde, was sie für Infos auf Englisch haben oder ob sie euch ein Angebot schicken können.*
*Und wir beide sehen uns in den Ferien? Ich freue mich darauf!*
*Liebe Grüße, Tobi*

b) Practise paraphrasing words you can't translate into English, such as
   *Abfahrt, Lernpiste, Rodelbahn, Kinderbetreuung, Therme, mithalten, Angebot.*
   – *Abfahrt:* That means skiing down a mountain, not like cross-country skiing.
   – *Lernpiste:* This is for …

c) Work in pairs.
   **Partner A:** you are the boy/girl in Germany who knows the family in Quebec.
   **Partner B:** you are the friend from Quebec.

   Talk to each other in a video chat. Partner A needs to give Partner B all the information he/she needs to decide whether 'Chalet Welcome' is a good option for the family's holiday in Germany.

d) **EXTRA** Now write an email to your friend in English and tell her about winter sports in Germany. Use paraphrasing for words that you can't translate.
   **More help** ➔ (p. 108)

➔ **Workbook** 22–23 (pp. 34–35)

### Mediation skills

This is what you need to do when you explain a German text to someone:
– decide which information is important.
– translate key words if you know them in English.
– paraphrase words that you don't know.
– use pictures and photos to help explain key information.
➔ SF 11: Finding key information (p. 125)
➔ SF 12: Paraphrasing (p. 126)

## 4 THINKING ABOUT LANGUAGE  Multilingualism

*Multilingual people are able to speak and understand two or more languages.*
*A person who can speak in two languages is bilingual. Most of the world's population is bilingual.*

a) Discuss different factors and situations which may play a role in the number of languages a person speaks. Use the words in the wordle for ideas.

b) Explain the ways in which multilingualism can be important in the different settings in a).

c) Read the information box about languages in Canada.
With your group, identify the languages that are spoken in Canada. Explain why English and French are the most commonly spoken languages.
Share your results with the class.

d) You are going to find out whether some of your classmates are bilingual or multilingual.
First, write down three questions you can ask to find out what languages they speak and when, where and how they learned them.

Mill about and ask a classmate your questions. Take notes on the answers.
You have 3-4 minutes to ask and answer questions.

When your teacher tells you to stop, end your conversation, mill about again and talk to a different partner.

After you have spoken with four partners, review your notes. Write down the three things which surprised you most and why.

Write down what you have learned about language learning. Share your thoughts with your class.

*Word cloud:* multilingual, border, government, internet, colonization, war, colony, international, French, business, indigenuous, bilingual, tourism, port, English, trade, diplomat, school, language

### LANGUAGES OF CANADA
The name "Canada" comes from the Iroquoian word "kanata" meaning "village" or "community". British and French colonists reached the land now called Canada in the 17th century. English and French are today Canada's official languages.
There are at least 58 different indigenous languages spoken in Canada. Some of these languages are slowly disappearing because they are no longer used by the indigenous population in daily life. In 1974, Quebec became the only province in Canada where French is the only official language as 95% of Quebec's population speak French.

**DANGER**
**FALLING ICE**
**CHUTE DE GLACE**

## The world behind the picture  2

### 1 A simple life

a) 👥 Look at the three film stills. Take turns and describe the activities and contexts you see. Exchange your ideas on what the film is about.

b) Now watch the film.
Were your ideas from a) correct?

c) List as many of the main actor's activities as you can. Then in a second list, write down as many of the backgrounds/locations/seasons and times of day you can remember.

d) Give the film a title. Then, in a few sentences, explain what the film is about.
👥 Read your partner's sentences. Say if you agree with them.

e) Watch the last minutes of the film. Say where the film was made. Can you name the province this city is located in? What does the film's location explain?

f) Evaluate the film. Give reasons for your opinion.

### 2 Making the film: Using music and a split screen

a) Watch the film without sound and then again with sound.
Make notes about:
- how your experience changes.
- the ways in which the music affects the image.
- when the music changes.

b) 👥 Compare your notes with a partner.
Discuss:
- which you think was created first, the music or the film.
- the ways the film is similar to and different from a music video.

c) The film sometimes uses a split screen: there are two or more separate images on the screen.

Watch the scenes when this happens and make notes about the characters in each image and what they do.

Discuss why the director chose to use a split screen for these scenes.

d) Write a text (about 150 words) in which you explain why you would or wouldn't recommend this film.

fifty-seven   57

# 2 Text

## ✋ Flash fiction: From an animal's perspective

Read the information box about flash fiction.
Then read the three stories below.

> **FLASH FICTION**
> One feature that all flash fiction stories have is length: flash fiction is very short. The length is usually from 50 to 1,000 words, but some have been written that are only six words long! Yes, a story in six words!
> Flash fiction writers try to tell a complete story in the fewest number of words. This means that every sentence counts.
>
> Flash fiction usually jumps right into the action without spending time introducing the characters or the setting. The story often presents a key scene or moment that suggests what has happened before and what may happen after the ending. Although flash fiction presents a complete story, many details are left to the reader to imagine, infer and interpret.

### *Awake*

Darker than my mother's black eyes: that's what it's like in here. My nose is awake. It sniffs, hungry. The more it sniffs, the hungrier it gets. It's so hungry that it pulls me out of this hole in the earth and down the snow-covered hill. The world was black; now it's white, only white light. My eyes feel like bouncing balls that can't stop bouncing. My black nose in the white snow leads the way. And slowly my back, my legs and my paws wake up. My body wants blood: living blood and quivering blubber. The memory of blood carries me across the ice. The soft white snow breathes in every living thing, sparkling with hunger for a beating heart. I follow my nose until I smell it: the blood of a seal – hot, living blood. The hunter in me waits, awake and still, for just the right moment to strike.

### *Wildlife Hotline*

Emory was the best howl, growl, and whine interpreter at the Toronto Wildlife Hotline. He was shy and felt more comfortable with dogs, coyotes, and foxes than with human beings. Emory's phone rang and he said hello to the caller with a few short whines. The caller whined back and explained with a series of barks, growls and a long howl that a large man was standing on a large rock near her den. He was banging on small pots. The man had put up a small tent the night before. The caller had not tried to scare him. She had simply been looking for food.
When she found a nice rabbit hole filled with animals for her family's next meal, she began to howl to let her family know. But then the wild man started banging on his pots and had even shot a gun in the air! This scared the other members of her family. They were very, very hungry, but they stayed back. Emory knew the caller – this wasn't the first time she had complained. She lived in the popular Beaumont Park, where visitors often reacted strangely when they noticed the local inhabitants.
Emory promised the caller he would send someone over to talk to the man. He also recommended that she should stay in her den until the wild man was quiet.
Emory checked the clock: time for lunch. He walked outside the office and noticed a lunch truck selling poutine. He started to howl – a friendly signal to his office friends that he'd found food.

# Text 2

## The Professor

Jamie turned off the TV. He had just watched a documentary about beavers. He left home, raced to the zoo and found the beaver area. He watched the animals until closing time. Before long, Jamie became Professor James Castor, an expert on beavers.

One day he was interviewed on a radio program. "You've spent your life studying beavers. Why did you do it?" the radio host asked.

"That's easy," said the Professor. "Beavers are the best teachers I've ever had. They're builders, you see, just like humans. They build dams in streams. These are safe environments where insects, fish, birds and plants can also live. The beaver doesn't eat any of these animals – they're vegetarians." Professor Castor was getting excited; his nose began to twitch. "Using its large front teeth, it can take down trees. It uses the trees to build its dams and for food. You could say it eats the waste products of its own production."

The Professor picked up a pencil from the table and played with it between his fingers as he spoke. "Now let's look at what humans did to this wonderful animal. From the 17th to the 19th century, European fur traders killed almost all of the beavers. And for what? They sold their skins which were then used to make top hats. Can you imagine? These stupid hats didn't even keep men's heads warm! They were worn for status." Professor Castor angrily bit off the pencil tip.

"Today, the beaver is one of Canada's official symbols," said the Professor. "The Canadian nation exists today because of the fur trade. I'm glad to say that the beaver hat went out of fashion by the end of the 19th century, so we humans now have a second chance to learn from these amazing animals. That is what I have spent my life doing." The Professor stopped talking. The pencil had disappeared.

## 1 Reading like a detective

a) Choose one of the stories. Read it again carefully.
   – Sum up the story in sentences that answer the five Ws (who, where, what happens, etc.)
   – Note down at least two questions about the story's events and/or characters.
   – Be a detective: note down what might have happened before or after the events described in the story.

b) Find two classmates who have chosen the same story and form a group. Read your text to your partners. Listen to theirs.
   Agree on the best answers to the five Ws. Make corrections to your sentences if necessary.
   Understand more of the story by discussing your group's questions and notes.

c) Now find two classmates that have read the other two stories and form a new group. Take turns, read your text to your new partners, share your understanding of the story and answer their questions.

## 2 Write a flash fiction story

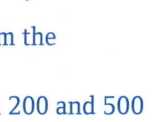

a) Write a flash fiction story from the perspective of an animal.
   Your story should be between 200 and 500 words. Try to create a story that has some of the features described in the information box.
   **More help** ➔ (p. 109)

b) Swap stories with a partner. Read your partner's text and make notes about how your partner can improve his/her text. Check spelling and grammar too.
   ➔ SF 23: Giving feedback (p. 133)

c) Think about your partner's comments and corrections. Decide what to change and write a final draft of your story.

**EXTRA** Put together a flash fiction magazine with the final drafts of all the stories your class has produced. Offer it to friends and family.

➔ **Workbook** 24 (p. 35)

fifty-nine 59

Workbook Checkpoint 2 (pp. 36–39)

# 2 Your task

## Film a sportscast

Imagine your class works for the Canadian kids' news channel 'It's up to us'. Your team has been asked to produce a sportscast about the All-Canada Youth Hockey Tournament in Quebec City.

### STEP 1
Form groups of at least five students. Each group member chooses one of these roles.
- hockey player, interviewer, camera person and two researchers

According to your role, follow Step 2, 3, or 4.

### STEP 2
Hockey player and researcher: prepare a profile of the player.
- Choose a name and hometown for the player.
- Develop a profile of the player's character, personal history and relationship to hockey.
- Find out interesting facts about the player's home town. Use information from this unit and find information on the internet.

### STEP 3
Interviewer and researcher: prepare for the interview.
- Put together a list of questions for the interview.
- Ask questions about the player's hometown, personal history, the tournament and the player's goals for the future.

### STEP 4
Camera person: prepare for the filming.
- Find a good location for the film. (Think about lights and background for the interview.) Arrange anything you need.
- Get information from the other members of your group about what they are planning.

### STEP 5
All: practise the interview and make the film.
- Practise the interview. The player should learn his/her role enough that he/she can answer questions without reading the information.
- Other members of the group should watch carefully and give feedback.
- Discuss ways to improve the interview.
- Make the film!

### STEP 6
Show your film to the class.
- Watch the films of other groups and give feedback.

**TIP**
- You can use camera apps on your phone to make simple videos.
- Make sure the light is good and hold the camera still while filming.

**TIP**
If you like your video a lot and are thinking of putting it online, remember:
- It's not always a good idea to put very personal information on the internet.
- Respect other people's rights. Get permission from everyone in the film before you post it online!

➡ SF 23: Giving feedback (p. 133)

# Checkpoint 2

## A

### 1 Canada's habitats

Name the habitat shown in the photos. Write three or four sentences about the geography, wildlife and climate of each habitat.

### 2 Paraphrases

Find the words that match these paraphrases. Write them in your exercise book.
1. The original inhabitants of a region.
2. People who move from place to place.
3. The person who makes sure all players follow the rules during a match.
4. A trip on foot or on skis across a long distance.
5. A prize given to the winning team or player.
6. A home made of snow.

### 3 Word families

Fill in as many of the gaps in these word families as you can. Write the words in your exercise book.

| Verb | Noun (person) | Noun (thing) |
|---|---|---|
| ... | competitor | ... |
| ... | ... | hunt |
| inhabit | ... | ... |
| coach | ... | ✗ |
| ... | ... | interpretation |
| ... | camper | ... |
| ... | producer | ... |
| build | ... | ... |

### 4 Collocations

a) Match the words/phrases in A and B and make collocations.
You can use some words/phrases more than once.

> get · have · make
>
> ready · an agreement · hungry · a fight · into an argument · a rule · fun · an argument · a goal · a promise · worried

b) Use the phrases in a) to write at least six sentences about Lauren, Maddie, Nukilik or Antoine.

### 5 The meaning changes

Complete the sentences about Nukilik, Antoine and Lauren with the correct form of the correct verb or collocation in brackets.

1. (keep · keep up · keep on · keep back · keep away from)
   You can ... my old skates, they're too small for me.
   If you ... hitting me, I'll get angry.
   Nukilik was too fast; Antoine couldn't ... with him.
   ...! Those coyotes look dangerous!
   ... your toys ... the dog, or he will chew them up.
2. (show to · show up for)
   Justin proudly ... the trophy ... his parents.
   Only two people ... the performance.
3. (turn back · turn around · turn sth. into sth. else · turn sth. on/off)
   We read a story about a wizard who could ... dirt ... gold.
   'It's 10 pm! Please ... the TV ...'
   It's getting dark, we had better ... .
   I ... when someone called my name.
4. (look for · look closely · look through)
   Lauren ... Antoine everywhere.
   If you ... this window, you'll see a beautiful view.
   If you ... , you can see a strange pattern.

sixty-one 61

# 2 Checkpoint

## 6 What has been done? (The present perfect passive)

Complete Antoine's homework with the right verb forms.

1  A wildlife park ... in Alberta to protect grizzly bears.
2  New laws ... to fight noise pollution that is killing orcas.
3  Reports ... about the need to protect the natural habitat of caribou.
4  Animals that are in danger, like the marmot and caribou, ... to zoos to breed.
5  Websites ... to teach people what they can do to help.
6  Research projects ... to better understand how to help wolverines.

> bring ·
> create · do ·
> make · set ·
> write ·

## 7 MIXED BAG  Global warming in the Arctic tundra

Complete the text about the Arctic tundra.

...¹ Arctic tundra ...² in the northern parts of North America, Europe and Asia. This habitat ... ...³ above the Arctic circle. Serious warnings ...⁴ by scientists around the world ...⁵ the ...⁶ Arctic regions are ...⁷ starting ...⁸ disappear forever. The ...⁹ danger is global ...,¹⁰ which ...¹¹ by greenhouse gases.
...¹² the Arctic tundra, ...¹³ of the ground is frozen ....¹⁴ In recent years, the three-month winter average temperatures were 8-11°C ... ...¹⁵ the temperatures from 1961–1990. And because of the temperatures, the frozen ground ... ...¹⁶ to melt, and as it ...,¹⁷ CO² and other gases ...¹⁸ into the atmosphere.
It ... ¹⁹ that there is 1,500 billion tons of CO² in the ...²⁰ permafrost. That is four times the amount of CO² that ...²¹ into the atmosphere ...²² the burning of all fossil fuel and other human activities ...²³ 1850! What ...²⁴ be done? Protected areas and park reserves ...²⁵ to protect the Arctic regions from human activities. The building ...²⁶ oil pipelines and mining ...²⁷ immediately. Fossil fuels ... ...²⁸ alternative energy, such ...²⁹ wind and solar energy.

## 8 MIXED BAG  Nukilik's uncle

Complete the text about Nukilik's uncle's new home in the tundra.

Nukilik ...¹ named after ...² uncle. His uncle ...³ always ...⁴ a traditional lifestyle in the Arctic tundra. He hunted ...⁵ of caribou in the fall and in the winter time. But ...⁶ uncle ... ...⁷ old. He isn't as ...⁸ as he used ...⁹ be. So last summer he ...¹⁰ a house in Nukilik ...¹¹ village Kuujjuaq.
...¹² Nukilik visited him, Uncle Nukilik told ...¹³ nephew what ... ...¹⁴ built and what still needed to be ....¹⁵ "All the walls ...¹⁶ painted, the windows and doors ...¹⁷ put in and the bathroom ...¹⁸ almost finished. Still, there is ... ...¹⁹ to do. Next week the kitchen equipment ... ...²⁰ delivered. The wood for the floor ...²¹ arrive ...²² days later. The roof ... ... ...²³ finished before the first ...²⁴ falls, or the new floor ...²⁵ get wet."
Nukilik wants to help his uncle, but that isn't p....²⁶ The school semester ...²⁷ over. Nukilik can't miss hockey ....²⁸ His uncle ...²⁹ accept that. To be on the hockey team and to take part in games, kids ... ...³⁰ come to training and go to all ...³¹ classes too.
"...³² w...,³³ Nukilik," says his uncle, "there ...³⁴ lots of work to ...³⁵ during the semester holidays."

# Checkpoint 2

## B

### 9 Competition in sports

a) Read the short article and write in one sentence what it is about.

> **KIDS' HOCKEY NEEDS CHANGE**
>
> In 2014, Brent Sutter coached the Canadian team at the World Junior Hockey Championships in Malmo, Sweden. His team finished fourth. This was a worse performance than expected and later Coach Sutter tried to understand what went wrong.
>
> Instead of finding reasons for the team's bad performance, he came up with ways to make hockey players better. He suggested that:
> – kids should play fewer games
> – winning or losing a game should be less important and not the focus of training
> – teams should take part in fewer tournaments and instead spend more time working on their skills and their speed
> – training should be more fun
> – there should be less emphasis on competition and more on simply loving the game.
>
> These recommendations are not likely to receive support from coaches and parents who usually push kids to compete. Although there is nothing wrong with wanting to win, Coach Sutter thinks that the focus should be in training kids to be hockey players for life.

b) Complete the sentences in your own words:
 1 The Canadian … 2 Brent Sutter is … 3 The performance of … 4 Coach Sutter tried …

c) Answer the questions.
 1 Why does Coach Sutter make suggestions?
 2 What are Coach Sutter's suggestions?
 3 Do parents agree with the suggestions?

d) Write a 200-word comment which expresses your opinion on this statement:
 *"There should be less emphasis on competition in team sports."*

## C

### 10 Explore Canada: Come to …

Imagine you work for the Canadian tourist bureau. Prepare a four-minute talk that describes the special sights, attractions and activities in one of Canada's provinces or territories to future visitors.

1 Choose one of Canada's provinces or territories to focus on.
2 Make notes about places, attractions, things to do that might be important for your talk.
3 Mark images of the places, attractions and activities in your book that you can look at during your talk.
4 Organize your information and plan your talk.
5 Give your talk to your group and answer your group's questions.

*Have you ever been to a place where … ?*
*XX province has the best … you can find in …*
*Wander through … Explore … Discover …*
*Here you can experience …*
*Get lost in …*
*Experience …*
*In … you'll find …*

# Access to cultures

# Canada: A quiz

Form teams of four. Find the correct answers to the questions.
Use a geography book or the internet if necessary.
The first team to answer all the questions correctly is the winner.

## Geography

1. *Canada's coast is longer than the coast of the USA.*
   a) true   b) false

2. *The US/Canada border is the second largest in the world after the Russia/Kazakhstan border.*
   a) true   b) false

3. *The whole of Canada has about three million fewer people than the US state of California.*
   a) true   b) false

4. *Order these countries from 1 to 4 on the size of their oil reserves.*
   a) Saudi Arabia   b) Venezuela   c) USA
   d) Canada

5. *Canada has more lakes than the rest of the world's lakes combined.*
   a) true   b) false

6. *The Atlantic Ocean in Newfoundland sometimes freezes over.*
   *When this happens, people play hockey on its frozen surface.*
   a) true   b) false

7. *What is the meaning of these Canadian place names?*
   a) Nunavut   b) Ontario   c) Saskatchewan
   d) Winnipeg   e) Quebec

## Society and culture

8. *Explain what these Inuit inventions do.*
   a) parka   b) kayak   c) toboggan

9. *Canada is maybe the most intelligent country in the world: over half its residents have been to university.*
   a) true   b) false

10. *Which funny facts about Canada are true?*
    a) Canada has maple syrup reserves to make sure the world will always have enough.
    b) There are 19 towns in Canada called Beaver and only two in the US.
    c) Licence plates in the Northwest Territories have the shape of polar bears.
    d) Licence plates in Ottawa have the shape of beavers.

11. *Which sport that is very popular in the US today was first developed in Canada?*
    a) ice hockey   b) football   c) basketball
    d) all of the above

12. *Which country has no weapons of mass destruction and has signed treaties condemning other countries who have them?*
    a) UK   b) US   c) Canada   d) France
    e) all of the above

13. *Canada is thought of as an especially nice place. Which of these facts are true?*
    a) People who live in Churchill, Canada, don't lock their cars – to offer an escape for people who might meet polar bears.
    b) Police departments in Canada give out 'positive tickets' when they see people doing something positive.
    c) When flights were not allowed during 9/11, Canada gave beds and food to over 33,000 passengers.
    d) all of the above

## Famous Canadians

**14** *Which of these singers is Canadian?*
 a) Daniel Caesar   b) Beyoncé   c) Drake   d) Justin Bieber   e) Jay-Z   f) all of the above

**15** *Which of these actors is Canadian?*
 a) Ryan Gosling   b) Rachel McAdams   c) Keanu Reeves   d) all of the above

**16** *Match quotes A-H to the person 1-8 who said them and match the person to their photo.*

**A** "Women are so capable of destroying girl on girl hate."

**B** "Canada was built on dead beavers."

**C** "Instead of kids just hearing about beads and baskets and fringe, and about what 'was' and 'were' we present Native American culture as a living contemporary culture."

**E** "The world needs more Canada."

**D** "Canadians are nice because they have Health Care."

**F** "We pride ourselves on our democratic traditions, but in Canada, women couldn't vote until 1918, Asians until 1948, and First Nations people living on reserves until 1960."

**G** "Canada and space are a natural fit."

**H** "We have created a society where individual rights and freedoms, compassion diversity are core to our citizenship. But underlying that idea of Canada is the promise that we all have a chance to build a better life for ourselves and our children."

1. Jim Carrey, Canadian actor
2. Margaret Atwood, Canadian environmental activist and novelist, author of *The Handmaid's Tale*
3. Marc Garneau, Canadian astronaut
4. Lilly Singh, Canadian entertainer, singer and educator
5. David Suzuki, Canadian scientist and environmental activist
6. Barack Obama, 44th President of the United States
7. Justin Trudeau, 23rd Prime Minister of Canada
8. Buffy Sainte-Marie, indigenous Canadian singer and educator

➔ **Workbook** 5–6 (pp. 62–63)

# Unit 3
# Faces of the Midwest

A

C

E

# Unit 3

## 1 Sounds and images 🎧 💬

a) Share your first impressions of the photos.

b) 🎧 You will hear different voices and sounds. Look at the photos (A–F) as you listen. Try to match the voices and sounds to the photos.
👥 Use your five senses and describe the photos in detail. Take turns. The words in the box may help you.

c) Find information about South Dakota. Have a look at the map in the back inside cover of your book. You can also use the internet. Take notes (size, landscapes, cities, people, etc.)

> Badlands · carve · dusty · rough · footsteps · cheering · motor · engine · smooth · gallop · Native American · prairie · reservation · rodeo · silence · tractor

## 2 A postcard home ✏️

Choose a photo. Imagine it is a postcard of South Dakota that you are sending to a friend.

Using your notes from 1c, write a text to go on the back of the postcard (about 50–100 words). Make sure you write something about the landscape.

➡ **Workbook** 1 (p. 40)

### Your task

**At the end of this unit:** You will give a presentation about the first confrontations between a Native American nation and European settlers.

## 3 Part A

### 1 A perfect morning

Look at the picture. Speculate about the relation between the picture and the title.

At 7:30 am, Drew Schmidt was sitting at the breakfast table when his dad entered the kitchen and slapped the keys on the counter.
"The truck's all yours, son. But drive carefully!"
5 Minutes later Drew was on the highway on the way to school. He was turning into the Mobridge-Pollock High School parking lot when the car behind his honked. It was Bobby Bauman, Drew's best friend.
10 "Hey buddy, where did you get the pickup?" asked Bobby.
"It's my dad's truck. He's away for the next two weeks and said I could use it while he was gone."
Bobby nodded his head. "Not bad! Not bad at all,"
15 he said. He then pulled out a large rolled-up map and a shoe box from the trunk of his car.
"Hey, what's with all the stuff?" asked Drew. "Is today show-and-tell?"
"Very funny, Drew. No, it's for my history
20 presentation on the Seven Years War."
Bobby lifted the roll into the air. "This," he said, "is a map and timeline. It shows all the battles between the French, British and Indians …"
"Native Americans —" corrected Drew.
25 "Right, sorry, Native Americans."
"And what's in the box?"
"Toy soldiers. I'm going to show how the British defeated the French at Fort Dusquene."
"Toy soldiers? Man, you're crazy! Why don't you
30 do a slide presentation like everyone else?"
"Trust me. It'll be awesome!" said Bobby excitedly.
They entered the school building. Drew had a big grin on his face. "And what are you so happy about?" asked Bobby.
35 "It looks like I'm going to the high school rodeo finals this June," said Drew.
"Awesome! How do you know?"
"Yesterday, Coach told me my times were really good. So, if I keep it up, I guess it's a sure thing."
40 As they were walking towards their classroom, Drew suddenly stopped.
There she was at the water fountain. She bent down for a drink and tucked her long black hair behind her ear.

Drew's eyes lit up. He leaned towards Bobby. 45
"The other reason I'm in such a good mood is standing right there …"
"What do you mean?" asked Bobby, but Drew was already walking towards Kaya Red Hawk.
"Hey! Kaya! I watched you during practice … 50
your riding is getting so good."
"Really? I wish Coach thought that. He said I was too slow. He told me to speed up if I wanted to qualify for the finals."
"It just takes practice," said Drew. "Uh, maybe we 55
could practice together if we could find some horses somewhere."
"You mean outside of school?" asked Kaya.
"Yeah, you know, we could help each other …"
"Well, my aunt has a ranch on the rez. They've 60
got horses …"
"Really?"
"Yeah, and she's always saying I can ride whenever I want. Problem is, I don't have a car."
"Well, I can drive you. How about this Saturday?" 65
Kaya smiled. The bell rang and Drew didn't hear her answer. Before he could ask again, one of her friends had pulled her away.

Bobby had been listening to Drew and Kaya.
"I don't believe it," he said. "Did you ask Kaya 70
Red Hawk for a date?"
"Yeah, so what?"
"Well, what did she say?"
Drew smiled: "Yes … I think."

## 2 Mobridge-Pollock High School

Take notes on the differences between your school and Mobridge-Pollock High School. Find sentences in the text that support your ideas and share your ideas in class.

## 3 What's in a name?

a) Say what you can guess about the characters from their names:
Drew Schmidt, Bobby Bauman, Kaya Red Hawk

b) Find these words in the text: 'buddy', 'pick-up', 'awesome', 'rez'. Re-read the sentences in which you found them and write down what you think each word means.

## 4 Drew's good mood

Give reasons why Drew is in such a good mood. Find the sentences in the text that support your ideas. Write down the lines.

👥 Compare your reasons and evidence with your partner.

## 5 Drew and Kaya

a) Explain how you know what Drew feels about Kaya. Find descriptive sentences and dialogue from the story to support your answers. Give the lines.

b) Kaya doesn't have time to answer Drew's question. Describe the effect this has on the reader.

## 6 What do they say? ✏️

**You choose**  Choose a) or b):

a) Imagine Kaya and Drew are texting after school. Continue the story by writing two texts for each character.

b) Imagine Kaya keeps a diary. Write her entry for this day.

➡ **Workbook** 2 (p. 40)

## 7 Toy soldiers

Read the info box about the Seven Years War. What are the three most important points Bobby should make in his presentation? Take notes.

### The Seven Years War

The Seven Years War was mainly fought between Britain and France from 1754 to 1763, for control over colonies in Asia, India, the Caribbean and North America. It is called The Seven Years War because it was only officially declared two years after the fighting began. After Britain lost several battles in the war's early years, its government sent many more troops and money and Britain finally won the war. Britain then became the most powerful empire in the world. Native American nations fought on both sides.

In 1763, Britain and France signed the Treaty of Paris, which gave the British control over parts of present-day Canada, Florida, and some important sugar-producing islands in the Caribbean. The British also signed the Proclamation of 1763, which declared the Appalachian Mountains as the boundary line of white settlement; the lands west of these mountains were reserved for Native Americans. White American settlers never respected this boundary and forced Native Americans further west.

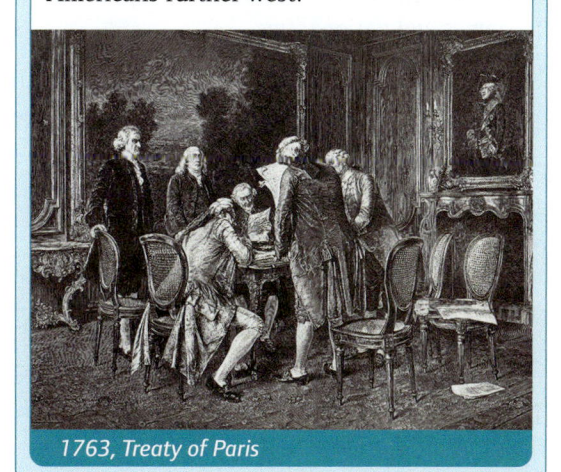

*1763, Treaty of Paris*

# 3 Part A Practice

## 1 THINKING ABOUT LANGUAGE  Varieties of English

Use the clues below and complete Jeff's story with the correct American English words and Abbie's story with the correct British English words.

*Hey dudes! I'm Jeff from Rapid City. I'm 15 and I just got my first job!*

I was driving down the ¹... in my ²... and saw a HELP WANTED sign at a big ³.... I saw the manager and he hired me on the spot. I get to wear an ⁴... uniform: blue ⁵..., white shirt, and basketball ⁶.... I make ten ⁷... an hour.
I'm sure that in a couple of weeks, I'll have enough cash to go to the movies on ⁸... with my ⁹....

My best ¹... was working at a big ².... He left for university and offered me the job. I earn ten ³... an hour, but I don't like the uniform: yellow ⁴..., black shirt, and jogging ⁵.... I look like a bumblebee! It's also a hard job. I sometimes have to park ⁶... in small spaces. I'm saving up the dosh to buy this ⁷... motorcycle. I'll tell you one thing – it's not yellow! When it's mine, I'll drive along ⁸... to show it off. Then I'll leave town and head into the sunset along the ⁹... .

*Hi …! I'm Abbie from Bristol. I just turned 18 and got a job doing what I love best: driving!*

### CLUES
- money
- a big vehicle used for transporting things
- a friend
- a big space for people to leave their cars
- a word to express 'wonderful'
- clothing for legs
- foot covering for sports
- the main street of a town
- a place where people buy things

## 2 Fizzy drink, soda or pop?

You are going to listen to a conversation between a British, an American and a Canadian speaker.

a) As you listen, take notes in your exercise book about where they are, what they are doing, their names and nationalities.

b) Copy the table. Listen again and note down the words they discuss and their definitions in the correct columns: British English (BE), American English (AE) or Canadian English (CaE).

| Definition | BE | AE | CaE |
| --- | --- | --- | --- |
| A place to store things in a car | boot | trunk | trunk |
| ... | ... | ... | sneakers |
| ... | ... | flashlight | ... |

c) Work in groups of four. Find reasons to explain why British and Canadian people are more familiar with American English words than the other way around.
Present your ideas to the class.

➜ Workbook  3 (p. 41)

## 3 REVISION  Yesterday in Mobridge  (Simple past or past progressive?)

Look at the pictures and complete the texts.
Use the correct form of the verbs: simple past or past progressive.

**A** *Hi Kaya.*

Bobby ¹… (see) Kaya while he ²… down Main Street in Mobridge yesterday.
He ³… and ⁴… hi, but Kaya ⁵… (not hear) him. She ⁶… to music and she ⁷… (not look) around when he ⁸… her.

**B** *Excuse me …*

Drew's mom ¹… down Main Street yesterday when a young exchange student ²… up to her.
He ³… for the post office and ⁴… Drew's mom for directions. She ⁵… towards the post office anyway, so she ⁶… (offer) to take him there.

➡ More help (p. 109)

➡ GF 12: Simple past / past progressive (p. 147)   ➡ Workbook 4 (p. 41)

---

### Language help

**Nominalized adjectives** are adjectives that are used as nouns. We can say:
*Young people often have fresh ideas* or *The young often have fresh ideas.*

The noun 'people' disappears and 'young' becomes a noun.
- We often use the form when talking about groups of people: *the rich / the poor / the healthy / the weak / the strong …*
- We also use it for some nationalities: *the British / the Irish / the French …*
- We put **the** before the noun, and although we are talking about a group, we do not use a plural 's'.

➡ GF 13: Adjectives used as nouns (p. 147)

---

## 4 The British defeated the French …  (Adjectives used as nouns)

a) Drew is telling a British visitor to Mobridge-Pollock High School about the history of different groups of people in America. Rewrite the sentences by using adjectives as nouns.

1. British people have a long history in North America.
2. In South America, Spanish people and Portuguese people had more power.
3. Today, young people are becoming more interested in Native American history.
4. Old people can remember a time when Native Americans were less respected.
5. A large number of poor people in the USA were Native Americans.
6. Luckily, rich people and educated people now come from all kinds of cultural backgrounds.

b) Is it true that some groups of people have an easier life than others?
Complete sentences using nominalized adjectives.
Then write three more sentences like the ones in b) with your own ideas.
Think about *the old / the young / the rich / the educated* etc. and use your own ideas.

1. The … have a more difficult life in some ways.
2. The … should do more to help the … .
3. The … really know how to enjoy life!
4. I want/don't want to be one of the … .

➡ GF 13: Adjectives used as nouns (p. 147)   ➡ Workbook 5 (p. 42)

# 3 Mediation course — Cultural differences

## How to get a driver's license

Bobby from Mobridge-Pollock High School is an exchange student at your school. He's very surprised that no one in the 8th, 9th or even 10th grade has a driver's license. You are going to answer his questions and respond to his comments, but first you need a little preparation.

a) Work in groups of four. Read the article. Each student writes down key information in English on two topics from the article about the process of getting a driver's license in Germany.

b) In English, tell your group what you found out.
Take notes in English on what each member of your group reports.

c) Now you are going to listen to Bobby's questions about getting a driver's license in Germany. There will be a pause after each question. Take turns and answer his questions as fully as you can.

d) Write an email (100-120 words) for Bobby and his high school website in English and explain how you can get a driver's license in Germany.

➡ *SF 13 Cultural differences (p. 126)* ➡ **Workbook** *6 (pp. 42–43)*

---

### In sieben Schritten zum Führerschein

**1. Die Anmeldung**
Gehen Sie zu Ihrer Fahrschule des Vertrauens und melden Sie sich an.

**2. Der Sehtest**
Bevor man mit der Ausbildung starten kann, muss man einen Sehtest und einen Erste-Hilfe-Kurs absolvieren.
Die Nachweise werden für den Antrag bei der Führerschein-Behörde benötigt.

**3. Der Antrag**
Im nächsten Schritt stellt man einen Antrag für den Führerschein.
Während der Bearbeitungszeit können Sie schon mit der Fahrausbildung beginnen, aber die Prüfung kann noch nicht gemacht werden.

**4. Der theoretische Unterricht**
Es gibt insgesamt 14 verschiedene Theorieeinheiten, von denen jede 90 Minuten dauert und alle wichtigen Bereiche zum Straßenverkehr und Autofahren abdeckt.
Zusatzstoff wird in zwei Veranstaltungen behandelt. In allen 14 Theorieeinheiten besteht Anwesenheitspflicht.

**5. Der praktische Unterricht**
Im Praxisunterricht lernt man, wie das Fahrzeug bedient wird und übt Situationen, die im Straßenverkehr vorkommen können. Für Fahrstunden gibt es keine geregelte Anzahl. Im Durchschnitt nehmen die Fahrschüler/innen mindestens 18 Stunden, es können aber auch weniger ausreichend sein. Verpflichtend sind jedoch die 12 Sonderfahrstunden: die fünf Überland-, vier Autobahn- und drei Nachtfahrten.

**6. Die theoretische Prüfung**
Wenn alle Stunden absolviert sind, kann man sich zur Theorieprüfung anmelden. Das ist höchstens drei Monate vor dem erlaubten Mindestalter möglich. Es gibt ca. 1.000 Prüfungsfragen, von denen 30 in der Prüfung vorkommen werden.

**7. Die praktische Prüfung**
Man kann die Praxisprüfung maximal einen Monat vor dem erlaubten Mindestalter absolvieren. Der/Die Prüfer/in sagt, was während der Prüfung gemacht werden muss: z.B. wo man abbiegen und wo und wie man einparken muss. Die Prüfung ist bestanden, wenn man 45 Minuten fehlerfrei gefahren ist.

**Die Kosten**
Die Kosten für einen Führerschein schwanken zwischen 1.500 und 2.000 Euro. Regional können die Gebühren für die Praxis- und Theoriestunden sehr unterschiedlich ausfallen.

**EXTRA**  Small town, big fun  **Background file 3**

South Dakota *News Magazine*

# Small town, big fun

What do teens do for fun in a town like Mobridge, South Dakota (population 3,500)?
We asked Keri Cox and Joey Beck about small town life in the Midwest.

When I'm home, I spend a lot of time on Twitter and Instagram. I also paint and draw because I want to be a graphic designer.
In the summer there's lots going on down at the Missouri River. We go swimming, but what I really love is tubing. You sit in the inner tube of a big truck tyre and get pulled downstream by a boat. It's amazing on a hot day.
I always look forward to the downtown dances on Main Street too. They put up a tent and we go in a big group and dance all evening.
I do a bit of fishing – everyone does – but my favorite is ice fishing in winter.

My buddies and I often just like driving around town, hanging out in our cars. Then in summer we watch movies at the Pheasant Drive-In. Mobridge has one of the last ones in South Dakota. It only costs five dollars and they show lots of good movies. The movie starts when it gets dark.
I also go hunting with my dad. I was only nine when I learned to shoot. I had to do a course with the Game, Fish and Parks Department before I was allowed to hunt. We mostly go after turkeys, but friends of mine hunt pheasant and deer too.

*Ice fishing*

We go out on the river when it freezes 4-feet thick. We make holes in the ice and catch lots of fish. There's a big ice-fishing tournament too, and people come from all over the world for that.

*Hunting*

In February, I love to go to the 'I Hate Winter' celebration in the Scherr-Howe Arena. They turn the heating up and we go in coats, then strip down to our bathing suits and pretend we're in Hawaii.

a) Compare Mobridge with your hometown. What can you do at different times of year?

b) Which social media would you use to contact Keri or Joey? Why?
Write a short message to one of them.
Say what interests you about Mobridge.

# 3  Part B

## 1 🔊 A day at the ranch

On Saturday Drew and Kaya drove to her aunt's ranch on the Standing Rock Reservation. They borrowed two horses, and, after practicing for an hour in the hot sun, they stopped for a water
5  break.

"I'm nervous about competing for a place in the high school finals," said Kaya. "I'm still not fast enough."

"Squeezing harder with your knees will give you
10  better control," suggested Drew. "That way, you and the horse will be a tighter, faster team."

"OK, I want to try that!"

They practiced for another hour and then began walking the horses back to the ranch.

15  "See, you're much faster now, Kaya. I'm sure you're going to make the finals."

"Yeah, I think I *am* faster, but I don't know about making the finals. Still, thank you so much for helping me."

20  "Riding with you is awesome. Hey, you know what? My brother is home from college. He brought his girlfriend and we're all going to Rapid City next weekend. Have you ever been there?"

Kaya shook her head.

25  "Then come with us! We're going to Mount Rushmore in the Black Hills!" said Drew excitedly. Just then they heard Cody shouting, "Kaya! Frybread is ready! Come and get it!"

"Ooh! Frybread! I really miss eating Aunt Jodi's
30  food." She turned to Drew. "Do you like frybread?"

"I don't know. What is it?"

Kaya smiled. "You'll see. Come on, let's hurry and bring the horses to the corral."

Aunt Jodi and Kaya's cousins were already sitting
35  around the kitchen table when she and Drew came in. "Hey guys, this is my friend Drew. Drew, these are my cousins Randall and Cody and my aunt Jodi. She's really good at making frybread. It's the best on the rez!"

40  "Nice to meet you, Drew," said Aunt Jodi. "Please, take a seat."

"Mmm, this is really delicious!" said Drew.

"Here, have another," offered Kaya's aunt.

"So how are your times, Cuz?" asked Randall.

45  "Much better. I'm more confident about trying out for the finals now. Drew helped me a lot."

"Next weekend, you two should try training with us," said Cody.

"I'd love to, but I'm going with my family to Mount
50  Rushmore" said Drew. "And I've just invited Kaya to come with us."

Cody shook his head in disbelief. "Mount Rushmore? Are you
55  serious?!"

## 2 Getting ready for the rodeo finals

a) Complete the sentences about Kaya, Drew and Aunt Jodi.
  1 Kaya is nervous …
  2 Drew says …
  3 They practise …
  4 Drew wants …
  5 Aunt Jodi …

b) Answer the questions.
  1 What do they eat?
  2 What are the names of Kaya's cousins?

c) Compare how Kaya feels about her riding skills after the first hour and second hour of practising. What changes and why? Find sentences in the text to support your answer.

d) Name a sport or activity in which you improved your skills. Write a short paragraph that describes how it happened.

### THE STANDING ROCK RESERVATION: PAST AND PRESENT

The Standing Rock Reservation covers an area of over nine thousand square kilometers in South Dakota and North Dakota. It is home to more than eight thousand people of the Lakota and Dakota nations. At its center are the Black Hills, which are sacred to these Native American peoples.

The reservation has had a troubled and often violent history. The Lakota and Dakota were traditionally a nomadic people. In the second half of the nineteenth century, as more and more of their territory was taken from them by the United States government, they were forced to live on reservation lands. They had to change their way of life from hunting to farming. Lakota and Dakota children were taken from their families and sent to boarding schools. They were forbidden to speak their own native language or to practice their traditional culture and were beaten whenever they did so.

The land in the reservation was too dry and the climate too hot for farming. By the end of the 19th century, many of the Native American inhabitants starved to death.

Today, the Standing Rock Reservation has its own schools, hospitals, and government or 'tribal council'. Yet it is still a site of bitter conflict. Despite Native American protest, an underground oil pipeline (NDAPL) was dug through sacred burial sites on the Standing Rock Reservation. The pipeline, which carries crude oil across six states, also threatens to pollute the reservation's fresh water supply.

*Lakota and Dakota children were forbidden to speak their own native language or to practice their traditional culture.*
*Talk about how this may have affected Lakota and Dakota children.*

## 3 Are they nervous or confident? ✎

Choose two to three adjectives from the box and write a short paragraph (about 60 words) that describes the attitude and behaviour of one character in the story.

> confident · welcoming · kind · nervous · satisfied ·
> dissatisfied · insulted · thankful · surprised ·
> shocked · helpful · polite

## 4 A trip to Mount Rushmore

Speculate about whether Kaya will accept Drew's invitation to go to Mount Rushmore with his family.
Is there any evidence in the text to suggest that she will or won't go?

## 5 Have a go

a) Say what each character is good at doing or not good at doing.
   eg. *Aunt Jodi is good at making frybread.*

b) 👥 Tell each other what you're good at doing.

➡ **Workbook** 7 (p. 43)

# 3 Part B Practice

## Looking at language

a) Which part of speech (verb, noun, adjective, etc.) are the words in **orange**?

> **Sport** is good for you. **Laughing** is good for you too.
> I love my **bed**. I don't like **getting up**.

b) Look at the words in **green** and complete:
The ing-form can be used like a … . When it is used like this, it is called a **gerund**.

Find sentences with gerunds on pp. 74–75. Put them in the right column.

| gerund as subject | gerund as object | gerund after prepositions |
|---|---|---|
| Riding with you is awesome | I miss eating Aunt Jodi's food | I'm nervous about competing |
| … | … | … |

➜ GF 14: The Gerund (pp. 148–149)

## 1 I don't mind doing that (Gerunds as object)

Say how much you like the activities in the box.
Use the phrases below with the gerund, e.g. I don't mind cleaning my room.

| 🙂 | 😐 | ☹️ |
|---|---|---|
| I love … | | I don't like … |
| I like … | I don't mind … | I can't stand … |
| I enjoy … | | I hate … |

clean your room · play computer games · shop for clothes · take out the rubbish · lie on the beach · go to the dentist · wash the dishes · stand in front of the class

**Early finisher** Make more sentences with your ideas, e.g. I hate queuing for a long time.

➜ **Workbook** 8 (p. 44)

## 2 Home huggers and sports sparks (Gerunds after prepositions)

a) Say what kind of people these phrases describe.

> home hugger · sports spark · music maniac · fashion follower · teenage Einstein

– I think a home hugger is someone who …

b) Make sentences about people you know.
You can use these ideas.

| be bad at | bake cakes |
| be good at | play football |
| be interested in | program computers |
| be keen on | solve maths problems |
| get excited about | go to a shopping mall |
| never get tired of | go to the gym |
| look forward to | … |

My uncle is a real home hugger. He's great at baking cakes. And he never gets tired of cleaning the kitchen.

**More help** ➜ (p. 109)   ➜ **Workbook** 9 (p. 44)

Part B  Practice  3

## 3 Living here is OK (Gerunds)

Write sentences about your neighbourhood: what you like / don't like, etc.
The great thing about living in our street is that it's really green.
I love going to the park because …

| The | good<br>best<br>bad<br>worst<br>… | thing about | live in our street<br>live near the station/park/…<br>live in a suburb …<br>have nice neighbours<br>… | is (that) … |
|---|---|---|---|---|
| I | like<br>don't like<br>don't mind<br>hate<br>… | talk to neighbours<br>live near the …<br>go …<br>play …<br>shop …<br>ride … | | because … |

More help ➔ (p. 110)
Early finisher ➔ (p. 112)

## 4 A day out in Mobridge

Imagine you both live in Mobridge. Your friends Max and Claire are visiting the town.
You're planning a day out with them. You want to find two activities both friends would enjoy, e.g.
- swimming and tubing in the Missouri River
- hunting turkeys and deer
- seeing a movie at the Pheasant Drive-in with friends
- going to a downtown dance on Saturday night
- an afternoon driving around in your family's pickup truck
- …

a) **Partner A:** Go to p. 115 and read about Claire.
   **Partner B:** Go to p. 264 and read about Max.

b) Ask and write down your partner's answers:
   What is Max/Claire interested in?
   What does he/she like doing?
   Is there anything he/she doesn't like doing?

c) Agree on two activities for the day out.
   Partner A: Well, Max likes …, so he might enjoy going to …
   Partner B: Yes, but he hates …, so …

Early finisher ➔ (p. 113)  ➔ Workbook  10–11 (p. 45)

# 3 Background file — Native American societies

EXTRA

## 1 Native American societies and cultures of the Great Plains

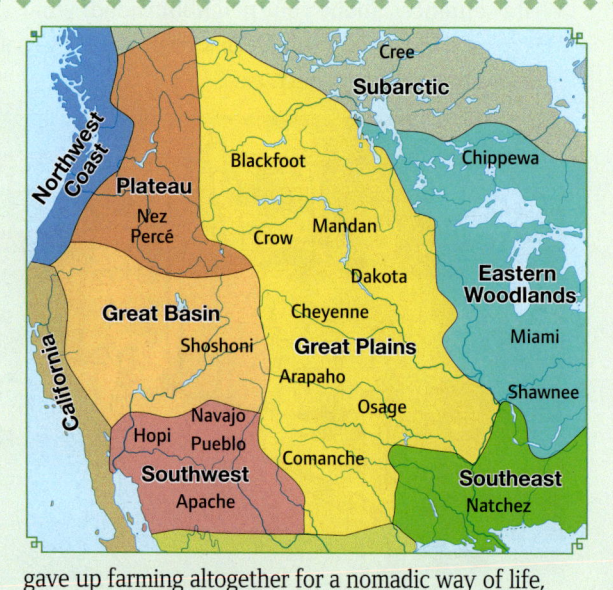

The yellow area in the map of North America shows the region known as the the Great Plains. As you have learned, this region of flatlands extends into present-day Canada and includes parts of ten states: Montana, South
5 Dakota, North Dakota, Minnesota, Wyoming, Nebraska, Colorado, Kansas, Oklahoma, New Mexico and Texas. By 1100 CE, many distinct groups farmed and hunted in this huge expanse of land, including the Pawnee, Mandan, Omaha, Wichita, Lakota, Dakota and Cheyenne
10 nations.

There were both nomadic and sedentary[1] communities in this region. Larger communities were able to lead a sedentary way of life by farming corn, beans and squash in small villages near rivers and lakes. In these
15 communities, the women tended[2] the crops[3], while the men hunted bison and small game. Other groups were nomadic - continually travelling across the Great Plains, often in 'bands' consisting of 12 to 300 people. They slept in teepees that could easily be set up and taken
20 down to be carried to the next location. Other communities lived both a sedentary and nomadic way of life. They planted crops and established villages in the spring, hunted in summer, harvested[4] their crops in the fall and hunted once again in winter.

25 Horses are not native to North America. Before the arrival of the Spanish conquistadores, men hunted on foot, using large spears with sharp points carved out of stone. With great skill and speed, they were able to hunt very large animals like buffalo. In 1519, the Spanish
30 explorer Hernán Cortés travelled by ship to the 'New World' with 600 horses. By the 1600s, horses were widely available and the Lakota and Cheyenne peoples gave up farming altogether for a nomadic way of life, hunting herds of buffalo on horseback.

The introduction of horses into Native American
40 communities had other social effects. Men who had a greater number of horses had a higher social status and greater political and economic power. As European colonists arrived, certain Native American nations – especially the Sioux – began to trade with them. They
45 exchanged buffalo robes, blankets and beads for guns and horses that were brought by the Europeans. Competition between communities increased: one group would steal the horses of other groups to have greater status and wealth[5]. Because some groups now possessed[6]
50 guns, these conflicts became violent as well. Native American nations were also continually threatened by the arrival of ever more European colonizers.

a) Reread the second paragraph of the text above. Make a Venn diagram. Add words and phrases that explain sedentary, nomadic, and sedentary-nomadic ways of life.

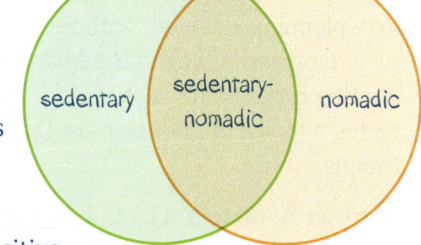

b) **Think**: Take notes on the effects of the introduction of horses to the nations of the Great Plains.

**Pair**: Compare your notes with your partner. Together, decide which effects are negative and which are positive.

**Share**: Meet with another pair, share notes, and make connections to what you've learned about the Standing Rock Reservation on p. 75 and report to the class.

---

1 **sedentary** ['sedntri] sesshaft · 2 **tend** [tend] sich um etwas/jmd. kümmern · 3 **crop** [krɒp] Ernte, Feldfrucht ·
4 **(to) harvest** ['hɑːvɪst] ernten, fangen · 5 **wealth** [welθ] Reichtum, Wohlstand · 6 **(to) possess** [pəˈzes] besitzen

## 2 Outcomes of western expansion

At the end of the 18th century, the United States was made up of 13 states on the eastern coast. Throughout the 19th century, European immigrants arrived in great numbers – primarily from Ireland and Germany.

The promise of good farmland led many of them to leave the established states and head westward. The discovery of gold in California and in the Black Hills of South Dakota in the late 1800s also drew others westward to seek[1] their fortune[2]. During this period, there were no roads, highways or trains. Thousands of European Americans, or 'pioneers', travelled overland in 'wagon trains', following trails through the wilderness. It took them about six months to cross over 3,000 kilometers. They began in springtime to avoid[3] being caught in the harsh winter. The crossing was extremely difficult - the pioneers were faced with disease, attacks by thieves, and clashes with Native Americans. European American settlers believed that they had been chosen by God to settle[4] the whole North American continent from the east coast to the west coast – from sea to shining sea. This belief had a name: 'Manifest Destiny'[5].

In 1830 the US government passed the Indian Removal Act. Native Americans from five different nations (Cherokee, Chickasaw, Choctaw, Creek, and Seminole) were forced to leave their ancestral lands in the south-east and migrate to territories or 'reservations' west of the Mississippi River.

During the forced march, which began in 1831, thousands of native people died from starvation[6], disease and exposure to harsh weather. Because of the great suffering[7], this forced migration became known as the 'Trail of Tears'.

Follow the link for a map of forced migration.

From 1831 to 1877, the US government pushed Native Americans off the best farmland, including territories west of the Mississippi River and the Great Plains, making it available for settlement by European Americans. New states were formed as settlers went westward and claimed land. The government set up a network of reservations where the displaced native nations were made to live.

In 1862, the US government passed the 'Homestead Act', which promised 160 acres (62 hectares) to all US citizens if they agreed to settle and farm the land for at least five years. By 1890, millions of new farms had been established in the Great Plains states, including North and South Dakota. Many of these farms were owned by German and Scandinavian immigrants. Native Americans of the Great Sioux nation fiercely resisted the occupation of their land by European American settlers. But in the end, the remaining Native Americans were forced to give up their land and move to the reservations. Their belief in Manifest Destiny led many settlers to feel justified[8] in taking land away from Native Americans and even killing them in order to do so.

a) A timeline
- Draw a timeline on a long piece of paper. Write important dates from the text on the timeline.
- Choose key events connected to the dates and write a short info note for each.
- Post the notes on the timeline. Be creative! Use arrows, draw pictures, add details and show connections between events.

b) What factors led the pioneers to steal land and kill native peoples? Discuss. ➡ Workbook 12 (p. 46)

---

1 **(to) seek** [siːk] suchen • 2 **fortune** [ˈfɔːtʃuːn] Schicksal, Glück • 3 **(to) avoid** [əˈvɔɪd] vermeiden • 4 **(to) settle** [ˈsetl̩] sich niederlassen, besiedeln • 5 **destiny** [ˈdestɪni] Schicksal • 6 **starvation** [staːˈveɪʃən] Hungertod, Verhungern • 7 **suffering** [ˈsʌfərɪŋ] Leiden • 8 **(to) justify** [ˈdʒʌstɪfaɪ] (sich) rechtfertigen

## 1 Bad news for Drew

Say what you think the bad news might be.

Friday afternoon. The school day was over. Even though it was already May, Drew felt a chill in the air as he walked through the high school's double doors. The night before, his dad had returned
5 from his trip and asked Drew for the keys to the truck. Now, whenever he wanted to go somewhere, Drew would have to ask someone for a ride.
Bobby slapped him on the back.
10 "Hey Buddy," he said, "Cheer up, it's the weekend! Let's celebrate with pizza at Joe's! Their pizza tastes great. Then I'll give you a ride home."
"OK," said Drew glumly.
Behind Drew, a group of students was talking and
15 laughing. He could hear Kaya's voice.
"Just a minute, Bobby, I have to ask Kaya something," said Drew and led Kaya away from her friends.
"So have you decided yet? Will you come with us
20 to Mount Rushmore?" he asked.
"I can't do it, Drew."
"Why not?" Drew looked confused.
"It would make my family really angry if I went with you."
25 Drew looked at Kaya, clueless. "Angry? But why?" he asked.
"Because Mount Rushmore is an insult to the Lakota people. The Black Hills are sacred to us. And those presidents – your heroes – stole our
30 land and killed so many of our people."
"But I just wanted to take a trip with you, Kaya, and I thought …"
"Drew, I know it's hard for you to understand. I just can't go there with you."
35 "But there are lots of other things we could do in Rapid City," Drew said.
Kaya sighed as she looked into Drew's disappointed face.
"Drew, I'd like to do something with you. But I
40 just can't go to the Black Hills. Why don't you stay here on the weekend?"
"You mean not go with my family?"
Bobby came up from behind. "Hey man, I can't wait any longer! I need that pizza now!"
45 "I've changed my mind … I'm going home."

Bobby looked surprised. "What? Are you sure?"
"Yeah, I'm sure."
"OK then. I'll give you a ride."
"No thanks. I'm going to walk."
50 "But it's over five miles, Drew!"
"Yeah, so what? I need to think."

## 2 Reasons

a) Complete the sentences:
   1 Bobby wants …   2 Drew hears …
   3 Kaya doesn't …

b) Answer the questions with one sentence.
   1 Why is Bobby happy?
   2 What is Kaya doing when Drew sees her?

c) Explain what decision Kaya has made and why. How does Drew react to this?

d) Compare Drew's mood here to his mood on p. 74. Give reasons for the change and support your ideas from the text.

## 3 Drew's thoughts

Imagine you are Drew. In a 100-word paragraph explain what you have decided to do at the weekend: go with your family to Rapid City or spend the weekend in Mobridge with Kaya.

More help ➔ (p. 110)

➔ Workbook 13 (p. 47)

**Part C** Practice  **3**

## 4 Mount Rushmore: For or against

The Mount Rushmore National Memorial – the faces of four presidents: George Washington, Thomas Jefferson, Abraham Lincoln and Theodore Roosevelt – was begun in 1927 and completed in 1941.
The sculptures were made to attract tourists to South Dakota, and today, nearly three million visit the site every year. But visitors can react very differently.

### Sarah Kelada

I have come to South Dakota to see the giant faces in the Black Hills. As I walk along Mount Rushmore's Avenue of Flags and see the four presidents' faces in the granite mountain before me, it is totally clear
5 what this place is: a symbol of American power, a monument to patriotism.
The memorial was paid for with taxpayers' money and it is looked after by the National Park Service. It is
10 one of the places where the country shows the world how great it is. It is in the Black Hills, Native American land that is sacred to the Lakota people.
15 The Black Hills that were promised to the Lakota forever in 1868, but were taken away from them a few years later when white people discovered gold there.
20 The presidents we see here only helped to steal that land and kill its people. How heartless to carve their giant heads on this sacred mountain! Quite a lot of Native Americans strongly criticize the memorial and
25 find it extremely offensive. I can fully understand that. How would people like it if they sprayed graffiti on the cathedral in Rapid City?

### Darren Wright

As I walked along Mount Rushmore's Avenue of Flags, I was blown away by one of the most wonderful sights in our country. This huge, awesome work of art made me proud to be an American! It is hardly surprising that it is found 5 on lists of the "Wonders of the Modern World".
These four presidents all played a part in the creation of the United States. That's why they were chosen for this memorial to our nation. Their 10 60-foot granite faces will gaze forever over the Black Hills as a symbol of the strength of our nation.
I stayed around for the evening 15 ceremony in the amphitheater. I thoroughly enjoyed the program. It began with a 20-minute movie about the monument's history. Then, as the national anthem played 20 in the background, huge floodlights lit up the presidents' faces against the cloudless night sky. As I watched, I felt tears of pride run down my face, like many other Americans in the crowd. 25
I firmly believe every American should visit this great monument.

Find out about the Crazy Horse monument near Mount Rushmore.

## 5 Different opinions

In a table, list the reasons the two writers give for liking or not liking Mount Rushmore. Compare your lists in class.

Would you visit Mount Rushmore? Prepare a short statement. Read it to the class.

## 6 Where's Drew?

Listen and find out where Drew is, and why. Say how Kaya finds out and how she reacts.

**EXTRA** Imagine Kaya and Drew's meeting at school next week. What will they say? Write their conversation and act it out.

➜ Workbook *14 (p. 48)*

# 3 Part C Practice

## 1 WORDS A colourful picture (Adjectives with *-ful* and *-less*)

a) Make adjectives from the nouns in the boxes.
Think of nouns that go with them and make a list.

**-ful**
colour · event · respect · rest · success · skill

**-less**
air · end · home · moon · rain · sleep

**TIP**
Recognizing suffixes like *-ful* or *-less* can help you to understand new words.

*-ful* = **full of** or **giving**, e.g. power*ful*, help*ful*
*-less* = **without**, e.g. cloud*less*, heart*less*

colourful: a colourful picture, a colourful …

More help ➜ (p. 111)

b) 👥 Compare your ideas.
Early finisher ➜ (p. 113)

c) Using the phrases in your list write six sentences.
👥 Read your sentences to your partner.

➜ Workbook 15 (p. 49)

### Language help

**Position of adverbs**
Different types of adverbs go in different places in a sentence.

**Adverbs of degree** are used to **stress** certain words in the sentence. They usually go between the subject and the verb:
When there is more than one verb, the adverb comes before the word it modifies.
I *really* like Drew.
Kaya's cousin was *totally* surprised that Drew invited Kaya to Mount Rushmore.

**Adverbs of manner** tell us the *way* something happened or is done. They usually go at the end of the sentence. Unlike in German, they cannot come between the main verb and the object:
She opened the door **quietly**.
Sie öffnete **leise** die Tür.

**Adverbs of time** tell us about *when* something happened. They come at the beginning or the end of a sentence:
I need that pizza **now**.
**Yesterday**, Coach told me my times were really good.

➜ GF 15 Adverbs and adverbials (pp. 150–151)

## 2 I ordered the words correctly (Adverb: word order)

a) Read the sentences about Kaya, Drew and Bobby and put the correct adverb at the right place.
1 Drew plays the guitar.
2 Everyone cheered 'Tigers' at the game.
3 Have you seen Kaya?
4 We have to leave to make the film.
5 She sang the second song.
6 You parked the car.
7 Drew's family left the house.
8 Kaya was tired after rodeo practice.
9 After his presentation Bobby answered Kaya's questions.

badly · beautifully · early · extremely · loudly · quickly · quietly · thoroughly · today · very

b) 👥 Choose four to five sentences from a) with adverbs and use them to write a dialogue between Drew and Kaya or Drew and Bobby.

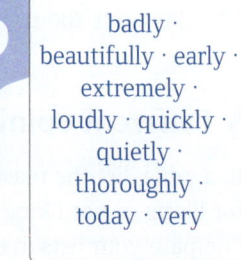

➜ Workbook 16 (p. 49)

## Part C Practice 3

### 3 Frybread on the Standing Rock Rez (Adjectives after verbs of perception)

Most verbs are described by adverbs, but verbs of perception *(look, feel, smell, taste, seem)* are followed by adjectives. Choose the correct word to fill in the blanks of the text about Mato.

Little Mato (his name means 'bear' in Lakota) lives on the Standing Rock Reservation and loves frybread. He wants to eat it every day, not just at powwows. His mother [1]... pats down the dough into flat circles. "Ah!" she says. "This dough feels [2]...!" She places the dough [3]... into the very hot oil as Mato watches. When they are brown, they are ready to eat with sugar or jam. Mato likes them with his mother's beef soup. "They smell [4]...," he tells his mother. He looks [5]..., waiting for her to give him one. He pauses and seems [6].... "And they taste [7]... too!"

> careful · delicious · excited · good · perfect · skilful · thoughtful

➜ Workbook 17 (p. 50)

### 4 A bit, completely, extremely ... (Adverbs of degree)

👥 Work with a partner and have a look at the following everyday sentences.
Take turns: Use the words in the box, make an adverb and put it in the correct position in the sentence. Then read the sentence to your partner.

> extreme · clear · total · thorough · quite · near · exact · hard · almost

1 I hadn't slept all night so I was tired.
2 I've finished. I need five more minutes.
3 That's perfect! It's what I wanted.
4 The exercise is difficult, but I think I can manage it.
5 They're friendly – the nicest people I've ever met.
6 It was cool in Iceland, but that was a surprise.
7 I love languages and I'm interested in English.
8 Please clean your room.

**Early finisher** Write more everyday sentences with adverbs.

➜ GF 15: Adverbs and adverbials (pp. 150–151)
➜ Workbook 18 (p. 51)

### 5 Say it with emphasis (Collocations with adverbs of degree)

a) Look at these sentences from the texts on p. 81.
The authors use collocations to give emphasis to their opinions.
1 It is *totally clear* what this place is: a symbol of American power.
2 Native Americans *strongly criticize* the memorial.
3 It is *hardly surprising* that it is found on lists of the "Wonders of the Modern World"
4 I *thoroughly enjoyed* the program.
5 I *firmly believe* every American should visit this great monument.

Make sure that you understand the meaning of the words marked in orange.
Use a dictionary if necessary.

b) Choose one of these topics below and express your opinion in a paragraph (about 60-80 words).
Use at least three of the collocations above to give emphasis to your ideas.
1 Eating meat should be against the law.
2 Summer holidays should be eight weeks long instead of six weeks long.
3 Fighting climate change should be the EU's number 1 priority.

c) 👥 Read your text to your group. Do they agree or disagree?
How effective do you think your argument was?

➜ GF 15: Adverbs and adverbials (pp. 150–151)
➜ Workbook 19 (p. 51)

# 3 Part C Practice

## 6 STUDY SKILLS  Making a slide for a presentation

On this page you will make a slide with important information and effectively integrate an image.

a) Select the important information.

Read the text about the Blackfoot nation's confrontation with European colonists.

These steps can help you take useful notes:
- On a copy of the text, underline or highlight key facts.
- Cover the text.
- Write down each key fact as a short note. **Use your own words!**

> - Blackfoot nation - Northern Plains - hunted buffalo
> - European American settlers - came with horses
> - Blackfoot - welcomed settlers why?
> - horses helped buffalo hunt
> - settlers brought disease -
> - by 1850s 2/3 Blackfoot Indians dead

👥 Compare your notes with a partner.

b) Review your notes, choose a key fact and write a one-line text for your slide.
Example:
Settlers introduce horses –
Blackfoot use them to hunt buffalo

c) Choose an image for your slide. Remember that it should give visual information for the text on your slide or other important facts.

Choose the image on the right that you think would work best with the bullet point in b).

👥 Compare your choice with a partner. Explain why you chose the image and how you would talk about it.

### THE BLACKFOOT OF THE NORTHERN PLAINS

The Blackfoot were a powerful buffalo-hunting society of the northern plains of present-day Montana, Idaho in the US, and Alberta, Canada. When European American settlers crossed into Blackfoot territory, they brought horses. At first, the Blackfoot welcomed the foreigners, whose horses greatly helped them in hunting buffalo. But the settlers also brought disease. In the mid-1800s several smallpox epidemics killed nearly two thirds of the Blackfoot population. There is even evidence that some European American settlers intentionally sold infected blankets to people of the Blackfoot nation.

In 1870, the US army attacked and killed a band of Blackfoot: a lot of women and children were among the dead. By the end of the 19th century, the white settlers had hunted down nearly all of the buffalo herds, the Blackfoot's main source of food. Hundreds of Blackfoot starved to death because of this. Those who survived were forced to give up their nomadic lifestyle and live on reservations established by the United States government.

d) Using your key fact from b) make a slide.

e) Choose an image for your slide or find an image on the internet.

**Early finisher** Follow steps b) and c) and make two or more slides.  ➜ SF 21: Making slides for a presentation (p. 131)

➜ **Workbook** 20 (p. 52)

# The world behind the picture 3

**1 *Bloodlines*** (by Christopher Nataanii Cegielski)

*Bloodlines is a short film which tells a story about relationships in a Native American family.*

a) Look at this still from the film and describe the mood between the characters.
Then watch the beginning of the film.
What else can you say about the family?

b) Now watch the rest of the film and take notes about what happens.
👥 Compare your ideas.

c) 👥 During the whole film, the characters never talk about their feelings.
Discuss how you think they feel towards each other as the story continues.

Now imagine what they are thinking in the stills on the right.
Write a short dialogue in which the father and the older boy say how they feel.

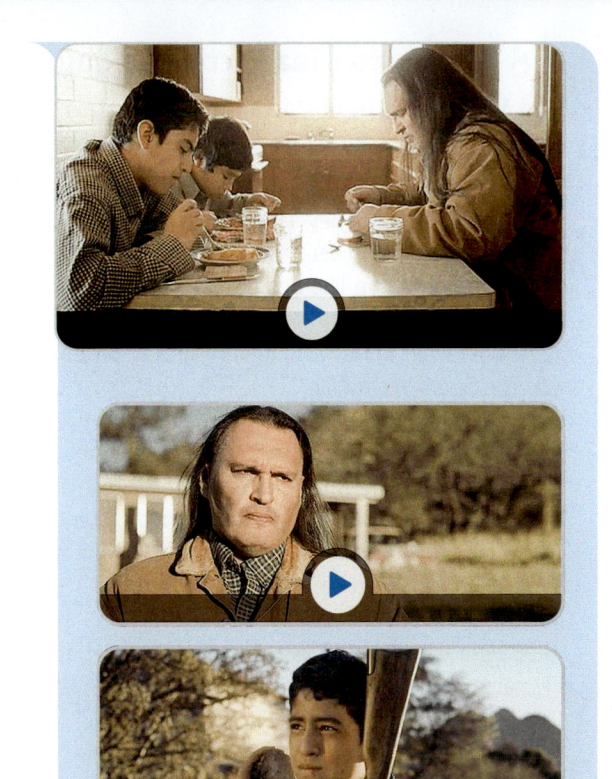

**2 Making the film: Shots**

a) Look at these stills from the film.
Describe what you can see in each shot.

b) Match the shots to the following definitions.
- This shot tells us more about the situation the characters are in.
- This shot helps you to understand where the action takes place.
- This shot shows the feelings of one of the characters.

Now watch some scenes from the film again and find examples of each kind of shot.

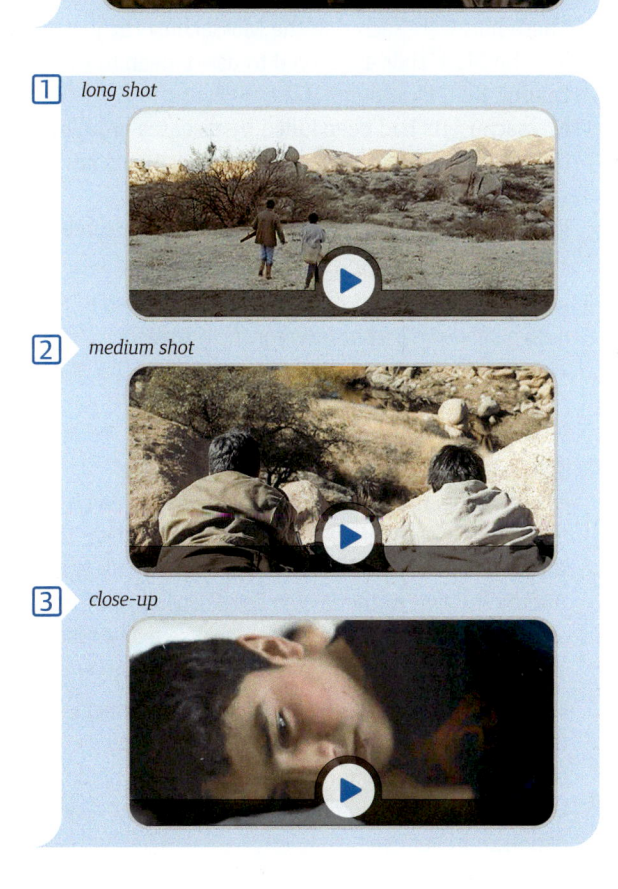

1 long shot

2 medium shot

3 close-up

eighty-five

# 3 Part D

## 1 🔊 The Boston Tea Party: Looking at history through a different lens

Find Massachusetts, Boston and the Blue Hills on the map of the United States on the back inside cover of your book.

On Tuesday, Drew and Kaya were working together in the school library. They sat across from each other, laptops back to back, doing the research for their presentation on The Boston Tea Party.
5 Drew suddenly got excited, "This is sooo cool! Remember what Bobby said about the way Britain won the Seven Years War?"
Kaya looked up. "Yeah, I remember hearing him say that they 'emptied their coffers' … I also remember
10 not knowing exactly what that means."
"It means that the British government put lots and lots of money into the war so they could send more troops to North America … to New York, New Jersey, Massachusetts and …"
15 "Stop right there!" said Kaya, "Do you know where the name Massachusetts comes from?"
"No …"
"It's the name of the indigenous community that had been living all around Boston Bay way before
20 the English immigrants arrived. Massachusetts is also the name of the Blue Hills around Boston Bay. These hills were sacred to the Massachusetts, just like the Black Hills are sacred to us - I mean to the Lakota. BUT, by around 1620, 90% of the
25 Massachusetts had been killed by diseases brought by the English. That's only part of it … it gets much worse. Let me read this to you:"
Kaya started to read the text she had on her screen:
*"'The English thought that the outbreak of disease
30 was a gift from God because it cleared the land of the native people in preparation for their arrival. The English colonists forced the remaining 10% of the Massachusetts off the best land into small villages. They were also forced to practice Christianity
35 and weren't allowed to follow their traditional customs. The Massachusetts barely survived. Even though they were treated so badly by the British, they still helped the colonists during the Seven Years War. And by the time of the Boston Tea Party, most of the
40 once powerful nation of the Massachusetts lived in 'prayer towns' in great poverty.'"*
Kaya's eyes narrowed. "What makes me so mad is that after the English colonists destroyed the Massachusetts' community, they stole their name!"
45 Drew was silent. He didn't know what to say. Kaya had tears in her eyes.

"I'm sorry," he said, and held out his hand to her. "I think what you're doing is really important."
"Yeah, but it hurts." Kaya sighed. "Now tell me what
50 you're going to talk about. You can practice what you are going to say."
"Are you sure?" asked Drew.
Kaya smiled. "Yeah, I'm sure. Just remember to talk slooooowly!"
55 "OK. But bring your chair around to this side. I want to show you the slides I've made."

## 2 Working together

a) Answer the questions.
1 What are Kaya and Drew doing in the library?
2 What does they *'emptied their coffers'* mean?

b) Complete the sentences with the correct information in your own words.
1 The Massachussetts are …
2 Kaya reads …   3 Drew is silent …

## 3 But it hurts … 💬

Explain why Kaya has tears in her eyes after reading the text about the Massachusetts to Drew. How does this information make you feel? Share your thoughts with the class.

## 4 Kaya's presentation

a) Speculate on what you think Kaya's presentation should be about.

b) Identify six points that you think Kaya's slides should show in her presentation.

c) 👥 Compare your points with your partner.

## 5 Actions and reactions

Study Drew's slides on p. 87. Name the British Empire's actions and the colonists' reactions before and after the Boston Tea Party.

### EXTRA The Boston Tea Party ✏️

Explain in a text (about 100-150 words) how the Seven Years War and the Boston Tea Party set the stage for the American War of Independence.

## 6 Drew's slides

Form groups. Discuss Drew's slides. Consider all of the following:

- Are they clear?
- Do they have too much/too little information?
- Do they have too many/too few illustrations?
- Are the illustrations effective?

**1** After the Seven Years War ... British Empire needs money !

Its coffers are empty ...

**2** British Empire taxes colonies in North America

Colonists are very angry !

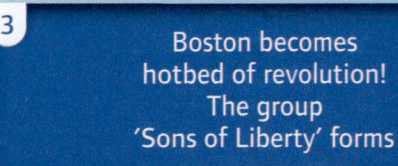

**3** Boston becomes hotbed of revolution! The group 'Sons of Liberty' forms

JOIN, or DIE.

**4** The Boston Tea Party
December 10, 1763

What kind of party was it???

**5** Bostonians disguised as Mohawks throw 342 crates of British Tea into Boston Harbor
Value: £10,000 / $ 1.7 million today

No Taxation without representation!

**6** British Empire reacts !!!
- shuts down → Boston Port
- shuts down → Boston's local government
- sends troops → to occupy Boston

**7** Colonists react !!!
- 1774 → Organize First Continental Congress
- Agree to boycott British goods

**8** Conclusion:

Boston Tea Party sets the stage for the

American War of Independence.

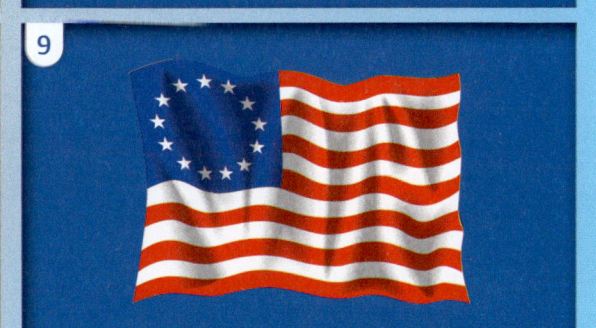

**9**

# 3  Part D  Practice

> **Language help**
>
> When you use two verbs together, the second verb is often an infinitive:
> e.g.: I *want to go* to Rapid City with you.
>   Have you *decided to try out* for the finals?
>   Yes, I *plan to practice* at the weekend.
>
> Some verbs, e.g. *forget, hate, like, love, start, stop, try* can be followed by either the infinitive or the gerund with a difference in meaning.
> *I hate doing presentations.*
> *I hate to do presentations.*
>
> The verb **remember** can be followed by either **the infinitive** or **the gerund** with a difference in **meaning.**
>
> 1  **Remember** *to speak* slowly.
> This form has a future meaning.
>
> 2  I **remember** *hearing* him say that they 'emptied their coffers'.
> This form is used when talking about the past.
> It is a 'memory', not a direction or request.
>
> ➡ *GF 14: The Gerund (p. 148)*

## 1  What came in last night? (Verb + infinitive)

Complete each short dialogue with the gerund or *to*-infinitive of one of the verbs from the box.

A: Were you there when it happened?
B: Yes, I remember ...¹ a loud crash.
A: How do you think it entered?
B: Jules didn't remember ...² the back door.
A: Is that all? Aren't there other reasons?
B: Well, there is a big sign on the back door which says: 'Remember ...³ all the lights, Remember ...⁴ all the windows, Remember ...⁵ all the food. When I entered the kitchen, I remember ...⁶ popcorn.
A: What happened after the crash?
B: I entered the kitchen. It was dark. I remember ...⁷ the light switch when I felt something touch my arm.

> turn off · smell · close · turn on ·
> hear · lock · put away

## 2  Where to go on Saturday night (Verb + gerund or *to*-infinitive)

Complete the text about Bobby, Drew and Kaya's night out.
Choose the right form for the verbs in the box: gerund or *to*-infinitive.
On Saturday night, Bobby, Drew and Kaya decided ...¹ together. Bobby wanted ...² an action movie at the local drive-in.
"I don't mind ...³ to see a movie, and I really enjoy ...⁴ to drive-ins," said Kaya,
"but look, it doesn't start until 10 pm. I hate ...⁵ so long."
"Yeah," said Drew. "Last time, I remember ...⁶ in your car for two hours, ...⁷ for the film to start."
Kaya nodded her head. "I tried ...⁸ warm, but I remember ...⁹ so cold that I drank four hot chocolates!"
"Well, do you have a better idea?" asked Bobby.
Kaya suggested going to the movie theater in town.
"I hate ...¹⁰ films at that theater! It's always filled with little kids!" said Bobby.
"That's not true! Not at night time," said Drew.
"Do you know what's playing?" asked Bobby.
"No, but I can try ...¹¹ ," said Kaya.
"OK," said Bobby glumly, "But remember ...¹² how much it costs.
Drive-ins are usually much cheaper and I don't feel like ...¹³ all of my allowance on a single movie!" said Bobby.

> ask · call · get ·
> go · go out · sit ·
> stay · use · wait ·
> watch

➡ *GF 14.2 The gerund as subject and object (p. 148)*
➡ **Workbook** *21 – 22 (pp. 53 – 54)*

## The Iroquois Confederacy: Roots of democracy

Iroquois (pronounced ir-uh-kwa) is the name the French colonists gave to the group of five nations who call themselves the Haudenosaunee (ho-dee-no-sho-nee), or 'People of the Long House'.
The five nations – Seneca, Cayuga, Onondaga, Oneida and Mohawk – each occupied a different geographical region of the Northeast woodlands. These individual nations had once fought against one another. But in about 1450, they agreed to form a confederacy based on peace, unity and mutual support. The Haudenosaunee developed a sophisticated political system that was one of the first examples of democracy in the world. The Iroquois Confederacy's form of government influenced the shaping of the democratic government of the United States three centuries later.

Each of the five member nations selected representatives to attend important political meetings. The representatives would discuss issues related to the welfare of the entire confederacy. The council passed laws and made decisions that would affect everyone. The Iroquois lived in wooden houses 30 to 90 meters long called 'longhouses'. These dwellings had two doors, one at each end. Inside the house, raised platforms were used for storage and sleeping. Many related families lived together in a longhouse and built fires in the middle for cooking and warmth. Villages often had twenty or more longhouses that were surrounded by a wall for protection.

But the longhouse was not only a dwelling, it also became a living symbol of the Iroquois Confederacy. Imagine a longhouse stretched over the geographical region where the five different nations lived. The Seneca, who lived farthest to the west, were known as the 'Keepers of the Western Door'. They made sure that no enemies attacked from the west. Moving eastward, the Cayuga were known as 'Little Brother', a name which emphasizes that one should treat and care for those of a different nation as if they were members of your own family. The Onondaga were the 'Keepers of the Fire'. They lived in the middle region. Their role was to keep the fire of the Great Peace burning. Continuing eastward, the Oneida were also known as 'Little Brother', while the Mohawks were known as 'Keepers of the Eastern Door'. It was their job to defend their people from attacks from the east.

The Iroquois are matrilineal: clans or families are traced back through the mother's line. The oldest and wisest women from each clan, known as clan mothers, were responsible for choosing the representatives to attend the meetings of the council.

*Exterior of an Iroquois longhouse*

👥 Using information from the text, draw a floor plan of a longhouse.
Write the name and role of each of the five nations in the correct position on your drawing.
Share your plan with your group.

➡ **Workbook** 23 (p. 54)

# 3 Text

## The Legend of the Great Peacemaker

There are over 500 Native American nations in North America. Their way of life, language and culture can be very different, but one thing they have in common is the oral tradition: the telling of stories passed on from generation to generation.

It was through storytellers that Native American children learned the history of their communities, how to behave, and how to understand the natural world. The oral tradition also helped to keep the native languages alive.

### 1 Words

Before you listen to the story, find the meaning of these words in a dictionary. Share what you found in class.

> legend · wampum · sorcerer · destiny · sorrow · needles · bundle · orator · faith · generation

### 2 The story

a) Listen to the story. Pay attention to the sequence of events.
Then, with your partner, arrange the story's events in the right order.
1. The sorcerer Tadodaho refuses the Peacemaker's message.
2. Peacemaker assembles the nations, speaks the Law of Peace, and throws all weapons under the roots of the Tree of Peace.
3. Hiawatha joins the Peacemaker on his journey to unify the five nations.
4. The Peacemaker uses wampum to heal Hiawatha removing his sorrow.
5. The Peacemaker promises Jigonsaseh that she will be the first Clan Mother of all the Nations.
6. The Mohawks test the Peacemaker by getting him to climb a tree, which they then cut down.
7. Tadodaho kills Hiawatha's family.

b) With your partner, write what you think is the meaning of each symbol.
 · Wampum belt  · Pine tree needles  · Tree of Peace
 · Five arrows  · Snake hair  · The eagle

c) Discuss your results in class.

*A wampum belt showing the five nations*

### 3 The characters

a) Listen to the story again and focus on the characters in the list below.
Write notes about each character's role and powers.
 · The Peacemaker  · Hiawatha  · Tadodaho  · Jigonsaseh

b) Share notes with your partner. Add more details.

c) As a class, discuss how the main characters achieved their goals.

d) **EXTRA** Find a story from your family's history.
Write it down (about 180 words) and tell it to your group. ➔ **Workbook** 24–25 (p. 55)

# The ways we learn history — The digital compass 3

On this page you will explore the ways you learn about the history of different cultures and nations, including your own.

## 1 How do you like to learn history best?

a) Choose your favourite ways to learn history and make notes about the reasons why.

- Reading history books/textbooks
- Listening to stories about the past from family members
- Reading novels and historical novels
- Watching films about the past
- Researching Wikipedia and other Internet sites
- Watching history videos online
- Visiting museums and historical sites
- Taking notes in history class
- Other ways: …

b) Compare your notes with your partner.
Talk about the advantages and disadvantages of these ways of learning history.

## 2 A closer look

You have learned about the Iroquois Confederacy in a background file from listening to the legend of The Great Peacemaker on p. 90.

a) Form groups and discuss these two questions:
- What did you learn about the Iroquois Confederacy from listening to the story?
- How did you learn it?

Think about image, language, sound, symbol and storytellers. Talk about the specific advantages, disadvantages, reliability and challenges of learning history in each way.

b) Work in groups of four. Do a placemat activity. In your corner, write down the informational science and history videos you watch regularly. Take turns.
Talk about what you learned from the videos in your list.
Write the names of the videos that two or more people in your group regularly watch in the middle of the placemat. Share your results in class.

**EXTRA** Choose a video from your list in 2b).
Say:
- if the video gives the answers you are looking for.
- if the video presents multiple perspectives on the topic.

Find out:
- who made the video and if they are an expert on the topic.
- when the video was made.
- what information is included and whether the information is different from other videos.

# 3 Your task

## Meeting of cultures

In this unit, you have learned about the Lakota, Dakota, and the five nations of the Iroquois Confederacy.

There were over 570 native nations who lived in North America before the European colonists arrived.

Your task is to give an electronic presentation about the first confrontations between a Native American nation and European settlers.

**STEP 1** Choose a nation
- The map on the right is divided into geographical/cultural regions. Each region has a different landscape and climate. Choose a Native American nation from the map.

**STEP 2** Research
- What happened when the colonists and your chosen native nation confronted each other?

These questions can guide you:
- When did the confrontation take place?
- Where was it?
- What changed?

You should think about:
- native culture at the time of confrontation
- settlers' goals and motivations
- the series of events leading up to and including an important confrontation

You can focus your presentation on:
- an actual battle
- a first encounter
- a person who played an important role in the confrontation

➡ SF 18: Internet research (p. 130)

**STEP 3** Find images
➡ SF 21: Making slides for a presentation (p. 131)

**STEP 4** Write the texts for your slides
**Remember:** Keep each text very short and to the point! ➡ SF 21: Making slides for a presentation (p. 131)

**STEP 5** Prepare note cards with key points to explain what is on the slides

**STEP 6** Give your presentation
- It's always a good idea to practice before you present.
- Be aware of the time you've been given for your presentation.
- Speak slowly and clearly.
- After your presentation, ask your audience for questions.

**STEP 7** Reflection
- Think about what you've learned about the meeting of cultures and what connections you can make to our society today.
- Write down your thoughts in a one-paragraph reflection (about 60 words).

# Checkpoint 3

## A

### 1 Stories from a British and an American teenager

Complete Jack's and Melanie's texts with the correct words.

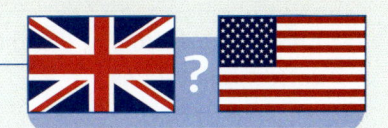

**1 Jack from Plymouth, UK**
"We were watching this really scary film. Something fell out of my [1]... pocket. What if it is a ten [2]... note, I thought. I just wasn't able to find it in the dark. I was going [3]... ! Finally, I used the [4]... on my [5]... phone. My [6]... Jason was really angry with me. But when I bought him a [7]... drink and a plate of [8]... at the snack bar, all was forgiven."

**2 Melanie from Mobridge, South Dakota, US**
"The weather has been really strange: Yesterday was so hot and today it's hard to believe its summer [1].... Yesterday, I drank a g [2]... of [3]... and had three orange-flavored [4]... . I was still hot, I guess that's because I was wearing [5]... instead of shorts and [6]... instead of sandals. But today is cool enough to wear a [7]... over my shirt. I'm meeting my friends on [8]... Street. We're going to get Chinese [9]... and eat it in the park."

### 2 Paraphrases

a) Find the words that match these paraphrases.
Write them in your exercise book.
1. A strong love and pride in your country.
2. A form of government in which leaders are elected by the people.
3. The song people sing to celebrate their nation or country, especially at international sports events.
4. The union of different peoples, states or tribes into one group.
5. A semicircular outdoor theater.
6. A disease that quickly spreads to many people.
7. A person or nation that has joined with another for a special purpose.

b) Paraphrase these words: wagon, salmon, powder, anticipation, revolutionary.

### 3 WORDS A restless night

Combine each word from box A with an ending from box B to form adverbs and adjectives.
Use the adverbs and adjectives to complete the sentences about everyday life.

**A**: home · peace · year · final · friend · silent · wonder · success · care · power · general · harm

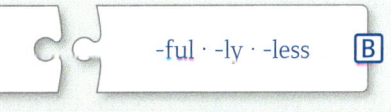

**B**: -ful · -ly · -less

1. A clan mother is a ... person in the Iroquois society.
2. That old man is always sitting on that street corner. He must be ... .
3. Yesterday, I had my ... check-up. My doctor said I was very healthy.
4. Please be ... ! The soup is very hot!.
5. I ... have a chance to call you back. I'm sorry it took so long.
6. Ted is always ... to the new kids in class.
7. The cat entered the room ... .
8. It's very ... out here in the desert.
9. I just listened to this ... song. I think you'll like it too.
10. Don't worry, that snake is ... . It doesn't bite.

# 3 Checkpoint

## 4 WORDS Looking forward to it

a) Choose words from A, B and C to form the correct collocations.

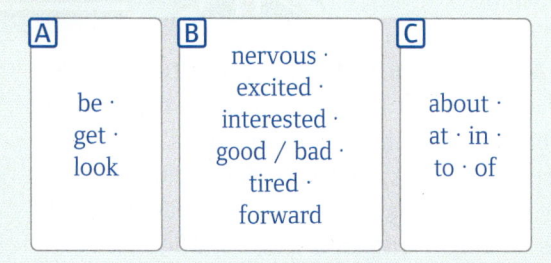

| A | B | C |
|---|---|---|
| be · get · look | nervous · excited · interested · good / bad · tired · forward | about · at · in · to · of |

b) Write a sentence for each collocation.

## 5 The Lakota and Dakota people

Complete the text about the Lakota and Dakota people with the correct words.

The Standing Rock ¹… is a large area of land in the US state of ²… and ³… . It is now home to the Lakota and Dakota people. Before the arrival of the ⁴… American ⁵…, the Lakota and Dakota were a ⁶… people who ⁷… buffalo to ⁸… . But in the second half of the 19th ⁹…, the United States ¹⁰… forced them to live on ¹¹… lands and change their way of life from ¹²… to ¹³… . But because the land was very dry, many Lakota and Dakota died of ¹⁴… .

## 6 Kaya's presentation: Before and after

Complete Kaya's and her mother's sentences with the right form of the verbs: gerund or *to*-infinitive.

be · bring · clap · do (2x) · learn · perform · practice (2x) · sing · speak · talk (3x) · understand

**The day before Kaya's presentation**

"I'm really nervous about ¹… my presentation tomorrow. I hate ²… in front of the whole class." complained Kaya.
"Do you remember ³… that old Lakota song at Cody's wedding? There were over 100 people there and you did a great job!"
"Thanks, Mom. But ⁴… is different than ⁵… about history.

The topic is important and I want ⁶… it right."
"Why don't you try ⁷… it in front of me? ⁸… is the best way to prepare yourself and to lose your fear."
"Now?"
"Yes, now. Just start ⁹… , but remember ¹⁰… clearly and slowly. I want ¹¹… every word."

**After Kaya's presentation**

"So, how did it go?" asked Kaya's mom.
"It was awesome! I totally forgot about ¹… nervous! There were lots of questions and after my talk, everyone started ²…! My teacher thanked me for ³… a Native American perspective to the class. Then he said, "⁴… about historical events from different perspectives is really important."

## 7 MIXED BAG

Complete the text about South Dakota with the correct words.

South Dakota, ¹… … its name from the Native American nation of the Dakotas, is the 17th ²… state ³… the US, but it is one of the least populated. It ⁴… an area of 199,729 km² but a population of only 882,235. Agriculture and tourism are the ⁵… important industries in South Dakota. Mount Rushmore, located ⁶… Keystone, South Dakota, is an ⁷… popular tourist attraction. Over two million people ⁸… the monumental sculpture ⁹… year. The memorial, ¹⁰… took ¹¹… 14 years to complete, ¹²… carved into ¹³… stone of the Black Hills. It ¹⁴… four US presidents, including George Washington, one ¹⁵… … 'Founding Fathers' of the nation. In South Dakota, you ¹⁶… … your driving licence ¹⁷… are 14 years and three months, which is ¹⁸… … age in the country. ¹⁹… do teenagers in South Dakota need ²⁰… at such a young age? They need ²¹… … to school ²²… areas where ²³… … no school buses. And they ²⁴… … be able to drive tractors to help ²⁵… families on farms and ranches. ²⁶… around town ²⁷… also a ²⁸… activity for South Dakota teens. Fishing and ²⁹… are also ³⁰… popular. ³¹… the winter, ³²… the Missouri River freezes over, ³³… kids ³⁴… … go ice skating.

# Checkpoint 3

## B

### 8 Koluscap and the water monster 🎧

The Mi'kmaq and the Maliseet tribes are from the north-eastern USA and eastern Canada. Before you listen to the story, look up the words in the box in a dictionary.

> bullfrog · creator · (to) crush · dam · drought · filthy · messenger · mud · (to) pray · prayers · (to) squeeze · (to) take pity (on sb.) · warrior

a) Listen to the story and complete the sentences with the correct information.
1. Once … … a … drought. The … stopped … and … … … dry.
2. …, the streams … stopped flowing.
3. There … a … … people … lived … … side … a stream, and life now … very … for … .

b) Listen to the story again. Then put these sentences in the right order: write down the sentence numbers in your exercise book.
1. The village people sent warriors to destroy the dam.
2. Koluscap squeezed the water monster.
3. There was a drought.
4. The Creator sent Koluscap to help the village people.
5. The warriors were killed by the monsters.
6. The village people sent a messenger to find out why there was no water.

c) Answer these questions in complete sentences.
1. What was the problem in this story?
2. Who was responsible for it?
3. What happened in the end?

## C

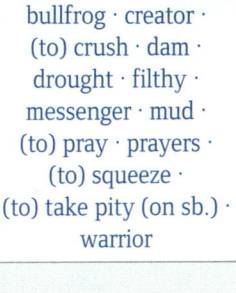

### 9 On the wagon train to Oregon ✏️

Read the diary entries from these pioneers travelling on the Oregon Trail. Imagine you are travelling westward to Oregon.
Write a letter (about 150-180 words) to a friend back home on the east coast telling them what you are experiencing on the trail.

> "Started at half past 4, after being up with team nearly all night. Came on to the good camp at spring. On our way here at Powder River we killed a noble salmon, taking breakfast out of him, and a fine dish it was."
> David Maynard, September 1, 1850

> "There are some of the largest rattlesnakes in this region I ever saw, being from 8 to 12 ft. long, and about as large as a man's leg about the knee. This is no fiction at all." Amelia Hadley, July 19, 1851

> Raining all day … and the boys are all soaking wet and look sad and comfortless. The little ones and myself are shut up in the wagons from the rain. Still it will find its way in and many things are wet; and take us all together we are a poor looking set, and all this for Oregon … I am thinking as I write, "Oh Oregon, you must be a wonderful country!"
> Amelia Stewart Knight, June 1, 1853

> "Left camp at 6 & traveled 9 miles when we laid by on the Little Blue to give the boys an opportunity to hunt Buffalo as they have been almost wild with excitement since they came into the Buffalo country. About 10 a.m. they started off with a good supply of powder shot & ball & great anticipations but poor fellows their feathers looked sadly drooping as they came straggling into camp near nightfall. Footsore & weary & having secured among them all one small Antelope."
> Louisa Cook, June 13, 1862

## Access to cultures

# Foundation of a new nation

## The Declaration of Independence
*A revolutionary document which laid down the foundation for a new democracy.*

### Why was it written?
The Declaration of Independence was written to explain to the rest of the world why the 13 colonies were declaring themselves independent from British rule. The Declaration was also a call for help. The newly formed 'United States' needed both economic and military support to be able to win a war against Great Britain, the most powerful empire in the world. The request for help was, above all, addressed to France, another world power and also Great Britain's long-time enemy.

*Signing of the Declaration of Independence, July 4th, 1776*

### When was it written?
The Declaration was written in 1776 by Thomas Jefferson, a rich farmer from Virginia, who would become the third president of the United States. It was revised and signed on July 4th, 1776, by representatives of all 13 states.

### What does it say?
The Declaration explains why the colonists were going to war against Great Britain. It lists their complaints against the British government. They were angry that Britain had collected taxes from the colonists without their consent. The Seven Years War had cost Great Britain a lot of money, so the British crown demanded much higher taxes from the colonists.
Britain also kept troops in the colonies. They prevented colonial governments from meeting and prevented the colonists from trading with other parts of the world.

### What was so new?
The Declaration of Independence states that government exists to serve the people and that the government should be elected by the people to represent them. If a government abuses its power, then the people have the right to change the government.
The Declaration also states that '… *all men are created equal*' and have the right to '*life, liberty and the pursuit of happiness.*'
These were revolutionary ideas which inspired other battles against the absolute rule of monarchs – most importantly the French Revolution of 1789-1799.

### What did it change?
The colonists received economic and military support from France, which helped them win the war against Great Britain in 1783.

The Declaration defined the path towards forming the government that the United States has today. Many of the men who signed the constitution, including Thomas Jefferson and George Washington, owned enslaved people of African descent. Jefferson owned over 100 enslaved people. So this important belief did not really apply to 'all men'. It only applied to 'white' men of European descent.
Secondly, although the Declaration states that 'the people' should elect their government only men who owned a lot of property were allowed to vote. Women, farm workers and the poor were not given this right.
The Declaration influenced democratic revolutions and civil rights movements in the US and throughout the world.

## Influence of the Declaration of Independence

The Women's Rights Movement, 1848

The French Revolution, 1789-1799

The Civil Rights Movement, 1954-1968

The US Constitution

a) Write down the events that answer each section's question.

Then write a headline for the five sections of the text on p. 96.

b) Set up a **'fishbowl' discussion** with 6-8 seats for the 'fishbowl' in the middle of your classroom and the rest of the desks in a circle around the inner circle.
Discuss the following statement:

*'All men are created equal'*
What did this mean for the people living in the new nation?
What does it mean for you today?

c) Use your feedback sheet to write a short paragraph (about 60 words) about your experience in the fishbowl and as a listener. What did you learn?

Suggest ideas for ways to improve a class discussion.

### Guidelines for a fishbowl discussion:

**In the fishbowl:**
1. Only one person speaks at a time.
2. Respond to what others have said.
3. Everyone in the fishbowl should speak at least once.

**In the outer circle:**
1. Listen actively (and fill in the feedback sheet).
2. To add to the discussion, tap on the shoulder of someone in the fishbowl who has already spoken. Switch places.

# Access to cultures

# Elections in the US and the UK

1) Read about the electoral system in the USA and note down important information about the political system. Then talk about it.
Give three important facts about the system.

---

*The electoral system in the USA uses the "first-past-the-post" system[1]. This means that voters must choose one candidate, and the candidate who receives more votes than any other candidate wins.*

### The two houses
The US Congress consists of the House of Representatives and the Senate.
5 Members of the House of Representatives are elected every two years. Each state is divided into districts and each district votes for one representative. The number of districts depends on a state's population, so the most highly populated state, California, has the biggest number of representatives (53) but the huge state of Alaska, which has a small population, has only one district and therefore only one representative in the House.
10 Members of the Senate are also elected by the public. Each state has two senators, no matter how big or small the state is. As with the House of Representatives, the first-past-the-post system is used, so the candidates with the most votes win.

### Presidential elections
Presidential elections take place every four years, and each President is limited to two terms of office[2], a
15 total of eight years. The President usually represents one of the two main parties in the US: the Democrats or the Republicans. Each party chooses its candidate in a first round of voting[3], known as primaries[4]. The two winners of the primaries – one for the Democrats, one for the Republicans – then begin massive election campaigns, travelling across the country for months before the election is finally held in November.

### The electoral college[5]
20 In the presidential election the people's votes are counted at state level, not at national level. Each of the 50 states has an electoral college with the same number of votes as its total
25 number of senators and representatives. For example, California has 2 + 53 = 55 electoral college votes; Alaska has 2 + 1 = 3 electoral college votes. The candidate who gets the highest number of votes in a state gets all of
30 that state's electoral votes. A total of 270 electoral votes is needed to win. It sometimes happens that the candidate wins 270 electoral votes, even though the other candidate received a higher total of votes nationally. This
35 was the case in 2000 and 2016.

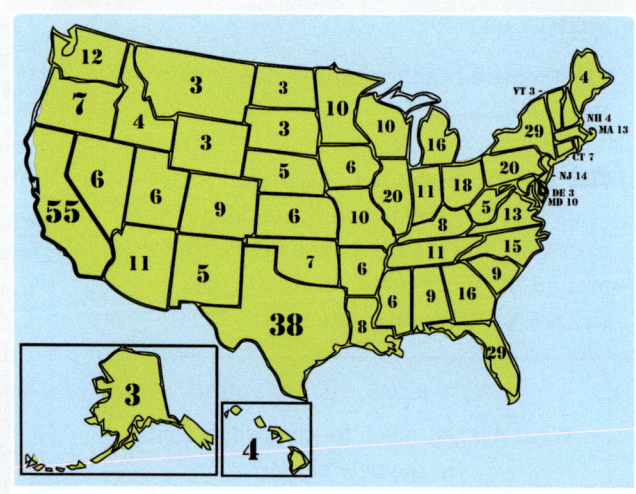

*Electoral map of the USA indicating the number of electoral college votes for each of the 50 US states*

**2 a)** 👥 Now read about elections in the UK and take notes about the important information. Then compare the US and UK systems. Discuss what is different and what is similar.

**b)** EXTRA ✏ Write a text (about 100-200 words) about the election systems in the US and the UK.

### A constitutional monarchy

The UK is a constitutional monarchy (with the monarch as head of state) and a parliamentary democracy. Parliament has two houses, the House of Lords and the House of Commons (with 600-650 elected members, each representing a constituency). The Prime Minister and cabinet lead the executive. Parliamentary elections are held at least every five years but only the House of Commons is elected.

### Elections

At election time, several candidates stand for election[6] in each constituency. They include members of the three main political parties, Labour, Conservative and Liberal Democrat. Other candidates represent[7] smaller or regional parties, or are independent. At the beginning of the election campaign, all parties publish statements about the policies they want to follow, and the candidates try to win public support for their party's ideas.

### Election Day

On election day, the votes are counted separately in each constituency and the candidate with the most votes there wins the election (first-past-the-post system). The winner does not need to have a majority of the votes, just a higher number than any other candidate. When the counting is finished, all the candidates of a constituency[8] stand on a stage, and an official reads out the number of votes received by each candidate. He or she then declares[9] the winner. After the votes have been counted, the party with the most MPs (Members of Parliament) forms the government, and their leader becomes the Prime Minister. If there is no clear winner, a coalition government can be formed, although this has not happened very often in the UK.

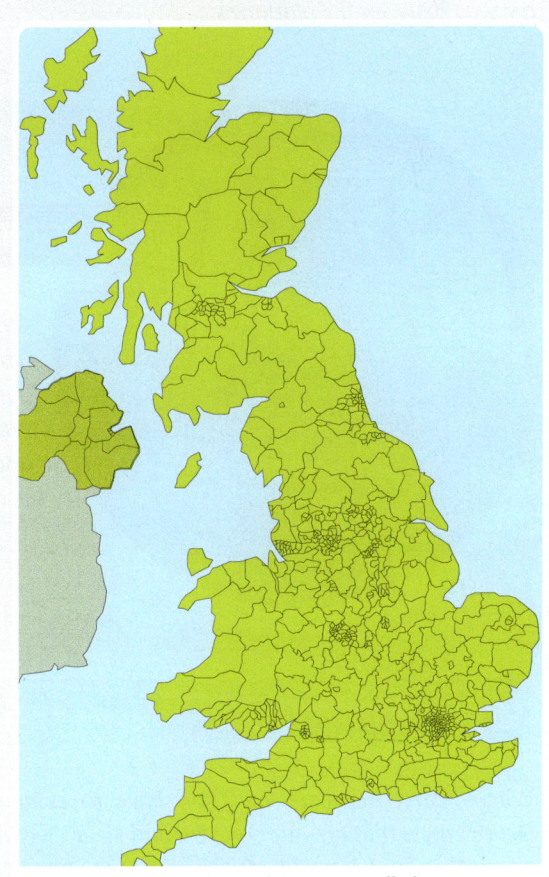

*Map showing the electoral areas, so-called constituencies, in the United Kingdom*

➔ **Workbook** *7 (pp. 64–65)*

---

1 **the "first-past-the-post" system** *wahlkreisbasiertes Wahlverfahren, bei dem der/die Kandidat/in die Wahl gewinnt, welche(r) die meisten Stimmen erhalten hat (eine absolute Mehrheit ist nicht erforderlich)* · 2 **term of office** *Amtsperiode* · 3 **round of voting** *Wahlgang* · 4 **primaries** *(pl)* [ˈpraɪməriz] *Vorwahl(en)* · 5 **electoral college** [ɪlektərəl kɒlɪdʒ] *Wahlmänner(gremium)/Wahlfrauen(gremium)* · 6 **stand for election** *zur Wahl stehen; sich zur Wahl stellen* · 7 **represent** *repräsentieren* · 8 **constituency** *Wahlkreis* · 9 **declare** [dɪˈkleə] *bekannt geben, verkünde*

# Text file

## Text 1: A guided tour to Harry Potter places in London

### 1 St. Pancras Station (Harry Potter and the Chamber of Secrets)

Harry Potter fans know it as the station where Harry and Ron take off in Mr Weasley's flying Ford Anglia because they missed the Hogwarts Express.

St. Pancras Station is one of the most beautiful train stations in the world, so it's not a surprise it was used in the Harry Potter movies. Platform 9 3/4, however, is at King's Cross Station, about a 15-minute walk away. There you can take a photo of yourself with a trolley that's just moving into the wall between the platforms.

### 2 Gringotts Bank (All movies)

Whenever you see Gringotts Bank in the Harry Potter movies, you actually see the inside of this building. Unfortunately, you can't just walk inside and visit the famous Goblin bank – it's Australia House on the Strand and not open to the public – but you can always go to the official Harry Potter Studio Tour and see it there.

### 3 Piccadilly Circus (Harry Potter and the Deathly Hallows Part 1)

When Harry, Hermione and Ron have to escape from the Death Eaters that are attacking Bill and Fleur's wedding, this is where they land: Piccadilly Circus, one of the busiest and most crowded places in London. From Piccadilly Circus the trio walk down Shaftesbury Avenue before turning into an alley (remember all the things that Hermione has in her bottomless purse?). And the café where they are attacked by two Death Eaters later is near Tottenham Court Road Tube station. Following in their footsteps should take you about 15 minutes.

## Text file

### 4 Millennium Bridge (Harry Potter and the Half-Blood Prince)

In the opening scenes of Harry Potter and the Half-Blood Prince you can see the Death Eaters flying around London. They do a lot of damage and one of the places they destroy is this bridge. The Millennium Bridge is a good place to cross the Thames when you find yourself walking along the river: on one side of the river you can see the Tate Modern museum with its lovely view over the city skyline from the top. And on the other side of the river is St. Paul's Cathedral, the world-famous church – and another Harry Potter filming site: the staircase that leads to the Divination Tower (you can see it in Harry Potter and the Prisoner of Azkaban) is actually inside St. Paul's. Unfortunately, the staircase is rarely open to the public – but you can always go in and try.

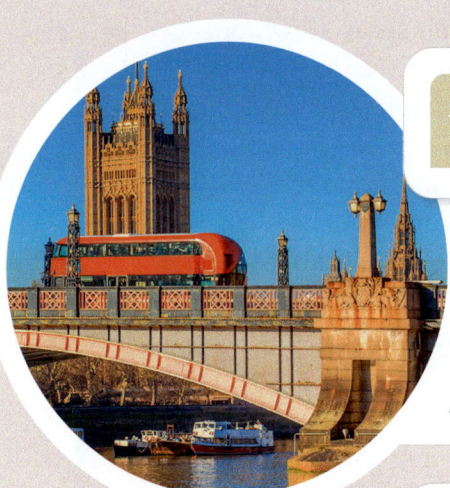

### 5 Lambeth Bridge – on the Knight Bus route (Harry Potter and the Prisoner of Azkaban)

Do you remember the moment when the Knight Bus is racing through London and has to squeeze between two red double-decker buses? This is the bridge where that scene takes place. You can see the bridge easily when you're walking around as it's very close to other attractions like Big Ben and the Houses of Parliament.

### 6 Other sites

You can find the headquarters of the Order of the Phoenix, 12 Grimmauld Place, in Islington (Claremont Square). You can find the entrance to The Leaky Cauldron (Harry Potter and the Philosopher's Stone) in Leadenhall Market. The entrance to the Ministry of Magic is at the intersection of Great Scotland Yard and Scotland Place. Unfortunately, there is no red phone booth to transport you inside …

a) Say which of these sites you would like to visit and why.
b) Look at a map of central London and plan the best route for your tour. Explain to a partner how to get from one site to the next (e.g. on foot, by bus, the Tube).

# Text file

## Text 2: The Amazing Adventures of Jack London

In this excerpt from *The Adventures of Jack London, Book 3: Forty Mile,* Jack and his friend Shania talk about First Nation languages. Find Dawson on a map of Canada and do some research on the First Nation people in the area.

### Chapter Four – Tr'ondëk Hwëch'in

Wherever I go, I always try to learn the language. I can speak pretty good Spanish and German, some French and a bit of Indonesian. I know a few phrases in Mandarin, Arabic and Swahili, and I can say 'hello' and 'thank you' in at
5 least ten other languages.

But I've never spoken a language like Hän.

Today we had Hän class in school. Hän is the language of the Tr'ondëk Hwëch'in, the First Nation people who lived in and around Dawson before the White Man came. Shania, a girl
10 from my class, is First Nation. She can only speak a few words of Hän, but her forefathers were Tr'ondëk Hwëch'in.

We sit on the swings at lunch break and she tells me about her people.

"The way I see it, it's like this," she says. "Europe and Canada
15 are about the same size, right? But in Europe you have all these nations, like the British and the Polish, and Greeks and Ukrainians. Sure, they moved around a lot, but most countries have their own identity. The First Nations were no different. Canada had people-nations just like Europe. They just
20 never made any borders. There was enough space for everybody."

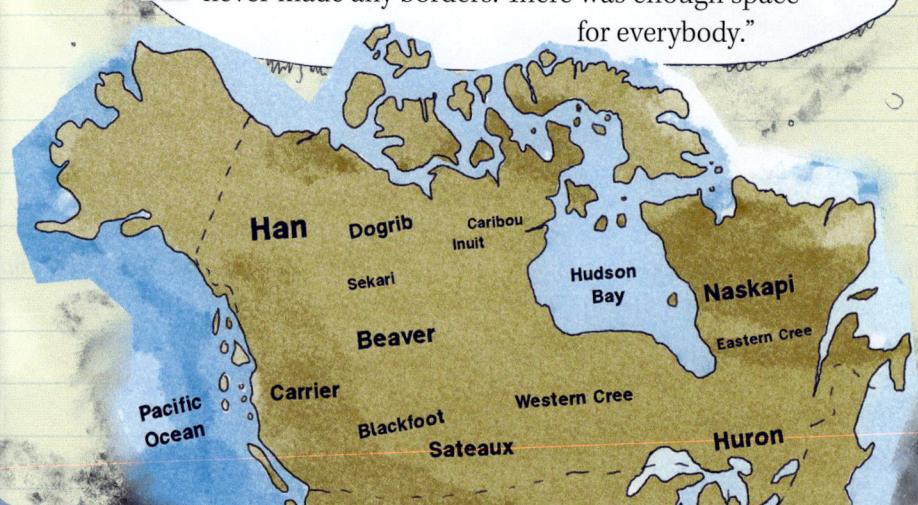

Back in Jack London's time, people called the First Nations 'Indians', but that word is out now. There are lots of different First Nation communities, each with their own culture or language.

5   Shania tells me that the Hän-speaking people lived on the River Yukon. The area around Dawson was called the 'Tr'ondëk' – the name given to the smaller of the two rivers. 'Tr'ondëk' means 'stone waters'. When the gold seekers came from America, they couldn't say 'Tr'ondëk', so they
10  changed it to Klondike. That's why it's still called the Klondike today.

During the Gold Rush, the First Nation people moved away from Dawson City, but now
15  they're back. They don't speak Hän anymore, but they have their own local government and are trying to keep their
20  culture alive.

Shania is nice. She's funny and smart and interesting. She laughs a lot and tells me stories about her family and life in Dawson. She likes living
25  here. She loves sport. She plays ice hockey in the winter and volleyball in the summer. She has two little brothers and a dog. She likes 'Lost City' as well. I tell her she can come over to my house at the weekend to watch Series Two.
30  She says she'll ask her parents. I'll have to put a few more pizzas onto that wish list of mine.

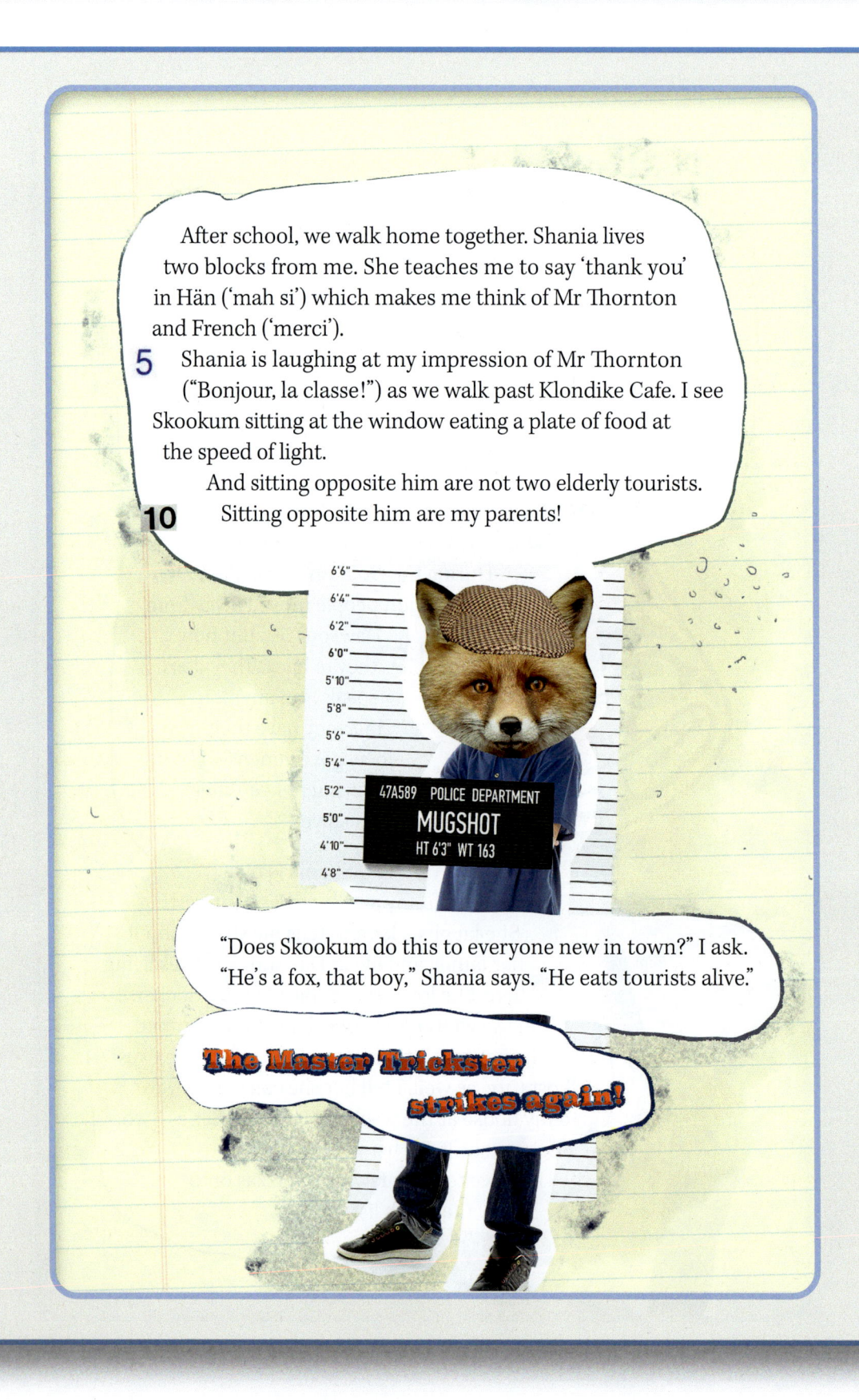

# Text file

After school, we walk home together. Shania lives two blocks from me. She teaches me to say 'thank you' in Hän ('mah si') which makes me think of Mr Thornton and French ('merci').

5   Shania is laughing at my impression of Mr Thornton ("Bonjour, la classe!") as we walk past Klondike Cafe. I see Skookum sitting at the window eating a plate of food at the speed of light.

    And sitting opposite him are not two elderly tourists.
10  Sitting opposite him are my parents!

"Does Skookum do this to everyone new in town?" I ask.
"He's a fox, that boy," Shania says. "He eats tourists alive."

**The Master Trickster strikes again!**

Skookum doesn't see me come into the restaurant. I hear his phone ring. He finishes eating, licks his knife and takes out his phone from under the table – exactly the same routine as the day before. The same panicked reaction to the call,
5 my parents looking shocked as they listen, Skookum trying not to cry. This guy could win an Oscar for Best Actor.

Skookum hangs up and says, "I'm really sorry. I've got to go. My dad … he just had …"

I finish his sentence: "A really bad accident."

10 Skookum turns around, but when he sees me, he doesn't look surprised. He just smiles and says, "Hi, Jack, what brings you here?"

"I'm on Trickster Patrol."

"Are you sure you're in the right place?"

15 Now it's me who smiles. Skookum is a cheat, but he is funny.

"Mum, Dad, this is Skookum from school. And this is Shania."

Mum and Dad stand up to shake Shania's hand. Mum looks confused. "What about your father?" she asks Skookum. "Can we drive you to the hospital?"

20 "That won't be necessary," I say. "The accident was ten years ago."

"Dad almost drowned," Skookum says. "Broke his ear drums trying to open the door. Deaf for the rest of his life."

Mum looks really shocked. "Oh. I'm sorry to hear that."

25 "Thanks."

"So who was that on the phone?" Dad asks.

"Skook called himself," I explain. "He was just about to leave and let you pay for his meal."

Dad thinks about this for a second. "Wow!" he says. "That's
30 so cool!"

---

Would you like to learn an unusual language? Say why/why not?
Which language would you like to learn?

# 1 More help

## Lead-in

### 3 Time traveller ✏︎  ← p. 9

You could write about:

- what/who you have come to see
- what you see, hear, feel
- who you meet and what you do
- the advantages and disadvantages of life in the city
- why you would/wouldn't like to stay longer
- …

## Part A Practice

### 3 EXTRA Panel discussion  ← p. 12

Think about:

- expressing opinions
- agreeing/disagreeing
- asking what somebody thinks will happen
- asking why somebody thinks something
- asking for clarification
- summing up
- asking audience for questions
- …

## Part B Practice

### 2 It wasn't founded by Britons (Passive: simple present and simple past)  ← p. 18

Correct the wrong information about London in each sentence.
You can check the facts on pages 16/17.

1. London was founded by Britons.
   – No, it wasn't founded by Britons. It was founded by …

2. The city was first named London.
   – No, it … first … London. It … Londinium.

3. The food in the Brixton café is cooked the night before.
   – No, it … in the mornings. It … there fresh every day.

4. The Huguenots were driven to London from Spain.
   – No, they … to London from Spain. They … to London from France.

5. London was burned by a Great Fire in 1665.
   – No, it … by a Great Fire in 1665. It … by a Great Fire in 1666.

6. After World War II, Europeans were brought to London to help rebuild the country.
   – No, after World War II Europeans … to London to help rebuild the country.
   Commonwealth people … to London to help rebuild the country.

# More help 1

## Part B Practice

### 4 *Romeo and Juliet* was written by Shakespeare (Passive with *by*)   ← *p. 19*

Complete the text about Shakespeare's Globe Theatre using the passive form of the verbs in brackets and *by*.

*Shakespeare's Globe:* England's most famous plays ¹written by (write / William Shakespeare). Many of his plays were ²... (perform) the actors of the Globe Theatre in London. The Globe was ³... (build) a group of actors called The Lord Chamberlain's Men in 1599. All actors were men in those days. Women's roles were ⁴... (play) boys. The Globe was ⁵... (destroy) a fire in 1613 but was rebuilt. In the year 1642 all theatres were ⁶... (close) the British government, which was very strict at that time. The theatre was built again in the late 20th Century and was ⁷... (open) the Queen in 1997. This event was ⁸... (celebrate) Shakespeare fans everywhere.

**TIP** With the passive, we use *by* ... if we want to say who did something.

## Part B Practice

### 7 A formal email ✎   ← *p. 21*

b) 🧩 Compare and explain your answers.
   Use a placemat to make a list of tips for writing a formal email.

- Always check you have the right email address.
- The subject is not clear enough./This makes it clear what you want.
- That's the most polite./That's not polite enough./That's how you write to a friend.
- Your language should be quite formal./That's too colloquial./You use that sort of language when you're talking, not writing.
- You have to say thank you at the end.
- That's how you end a letter to a friend/soeone you don't know/…
- Give all your contact details in case they want to contact you by letter or phone.

# 2 More help

## Part A

### 3 Alyssa's friend Lauren ✏️
← p. 41

a) Write a profile of Lauren. Use any of the adjectives in the box that you need.

> friendly · curious · silly · angry · proud · careful · generous · funny · kind · strong · shy · thankful

b) 👥 Read your profile to your group.

c) Here is a box with descriptive language to describe the style of Lauren's blog.

> informal · formal · colloquial · informational · personal · descriptive · humorous · funny · silly · upbeat

## Part B Practice

### 4 After the final (The passive with *will*)
← p. 49

Read the note from the tournament organizers that describes what will happen after the final. Complete the text with the *will*-future passive. You can use the verbs in the box.

> hold · ask · offer · serve · give · show · present

The award ceremony will be held[1] tomorrow night after the tournament final in the Quebec City Youth Centre. First, second and third-place trophies ...[2] (present) to the winning teams. Official "All-Canada Ice Hockey" T-shirts ...[3] (offer) to every player. Following a two-hour break, a special three-course dinner ...[4] (serve) in the restaurant. Transport ...[5] (give) for $2.50. Speeches ...[6] (give) by the Minister of Education and Sports of Quebec City and hockey star Patrick Roy. Players ...[7] (ask) to share their stories and impressions of the tournament. To end the evening, a short film of the best moments of the tournament ...[8] (present) on a large screen. We're looking forward to seeing all of you!

## Part C

### 6 Fight for fun ✏️
← p. 53

a) 👥 Work in groups. Discuss the differences between the fight on the ice and the snowball fight at the end of the story. These questions can help guide your discussion:

- How do you think Antoine felt when he hit number 11 in the chest? Why do you think Lauren threw the first snowball at Antoine? Were Antoine and Lauren's feelings different?
- When the other players saw Antoine's action, what did they do? Contrast their reactions with the reaction of the students watching Nukilik, Lauren and Antoine's snowball fight from the hostel windows.
- Why did both group of kids join the 'fight'?
- How did the fight in the final game of the tournament end? Did anyone get hurt? What about in the snowball fight?
- Find three adjectives to describe the fight during the hockey game and three more adjectives to describe the snowball fight. Compare your words in your group.

### Mediation course
← p. 55

c) **Partner A:** You are the boy/girl in Germany. Before you talk to your friend in Quebec, make a list of reasons why 'Chalet Welcome' is a good option for her family. Then list anything that is not good. How will you introduce the hotel? You can say *'I've found the perfect hotel for you,'* or *'I've found a hotel, but I'm not sure if you'll like it.'*

**Partner B:** You are the friend from Quebec. Your partner has found a hotel with a ski school for you and your family. What questions do you have? Write them down and then begin the video chat. At the end of the chat, decide whether you want to recommend the hotel to your family.

# More help 2

### Text

## 2 ✎ Write a flash fiction story  ← *p. 59*

a) Write a flash fiction story from the perspective of an animal. The animal can be one that lives wild, or a pet … it can even be a noisy insect. How does the world change from this perspective?

# More help 3

### Part A Practice

## 3 REVISION Yesterday in Mobridge (Simple past or past progressive?)  ← *p. 71*

Look at the pictures and complete the texts. Use the correct form of the verb: simple past or past progressive.

**A**

Bobby ¹ saw / was seeing Kaya while he ² walked / was walking down Main Street in Mobridge yesterday. He ³ smiled / was smiling and ⁴ said / was saying hi, but Kaya ⁵ didn't hear / wasn't hearing him. She ⁶ listened / was listening to music and she ⁷ didn't look / wasn't looking around when he ⁸ called / was calling her.

**B**

Drew's mom ¹ walked / was walking down Main Street yesterday when a young exchange student ² came / was coming up to her. He ³ looked / was looking for the post office and ⁴ asked / was asking Drew's mom for directions. She ⁵ went / was going towards the post office anyway, so she ⁶ offered / was offering to take him there.

### Part B Practice

## 2 Home huggers and sports sparks (Gerunds after prepositions)  ← *p. 76*

b) Make sentences about people you know. You can use the ideas from the boxes.
Remember to change the infinitive to a **gerund**.

| best friend · maths teacher · mum · dad · sister · brother · neighbour · favourite sportsperson … |
|---|

| bad at · excited about · good at · happy about · interested in · keen on · tired of · unhappy about |
|---|

1 *My dad* is good at (bake) *baking* cakes.
2 … isn't keen on (go) *going* outside.
3 … is good at (play) football.
4 … is unhappy about (buy) clothes.
5 … is … (clean) his/her room.
6 … is … (program) computers.
7 … is … (follow) news about famous people.
8 … is … (solve) maths problems.

# 3 More help

## 3 Living here is OK (Gerunds)
← p. 77

Write sentences about your neighbourhood: what you like / don't like, etc.
*The great thing about living in our street is that it's really green. I love going to the park because …*

| The | good<br>best<br>bad<br>worst<br>… | thing<br>about | live in our street<br>live near the station/<br>park/…<br>live in a suburb …<br>have nice neighbours<br>… | is … | that we are close to a great museum.<br>that we can eat food together.<br>that you can hang out in the …<br>that you can play football.<br>the fast cars.<br>the neighbours who aren't nice.<br>the noisy dogs.<br>the older kids who are looking for a fight.<br>the rubbish at the bus stop. |
|---|---|---|---|---|---|
| I | love<br>like<br>don't like<br>don't mind<br>hate<br>… | | talk to neighbours<br>go to the park<br>have lots of shops<br>live near the pool<br>have no shops<br>… | because … | they are so interesting/boring/…<br>you can play there or just hang out.<br>there are lots of things to buy.<br>you can swim whenever you want.<br>you have to go to a big city to buy things. |

## Part C

### 3 Drew's thoughts
← p. 80

Imagine you are Drew. Will you go with your family or spend the weekend in Mobridge with Kaya? Write down some of your thoughts on your walk home. Use these ideas to start your thoughts:

| | | Mount Rushmore | Mobridge |
|---|---|---|---|
| for | | interesting monument | be with Kaya! |
| | | see brother + girlfriend | spend time riding |
| | | … | … |
| against | | miss Kaya | no car |
| | | insult the Lakota | town is boring |
| | | … | … |

Then complete your thoughts.
Use the conditional sentence I.
- *If I go to Mount Rushmore with my family, …*
- *If I spend the weekend in Mobridge, …*

110  one hundred and ten

# More help 3

## Part C Practice

### 1 WORDS A colourful picture (Adjectives with *-ful* and *-less*) ← p. 82

a) Make adjectives from the nouns in the boxes.

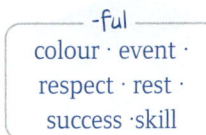

— *-ful* —
colour · event ·
respect · rest ·
success · skill

— *-less* —
air · end ·
home · moon ·
rain · sleep

**TIP**
Recognizing suffixes like *-ful* or *-less* can help you to understand new words.
*-ful* = **full of** or **giving**, e.g. power<u>ful</u>, help<u>ful</u>
*-less* = **without**, e.g. cloud<u>less</u>, heart<u>less</u>

Which nouns from the box on the right go well with the adjectives? Try to use the adjectives and nouns as often as you can.

colourful: a colourful picture, a colourful ...

actor · behaviour · bird · clothes ·
day · desert · furniture · garden · history · list ·
man · manager · night · people · picture · report ·
room · sky · story · teenager · trip · week

## Early finisher 1

### How much do you know about the Commonwealth? ← p. 11, 4 Visitors from …

Answer the following questions about the Commonwealth.
You might have to do some more research for some of the answers.

**1** How many independent countries are in the Commonwealth?
   a) 53   b) 63   c) 43

**2** Which Commonwealth country has the biggest population?
   a) South Africa   b) Australia   c) India

**3** When was the Commonwealth founded?
   a) 1890   b) 1949   c) 1930

**4** Which of these countries is not a member of the Commonwealth?
   a) Australia   b) Canada   c) United States

**5** Which country is the only Commonwealth member in South America?
   a) Brazil   b) Guyana   c) Chile

**6** How many people live in the Commonwealth?
   a) 1.2 billion   b) 2.4 billion   c) 3.6 billion

# 2  Early finisher

## Canadian food

← *p. 41,* **4 Write a blog post**

Match the pictures to the descriptions of these Canadian specialties. Which one would you like to try?

1. **Nanaimo Bars** are made from a thick, buttery cream sandwiched between two kinds of chocolate.
2. **Timbits** are bite-sized balls of fried dough. They're also called 'donut holes'.
3. **Tourtiere** is a meat pie made with ground beef and spices.
4. **Hawaiian Pizza**, made with ham and pineapple, was invented in Canada.

A  B  C  D

Find out more about these Canadian specialties on the internet.

## American city quiz

← *p. 77,* **3 Living here is OK**

Match each description (A–E) to a city (1–6). Write a short text for the missing description.

**A**
- founded 1790
- named after a famous president
- city of politics
- lots of museums and monuments

**B**
- founded 1781
- close to the Pacific
- second-largest city in the USA
- famous for smog
- home to the entertainment industry

**C**
- founded 1869
- on the Pacific coast
- Boeing planes are made here
- famous building: Space Needle, a 184-metre viewing tower

**D**
- founded 1819
- on the Mississippi
- famous for rock and roll
- home of Elvis Presley
- city where Martin Luther King was killed in 1968

**E**
- founded 1630
- close to the Atlantic
- has a big harbour
- home to the famous Harvard university
- baseball team: Red Sox

1 Boston
2 New York City
3 Memphis
4 Washington
5 Seattle
6 Los Angeles

# Early finisher 3

## A capital city

← p. 77, 4 A day out in Mobridge

a) 14,000 people live in the capital city of South Dakota.
   To find the name of this city, solve this puzzle.
   1 Another word for *answer* (5). Use letter 3.
   2 The Golden State (10). Use letter 4
   3 A famous New York skyscraper (6,5,8). Use letter 11.
   4 It grows on your head (4). Use letter 4.
   5 You can … in South Dakota when you're 14. (5). Use letter 2.
   6 A competition for a cowboy (5). Use letter 4.

b) Make a similar puzzle and give it to another early finisher.

*A large building in a small town. Dakota's State Capitol in the city of …?*

## Good adjectives

← p. 82, 1 WORDS A colourful picture

Do a) or b).

a) In the news
   Complete the newspaper headlines with adjectives.

   1 … night for parents of missing child
   2 … weekend in Berlin
     Hollywood star visits five different nightclubs
   3 Smiling tourists, but worried farmers after a … summer
   4 … man attacked as he slept on park bench
   5 … parade brightens up rainy Sunday
   6 New cover version of '… Love' hits number 1 in US charts

b) Find the synonym.
   Find a word with a similar meaning to the **blue** words.
   For each word, choose one of the nouns on the right and add *-ful* or *-less*.

| | | | | | |
|---|---|---|---|---|---|
| 1 | a **cruel** man | arm | head | heart | face |
| 2 | **calm** water | silence | peace | love | rest |
| 3 | a **boring** film | smile | interest | hour | end |
| 4 | a **clean** kitchen | spot | mark | dark | mud |
| 5 | a **quiet** machine | noise | shout | roar | talk |
| 6 | a **busy** day | action | activity | event | story |
| 7 | a **relaxing** weekend | break | rest | pause | sleep |
| 8 | a **kind** person | heart | idea | thought | head |
| 9 | a **dry** summer | drink | rain | plant | juice |

# Partner pages

## Unit 1

### 4 REVISION 👥 London and Ottawa (Simple present) → p. 13

a) Partner B: Imagine you're Alyssa.
   Use the prompts below to write down questions for Lauren about life back in Ottawa.
   Add two or three more questions of your own.

   Use the simple present.

   - how: your family
   - weather: what like?
   - snow on the ground?
   - new teachers: like?
   - miss me?
   - …

   Example: Do you have a ticket for the Senators game at the weekend?
   Is your brother still at school?
   …

b) Give your questions to your partner. Take the questions they give you and write down answers to them (use your imagination).

c) Return your partner's questions and your answers. Look at them together.
   Exchange your opinions on the questions and answers.

### 9 Role play 💬 → p. 14

a) 👥 Work in groups of three. Two of you play Tourists A and B, two English-speaking tourists to your area.
The third plays a tourist information worker (TIW) at your local visitor centre.

b) 👥 Study your role cards carefully. Make notes on language you might need and information about your area.

c) 👥 Use your notes to act out a conversation at the tourist information office.

---

**Tourist A**

- You are a tourist from an EU country but do not speak German.
- You are here with your child and have two days to look at the area.
- You like history and would enjoy going on a guided walking tour if there is one.
- You also want to try out the local food and are looking for a nice restaurant for the evening.
- You also need to book a hotel for the night.
- You have a rental car.

Partner pages

## 3 Which is the oldest? (Passive: simple past) ← p. 19

b) Partner A: Ask the questions about 1, 3 and 5.

*When was Liverpool Cathedral started?*

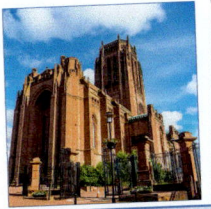

**Liverpool Cathedral** — start finish

**Mona Lisa** — 2 paint 1503–1507

**Berlin Underground** — 3 open

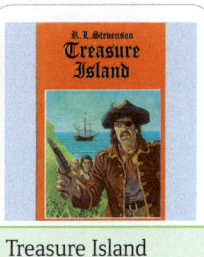

**Treasure Island** — write 1881–1883

**Lift** — invent

**1 Cologne Cathedral** — start finish

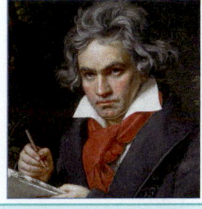

**Portrait of Ludwig van Beethoven** — paint 1820

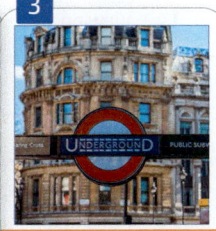

**London Underground** — open

**4 Oliver Twist** — write 1837–1839

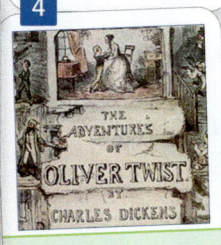

**5 Escalator** — invent

## 5 THINKING ABOUT LANGUAGE  Idioms ← p. 25

Explain to your partner in English what the German idioms mean.

Den Braten riechen

Ich hab die Nase voll.

### Unit 3

## 4 A day out in Mobridge ← p. 77

Partner A:

### Claire

Claire is very social. She worked hard during the school year and wants to have fun during her summer vacation in the states. Claire loves outdoor activities like swimming and hiking. She hates sitting without doing anything active. She is a vegetarian and cares a lot about the well-being of animals. She doesn't have a drivers licence yet and probably won't get one, because she thinks cars make too much pollution. At home, she takes dance classes and likes dancing to all kinds of music.

# Skills File

## Skills File – Inhalt                                                                 Seite

| | | | |
|---|---|---|---|
| **READING SKILLS** | SF 1 | Skimming and scanning | 116 |
| | SF 2 | Marking up a text | 117 |
| **WRITING SKILLS** | SF 3 | The stages of writing | 118 |
| | SF 4 | Structuring texts | 119 |
| | SF 5 | Writing good sentences | 120 |
| | SF 6 | Writing a formal letter or email | 121 |
| | SF 7 | Writing a comment / opinion piece | 122 |
| | SF 8 | Summing up a text | 123 |
| | SF 9 | Revising texts | 124 |
| **MEDIATION SKILLS** | SF 10 | Mediating written or spoken information | 125 |
| | SF 11 | Finding key information | 125 |
| | SF 12 | Paraphrasing | 126 |
| | SF 13 | Cultural differences | 126 |
| **VIEWING SKILLS** | SF 14 | Viewing | 127 |
| **LISTENING AND SPEAKING SKILLS** | SF 15 | Speaking | 128 |
| | SF 16 | Listening | 129 |
| **PROJECT AND PRESENTATION SKILLS** | SF 17 | Teamwork | 129 |
| | SF 18 | Internet reserach | 130 |
| | SF 19 | Describing and presenting pictures | 130 |
| | SF 20 | Putting a page together | 131 |
| | SF 21 | Making slides for a presentation | 131 |
| | SF 22 | Giving a presentation | 132 |
| | SF 23 | Giving feedback | 133 |
| **STUDY SKILLS** | SF 24 | Dealing with unknown words | 133 |
| | SF 25 | Using a dictionary | 134 |
| | SF 26 | Study posters | 135 |
| | SF 27 | Making and taking notes | 135 |

In diesem **Skills File** findest du **Lernhilfen und Methoden,** die dir z. B. den Umgang mit Texten erleichtern, beim Schreiben von eigenen Texten und bei der Sprachmittlung helfen oder Tipps zum Vorbereiten von Präsentationen geben.

## READING SKILLS

### SF 1  Skimming and scanning  (Media skills)

Skimming *(reading for gist)* und Scanning *(reading for specific information)* sind Lesetechniken, die viel Zeit sparen, v. a. beim Lesen von langen Texten.

**SKIMMING**
Angenommen, du suchst Informationen zu einem bestimmten Thema, z. B. für ein Referat oder als Antwort für eine Hausaufgabe. Deine Suche im Internet liefert eine Vielzahl an Ergebnissen, die für dein Thema relevant sein könnten. Die alle gründlich zu lesen, würde zu viel Zeit kosten. Hier hilft das Skimming.

# Skills File

Step 1: Siehe dir die folgenden Textteile an, um zu sehen, worum es im Text geht:
- Überschrift und Unterüberschriften
- Bilder und Bildunterschriften
- den ersten Satz jedes Absatzes – dieser Satz ist meist der *topic sentence*, der die Hauptidee des Absatzes nennt
- den letzten Absatz des Textes, der oft eine Zusammenfassung des Textes enthält

Step 2: Fasse für dich selbst den Text in ein paar Worten zusammen. Wenn dir das ohne Probleme gelingt, dann weißt du, um was es in dem Text geht – und dass dein Skimming erfolgreich war.

> **TIPP**
> Mache dir um unbekannten Wortschatz erstmal keine Gedanken – dafür ist Zeit, wenn du feststellst, dass der Text für dich geeignet ist.

## SCANNING

Wenn du in einem Text nach Informationen oder Antworten auf eine Frage suchst, aber nicht den ganzen Text lesen willst, reicht es oft, wenn du den Text nach Schlüsselwörtern *(keywords)* absuchst und nur dort genauer liest, wo du sie findest.

Step 1: Überlege dir *keywords*, die für dein Thema oder deine Frage relevant sind. Wenn du z. B. nach den Öffnungszeiten eines Museums usw. suchst, dann könnten das Wörter (oder Symbole) sein wie *open, (opening) hours, days,* oder Zahlen wie *8am–5pm*.

Step 2: Gehe mit deinen Augen sehr schnell durch den Text und suche nach deinen *keywords*. Du kannst auch mit dem Finger in breiten Bewegungen wie bei einem „S" von oben bis unten durch den Text gehen, bis du eines oder mehrere deiner *keywords* gefunden hast.

Step 3: Lies die Textstelle, die dein *keyword* enthält, um zu sehen, ob sie die gewünschten Informationen enthält. Wenn nicht, scanne weiter.

> **TIPP**
> Wenn du mit Texten im Internet arbeitest, kann dein Browser dir viel Arbeit abnehmen.
> Mit Strg+F (Cmd+F am Mac) kannst du nach deinen *keywords* suchen und nur die Textstellen lesen, in denen ein *keyword* markiert ist.

## SF 2  Marking up a text

Wenn du mit Kopien von Texten arbeitest, kannst du wichtige Informationen darin markieren, um sie einfacher wiederzufinden oder als Grundlage für die Weiterarbeit zu verwenden, z. B. wenn du eine Zusammenfassung schreiben oder mit Hilfe des Textes eine inhaltliche Frage beantworten sollst.

Step 1: Lies dir die Aufgabe genau durch und überlege, welche Informationen du zur Beantwortung brauchst. Behalte dies im Kopf, während du den Text liest.

Step 2: Lies den Text und markiere nur Informationen, die wichtig sind. Nicht jeder Satz enthält Wichtiges, und oft reicht es aus, nur ein oder zwei Wörter in einem Satz zu markieren. Hebe wichtige Informationen hervor, z. B. durch Unterstreichen, Einkreisen oder Markieren mit einem Textmarker.

Step 3: Mache dir kurze Notizen am Rand – z. B. kurze Überschriften oder Stichwörter –, die den Inhalt kurz zusammenfassen. (➜ *SF 27*)

> **TIPP**
> 1. Verwende unterschiedliche Farben für unterschiedliche Aufgaben/Fragestellungen.
> 2. Markiere wirklich nur Stichwörter, sonst wird es unübersichtlich.

An exhibition at the Black Cultural Archives recently took me back to my childhood haunts in Brixton. As I wandered the colourful South London streets where I grew up, my senses were treated to the sounds of many different languages For centuries, foreigners have arrived here through the Port of London. Some came from not so far away: Irish, Welsh, Scots. At the time of the Great Fire in 1666 a majority of Londoners had been born abroad, like protestant Huguenots

# Skills File

## WRITING SKILLS

### SF 3  The stages of writing

Wenn deine Texte präzise und gut lesbar sind, machst du es deinen Lesern leichter, deinen Gedanken zu folgen, egal ob du eine Geschichte, einen Kommentar oder eine Zusammenfassung schreibst.

Du solltest deine Texte stets gut planen und zuerst einen Entwurf erstellen, den du dann überarbeitest, bis das Ergebnis so ist, wie du es haben willst – gut lesbar, leicht zu verstehen und ohne Fehler. Dieses Vorgehen braucht Zeit, aber es macht deine Texte besser.

#### PLANUNGSPHASE
Step 1: Plane für diese Phase ausreichend Zeit ein und denke über folgende Fragen nach:

- über welches Thema willst du schreiben?
- was genau sollst du tun (beschreiben, erläutern, zusammenfassen …)?
- welche Dinge musst du für den geforderten Text beachten?

Step 2: Dann solltest du

- alle nötigen Informationen für dein Thema recherchieren (➜ SF 18),
- Ideen/Argumente sammeln und sortieren
- Notizen anfertigen zu dem, was du schreiben willst (➜ SF 27)

#### ENTWURFSPHASE
Jetzt schreibe deinen ersten Entwurf:

- Füge deinen Notizen linking words (➜ SF 5) und topic sentences hinzu (➜ SF 4).
- Beginne für jede neue Idee einen neuen Absatz.
- Führe deine Ideen aus und gib Beispiele (wenn das die Textsorte erfordert).
- Denke über das Ende deines Textes nach. Wenn du weißt, wie dein Text endet, ist es leichter, eine gute Einleitung zu schreiben, die darauf hinführt. (➜ SF 4)

#### ÜBERARBEITUNGSPHASE
Wenn dein Entwurf fertig ist, heißt das leider noch nicht, dass dein Text auch schon so weit ist. Jetzt ist es an der Zeit, dass du oder jemand anderes deinen Text noch einmal kritisch durchliest. Am besten ist es, wenn du den Text mehrmals liest, jedes Mal mit einem anderen Schwerpunkt:

- Liest sich der Text gut? Ist er logisch aufgebaut und hat eine gute Struktur? (➜ SF 4)
- Sieh dir die verschiedenen sprachlichen Aspekte deines Textes an: Grammatik, Rechtschreibung, Zeichensetzung, Ausdruck, linking words, time markers etc. (➜ SF 5, SF 9)
- Schreibe deinen Text noch einmal. Verbessere alles, was im ersten Entwurf noch nicht ganz gepasst hat. Wenn du Feedback von jemand anderem bekommen hast, sieh es dir genau an und entscheide dann, was davon du für deinen Text übernehmen möchtest.

> **TIPP**
> Wenn du mehr Informationen zum Verfassen guter Texte haben möchtest, sieh dir auch die folgenden Skills files an:
> - SF 18: Internet research
> - SF 4: Structuring texts
> - SF 5: Good sentences
> - SF 6: Writing a formal letter or email
> - SF 7: Writing a comment
> - SF 8: Summing up a text
> - SF 9: Revising texts

# SF 4 Structuring texts

## STRUCTURE
Ein guter Text besteht in der Regel aus den folgenden drei Teilen:

- Einleitung *(introduction)*:
  Hier steht, worum es in dem gesamten Text geht. An dieser Stelle kann auch ein Problem genannt werden, das in dem Text erörtert werden soll.

- Hauptteil *(main body)*:
  Dieser Teil ist in mehrere Absätze gegliedert und präsentiert die Details (Fakten, Beispiele etc.) zu deinem Thema.

- Schluss *(conclusion)*:
  Hier gibst du deinem Text ein passendes, interessantes Ende.

## PARAGRAPHS
Längere Texte sind einfacher zu lesen und schneller zu verstehen, wenn sie in Absätze eingeteilt sind. Dabei solltest du folgende Dinge beachten:

- Fange für jeden neuen Aspekt einen neuen Absatz an.
- Beginne mit einem interessanten *topic sentence*.
- Beende deinen Text im letzten Absatz mit einer Zusammenfassung oder etwas Persönlichem.

## TOPIC SENTENCES
Jeder Absatz sollte mit einem Einleitungssatz beginnen.

Dieser *topic sentence* beschreibt, worum es in dem Absatz geht. Wichtige Dinge, die du in einem *topic sentence* ansprechen kannst, sind z. B.

- **Orte:** My trip to Berlin was exciting.
- **Personen:** The Beatles are one of the most famous bands in the world.
- **Aktivitäten:** Lots of people ride their bike every day.

---

My Trip to Wales

Last summer I wanted to go to Wales because I like the mountains.

First I had to find some information on Wales. So I went to the library and looked for books about Wales. I found a book with some interesting information on hiking tours and I also found a camping guide for Wales. I went home with three books under my arm.

At home I started to plan for my trip. I read all the books and took notes on hiking trails, the weather and the equipment I would need for camping and hiking. After a few days I knew where I wanted to go and what I wanted to do there.

I did not want to go to Wales alone, so I had to find someone to go with me. I called most of my friends and told them about my plan. Some of them did not want to go hiking and others had no money for the trip. But my friend Judith agreed to go with me. We decided to go in late August.

Judith and I spent two lovely weeks in Wales. We went to Snowdonia and enjoyed the fantastic mountains. We stayed in a lovely bed and breakfast and met lots of really nice people. Before we went home we spent two very interesting days in Cardiff.

This was one of the best summer holidays I ever had. Go to Wales – it's fantastic!

# Skills File

## SF 5 Writing good sentences

Gute Texte bestehen aus wohlformulierten, abwechslungsreichen Sätzen. Die folgenden Techniken helfen dir, dich variabel auszudrücken und damit den Stil deiner Texte zu verbessern.

### ADJEKTIVE
Verwende Adjektive, wenn du Dinge, Orte und Menschen näher beschreiben möchtest:
- a bright face
- a fantastic trip

Stell aber sicher, dass du die Adjektive good, bad and nice nicht zu häufig einsetzt. Ersetze sie durch andere Adjektive mit einer ähnlichen bzw. genaueren Bedeutung:
- a nice teacher: a friendly teacher, a helpful teacher, …
- a good book: an interesting book, a funny book, …

### ADVERBIEN
Verwende Adverbien, um Handlungen näher zu beschreiben:
- They walked home slowly.
- She talked quietly.

Verwende Ausdrücke wie really, very, a bit etc., um Aussagen zu verdeutlichen oder zu verstärken:
- It was a really sad story.
- The houses are very high.

### KONJUNKTIONEN
Konjunktionen wie and, but oder because geben deinen Sätzen eine klare, gut nachvollziehbare Struktur:
- We went to the London Eye, but it was very expensive.

### RELATIVSÄTZE
Relativsätze verbinden Sätze oder geben mehr Informationen zu einer Sache oder einer Person:
- This is the shop which sells the best ice cream in Berlin.

### ZEITANGABEN
*Time markers* / adverbiale Bestimmungen der Zeit helfen dem Leser, sich in einem Text oder einer Geschichte zeitlich zurechtzufinden. Verwende *time markers*, um …
- die Reihenfolge von Ereignissen zu verdeutlichen:
  *at first, next, finally, …*
- zu zeigen, wie viel Zeit zwischen einzelnen Ereignissen vergeht:
  *for half an hour, just two minutes later, …*
- zu verdeutlichen, wie langsam oder schnell etwas passiert:
  *immediately, it took hours, faster than I could look, …*
- zu sagen, wenn etwas zeitgleich passiert:
  *while I was waiting, during the lesson, as we came round the corner, …*
- die Ereignisse eines Textes/einer Geschichte zeitlich einzuordnen:
  *two summers ago, last Halloween, on my way home from school yesterday, …*

## SF 6  Writing a formal letter or email

→ p. 21

Wenn du einen Brief oder eine Mail an eine Organisation, einen potenziellen Arbeitgeber oder Ähnliches schreibst, sollte dein Schreiben gewissen formalen Regeln folgen.

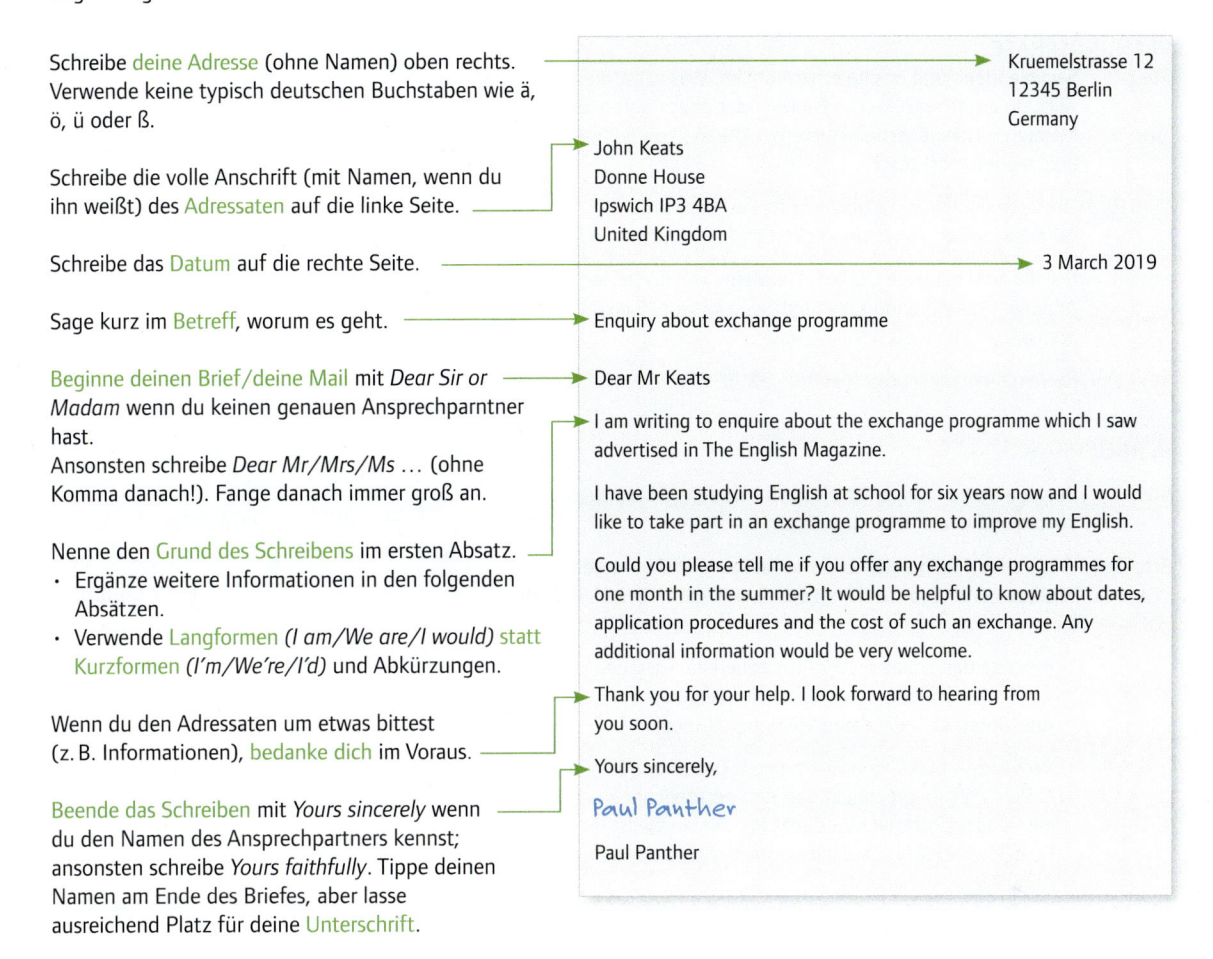

Schreibe deine Adresse (ohne Namen) oben rechts. Verwende keine typisch deutschen Buchstaben wie ä, ö, ü oder ß. → Kruemelstrasse 12 / 12345 Berlin / Germany

Schreibe die volle Anschrift (mit Namen, wenn du ihn weißt) des Adressaten auf die linke Seite. → John Keats / Donne House / Ipswich IP3 4BA / United Kingdom

Schreibe das Datum auf die rechte Seite. → 3 March 2019

Sage kurz im Betreff, worum es geht. → Enquiry about exchange programme

Beginne deinen Brief/deine Mail mit *Dear Sir or Madam* wenn du keinen genauen Ansprechparntner hast.
Ansonsten schreibe *Dear Mr/Mrs/Ms …* (ohne Komma danach!). Fange danach immer groß an. → Dear Mr Keats

Nenne den Grund des Schreibens im ersten Absatz. →
- Ergänze weitere Informationen in den folgenden Absätzen.
- Verwende Langformen (*I am/We are/I would*) statt Kurzformen (*I'm/We're/I'd*) und Abkürzungen.

I am writing to enquire about the exchange programme which I saw advertised in The English Magazine.

I have been studying English at school for six years now and I would like to take part in an exchange programme to improve my English.

Could you please tell me if you offer any exchange programmes for one month in the summer? It would be helpful to know about dates, application procedures and the cost of such an exchange. Any additional information would be very welcome.

Wenn du den Adressaten um etwas bittest (z. B. Informationen), bedanke dich im Voraus. → Thank you for your help. I look forward to hearing from you soon.

Beende das Schreiben mit *Yours sincerely* wenn du den Namen des Ansprechpartners kennst; ansonsten schreibe *Yours faithfully*. Tippe deinen Namen am Ende des Briefes, aber lasse ausreichend Platz für deine Unterschrift. →

Yours sincerely,

*Paul Panther*

Paul Panther

---

**TIPP**
Bei einer formellen E-Mail brauchst du Datum und Adressaten nicht zu nennen. Ansonsten gelten dieselben Regeln wie bei einem formellen Brief. Liste am Ende der Mail deine Kontaktdaten auf (Name, Adresse, ggf. Telefonnummer). Ganz wichtig: verwende auf keinen Fall Emoticons oder Smileys.

# Skills File

## SF 7 Writing a comment / opinion piece

→ p. 45

In einem Meinungsartikel oder Kommentar (*opinion piece/comment*) geht es darum, deine persönliche Meinung zu präsentieren und mit Argumenten zu stützen.

### PLANUNGSPHASE

**Step 1:** Sammle Ideen und mache erste Notizen. Was willst du sagen? Was willst du erreichen? Welche Fakten oder Zitate unterstützen deine Meinung? Hast du schon eine Lösungsidee, von der du andere überzeugen möchtest?

**Step 2:** Überlege dir eine gute Überschrift. Sie sollte die Aufmerksamkeit der Leser wecken und sie neugierig machen.

**Step 3:** Erstelle Notizen/eine Outline. Überlege, wie du deine Argumentation/Meinung unterstützen kannst (Fakten, Statistiken, Zitate etc.).

**Step 4:** Recherchiere passendes Material. (→ *SF 18*)

### SCHREIBPHASE

**Step 1:** Beginne deinen *comment* mit einem kurzen Absatz zu dem Thema und deiner Meinung dazu.

**Step 2:** Präsentiere Argumente für deine Meinung in den folgenden Absätzen und ergänze sie mit weiteren Fakten, Beispielen oder Zitaten.

- Benutze das simple present für generelle Aussagen und das simple present oder simple past für die Beispiele, Anekdoten etc., die deine Meinung stützen.

- Verwende Überzeugungstechniken. Das sind z.B
  – Personalpronomen, um den Text persönlicher zu machen: mit you sprichst du Leser direkt an, mit we stellst du eine Gemeinsamkeit her und mit I unterstreichst du, dass es sich um deine Meinung handelt.
  – Zitate, Anekdoten, Statistiken stützen deine Meinung: Zitate zeigen, dass andere Menschen deine Meinung teilen, Anekdoten bringen deine Punkte den Lesern näher und Statistiken belegen, dass deine Meinung auf Fakten beruht.
  – Ausdrucksstarke Sprache: schreibe abwechslungsreich (→ *SF 5*) und verwende Wörter, die emotional ansprechen, wie z. B. Adjektive und Adverbien, die den Leser wütend oder glücklich, traurig oder fröhlich machen
  – Rhetorische Fragen: mit Fragen, auf die eigentlich keine Antwort erwartet wird, kannst du deine Aussage nochmal unterstreichen: Is climate change real? Is killing wrong? Who can deny this?

**Step 3:** Im letzten Absatz, der *conclusion*, wiederholst du noch einmal deine Meinung und schlägst entweder eine Lösung vor (wenn es sich z. B. um ein Problem handelt) oder forderst deine Leser auf, etwas zu tun.

---

**Outline / Notes**

1. Headline
   - catch your readers' attention (clear statement, provocative question etc.)

2. First paragraph
   - state your topic AND your opinion clearly (keep it short!)
   - keep your readers interested

3. Supporting paragraphs
   use statistics, facts, quotes etc. to back up your main statement

4. Final paragraph / Conclusion
   - restate your opinion
   - suggest a solution or call for action

---

**TIPP**

Übertreibe es nicht mit den Statistiken, Anekdoten und Zitaten, sondern konzentriere dich auf besonders interessante oder spannende Punkte wie z. B. Zahlen, die dich in einer Statistik selber überrascht haben.

# SF 8 Summing up a text

→ *p. 20*

Wenn du eine Zusammenfassung schreiben sollst, ist es wichtig, den Text gut zu verstehen. Erst dann kannst du entscheiden, welche Aspekte so wichtig sind, dass sie in deiner Zusammenfassung erwähnt werden sollten – und welche nicht. Die folgenden Schritte können beim Schreiben einer Zusammenfassung helfen:

## PLANUNGSPHASE

**Step 1:** Lies den Text genau. Mache dir Notizen (→ *SF 27*) oder markiere wichtige Stellen im Text (→ *SF 2*).

**Step 2:** Beantworte die *wh*-Fragen Who? What? Where? When? Why? zum Text. Du kannst dir dazu Stichworte am Rand machen.

- Who? Who does something? Who is the text about?
- What? What happens? What does person X do?
- Where? Where does it take place?
- When? When does it take place?
- Why? Why does person X act this way? Why does something happen?

**Step 3:** Entscheide, welche Textteile wichtige Informationen enthalten. Beispiele, Vergleiche, direkte Rede oder Zahlen und Ähnliches gehören nicht in eine Zusammenfassung.

> **TIPP**
> Du kannst Teile, die für deine Zusammenfassung überflüssig sind, im Text einklammern.

## SCHREIBPHASE

**Step 1:** Schreibe einen ersten Entwurf.

- Beginne mit der Einleitung, in der wichtige Informationen wie Titel, Autor/in, Thema und Hauptaussage des Textes stehen. Wenn du einen Artikel zusammenfasst, solltest du hier die Quelle nennen.
- Verwende immer das *simple present*.
- Kopiere nicht den Text, sondern benutze deine eigenen Worte.
- Wichtig: gib nie deine eigene Meinung oder Wertung.

**Step 2:** Überarbeite deine Zusammenfassung.

- Hast du alle wichtigen Aspekte genannt und unwichtige Details weggelassen?
- Ist der Text durchgängig im *simple present*?
- Vergiss nicht, Rechtschreibung/Grammatik zu prüfen. (→ *SF 9*)

> **LANGUAGE HELP**
> Folgende *phrases* können dir bei der Einleitung helfen:
> - The story/text is about …
> - The text deals with …
> - The topic of the text is …
> - The article/text shows …

# Skills File

## SF 9 Revising texts

Egal, ob du eine Rückmeldung von einem Partner/einer Partnerin bekommen hast oder nicht – einen Text solltest du auf jeden Fall noch einmal gut prüfen, bevor du ihn deinem Lehrer/deiner Lehrerin übergibst.

### TEXTÜBERARBEITUNG

1. **Stimmt die Struktur?**
   Jeder Text braucht
   - eine Einleitung, die in das Thema einführt,
   - einen Hauptteil, der das Thema ausführt,
   - einen Schluss, der alles auf den Punkt bringt.
   (➜ *SF 4*)

2. **Stimmt der Aufbau der Absätze?**
   Jeder Absatz
   - befasst sich mit einem zusammenhängenden Gedanken,
   - beginnt mit einem **topic sentence**, der diesen Gedanken einführt.
   (➜ *SF 4*)

3. **Stimmen die Verknüpfungen?**
   Gute *linking words*
   - schaffen Verbindungen zwischen Sätzen oder Satzteilen,
   - helfen, Zusammenhänge besser darzustellen und verständlich zu machen.
   (➜ *SF 5*)

4. **Sind die Zeitangaben richtig gesetzt?**
   *Time markers*
   - helfen, sich z. B. in einer Geschichte zurechtzufinden,
   - machen das Geschehen anschaulicher.
   (➜ *SF 5*)

5. **Enthält der Text Adjektive und Adverbien?**
   Adjektive und Adverbien
   - erlauben nähere Beschreibungen von Personen und Dingen,
   - machen Texte anschaulicher.
   (➜ *SF 5*)

6. **Hat der Text sprachliche/grammatikalische Fehler?**
   Überprüfe deinen Text
   - auf Rechtschreibung,
   - auf grammatische Formen, z. B. Verbformen, Satzbau (*word order*) usw.

### FEHLERPROTOKOLL

Die Fehler in einem Text zu finden und zu korrigieren ist eine Sache, aber es wäre natürlich noch viel besser, dieselben Fehler nicht wieder zu machen.

Dabei hilft ein Fehlerprotokoll, in dem du dir die wichtigsten Fehler – diejenigen, die du immer wieder machst – notierst und dir immer wieder veranschaulichst. Dieses Fehlerprotokoll kann ein kleines Extra-Heft sein oder auch eine Sammlung von Klebezetteln, die du dir über deinen Schreibtisch hängst.

Hauptsache, es ist etwas, das du dir immer wieder schnell angucken kannst, wenn du einen Text schreiben sollst.

> **TIPP**
> Häufige Fehlerquellen sind z. B.
> - Groß-/Kleinschreibung
> - Wörter, die gleich klingen, aber unterschiedlich geschrieben werden: *their/there/they're*
> - Verwendung des Apostrophs
> - Bildung der Zeitformen der Verben: *stop* ➜ *stopping*, *try* ➜ *tries*
> - Wörter mit „stummen" Buchstaben: *walk, talk, know*

# Skills File

## MEDIATION SKILLS

### SF 10 Mediating written or spoken information

Nicht jeder spricht und versteht sowohl Deutsch als auch Englisch; daher kann es vorkommen, dass du in bestimmten Situationen für Andere zwischen den Sprachen vermitteln musst – das nennt man dann Mediation.

Wie und was genau du vermitteln musst, hängt von der Situation ab und auch davon, ob du den Inhalt eines geschriebenen Textes wiedergeben oder zwischen zwei Sprechern vermitteln sollst.

Sprachmittlung bedeutet nicht Übersetzen (von Texten) oder Dolmetschen (bei Unterhaltungen), sondern das sinngemäße Übertragen von Inhalten in die andere Sprache.

#### MEDIATION VON SCHRIFTLICHEN ODER MÜNDLICHEN INFORMATIONEN
Wenn du Informationen in einer anderen Sprache wiedergeben sollst, geht es nicht darum, alles zu übersetzen, sondern es kommt darauf an, die wichtigsten Informationen herauszusuchen. Oft stellt dir die Person, für die du die Informationen wiedergibst, gezielte Fragen – so weißt du, worauf du achten musst.

#### Schriftliche Informationen
- Scanne den Text gezielt nach den geforderten Informationen. (➜ *SF 1*)
- Mach dir keine Sorgen, wenn du nicht jedes Wort verstehst. Das ist oft nicht nötig, um die wichtigen Punkte zu verstehen und wiederzugeben.
- Wenn der Text länger ist und du viele Informationen im Blick behalten musst, markiere die wichtigsten Textstellen. (➜ *SF 2*)
- Mach dir Notizen in deinen eigenen Worten. (➜ *SF 27*)

#### Mündliche Informationen
- Achte beim Hören gezielt auf die gesuchten Informationen. (➜ *SF 16*)
- Mach dir Notizen. (➜ *SF 27*)
- Überlege, wie du deine Notizen am besten in der anderen Sprache wiedergeben kannst.

> **TIPP**
> Bei Mediation im Unterricht hast du in der Regel eine Aufgabenstellung, die dir sagt, worauf du beim Lesen oder Hören achten musst bzw. welche Stellen du wiedergeben sollst. Konzentriere dich beim Lesen des Textes auf diese Stellen (*scanning*) bzw. mache dir gezielt zu diesen Stellen Notizen.

> **TIPP**
> Wenn du den Inhalt eines Texts schriftlich in einer anderen Sprache wiedergeben sollst, achte darauf, dass deine Mediation nicht länger ist als ca. 35-40% des Originaltextes, ähnlich wie bei einer *summary*. (➜ *SF 8*)

### SF 11 Finding key information ➜ *p. 23*

Manchmal gibt es keine gezielten Fragen oder Aufgabenstellungen, die dir sagen, welche Informationen du aus einem Text heraussuchen und wiedergeben sollst. In der Regel hast du aber trotzdem Anhaltspunkte, die sich aus der Situation ergeben oder aus dem, was dir dein Gegenüber erzählt hat.

Wenn du in einer solchen Situation bist, helfen folgende Hinweise:

- Analysiere die Situation, um abzuschätzen, um welche Informationen es gehen könnte (Restaurant, Bahnhof, Flughafen usw.).
- Wenn du unsicher bist, frage nach.
- Übersetze wichtige Stichworte direkt, wenn du die Wörter kennst.
- Umschreibe Begriffe, die du nicht kennst.

> **TIPP**
> Wenn du Informationen wiedergibst, kannst du oft Details zu einem Begriff zusammenfassen. Wenn z. B. in einem Text *twitter*, *Facebook*, *tumblr* und *Pinterest* vorkommen, kannst du *social media* sagen anstatt alle aufzuzählen.

# Skills File

## SF 12 Paraphrasing
→ p. 55

Es fällt dir eventuell manchmal schwer, mündliche Aussagen oder Texte in Englisch wiederzugeben, z. B. weil

- dein Wortschatz nicht ausreicht
- dir bekannte Wörter "im Eifer des Gefechts" nicht einfallen
- oder spezielle Fachbegriffe auftauchen.

Wenn dir das passiert, dann solltest du versuchen, diese Wörter zu umschreiben, z. B. mithilfe von Relativsätzen wie:

*It's somebody/a person who …*
*It's something that you use to …*
*It's an animal that …*
*It's a place that/where …*

> Oh, sure. There's a drugstore down the street. Come on, I'll show you.

> Ich hab Kopfschmerzen. Kannst du Marcus mal fragen, wo hier eine Apotheke ist?

> Apotheke? Er … OK … Marcus, is there a place nearby where Lukas can buy something for his headache?

### TIPP
Oft helfen beim Umschreiben auch Synonyme (gleiche Bedeutung) oder Antonyme (gegenteilige Bedeutung). Wenn du die weißt, kannst du z. B. sagen:
- It's the same as …
- It's the opposite of …

## SF 13 Cultural differences
→ p. 72

Wenn du anderen Menschen hilfst, Texte oder Gehörtes zu verstehen, kann es neben Wortschatzproblemen auch noch andere Schwierigkeiten geben. Diese sind häufig in kulturellen Unterschieden begründet. Um hier helfen zu können, musst du dir beim Sprachmitteln bewusst machen, dass dein Gegenüber evtl. bestimmte Dinge nicht weiß, die für dich selbstverständlich sind, oder dass er/sie dich nicht sofort versteht, obwohl du den Inhalt korrekt übertragen hast.

Dinge, die häufig zu Missverständnissen führen, sind z. B.
- Temperaturen: 30 Grad bei uns sind heiß, in den USA eher kalt, weil in den USA Temperaturen in Fahrenheit angegeben werden, nicht in Celsius.
- Längenangaben/Geschwindigkeit: Bei uns wird das metrische System verwendet (Meter, Kilometer usw.), in den USA das *imperial system* mit *inch*, *yard* und *mile*. Das kann auch bei Geschwindigkeitsangaben zu Verwirrung führen, denn 75 *mph* (Meilen pro Stunde) sind z. B. ca. 120 km/h.

Am besten ist es, wenn du immer noch mal höflich nachfragst, ob dein Gegenüber alles verstanden hat. Wenn du dann feststellst, dass es zu einem Missverständnis gekommen ist, dann kannst du folgende Dinge probieren:
- Frage höflich nach, wo das Missverständnis ist.
- Versuche, das Missverständnis durch eine neue Erklärung zu beseitigen.
- Ergänze deine Erläuterung evtl. mit Hintergrundinformationen: Es kann sein, dass du bestimmte Dinge, die für dich völlig normal sind, erklären musst (wie z. B. Mülltrennung oder das Benutzen des Nahverkehrs).
- Sei auch offen für die Erklärungen, die du evtl. im Gegenzug bekommst – hier kannst du Dinge über das Land deines Gegenübers lernen.

# Skills File

## VIEWING SKILLS

### SF 14 Viewing (Media skills)

Wenn du verstehst, wie Filmtechniken eingesetzt werden, um beim Zuschauer z. B. Angst, Freude, Spannung oder Lachen auszulösen, bekommst du ein besseres Verständnis dafür, wie Filme funktionieren.

Es gibt viele verschiedene Elemente, die die Atmosphäre und die Wirkung eines Filmes beeinflussen:

- Genre: Handelt es sich um einen Dokumentarfilm (documentary), einen Spielfilm (feature film) wie z. B. thriller, science-fiction/sci-fi movie, comedy oder ein drama? Oder ist es ein Videoclip oder ein Werbefilm?
- Story: Wo und wann spielt der Film (setting)? Besetzung der Rollen (cast), Schauplatz (location), Handlung (plot).
- Camera: Erst durch die Bilder der **Kamera** ist der Zuschauer in der Lage, einen Film wahrzunehmen. Die Kamera stellt das Blickfeld her und begrenzt es gleichzeitig, z. B. hinsichtlich der Beziehung der Charaktere zueinander. Auch die Stimmung oder Spannung in einer Szene wird von der Kameraführung beeinflusst. Dafür gibt es z. B. folgende Mittel:
  - Shots: Die **Kameraeinstellung** beeinflusst, wie man Szenen wahrnimmt, ob z. B. Personen oder Objekte als Nahaufnahme (close-up), aus der mittleren Distanz (medium shot) oder als Totale (long shot) gefilmt sind.
  - Editing: Filme werden in der Regel nicht chronologisch gedreht und auch nicht nur mit einer einzigen Kamera, d. h. am Ende der Dreharbeiten müssen viele einzelne Shots zu einem Film zusammengefügt werden. Dieser **Filmschnitt** bestimmt, wie eine Szene wirkt. Er bestimmt den Rhythmus – lange Einstellungen mit wenigen Schnitten wirken eher ruhig, können aber auch große Spannung erzeugen, während schnelle, harte Schnitte eher actiongeladen wirken. Wie genau eine Szene wirkt, hängt oft auch vom Zusammenspiel von Schnitt und Musik ab.
- Soundtrack: Die **Musik**, die für eine Szene gewählt wird, hat großen Einfluss darauf, wie man die Szene wahrnimmt. Eine Actionszene wird meist mit schneller, lauter Musik unterlegt, eine romantische Szene eher mit ruhiger, leiser Musik. Dies geschieht, um die Wirkung des Gesehenen zu verstärken.

*long shot*

*medium shot*

*close-up*

### VIEWING LOG

Wenn du eine Szene oder einen ganzen Film sehr intensiv analysieren möchtest, hilft es, ein Filmtagebuch (viewing log) anzulegen, in dem du die Handlung oder einzelne wichtige Szenen sowie deine Reaktion darauf festhältst.

Das Filmtagebuch kann z. B. eine simple, zweispaltige Tabelle sein:

Spalte 1: What you noticed – images, sounds, dialogue, lighting, costumes, mood, characterization, plot, etc.

Spalte 2: Your reaction – What did you think? How did the scene make you feel?

---

**TIPP**

Wenn du über Filme sprechen möchtest, können dir folgende Redewendungen helfen:

- The film is about … / shows … / tells the story of …
- The music creates/builds/supports tension/ suspense/joy …
- The actor's body language helps to create a feeling of happiness/joy/anger/suspense …
- In this scene the music/effects/camera angle … supports the plot /mood of the scene / …
- The camera movement creates a feeling of …
- The camera work/soundtrack helps to …
- The close-ups show his/her feelings.

# Skills File

## LISTENING AND SPEAKING SKILLS

### SF 15  Speaking

Es ist nicht immer einfach, sich mit Menschen aus anderen Ländern zu unterhalten. Neben der Sprachbarriere gibt es oft auch kulturelle Unterschiede, wie das folgende Beispiel zeigt.

Lies dieses Gespräch zwischen Paul, einem deutschen Schüler, und seinem Austauschpartner Jack in den USA:

> **Jack:** How's your school at home?
> **Paul:** It's okay.
> **Jack:** Oh … good. What are your favorite subjects?
> **Paul:** Er, I don't know.
> **Jack:** Oh, well. Maybe you'll enjoy our school too.
> **Paul:** Maybe.
> **Jack:** Er … want to play a game?

Das Gespräch kommt nicht so richtig in Gang, und Jack gibt irgendwann auf. Wenn man aber einige Regeln beachtet, werden Unterhaltungen einfacher und für beide Parteien erfreulicher. Vergleiche das folgende Gespräch mit dem obigen:

> **Jack:** How's your school at home?
> **Paul:** I like it … but of course I don't like all my teachers.
> **Jack:** Yeah, I think that's normal. What are your favorite subjects?
> **Paul:** I'm not sure. I like history and maths, but art and German are okay, too.
> **Jack:** Ah, my favorite subject is English. Anyway, I'm sure you'll enjoy our school too. Our history teacher is pretty cool. Have you met any of the teachers yet?
> **Paul:** No, not yet, but I think …

Die folgenden Schritte helfen dir, wenn du dich freundlich und flüssig unterhalten willst:

**Step 1:** Beginne freundlich, z. B. mit etwas, was beide Gesprächspartner verbindet (der Ort, die Situation usw.).

**Step 2:** Halte die Unterhaltung am Laufen:
- zeige dein Interesse, indem du Fragen stellst
- vermeide einsilbige Antworten, um nicht desinteressiert oder unfreundlich zu wirken
- wenn du etwas nicht verstehst, frage nach
- wenn du etwas nicht sagen kannst, versuche es zu umschreiben oder bitte deinen Gesprächspartner um Hilfe

**Step 3:** Beende das Gespräch so freundlich, wie du es angefangen hast:
- bedanke dich, wenn du um Hilfe gebeten hast
- verabschiede dich freundlich

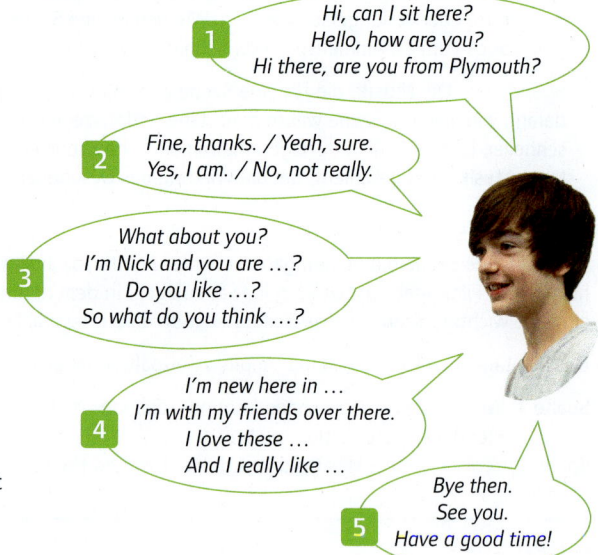

**1** Hi, can I sit here?
Hello, how are you?
Hi there, are you from Plymouth?

**2** Fine, thanks. / Yeah, sure.
Yes, I am. / No, not really.

**3** What about you?
I'm Nick and you are …?
Do you like …?
So what do you think …?

**4** I'm new here in …
I'm with my friends over there.
I love these …
And I really like …

**5** Bye then.
See you.
Have a good time!

> **TIPP**
> Mache dir vor dem Gespräch klar, mit wem du redest. Wenn du mit einem gleichaltrigen Jugendlichen sprichst, kannst du viel informeller sprechen als wenn du mit jemand Älterem sprichst. Überlege auch, ob es kulturelle Unterschiede gibt und passe deine Sprache entsprechend an (➜ *SF 13*).

# Skills File

## SF 16 Listening

Wenn du Englisch hörst, kann es sein, dass du entweder Details heraushören musst (listening for detail), z. B. bei Ansagen am Bahnhof, oder generell verstehen musst, um was es geht (listening for gist) wie z. B. bei einem Film oder Hörbuch.

### LISTENING FOR DETAIL

- Wenn du Details heraushören sollst, überleg dir vorher, welche Informationen du verstehen musst. Bei einem Wetterbericht sind das z. B. Beschreibungen wie sunny, dry, cloudy, chance of rain etc., bei Bahnhofsansagen z. B. Wörter wie train, platform oder Orte und Zeiten. Achte beim Hören dann verstärkt auf diese Wörter und notiere sie. (→ SF 27)

- Je nachdem, welche Details du heraushören sollst, können auch Signalwörter helfen, dem Inhalt zu folgen und dich auf die Details zu konzentrieren:
  - Gründe, Folgen: because, so, so that, …
  - Vergleiche: larger/older/… than, as … as, more, most, …
  - Reihenfolge: before, after, then, next, later, …

> **TIPP**
> - Oft kannst du die Menschen um dich herum fragen, wenn du nicht alles richtig verstanden hast – z. B. bei Durchsagen am Bahnhof.
> - In einer Unterhaltung kannst du deinen Gesprächspartner bitten, Sachen zu wiederholen oder zu erklären.

### LISTENING FOR GIST

- Wenn du verstehen sollst, worum es generell geht, dann brauchst du dir keine Sorgen zu machen, wenn du nicht jedes Wort verstehst – du musst nicht alles verstehen, um der Grundaussage folgen zu können.

- Überlege dir im Vorfeld, um was es gehen könnte (z. B. anhand einer Aufgabenstellung oder anhand des Themas) und konzentriere dich darauf.

- Versuche, von den Sachen, die du verstehst, auf Sachen zu schließen, die noch kommen könnten.

> **TIPP**
> Beim Listening im Unterricht kannst du Texte oft zweimal hören und hast weitere Hilfen:
> - Sieh dir die Aufgabenstellung an: Was sollst du heraushören?
> - Sieh dir Titel und Bilder an.
> - Vergleiche nach dem Hören mit einem Partner, was ihr verstanden habt.
> - Vervollständige deine Notizen sofort.

## PROJECT AND PRESENTATION SKILLS

## SF 17 Teamwork

Bei Projekten arbeitet ihr oft im Team. Dabei solltet ihr eure unterschiedlichen Fähigkeiten und Talente einbringen und bestimmte Regeln beachten. Folgende Schritte können helfen, die Arbeit zu organisieren:

Step 1: Legt Regeln für die Arbeit in der Gruppe fest, z. B. gegenseitige Unterstützung, pünktliches und zügiges Arbeiten, einander zuhören oder verschiedene Lösungen diskutieren usw.

Step 2: Sammelt Ideen für die Bearbeitung eures Themas (z. B. in einer Mindmap). Wählt gemeinsam Unterthemen aus und legt die Arbeitsschritte fest, die für die Bearbeitung nötig sind.

Step 3: Verteilt Rollen und Aufgaben nach euren Interessen und Fähigkeiten. Wenn ihr euch nicht einigen könnt, hilft Auslosen oder Würfeln. Folgende Rollen solltet ihr auf jeden Fall verteilen:
- coordinator
- writer
- researcher

Step 4: Macht einen Zeitplan für eure Arbeiten, an den sich alle halten.

Step 5: Am Ende der Arbeit sollte ein Rückblick stehen: Besprecht, was gut war und wo ihr Verbesserungsmöglichkeiten seht.

# Skills File

## SF 18 Internet research (Finding information for a presentation) [Media skills] → p. 44

Das Internet ist voller Informationen, aber es ist nicht immer einfach, genau die Informationen zu finden, die du benötigst.

Step 1: Überlege dir gute Stichwörter für dein Thema. Für „Music in New Orleans" wären *music* und „*New Orleans*" ein guter Start.

Step 2: Gib deine Stichwörter in eine Suchmaschine ein. Je mehr gute Stichwörter du eingibst, desto genauer sind die Ergebnisse. Die Infografik rechts hilft dir, wenn du ganz spezielle Informationen suchst.

Step 3: Sieh dir mehrere Suchergebnisse an, um zu sehen, ob sie passen (→ SF 1).

Step 4: Achte darauf, wer die Webseite erstellt hat, um die Qualität der Suchergebnisse einzuschätzen. Sind sie eher zuverlässig (Online-Lexikon, Medien, …) oder eher persönliche Meinungen (Forum, Fan-Seite, …)?

Step 5: Kopiere nicht einfach ganze Artikel aus dem Internet. Mach dir Notizen und verwende deine eigenen Worte, um die Inhalte wiederzugeben. (→ SF 27)

Step 6: Setze dir ein Zeitlimit für deine Recherche und ordne dann dein Material. Prüfe, ob etwas fehlt, und suche dann ggf. gezielt nach diesen Informationen.

Step 7: Lege alle interessanten Materialien zu deinem Thema in einem eigenen Ordner ab. Dann kannst du sie dir später genauer ansehen und auswählen, was du nutzen möchtest.

### Internet research — Tipps und Tricks

**Wenn du ganz spezifische Informationen suchst, helfen diese Tricks:**

**Was du suchst:** Artikel aus dem *Guardian* von 2010–2020 über den FC Liverpool in der Champions League.

**Wie du danach suchst:**

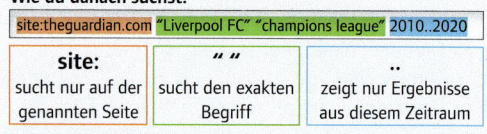

`site:theguardian.com "Liverpool FC" "champions league" 2010..2020`

| site: | " " | .. |
|---|---|---|
| sucht nur auf der genannten Seite | sucht den exakten Begriff | zeigt nur Ergebnisse aus diesem Zeitraum |

**Was du suchst:** Einen englischsprachigen Bericht, am liebsten als PDF, über den Lebensraum von Füchsen.

**Wie du danach suchst:**

`filetype:pdf intitle:habitat of *fox`

| filetype: | intitle: | * |
|---|---|---|
| sucht nur diesen Dateityp (pdf, doc, jpg usw.) | zeigt nur Ergebnisse, in denen dieses Wort im Titel auftaucht | sucht auch Worte wie Red Fox, Black Fox, Desert Fox usw. |

## SF 19 Describing and presenting pictures [Media skills]

Manchmal sollst du ein Foto vor der Klasse vorstellen. Hier sind ein paar Hilfen.

Step 1: Stelle das Foto vor und sage, woher es kommt.

Step 2: Beschreibe das Foto:
- Sage, was wo zu sehen ist: at the top/bottom · in the foreground/background · in the middle · on the left/right
- Diese Präpositionen sind auch hilfreich: behind · between · in front of · next to · under · above
- Geh bei der Beschreibung in einer bestimmten Reihenfolge vor, z. B. von links nach rechts oder von oben nach unten.

Step 3: Sage, was dir an dem Foto gefällt oder nicht.

Step 4: Wenn du fertig bist, bedanke dich fürs Zuhören und frage, ob noch jemand Fragen hat.

**1** *I'd like to talk about this photo of … I found it on the internet/in a magazine/…*

**2** *In the foreground you can see … I think the people in the photo are talking about …/having fun/ celebrating/…*

**3** *I really like/don't like the photo because … It's interesting/boring/exciting/… because …*

**4** *Thank you for listening. Do you have any questions?*

# Skills File

## SF 20 Putting a page together (Media skills)

Wenn du einen Text gestalten möchtest, z. B. für einen Vortrag, einen Blog oder als Poster für eine Präsentation, können dir folgende Hinweise helfen:

- Sortiere die Informationen, die du vermitteln willst: Was ist wichtig? Was ist ein Unterpunkt? Hast du Beispiele für Thesen/ Argumente?

- Gib deinem Produkt eine klare Struktur: Texte haben meist drei Teile (Einleitung, Hauptteil, Schluss), während Poster häufig aus Aufzählungen wichtiger Punkte bestehen. Beginne für jeden neuen Gedanken einen neuen Absatz bzw. einen neuen Stichpunkt.

- Eine Überschrift verdeutlicht, worum es in deinem Text geht. Sie soll Leser auch neugierig machen auf das, was kommt. Wenn es in deinem Produkt um mehrere Themen/Aspekte eines Themas geht, dann kannst Du für einzelne Abschnitte auch Zwischenüberschriften verwenden. Das gibt dem Ganzen eine klare Struktur und hilft dem Leser, sich schnell zu orientieren.

- Ergänze dein Produkt mit passenden Fotos, Videos, Audios, Statistiken etc. Vergiss nicht anzugeben, woher die Medien stammen (➡ *SF 21*).

- Wenn nicht auf den ersten Blick erkennbar ist, was z. B. ein Bild zeigt, füge Bildunterschriften ein.

- Formatiere dein Produkt so, dass es gut lesbar ist. Dabei ist das Medium wichtig – für einen ausgedruckten Handzettel kannst du andere Schriftarten wählen als für einen Text, der am Bildschirm gelesen wird. (➡ *SF 21*) Für ein Poster (z. B. für einen *gallery walk*) muss die Schriftgröße größer sein als für einen Ausdruck. Eine große Schriftgröße hilft dir auch, nicht zu viele Punkte auf dem Poster unterzubringen – hier ist weniger mehr.

## SF 21 Making slides for an electronic presentation (Media skills) ➡ p. 84

Vieles, was für das Layout von Texten/Postern gilt, kannst du auch auf Folien für Präsentation anwenden. Es gibt aber einige Besonderheiten zu beachten. Generell gilt: gut ist, was deine Folien übersichtlich und leicht zu lesen macht.

### TEXT
- Verwende möglichst wenige Folien.

- Nutze Aufzählungen mit *keywords*, keine ganzen Sätze und schreibe nicht mehr als sechs Zeilen auf eine Folie.

- Wähle eine ausreichende Schriftgröße (mindestens 30pt, gerne mehr) und eine gut lesbare Schrift und gehe sparsam mit Texthervorhebungen wie fett, kursiv, Unterstreichung um; lass einen ausreichend großen Abstand zwischen den Zeilen.

- Richte den Text linksbündig aus, außer du verfolgst ein ganz besonderes Ziel damit (z. B. zentriert zum Herausheben eines Zitats), aber mische die Ausrichtung nicht auf einer Folie. Zitate z. B. wirken oft am besten, wenn sie zentriert alleine auf einer Folie stehen.

> **TIPP**
> - Eine gute Faustregel lautet 6 x 6: pro Folie maximal 6 Zeilen mit je maximal 6 Wörtern
> - Bedenke: Folien sind eine visuelle Unterstützung für eine Präsentation, keine Zusammenfassung. Die Zuhörer sollen hören, nicht lesen – die Texte sollten daher auf das Wichtigste reduziert sein.
> - Vermeide Spezialeffekte wie verspielte Übergänge, tanzende Buchstaben etc. Sie kosten viel Zeit und helfen den Zuhörern nicht.

# Skills File

**FARBE UND KONTRAST**
- Du kannst einzelne Wörter in einer anderen Farbe setzen, um sie hervorzuheben. Aber auch hier gilt: weniger ist mehr – mehrere Wörter in unterschiedlichen Farben zu setzen, kann beim Lesen eher hinderlich sein.
- Wenn du mit farbigem Untergrund oder Fotos als Hintergrund arbeitest, solltest du darauf achten, dass dein Text in einer Farbe ist, die ausreichend Kontrast zum Hintergrund bietet – je stärker der Kontrast, desto besser die Lesbarkeit.

**ABBILDUNGEN**
- Ein Bild sagt mehr als tausend Worte – das gilt auch für Folien: manche Inhalte kannst du ebenso mit einem passenden Bild oder einer Grafik ausdrücken.
- Suche ein Bild, dass die Aussage deines Vortrages unterstreicht: z. B. ein Foto, das eine Fragestellung gut illustriert oder eines, das das Problem gut darstellt. Es muss auch kein Foto sein – manchmal ist eine passende Grafik genauso gut, um z. B. statistische Aussagen auf den Punkt zu bringen.
- Wichtig: bei allen Bildern, die du verwendest, musst du die Quelle angeben, d.h. der Fotograf/die Fotografin, Illustrator/Illustratorin etc. sowie der Ort, wo du das Bild gefunden hast (eine Suchmaschine im Internet ist keine Quellenangabe!).

> **TIPP**
> Wenn du deine Folien/Poster nur vor der Klasse zeigst, darfst du Bilder verwenden, ohne die Urheber um Erlaubnis zu fragen, weil es sich um eine begrenzte Öffentlichkeit handelt. Wenn die Folien aber öffentlich zugänglich sind (z. B. auf einer Webseite oder der Schulzeitung), musst du die Urheber unbedingt um Erlaubnis fragen.
> Als Faustregel gilt: veröffentliche kein Bild ohne Erlaubnis, das du nicht selbst gemacht hast.

## SF 22 Giving a presentation

Ob in der Schule oder später im Beruf, die Kunst, eine gut vorbereitete und gut strukturierte Präsentation halten zu können, ist sehr wichtig. Die folgenden Schritte helfen dir dabei.

**PLANUNGSPHASE**

Step 1: Recherchiere dein Thema (➔ SF 18) und mach dir Notizen, am besten gleich auf Englisch (➔ SF 27).

Step 2: Strukturiere die Informationen, z. B. mihilfe von Notizen. (➔ SF 27)

Step 3: Wähle eine Form der Präsentation aus, die das Thema gut veranschaulicht (Poster, Folie, …). Gestalte dein Poster/deine Folie.

Step 4: Bereite deine Notizen für die Präsentation vor, z. B. auf nummerierten Karteikarten. Verwende nur Stichworte.

Step 5: Wenn du in einem Team arbeitest, entscheidet gemeinsam, wer welchen Teil der Präsentation übernimmt. (➔ SF 17)

Step 6: Übe deine Präsentation zu Hause vor einem Spiegel oder vor einem kleinen Publikum (Eltern, Großeltern, Freunde).

**HALTEN DER PRÄSENTATION**

Step 1: Warte, bis es ruhig ist. Schau die Zuhörer/innen an. Erkläre, worüber du sprechen wirst und wie deine Präsentation aufgebaut ist.

Step 2: Sprich langsam und deutlich und möglichst frei. Lies nicht von deinen Notizen ab.

Step 3: Beende deine Präsentation mit einer kleinen Zusammenfassung der wichtigsten Punkte. Bedanke dich fürs Zuhören und frag, ob jemand Fragen hat.

> *My presentation is about …*
> *First I'd like to talk about …*

> *Here's a new word. It is … in German.*

> *On my poster you can see a photo of … The mind map shows …*

> *That's the end of my presentation. Do you have any questions?*

# Skills File

## SF 23 Giving feedback

Gegenseitige Rückmeldungen sind wichtig, damit du siehst, was gut gelungen ist und woran du noch arbeiten musst. Wenn du eine Rückmeldung gibst, solltest du grundsätzliche Regeln beachten, die für einen geschriebenen Text genauso gelten wie für eine Präsentation.
Diese Dinge solltest du beachten:

- Lies den Text sorgfältig durch oder höre der Präsentation gut zu.

- Bei Feedback zu einer Präsentation mache dir Notizen zu den Punkten, auf die du achten sollst, z. B. Inhalt, Struktur, Sprache, Verständlichkeit des Vortrags. Wenn du einen Feedbackbogen hast, kannst du deine Notizen gleich darauf festhalten.

- Bei Feedback zu einem Text lies den Text genau und achte dabei besonders auf Inhalt, Struktur, Wortwahl, Grammatik und Rechtschreibung. Wenn du einen Feedbackbogen hast, mache dir darauf Notizen (siehe rechts).

- Begründe deine Einschätzungen.

- Gib dein Feedback mit Respekt – niemand soll sich angegriffen fühlen. Nenne erst Gelungenes und mache dann Verbesserungsvorschläge zu Punkten, die aus deiner Sicht nicht so gelungen sind.

- Wenn du Feedback bekommst, überdenke die Vorschläge gut. Korrigiere die Fehler, die andere gefunden haben, und arbeite an den Stellen nach, wo du eventuell Probleme hattest.

| PEER FEEDBACK CHECKLIST | ☺☺☺ | ☺☺ | ☺ | ☹ |
|---|---|---|---|---|
| **Content** | | | | |
| _Lena's_ text is: | | | | |
| · interesting | | | ✓ | |
| · exciting | | | | ✓ |
| · funny | | | | ✓ |
| · easy to understand. | | ✓ | | |
| **Language** | | | | |
| You connected short sentences with linking words. | | ✓ | | |
| You connected short sentences with relative clauses. | | ✓ | | |
| You used different adjectives in your description of places, people and things. | | | ✓ | |
| You used time phrases to show the order of events. | | ✓ | | |
| You chose interesting words. | | | | ✓ |
| You used adverbs. | | | ✓ | |

## STUDY SKILLS

## SF 24 Understanding new words

Das Nachschlagen unbekannter Wörter kostet Zeit und ist auch nicht immer nötig. Oft geht es auch ohne den Einsatz eines Wörterbuches.

### Immer gleich im Wörterbuch nachschlagen?

- Viele englische Wörter werden ähnlich wie im Deutschen geschrieben oder klingen ähnlich (z.B. *brochure, statue, insect*). Manche sehen auch einem Wort aus anderen Sprachen ähnlich, z.B. *voice (French: voix; Latin: vox)*.

- In manchen Wörtern stecken bekannte Teile, z. B. *bottle opener, snowshoe*.

- Präfixe und Suffixe wie *un-*, *re-* und *-er* helfen beim Erschließen: *listener (sb. who listens)*, **un**happy <> happy, **re**pay *(pay sb. back)*.

- Bilder zum Text zeigen oft Dinge, die du im Text vielleicht nicht verstehst.

- Der Kontext, also die Wörter und Sätze um das Wort herum, kann beim Verstehen helfen, z.B. *Let's hurry. The train **departs** in ten minutes.*

> **TIPP**
> Nicht alle Wörter, die im Deutschen und Englischen ähnlich sind, haben auch dieselbe Bedeutung.
> Achte daher auf false friends:
> *handy* = praktisch, *nicht* Handy

# Skills File

## SF 25 Using a dictionary

Es gibt unterschiedliche Wörterbücher, in denen du nachschlagen kannst. Wenn du die Bedeutung eines unbekannten Wortes nachschlagen willst, dann benutzt du am besten ein zweisprachiges Wörterbuch (Englisch-Deutsch).
Wenn du mehr Informationen zu englischen Wörtern haben möchtest, etwa Beispielsätze, Definitionen oder Alternativen, dann bietet sich ein einsprachiges Wörterbuch an.

### ZWEISPRACHIGE WÖRTERBÜCHER

Die Leitwörter (running heads) oben auf der Seite helfen dir, schnell zu finden, was du suchst. Auf der linken Seite steht das erste Stichwort, auf der rechten Seite das letzte Stichwort der Doppelseite.

- resign ist das Stichwort (headword). Stichwörter sind alphabetisch geordnet: r vor s, ra vor re, rhe vor rhi usw.

- Die kursiv gedruckten Hinweise helfen dir, die für deinen Text passende Bedeutung zu finden.

- Die Ziffern 1, 2 usw. zeigen, dass ein Stichwort unterschiedliche Bedeutungen haben oder unterschiedlichen Wortarten angehören kann (z. B. Adjektiv, Nomen, Verb).

- Beispielsätze und Redewendungen sind dem Stichwort zugeordnet.

- Unregelmäßige Verbformen, besondere Pluralformen, die Steigerungsformen der Adjektive und ähnliche Hinweise stehen oft in Klammern oder sind kursiv gedruckt.

- Die Lautschrift gibt Auskunft darüber, wie das Wort ausgesprochen und betont wird.

---

**resort**

**resign** /rɪˈzaɪn/
**1** BERUF • *als Vorsitzender usw* zurücktreten: *He resigned from the company.* Er verließ das Unternehmen.
**2** (*job, post*) aufgeben (*Stelle, Posten*)
**3** **resign oneself to something** sich mit etwas abfinden
**resignation** /ˌrezɪɡˈneɪʃn/
**1** BERUF • *bei Unternehmen* Kündigung; *von Minister usw* Rücktritt
**2** **hand in one's resignation** *von Angestelltem* kündigen; *von Minister usw* sein Amt niederlegen
**3** *Gemütszustand* Resignation
**resigned** /rɪˈzaɪnd/ (*look, sigh*) resigniert

**resit¹** /ˌriːˈsɪt/ *Verb* (→ *sit*) *BE* (*exam*) wiederholen (*Prüfung*)
**resit²** /ˈriːsɪt/ *Substantiv* • *BE* Wiederholungsprüfung
**resolution** /ˌrezəˈluːʃn/
**1** POLITIK Beschluss, Resolution
**2** *bei Problem, Streit* Lösung
**3** ≈ *Entschiedenheit* Entschlossenheit

---

> **TIPP**
> Wenn du ein Online-Wörterbuch verwenden möchtest, erkundige dich vorher bei deinem Lehrer/deiner Lehrerin, welche zu empfehlen sind, denn nicht alle sind gleich gut. Fast alle funktionieren aber nach den gleichen Prinzipien wie gedruckte Wörterbücher.

### EINSPRACHIGE WÖRTERBÜCHER

Wenn du selbst einen englischen Text schreibst, kannst du ein einsprachiges englisches Wörterbuch zu Hilfe nehmen. Hier findest du mehr über ein englisches Wort heraus als in einem zweisprachigen Wörterbuch:

- Ein einsprachiges Wörterbuch erklärt die Bedeutung eines englischen Wortes auf Englisch. Da manche Wörter mehrere Bedeutungen haben, ist es wichtig, alle Einträge und Beispielsätze zu einem Wort zu lesen und mit deinem englischen Text zu vergleichen, um die korrekte Bedeutung herauszufinden.

- Das Wörterbuch hilft dir, die passende Verbindung mit anderen Wörtern zu finden, z. B. zu Verben, Präpositionen oder in bestimmten feststehenden Wendungen. Das ist nützlich, wenn du selbst einen englischen Text schreiben willst und nach den richtigen Wörtern suchst.

---

**deadly** [ˈdedli] *adj*
**1** *able or likely to kill people* (= lethal): This is no longer a deadly disease.
**deadly to** The HSN virus is deadly to chickens.
**a deadly weapon** The new generation of biological weapons is more deadly than ever.
**2** (*only before noun*) (= complete):
**deadly silence** There was deadly silence after his speech.
**a deadly secret** Don't tell anyone – this is a deadly secret.
**deadly serious** *completely serious:* Don't laugh – I am deadly serious!
**3** (*informal*) *very boring*: Many TV programmes are pretty deadly!

# Skills File

## SF 26 Study posters

Lernplakate sind ein gutes Hilfsmittel, um Informationen darzustellen, die du dir merken möchtest wie z. B. Grammatikregeln.

### Was muss ich beachten, wenn ich ein Lernposter erstelle?

- Sammle und notiere alle Informationen zum Thema, die du auf dem Poster darstellen willst.

- Überlege, wie du das, was du dir merken willst, am besten darstellen kannst. Du kannst z. B. Kästen oder Tabellen verwenden, aber auch kleine Zeichnungen.

- Finde einen guten Titel für dein Plakat.

- Gestalte dein Plakat. Schreibe groß und gut leserlich.

- Hebe wichtige Punkte hervor, z. B. durch Unterstreichen oder durch unterschiedliche Farben. Verwende aber nicht zu viele verschiedene Farben, denn sonst wird dein Lernposter unübersichtlich.

- Wenn du ein Lernposter zu einer Grammatikregel machst, kannst du auch ein paar Beispielsätze aufschreiben. Am Besten kannst du dir die Regel merken, wenn du dir zwei oder drei eigene Beispielsätze ausdenkst.

- Häng dein Poster zu Hause oder in der Schule an einer Stelle auf, an der du es häufig siehst, so dass sich dir der Inhalt ganz automatisch einprägen kann.

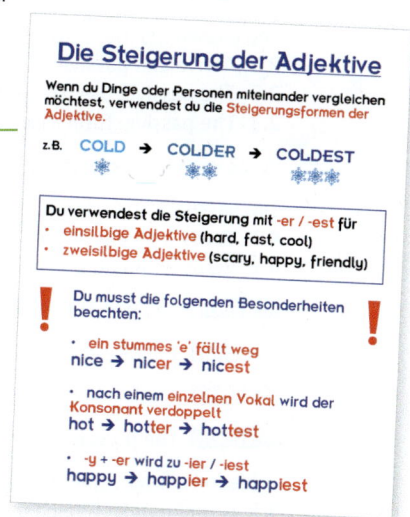

## SF 27 Making and taking notes

Wenn du Informationen oder eigene Gedanken kurz für dich notierst – z. B. als Vorbereitung auf einen eigenen Vortrag oder eine Präsentation –, heißt das im Englischen making notes. Wenn du dir Notizen beim Lesen oder Zuhören machst, heißt das taking notes. Für beide Varianten gelten aber die gleichen Grundsätze.

Step 1: Achte auf keywords, die die wichtigsten Informationen enthalten, um deine Frage/Aufgabe zu beantworten oder den Inhalt eines Textes grob zu verstehen.

Step 2: Notiere nur die wichtigsten Informationen. Verwende Abkürzungen und Symbole, aber achte darauf, dass du ein System hast und immer dieselben verwendest, damit du deine Notizen auch später noch verstehst. Markiere offene Fragen.

Step 3: Geh im Anschluss an das Lesen oder Hören nochmal durch deine Notizen und ergänze evtl. noch fehlende Informationen.

> **TIPP**
> Wenn du kein eigenes System von Abkürzungen hast, kannst du z. B. auch diese verwenden:
>
> | | | | | |
> |---|---|---|---|---|
> | · the same as | = | | · for example | e.g. |
> | · not the same as | ≠ | | · important | ! |
> | · about the same as | ≈ | | · not | x |
> | · and | + | | · with | w/ |
> | · becomes/will be | -> | | · without | w/o |
> | · between | b/w | | · open question | ?? |

# Grammar File

## Grammar File – Inhalt                                                                                 Seite

| | | |
|---|---|---|
| GF 1 | **REVISION** **Simple present / simple past** Die einfache Form der Gegenwart / der Vergangenheit | 137 |
| GF 2 | **The passive (I)** Das Passiv (I) | 138 |
| | 2.1 **Active and passive** Aktiv und Passiv | 138 |
| | 2.2 **The passive: use** Das Passiv: Gebrauch | 138 |
| | 2.3 **The passive: form** Das Passiv: Form | 138 |
| GF 3 | **Verbs with two objects** Verben mit zwei Objekten | 139 |
| GF 4 | **The passive (II): Different kinds of verbs** Das Passiv (II): Verschiedene Arten von Verben | 140 |
| | 4.1 **Verbs with one object** Verben mit einem Objekt | 140 |
| | 4.2 **Verbs with two objects** Verben mit zwei Objekten | 140 |
| GF 5 | **REVISION** **The *will*-future** Das Futur mit *will* | 141 |
| GF 6 | **REVISION** **Conditional sentences** Bedingungssätze | 141 |
| GF 7 | **REVISION** **Modal verbs** Modalverben | 143 |
| GF 8 | **REVISION** **The present perfect** Das *present perfect* | 143 |
| GF 9 | **Subject-verb agreement** Subjekt-Verb-Kongruenz | 144 |
| | 9.1 **Group nouns** Gruppenbezeichnungen | 144 |
| | 9.2 **Singular nouns ending in -s** Singularnomen auf *-s* | 144 |
| GF 10 | **The passive (III): Present perfect / will-future / modal verbs** Das Passiv (III): Present perfect / *will*-future / Modalverben | 145 |
| | 10.1 **The present perfect passive** Das Passiv des *present perfect* | 145 |
| | 10.2 **The will-future and modal verbs in the passive** Das *will*-future und Modalverben im Passiv | 145 |
| GF 11 | **The definite article** Der bestimmte Artikel | 146 |
| GF 12 | **REVISION** **Simple past / past progressive** Einfache Form / Verlaufsform der Vergangenheit | 147 |
| GF 13 | **Adjectives used as nouns** Das Adjektiv als Nomen | 147 |
| GF 14 | **The gerund** Das Gerundium | 148 |
| | 14.1 **Use and form** Gebrauch und Form | 148 |
| | 14.2 **The gerund as subject and object** Das Gerundium als Subjekt und als Objekt | 148 |
| | 14.3 **The gerund after prepositions** Das Gerundium nach Präpositionen | 149 |
| GF 15 | **Adverbs and adverbials** Adverbien und Adverbialbestimmungen | 150 |
| **Grammatical terms** (Grammatische Fachbegriffe) | | 152 |
| **Lösungen der Grammar-File-Aufgaben** | | 153 |

Das **Grammar File** (S. 136–153) fasst die in diesem Buch behandelten grammatischen Themen zusammen.

**In English**

Die **In English**-Abschnitte enthalten kurze Zusammenfassungen der wichtigsten grammatischen Regeln auf Englisch.

Verweise wie ➡ *Unit 1: p. 15, exercises 4, 6* zeigen dir, welche **Übungen** zum gerade behandelten Thema gehören.

Die **grammatischen Fachbegriffe** (*grammatical terms*) kannst du auf den Seiten 152–153 nachschlagen.

Hier stehen kleine **Aufgaben** zur **Selbstkontrolle**. Damit kannst du überprüfen, ob du das behandelte Thema verstanden hast. Auf S. 153 kannst du nachsehen, ob deine Lösungen richtig sind.

# Grammar File

## GF 1 REVISION Simple present / simple past
### Die einfache Form der Gegenwart / der Vergangenheit

### 1.1 The simple present — Die einfache Form der Gegenwart

Das **simple present** wird verwendet,

1 We **often visit** museums **at the weekend**.
I **usually do** my homework **in the evenings**.

1 um über Handlungen und Ereignisse zu sprechen, die **wiederholt, regelmäßig, immer** oder **nie** geschehen. Signalwörter für das *simple present* sind Angaben wie *always, usually, often, sometimes, at the weekend, in the evenings, never* u.Ä.

2 The Robertsons **live** in Ottawa, Canada.
Lots of Canadians **play** ice hockey.
My aunt **works** at an embassy.

2 um über **Dauerzustände** sowie über **Hobbys und Berufe** zu sprechen.

| I/you/we/you/they | **visit**/**try**/**play**/… |
| He/she/it | **visits**/**tries**/**plays**/… |

◁ Das *simple present* hat die Form des Infinitivs. Nur bei der **3. Person Singular** (*he, she, it*) wird **-(e)s** angehängt.

Canadians **don't call** their diplomatic places embassies.
My uncle **doesn't work** at weekends.

◁ **Verneinte Sätze** werden mit **don't** bzw. **doesn't** gebildet.

**Do** you **know** anyone from Canada?
**Does** your aunt **work** at an embassy?

◁ **Fragen** werden mit **do** bzw. **does** gebildet

(**Ausnahme**: Verneinungen und Fragen mit dem Verb **be** werden nicht mit einer Form von **do** gebildet.)

➡ Unit 1: p. 13, exercises 4, 6

### 1.2 The simple past — Die einfache Form der Vergangenheit

Das **simple past** wird verwendet,

1 **Last Saturday**, we **went** to St Paul's Cathedral.
The first Caribbean workers **arrived** in Britain **in the 1940s**.

1 um über **abgeschlossene Handlungen und Ereignisse** zu sprechen, die zu einem bestimmten Zeitpunkt in der Vergangenheit stattfanden. Signalwörter für das *simple past* sind genaue Zeitangaben wie *last Saturday, twenty years ago, yesterday, in the 1940s* u.Ä.

2 **First**, we **visited** the Whispering Gallery. **Then** we **went** to the outdoor markets in Brixton. **After that**, we **took** a boat to Greenwich.

2 wenn man über vergangene Ereignisse berichtet oder eine Geschichte erzählt (oft mit *first …, then …, after that …*).

The Robertsons **flew** to London a couple of weeks ago.
Die Robertsons **sind** … nach London **geflogen**.

❗ Im Deutschen steht oft das Perfekt, wo im Englischen das *simple past* stehen muss.

| want → want**ed** | arrive → arriv**ed** |
| stop → stopp**ed** | try → tr**ied** |
| fly → flew | meet → met |
| go → went | take → took |

◁ Bei **regelmäßigen** Verben wird **-ed** an den Infinitiv gehängt, um das *simple past* zu bilden.

◁ **Unregelmäßige** Verben haben eine eigene Form für das *simple past*.

➡ *Liste der unregelmäßigen Verben, S. 268–270*

We **didn't go** to the silent disco.
What **did** you **do** during your stay in London? **Did** you **visit** the Houses of Parliamen? — No, we **didn't**.

◁ **Verneinte Aussagesätze** im *simple past* werden mit **didn't** gebildet, **Fragen** mit **did**.

(**Ausnahme**: Verneinungen und Fragen mit dem Verb **be** werden nicht mit **did** gebildet.)

➡ Unit 1: p. 13, exercises 5–6

# Grammar File

## GF 2 The passive (I)  Das Passiv (I)

### 2.1 Active and passive — Aktiv und Passiv

| | | |
|---|---|---|
| **Active** | Alyssa **took** some photos at the outdoor market in Brixton. | **Aktivsätze** drücken aus, **wer oder was etwas tut**. Das Subjekt des Aktivsatzes führt die Handlung aus. Der Beispielsatz sagt etwas über Alyssa aus – nämlich, dass sie auf dem Markt in Brixton Fotos gemacht hat. |
| **Passive** | These photos **were taken** at the outdoor market in Brixton. | **Passivsätze** drücken aus, **mit wem oder womit etwas geschieht**. Der Beispielsatz sagt etwas über Fotos aus – nämlich, dass sie auf dem Markt in Brixton gemacht wurden. |

### 2.2 The passive: use — Das Passiv: Gebrauch

This windmill **was built** in 1816.
Diese Windmühle wurde 1816 erbaut.

Our snacks **are made** fresh every day.
Unsere Snacks werden jeden Tag frisch zubereitet.

On the anniversary of David Bowie's death, lots of flowers **are laid** on the ground at the mural.
An David Bowies Todestag werden viele Blumen … abgelegt.

Mit Passivsätzen kannst du Handlungen beschreiben, ohne zu sagen, wer die Handlung ausführt.

Oft ist nicht bekannt oder nicht wichtig, wer die Handlung ausführt, manchmal ist es auch offensichtlich und wird daher nicht erwähnt.

London **was founded by** the Romans.
London wurde von den Römern gegründet.

The mural **is protected by** a cover.
Das Wandbild wird durch eine Abdeckung geschützt.

◂ Wenn man in einem Passivsatz „Täter" oder „Verursacher" nennen will, kann man die Präposition **by** verwenden.

### 2.3 The passive: form — Das Passiv: Form

The David Bowie mural **is visited** by thousands of fans each year.

People from all over the world **are attracted** to London.

The river **was covered up** in the 19th century.

After the Second World War, people from places like India **were invited** to help rebuild Britain.

Das Passiv bildest du mit einer **Form von be** und der **3. Form des Verbs** (Partizip Perfekt; past participle).

**Simple present:**  **am/are/is** + **past participle**
The mural is visited …
People are attracted …

**Simple past:**  **was/were** + **past participle**
The river was covered up …
People were invited …

➡ Unit 1: pp. 18–19, exercises 1–5

➡ Liste der unregelmäßigen Verben, S. 268–270

---

**In English** 🇺🇸 🇬🇧

**The passive (I)**

- An **active** sentence describes what somebody (or something) does.

  *Alyssa took* some photos at the market.
  (You are talking about what Alyssa did.)

- A **passive** sentence describes what is done or what happens to people or things; often we do not say who does the action. Passive sentences are made with a **form of be** + **past participle**.

  *These photos were taken* at the market.
  (You are talking about photos and where they were taken.)

- You can use **by** if you want to say who does the action.

  *London was founded by the Romans*.

# Grammar File

Bilde Passivsätze wie im Beispiel. Achte auf die richtige Zeitform – *simple present* oder *simple past*.

1 *No, we didn't win. (beat / 4 : 1)* – We were beaten 4 : 1.
2 *We don't use plastic for our steering wheels. (make / of wood)* – They …
3 *We don't buy our vegetables at the supermarket. (grow / on local farms)* – They …
4 *It's not our flat. (own / large building company)*
5 *The terrorists didn't escape. (catch / at the border)*
6 *We specialize in traditional English food. (prepare / fresh / every day)*

## GF 3  Verbs with two objects — Verben mit zwei Objekten

I'll **show** *you the view* and **tell** *you some stories*.
Ich zeige euch die Aussicht und erzähle euch ein paar Geschichten.

The tour guide **gave** *the Robertsons a tour of the city*.

Alyssa **sent** *her parents a list of things to bring*.

1 Alyssa wrote a list of things she needed.
   Then she **sent** *it to her parents*.
   … Dann schickte sie sie ihren Eltern.

2 The Robertsons **suggested** *a walking tour to Alyssa*.
   … schlugen Alyssa einen Stadtrundgang vor.

   **Describe/Explain** *the table to your group*.
   Beschreibe/Erkläre deiner Gruppe die Tabelle.

   ➡ Unit 1: p. 24, exercise 1

Wenn ein Verb **zwei Objekte** hat, dann ist die normale Wortstellung wie im Deutschen:
Das **indirekte Objekt** (meist eine **Person**, daher auch „Personenobjekt") steht vor dem **direkten Objekt** (meist eine **Sache**, daher auch „Sachobjekt").
Also wie im Alphabet: **P**erson vor **S**ache.

❗ Die Wortstellung ändert sich:

1 Wenn das **Sachobjekt** ein **Pronomen** ist *(it; them)*, dann steht es direkt hinter dem Verb, und das **Personenobjekt** wird mit *to* angehängt.

2 Bei einigen Verben wird das Personenobjekt immer mit *to* angehängt. Beispiele:
   *describe/explain/introduce/present/report/say/suggest* **something** *to* **somebody**.

### In English

**Verbs with two objects**

- When a verb has two objects, the normal word order is **indirect object ("person object") – direct object ("thing object")**.
- When the direct object is a pronoun, the word order is **direct object** *(it; them)* + *to* + **indirect object**.
- There are some verbs where we always use *to* with the indirect object; examples:
  *describe/explain/introduce/present/report/say/suggest something to somebody*.

Bilde Sätze wie im Beispiel.
(Denke daran, dass bei manchen Verben das Personenobjekt immer mit *to* angehängt wird.)

1 *(English teachers / teach English / their students)*
   English teachers teach their students English.
2 *(Tour guides / show interesting sights / tourists)* – Tour guides …
3 *(He tried to / explain his feelings / her)* – He …
4 *(Last weekend she / introduce her boyfriend / her parents)*
5 *(When we arrived, a woman / give the room keys / us)*
6 *(You should / report the accident / the police)*

# Grammar File

## GF 4 The passive (II): Different kinds of verbs
Das Passiv (II): Verschiedene Arten von Verben

### 4.1 Verbs with one object — Verben mit einem Objekt

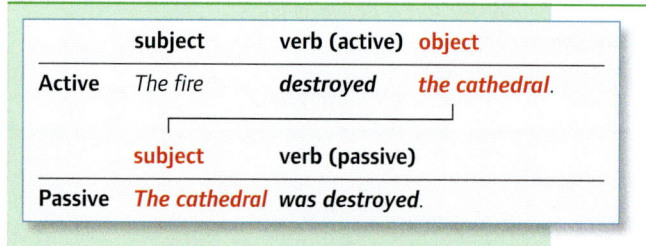

|        | subject      | verb (active) | object         |
|--------|--------------|---------------|----------------|
| Active | The fire     | **destroyed** | the cathedral. |
|        | subject      | verb (passive)|                |
| Passive| The cathedral| **was destroyed**. |           |

Das Passiv kann von Verben gebildet werden, die im Aktiv ein **Objekt** haben.
Das Objekt des Aktivsatzes entspricht dem Subjekt des Passivsatzes.

|        | subject   | verb (active) | object |                 |
|--------|-----------|---------------|--------|-----------------|
| Active | The mayor | **thanked**   | them   | for their help. |
|        | subject   | verb (passive)|        |                 |
| Passive| They      | **were thanked** |     | for their help. |

**Ihnen** *(Dativobjekt)* wurde für ihre Hilfe gedankt. / Man dankte **ihnen** für ihre Hilfe.

Das **Subjekt des englischen Passivsatzes** (im Beispiel: *They*) kann auch einem **deutschen Dativobjekt** (hier: „**ihnen**") entsprechen.

**We were joined** by a group of Spanish tourists.
Eine Gruppe spanischer Touristen schloss sich **uns** an.

**He was told** to wait outside.
**Ihm** wurde gesagt, er solle draußen warten. / Man sagte **ihm**, er solle draußen warten.

**The thieves were helped** by one of the office workers.
**Den Dieben** wurde von einem der Büroangestellten geholfen. / Die Diebe hatten Hilfe von …

◀ Hier findest du drei weitere Beispiele dieses sogenannten „persönlichen Passivs" *(personal passive)*, bei denen das **Subjekt** des englischen Passivsatzes einem deutschen **Dativobjekt** entspricht.

### 4.2 Verbs with two objects — Verben mit zwei Objekten

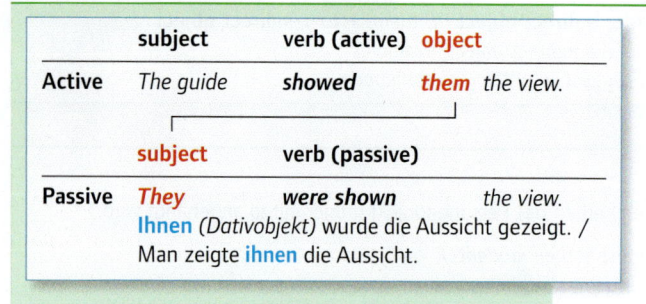

|        | subject   | verb (active) | object |           |
|--------|-----------|---------------|--------|-----------|
| Active | The guide | **showed**    | them   | the view. |
|        | subject   | verb (passive)|        |           |
| Passive| They      | **were shown**|        | the view. |

**Ihnen** *(Dativobjekt)* wurde die Aussicht gezeigt. / Man zeigte **ihnen** die Aussicht.

Auch von **Verben mit zwei Objekten** *(give/offer/ pay/promise/send/show/… sb. sth.)* kann ein Passiv gebildet werden.

– Im Englischen wird meist das **indirekte Objekt (Personenobjekt)** zum Subjekt des Passivsatzes („persönliches Passiv").
– Im Deutschen bleibt die Dativform des Personenobjekts im Passivsatz erhalten: „**Ihnen** wurde … gezeigt".

**She was offered/paid/promised** a lot of money for her new book.
**Ihr** wurde viel Geld angeboten/gezahlt/versprochen … / Man bot **ihr** viel Geld an / zahlte **ihr** viel Geld / versprach **ihr** viel Geld …

**We were given** the keys and **shown** up to our rooms.
Man gab **uns** die Schlüssel und führte **uns** zu unseren Zimmern.

➡ Unit 1: p. 24, exercises 2 – 3

◀ Hier findest du weitere Beispiele für das *personal passive*.

Passivsätze dieser Art sind im Englischen sehr häufig. Im Deutschen müssen andere Konstruktionen verwendet werden.

# Grammar File

**In English**

**The passive (II)**
In English, the **indirect object (the 'person object')** of an active sentence can be the subject of a passive sentence. We call this structure the **personal passive**.
(This kind of passive sentence is not possible in German.)

Active: Two Swedes joined **us**.
Passive: **We** were joined by two Swedes.
(Zwei Schweden schlossen sich **uns** an.)
Active: They offered **her** a job in Bristol.
Passive: **She** was offered a job in Bristol.
(**Ihr** wurde ein Job in Bristol angeboten.)

---

Sieh dir Beispiel 1 an. Vervollständige dann die *Personal passive*-Sätze 2 bis 6. Achte auf die richtige Zeitform.

1 (Someone **gave us** the key)    We … key and went up to our room.
    *We were given the key and went up to our room.*

2 (They **gave us** ten minutes)    We … ten minutes to read the questions.
3 (They **offered me** a job)    I … a job at the local radio station.
4 (Someone **told him** the news)    He was shocked when he …
5 (They **promised her** a TV role)    She … a TV role.
6 (Someone **sent him** a letter bomb)    He …

---

## GF 5 `REVISION` The *will*-future   Das Futur mit *will*

*In a few years I'**ll be** old enough to drive a car.*

*When **will** Dad **come** back?*
*– I think he'**ll be** back on Friday.*

*Wales **will get** a lot of rain tomorrow, and it **will be** very windy in Scotland.*

*Get a good night's sleep, then you'**ll feel** better.*
Schlaf dich mal richtig aus, dann **fühlst** du dich besser.

➡ Unit 2: p. 42, exercise 2

Mit **will/won't + Infinitiv** sagst du, was in der Zukunft geschehen bzw. nicht geschehen wird.

◀ Wenn **Vermutungen** geäußert werden, steht häufig *I (don't) think*, *I'm (not) sure*, *maybe* oder *probably*.

◀ Oft geht es um Dinge, die man nicht beeinflussen kann, z.B. **Vorhersagen** über das Wetter.

❗ Im Deutschen benutzen wir oft das Präsens, wenn wir Vermutungen äußern oder Vorhersagen machen. Im Englischen steht das *will*-future.

---

## GF 6 `REVISION` Conditional sentences   Bedingungssätze

### 6.1 Type 1     Typ 1

*Your parents **will be** very angry if they **find** out you didn't go to school.*
Deine Eltern werden sehr wütend sein, wenn sie herausfinden, dass du nicht zur Schule gegangen bist.

*If you **don't get** enough sleep, you **won't be** able to work hard.*
Wenn du nicht genug Schlaf bekommst, kannst du nicht hart arbeiten / wirst du nicht hart arbeiten können.

*I **can't concentrate if** I don't get enough sleep.*

*If your teachers speak too fast, **ask** them to slow down.*

➡ Unit 2: p. 42, exercise 3

Bedingungssätze vom Typ 1 sind „Was ist, wenn …"-Sätze: Sie beschreiben, was unter bestimmten Bedingungen geschieht oder nicht geschieht.

Die Bedingung steht im *if*-Satz. Der Hauptsatz sagt aus, was passiert, wenn die Bedingung erfüllt wird.

Im *if*-Satz steht das **simple present**. Im Hauptsatz steht meist das **will-future**.

◀ Im Hauptsatz können auch *can, must, could, might, should* + Infinitiv oder ein Imperativ stehen.

# Grammar File

## 6.2 Type 2 — Typ 2

1 **If** he **gave** me his phone number, I **would call** Mike.
Wenn er mir seine Telefonnummer geben würde, dann würde ich ihn anrufen.

❗ Kein *would* im *if*-Satz! Nicht: *If I would have* …

2 **If** I **were** you, I**'d ask** him for his phone number.
Wenn ich du wäre, würde ich ihn nach seiner Telefonnummer fragen.

*If he gave me his phone number, I could call him.*
… könnte ich ihn anrufen.

*If I were the president, I would make a lot of changes.*
Wenn ich Präsident/in wäre, …

➡ Unit 2: p. 42, exercise 3

**Bedingungssätze vom Typ 2** sind „Was wäre, wenn …"-Sätze: Sie drücken aus, dass etwas nicht sehr wahrscheinlich oder sogar unmöglich ist.

Die Sprecherin hält es für unwahrscheinlich, dass Mike ihr seine Nummer gibt (Satz 1), und „ich" bin nun einmal nicht „du" (Satz 2).
Die Sprecher/innen sagen nur, was geschehen würde oder der Fall wäre, wenn …

Im *if*-Satz steht das **simple past**. Im Hauptsatz steht meist **would** + **Infinitiv** (Kurzform: **'d**).

◀ Im Hauptsatz kann auch *could* („könnte") + Infinitiv stehen.

❗ Beachte, dass nach *I* im *if*-Satz oft *were* statt *was* steht:
***If I were the president …***
(*If I was …* ist aber ebenfalls möglich.)

## 6.3 Type 3 — Typ 3

1 She **would have called** Mike **if** he **had given** her his phone number.
Sie hätte Mike angerufen, wenn er ihr seine Telefonnummer gegeben hätte.

2 **If** she **had asked** him, he **would have given** her his phone number.
Wenn sie ihn gefragt hätte, dann hätte er ihr seine Telefonnummer gegeben.

*If she **'d** asked me,    I**'d** have helped her.*
*If she **had** asked me,    I **would** have helped her.*

*If it hadn't rained, we **could** have gone swimming /*
                            *we **might** have gone swimming.*
…, hätten wir schwimmen gehen können /
     wären wir vielleicht schwimmen gegangen.

➡ Unit 2: p. 42, exercise 3

**Bedingungssätze vom Typ 3** sind „Was wäre gewesen, wenn …"-Sätze.
Sie beziehen sich auf die **Vergangenheit**.

Sie drücken aus, was unter bestimmten Bedingungen geschehen oder nicht geschehen **wäre**.

– Der *if*-Satz nennt eine **nicht** erfüllte Bedingung:
  Satz 1: Er hat ihr seine Nummer nicht gegeben.
  Satz 2: Sie hat ihn nicht danach gefragt.

– Der **Hauptsatz** drückt aus, was gewesen wäre, wenn die Bedingung im *if*-Satz doch erfüllt worden wäre:
  Satz 1: Sie hätte ihn angerufen.
  Satz 2: Er hätte ihr seine Nummer gegeben.

Im *if*-Satz steht das **past perfect**.
Im Hauptsatz steht meist **would have** + **past participle**.

❗ Beachte: Die Kurzform **'d** steht im *if*-Satz für *had*, im Hauptsatz aber für *would*.

◀ Im Hauptsatz können auch **could have** + **past participle** oder **might have** + **past participle** stehen.

# Grammar File

## GF 7  REVISION  Modal verbs  Modalverben

1 *I think you **can/may/must/should** leave now.*
   Ich denke, Sie **können/dürfen/müssen/sollten** jetzt gehen.

2 *Be careful, the roads **might** be slippery.*
   Sei vorsichtig, die Straßen könnten glatt sein.
   *The Millers **should** be here by now.*
   Die Millers sollten (eigentlich) inzwischen hier sein.

*I **can clear** the table. **Can** you **wash** the dishes? –
Yes, I **can**. / No, I **can't**.*
Ich kann den Tisch abräumen. Kannst du den Abwasch machen? …

*You **must feed** the cats. They're hungry.*

*You **needn't feed** the dogs. Mum has fed them already.*

*You **mustn't feed** the birds. Bread is bad for them.*

➡ Unit 2: p. 43, exercise 4

Die **modalen Hilfsverben** (*modal verbs*, kurz: *modals*) *can, may, might, must, should* usw. werden verwendet,

1 um zu sagen, was jemand
   – tun **kann** (Fähigkeit, englisch: *ability*),
   – tun **darf** (Erlaubnis, englisch: *permission*),
   – tun **muss** (Verpflichtung, englisch: *obligation*),
   – tun **sollte** (Ratschlag, englisch: *advice*),

2 um **Vermutungen** ausdrücken und zu sagen, für wie **wahrscheinlich** oder **möglich** man etwas hält.

**Eigenschaften der Modalverben:**

– Modale Hilfsverben werden zusammen mit dem Infinitiv eines Vollverbs verwendet. (Nur in Kurzantworten können modale Hilfsverben allein stehen.)

– Frage und Verneinung werden ohne *do/does/did* gebildet.

❗ Vorsicht bei **must**, **mustn't** und **needn't**:
- Mit **must** drückt man aus, dass jemand etwas **tun muss**.
- Mit **needn't** drückt man aus, dass jemand etwas **nicht tun muss**.
- Mit **mustn't** drückt man aus, dass jemand etwas **nicht tun darf**.

## GF 8  REVISION  The present perfect  Das *present perfect*

1 *We **have often been** to England.*
   *Have you **ever been** to England?*
   *– No, I've **never been** to a foreign country.*

   *Have you **done** your homework **yet**?*
   *– Yes, I've **just finished**.*

2 *I've **lived** here **all my life**.*
   Ich lebe schon mein ganzes Leben hier.
   *We've **always wanted** to go to New Zealand.*
   Wir wollten schon immer nach Neuseeland reisen.

   *She's **had** her dog **for ages**.*
   Sie hat ihren Hund schon seit einer Ewigkeit.

*I've / You've / We've / They've **had** …*
*He's / She's / It's **had** …*

*We've **had** this car **since 2015** / **for six years**.*
… seit 2015 / seit sechs Jahren.

➡ Unit 2: p. 43, exercises 5

Das *present perfect* drückt aus,

1 dass jemand **irgendwann** etwas getan hat oder dass **irgendwann** etwas geschehen ist. Es ist nicht wichtig (oder nicht bekannt), wann das war – deshalb wird auch **kein genauer Zeitpunkt** genannt. Aber es stehen oft unbestimmte Zeitangaben wie **already, before, ever, just, often, never, yet**.

2 dass ein **Zustand in der Vergangenheit begonnen** hat und jetzt **noch andauert**. Oft enthalten diese Sätze Angaben, wie lange der Zustand schon andauert (z.B. *all my life, a long time, for ages, since/for …*).

❗ Im **Deutschen** benutzen wir in diesen Fällen meist einen Satz im Präsens (oft mit „schon"):
   Ich **kenne** ihn schon ewig.
   Im **Englischen** steht das *present perfect*:
   I've **known** him forever.

◀ Das *present perfect* wird mit **have/has** + **Partizip Perfekt** gebildet. (Kurzform: **'ve** / **'s** + Partizip Perfekt)

❗ **since** gibt einen **Zeitpunkt** an: *since 10 o'clock; since 2012; since Friday evening; since I was born*.

**for** gibt einen **Zeitraum** an: *for hours; for 14 years; for five minutes; for a long time*.

# Grammar File

## GF 9 Subject-verb agreement  Subjekt-Verb-Kongruenz

### 9.1 Group nouns — Gruppenbezeichnungen

The **band has** / **have** finished playing.

His **family wants** / **want** to move to Bristol.

The **government has** / **have** introduced a new tax.

The **team was** / **were** sure **it** / **they** would win.

| More group nouns | |
|---|---|
| audience | Publikum, Zuhörer/innen |
| choir | Chor |
| class | Klasse |
| club | Klub, Verein |
| crowd | (Menschen-)Menge |
| enemy | Feind |
| majority | Mehrheit |
| minority | Minderheit |

The **police are** on **their** way.

➡ Unit 2: p. 43, exercise 6

Nomen wie **band**, **family**, **government**, **group**, **team** bezeichnen **Gruppen** von Menschen.
Man kann bei diesen Nomen entweder an die **Gruppe als Ganzes** denken (die Band/Familie/… als **eine Einheit**) oder aber die **einzelnen, individuellen Mitglieder der Gruppe** vor Augen haben.
Daher können zugehörige **Verben** und **Pronomen** entweder **im Singular** oder **im Plural** stehen:

– Die **Singularform** des Verbs steht, wenn man an die **Gruppe als Einheit** denkt; die zugehörigen Pronomen stehen dann ebenfalls im Singular: **it**, **its**.

– Die **Pluralform** des Verbs steht, wenn man an die **einzelnen Mitglieder der Gruppe** denkt; die Pronomen stehen dann ebenfalls im Plural: **they**, **their**.

(Im **amerikanischen Englisch** ist bei Gruppenbezeichnungen generell der Singular gebräuchlicher.)

❗ Nach der Gruppenbezeichnung **police** stehen Verb und Pronomen immer im Plural!

### 9.2 Singular nouns ending in –s — Singularnomen auf –s

**Economics is** an interesting subject.

**Maths was** my best subject at school.

Fake **news has** become a big problem.

**Politics plays** an important role in my life.

**The United States** / **The USA consists** of 50 states.
Die Vereinigten Staaten / Die USA bestehen aus 50 Staaten.

➡ Unit 2: p. 43, exercise 6

Es gibt eine Reihe von **Nomen**, die zwar **auf –s enden**, aber dennoch mit einem **Verb im Singular** verwendet werden.
Dazu gehören **economics** („Wirtschaft"), **maths/mathematics**, **news**, **physics**, **politics**.

❗ Auch nach **the United States (the USA, the US)** steht das Verb im Singular!

---

**In English**

**Subject-verb agreement**
- Nouns like *band, family, government, team* are called **group nouns**.
  As we can think of a group of people either as a **number of individuals** or as a **single unit**, we can use a **plural verb and pronoun** or a **singular verb and pronoun** after these nouns.
  (Note that the noun *police* is always plural.)
- Some nouns end in **–s** but still take a singular verb, e.g. **economics, maths/mathematics, news, physics, politics** and **the United States (the USA, the US)**.

---

Vervollständige die Sätze mit der richtigen Form des Verbs in Klammern.

1 The USA … (play) an important role for the German manufacturing industry.
2 The news from the Middle East … (be) getting better.
3 The politics of a country … (have) an influence on the happiness of its population.
4 Of course, the economics of a country … (be) important, but money isn't everything.
5 Physics … (have) always been my brother's favourite subject.

# Grammar File

## GF 10 The passive (III): Present perfect / *will*-future / modal verbs
### Das Passiv (III): Present perfect / *will*-future / Modalverben

### 10.1 The present perfect passive | Das Passiv des *present perfect*

Jonathan **has been invited** to Bristol.
Jonathan ist nach Bristol eingeladen worden.

These windows **haven't been cleaned** for years.
Diese Fenster sind seit Jahren nicht mehr geputzt worden.

She**'s been given** a pair of skates for her birthday.
Sie hat Inlineskates zum Geburtstag bekommen.

➡ Unit 2: p. 48, exercise 1

Das **Passiv des *present perfect*** wird mit **have been** / **has been** + **Partizip Perfect** gebildet.

Zum Aktiv des *present perfect* vergleiche GF 8, S. 143.

Zum Gebrauch des Passiv vergleiche auch GF 2 und GF 4 auf den Seiten 138 und 140.

### 10.2 The *will*-future and modal verbs in the passive | Das *will*-future und Modalverben im Passiv

They're building a new bridge over the river. It **will be completed** next year.
… Sie wird nächstes Jahr fertiggestellt (werden).

This dress **cannot be washed**. It **must be dry-cleaned**.
Dieses Kleid kann nicht gewaschen werden. Es muss gereinigt werden.

Fireworks **may** only **be lit** from midnight to 3 am.
Feuerwerkskörper dürfen nur von Mitternacht bis 3 Uhr gezündet werden.

Jackets and coats **should be left** at the door.
Jacken und Mäntel sollten an der Tür abgegeben werden.

➡ Unit 2: pp. 48–49, exercises 2–5

Nach **will** und **Modalverben** wird das Passiv mit **be** + **Partizip Perfekt** gebildet:

| I/you/he/she/it we/you/they | will can could may might must should | be + Partizip Perfekt |
|---|---|---|

Zu den Modalverben vergleiche GF 7, S. 143.

Zum Gebrauch des Passiv vergleiche auch GF 2 und GF 4 auf den Seiten 138 und 140.

### The passive

| | | | |
|---|---|---|---|
| Simple present | Lots of cars / Viele Autos | **are** stolen. | … werden gestohlen. |
| Simple past | | **were** stolen. | … wurden gestohlen. |
| Present perfect | | **have been** stolen. | … sind gestohlen worden. |
| *will*-future | | **will be** stolen. | … werden gestohlen werden. |
| Modal verbs | | **could be** stolen / **might be** stolen. | … könnten gestohlen werden. |

🇺🇸 🇬🇧 **In English**

### The passive (III)
The present perfect passive is made with **have been** / **has been** + **past participle**: *A bridge has been built.*
The *will*-future passive is made with **will** + **be** + **past participle**: *A bridge will be built.*
The passive with modal verbs is made with **modal verb** + **be** + **past participle**: *A bridge might/must be built.*

---

Bilde Passivsätze in der richtigen Zeitform. (Manchmal musst du ein Modalverb ergänzen.)

1 Work on the new gym has finished. (It / open / tomorrow)
2 Snowboarding is dangerous. (Helmets / wear / at all times)
3 It was quiet during the day. But at night, (barking dogs / hear)
4 Mr Brown is angry. (One of his windows / break)
5 There's been a hurricane. (Hundreds of homes / destroy)

# Grammar File

## GF 11 The definite article  Der bestimmte Artikel

1  *Life* in the Arctic tundra can be hard.
Das Leben in der arktischen Tundra kann hart sein.

*Pollution* is a big problem.
Die Umweltverschmutzung …

2  What will happen if we run out of *oil / water*?
…, wenn uns das Öl / das Wasser ausgeht?

3  Most *people* are worried about climate change.
Die meisten Menschen …

*Rules* are important in competitive sports.
Regeln sind wichtig …

House *prices* have gone up again.
Die Hauspreise sind wieder gestiegen.

4  Hunting is important in **the life** <u>of the Inuit</u>.
… im Leben der Inuit.

What can we do to stop **the pollution** <u>of our oceans</u>?
… die Verschmutzung unserer Ozeane …

5  **The oil** <u>that was found on his land</u> made him rich.
Das Öl, das auf seinem Land gefunden wurde …

6  **The people** <u>who live here</u> all help each other.
Die Menschen, die hier leben, …

**The prices** <u>you have to pay in this area</u> are shocking.
Die Preise, die man bezahlt …

◂ Wenn ein Nomen **ganz allgemein** gebraucht wird, steht es **ohne bestimmten Artikel** (auch, wenn ein Adjektiv davor steht). Das gilt insbesondere für

1  **abstrakte Begriffe** wie *death, history, life, music, nature, noise, peace, pollution, research, sport(s), winter,*

2  **Stoffbezeichnungen** wie *air, oil, gold, tea, glass, snow, water,*

3  **Nomen im Plural** (hier: *people, rules, prices*).

◂ Solche Nomen stehen jedoch **mit bestimmtem Artikel**, wenn sie **näher bestimmt** sind, z.B. durch eine *of*-Fügung (**4**) oder einen Relativsatz (**5, 6**).

Vergleiche die Sätze **1 – 3** mit den Sätzen **4 – 6**. In 4 – 6 geht es nicht um das Leben, die Umweltverschmutzung, das Öl usw. im Allgemeinen, sondern um das Leben der Inuit, die Verschmutzung der Ozeane, das Öl auf jemandes Land usw.

❗ Vorsicht bei den **Gebäudebezeichnungen** *church, hospital, prison, school, college, university.*

1  We go to **church** every Sunday.
… in die Kirche *(zum Gottesdienst)*
He spent two years in **prison**.
… im Gefängnis *(um eine Strafe zu verbüßen)*
I know her from **school**.
… aus der Schule *(vom gemeinsamen Unterricht)*
Dad's ill. He's in **hospital**. *(AE: in the hospital)*
… im Krankenhaus *(zur Behandlung)*

2  There's a concert in **the church** on Friday.
He works in one of the shops behind **the prison**.
Go straight on till you get to **the school**, then turn left.

1  Sie stehen **ohne bestimmten Artikel**, wenn die **Funktion** / der **Zweck** des Gebäudes im Vordergrund steht.

2  Sie stehen **mit bestimmtem Artikel**, wenn es um den **Ort** / das **Bauwerk** geht.

➡ Unit 2: p. 54, exercise 1

### In English 🇺🇸 🇬🇧
**The definite article**

- We do not use **the** with **abstract nouns** (*life, death, history, …*), **material nouns** (*air, oil, gold, tea, …*) and **plural nouns** (*people, prices, …*) when they are used **in a general sense**.

- But we use **the** with these nouns when they are used **in a specific sense**, for example when they are followed by an *of*-phrase or a relative clause.

- The nouns *church, hospital, prison, school, college, university* are used **without the** when we have the **purpose of the building** in mind. They are used **with the** when we are thinking of the **building** itself.

*Life* is full of surprises.
*Gold* is expensive.
*Prices* keep going up.

**The life** of the Inuit …
**The gold** that was found here …
**The prices** we had to pay …

We always go to **church** on Sundays.

Don't miss the concert in **the church**.

# Grammar File

Mit oder ohne *the*? Schreib die Sätze in dein Heft.

1 We can learn a lot from … history.
2 What do you know about … history of Canada?
3 Mr Jones takes the bus to … church every Sunday morning.
4 What's the name of … school you go to?
5 She's always friendly and helpful. That's why … people love her.
6 … scientists agree that we have to do something against … pollution.
7 I'm reading a book about … history of … architecture.
8 I think … life in … prison can be worse than … death.

## GF 12 REVISION Simple past / past progressive
### Einfache Form der Vergangenheit / Verlaufsform der Vergangenheit

I **went** to a party last Friday. My friend **was invited** too, but she **wasn't allowed** to go. She **had to** stay at home.

Das *simple past* verwendet man, um über **abgeschlossene Handlungen und Ereignisse** zu sprechen, die zu einem bestimmten Zeitpunkt in der Vergangenheit stattfanden.

Jonathan **got** a bike for Christmas.
Jonathan **hat** zu Weihnachten ein Fahrrad **bekommen**.

! Im Deutschen verwenden wir oft das Perfekt in Situationen, in denen im Englischen das *simple past* stehen muss.

Siehe auch GF 1.2, S. 137.

The party guests **were laughing** and **talking** when the DJ started to play music. Soon everybody **was dancing**.

◀ Mit dem *past progressive* sagt man, dass etwas zu einem bestimmten Zeitpunkt in der Vergangenheit **im Gange** und **noch nicht abgeschlossen** war.

Everybody **was dancing** and **having** a good time when suddenly the lights **went** out.

Das *past progressive* wird oft benutzt, um zu sagen, was gerade vor sich ging, als etwas anderes passierte. (Das neu einsetzende Ereignis steht im *simple past*.)

➡ Unit 3: p. 71, exercise 3

## GF 13 Adjectives used as nouns Das Adjektiv als Nomen

Do you think **the rich** should pay higher taxes?
… die Reichen / reiche Leute …

**The homeless** need our help.
Die Obdachlosen / Obdachlose Meschen …

◀ Englische **Adjektive** können **als Nomen** verwendet werden, um über eine **Gruppe von Menschen** zu sprechen, die eine Eigenschaft gemeinsam haben: *the rich* („reiche Menschen im Allgemeinen", „alle Reichen"), *the homeless*, *the young*, *the Irish*, …

Amelia helped **the blind man** at the ticket office.
… dem Blinden / dem blinden Mann …

**A lot of rich people** live in this area.

! Wenn man über eine oder mehrere **Einzelpersonen** spricht, muss im Englischen – anders als im Deutschen – ein Nomen folgen, z.B. *girl(s), boy(s), man/men, woman/women, people*.

It is a journey into **the unknown**.   … ins Unbekannte …
Always expect **the unexpected**.   … das Unerwartete …

◀ **The** + **Adjektiv** kann auch für **allgemeine, abstrakte Begriffe** verwendet werden, etwa *the unknown, the unexpected, the impossible, the good, the evil*, …

**The good thing** about school is that you meet your friends there.

! Wenn es um eine **bestimmte** Sache oder Situation geht, muss auf das Adjektiv ein Nomen wie *thing* folgen.

➡ Unit 3: p. 71, exercise 4

# Grammar File

## GF 14 The gerund  Das Gerundium

### 14.1 Use and form — Gebrauch und Form

*Travelling* can be expensive.
Reisen kann teuer sein.

*Surfing* isn't easy.
Surfen ist nicht einfach.

Emily likes *playing* chess.
Emily spielt gern Schach.

*Chilling* in the park is fun.
Chillen im Park macht Spaß. /
Es macht Spaß, im Park zu chillen.

Wenn die **-ing-Form** eines Verbs die Funktion eines **Nomens** hat, wird sie **Gerundium (gerund)** genannt.

Vergleiche:  I love **pop music**.    (I love + Nomen)
                      I love **surfing**.       (I love + -ing-Form)

◂ Wie ein Verb kann das Gerundium erweitert werden, z. B. durch ein Objekt *(comics; chess)* oder eine Orts- oder Zeitangabe *(here; in the park)*.

Im Deutschen wird das Gerundium oft durch einen Infinitiv mit „zu" oder durch ein Nomen wiedergegeben.

### 14.2 The gerund as subject and object — Das Gerundium als Subjekt und als Objekt

**subject**
*Surfing* isn't easy.
*Playing chess* is fun.

**object**
I love *surfing*.
Emily is good at *playing chess*.

◂ Das Gerundium (und seine Erweiterung) kann wie ein Nomen **Subjekt** oder **Objekt** eines Satzes sein.

**1** I **enjoy** *living* in South Dakota.
Ich wohne gern in South Dakota. /
Ich genieße es, in South Dakota zu wohnen.

I can't **imagine** *living* anywhere else.
Ich kann mir nicht vorstellen, woanders zu wohnen.

I don't **mind** *having* to help on the farm.
Es macht mir nichts aus, … helfen zu müssen.

**2** She **began** *learning* judo when she was eight.
          *to learn*

I **hate** / I don't **like** *getting up* when it's still dark.
                          *to get up*

**3** I mustn't **forget** *to call* Ava – it's her birthday.
I'll never **forget** *kissing* Ava for the first time.

**Remember** *to turn off* the lights when you leave.
I **remember** *closing* the window before going to bed.

He **tried** *to kick* the door open but only hurt his foot.
I can't open the door. – **Try** *kicking* it.

I **stopped** *to buy* a hamburger.
I've **stopped** *eating* meat.

❗ Beachte:

**1** Nach einigen Verben – z.B. **enjoy, finish, imagine, mind, miss, practise, suggest** – kann (anders als im Deutschen) kein Infinitiv stehen.
Stattdessen muss man ein Gerundium verwenden.

          Also nicht: I ~~enjoy to live~~ …,
                              I ~~can't imagine to live~~ …

**2** Nach **begin/start, continue, hate, like, love** kann ein Gerundium oder ein *to*-Infinitiv stehen.
(Aber nach **would like, would love, would hate** kann nur der *to*-Infinitiv stehen!)

**3** Bei manchen Verben hängt es von der Bedeutung ab, ob sie mit *to*-Infinitiv oder mit Gerundium stehen. Zu diesen Verben gehören **forget, remember** und **try**:

- **forget to do sth.**  = vergessen, (später) etwas zu tun
  **forget doing sth.** = vergessen, dass man (in der Vergangenheit) etwas getan hat

- **remember to do sth.** = daran denken, (später) etwas zu tun
  **remember doing sth.** = sich daran erinnern, dass man etwas getan hat

- **try to do sth.** = versuchen, etwas zu tun
  **try doing sth.** = etwas ausprobieren

- **stop to do sth.** = anhalten, um etwas zu tun
  **stop doing sth.** = aufhören, etwas zu tun

➡ Unit 3: p. 76, exercise 1/ p. 88, exercise 2

# Grammar File

## 14.3 The gerund after prepositions — Das Gerundium nach Präpositionen

1. *Never cross a street **without looking**.*
   Überquere nie eine Straße, ohne zu schauen.

2. ***Instead of walking** home, they went into the park and played football.*
   Anstatt / Statt nach Hause zu gehen, …

3. *You can improve your English **by watching** British or American films.*
   …, indem du britische oder amerikanische Filme anschaust.

4. *Mike is **interested in taking** photos.*
   Mike interessiert sich fürs Fotografieren / ist am Fotografieren interessiert.

5. *Mr Jones talked about the **danger of losing** money.*
   Mr Jones sprach von der Gefahr, Geld zu verlieren.

6. *She **was looking forward to meeting** her friends.*
   Sie freute sich darauf, ihre Freunde zu treffen.

Wenn auf eine **Präposition** (about, at, for, in, instead of, of, without, …) ein **Verb** folgt, dann steht dieses Verb als Gerundium.

◄ Die Präposition kann

– allein stehen (Sätze **1–3**) oder

– mit einem anderen Wort fest verbunden sein (Sätze **4–6**).

Im Kasten findest du eine Reihe von nützlichen Wendungen mit **Präposition + Gerundium**.

---

**Adjektiv + Präposition + Gerundium:**

| (to) be | afraid of | doing sth. | Angst haben vor |
| | excited about | | gespannt sein auf; aufgeregt sein wegen |
| | good/bad at | | gut/schlecht sein in; etwas gut/schlecht können |
| | interested in | | interessiert sein an, sich interessieren für |
| | keen on | | begeistert sein von; interessiert sein an |
| | tired of | | genug haben von; etwas über/satt haben |

**Nomen + Präposition + Gerundium:**

| the | chance of | doing sth. | Chance, (günstige) Gelegenheit (zu) |
| | danger of | | Gefahr (zu) |
| | hope of | | Hoffnung (zu/auf) |
| | idea of | | Idee, Gedanke (zu) |
| | reason for | | Grund für |
| | way of | | Art und Weise, Weg (zu) |

**Verb + Präposition + Gerundium:**

| (to) | believe in | doing sth. | glauben an |
| | decide against | | sich entscheiden gegen |
| | dream of/about | | träumen von |
| | look forward to | | sich freuen auf |
| | talk about/of | | reden von |
| | think of | | denken an; in Betracht ziehen |
| | worry about | | sich Sorgen machen wegen/um |

➜ Unit 3: pp. 76–77, exercises 2–4

**In English**

### The gerund

- An *-ing* form which is used like a noun is called a **gerund**.
- Gerunds can be
  - the **subject** of a sentence: ***Surfing** / **Playing tennis** is fun.*
  - the **object** of a sentence: *I love **surfing** / **playing tennis**.*
- Verbs which follow a **preposition** take the form of a gerund: *He left the shop **without paying**.*

# Grammar File

Wähle ein passendes Verb aus dem Kästchen und vervollständige die Sätze in deinem Heft. Achte auf die richtige Form.

*fly · go · lie · notice · spend · surf · travel*

1. We're going to fly to California next summer. I'll enjoy … the waves.
2. My parents have decided against … camping this year.
3. We want to spend our holidays in Spain. I'm looking forward to … on the beach all day.
4. … alone to New York was very exciting for me.
5. I like the idea of … through Australia.
6. I'm so tired of … my holidays on a farm in the south of Germany year after year.
7. I remember … a man in black clothes in front of the bank.

## GF 15 Adverbs and adverbials — Adverbien und Adverbialbestimmungen

### 15.1 Word order — Wortstellung

**Luckily** we had our umbrellas with us.
**Suddenly** the car stopped and two men got out.
**Maybe** you can use your sister's bike.

◀ **Satzadverbien** (sentence adverbs) wie etwa *luckily, maybe, of course, suddenly, at first, then, finally* beziehen sich auf den ganzen Satz. Sie stehen in der Regel am Satzanfang **(front-position)**.

1. My brother **is always** late.
   It was only 11 o'clock, but we **were already** hungry.
2. I **often make** breakfast on Sundays.
   They didn't have a map and **soon got** lost.
3. Emma **doesn't usually** take the bus to school.
   Your uncle **has just** phoned.
   That story **will never** be forgotten.

Have you been here **before**? (schon mal)
Have you cleaned the kitchen **yet**? (schon)
The play hasn't started **yet**. (noch nicht)

◀ **Adverbien** wie *already, always, ever, just, never, often, sometimes, soon, usually* beschreiben eine **unbestimmte Zeit oder Häufigkeit** (adverbs of frequency / of indefinite time).
Sie haben meist **mid-position**, stehen also
1. nach *am/are/is/was/were*
2. direkt vor dem Vollverb (simple present, simple past)
3. nach dem Hilfsverb.

❗ **Ausnahmen:** *before* und *yet* stehen am Satzende.

4. Jeremy scored a goal, and everyone **cheered loudly**.
   My cousin **speaks Spanish well**.
5. Can we go and **play outside**?
   I first **met my girlfriend in Mobridge**.
6. Sally **sold her motorbike yesterday**.
   My grandmother **died two years ago**.

◀ Nach dem Vollverb bzw. nach dem Objekt **(end-position)** stehen
4. **Adverbien der Art und Weise** (adverbs of manner) wie etwa *loudly, quickly, well*
5. **Adverbien und Adverbialbestimmungen des Ortes** wie etwa *outside, there, in Mobridge, on the beach*
6. **Adverbien und Adverbialbestimmungen der Zeit** wie etwa *yesterday, two years ago, in 2016*.

I **really** like Drew.
We were **totally** surprised.
Mr Walter was **very/quite/extremely** angry.

◀ **Gradadverbien** (adverbs of degree) wie etwa *very, quite, too, really, hardly, nearly, especially, totally* stehen in der Regel direkt vor dem Wort, auf das sie sich beziehen.

❗ Beachte:
– **Zeitangaben** können auch **front-position** haben. Die Wortstellung bleibt dann trotzdem **S – V – O**.

**Every Saturday morning** my father does the shopping.
Jeden Samstagmorgen erledigt mein Vater die Einkäufe.

She **opened the door quietly**.
Sie **öffnete leise die Tür**.

We're **going to buy a new computer next Friday**.
Wir **kaufen nächsten Freitag einen neuen Rechner**.

– Anders als im Deutschen dürfen englische Adverbien der Art und Weise und Orts- und Zeitangaben **nicht zwischen Prädikat und Objekt** stehen.

➡ Unit 3: pp. 82–83, exercises 2, 4–5

# Grammar File

## 15.2 REVISION Adverb or adjective after certain verbs?

Adverb oder Adjektiv nach bestimmten Verben?

She **shouted** *angrily* at me. ... schrie mich wütend an.
He **greeted** us *nervously*. ... begrüßte uns nervös.

She **looked** very *angry*. ... sah sehr wütend aus.
He **felt** a bit *nervous* when the guests arrived.
Er war ein bisschen nervös, als die Gäste eintrafen.
She **seemed** very *sad*. What happened?
The soup **smelled** *wonderful* and **tasted** *great*.
Fresh strawberries? **Sounds** *nice*!

Wie du weißt, drücken **Adverbien der Art und Weise** aus, **wie** – auf welche Art und Weise – **jemand etwas tut**.

◀ Bei manchen Verben geht es aber nicht darum, wie jemand etwas tut, sondern darum, **wie jemand oder etwas ist** – sie beschreiben einen **Zustand** oder eine **Eigenschaft**.
Nach solchen Verben steht nicht ein Adverb, sondern ein **Adjektiv**. Beispiele:

*(to)* **feel** (sich fühlen), *(to)* **look** (aussehen),
*(to)* **sound** (klingen), *(to)* **seem** (scheinen),
*(to)* **smell** (riechen), *(to)* **taste** (schmecken)

**1** The doctor **felt** my arm *carefully*. betasten
He **looked** *nervously* at his watch. schauen
The dog **smelled** the shoe *carefully*. riechen an
She **tasted** the meat *slowly*. kosten, probieren

**2** My arm **felt** *heavy* and a bit *sore*. sich anfühlen
He **looked** *scared*. aussehen
The shoe **smelled** *awful*. riechen, stinken
The meat **tasted** *delicious*. schmecken

➡ Unit 3: p. 83, exercise 3

❗ Bei den Verben der Wahrnehmung **feel, look, smell, taste** kann – je nach Bedeutung – ein **Adverb** oder ein **Adjektiv** stehen:

1 Ein **Adverb** steht, wenn eine **Tätigkeit** beschrieben wird.

2 Ein **Adjektiv** steht, wenn ein **Zustand** oder eine **Eigenschaft** beschrieben wird.

### In English

**Adverbs and adverbials – word order**
Different kinds of adverbs and adverbials have different positions in a sentence:
- **Sentence adverbs** like *luckily, maybe, suddenly, at first* usually go in **front-position**.
- **Adverbs of frequency /of indefinite time** like *already, always, ever, just, never* usually go in **mid-position**.
- **Adverbs of manner** like *quickly, well* and **adverbs and adverbials of place and time** like *outside, on the beach, yesterday, two years ago* usually go in **end-position**.
- **Adverbs of degree** like *very, too, really, extremely, nearly, especially* usually go before the word they refer to.

After a verb which describes a **state** or a **quality** – e.g. *feel, look, sound, seem, smell, taste* –, we use an **adjective**, not an adverb.

Schreibe die Sätze in dein Übungsheft. Füge die Adverbien und Adverbialbestimmungen an den richtigen Stellen ein. (Manchmal gibt es mehr als eine mögliche Lösung.)

1 We moved (**to a new house / last month**).
2 I liked our old house (**quite**). We went (**often / outside**) and played (**in the garden**).
3 We can't go (**now / as easily as before / outside**).
4 It was busy (**really / on the moving day**).
5 Our cat Teddy was getting (**all the time / in the way**).
6 Dad broke his neck when he fell over Teddy (**nearly**). He shouted at him (**very / loudly**).
7 Teddy ran and disappeared (**away**).
8 Teddy hadn't come back and we had to look for him (**everywhere / after a few hours / still**).
9 I went and found him (**outside / under the balcony**).
10 He wasn't hurt (**luckily**).

# Grammar File

## Grammatical terms (Grammatische Fachbegriffe)

| English | Deutsch | Beispiel |
|---|---|---|
| active ['æktɪv] | Aktiv | A heavy storm **destroyed** twelve houses. |
| adjective ['ædʒɪktɪv] | Adjektiv (Eigenschaftswort) | good, new, green, interesting, … |
| adverb ['ædvɜːb] | Adverb | today, there, outside, very, … |
| adverb of degree [dɪ'griː] | Gradadverb | very, quite, really, extremely, totally |
| adverb of frequency ['friːkwənsi] | Häufigkeitsadverb | always, usually, often, sometimes, never |
| adverb of indefinite time [ɪn'defɪnət] | Adverb der unbestimmten Zeit | already, ever, just, never, before, yet, … |
| adverb of manner ['mænə] | Adverb der Art und Weise | nicely, happily, quietly, slowly, well, fast, … |
| adverbial [æd'vɜːbiəl] | Adverbilbestimmung | two years ago, on the beach |
| article ['ɑːtɪkl] | Artikel | the, a, an |
| auxiliary (verb) [ɔːg'zɪliəri] | Hilfsverb | |
| comparative [kəm'pærətɪv] | Komparativ (1. Steigerungsform) | older; more expensive |
| comparison [kəm'pærɪsn] | Steigerung | old – older – oldest; expensive – more expensive – most expensive |
| conditional sentence [kən'dɪʃənl] | Bedingungssatz | If I see Sam, I'll tell him. |
| conjunction [kən'dʒʌŋkʃn] | Konjunktion | and, but, …; because, when, … |
| definite article [ˌdefɪnət_'ɑːtɪkl] | bestimmter Artikel | the |
| gerund ['dʒerənd] | Gerundium | I like **dancing**. **Dancing** is fun. |
| going to-future ['fjuːtʃə] | Futur mit going to | I**'m going to watch** TV tonight. |
| imperative [ɪm'perətɪv] | Imperativ (Befehlsform) | Open your books. Don't talk. |
| infinitive [ɪn'fɪnətɪv] | Infinitiv (Grundform des Verbs) | (to) open, (to) go, … |
| irregular verb [ɪ'regjələ] | unregelmäßiges Verb | (to) go – went – gone, (to) see – saw – seen |
| modal auxiliary [ˌməʊdl_ɔːg'zɪliəri] | modales Hilfsverb, Modalverb | can, may, might, needn't, should, must, … |
| negative statement ['negətɪv] | verneinter Aussagesatz | I don't like oranges. |
| noun [naʊn] | Nomen, Substantiv | Justin, girl, man, time, name, … |
| object ['ɒbdʒɪkt] | Objekt | Justin has **a new camera**. |
| object question | Objektfrage, Frage nach dem Objekt | **Who** did Mrs Pascoe **invite** to tea? |
| passive ['pæsɪv] | Passiv | Twelve houses **were destroyed** by a storm. |
| past participle [ˌpɑːst 'pɑːtɪsɪpl] | Partizip Perfekt | checked, phoned, tried, gone, eaten, … |
| past perfect [ˌpɑːst 'pɜːfɪkt] | past perfect (Vorvergangenheit, Plusquamperfekt) | I **had** already **gone** to bed when they arrived. |
| past progressive [ˌpɑːst prə'gresɪv] | Verlaufsform der Vergangenheit | Olivia **was playing** cards. |
| personal passive [ˌpɜːsənl 'pæsɪv] | persönliches Passiv | She was offered a job. |
| personal pronoun [ˌpɜːsənl 'prəʊnaʊn] | Personalpronomen (persönliches Fürwort) | I, you, he, she, it, we, they; me, you, him, her, it, us, them |
| plural ['plʊərəl] | Plural, Mehrzahl | |
| positive statement ['pɒzətɪv] | bejahter Aussagesatz | I like oranges. |
| possessive determiner [pə'zesɪv dɪ'tɜːmɪnə] | Possessivbegleiter (besitzanzeigender Begleiter) | my, your, his, her, its, our, their |
| possessive form [pə'zesɪv 'fɔːm] | s-Genitiv | Sam's sister, the Blackwells' house, … |
| possessive pronoun [pə'zesɪv 'prəʊnaʊn] | Possessivpronomen | mine, yours, his, hers, ours, theirs |
| prefix ['priːfɪks] | Präfix, Vorsilbe | un-, in-, re-, dis-, … |
| preposition [ˌprepə'zɪʃn] | Präposition | after, at, in, into, near, next to, … |
| present perfect [ˌpreznt 'pɜːfɪkt] | present perfect | We**'ve made** some scones for you. |
| present perfect progressive [ˌpreznt ˌpɜːfɪkt prə'gresɪv] | Verlaufsform des present perfect | He**'s been watching** TV for hours. |
| present progressive [ˌpreznt prə'gresɪv] | Verlaufsform der Gegenwart | Olivia **is playing** cards. |
| pronoun ['prəʊnaʊn] | Pronomen (Fürwort) | |
| prop-word ['prɒp wɜːd] | Stützwort | one, ones |
| question tag ['kwestʃn tæg] | Frageanhängsel | isn't he?, are you?, can't we?, … |
| question word ['kwestʃn wɜːd] | Fragewort | who?, what?, when?, where?, how?, … |
| reciprocal pronoun [rɪ'sɪprəkl 'prəʊnaʊn] | reziprokes Pronomen | each other, one another |
| reflexive pronoun [rɪˌfleksɪv 'prəʊnaʊn] | Reflexivpronomen | myself, yourself, themselves, … |
| regular verb ['regjələ] | regelmäßiges Verb | (to) help – helped, (to) look – looked, … |
| relative clause [ˌrelətɪv 'klɔːz] | Relativsatz | I like teachers **who laugh a lot**. |
| relative pronoun [ˌrelətɪv 'prəʊnaʊn] | Relativpronomen | who – which – that |
| short answer [ˌʃɔːt_'ɑːnsə] | Kurzantwort | Yes, I am. / No, we don't. / … |
| simple past [ˌsɪmpl 'pɑːst] | einfache Form der Vergangenheit | Olivia **played** cards last Friday. |
| simple present [ˌsɪmpl 'preznt] | einfache Form der Gegenwart | Olivia **plays** cards every Friday evening. |

# Grammar File

| | | |
|---|---|---|
| **singular** [ˈsɪŋgjələ] | Singular, Einzahl | |
| **statement** [ˈsteɪtmənt] | Aussage(satz) | *I like Plymouth **because I like the sea**.* |
| **sub-clause** [ˈsʌbklɔːz] | Nebensatz | *Justin/**He** has a new camera.* |
| **subject** [ˈsʌbdʒɪkt] | Subjekt | *Who invited the Coopers to tea?* |
| **subject question** | Subjektfrage, Frage nach dem Subjekt | |
| **substitute** [ˈsʌbstɪtjuːt] | Ersatzverb (eines Modalverbs) | be able to, be allowed to, have to |
| **suffix** [ˈsʌfɪks] | Suffix, Nachsilbe | -er, -able, -ity, -ness, … |
| **superlative** [suˈpɜːlətɪv] | Superlativ (2. Steigerungsform) | (the) oldest; (the) most expensive |
| **verb** [vɜːb] | 1. Verb; 2. Prädikat | go, help, look, see, … *Reading **can be** fun.* |
| **verb of perception** [ˌvɜːb əv pəˈsepʃn] | Verb der (sinnlichen) Wahrnehmung; | look, feel, smell, … |
| **will-future** [ˈfjuːtʃə] | Futur mit *will* | *I'm sure **you'll like** the new maths teacher.* |
| **yes/no question** | Entscheidungsfrage | *Are you 14? Do you like oranges?* |

## Lösungen der Grammar-File-Aufgaben

**p. 139/1**
1 *We were beaten 4 : 1.*
2 *They are made of wood.*
3 *They are grown on local farms.*
4 *It's owned by a large building company.*
5 *They were caught at the border.*
6 *It's prepared fresh every day.*

**p. 139/2**
1 *English teachers teach their students English.*
2 *Tour guides show tourists interesting sights.*
3 *He tried to explain his feelings to her.*
4 *Last weekend she introduced her boyfriend to her parents.*
5 *When we arrived, a woman gave us the room keys.*
6 *You should report the accident to the police.*

**p. 141**
1 *We were given the key …*
2 *We were given ten minutes …*
3 *I was offered a job …*
4 *He was shocked when **he was told the news**.*
5 *She was promised a TV role.*
6 *He was sent a letter bomb.*

**p. 144**
1 *The USA plays an important role …*
2 *The news from the Middle East is getting better.*
3 *The politics of a country has an influence …*
4 *Of course, the economics of a country is important, but …*
5 *Physics has always been my brother's favourite subject.*

**p. 145**
1 *… It will be opened tomorrow.*
2 *… Helmets should be / must be worn at all times.*
3 *… barking dogs could be heard.*
4 *… One of his windows has been broken.*
5 *… Hundreds of homes have been destroyed.*

**p. 147**
1 *We can learn a lot from history.*
2 *What do you know about **the** history of Canada?*
3 *Mr Jones takes the bus to church every Sunday morning.*
4 *What's the name of **the** school you go to?*
5 *She's always friendly and helpful. That's why people love her.*
6 *Scientists agree that we have to do something against pollution.*
7 *I'm reading a book about **the** history of architecture.*
8 *I think life in prison can be worse than death.*

**p. 150**
1 *… I'll enjoy **surfing** the waves.*
2 *My parents have decided against **going** camping this year.*
3 *… I'm looking forward to **lying** on the beach all day.*
4 ***Flying** alone to New York was very exciting for me.*
5 *I like the idea of **travelling** through Australia.*
6 *I'm so tired of **spending** my holidays on a farm in the south of Germany year after year.*
7 *I remember **noticing** a man in black clothes in front of the bank.*

**p. 151**
1 *We moved **to a new house last month**.*
2 *I **quite** liked our old house. We **often** went **outside** and played **in the garden**.*
3 ***Now** we can't go **outside** as easily as **before**. / We can't go **outside** as easily as **before now**.*
4 *It was **really** busy **on the moving day**.*
5 *Our cat Teddy was getting **in the way all the time**.*
6 *Dad **nearly** broke his neck when he fell over Teddy. He shouted at him **very loudly**.*
7 *Teddy ran **away** and disappeared.*
8 ***After a few hours** Teddy **still** hadn't come back and we had to look for him **everywhere**. / Teddy **still** hadn't come back **after a few hours** and we had to look for him **everywhere**.*
9 *I went **outside** and found him **under the balcony**.*
10 ***Luckily** he wasn't hurt.*

# Vocabulary

Das **Vocabulary** (S.154–193) enthält alle Wörter und Wendungen deines Englischbuches, die du lernen musst. Sie stehen in der Reihenfolge, in der sie im Buch zum ersten Mal vorkommen.

Hier siehst du, wie das **Vocabulary** aufgebaut ist:

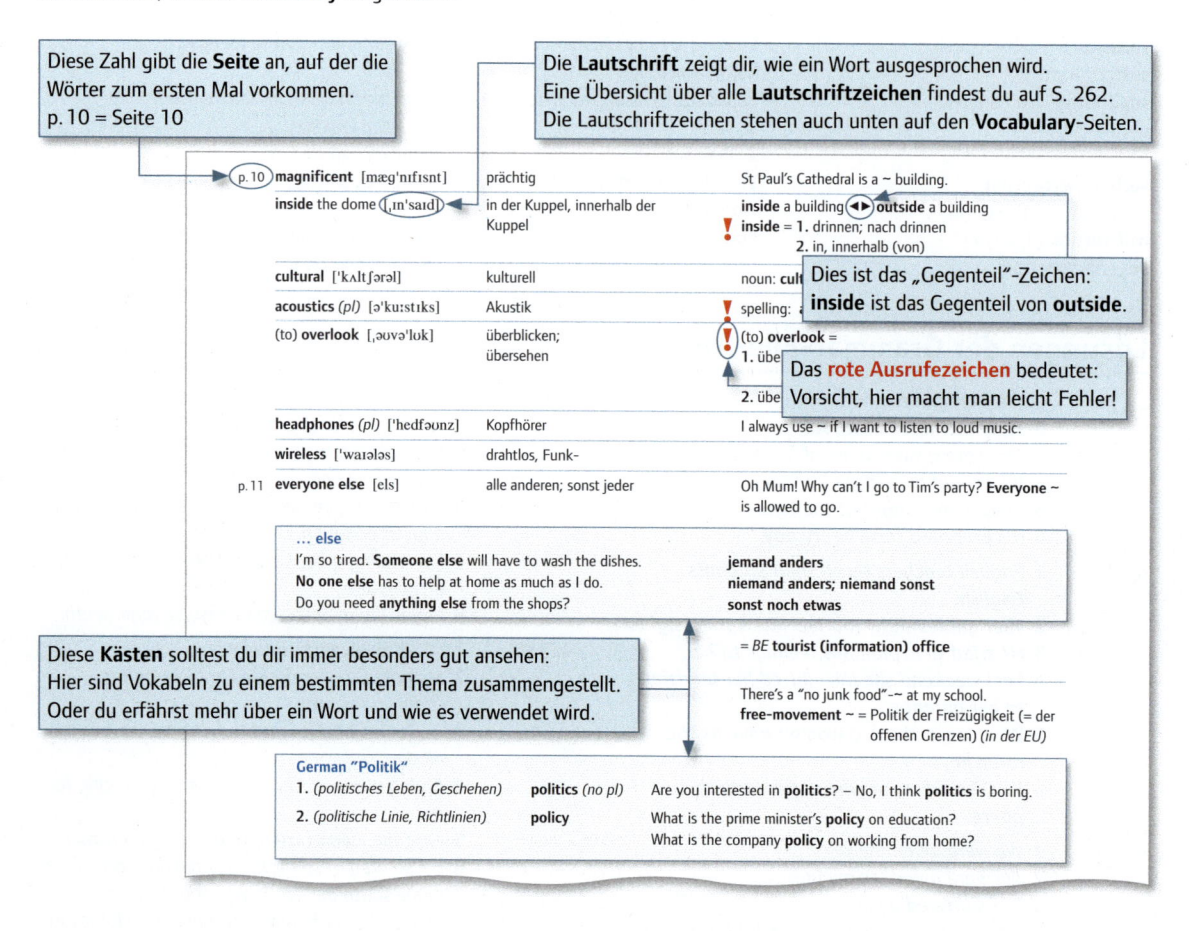

Diese Zahl gibt die **Seite** an, auf der die Wörter zum ersten Mal vorkommen.
p. 10 = Seite 10

Die **Lautschrift** zeigt dir, wie ein Wort ausgesprochen wird. Eine Übersicht über alle **Lautschriftzeichen** findest du auf S. 262. Die Lautschriftzeichen stehen auch unten auf den **Vocabulary**-Seiten.

| | | | |
|---|---|---|---|
| p.10 **magnificent** [mægˈnɪfɪsnt] | prächtig | | St Paul's Cathedral is a ~ building. |
| **inside** the dome [ˌɪnˈsaɪd] | in der Kuppel, innerhalb der Kuppel | | **inside** a building ◄► **outside** a building<br>❗ **inside** = 1. drinnen; nach drinnen<br>2. in, innerhalb (von) |
| **cultural** [ˈkʌltʃərəl] | kulturell | | noun: cul... |
| **acoustics** (pl) [əˈkuːstɪks] | Akustik | | ❗ spelling: a... |
| (to) **overlook** [ˌəʊvəˈlʊk] | überblicken; übersehen | | ❗ (to) **overlook** =<br>1. übe...<br>2. übe... |
| **headphones** (pl) [ˈhedfəʊnz] | Kopfhörer | | I always use ~ if I want to listen to loud music. |
| **wireless** [ˈwaɪələs] | drahtlos, Funk- | | |
| p.11 **everyone else** [els] | alle anderen; sonst jeder | | Oh Mum! Why can't I go to Tim's party? Everyone ~ is allowed to go. |

Dies ist das „Gegenteil"-Zeichen: **inside** ist das Gegenteil von **outside**.

Das rote Ausrufezeichen bedeutet: Vorsicht, hier macht man leicht Fehler!

| ... **else** | | |
|---|---|---|
| I'm so tired. **Someone else** will have to wash the dishes. | jemand anders | |
| **No one else** has to help at home as much as I do. | niemand anders; niemand sonst | |
| Do you need **anything else** from the shops? | sonst noch etwas | |

Diese **Kästen** solltest du dir immer besonders gut ansehen: Hier sind Vokabeln zu einem bestimmten Thema zusammengestellt. Oder du erfährst mehr über ein Wort und wie es verwendet wird.

| | | |
|---|---|---|
| | | = BE **tourist (information) office** |
| | | There's a "no junk food"-~ at my school. |
| | | **free-movement** ~ = Politik der Freizügigkeit (= der offenen Grenzen) (in der EU) |

| German "Politik" | | |
|---|---|---|
| 1. (politisches Leben, Geschehen) | **politics** (no pl) | Are you interested in **politics**? – No, I think **politics** is boring. |
| 2. (politische Linie, Richtlinien) | **policy** | What is the prime minister's **policy** on education?<br>What is the company **policy** on working from home? |

---

Im **Vocabulary** werden folgende **Abkürzungen** verwendet:

p. = page • pp. = pages

adj = adjective • adv = adverb

conj = conjunction • prep = preposition

sth. = something (etwas) • sb. = somebody (jemand)

jn. = jemanden • jm. = jemandem

pl = plural (Mehrzahl)

infml = informal (umgangssprachlich) • fml = formal (formell, förmlich)

BE = British English • AE = American English

Ⓕ = verwandtes Wort im Französischen • Ⓛ = verwandtes Wort im Lateinischen

---

Wenn du **nachschlagen** möchtest, was ein englisches Wort bedeutet oder wie man es ausspricht, dann verwende das **English – German Dictionary** auf den Seiten 194–228.
Und wenn du vergessen hast, wie etwas auf Englisch heißt, dann kann dir das **German – English Dictionary** auf den Seiten 229–262 eine erste Hilfe sein.

---

[iː] green • [i] happy • [ɪ] big • [e] red • [æ] cat • [ɑː] class • [ɒ] song •
[ɔː] door • [uː] blue • [ʊ] book • [ʌ] mum • [ɜː] girl • [ə] a partner

# Unit 1 Vocabulary

## Unit 1 London changing

| pp. 8/9 | **Victorian** [vɪkˈtɔːriən] | viktorianisch; Viktorianer/in | |
|---|---|---|---|
| | **circa (c.)** [ˈsɜːkə] | zirka (ca.) | I'm not sure of the exact year, but it was ~ 1350.<br>❗ **circa/c.** is only used with dates.    (L) circa |
| | **era** [ˈɪərə] | Ära, Epoche | the post-war ~; an ~ of peace<br>(F) l'ère    (L) aera |
| | **advantage** [ədˈvɑːntɪdʒ] | Vorteil | (F) l'avantage (m) |
| | **disadvantage** [ˌdɪsədˈvɑːntɪdʒ] | Nachteil | **advantage ◄► disadvantage**<br>Not being able to drive can be a ~ when you're looking for a job.    (F) le désavantage |

## Part A

| p. 10 | **magnificent** [mægˈnɪfɪsnt] | prächtig | St Paul's Cathedral is a ~ building.<br>(F) magnifique    (L) magnificus, a, um |
|---|---|---|---|
| | **inside** the dome [ˌɪnˈsaɪd] | in der Kuppel, innerhalb der Kuppel | **inside** a building ◄► **outside** a building<br>❗ **inside** = 1. drinnen; nach drinnen<br>             2. in, innerhalb (von) |
| | **opposite** [ˈɒpəzɪt] | gegenüberliegende(r, s); entgegengesetzte(r, s) | You'll find the answers to our quiz on the ~ page.<br>❗ **opposite** =<br>1. (n) Gegenteil; 2. (prep) gegenüber (von);<br>3. (adj) gegenüberliegende(r, s); entgegengesetzte(r, s)    (L) oppositus, a, um |
| | **acoustics** (pl) [əˈkuːstɪks] | Akustik | ❗ spelling: ac<u>ou</u>stics    (F) l'acoustique (f) |
| | **How's that for** acoustics? | Ist das nicht eine tolle Akustik? / Das nennt man tolle Akustik! | Three bedrooms, a large garden and a swimming pool on the roof – **how's that for** a holiday home for you and your family? |
| | **cultural** [ˈkʌltʃərəl] | kulturell | noun: **culture** – adj: **cultural**<br>(F) culturel, le    (L) cultura (Pflege, Kultur) |
| | **archive** [ˈɑːkaɪv] | Archiv | ❗ stress and pronunciation: <u>**ar**</u>chive [ˈɑːkaɪv]<br>(F) l'archive (f) |
| | **in the 1940s** | in den 40er-Jahren (des 20. Jahrhunderts) | |
| | **origin** [ˈɒrɪdʒɪn] | Ursprung, Herkunft | *English:* … of African origin<br>*German:* … afrikanischer Herkunft<br>(F) l'origine (f)    (L) origo, inis f |
| | **destination** [ˌdestɪˈneɪʃn] | Reiseziel, Fahrtziel; Bestimmungsort | We offer cheap hotel rooms at popular holiday ~s.<br>(F) la destination |
| | **audio** [ˈɔːdiəʊ] | Audio-, Ton- | (F) audio    (L) audire (hören) |
| | **(to) overlook** [ˌəʊvəˈlʊk] | überblicken; übersehen | ❗ **(to) overlook** =<br>1. überblicken – a room **overlooking** the Thames<br>               (ein Raum mit Blick auf die Themse)<br>2. übersehen – (to) **overlook** a question / a mistake |
| | **headphones** (pl) [ˈhedfəʊnz] | Kopfhörer | I always use ~ if I want to listen to loud music. |
| | **wireless** [ˈwaɪələs] | drahtlos, Funk- | |
| | **channel** [ˈtʃænl] | Kanal; Sender | In the evenings, we watch the news on **Channel** 5. |
| p. 11 | **chat** [tʃæt] | Chat; Unterhaltung (Gespräch) | |

[eɪ] name · [aɪ] time · [ɔɪ] boy · [əʊ] old ·
[aʊ] town · [ɪə] here · [eə] where · [ʊə] tour

# Vocabulary Unit 1

| | | |
|---|---|---|
| **pretty** old/expensive/… ['prɪti] | ziemlich alt/teuer/… | ❗ **pretty** = 1. (*adj*) hübsch; 2. (*adv*) ziemlich<br>£ 220? That's ~ expensive for a pair of jeans, isn't it? |
| **mom** [mɒm], [mɑːm] (*AE*) | Mutti, Mama | |
| **round** … [raʊnd] | um (… herum); in (… umher) | = **around** …<br>Let's walk ~ the lake / ~ the West End.<br>(um … herum / in … umher) |
| **tourist (information) bureau** ['tʊərɪst ˌbjʊərəʊ] (*AE*) | Touristeninformation, Fremdenverkehrsbüro | = *BE* **tourist (information) office** |
| **No idea.** (*infml*) | Keine Ahnung. | Do you know where the tourist office is?<br>– **No ~**, sorry. |
| (to) **consult with** sb. [kən'sʌlt] (*AE*) | sich mit jm. beraten | (to) **consult** sb. = jn. fragen, jn. konsultieren<br>(F) consulter   (L) consulere |
| **high commission** [ˌhaɪ kə'mɪʃn] | Diplomatische Vertretung eines Commonwealth-Landes in einem anderen Commonwealth-Land | |
| **embassy** ['embəsi] | Botschaft (*diplomatische Vertretung*) | (F) l'ambassade (f) |
| **because of** [bɪ'kɒz_əv] | wegen | ❗ • **because of** (*prep*) = wegen<br>We stayed at home **because of** the rain.<br>• **because** (*conj*) = weil<br>We stayed at home **because** it rained. |
| **Commonwealth** ['kɒmənwelθ] | Gemeinschaft der Länder des ehemaligen britischen Weltreichs | |
| **member** ['membə] | Mitglied | **Nur für Mitglieder!**<br>(F) le membre |
| **organization** [ˌɔːɡənaɪ'zeɪʃn] | Organisation | noun: **organization** – verb: (to) **organize**<br>(organisieren; ordnen)<br>(F) l'organisation (f) |
| **diplomatic** [ˌdɪplə'mætɪk] | diplomatisch, Diplomaten- | (F) diplomatique |
| **everyone else** [els] | alle anderen; sonst jeder | Oh Mum! Why can't I go to Tim's party? **Everyone ~** is allowed to go. |

> **… else**
> I'm so tired. **Someone else** will have to wash the dishes.   jemand anders
> **No one else** has to help at home as much as I do.   niemand anders; niemand sonst
> Do you need **anything else** from the shops?   sonst noch etwas

| | | |
|---|---|---|
| **Catch you later.** (*infml*) | Bis später dann! | = See you later. |
| p.12 **greeting** ['ɡriːtɪŋ] | Gruß(formel), Begrüßung | |
| **act** [ækt] | Tat, Akt, Handlung | (F) l'acte (m)   (L) acta n pl |
| **Goodnight.** [ˌɡʊd'naɪt] | Gute Nacht! | |
| **Hi.** [haɪ] | Hallo. | |
| (to) **share** sth. [ʃeə] | (sich) etwas teilen | My sister and I ~ a room. = I ~ a room with my sister. |
| (to) **subscribe to** sth. [səb'skraɪb] | etwas abonnieren | (to) **subscribe to** ◄▶<br>(to) **unsubscribe from** [ˌʌnsəb'skraɪb]<br>(abbestellen, kündigen; sich aus einer Mailingliste austragen lassen)<br>(L) subscribere (*unterschreiben*) |

[b] boat · [p] pool · [d] dad · [t] ten · [g] good · [k] cat ·
[m] mum · [n] no · [ŋ] song · [l] hello · [r] red · [w] we · [j] you

# Unit 1 Vocabulary

| | | |
|---|---|---|
| (to) email (sb. sth.) [ˈiːmeɪl] | (jm. etwas) mailen | noun: **email** – verb: (to) **email** |
| **How's things?** (infml) | Wie geht's? | |
| **messenger service** [ˈmesɪndʒə sɜːvɪs] | Messenger (Dienst zur Nachrichtenübermittlung im Internet) | **messenger** = Kurier/in, Bote/Botin |
| (to) **trend** [trend] | im Trend liegen, angesagt sein | Last week, the news story about Prince William was ~ing on Twitter. This week no one is talking about it. verb: (to) **trend** – noun: **trend** |
| (to) **message** (sb.) [ˈmesɪdʒ] | (jm.) eine (elektronische) Nachricht schicken/übermitteln | verb: (to) **message** – noun: **message** (Nachricht; Botschaft, Aussage) |
| **contact** [ˈkɒntækt] | Kontakt | ❗ stress: **contact** [ˈkɒntækt] noun: **contact** – verb: (to) **contact sb.** (Kontakt mit jm. aufnehmen, sich mit jm. in Verbindung setzen) (F) le contact (L) contingere (berühren) |
| **face to face** | von Angesicht zu Angesicht | I would rather meet her ~ **to** ~ than write to her. |
| p. 13 (to) **express** sth. [ɪkˈspres] | etwas ausdrücken, zum Ausdruck bringen | "In my view" is a useful phrase to ~ your opinion. verb: (to) **express** – noun: **expression** (L) exprimere |
| p. 15 **absurd** [əbˈsɜːd] | absurd | (F) absurde (L) absurdus, a, um (widersinnig) |
| **humorous** [ˈhjuːmərəs] | humorvoll, witzig | ❗ spelling: **humour** (noun) – **humorous** (adj) (F) humoristique |
| **realistic** [ˌriːəˈlɪstɪk] | realistisch | I want to see all the sights! – Come on, be ~. We only have two days in London. adj: **realistic** – adv: **realistically** [ˌriːəˈlɪstɪkli] (F) réaliste |
| **feature** [ˈfiːtʃə] | Merkmal, Eigenschaft | This car has an interesting ~: it can park itself automatically. |
| **titanium** [tɪˈteɪniəm] | Titan (Metall) | |
| **frame** [freɪm] | Rahmen; Gestell, Fahrgestell | This bike is cheaper, but its ~ is much heavier. |
| (to) **fire** [ˈfaɪə] | (ab)schießen, (ab)feuern | The two men shot at each other, but nobody knows who ~d first. |
| **horn** [hɔːn] | Horn; Hupe | horn She's blowing the horn. |
| **reaction (to)** [riˈækʃn] | Reaktion (auf) | ❗ stress: **reaction** [riˈækʃn] verb: (to) **react (to)** – noun: **reaction (to)** (F) la réaction (à) |
| **unicorn** [ˈjuːnɪkɔːn] | Einhorn | (L) unus (ein) + cornus (Horn) |
| **credits** (pl) [ˈkredɪts] | Credits (Vor- oder Nachspann, z.B. eines Films) | The ~ usually come at the end of the film. |
| **long shot** [ˈlɒŋ ʃɒt] | Totale (Film) | |
| **close-up** [ˈkləʊs ʌp] | Nahaufnahme (Film) | |

[f] father • [v] river • [s] sister • [z] please • [ʃ] shop • [ʒ] television •
[tʃ] teacher • [dʒ] Germany • [θ] thanks • [ð] this • [h] here

# Vocabulary Unit 1

## Part B

| | | | |
|---|---|---|---|
| p. 16 | **trendy** ['trendi] | modisch, trendy, „angesagt" | noun: **trend** – adj: **trendy** |
| | **exhibition** [ˌeksɪ'bɪʃn] | Ausstellung; Messe | I want to see the Chagall ~ at the museum.<br>This new machine was presented at last month's technology ~.    (L) exhibere *(vorführen)* |
| | **windmill** ['wɪndmɪl] | Windmühle | |
| | **wheat** [wiːt] | Weizen | |
| | (to) **grind** [graɪnd], **ground**, **ground** [graʊnd] | (zer)mahlen | |
| | **mural** ['mjʊərəl] | Wandgemälde | a large painting on a wall    (L) murus *(Mauer)* |
| | (to) **cover** sth. **up** [ˌkʌvər_'ʌp] | etwas abdecken, zudecken | There's a river under our house. It was ~ed up before the house was built.<br>(F) couvrir    (L) cooperire |
| | (to) **flow** [fləʊ] | fließen, strömen | The River Thames ~s into the North Sea.<br>verb: (to) **flow** – noun: **flow** *(Fließen, Fluss, Strom)* |
| | **well** [wel] | Quelle, Brunnen | My great-grandfather grew up on a farm. They had to get water from a ~ behind the house. |
| | **cellar** ['selə] | Keller | (L) cella *(Kammer, Zelle)* |
| | **anniversary** [ˌænɪ'vɜːsəri] | Jahrestag | Last weekend, my parents celebrated their 25th wedding ~.<br>(F) l'anniversaire *(m)*    (L) anniversaria *n pl* |
| | (to) **protect** sb./sth. **(from** sb./sth.**)** [prə'tekt] | jn./etwas (be)schützen (vor jm./etwas) | Wear a hat to ~ your head **from** the sun.<br>Animals might get dangerous if they're trying to ~ their young.    (F) protéger    (L) protegere |
| p. 17 | **opinion piece** [ə'pɪnjən piːs] | Stellungnahme | an article in which the writer expresses a personal opinion<br>(F) l'opinion *(f)*    (L) opinio, onis *f (Meinung)* |
| | **recently** ['riːsntli] | in letzter Zeit; vor Kurzem | There have been a lot of accidents in our street ~.<br>(F) récemment    (L) recens |
| | **childhood** ['tʃaɪldhʊd] | Kindheit | the time in your life when you are a child |
| | **haunt** [hɔːnt] | Lieblingsort | a place where you spend a lot of time:<br>This park was our favourite ~ when we were young. |
| | (to) **treat** sb. **to** sth. ['triːt] | jn. zu etwas einladen; jm. etwas spendieren | The special guests were ~ed **to** a magnificent show.<br>verb: (to) **treat sb. to sth.** –<br>noun: **treat** *(Hochgenuss, besonderes Vergnügen; (besondere) Leckerei)* |

*a **windmill***    *wheat*

*He's grinding coffee beans.*

# Unit 1  Vocabulary

| | | |
|---|---|---|
| **dialect** [ˈdaɪəlekt] | Dialekt | ❗ stress: **dialect** [ˈdaɪəlekt]<br>Ⓕ le dialecte   Ⓛ dialectus |
| **aroma** [əˈrəʊmə] | Duft, Aroma | Ⓕ l'arôme *(m)*   Ⓛ aroma *n* |
| **multicultural** [ˌmʌltiˈkʌltʃərəl] | multikulturell | adj: **multicultural** –<br>noun: **multiculturalism** [ˌmʌltiˈkʌltʃərəlɪzm]<br>(Multikulturismus, kulturelle Vielfalt)<br>Ⓕ multiculturel   Ⓛ multi *(viele)* + cultura *(Kultur)* |
| **vibe** [vaɪb] *(infml)* | Ausstrahlung, Atmosphäre | I love that club. It has such a cool ~. |
| **nationalist** [ˈnæʃnəlɪst] | Nationalist/in; nationalistisch | The Scottish ~s want Scotland to become independent from the UK.   Ⓕ le/la nationaliste |
| **(to) claim** [kleɪm] | angeben, behaupten | He looks about 15, but ~s he's 18.<br>verb: (to) **claim** – noun: **claim** (Behauptung) |
| **failure** [ˈfeɪljə] | Misserfolg, Fehlschlag | It was a ~. = It wasn't successful.<br>noun: **failure** – verb: (to) **fail** [feɪl]<br>(scheitern; (es) nicht schaffen) |
| **inhabitant** [ɪnˈhæbɪtənt] | Einwohner/in, Bewohner/in | In 1750, Munich had about 32,000 ~s.<br>Ⓕ l'habitant/e   Ⓛ inhabitantes *m pl* |
| **CE** [ˌsiːˈiː] (= **Common Era** [ˌkɒmən ˈɪərə]) | Christliche Zeitrechnung | 43 CE ◄► 43 BCE (= before the Common Era) |
| **immigrant** [ˈɪmɪɡrənt] | Einwanderer/Einwanderin | ❗ stress: **immigrant** [ˈɪmɪɡrənt]<br>Ⓕ l'immigré/e   Ⓛ immigrare *(einwandern)* |
| **province** [ˈprɒvɪns] | Provinz | ❗ stress: **province** [ˈprɒvɪns]<br>Ⓕ la province   Ⓛ provincia |
| **(ever) since** [ˌevə ˈsɪns] | seitdem, seither; seit | ❗ since =<br>1. *(prep)* seit – **since** 10 o'clock<br>2. *(adv)* seitdem, inzwischen – We saw Jill last May, but haven't seen her **(ever) since**. |
| **foreigner** [ˈfɒrənə] | Ausländer/in; Fremde(r) | noun: **foreigner** – adj: **foreign** [ˈfɒrən]<br>(ausländisch, fremd)<br>**foreign language** = Fremdsprache |
| **majority** [məˈdʒɒrəti] | Mehrheit, Mehrzahl | There are 16 girls and 13 boys in my class. The girls are in the ~.<br>Ⓕ la majorité   Ⓛ maior *(größer)* |
| **abroad** [əˈbrɔːd] | im/ins Ausland | = in or to another country |
| **(to) drive** [draɪv], **drove** [drəʊv], **driven** [ˈdrɪvn] | treiben; antreiben | The farmer **drove** the cows into another field.<br>Famine **drove** millions of people to leave the country.<br>❗ (to) **drive, drove, driven** =<br>1. fahren *(mit dem Auto)*; 2. treiben; antreiben |
| **persecution** [ˌpɜːsɪˈkjuːʃn] | Verfolgung | The ~ of Native Americans led to the deaths of millions.   Ⓕ la persécution   Ⓛ persequi *(verfolgen)* |
| **Jew** [dʒuː] | Jude/Jüdin | noun: **Jew** – adj: **Jewish** [ˈdʒuːɪʃ] *(jüdisch)*<br>Ⓕ le juif / la juive |
| **(to) flee (from)** [fliː], **fled, fled** [fled] | flüchten (aus), fliehen (vor) | Thousands of people **fled** their country.<br>They tried to ~ from the war. |
| **pogrom** [ˈpɒɡrəm] | Pogrom | ❗ stress and pronunciation: **pogrom** [ˈpɒɡrəm]<br>Ⓕ le pogrom |
| **the more …, the more …** | je mehr …, desto mehr … | **The** ~ you work here, **the** ~ money you can make. |

[eɪ] name · [aɪ] time · [ɔɪ] boy · [əʊ] old ·
[aʊ] town · [ɪə] here · [eə] where · [ʊə] tour

# Vocabulary Unit 1

| | | | |
|---|---|---|---|
| **people** [ˈpiːpl], *pl* **peoples** | Volk | | ❗ **people** =<br>1. Menschen – A lot of **people** are afraid of dogs.<br>2. Volk – the Zulu **people** (das Volk der Zulu)<br>the native **peoples** of Africa<br>(die Urvölker Afrikas)<br>ⓛ populus |
| (to) **attract** [əˈtrækt] | anziehen, anlocken | | London ~s millions of tourists every summer. |
| **war** [wɔː] | Krieg | | *German:* der **erste/zweite Weltkrieg**<br>*English:* the **First/Second World War** *or*<br>**World War I / World War II** |
| **policy** [ˈpɒləsi] | Politik *(politische Linie)*,<br>Richtlinie(n), Bestimmung(en) | | There's a "no junk food"-~ at my school.<br>**free-movement** ~ = Politik der Freizügigkeit (= der offenen Grenzen) *(in der EU)* |

> **German "Politik"**
> 1. *(politisches Leben, Geschehen)*    **politics** *(no pl)*    Are you interested in **politics**? – No, I think **politics** is boring.
> 2. *(politische Linie, Richtlinien)*    **policy**    What is the prime minister's **policy** on education?
> What is the company **policy** on working from home?

| | | |
|---|---|---|
| **mixture** [ˈmɪkstʃə] | Mischung | = mix     ⓛ mixtura |
| **unique** [juˈniːk] | einmalig, einzigartig | Our ketchup has a ~ and special taste.<br>Ⓕ unique    ⓛ unicus, a, um |
| **diversity** [daɪˈvɜːsəti] | Vielfalt | In London, you'll experience a unique ~ of people and cultures.<br>noun: **diversity** – adj: **diverse**<br>Ⓕ la diversité    ⓛ diversitas f *(Verschiedenheit)* |
| **race** [reɪs] | Rasse | noun: **race** – adj: **racial** [ˈreɪʃl]<br>(ethnisch, rassisch; Rassen-)<br>Big cities have lots of problems, some of them **racial** / some of them connected with **race**.<br>Ⓕ la race |
| **mythical** [ˈmɪθɪkl] | mythisch; fiktiv | Ⓕ mythique |
| **nostalgic** [nɒˈstældʒɪk] | nostalgisch | When I saw my old school, I felt very ~.<br>Ⓕ nostalgique |
| (to) **exist** [ɪɡˈzɪst] | existieren | Do you believe that life ~s on Mars?<br>Ⓕ exister    ⓛ exsistere |
| **tolerance (of/for)** [ˈtɒlərəns] | Toleranz (für/gegenüber) | noun: **tolerance** –<br>adj: **tolerant (of/towards)** [ˈtɒlərənt]<br>(tolerant (gegenüber))<br>❗ stress: **tolerance** [ˈtɒlərəns], **tolerant** [ˈtɒlərənt]<br>Ⓕ la tolérance    ⓛ tolerare *(ertragen, aushalten)* |
| (to) **transform** [trænsˈfɔːm] | (sich) verwandeln; umwandeln | They're planning to ~ the station into an art gallery.<br>Ⓕ transformer    ⓛ transformare |
| **brand** [brænd] | Marke, Markenname *(bei Produkten)* | My bike is from *RACERS*. What ~ is yours? |
| **byline** [ˈbaɪlaɪn] | Zeile mit Angabe des Verfassers/der Verfasserin eines Zeitungsartikels | |
| **headline** [ˈhedlaɪn] | Überschrift; Schlagzeile | |

# Unit 1 Vocabulary

| | | | |
|---|---|---|---|
| illustration [ˌɪləˈstreɪʃn] | Abbildung, Illustration | (F) l'illustration (f) | |
| immigration [ˌɪmɪˈgreɪʃn] | Einwanderung | (F) l'immigration (f) | |

**Auswanderung – Einwanderung**
| (to) emigrate | [ˈemɪgreɪt] | auswandern | (to) immigrate | [ˈɪmɪgreɪt] | einwandern |
|---|---|---|---|---|---|
| emigration | [ˌemɪˈgreɪʃn] | Auswanderung | immigration | [ˌɪmɪˈgreɪʃn] | Einwanderung |
| emigrant | [ˈemɪgrənt] | Auswanderer/Auswanderin | immigrant | [ˈɪmɪgrənt] | Einwanderer/Einwanderin |

| | | | | |
|---|---|---|---|---|
| p. 18 | active [ˈæktɪv] | aktiv | (F) actif/active (L) agere (handeln) | |
| | passive [ˈpæsɪv] | passiv | **active ◀▶ passive** (F) passif/passive (L) pati (ertragen) | |
| | (to) hold [həʊld], held, held [held] | abhalten (Veranstaltung) | Our next meeting will be **held** on the first Saturday in July. | |
| | (to) name [neɪm] | (be)nennen | We ~d our cat Blueberry. (= Her name is Blueberry.) noun: **name** – verb: (to) **name** | |
| | (to) burn [bɜːn] | brennen; verbrennen | The lights in the flat are ~**ing**. They must be in. Don't ~ the magazines. Recycle them instead. | |
| p. 19 | (to) design [dɪˈzaɪn] | entwerfen, konstruieren, entwickeln | What's your aunt's job? – She ~**s** cars. verb: (to) **design** – noun: **design** | |
| | escalator [ˈeskəleɪtə] | Rolltreppe | **an escalator** (F) l'escalier (mécanique) (m) | |
| p. 20 | formal [ˈfɔːml] | formell, förmlich | When you write a letter to your bank, it should be quite **formal**, but your emails to your friends can be **informal**.     **formal ◀▶ informal** ❗ stress: **formal** [ˈfɔːml] | |
| | fabulous [ˈfæbjələs] | sagenhaft, fabelhaft | | |
| | site [saɪt] | Ort, Platz, Stelle, Stätte | the ~ of the accident (Unfallstelle) a tourist ~ (touristischer Ort) | |
| | anywhere [ˈeniweə] | überall(hin) | Accidents can happen ~. | |
| | discovery [dɪˈskʌvəri] | Entdeckung | noun: **discovery** – verb: (to) **discover** [dɪˈskʌvə] (entdecken) | |
| | district [ˈdɪstrɪkt] | Bezirk, Gebiet, (Stadt-)Viertel | ❗ stress: **district** [ˈdɪstrɪkt] | |
| | bakery [ˈbeɪkəri] | Bäckerei | = baker's shop     **baker** [ˈbeɪkə] = Bäcker/in | |
| | loads of … [ləʊdz] (infml) | eine Menge (von) … | = lots of | |
| | neighbourhood (AE: neighborhood) [ˈneɪbəhʊd] | Viertel, Gegend, Umgebung; Nachbarschaft | Do you live in a poor or rich ~? | |
| | lively [ˈlaɪvli] | lebendig, lebhaft | My grandma is still very ~ at 75. She goes dancing twice a week. | |
| | case [keɪs] | Fall | In ~ of fire do not use the elevator! Take an umbrella **in** ~ it rains. (… falls es regnet.) | |

# Vocabulary Unit 1

| | | |
|---|---|---|
| **absolute** [ˈæbsəluːt] | absolut | ❗ stress: **absolute** [ˈæbsəluːt]<br>adj: **absolute** – a monarch's **absolute** power<br>adv: **absolutely** [ˈæbsəluːtli]<br>(absolut, vollkommen, total)<br>I wasn't just hungry, I was **absolutely** starving.<br>The show was **absolutely** fantastic.<br>❗ Wenn **absolutely** als zustimmende Antwort benutzt wird, liegt die Hauptbetonung auf der 3. Silbe:<br>The show was fantastic, wasn't it?<br>– **Absolutely**! [ˌæbsəˈluːtli]<br>Ⓕ absolu   Ⓛ absolutus, a, um |
| p.21 **volunteer** [ˌvɒlənˈtɪə] | Freiwillige(r), Ehrenamtliche(r) | ❗ • **volunteer** *(noun)* – I work as a **volunteer** for a charity.<br>• (to) **volunteer** *(verb)* – I **volunteer** for a charity. (freiwillig/ehrenamtlich arbeiten *(unbezahlt)*)<br>• **volunteer** *(adj)* – I do **volunteer** work for a charity.<br>Ⓕ le/la volontaire   Ⓛ voluntarius |
| **subject** [ˈsʌbdʒɪkt] | Thema; *(in E-Mails)* Betreff | I'm reading a book on the ~ of terrorism.   Ⓕ le sujet<br>❗ **subject** = 1. Schulfach<br>2. Thema; *(in E-Mails)* Betreff |
| **contact details** *(pl)* [ˈkɒntækt ˌdiːteɪlz] | Kontaktdaten | |
| **grateful** [ˈgreɪtfl] | dankbar | We are ~ for the help they offered.<br>Ⓛ gratus, a, um |
| **in advance** [ədˈvɑːns] | im Voraus | I've already made tomorrow's lunch in ~. |
| **Yours sincerely** [ˌjɔːz sɪnˈsɪəli] | Mit freundlichen Grüßen *(Briefschluss)* | |
| **All the best** [ˌɔːl ðə ˈbest] | Mit besten Grüßen / Alles Gute *(Briefschluss)* | |
| **Yours, Finn** [jɔːz] | Dein/Euer Finn *(Briefschluss)* | |

## Part C

| | | |
|---|---|---|
| p.22 **monument (to)** [ˈmɒnjumənt] | Monument, Denkmal (für/zum Gedenken an) | ❗ stress: **monument** [ˈmɒnjumənt]<br>Ⓕ le monument   Ⓛ monumentum |
| **spiral** [ˈspaɪrəl] | spiralförmig | ❗ stress: **spiral** [ˈspaɪrəl]<br>Ⓕ en spirale   Ⓛ spira *(Spirale)* |
| **staircase** [ˈsteəkeɪs] | Treppe; Treppenhaus | a **spiral staircase** *(eine Wendeltreppe)* |
| (to) **regret** [rɪˈgret] | bedauern, bereuen | I'm so sorry! I really ~ what I did to you.<br>verb: (to) **regret** – noun: **regret** (Bedauern)<br>Ⓕ regretter |

[iː] green · [i] happy · [ɪ] big · [e] red · [æ] cat · [ɑː] class · [ɒ] song · [ɔː] door · [uː] blue · [ʊ] book · [ʌ] mum · [ɜː] girl · [ə] a partner

# Unit 1  Vocabulary

| | | |
|---|---|---|
| (to) **emerge (from …)** [ɪˈmɜːdʒ] | herauskommen, hervortreten, auftauchen (aus …) | Suddenly three men ~d from the forest. She came up the dark staircase and ~d into the light. Give me a call if problems ~. ⓛ emergere |
| **daylight** [ˈdeɪlaɪt] | Tageslicht | |
| (to) **be all ears** [ˌɔːl ˈɪəz] (infml) | ganz Ohr sein (gespannt zuhören) | We were all ~ as Grandpa told his story. |
| (to) **commemorate** sb./sth. [kəˈmeməreɪt] | jemandes/einer Sache gedenken | The monument ~s the Battle of Trafalgar and all the people that died there. ⓛ commemorare |
| (to) **last (for)** [lɑːst] | (an)dauern; halten (von Bestand sein) | The concert will ~ (for) about an hour. Cheap toys often don't ~ very long. |
| **nickname** [ˈnɪkneɪm] | Spitzname | |

p. 23

> **so**
> - In Antworten auf Entscheidungsfragen wird nach Verben wie **think**, **hope**, **guess**, **expect** oft **so** verwendet:
>   Is Evie home? – I **think so**. / I **don't think so**. / I **guess so**. / I **expect so**.   Will she get the job? – I **hope so**.
> - Um die Wiederholung von Informationen aus der vorhergehenden Äußerung zu vermeiden, steht **so** …
>   – nach **say** und **tell sb.**:
>   They're going to win the match. Everybody **says so**.   Emily is getting married. Her mother **told me so**.
>   That's a stupid idea. – Who **says so**?   If you don't want to join us, just **say so**.
>   – nach **if**:
>   Would you like to visit London? **If so**, what would you do there?

| | | |
|---|---|---|
| **role-play** [ˈrəʊl pleɪ] | Rollenspiel | |
| p. 24 **normal** [ˈnɔːml] | normal | |
| **bill** [bɪl] | Rechnung | the bill |

p. 25

| | | |
|---|---|---|
| **brick** [brɪk] | Ziegelstein; Ziegel- | |
| **upwards** [ˈʌpwədz] | nach oben | A spiral staircase leads ~ to the top of the tower. |
| **idiom** [ˈɪdiəm] | Redewendung | a phrase whose meaning you can't guess from the meanings of the words that make up the phrase Ⓕ l'idiome (m)  ⓛ idioma n |
| (to) **pull** sb.'s **leg** (infml) | jn. auf den Arm nehmen (veräppeln) | He's not serious – he's just **pulling your** ~. |
| (to) **mind** [maɪnd] | aufpassen auf, achten auf | **Mind the doors.** (im Bahnhof: Vorsicht an den Türen!) **Mind your head.** (Pass auf deinen Kopf auf! / Kopf weg!) |
| **Congratulations (on** sth.**)!** [kənˌɡrætʃʊˈleɪʃnz] | Herzlichen Glückwunsch (zu etwas)! | ~ **on** finding a new job! ⓛ congratulari (beglückwünschen) |

[eɪ] name · [aɪ] time · [ɔɪ] boy · [əʊ] old ·
[aʊ] town · [ɪə] here · [eə] where · [ʊə] tour

# Vocabulary Unit 1

## Text: Escape from Uncle Jack

| p.26 | Latin ['lætɪn] | lateinisch; Latein | |
| | (to) steal [stiːl], stole [stəʊl], stolen ['stəʊlən] | stehlen, rauben | My bike is gone! Someone has **stolen** my bike! |
| | (to) abandon [əˈbændən] | zurücklassen, verlassen, im Stich lassen | I think it's terrible how people ~ dogs on busy roads. (F) abandonner |
| | (to) separate ['sepəreɪt] | trennen | It's not right to ~ children from their parents. (F) séparer (L) separare |
| | (to) freeze [friːz], froze [frəʊz], frozen ['frəʊzn] | (ge)frieren; erstarren | Rivers and lakes sometimes ~ in winter. Suddenly the lights went out, and I **froze**. |
| | (to) search for sth. [sɜːtʃ] | (nach) etwas suchen | The police ~ed for clues, but they couldn't find any. verb: (to) search – noun: search (Suche) |
| | pain [peɪn] | Schmerz(en) | The doctor asked me where the ~ was exactly. |
| | (to) stumble ['stʌmbl] | stolpern; torkeln | As I was coming in, I ~d over the dog. That man is **stumbling** terribly – is he ill, perhaps? |
| | backwards ['bækwədz] | rückwärts, nach hinten | Dad still finds it difficult to drive ~. He stumbled ~ and fell down the stairs. |
| | On the one hand … On the other hand … | Einerseits … Andererseits … | On the one ~, Australia is close to Asia. On the other ~, it has a strong British tradition. |
| | cry [kraɪ] | Schrei, Ruf | verb: (to) cry – noun: cry |
| | direction [dəˈrekʃn] | Richtung | That's the wrong way. We must go in the opposite ~. (F) la direction |
| | frequent [ˈfriːkwənt] | häufig | Mum ~**ly** flies to the USA, about 10 times a year. (F) fréquent |
| | (to) lift sth. up [ˌlɪft ˈʌp] | etwas hochheben | Can you ~ this rock **up**? It's very heavy. |
| | (to) prove [pruːv] | nachweisen, beweisen | Is that right? Can you ~ it? (F) prouver (L) probare |
| p.27 | support [səˈpɔːt] | Unterstützung | verb: (to) support – My parents always **support** my dreams and plans. noun: support – My parents are a great **support**. |
| | (to) be trapped [træpt] | gefangen sein, in der Falle sitzen | The dog **was** ~ in the attic for five hours. |
| | heat [hiːt] | Hitze, Wärme | noun: heat verb: (to) heat (erwärmen, erhitzen) adj: hot |
| | smoke [sməʊk] | Rauch | verb: (to) smoke (rauchen) – noun: smoke |
| | (to) trust [trʌst] | trauen, vertrauen | She's a friend of the family. You can ~ her. verb: (to) trust – noun: trust (Vertrauen) |
| | repeatedly [rɪˈpiːtɪdli] | wiederholt | We have ~ pointed out that problems might emerge. |
| | distance ['dɪstəns] | Distanz, Entfernung; Strecke | (to) keep your distance (from) = Abstand halten (zu/von) (F) la distance (L) distantia |
| | certain ['sɜːtn] | sichere(r, s); gewisse(r, s), bestimmte(r, s) | That would mean ~ disaster / ~ death. Try to learn a ~ number of new words each week. A ~ Mr Davidson called this morning. (F) certain (L) certus |
| | (to) creep [kriːp], crept, crept [krept] | schleichen; kriechen | A man **was** ~**ing** quietly along the wall outside our house. |

# Unit 1  Vocabulary

| | | | |
|---|---|---|---|
| | **protective** [prəˈtektɪv] | schützend, beschützend, Schutz- | verb: (to) **protect** – Animals usually try to **protect** their young.<br>adj: **protective** – We had to wear a **protective** jacket.<br>adv: **protectively** – She stepped **protectively** in front of her children.<br>Ⓛ protegere *(schützen)* |
| p. 28 | (to) **reach out a hand (to** sb.**)** [ˌriːtʃ ˈaʊt] | die Hand ausstrecken (nach jm.) | Dad ~ed out a hand to Mum to help her to the top of the mountain. |
| | (to) **bend over** [ˌbend ˈəʊvə], **bent, bent** [bent] | sich bücken, sich vorbeugen | The door was so small that I had to ~ **over** to get in. |
| | **sweat** [swet] | Schweiß | noun: **sweat** – verb: (to) **sweat** (schwitzen)<br>❗ pronunciation: **sweat** [swet] |
| | (to) **be frightened of** sth. [ˈfraɪtnd] | Angst haben vor etwas | Don't **be** ~ of the thunder. It sounds scary but isn't dangerous.<br>**frightened** *(adj)* = verängstigt |
| | (to) **swallow** [ˈswɒləʊ] | (ver)schlucken | He thought he was going to be sick when he realized that he had ~ed a spider. |
| | **weak** [wiːk] | schwach | **weak** ◀▶ **strong** |
| p. 29 | (to) **float** [fləʊt] | schwimmen, *(auf der Wasseroberfläche)* treiben | Wood ~s on water; stones don't. |
| | **by the time** [ˌbaɪ ðə ˈtaɪm] | als; wenn | ❗ **by the time** =<br>1. als – **By the time** we arrived, the concert had already started.<br>2. wenn – I'll have dinner ready **by the time** you get back. |
| | (to) **stink** [stɪŋk], **stank** [stæŋk], **stunk** [stʌŋk] | stinken | The water looked dirty and **stank**.<br>His breath **stank** of onions. |
| | (to) **hesitate** [ˈhezɪteɪt] | zögern | Don't ~ to get in touch if there is anything I can do.<br>Ⓕ hésiter  Ⓛ haesitare |

## Checkpoint

| | | | |
|---|---|---|---|
| p. 31 | **financial** [faɪˈnænʃl] | finanziell | ❗ stress: fi**na**ncial [faɪˈnænʃl] |
| p. 32 | (to) **employ** sb. [ɪmˈplɔɪ] | jn. anstellen, beschäftigen | My uncle's company ~s over 1,000 people. |
| | **flight** [flaɪt] | Flug | noun: **flight** – verb: (to) **fly, flew, flown** |
| | **hub** [hʌb] | Mittelpunkt, (Verkehrs-)Knotenpunkt | |
| p. 33 | **hide-and-seek** [ˌhaɪd ən ˈsiːk] | Versteckspiel | |

## Access to cultures: Guy Fawkes

| | | | |
|---|---|---|---|
| p. 34 | **gunpowder** [ˈgʌnpaʊdə] | Schießpulver | |
| | **plot** [plɒt] | Verschwörung | noun: **plot** – verb: (to) **plot** (sich verschwören) |
| | **conspirator** [kənˈspɪrətə] | Verschwörer/in | Over 20 ~s took part in the plot.  Ⓛ conspiratus |

[f] **f**ather · [v] ri**v**er · [s] **s**ister · [z] plea**s**e · [ʃ] **sh**op · [ʒ] televi**s**ion ·
[tʃ] **t**eacher · [dʒ] **G**ermany · [θ] **th**anks · [ð] **th**is · [h] **h**ere

# Vocabulary Unit 1

| | | | |
|---|---|---|---|
| **bonfire** [ˈbɒnfaɪə] | (großes Freuden-)Feuer | | a **bonfire** |
| **guy** [gaɪ] | Guy-Fawkes-Puppe | ❗ **guy** = 1. Typ, Kerl; 2. **guys** *(pl)* Leute; 3. Guy-Fawkes-Puppe | |
| (to) **part with** sth. [ˈpɑːt wɪð] | sich von etwas trennen | I love my dog so much. I could never ~ **with** him. | |
| **vendetta** [venˈdetə] | Blutrache; Hetzkampagne | The two families hate each other and have had a ~ for 20 years. | |
| **graphic** [ˈgræfɪk] | grafisch; anschaulich | The news reported about the plane crash in ~ detail. **graphic novel** = Bildroman, Comicroman | |
| **nuclear** [ˈnjuːklɪə] | Kern-, Atom-, Nuklear- | ~ **power** = Atomenergie, Kernenergie  (F) nucléaire  (L) nucleus *(Kern)* | |
| **fascist** [ˈfæʃɪst] | faschistisch | adj: **fascist** – noun: **fascist** (Faschist/in) | |
| **rebel** [ˈrebəl] | Rebell/in | ❗ stress: **rebel** [ˈrebəl] | |
| **explosive** [ɪkˈspləʊsɪv] | Sprengstoff; Sprengsatz | noun: **explosive** – adj: **explosive** (explosiv) | |
| p. 35  **anonymous** [əˈnɒnɪməs] | anonym | ❗ stress: **anonymous** [əˈnɒnɪməs] | |
| (to) **admire** [ədˈmaɪə] | bewundern | She's a great artist. I ~ her paintings and sculptures.  (F) admirer  (L) admirari | |
| **identity** [aɪˈdentəti] | Identität | ❗ stress: **identity** [aɪˈdentəti] | |
| **resistance** [rɪˈzɪstəns] | Widerstand | This is an unusual plan. Do you expect ~?  (F) la résistance  (L) resistere *(Widerstand leisten)* | |
| **somehow** [ˈsʌmhaʊ] | irgendwie | **Somehow** they managed to escape from prison. | |
| **barrel** [ˈbærəl] | Fass | | a **barrel** |
| **complete** [kəmˈpliːt] | vollständig, komplett | adj: **complete** –  (F) complet/complète  verb: (to) **complete** (vervollständigen) | |
| (to) **blow** sth. **up** [ˌbləʊ ˈʌp] | etwas in die Luft sprengen | Terrorists tried to ~ **up** the local police station this morning. | |
| (to) **invent** [ɪnˈvent] | erfinden | (F) inventer  (L) invenire  verb: (to) **invent** – noun: **invention** (Erfindung) | |
| (to) **torture** [ˈtɔːtʃə] | foltern, quälen | verb: (to) **torture** – noun: **torture** (Folter)  (F) torturer  (L) torquere | |
| **rebellion** [rɪˈbeljən] | Rebellion, Aufstand | ❗ stress: **rebellion** [rɪˈbeljən]  (F) la rébellion | |
| (to) **execute** [ˈeksɪkjuːt] | hinrichten | verb: (to) **execute** –  noun: **execution** [ˌeksɪˈkjuːʃn] (Hinrichtung)  (F) exécuter  (L) exsequi, exesecutus sum *(strafen)* | |
| **pike** [paɪk] | Spieß | | a **pike** |

[iː] green · [i] happy · [ɪ] big · [e] red · [æ] cat · [ɑː] class · [ɒ] song ·
[ɔː] door · [uː] blue · [ʊ] book · [ʌ] mum · [ɜː] girl · [ə] a partner

# Unit 2  Vocabulary

## Unit 2  Canada

| | | | |
|---|---|---|---|
| pp. 38/39 | **rink** [rɪŋk]<br>(*kurz für* **ice rink, skating rink**) | Eisbahn; Rollschuhbahn | an **ice rink** |
| | **polar bear** [ˈpəʊlə beə] | Eisbär | ❗ stress: **polar** [ˈpəʊlə] (= polar) |
| | **chart** [tʃɑːt] | Diagramm; Tabelle | 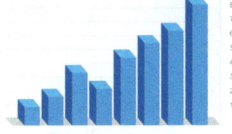 a **bar chart** (ein Balkendiagramm)   **pie charts** (Tortendiagramme) |
| | **sportscast** [ˈspɔːtskɑːst] *(AE)* | Sportsendung | |
| | **tournament** [ˈtʊənəmənt], [ˈtɔːnəmənt] | Turnier | Ⓕ le tournoi |

## Part A

| | | | |
|---|---|---|---|
| p. 40 | **eager** [ˈiːɡə] | eifrig; begeistert | (to) **be eager to do** sth. = etwas unbedingt tun wollen |
| | **beaver** [ˈbiːvə] | Biber |  a **beaver**<br>an **eager beaver** = *jemand, der eifrig und fleißig ist* |
| | (to) **compete (with)** [kəmˈpiːt] | *(in Wettbewerben)* antreten *(gegen);* konkurrieren *(mit)* | He ~d for Germany against England.<br>verb: (to) **compete** – noun: **competition**<br>Ⓛ competere *(etwas zugleich wollen)* |
| | (to) **bake** [beɪk] | backen | a **bake sale** = ein Kuchenbasar |
| | **spirit** [ˈspɪrɪt] | Geist, Seele; Stimmung; Einstellung | ❗ German **Geist** = 1. *(Gespenst)* **ghost**;<br>                         2. *(Seele)* **spirit**   Ⓛ spiritus *m*<br>They won the match because their team ~ was better.<br>I'll have a go. – That's the ~!<br>(to) **lift sb.'s spirits** = jn. aufmuntern |
| | **case** [keɪs] | Kiste *(Getränke)*; Behälter, Kasten, Gehäuse | a ~ of orange juice/beer/wine   (Kiste, Kasten)<br>a pencil ~                         (Federmäppchen)<br>a glass ~ *(in a shop/museum)*    (Vitrine) |
| | (to) **turn** sb./sth. **into** sth. /<br>(to) **turn into** sth. | jn./etwas in etwas verwandeln / sich in etwas verwandeln, zu etwas w**e**rden | Jesus ~ed water **into** wine.<br>Do you know why water ~s **into** ice when it's cold? |
| | **coach** [kəʊtʃ] | Trainer/in | |
| | **coed** [ˌkəʊˈed]<br>(= **co-educational** [ˌkəʊ_edʒuˈkeɪʃənl]) | koedukativ, gemischt *(mit beiden Geschlechtern; z.B. Schulen)* | Very few boarding schools are ~. Most are just for boys or for girls. |
| | (to) **keep up (with** sb.**)** [ˌkiːp_ˈʌp] | *(mit jm.)* Schritt halten | I've stopped going jogging with my older brother. He's too fast for me, and I can't ~ **up with** him. |
| p. 41 | **primary school** [ˈpraɪməri skuːl] | Grundschule | |

[eɪ] n**a**me · [aɪ] t**i**me · [ɔɪ] b**oy** · [əʊ] **o**ld ·
[aʊ] t**ow**n · [ɪə] h**e**re · [eə] wh**e**re · [ʊə] t**ou**r

# Vocabulary Unit 2

| | | |
|---|---|---|
| **middle school** [ˈmɪdl skuːl] (AE) | Mittelschule *(für 11- bis 14-Jährige)* | |
| **Inuit** [ˈɪnjuɪt] | Inuit *(kanadische Ureinwohner/innen)* | |
| **Inuktitut** [ɪˈnʊktɪtʊt] | Inuktitut *(Sprache der Inuit)* | |
| **igloo** [ˈɪgluː] | Iglu | an **igloo** |
| **stereotype** [ˈsteriətaɪp] | Stereotyp, Klischee(vorstellung) | The film's main character doesn't seem real to me. She's just the ~ of a schoolgirl in love. noun: **stereotype** – adj: **stereotypical** [ˌsteriəˈtɪpɪkl] *(stereotyp, klischeehaft)* (F) le stéréotype |
| **elder** [ˈeldə] | Älteste(r) *(z.B. eines Stammes)* | |
| **community** [kəˈmjuːnəti] | Gemeinschaft, Gemeinde | Bayern Munich have a big ~ of fans all over Germany. (F) la communauté (L) communis, -e *(gemeinsam)* |
| **mostly** [ˈməʊstli] | größtenteils, hauptsächlich; meistens | We ~ grow potatoes in our garden. The milk we drink is ~ from cows. |
| **frosting** [ˈfrɒstɪŋ] | Zuckerguss | |
| **skin** [skɪn] | Haut; Fell | People shouldn't have disadvantages because of the colour of their ~. |
| **blubber** [ˈblʌbə] | Tran *(aus dem Speck von Walen, Robben o. Fischen gewonnenes Öl)* | |
| **order** [ˈɔːdə] | Bestellung | noun: **order** – verb: (to) **order** |
| **poutine** [puːˈtiːn] | Poutine *(Pommes frites mit Käse in Bratensoße)* | |
| (to) **serve** [sɜːv] | servieren *(Essen, Getränke)*; bedienen *(Kundschaft)*; dienen | Who can ~ the drinks at our party? I want to work at a pub. It must be fun to ~ people. I think it's a mayor's job to ~ the community. verb: (to) **serve** – noun: **service** *(Dienst(leistung), Service)* (F) servir (L) servire |
| (to) **fry** [fraɪ] | braten *(in der Pfanne)* | **fried eggs** |
| **curds** *(pl)* [kɜːdz] | Quark | |
| **gravy** [ˈgreɪvi] | Bratensoße | |
| **personal** [ˈpɜːsənl] | persönlich | Could we meet? I need to talk about a ~ problem. (F) personnel, le (L) personalis, e |
| **thankful** [ˈθæŋkfl] | dankbar | The accident was terrible, but he was ~ he was still alive. |
| **colloquial** [kəˈləʊkwiəl] | umgangssprachlich | "Kids" is a ~ word for "children". (L) colloqui *(sich unterhalten)* |
| **informational** [ˌɪnfəˈmeɪʃnl] | Informations- | |
| **descriptive** [dɪˈskrɪptɪv] | beschreibend | verb: (to) **describe** – adj: **descriptive** (F) descriptif/-ive (L) describere *(beschreiben)* |

# Unit 2 Vocabulary

| | | | |
|---|---|---|---|
| p. 42 | **agreement** [ə'gri:mənt] | Einigung; Zustimmung; Vereinbarung, Absprache | We reached ~ after five hours.<br>Do I have your ~ on my plan?<br>No, the ~ was that we are staying home tonight.<br>verb: (to) **agree on** sth. / **with** sb. –<br>noun: **agreement** |
| | **exit** ['eksɪt] | Ausgang; Ausfahrt | **entrance** ◄► **exit**    Ⓛ *exitus m* |
| p. 43 | **optional** ['ɒpʃənl] | wahlweise, freiwillig | adj: **optional** – noun: **option** ['ɒpʃn]<br>(Wahl(möglichkeit), Option) |
| | **unhealthy** [ʌn'helθi] | ungesund | **healthy** ◄► **unhealthy**<br>adj: **(un)healthy** – noun: **health** (Gesundheit) |
| | **grade** [greɪd] *(AE)* | Klasse, Jahrgang(sstufe); (Schul-)Note, Zensur | = BE 1. **(school) year**;<br>2. **mark** [mɑːk] (Schulnote, Zensur)<br>I'm in third **grade** *(AE)* / in the third **year** *(BE)*.<br>This year I'll get good **grades** *(AE)* / **marks** *(BE)* in maths and science. |
| | **exception** [ɪk'sepʃn] | Ausnahme | noun: **exception** – adj: **exceptional** [ɪk'sepʃənl]<br>(außergewöhnlich) |
| p. 44 | **description** [dɪ'skrɪpʃn] | Beschreibung | verb: (to) **describe** – noun: **description** –<br>adj: **descriptive**<br>Ⓕ *la description*   Ⓛ *describere (beschreiben)* |
| | **bookmark** ['bʊkmɑːk] | Lesezeichen | noun: **bookmark** – verb: (to) **bookmark** (markieren; zu den Lesezeichen hinzufügen *(Computer)*) |
| | **guideline** ['gaɪdlaɪn] | Richtlinie | These are just ~s and not the law. |
| p. 45 | **statistics** *(pl)* [stə'tɪstɪks] | Statistik(en) | ❗ The **statistics show** that … =<br>die Statistik zeigt / die Statistiken zeigen, dass …<br>noun: **statistics** – adj: **statistical** [stə'tɪstɪkl]<br>(statistisch) |
| | **competitive** [kəm'petətɪv] | leistungsorientiert, ehrgeizig; wettbewerbsorientiert | Olivia is very ~ and always wants to win.<br>This isn't a ~ race – it's just for fun.<br>verb: (to) **compete** – noun: **competition** –<br>adj: **competitive** |
| | (to) **state** [steɪt] | darlegen, erklären | The president ~d that he would introduce a new law.<br>verb: (to) **state** – noun: **statement** ['steɪtmənt]<br>(Aussage(satz); Feststellung, Behauptung) |
| | **evidence** *(no pl)* ['evɪdəns] | Nachweis(e), Beweis(e) | There was no ~ that Mr Wainwright was the thief. |
| | (to) **back** sth. **up** [ˌbæk _'ʌp] | etwas belegen; etwas untermauern, etwas bekräftigen | That sounds unlikely. Do you have facts to ~ **up** your opinion? |
| | **solution (to)** [sə'luːʃn] | Lösung (für) *(Problem; Aufgabe)* | noun: **solution (to)** –     Ⓕ *la solution*   Ⓛ *solutio*<br>verb: (to) **solve** [sɒlv] (lösen *(Problem)*, lüften) |
| | **reality** [ri'ælɪti] | Realität, Wirklichkeit | ❗ stress: re**a**lity [ri'ælɪti]    Ⓕ *la réalité*<br>adj: **real** – noun: **reality** |
| | **comparison** [kəm'pærɪsn] | Vergleich | On this website you can **make** ~s between different schools.    Ⓕ *la comparaison*   Ⓛ *comparare*<br>English:  (to) **make comparisons**<br>German:  **Vergleiche anstellen**<br>verb: (to) **compare** – noun: **comparison** |
| | (to) **order** ['ɔːdə] | ordnen, anordnen | verb: (to) **order** – noun: **order** (Reihenfolge) |

[f] **f**ather · [v] ri**v**er · [s] **s**ister · [z] plea**s**e · [ʃ] **sh**op · [ʒ] televi**s**ion ·
[tʃ] **t**eacher · [dʒ] **G**ermany · [θ] **th**anks · [ð] **th**is · [h] **h**ere

# Vocabulary Unit 2

| | | |
|---|---|---|
| in the first place | erstens, in erster Linie; überhaupt | In the first ~, you need to get your facts right. But why did she marry him in the first ~? |
| **Firstly** ['fɜːstli], … **Secondly** ['sekəndli], … **Thirdly**, … ['θɜːdli] | Erstens … Zweitens … Drittens … | There's a lot of shopping to do: **firstly**, we need something to eat. **Secondly**, we have to get some drinks. And **thirdly**, … |

## Part B

| | | | |
|---|---|---|---|
| p. 46 | (to) **come true** | wahr werden | I hope all your dreams will ~ **true**. *English:* a dream **come true** *German:* ein **wahr gewordener** Traum |
| | (to) **ski** [skiː] | Ski laufen, Ski fahren | verb: (to) **ski** – nouns: 1. *(equipment)* **ski(s)** 2. *(person)* **skier** (Skiläufer/in) |
| | (to) **inspire** [ɪnˈspaɪə] | inspirieren | It was the pope who ~**d** her to work in Africa. (F) inspirer (L) inspirare |
| | **territory** ['terətri] | Gebiet, Territorium | |
| | (to) **set out** [ˌset ˈaʊt] | aufbrechen, sich auf den Weg machen | |

| (to) **set, set, set** | | | |
|---|---|---|---|
| 1. (to) **set, set, set** | legen, stellen, setzen; untergehen *(Sonne)* | Shall we **set** the presents on the table over there? The sun **set** at 9 pm last night. | |
| 2. (to) **set** sth. **up** | etwas aufstellen, aufbauen, errichten; etwas einrichten | It took half an hour to **set up the tent**. It took me 20 minutes to **set up** my new computer. They want to **set up** a national park near our home. | |
| 3. (to) **set out** | aufbrechen, sich auf den Weg machen | It's a long walk, so let's **set out** early. | |

| | | |
|---|---|---|
| **cross-country** [ˌkrɒs ˈkʌntri] | Skilanglauf; Querfeldeinrennen | |
| **gear** [gɪə] | Ausrüstung | You don't need a lot of ~ to go swimming. |
| **version** ['vɜːʃn] | Version | ❗ stress: **version** ['vɜːʃn]   (F) la version |
| (to) **be made up of** | sich zusammensetzen aus; gebildet sein/werden aus | The group **is** ~ **up of** students from different schools. |
| **expedition** [ˌekspəˈdɪʃn] | Expedition | ❗ stress: **expedition** [ˌekspəˈdɪʃn] (F) l'expédition (f)   (L) expeditio f |
| (to) **witness** sth. ['wɪtnəs] | etwas (mit)erleben, Zeuge/Zeugin werden von etwas | verb: (to) **witness** – noun: **witness** (Zeuge/Zeugin) |
| (to) **recreate** sth. [ˌriːkriˈeɪt] | etwas nachbilden, nachmachen | = (to) do sth. again, (to) create sth. again |
| (to) **rename** sth. [ˌriːˈneɪm] | etwas umbenennen, umtaufen | = (to) give sth. a new name |
| **fellow** ['feləʊ] | Mit- | your **fellow** students = the other students from your class/course (deine Mitschüler/innen) |
| **terrain** [təˈreɪn] | Terrain, Gelände | (F) le terrain |
| **recent** ['riːsnt] | aktuell, jüngst; kürzlich geschehen/erfolgt | (F) récent   (L) recens |

| **recent** *(adj)* – **recently** *(adv)* | |
|---|---|
| **Recent** research shows that … | **Jüngste** Forschungen zeigen, dass … |
| In the light of **recent** events … | Im Licht der **aktuellen** Ereignisse, … |
| I've done a lot of sport in **recent** weeks. | In den **letzten** Wochen habe ich viel Sport gemacht. |
| I talked to them just **recently**. | Ich habe erst **vor Kurzem** mit ihnen gesprochen. |
| There've been a lot of accidents in our street **recently**. | Es hat **in letzter Zeit** viele Unfälle … gegeben. |

## Unit 2 Vocabulary

| | | | |
|---|---|---|---|
| **dozen** [ˈdʌzn], *pl* **dozen** | Dutzend | ❗ | two **dozen** eggs = zwei Dutzend Eier<br>*but:* **dozens** of people = dutzende Leute |
| **hall** [hɔːl] | Halle, Saal | | Our town has a new concert ~.<br>Our school band played in the **school** ~. (Aula) |
| (to) **head out** [ˌhed ˈaʊt] | aufbrechen, sich auf den Weg machen | | = (to) set out |
| (to) **sign up (for)** [ˌsaɪn ˈʌp] | sich anmelden (für) | | Dad has just ~**ed up** for a cooking class.<br>(to) **sign** sth. = etwas unterschreiben |
| **tough** [tʌf] | (knall)hart; zäh, robust | | Rugby is a ~ game, and rugby players are ~ people. |
| p. 47 **protection** [prəˈtekʃn] | Schutz | | A hat is good ~ against the sun.<br>(F) la protection   (L) protegere *(schützen)* |
| **lack (of)** [læk] | Mangel (an) | | noun: **lack** – Why didn't you help? Was it for ~ of courage? (aus Mangel an)<br>verb: (to) **lack** – Why didn't you help? Was it because you ~**ed** courage? (weil dir/euch der Mut fehlte) |
| **hilly** [ˈhɪli] | hügelig | | It's a ~ area. = There are a lot of hills in the area. |
| (to) **sit** sb. **down** | jn. bitten, sich hinzusetzen | | The secretary **sat** me ~ and told me to wait. |
| (to) **encourage** [ɪnˈkʌrɪdʒ] | ermutigen, ermuntern | | My friends ~**d** me to look for a new job.<br>verb: (to) **encourage** – noun: **courage**<br>(F) encourager |
| **at a time** | gleichzeitig, auf einmal; jeweils | | |

| **... at a time** | | |
|---|---|---|
| **one at a time** | Don't panic. Just try and do the tasks **one at a time**.<br>Please enter **one at a time**.<br>We'll have to check the whole building, **one floor at a time**. | einzeln, nacheinander<br>einzeln, einer nach dem anderen<br>Stockwerk für Stockwerk |
| **two/three at a time** | She took the stairs **two at a time**.<br>The actors entered the stage **two at a time**.<br>My violin teacher always teaches **three students at a time**. | zwei Stufen auf einmal<br>jeweils zu zweit<br>drei Schüler/innen gleichzeitig |

| | | | |
|---|---|---|---|
| **lens** [lenz] | (Kamera-)Objektiv, Linse *(Optik)* | | |
| (to) **interact** [ˌɪntərˈækt] | (miteinander) interagieren, kommunizieren | | verb: (to) **interact** – noun: **interaction** –<br>adj: **interactive** |
| **ideal** [aɪˈdɪəl] | ideal | ❗ | stress: **ideal** [aɪˈdɪəl]   (F) idéal |
| (to) **frustrate** [frʌˈstreɪt] | frustrieren | ❗ | • **frustrating** – We weren't successful. It was very **frustrating**. (frustrierend)<br>• **frustrated** – We were very **frustrated**. (frustriert)<br>(L) frustra *(vergeblich)* |
| **perseverance** [ˌpɜːsɪˈvɪərəns] | Ausdauer, Beharrlichkeit | | You can't stop yet! Don't you have any ~?<br>(L) perseverare *(beharrlich sein)* |
| (to) **recall** sth. [rɪˈkɔːl] | sich an etwas erinnern | | = (to) remember sth. |
| (to) **develop** [dɪˈveləp] | (sich) entwickeln | | verb: (to) **develop** –<br>noun: **development** [dɪˈveləpmənt] (Entwicklung) |
| **blister** [ˈblɪstə] | Blase (z.B. auf der Haut) | | |

a **blister**

[eɪ] name · [aɪ] time · [ɔɪ] boy · [əʊ] old ·
[aʊ] town · [ɪə] here · [eə] where · [ʊə] tour

# Vocabulary Unit 2

**yet** [jet]      (und) doch, dennoch

> **yet**
> 1. He was handsome and successful, and **yet** he often felt unhappy.     (und) doch, dennoch
> 2. Have you done your homework **yet**?     schon?
> 3. No, I haven't. I have**n't** even started **yet**.     noch nicht

**(to) make it**      es schaffen, Erfolg haben

> **(to) make it / (to) make sth.** („es schaffen" / „etwas schaffen")
> - Don't give up! You'll **make it**!     … Du schaffst es!
> - I'm sure our team will **make the finals**.     … unsere Mannschaft wird es ins Finale schaffen / wird ins Finale kommen.
> - I'm sorry I couldn't **make your party**.     Es tut mir leid, dass ich es nicht geschafft habe, zu eurer Party zu kommen.

| | | |
|---|---|---|
| **mathematics** [ˌmæθəˈmætɪks] | Mathematik | = maths |
| **(to) suffer (from)** [ˈsʌfə] | leiden (an); erleiden | I often ~ **from** headaches. <br> He ~**ed** a heart attack. (Er erlitt einen Herzinfarkt.) <br> (F) souffrir    (L) sufferre |
| **(to) vacate** [vəˈkeɪt] *(fml)* | räumen *(Zimmer, Gebäude)* | Please ~ your room before 10 am tomorrow. <br> (L) vacare *(leer sein)* |
| **by** 8 am [baɪ] | bis (spätestens) 8 Uhr morgens | We should be there ~ 6 o'clock. <br> (= not later than 6 o'clock) |
| **(to) respect** [rɪˈspekt] | respektieren, achten | verb: (to) **respect** – noun: **respect** (Respekt) <br> (F) respecter    (L) respicere *(beachten)* |
| **(to) fine** sb. [faɪn] | jn. zu einer Geldstrafe verurteilen | verb: (to) **fine** – Don't do this! You might be **fined**. <br> noun: **fine** – Don't do this! You might have to pay **a fine**. (Geldstrafe) |
| **anyway** [ˈeniweɪ] | sowieso | Why invite the Millers? They won't come ~. |

> **anyway**
> 1. Jedenfalls … /    Is her mother American? – I don't really know. But **anyway**, she lives in California now.
>      Wie dem auch sei … /    We'll arrive at 7:35 or 7:45, I'm not sure. **Anyway**, we'll be there before 8.
>      Aber egal …
> 2. Und überhaupt, …    I don't have the time to go on holiday. **And anyway**, it's too expensive.
> 3. sowieso    I can give you a lift. I'm going there **anyway**.

| | | |
|---|---|---|
| **(to) put** sth. **up** | etwas aufstellen, aufbauen *(Zelt)* | It took half an hour to ~ up the tent. |
| **smelly** [ˈsmeli] | stinkend | (to) **be smelly** = stinken <br> adj: **smelly** – verb: (to) **smell** – noun: **smell** |
| **on time** | pünktlich | We won't be late. Our train will arrive **on** ~. |
| **principal** [ˈprɪnsəpl] *(AE)* | Schulleiter/in | = BE **head teacher** |
| **(to) pass (a test / an exam)** [pɑːs] | (einen Test / eine Prüfung) bestehen, schaffen | Julia is happy: she's just heard that she ~**ed** her history exam. <br> (to) **take a test / an exam / a course** = einen Test / eine Prüfung / einen Kurs machen <br> **a passing grade** = eine Note/Zensur, mit der man bestanden hat |
| p. 48 **Arctic** *(adj; n)* [ˈɑːktɪk] | arktisch, Polar-; die Arktis | (F) l'Arctique (m), arctique    (L) Arctus f *(Norden)* |

# Unit 2  Vocabulary

| | | | |
|---|---|---|---|
| | **topping** ['tɒpɪŋ] | Überzug, Belag; Soße | with a cheese **topping** = mit Käse überbacken |
| p. 49 | **national park** [ˌnæʃnəl 'pɑːk] | Nationalpark *(staatliches Naturschutzgebiet)* | |
| | **campfire** ['kæmpfaɪə] | Lagerfeuer | *a campfire* |
| | **(to) put out a fire** [ˌpʊt ˈaʊt] | ein Feuer löschen | |
| | **(to) prevent** [prɪ'vent] | verhindern, vorbeugen | Help to ~ fires! No smoking, no campfires! verb: (to) **prevent** – noun: **prevention** [prɪ'venʃn] (Vermeidung, Vorbeugung)  (F) prévenir  (L) praevenire *(zuvorkommen)* |
| | **(to) prevent** sb. **from doing** sth. | jn. daran hindern, etwas zu tun | A police officer ~**ed us from entering** the building. |
| | **licence** ['laɪsns] | Genehmigung, Lizenz | You need a ~ to fish here.  (L) licentia *(Erlaubnis)* |
| | **award** [ə'wɔːd] | Preis *(Auszeichnung)* | noun: **award** – verb: (to) **award sb. sth.** *or* **sth. to sb.** (jm. etwas zuerkennen, zusprechen, verleihen) |
| | **ceremony** ['serəməni] | Feier, Zeremonie | ❗ stress: **cere**mony ['serəməni]  (F) la cérémonie |
| | **final** ['faɪnl] | letzte(r, s) | ❗ **final** = 1. letzte(r, s); 2. Finale, Endspiel  (L) finalis, e *(endgültig)* |

## Part C

| | | | |
|---|---|---|---|
| p. 52 | **(to) dress** [dres] | sich kleiden, sich anziehen | She has very nice clothes and always ~**es** well. ❗ Meist verwendet man **get dressed** für das deutsche „sich anziehen": After I got up, I **got dressed** and went to school. |
| | **stadium** ['steɪdiəm] | Stadion | (F) le stade  (L) stadium *(Rennbahn)* |
| | **tension** ['tenʃn] | Spannung; Verspannung(en) | The ~ in the film was too much for me and I turned the TV off.  (F) la tension  (L) tendere *(spannen)* |
| | **shiny** ['ʃaɪni] | glänzend | What has she put on her hair? It's so nice and ~. |
| | **familiar (to** sb. **/ with** sth.**)** [fə'mɪliə] | (jm. / mit etwas) vertraut | Who's that guy over there? He looks ~, but I can't think of how I might know him.  (L) familiaris, e |
| | **score** [skɔː] | Spiel-/Punktestand; *(im Spiel/Sport erzielter)* Punkt | *English:* What's the **score**? *German:* Wie steht es? |
| | **(to) slide** [slaɪd], **slid, slid** [slɪd] | gleiten, rutschen; schieben, gleiten lassen | I **slid** down the bank into the river. Can you help me to ~ this box into my room? |
| | **(to) strike** [straɪk], **struck, struck** [strʌk] | schießen *(Ball, Puck)*; schlagen; treffen; zuschlagen | Klmmich **struck** the ball into the goal. You must never ~ a child. A flash of lightning **struck** the farm. Terrorists have **struck** again, this time in Paris. |
| | **(to) skate** [skeɪt] | Schlittschuh laufen, eislaufen | |
| | **referee** [ˌrefə'riː] | Schiedsrichter/in | |
| | **penalty** ['penəlti] | Strafe | **penalty box** = Strafbank *(Eishockey)*  (L) poenalis, e *(der Strafe dienend)* |

---

[f] **f**ather · [v] ri**v**er · [s] **s**ister · [z] plea**s**e · [ʃ] **sh**op · [ʒ] televi**s**ion · [tʃ] **t**eacher · [dʒ] **G**ermany · [θ] **th**anks · [ð] **th**is · [h] **h**ere

# Vocabulary Unit 2

| | | |
|---|---|---|
| (to) **joke** [dʒəʊk] | Witze machen, scherzen | *English:* You're **joking**! / You must be **joking**! <br> *German:* Du machst wohl Witze! / Das kann doch nicht dein Ernst sein! <br> (to) **joke around** = herumscherzen |
| (to) **be about to do** sth. | im Begriff sein, etwas zu tun | I **was ~ to go** to bed when the doorbell rang. |
| p. 53 **outcome** [ˈaʊtkʌm] | Ausgang *(einer Geschichte)*; Ergebnis, Resultat | |
| (to) **contrast** [kənˈtrɑːst] | gegenüberstellen, vergleichen | verb: (to) **contrast** [kənˈtrɑːst] – <br> noun: **contrast** [ˈkɒntrɑːst] (Kontrast, Gegensatz) |
| (to) **be hurt**, <br> (to) **get hurt** | verletzt sein, <br> sich verletzen | There's been an accident. <br> – **Is** anybody **hurt**? / **Did** anybody **get hurt**? |
| p. 54 **indigenous (to)** [ɪnˈdɪdʒənəs] | einheimisch (in) | **indigenous people** = ⓁＬ indigenus, a, um <br> Einheimische, Ureinwohner/innen |
| **ancestry** [ˈænsestri] | Abstammung | Donald was born in the USA but has German ~. |
| **pollution** [pəˈluːʃn] | (Umwelt-)Verschmutzung | noun: **pollution** – Ⓕ la pollution <br> verb: (to) **pollute** [pəˈluːt] <br> ((*die Umwelt*) verschmutzen) <br> Ⓛ polluere (beschmutzen) |
| **separate** [ˈseprət] | getrennt, separat | The library has a ~ room for children's books. <br> They didn't drive there together (= in the same car); they drove there **~ly** (= in different cars). <br> Ⓛ separatus, a, um |
| p. 55 **resort** [rɪˈzɔːt] | Ferienanlage; Ferienort | |
| (to) **recommend** sth. **(to** sb.**)** [ˌrekəˈmend] | (jm.) etwas empfehlen | I can ~ the store on 3rd Street. They have great stuff! <br> verb: (to) **recommend** – <br> noun: **recommendation** [ˌrekəmənˈdeɪʃn] (Empfehlung) <br> Ⓕ recommander   Ⓛ commendare |
| p. 56 **multilingualism** [ˌmʌltiˈlɪŋgwəlɪzm] | Mehrsprachigkeit | noun: **multilingualism** – <br> adj: **multilingual** [ˌmʌltiˈlɪŋgwəl] (mehrsprachig) <br> Ⓛ multi (*viele*) + lingua (*Sprache*) |
| **no longer** <br> (*auch:* **not any longer**) | nicht mehr, nicht länger | I have to go now. I can stay **no longer**. / <br> I can't stay **any longer**. |
| p. 57 (to) **split** [splɪt], split, split | aufteilen; (sich) trennen; spalten | Please ~ the cake fairly. <br> Please ~ into groups of four. <br> You'll have to ~ that wood if you want to light a fire. <br> **split screen** = geteilter Bildschirm; Bildschirm(auf)teilung |
| (to) **affect** [əˈfekt] | beeinflussen, betreffen, sich auswirken auf | Climate change will ~ all of us. <br> Ⓕ affecter   Ⓛ afficere |

## Text: From an animal's perspective

| | | |
|---|---|---|
| p. 58 **perspective** [pəˈspektɪv] | Perspektive | ❗ stress: per**spec**tive [pəˈspektɪv] <br> Ⓕ la perspective   Ⓛ perspicere (durchschauen) |
| **awake** [əˈweɪk] | wach | **awake** ◄► **asleep** |
| (to) **sniff** [snɪf] | schnüffeln, schnuppern; schniefen | My dog loves **~ing** around bushes. <br> Stop **~ing**. It sounds awful. |

[iː] green · [i] happy · [ɪ] big · [e] red · [æ] cat · [ɑː] class · [ɒ] song · [ɔː] door · [uː] blue · [ʊ] book · [ʌ] mum · [ɜː] girl · [ə] **a** partner

## Unit 2 Vocabulary

| | | |
|---|---|---|
| (to) bounce [baʊns] | aufspringen (lassen), hüpfen (lassen), prellen *(Ball)* | Josie can spend hours **bouncing** her ball against the wall. |
| paw [pɔː] | Pfote | a **paw** |
| (to) quiver [ˈkwɪvə] | zittern | I ~**ed** in fright when I saw the dark shape. |
| (to) breathe (in/out) [briːð] | (ein-/aus-)atmen | verb: (to) **breathe** [briːð] – noun: **breath** [breθ] |
| (to) sparkle [ˈspɑːkl] | funkeln, glitzern, glänzen | She smiled sadly and her eyes ~**d** beautifully. |
| hunter [ˈhʌntə] | Jäger/in | = a person or an animal that hunts |
| wildlife [ˈwaɪldlaɪf] | Tiere *(in freier Wildbahn)*, Tierwelt | The ~ of Africa is very different from the ~ in Europe. You can find all kinds of ~ in our national parks. |
| (to) howl [haʊl] | heulen | Tom's dog always ~**s** when he hears a siren. |
| (to) whine [waɪn] | winseln; jammern | My little brother always ~**s** when he's tired. |
| interpreter [ɪnˈtɜːprɪtə] | Dolmetscher/in | verb: (to) **interpret** [ɪnˈtɜːprɪt] (interpretieren; dolmetschen *(gesprochenen Text mündlich wiedergeben)*) <br> nouns: 1. **interpretation** [ɪnˌtɜːprɪˈteɪʃn] (Interpretation; *(das)* Dolmetschen) <br> 2. *(person)* **interpreter** |
| coyote [kaɪˈəʊti] | Kojote | a **coyote** |
| fox [fɒks] | Fuchs | a **fox** |
| series [ˈsɪəriːz], *pl* series | Serie; (Sende-)Reihe | It's my favourite ~. I watch it every week. <br> ⓛ series *f* |
| den [den] | Bau, Höhle *(z.B. von Raubtier)* | |
| (to) bang (on) sth. [bæŋ] | auf etwas schlagen | Stop ~**ing** that drum! I can't concentrate. |
| gun [gʌn] | Schusswaffe | |
| professor [prəˈfesə] | Professor/in | Ⓕ le/la professeur *(auch: der/die Lehrer/in)* <br> ⓛ professor *m* |
| (to) interview [ˈɪntəvjuː] | befragen, interviewen | verb: (to) **interview** – noun: **interview** |
| builder [ˈbɪldə] | Bauarbeiter/in; Bauunternehmer/in | |

[eɪ] name · [aɪ] time · [ɔɪ] boy · [əʊ] old · [aʊ] town · [ɪə] here · [eə] where · [ʊə] tour

## Vocabulary Unit 2

| | | | |
|---|---|---|---|
| **dam** [dæm] | | Damm, Staudamm | |
| | | | a huge **dam** |
| **environment** [ɪnˈvaɪrənmənt] | | Umwelt; Umfeld, Umgebung | Cycling isn't just good for you. It's good for the ~ too. (F) l'environnement (m) <br> a good **working/learning environment** <br> noun: **environment** – <br> adj: **environmental** [ɪnˌvaɪrənˈmentl] (Umwelt-) |
| **insect** [ˈɪnsekt] | | Insekt | ❗ stress: **insect** [ˈɪnsekt] <br> (F) l'insecte (m)   (L) inscectum |
| (to) **twitch** [twɪtʃ] | | zucken | The dog's nose was ~**ing**: he had smelled something. |
| **waste** [weɪst] | | Müll, Abfall | **waste product** = Abfallprodukt |
| **product** [ˈprɒdʌkt] | | Produkt | verb:   (to) **produce** [prəˈdjuːs] (produzieren, herstellen) <br> nouns: 1. **product** [ˈprɒdʌkt] (Produkt) <br>         2. **production** [prəˈdʌkʃn] (Produktion) <br>         3. (person) **producer** [prəˈdjuːsə] (Produzent/in) <br> (F) produire; le produit; la production <br> (L) producere (herstellen) |
| p.59 **fur** [fɜː] | | Fell | |
| **trader** [ˈtreɪdə] | | Händler/in | verb:   (to) **trade** [treɪd] (Handel treiben) <br> nouns: 1. **trade** (Handel) <br>         2. (person) **trader** |
| **top hat** [ˌtɒp ˈhæt] | | Zylinder (Hut) | |
| **status** [ˈsteɪtəs] | | Status | (F) le statut   (L) status m (Stellung, Rang) |
| **few** [fjuː] | | wenige | |

> **(a) little – (a) few**
>
> **little / a little** steht mit nicht zählbaren Nomen wie *cheese, milk, money, time, traffic*.
> **few / a few** steht mit dem Plural von zählbaren Nomen.
>
> ❗ Beachte die Unterschiede zwischen **little** und **a little** und **few** und **a few**.
>
> | | | |
> |---|---|---|
> | | We had very **little** money (= *not much money*) when we were young. | wenig/nicht viel Geld |
> | | Dad gave me **a little** money (= *some money*) and sent me to the shops. | etwas/ein bisschen Geld |
> | | There were **few** people (= *not many people*) in the streets, so I felt a bit scared. | wenige/nicht viele Leute |
> | | There were **a few** people (= *some people*) at the ticket office, but I didn't have to wait long. | einige/ein paar Leute |
>
> ❗ Deutsch „weniger"
> „less" mit nicht zählbaren Nomen:       My grandparents had even **less** money.
> „fewer" mit dem Plural von zählbaren Nomen:   There were **fewer** people than usual in the cinema.

| | | | |
|---|---|---|---|
| (to) **infer** sth. (**from** sth.) [ɪnˈfɜː] (fml) | | etwas (aus etwas) folgern, schließen | We could ~ from his tone of voice that he didn't like the idea. (F) inférer   (L) inferre |
| **detective** [dɪˈtektɪv] | | Detektiv/in | ❗ stress: **detective** [dɪˈtektɪv] <br> (F) le détective   (L) detegere (aufdecken) |
| (to) **note** sth. **down** [ˌnəʊt ˈdaʊn] | | (sich) etwas notieren; etwas aufschreiben | (L) notare |

# Unit 2  Vocabulary

## Checkpoint

| p. 61 | habitat ['hæbɪtæt] | Lebensraum | The natural ~ of the panda is China. (F) l'habitat (m)  (L) habitare (bewohnen) |
| --- | --- | --- | --- |
| | competitor [kəm'petɪtə] | Wettbewerbsteilnehmer/in; Konkurrent/in, Konkurrenz | I defeated 14 other ~s to win the race. (L) competere (etwas zugleich wollen) |
| | (to) inhabit (a region) [ɪn'hæbɪt] | (eine Region) bewohnen | Few people ~ Alaska: it's too cold! (F) habiter (wohnen)  (L) habitare (bewohnen) |
| | collocation [ˌkɒlə'keɪʃn] | Kollokation (Wörter, die oft zusammen vorkommen) | words that are often used together, for example: strong wind, heavy rain (L) collocatio f (Stellung, Anordnung) |
| | (to) keep back [ˌkiːp 'bæk] | fernbleiben, zurückbleiben | Keep ~. The horses bite. |
| | (to) chew [tʃuː] | kauen | (to) chew sth. up = etwas zerkauen |
| | wizard ['wɪzəd] | Zauberer | |
| | (to) look closely ['kləʊsli] | genau/näher hinschauen | ❗ (to) look closely at = (to) take a close look at (einen genauen Blick werfen auf) |
| p. 62 | grizzly (bear) [ˌgrɪzli 'beə] | Grizzlybär | |
| | marmot ['mɑːmət] | Murmeltier | |

a **grizzly (bear)**     a **marmot**  (F) la marmotte

| | (to) breed [briːd], bred, bred [bred] | brüten, Junge bekommen, sich vermehren; hervorrufen | breeding ground = Brutplatz, Brutstätte Female pigs are ready to ~ when they are 5 months old. The new policy has bred a lot of bad feeling. |
| --- | --- | --- | --- |
| | wolverine ['wʊlvəriːn] | Bärenmarder | |

a **wolverine**

| | global warming [ˌgləʊbl 'wɔːmɪŋ] | Erderwärmung | global = global, weltweit |
| --- | --- | --- | --- |
| | (to) be located (in …) [ləʊ'keɪtɪd] | (in …) liegen, sich (in …) befinden | verb: (to) be located (in …) – noun: location [ləʊ'keɪʃn] (Ort, Platz, Lage; Drehort (z.B. von Filmen)) (L) locus |
| | greenhouse gas [ˌgriːnhaʊs 'gæs] | Treibhausgas | gas = 1. Gas; 2. (AE) Benzin |
| | tonne [tʌn] | Tonne (= 1.000 kg) | ❗ pronunciation: tonne [tʌn] |
| | amount [ə'maʊnt] | Menge; Betrag (Geld) | ❗ • Mit dem Plural von zählbaren Nomen: **number** a large **number** of cars/students/dogs/… • Mit nicht zählbaren Nomen: **amount** a large **amount** of money/water/snow/… |
| | such as ['sʌtʃ_əz] | wie zum Beispiel | I like ball sports such ~ football, basketball or hockey. (= … like football, basketball or hockey) |
| | (to) deliver [dɪ'lɪvə] | (aus)liefern | "Stay at home for a delicious dinner – we ~ pizzas to your door!" |

[f] father · [v] river · [s] sister · [z] please · [ʃ] shop · [ʒ] television · [tʃ] teacher · [dʒ] Germany · [θ] thanks · [ð] this · [h] here

# Vocabulary Unit 2

| | | | |
|---|---|---|---|
| p. 63 | (to) **coach** sb. [kəʊtʃ] | jn. trainieren, jm. Unterricht geben | |
| | **focus** [ˈfəʊkəs] | Mittelpunkt, Hauptpunkt, Schwerpunkt | noun: **focus** – verb: (to) **focus on sth.** (sich auf etwas konzentrieren) <br> (L) focus (Herd, als Mittelpunkt des Hauses) |
| | (to) **be likely to do** sth. [ˈlaɪkli] | wahrscheinlich etwas tun (werden) | I would take an umbrella. It's ~ **to** rain at this time of the year. |
| | (to) **receive** [rɪˈsiːv] | erhalten, empfangen | a more formal word for "(to) **get**" <br> **receive** a letter ◄► **send** a letter <br> (F) recevoir  (L) recipere |

## Access to cultures: Canada: a quiz

| | | | |
|---|---|---|---|
| p. 64 | **reserve** [rɪˈzɜːv] | Reserve | (F) la réserve   (L) reservare (aufbewahren) |
| | (to) **combine** [kəmˈbaɪn] | verbinden, kombinieren | verb: (to) **combine** –   (F) combiner <br> noun: **combination** [ˌkɒmbɪˈneɪʃn] (Kombination, Verbindung) |
| | **society** [səˈsaɪəti] | (die) Gesellschaft | ❗ *No article:* **in** (modern) **society** <br> **in der** (modernen) **Gesellschaft** <br> (F) la société   (L) societas f |
| | **toboggan** [təˈbɒɡən] | Schlitten | a **toboggan** |
| | **weapon** [ˈwepən] | Waffe | |
| | **mass destruction** [ˌmæs dɪˈstrʌkʃn] | Massenvernichtung | verb: (to) **destroy** – noun: **destruction** (Zerstörung, Vernichtung) |
| | **treaty** [ˈtriːti] | (Staats-)Vertrag, Abkommen | The enemies stopped fighting after the peace ~ of 1977. |
| | (to) **condemn** [kənˈdem] | verurteilen, verdammen | The school ~**s** all forms of bullying. |
| | **maple syrup** [ˌmeɪpl ˈsɪrəp] | Ahornsirup | **maple** = Ahorn  –  **syrup** = Sirup |
| | **licence plate** [ˈlaɪsns pleɪt] (AE) | Nummernschild, Autokennzeichen | = BE **number plate** |
| | (to) **be thought of as …** | angesehen werden als … | Everybody wants to **be** ~ **of as** intelligent. |
| | (to) **lock** [lɒk] | abschließen (z.B. Tür) | (to) **lock** ◄► (to) **unlock** (aufschließen, entsperren) <br> verb: (to) **lock** – noun: **lock** ((Tür-)Schloss) |
| | **police department** [pəˈliːs dɪˌpɑːtmənt] | Polizei(behörde) | |
| | **positive** [ˈpɒzətɪv] | positiv | **positive** ◄► **negative** [ˈneɡətɪv] <br> (F) positif / positive   (L) positivus, a, um |
| | **ticket** | Strafzettel | ❗ **ticket** = 1. Eintrittskarte; 2. Fahrkarte; 3. Strafzettel |
| p. 65 | **intelligent** [ɪnˈtelɪdʒənt] | intelligent | ❗ stress: **intelligent** [ɪnˈtelɪdʒənt] <br> (F) intelligent   (L) intellegens |
| | **resident** [ˈrezɪdənt] | Anwohner/in, Bewohner/in | There are 50 ~**s** in the building. <br> (F) le/la résident/e   (L) residere (sich niederlassen) |
| | **quote** [kwəʊt] | Zitat | I find ~**s** from famous people interesting. |
| | **capable (of)** [ˈkeɪpəbl] | fähig (zu), imstande (zu) | She wanted to show her family what she was ~ **of**. <br> (F) capable   (L) capax (geeignet) |

[iː] green · [i] happy · [ɪ] big · [e] red · [æ] cat · [ɑː] class · [ɒ] song ·
[ɔː] door · [uː] blue · [ʊ] book · [ʌ] mum · [ɜː] girl · [ə] a partner

# Unit 3 Vocabulary

| | | |
|---|---|---|
| **hate** [heɪt] | Hass | noun: **hate** – verb: (to) **hate** (hassen) |
| **fringe** [frɪndʒ] | Fransen; Pony(fransen) | Her ~ was too long and needed to be cut. |
| **contemporary** [kən'temprəri] | modern, zeitgenössisch | I like ~ art more than older art.<br>Ⓕ contemporain  Ⓛ con *(mit)* + tempus *(Zeit)* |
| **health care** [ˈhelθ keə] | Gesundheitsfürsorge, medizinische Versorgung | |
| (to) **pride oneself on** sth. [praɪd] | stolz sein auf etwas | adj: **proud (of)** – verb: (to) **pride oneself** – noun: **pride** (Stolz) |
| **democratic** [ˌdeməˈkrætɪk] | demokratisch | adj: **democratic** –  Ⓕ démocratique<br>noun: **democracy** [dɪˈmɒkrəsi] (Demokratie) |
| (to) **vote** [vəʊt] | wählen, zur Wahl gehen; (ab)stimmen | verb: (to) **vote**<br>In most countries you have to be 18 before you can ~.<br>Who did you ~ for as band of the year?<br>noun: **vote** (Stimmrecht)<br>In what year did women get the ~ in this country?<br>Ⓕ voter  Ⓛ vovere *(versprechen; wünschen)* |
| **fit** [fɪt] | Übereinstimmung; Passform, Sitz | The dress is a very good ~.<br>English: … are a natural fit<br>German: … passen von Natur aus gut zusammen |
| **individual** [ˌɪndɪˈvɪdʒuəl] | individuell, Individual- | adj: **individual** – noun: **individual** (Einzelne/r, Individuum; Person)<br>Ⓕ individuel, le  Ⓛ individuus, a, um |
| **right** [raɪt] | Recht | |
| **freedom** [ˈfriːdəm] | Freiheit | |
| **compassion (for)** [kəmˈpæʃn] | Mitleid (mit); Mitgefühl; Barmherzigkeit | It's important to have ~ for the sick.<br>Ⓛ compati, compassus sum *(Mitleid haben)* |
| **core** [kɔː] | Kern; Basis | His lack of money is the ~ of the problem.<br>English: … are core to …<br>German: … bilden den Kern von …;<br>… sind zentral für … |
| **citizenship** [ˈsɪtɪzənʃɪp] | Staatsbürgerschaft | **citizen** [ˈsɪtɪzn] = Staatsbürger/in<br>Ⓛ civis m/f *(Bürger/in)* |
| **activist** [ˈæktɪvɪst] | Aktivist/in | ❗ stress: **act**ivist [ˈæktɪvɪst] |
| **novelist** [ˈnɒvəlɪst] | Romanautor/in | |
| **educator** [ˈedʒukeɪtə] | Pädagoge/Pädagogin | Ⓕ l'éducateur, l'éducatrice  Ⓛ educator *m* |

## Unit 3  Faces of the Midwest

| pp. 66/67 | | | |
|---|---|---|---|
| | **the Midwest** [ˈmɪdˈwest] | der Mittlere Westen *(der USA)* | |
| | **badlands** *(pl)* [ˈbædlændz] | Ödland | **Badlands** National Park is a national park in South Dakota. |
| | (to) **carve** [kɑːv] | meißeln, schnitzen; *(in Stein)* hauen | The teacher was angry when the boy ~d his name into the table. |
| | **dusty** [ˈdʌsti] | staubig | noun: **dust** – adj: **dusty** |
| | **footstep** [ˈfʊtstep] | Schritt *(Geräusch)*; Fußabdruck | We could hear ~s, but it was too dark to see anything. |

[eɪ] name · [aɪ] time · [ɔɪ] boy · [əʊ] old ·
[aʊ] town · [ɪə] here · [eə] where · [ʊə] tour

# Vocabulary Unit 3

| | | |
|---|---|---|
| **engine** [ˈendʒɪn] | Motor, Maschine | Car **~s** that run on petrol or diesel are bad for the environment.<br>**search engine** = Suchmaschine |
| **smooth** [smuːð] | glatt, eben, ruhig | Our trip was very ~. |
| **gallop** [ˈgæləp] | Galopp | ❗ noun: **gallop** – verb: (to) **gallop**<br>stress: **gallop** [ˈgæləp]<br>*English spelling:* **gallop**<br>*German spelling:* **Galopp; galoppieren** |
| **prairie** [ˈpreəri] | Prärie | ❗ stress: **prairie** [ˈpreəri] |
| **rodeo** [ˈrəʊdiəʊ] | Rodeo | ❗ stress: **rodeo** [ˈrəʊdiəʊ] |
| **silence** [ˈsaɪləns] | Stille; Schweigen | noun: **silence** – verb: (to) **silence** (zum Schweigen bringen)<br>Ⓕ le silence  Ⓛ silentium |
| **confrontation** [ˌkɒnfrʌnˈteɪʃn] | Konfrontation, Auseinandersetzung | noun: **confrontation** [ˌkɒnfrʌnˈteɪʃn] – verb: (to) **confront sb. (with)** [kənˈfrʌnt] (jn. konfrontieren (mit)) |

## Part A

| | | | |
|---|---|---|---|
| p. 68 | (to) **slap** [slæp] | knallen, schlagen (auf); klatschen *(z.B. Regen)* | "Have you seen this?" he shouted and **~ped** the paper on the table.<br>We could hear the heavy rain **~ping** on the ground.<br>(to) **slap sb.'s face** = jm. eine Ohrfeige verpassen *(ins Gesicht schlagen)*<br>verb: (to) **slap** – noun: **slap** (Schlag) |
| | **counter** [ˈkaʊntə] | Theke; Ladentisch | |
| | **highway** [ˈhaɪweɪ] *(AE)* | Fernstraße *(in den USA; oft mit vier oder mehr Spuren)* | |
| | **parking lot** [ˈpɑːkɪŋ lɒt] *(AE)*,<br>**car park** [ˈkɑː pɑːk] *(BE)* | Parkplatz *(Gelände zum Abstellen von mehreren Autos)* | **car park** *(BE)* / **parking lot** *(AE)*<br>**parking space** |
| | (to) **honk** [hɒŋk] | hupen | |
| | **buddy** [ˈbʌdi] *(infml)* | Freund/in, Kumpel | |
| | **pickup (truck)** [ˈpɪkʌp] | Pritschenwagen | a **pickup (truck)** |
| | **trunk** [trʌŋk] *(AE)* | Kofferraum | = *BE* **boot**<br>❗ **boot** = 1. Stiefel; 2. *(BE)* Kofferraum |
| | **roll** [rəʊl] | Rolle | noun: **roll** – verb: (to) **roll** |
| | **slide** [slaɪd] | Dia; Folie *(Präsentationssoftware)* | |
| | **grin** [grɪn] | (ein/das) Grinsen | English: a **grin on** sb.'s face<br>German: ein Grinsen **in** jemandes Gesicht<br>noun: **grin** – verb: (to) **grin** |
| | (to) **keep** sth. **up** [ˌkiːp ˈʌp] | etwas aufrechterhalten, fortsetzen; weitermachen mit etwas | Dad goes to evening classes to **keep up** his English.<br>You're doing good work. **Keep** it **up**! (Weiter so!) |

# Unit 3 Vocabulary

| | | | |
|---|---|---|---|
| | **(water) fountain** [ˈfaʊntən] | (Spring-)Brunnen; Trinkbrunnen | (F) la fontaine (L) fons f (Quelle) |
| | **(to) tuck** [tʌk] | stecken, klemmen | He ~ed his books under his arm and left. She ~ed her hair behind her ear and started writing. He'd look much better if he ~ed his shirt in. (… wenn er sein Hemd in die Hose stecken würde.) |
| | **mood** [muːd] | Stimmung, Laune | English: I'm in a terrible **mood** early in the morning. German: Frühmorgens **habe ich schlechte Laune**. |
| | **(to) speed up** [ˌspiːd_ˈʌp], **sped, sped** [sped] | beschleunigen; schneller werden/ machen | You're so slow! Can't you ~ up a bit? Would it ~ up the work if I helped? |
| | **(to) qualify** [ˈkwɒlɪfaɪ] | (sich) qualifizieren | If we win this match, we'll ~ for the finals. (F) se qualifier |
| | **outside of** [aʊtˈsaɪd_əv] | außerhalb (von) | |
| | **whenever** [ˌwenˈevə] | wann (auch) immer | You can come and visit us ~ you like. |
| | **So what?** [ˌsəʊ ˈwɒt] | Na und? | "We won't know anyone at the party." – "So what?" |
| p. 69 | **mainly** [ˈmeɪnli] | hauptsächlich, vorwiegend | The hotel was full of tourists, ~ from Germany. |
| | **control** [kənˈtrəʊl] | Kontrolle | noun: **control** The driver **lost ~ of** his car in the snow. (… verlor die Kontrolle über …) verb: (to) **control** (kontrollieren, regulieren) Should parents ~ how much TV their kids watch? |
| | **(to) declare** [dɪˈkleə] | verkünden, erklären | English: (to) **declare** war **on** a country German: **einem Land den Krieg erklären** (F) déclarer (L) declarare |
| | **troop** [truːp] | Truppe *(Militär)* | |
| | **sugar** [ˈʃʊgə] | Zucker | **sugar**-producing countries (Zucker produzierende Länder) |
| | **proclamation** [ˌprɒkləˈmeɪʃn] | Proklamation, Ankündigung, Bekanntmachung | The King will read the ~ at 11am. (F) la proclamation (L) proclamare *(laut rufen)* |
| | **boundary (line)** [ˈbaʊndri] | Grenze; Trennlinie | Music crosses cultural **boundaries**. |
| | **settlement** [ˈsetlmənt] | (Be-)Siedlung | verb: (to) **settle** – nouns: 1. **settlement**; 2. *(person)* **settler** |
| | **(to) force** sb. **to do** sth. [fɔːs] | jn. zwingen, etwas zu tun | The kids aren't hungry. Don't ~ them **to** eat. English: They were **forced further west / from** their land. German: Sie wurden **weiter nach Westen / von ihrem Land vertrieben**. |
| p. 70 | **variety** [vəˈraɪəti] | Variante, Sorte, Art | Germany is known for the ~ of its bread. (F) la variété (L) varietas, atis f *(Verschiedenheit)* |
| | **(to) hire** [ˈhaɪə] | *(Person)* einstellen; mieten, leihen | We need to ~ three more people for the project. They ~d a car and drove to the coast. |
| | **on the spot** [spɒt] | an Ort und Stelle, sogleich | She offered him the job **on the ~**. |

# Vocabulary Unit 3

| | | |
|---|---|---|
| (to) **get to do** sth. | etwas tun können/dürfen; die Möglichkeit haben/bekommen, etwas zu tun | If I finish my homework, I ~ **to go** to the party tonight. (= I will be allowed to go to the party) Did you ~ **to visit** Buckingham Palace when you were in London? |
| (to) **make (money)** | (Geld) verdienen | |
| **cash** [kæʃ] | Bargeld; *(infml auch:)* Geld | You have to pay ~ in this shop – you can't use a card. *English:* (to) **pay cash** – *German:* **bar bezahlen** |
| (to) **earn** [ɜːn] | verdienen *(Geld)* | ❗ German "Geld verdienen": 1. *(Gehalt bekommen)* (to) **earn money** 2. *(Profit machen)* (to) **make money** |
| **bumblebee** ['bʌmblbiː] | Hummel | a **bumblebee** |
| (to) **save (up)** [seɪv] | *(z.B. Geld)* sparen | How can we ~ energy? I'm **saving up** for a new bike. ❗ (to) **save** = 1. sparen; 2. retten |
| **dosh** [dɒʃ] *(infml)* | Knete *(infml für Geld)* | an informal word for **money** |
| **motorcycle** ['məʊtəsaɪkl] *(BE auch:* **motorbike** ['məʊtəbaɪk]*)* | Motorrad | a **motorcycle / motorbike** Ⓕ la motocyclette |
| (to) **show off** [ˌʃəʊ ˈɒf] | angeben, prahlen | Stop ~**ing off**! We know you're the best! *English:* (to) **show sth. off** *German:* **mit** etwas angeben, prahlen |
| (to) **head** + *prep/+ adv* [hed] | Richtung … gehen, fahren; sich nach … aufmachen; zusteuern auf … | When we arrived at the coast, we ~ed straight **for** the beach. I'm going to ~ **home**. I'm very tired. |
| **sunset** ['sʌnset] | Sonnenuntergang | **sunset** ◀▶ **sunrise** ['sʌnraɪz] (Sonnenaufgang) |
| **vehicle** ['viːəkl] | Fahrzeug | Cars and buses, for example, are ~s. ❗ stress: **ve**hicle ['viːəkl] Ⓕ le véhicule Ⓛ vehiculum |
| (to) **transport** [træn'spɔːt] | transportieren, befördern | ❗ verb: (to) **trans**port [træn'spɔːt] – noun: **trans**port ['trænspɔːt] Ⓕ transporter Ⓛ transportare |
| **clothing** *(no pl)* ['kləʊðɪŋ] | Kleidung | *English:* **a piece of clothing** *German:* **ein Kleidungsstück** ❗ The word **clothing** is more formal than **clothes**. |
| **fizzy drink** [ˌfɪzi ˈdrɪŋk] | kohlensäurehaltiges Erfrischungsgetränk | |
| **soda** ['səʊdə] *(AE)* *(auch:* **soda pop***)* | Limonade | |
| (to) **store** [stɔː] | aufbewahren, lagern; speichern | We use the attic to ~ old books and clothes and stuff. Do you ~ your photos on your computer or in the cloud? |
| **sneakers** *(pl)* ['sniːkəz] *(AE)* | Sportschuhe, Turnschuhe | = *BE* **trainers** |
| **nationality** [ˌnæʃəˈnæləti] | Staatsangehörigkeit, Nationalität | |

## Unit 3 Vocabulary

| | | | |
|---|---|---|---|
| | (to) **educate** sb. [ˈedʒukeɪt] | jn. ausbilden, unterrichten, erziehen | verb: (to) **educate** sb. – noun: **education** **uneducated** = ungebildet |
| p. 72 | **driver's license** [ˈdraɪvəz laɪsns] *(AE)* | Führerschein | = *BE* **driving licence** You need a **driver's license** *(AE)* / **driving licence** *(BE)* if you want to drive a car. |

### Part B

| | | | |
|---|---|---|---|
| p. 74 | (to) **borrow** [ˈbɒrəʊ] | (aus)leihen, sich borgen | Can I ~ your bike tomorrow? Mine is broken. |
| | (to) **practice** [ˈpræktɪs] *(AE)* | praktizieren; üben, trainieren | = *BE* (to) **practise** |
| | (to) **squeeze** [skwiːz] | drücken, pressen; (sich) zwängen, (sich) quetschen | **Squeeze** the bottle to get the honey out. She **~d** herself into the skirt. |
| | **tight** [taɪt] | fest, eng; knapp, eng anliegend *(Kleidung)* | We were a very ~ team from the beginning. This dress is too ~. I need a bigger size. |
| | (to) **walk** sb. **somewhere** | jn. irgendwohin begleiten/führen *(zu Fuß)* | The lady needed help, so I **~ed** her **to** the bus stop. |
| | **college** [ˈkɒlɪdʒ] | Hochschule | |
| | **corral** [kəˈrɑːl] | Gehege; (Vieh-)Pferch | |
| | **confident** [ˈkɒnfɪdənt] | (selbst)sicher; zuversichtlich | He's very shy. He'd like to become more ~. The interview went very well. I'm ~ I'll get the job. |
| | (to) **try out for** sth. *(AE)* | sich bewerben um etwas *(einen Platz, eine Rolle etc.)* | I'm going **to** ~ **out for** the school play. |
| p. 75 | **sacred (to)** [ˈseɪkrɪd] | heilig (für) | Uluru is a famous rock in Australia. It is ~ **to** the indigenous Australian people. (… ist ihnen heilig) *(F)* sacré  *(L)* sacer |
| | **troubled** [ˈtrʌbld] | unruhig, mit Problemen belastet; beunruhigt, bekümmert, besorgt | He bit his lip and looked very ~. The president brought peace to the ~ country. |
| | **violent** [ˈvaɪələnt] | gewalttätig; gewaltsam | adj: **violent** – noun: **violence** [ˈvaɪələns] (Gewalt; Gewalttätigkeit) *(F)* violent  *(L)* violentus, a, um |
| | **nomadic** [nəʊˈmædɪk] | nomadisch, Nomaden- | |
| | **farming** [ˈfɑːmɪŋ] | Landwirtschaft | They are **farmers**. = They have a **farm**. = They live from **farming**. |
| | (to) **forbid** [fəˈbɪd], **forbade** [fəˈbæd], **forbidden** [fəˈbɪdn] | verbieten, untersagen | I am **forbidden** from going home on the bus alone. |
| | **bitter** [ˈbɪtə] | erbittert; verbittert; bitter | When I see happy couples I feel ~. I don't like coffee. I think it tastes ~. |
| | **conflict** [ˈkɒnflɪkt] | Konflikt, Auseinandersetzung, Streit | ❗ stress: **conflict** [ˈkɒnflɪkt] *(F)* le conflit  *(L)* conflictus |
| | **despite** [dɪˈspaɪt] | trotz | **despite** the dangers = although it is/was dangerous |
| | (to) **dig** [dɪg], **dug, dug** [dʌg] | graben | **digging** a hole in the sand |
| | **burial** [ˈberiəl] | Beerdigung, Begräbnis | noun: **burial** – verb: (to) **bury** (begraben, beerdigen) **burial site** = Begräbnisstätte |

[eɪ] name · [aɪ] time · [ɔɪ] boy · [əʊ] old ·
[aʊ] town · [ɪə] here · [eə] where · [ʊə] tour

# Vocabulary Unit 3

| | | |
|---|---|---|
| **crude** [kruːd] | roh, grob | **crude oil** = Rohöl   (L) crudus, a, um |
| (to) **threaten** ['θretn] | (be)drohen | They ~ed him with a knife and he ran away.<br>verb: (to) **threaten** – noun: **threat** [θret]<br>((Be-)Drohung) |
| **supply** [sə'plaɪ] | Versorgung, Lieferung; Vorrat | Wars make the ~ of food to the population difficult.<br>noun: **supply** –<br>verb: (to) **supply**  (liefern, bereitstellen, zur Verfügung stellen)<br>(L) supplere (nachfüllen) |
| (to) **welcome** sb. **(to)** ['welkəm] | jn. begrüßen (in), jn. willkommen heißen (in) | **welcoming** = friendly towards visitors (freundlich, gastfreundlich) |
| (to) **satisfy** sb. ['sætɪsfaɪ] | jn. zufriedenstellen, jn. befriedigen | **satisfied** = zufrieden(gestellt)<br>**dissatisfied** = unzufrieden<br>(F) satisfaire   (L) satisficere |
| **helpful** ['helpfl] | hilfsbereit; hilfreich, nützlich | |
| p.76 **I can't stand ...** | Ich kann … nicht ausstehen/ertragen. | **I can't** ~ reggae music. Could you turn it off, please?<br>I'm a very active person. **I can't** ~ doing nothing. |
| (to) **program** ['prəʊgræm] | programmieren | verb: (to) **program** – noun: **program**<br>❗ • **programme** (BE) / **program** (AE) =<br>    1. Programm; 2. (Fernseh-/Radio-)Sendung<br>• **program** (BE, AE) = (Computer-)Programm |
| p.77 **suburb** ['sʌbɜːb] | Vorstadt, Vorort | It's so noisy in the town centre that we have moved to a ~.   (L) sub (unter), urbs f (Stadt) |
| (to) **hike** [haɪk] | wandern | (to) go for long walks in the country<br>**Hiking** in the mountains is fun.<br>We often go **hiking** at the weekend. |
| **outdoors** [ˌaʊt'dɔːz] | im Freien, draußen | adj: **outdoor**  –  **outdoor** activities/sports<br>adv: **outdoors**  –  I like to be **outdoors**. |
| **of one's own** | eigene(r, s) | She wants to make a film **of her own**. (= her own film) |
| **golden** ['gəʊldn] | golden, aus Gold | |

## Part C

| | | |
|---|---|---|
| p.80 **though** [ðəʊ]<br>(kurz für: **although**) | obwohl | I really liked my host family, ~ (= **although**) it was hard to understand them at first.<br>**even though** = selbst wenn, obwohl (betont)<br>**Even** ~ it was already 9 am, it was still dark outside. |
| **chill** [tʃɪl] | Kühle, Kälte | There was a ~ in the air and I put on a pullover. |
| (to) **return** [rɪ'tɜːn] | zurückkehren, zurückkommen | verb: (to) **return** – noun: **return**   (F) retourner |
| (to) **give** sb. **a ride** | jn. (im Auto) mitnehmen | (to) **ask sb. for a ride** =<br>jn. um eine Mitfahrgelegenheit bitten |
| (to) **cheer** sb. **up** [ˌtʃɪər_'ʌp] | jn. aufheitern | **Cheer up!**<br>(Kopf hoch! / Lass den Kopf nicht hängen!) |
| **glum** [glʌm] | niedergeschlagen, bedrückt, mürrisch | adj: **glum**   – Don't be ~. Try to be more optimistic.<br>adv: **glumly** – "We lost again," he said ~**ly**. |
| (to) **confuse** [kən'fjuːz] | verwirren; verwechseln | I was ~d when I got the strange message.<br>I always ~ right with left / right and left.<br>(L) confundere |

# Unit 3 Vocabulary

| | | | |
|---|---|---|---|
| clueless [ˈkluːləs] | ratlos; ahnungslos, unbedarft | He was ~ about what he wanted in life.<br>They had organized a party for me but I was ~. | |
| insult [ˈɪnsʌlt] | Beleidigung | I take your comment as a personal ~ to me.<br>❗ noun: **insult** [ˈɪnsʌlt] – verb: (to) **insult** sb. [ɪnˈsʌlt]<br>(jn. beleidigen)<br>(F) insulter – l'insulte (f)　(L) insultare | |
| (to) disappoint sb. [ˌdɪsəˈpɔɪnt] | jn. enttäuschen | He didn't get the job and that ~ed all of us.<br>**disappointing** = enttäuschend<br>**disappointed** = enttäuscht | |
| (to) come up [ˌkʌm‿ˈʌp] | auftauchen; vorkommen, erwähnt werden | She came ~ behind me and slapped me on the back.<br>The question came ~ when we were talking about education. | |
| mind [maɪnd] | Verstand, Sinn, Geist | Grandpa is very old, but his ~ is still very active.<br>(to) **change your mind** =<br>seine Meinung ändern, es sich anders überlegen<br>Daniel had wanted to go out, but then he ~d his **mind** and stayed home. | |
| p. 81　sculpture [ˈskʌlptʃə] | Skulptur | making a **sculpture**<br>❗ stress: **sculp**ture [ˈskʌlptʃə]<br>(F) la sculpture | |
| giant [ˈdʒaɪənt] | riesige(r, s) | (F) géant, e　(L) Gigas m (Gigant, Riese) | |
| granite [ˈgrænɪt] | Granit | ❗ stress: **granite** [ˈgrænɪt]　(F) le granit(e) | |
| patriotism [ˈpeɪtriətɪzəm] | Patriotismus | ❗ stress: **patriotism** [ˈpeɪtriətɪzəm]<br>(F) le patriotisme | |
| taxpayer [ˈtækspeɪə] | Steuerzahler/in | **tax** = (die) Steuer | |
| heartless [ˈhɑːtləs] | herzlos | | |
| strongly [ˈstrɒŋli] | heftig, entschieden, voll und ganz | I'm ~ against the new plan.<br>(to) criticize sth. **strongly**; (to) (dis)agree **strongly** | |
| (to) criticize sb. (for) [ˈkrɪtɪsaɪz] | jn. kritisieren (wegen) | She was ~d for her article in the school magazine.<br>❗ stress: **criticize** [ˈkrɪtɪsaɪz]　(F) critiquer | |
| extreme [ɪkˈstriːm] | extrem; Extrem | • adj: **extreme** temperatures<br>• adv: **extremely** hot (äußerst, höchst, extrem)<br>• noun: The weather went from one **extreme** to the other: first it was sunny and hot, then it was cold and rainy.<br>(F) extrême, l'extrême (m)<br>(L) extremus (der äußerste) | |
| offensive [əˈfensɪv] | beleidigend, anstößig | My grandma finds some words very ~.<br>adj: **offensive** – verb: (to) **offend** sb. [əˈfend]<br>(jn. beleidigen; jn. stören)<br>(L) offendere (beleidigen) | |
| fully [ˈfʊli] | völlig, vollkommen | I can ~ understand that he feels insulted. | |
| (to) spray [spreɪ] | (be)sprühen, sprayen | **Spraying** graffiti is illegal. | |

[f] father · [v] river · [s] sister · [z] please · [ʃ] shop · [ʒ] television ·
[tʃ] teacher · [dʒ] Germany · [θ] thanks · [ð] this · [h] here

## Vocabulary Unit 3

| | | |
|---|---|---|
| (to) **blow** sb. **away** [ˌbləʊ_əˈweɪ] *(AE, infml)* | jn. total umhauen | When she first saw her she was **blown** ~. |
| **hardly** [ˈhɑːdli] | kaum | There was ~ anyone in the streets. It was very quiet.<br>❗ They work **hard**. \| They **hardly** work.<br>Sie arbeiten **hart**. \| Sie arbeiten **kaum**. |
| (to) **surprise** [səˈpraɪz] | überraschen | ❗ **surprised** – Are you **surprised**? (überrascht)<br>**surprising** – It's **surprising** that … (überraschend)<br>**surprisingly** – **Surprisingly**, he agreed. (überraschenderweise) |
| **wonder** [ˈwʌndə] | Wunder *(etwas Außergewöhnliches/Erstaunliches)* | The Grand Canyon is one of the natural ~s of the world. |
| **creation** [kriˈeɪʃn] | Schaffung; Kreation, Werk | noun: **creation** – verb: (to) **create** –<br>adj: **creative** [kriˈeɪtɪv]<br>Ⓕ la création   Ⓛ creare *(erschaffen)* |
| **strength** [streŋθ] | Stärke, Kraft | adj: **strong** – noun: **strength** |
| **amphitheatre** [ˈæmfɪθɪətə] | Amphitheater | an **amphitheatre** *(BE)* / **amphitheater** *(AE)*<br>❗ stress: **amphitheatre** [ˈæmfɪθɪətə]<br>Ⓕ l'amphithéâtre *(m)*   Ⓛ amphitheatrum |
| **thorough** [ˈθʌrə] | gründlich; sorgfältig | adj: **thorough**   They did very **thorough** research.<br>adv: **thoroughly**   1. gründlich, sorgfältig<br>    Please read the text **thoroughly**.<br>   2. völlig, total<br>    I **thoroughly** enjoyed the show. |
| **floodlight(s)** [ˈflʌdlaɪt] | Flutlicht | **floodlights** |
| **cloudless** [ˈklaʊdləs] | wolkenlos | |
| **firm** [fɜːm] | fest, sicher; verbindlich | adj: **firm**   **firm** ground, a **firm** decision<br>adv: **firmly**   I **firmly** believe that …<br>(Ich glaube ganz sicher/ganz fest/entschieden daran, dass …) |
| p.82 **success** [səkˈses] | Erfolg | noun: **success** – adj: **successful**<br>Ⓕ le succès   Ⓛ successus |
| **position** [pəˈzɪʃn] | Position, Standort, Platz; (Arbeits-)Stelle | From this ~, you can see the whole city.<br>He called me to offer me the ~.<br>❗ stress: **position** [pəˈzɪʃn]<br>Ⓕ la position   Ⓛ positio f |
| (to) **stress** [stres] | betonen | verb: (to) **stress** – noun: **stress** |
| **unlike** [ˌʌnˈlaɪk] | anders als, im Gegensatz zu | I'm not a good swimmer, ~ my sister. She swims like a fish.<br>**like** my sister ◄► **unlike** my sister |
| p.83 **skilful** [ˈskɪlfl] *(AE auch: **skillful**)* | geschickt, gut | She is a very ~ musician. |
| **dough** [dəʊ] | Teig *(Hefeteig)* | |

[iː] green · [i] happy · [ɪ] big · [e] red · [æ] cat · [ɑː] class · [ɒ] song ·
[ɔː] door · [uː] blue · [ʊ] book · [ʌ] mum · [ɜː] girl · [ə] a partner

# Unit 3 Vocabulary

| | | | |
|---|---|---|---|
| | **flat** [flæt] | flach; eben | It's easier to ride a bike in a ~ city like Berlin than in a hilly city like Stuttgart.  **hilly** ◄► **flat**  ❗ **flat** = 1. *(n)* Wohnung; 2. *(adj)* flach; eben |
| | **priority** [praɪˈɒrəti] | Priorität | ❗ stress: **priority** [praɪˈɒrəti] |
| p. 84 | **buffalo** [ˈbʌfələʊ], *pl* **buffalo** *or* **buffaloes** | Büffel; Bison | a **buffalo** |
| | **plains** *(pl)* [pleɪnz] | Ebene | |
| | **greatly** [ˈgreɪtli] | stark, erheblich | Speaking four languages has ~ helped him in his career. |
| | **the mid-1800s** [mɪd] | Mitte des 19. Jahrhunderts | He's in his **mid**-thirties. (Er ist Mitte dreißig.)  She's in her **early** thirties. (… Anfang dreißig.)  They're in their **late** thirties. (… Ende dreißig.) |
| | **smallpox** [ˈsmɔːlpɒks] | Pocken *(Erkrankung)* | |
| | **epidemic** [ˌepɪˈdemɪk] | Epidemie; epidemisch | Over 50 million people died in the **flu** ~ of 1918–1919. (Grippeepidemie) |
| | **one third** [θɜːd] | ein Drittel | 1/2 = a/one **half** *(pl.* **halves***)*  1/3 = a/one **third**  1/4 = a/one **quarter**; a/one **fourth** *(AE)*  1/5 = a/one **fifth**  1/6 = a/one **sixth** |
| | **intentional** [ɪnˈtenʃənl] | absichtlich, vorsätzlich | I'm sorry, this wasn't **intentional** *(adj)* /  I didn't do this **intentionally** *(adv)*. |
| | **(to) infect** [ɪnˈfekt] | infizieren; verseuchen | verb: (to) **infect** – noun: **infection** [ɪnˈfekʃn]  (Infektion)  *L* inficere *(vergiften)* |
| | **army** [ˈɑːmi] | Armee | ❗ stress: **army** [ˈɑːmi]  *F* l'armée *(f)*   *L* arma *n pl (Waffen)* |
| | **herd** [hɜːd] | Herde, Rudel | |
| | **source** [sɔːs] | Quelle *(auch:* Textquelle*)* | Fish is the main ~ of food for the people here.  I think books are better for research than online ~s.  *F* la source |
| | **lifestyle** [ˈlaɪfstaɪl] | Lebensstil | |
| | **(to) establish** [ɪˈstæblɪʃ] | etablieren, gründen, aufbauen, einrichten | Munich was ~ed in 1158.  The film ~ed her as a famous actor. |
| p. 85 | **bloodline** [ˈblʌdlaɪn] | Stammbaum | a person's or an animal's ancestors |
| | **across from each other** [əˈkrɒs] | einander gegenüber | They're sitting **across from each other.** |
| | **back to back** | Rücken an Rücken | They're sitting **back to back.** |
| | **(to) empty** [ˈempti] | leeren | **emptying** the dishwasher  verb: (to) **empty** –  adj: **empty** |

[eɪ] **n**a**me** · [aɪ] **t**i**me** · [ɔɪ] **b**oy · [əʊ] **o**l**d** ·
[aʊ] **t**ow**n** · [ɪə] **h**e**re** · [eə] **wh**e**re** · [ʊə] **t**ou**r**

# Vocabulary Unit 3

| | | |
|---|---|---|
| **bay** [beɪ] | Bucht | a beautiful **bay**<br>(F) la baie |
| **way before ...** | lange/weit vor ... | I knew Sophie ~ **before** her boyfriend met her. |
| **outbreak** [ˈaʊtbreɪk] | Ausbruch *(z.B. Krankheit, Regenschauer)* | At the ~ of war, they left the country. |
| **gift** [ɡɪft] | Geschenk; Gabe; Talent | She has a ~ for understanding things very quickly. |
| **Christianity** [ˌkrɪstiˈænəti] | Christentum | |
| **customs** *(pl)* [ˈkʌstəmz] | Bräuche, Gebräuche, Sitten | In foreign countries people have different habits and ~. |
| **barely** [ˈbeəli] | kaum | = **hardly** |
| **poverty** [ˈpɒvəti] | Armut | adj: **poor** – noun: **poverty**<br>(F) la pauvreté   (L) paupertas f |
| **(to) narrow** [ˈnærəʊ] | (sich) verengen | His eyes ~**ed** as he looked at me.<br>adj: **narrow** – verb: (to) **narrow**<br>(to) **narrow sth. down (to sth.)** =<br>    etwas eingrenzen; etwas (auf etwas) reduzieren<br>We ~**ed down** the list to just three people. |
| **mad (at** sb./**about** sth.**)** [mæd] *(AE, infml)* | wütend (auf jn./wegen etwas) | When I came home late my parents were ~ **at** me.<br>❗ **mad** = 1. *(bes. BE)* verrückt; 2. *(bes. AE)* wütend |
| p. 87 **hotbed** [ˈhɒtbed] | Nährboden | Airports are a ~ of disease. |
| **revolution** [ˌrevəˈluːʃn] | Revolution | ❗ stress: rev**o**lution [ˌrevəˈluːʃn]   (F) la révolution |
| **(to) disguise** [dɪsˈɡaɪz] | (sich) verkleiden; (sich) tarnen | He tried to ~ his voice on the phone. |
| **crate** [kreɪt] | Kiste; Kasten *(für Getränke)* | bottles in **crates** |
| **value** [ˈvæljuː] | Wert | • The ~ of our car has gone down by £ 2000 since we bought it.<br>• **values** *(pl)* = Werte, Wertvorstellungen<br>  Do young people share older people's ~**s**?<br>• It's good ~ (for money). =<br>  Es ist sein Geld wert. / Es ist preiswert.<br>(F) la valeur   (L) valere *(wert sein)* |
| **taxation** [tækˈseɪʃn] | Besteuerung, Steuern | |
| **representation** [ˌreprɪzenˈteɪʃn] | (Interessens-)Vertretung, Repräsentanz | We want to improve the ~ of minorities in parliament.   (F) la représentation |
| **(to) shut** sth. **down** [ˌʃʌt ˈdaʊn], **shut, shut** | etwas schließen | You should always ~ **down** your computer at the end of the day. |
| **continental** [ˌkɒntɪˈnentl] | kontinental | There are some differences between the UK and **Continental** Europe.<br>(F) continental, e   (L) continens f *(Kontinent)* |
| **congress** [ˈkɒŋɡres] | Kongress | ❗ stress: **c**ongress [ˈkɒŋɡres] |
| **(to) boycott** [ˈbɔɪkɒt] | boykottieren | ❗ stress: (to) **b**oycott [ˈbɔɪkɒt]   (F) boycotter<br>verb: (to) **boycott** – noun: **boycott** |
| **(to) set the stage (for)** | den Weg bereiten (für) | Their argument at Christmas **set the** ~ **for** their fight at New Year. |

[b] **b**oat · [p] **p**ool · [d] **d**ad · [t] **t**en · [ɡ] **g**ood · [k] **c**at ·
[m] **m**um · [n] **n**o · [ŋ] so**ng** · [l] **h**ello · [r] **r**ed · [w] **w**e · [j] **y**ou

# Unit 3 Vocabulary

## Part D

| | | | |
|---|---|---|---|
| p. 88 | **request** [rɪˈkwest] | Wunsch, Bitte; Anfrage | Nobody reacted to their ~ for help. *(L) requirere (fragen)* |
| | **crash** [kræʃ] | Krachen; Unfall, Zusammenstoß | Four people died in the car ~. |
| | **movie theater** [ˈmuːvi θɪətə] *(AE)* | Kino | = *BE* **cinema** |
| | **allowance** [əˈlaʊəns] *(AE)* | Taschengeld | = *BE* **pocket money** |

## Text: The Legend of the Great Peacemaker

| | | | |
|---|---|---|---|
| p. 90 | **peacemaker** [ˈpiːsmeɪkə] | Friedensstifter/in | |
| | **way of life** [ˌweɪ_əv ˈlaɪf] | Lebensweise | I love the relaxed **way of** ~ in Ireland. |
| | **(to) have** sth. **in common** | etwas gemeinsam haben, etwas miteinander gemein haben | We're the same age, but we don't **have** much **in** ~. |
| | **oral** [ˈɔːrəl] | mündlich | We have two exams next week: a written one and an ~ one. *(F) oral, e (L) os, oris n (Mund)* |
| | **(to) pass** sth. **on (to** sb.**)** [ˌpɑːs_ˈɒn] | (jm.) etwas weitergeben, weitersagen, weiterleiten | I'll read the book and ~ it **on** to my sister. Please ~ **on** this news to all your friends. |
| | **storyteller** [ˈstɔːrɪtelə] | (Geschichten-)Erzähler/in | |
| | **It was** through storytellers **that** they learned ... | Durch Geschichtenerzähler/innen lernten sie ... | |

> **"It is ... / It was ..." zur Hervorhebung**
>
> Die Konstruktion **It is ... / It was ...** + **Relativsatz** oder **that**-Satz wird verwendet, um etwas hervorzuheben.
>
> **It was** through my yoga teacher **that** I got to know my wife. — Durch meinen Yogalehrer habe ich meine Frau kennengelernt.
> **It's** Sophie **who** is often late, not her sister. — Es ist Sophie, die oft zu spät kommt, nicht ihre Schwester.
>
> ❗ Beachte, dass ein **hervorgehobenes Personalpronomen** in der **Objektform** steht:
> It's <u>him</u> **that** I'm talking about, not you. (*nicht: It's he that...*)
> It was <u>me</u> who found the keys under the sofa.

| | | |
|---|---|---|
| **sorcerer** [ˈsɔːsərə] | Zauberer, Hexenmeister | a man with magic powers |
| **(to) refuse** [rɪˈfjuːz] | sich weigern, ablehnen | • I asked him to help me, but he ~d. <br>• She was very proud and ~d her friend's help. <br>• (to) **refuse to do** sth. = sich weigern / es ablehnen, etwas zu tun <br> He ~d **to help** his brother with his homework. <br>*(F) refuser (L) refutare* |
| **(to) assemble** [əˈsembl] | (sich) versammeln; zusammen-kommen; zusammenbauen, montieren | They ~d a team of scientists to study the problem. We ~d in front of the church. Her mother helped her to ~ her new bike. |
| **root** [ruːt] | Wurzel | roots |
| **(to) unify** [ˈjuːnɪfaɪ] | (ver)einen, vereinigen | In 1871 most of the German states were **unified** to become the German empire. |
| **(to) heal** [hiːl] | heilen | I need to give my foot time to ~. |

---

[f] **f**ather · [v] ri**v**er · [s] **s**ister · [z] plea**s**e · [ʃ] **sh**op · [ʒ] televi**s**ion ·
[tʃ] **t**eacher · [dʒ] **G**ermany · [θ] **th**anks · [ð] **th**is · [h] **h**ere

# Vocabulary Unit 3

| | | | |
|---|---|---|---|
| (to) **remove** [rɪˈmuːv] | entfernen, beseitigen; ausziehen *(Kleidung)* | (to) take sth. away; (to) take off (clothes) | |
| **sorrow** [ˈsɒrəʊ] | Kummer, Leid | the feeling of being very sad | |
| **clan** [klæn] | Clan, Sippe | | |
| (to) **get** sb. **to do** sth. | jn. dazu bringen, etwas zu tun | My brother always tries to ~ **me to** clean his room. | |
| **belt** [belt] | Gürtel; Band *(zum Transport)* | The dress looks better with a ~. | |
| **pine (tree)** [paɪn] | Kiefer *(Baum)* | | |
| **needle** [ˈniːdl] | Nadel | | |
| **arrow** [ˈærəʊ] | Pfeil | an **arrow**: ⟶ | |
| **eagle** [ˈiːgl] | Adler | | |

## The digital compass: The ways we learn history

p. 91 **compass** [ˈkʌmpəs]  Kompass

a **compass**

| | | |
|---|---|---|
| **historical** [hɪˈstɒrɪkl] | historisch, geschichtlich | The town's main ~ attraction is a 12th century castle.  *F* historique   *L* historia, -ae f |
| (to) **research** [rɪˈsɜːtʃ] | erforschen, untersuchen, recherchieren | verb: (to) **research** [rɪˈsɜːtʃ] – noun: **research** [ˈriːsɜːtʃ, rɪˈsɜːtʃ] |
| **confederacy** [kənˈfedərəsi] | Bund, Bündnis, Konföderation | *F* la confédération   *L* confoederatio f |

## Checkpoint

| | | |
|---|---|---|
| p. 93 (to) **forgive** [fəˈgɪv], **forgave** [fəˈgeɪv], **forgiven** [fəˈgɪvn] | verzeihen | I know that he has hurt you, but try to ~ him. |
| (to) **flavour** sth. **with** sth. [ˈfleɪvə] | etwas mit etwas aromatisieren, würzen | **orange-flavoured** = mit Orangen-Geschmack |
| **sandals** *(pl)* [ˈsændlz] | Sandalen | a pair of **sandals**  *F* la sandale  *L* sandalium |
| (to) **elect** sb. **(to be)** sth. [ɪˈlekt] | jn. zu etwas wählen | *English:* They **elected her (to be)** president.  *German:* Sie **wählten sie zur** Präsidentin.  verb: (to) **elect** – noun: **election**  *F* élire   *L* eligere, electum *(auswählen)* |
| **union** [ˈjuːniən] | Union; Vereinigung, Verband | When I became a teacher I joined the teachers' ~.  *F* l'union (f)   *L* unire *(vereinigen)* |
| **circular** [ˈsɜːkjələ] | rund | **semicircular** = halbrund  *F* circulaire   *L* circulus *(Kreis)* |
| **purpose** [ˈpɜːpəs] | Absicht, Sinn, Zweck, Ziel | **on purpose** = intentionally  I think Dad lost our last chess match **on purpose**. (mit Absicht, absichtlich) |
| **restless** [ˈrestləs] | unruhig, rastlos | I get ~ when I have to sit down for more than an hour. |

[iː] green · [i] happy · [ɪ] big · [e] red · [æ] cat · [ɑː] class · [ɒ] song ·
[ɔː] door · [uː] blue · [ʊ] book · [ʌ] mum · [ɜː] girl · [ə] a partner

# Unit 3  Vocabulary

| | | |
|---|---|---|
| **general** ['dʒenrəl] | allgemein | **in general** = im Allgemeinen, generell<br>(F) général, e   (L) generalis, e |
| **harm** *(no pl)* [hɑːm] | Schaden, Schäden, Verletzung | noun: **harm**<br>I would never do (any) **harm** to another person / do another person (any) **harm**.<br>verb: (to) **harm**  (schaden, schädigen, verletzen)<br>I would never **harm** another person. |
| **desert** ['dezət] | Wüste | (F) le désert   (L) deserere *(verlassen)* |
| p. 94  **forward(s)** ['fɔːwəd(z)] | nach vorne; vorwärts | **forward(s)** ◄► **backward(s)**<br>It's easier to count **forwards** from 1 to 100 than to count **backwards** from 100 to 1. |
| **fear (of)** [fɪə] | Angst (vor) | verb: (to) **fear**   The workers **feared** their boss.<br>noun: **fear (of)**   I have a **fear of** rats.<br>(= I'm afraid of /scared of rats) |
| **low** [ləʊ] | niedrig, tief | **low** ◄► **high** |
| (to) **populate** ['pɒpjuleɪt] | bevölkern, besiedeln | English people moved there and began to ~ the area.<br>verb: (to) **populate** – noun: **population**<br>(F) peupler   (L) populus *(Volk)* |
| (to) **freeze over** [ˌfriːz ˈəʊvə] | vereisen, zufrieren, überfrieren | |
| p. 95  **north-eastern** [ˌnɔːθ'iːstən] | nordöstlich, Nordost- | |
| (to) **crush** [krʌʃ] | (zer)quetschen; (aus)pressen | The car **~ed** the bicycle against the wall. |
| **wagon** ['wægən] | Planwagen, (Pferde-)Fuhrwerk | Two horses are pulling the **wagon**.<br>**wagon train** = Planwagenkolonne |
| **noble** ['nəʊbl] | stattlich, prächtig; edel; adlig | She comes from a ~ family and is very rich.<br>(F) noble   (L) nobilis, e |
| **salmon** ['sæmən], *pl* **salmon** | Lachs | ❗ Silent letter **l**: salmon ['sæmən]   (F) le saumon |
| **dish** [dɪʃ] | Gericht *(Mahlzeit)*; Schüssel, Schale | Lasagne is an Italian ~.<br>a lasagne **dish**<br>❗ **dish** = 1. Gericht; 2. Schüssel, Schale; 3. dishes *(pl)* Abwasch |
| **soaking wet** [ˌsəʊkɪŋ 'wet] | völlig durchnässt, klitschnass | It was raining heavily and we were ~ **wet**. |
| (to) **shut** sb. **up** [ˌʃʌt ˈʌp], shut, shut | jn. einsperren | I hate being ~ **up** inside when it's snowing. |

[eɪ] n**a**me · [aɪ] t**i**me · [ɔɪ] b**oy** · [əʊ] **o**ld ·
[aʊ] t**ow**n · [ɪə] h**ere** · [eə] wh**ere** · [ʊə] t**our**

# Vocabulary Unit 3

| | | | |
|---|---|---|---|
| **fiction** [ˈfɪkʃn] | Belletristik, Prosa(literatur); Märchen, Fiktion | Do you only read history and science books? – No, I like ~ too, like the Harry Potter series. Don't believe him … everything he says is ~. | |
| **opportunity** [ˌɒpəˈtjuːnəti] | Gelegenheit, Möglichkeit, Chance | I think you'll have better job **opportunities** if you speak more than one language. (L) opportunus (*gelegen*) | |
| **powder** [ˈpaʊdə] | Pulver | We haven't got any fresh milk, but we've got some milk ~. (F) la poudre | |
| **shot** [ʃɒt] | Schuss; Geschoss, Schrot | ❗ **shot** = 1. Schuss; 2. Geschoss, Schrot; 3. Aufnahme, Foto; (*Film*) Einstellung, Szene | |
| **anticipation** [ænˌtɪsɪˈpeɪʃn] | Vorfreude, Erwartung; Vorausahnung | He looked forward to the party with ~. (L) anticipare (*vorwegnehmen*) | |

## Access to cultures: Foundation of a new nation

| | | | |
|---|---|---|---|
| p. 96 **foundation** [faʊnˈdeɪʃn] | Gründung; Fundament, Grundlage | The school has been just for girls since its ~ in 1961. The course gives students a ~ in mathematics. (F) la fondation (L) fundare (*gründen*) | |
| **revolutionary** [ˌrevəˈluːʃənəri] | revolutionär; Revolutionär/in | ❗ stress: **revolutionary** [ˌrevəˈluːʃənəri] (F) révolutionnaire | |
| **document** [ˈdɒkjumənt] | Dokument; Text(datei) | ❗ stress: **document** [ˈdɒkjumənt] (F) le document | |
| (to) **lay** sth. **down** [ˌleɪ ˈdaʊn] | etwas festsetzen, festlegen | She's the one who ~s **down** the rules for the company. | |
| **economic** [ˌiːkəˈnɒmɪk] | wirtschaftlich, Wirtschafts- | The ~ situation was a lot worse after the war. (F) économique (L) oeconomicus, a, um | |
| **military** [ˈmɪlətri] | militärisch; Militär | He left the ~ because he didn't want to kill anybody. (F) militaire (L) militaris, e | |
| (to) **address** sth. **to** sb. [əˈdres] | etwas an jn. richten | The letter is ~ed **to** me. (to) **address sb.** = jn. ansprechen, anreden I always ~ him as 'Sir'. (F) adresser | |
| **representative** [ˌreprɪˈzentətɪv] | Repräsentant/in, Abgeordnete(r) | **Representatives** from all of the age groups made the decision. (F) le représentant / la représentante | |
| (to) **go to war** | in den Krieg ziehen | | |
| **complaint** [kəmˈpleɪnt] | Beschwerde | The shop assistant listened to my ~ and said sorry. (to) **make a complaint (about sth.)** = eine Beschwerde vorbringen (über etwas), etwas beanstanden verb: (to) **complain** – noun: **complaint** | |
| **consent** [kənˈsent] | Einwilligung, Zustimmung; Genehmigung | verb: (to) **consent** (einwilligen, zustimmen) At first he wasn't sure but finally he ~ed. noun: **consent** She did not give her ~ for her name to be used. (F) le consentement (L) consentire (*zustimmen*) | |
| (to) **demand** [dɪˈmɑːnd] | fordern, verlangen | The workers ~ed more money. (F) demander verb: (to) **demand** – noun: **demand** (Forderung, Anforderung) | |

# Unit 3  Vocabulary

| | | |
|---|---|---|
| **colonial** [kəˈləʊniəl] | kolonial, Kolonial- | (F) colonial   (L) colonia (Kolonie) |
| (to) **trade** [treɪd] | handeln, Handel (be)treiben | Germany ~s a lot with China.   (L) tradere<br>verb: (to) **trade** – noun: **trade** |
| (to) **represent** [ˌreprɪˈzent] | vertreten, repräsentieren | It's an honour to ~ your country in the Olympic Games. |
| **civil rights** (pl) [ˌsɪvl ˈraɪts] | Bürgerrechte | |
| **constitution** [ˌkɒnstɪˈtjuːʃn] | Verfassung | (F) la constitution   (L) constitutio f |
| p.97 (to) **abuse** [əˈbjuːz] | missbrauchen | verb: (to) **abuse** [əˈbjuːz]<br>    He ~d his friend's trust.<br>noun: **abuse** [əˈbjuːs]  (Missbrauch)<br>    This car has taken a lot of ~.<br>(L) abuti, abusus sum |
| **equal** [ˈiːkwəl] | gleich, gleichgestellt | Do men and women really have ~ rights?<br>adj: **equal** – noun: **equality** [iˈkwɒləti]<br>    (Gleichheit, Gleichberechtigung)<br>(F) égal, e   (L) aequus, -a, -um (gleich) |
| **pursuit (of)** [pəˈsjuːt] | Streben (nach); Jagd (auf) | (F) la poursuite |
| **happiness** [ˈhæpinəs] | Glück, Zufriedenheit | adj: **happy** – noun: **happiness** |
| **nature** [ˈneɪtʃə] | (die) Natur | English:  (to) **protect nature**<br>German:  **die Natur beschützen**<br>❗ stress: **nature** [ˈneɪtʃə]   (F) la nature<br>noun: **nature** – adj: **natural**   (L) natura |
| **rule** [ruːl] | Herrschaft | verb:  (to) **rule**  (beherrschen, herrschen über) –<br>noun: **rule**<br>    British ~ ended in Hong Kong in 1997. |
| (to) **enslave** sb. [ɪnˈsleɪv] | jn. versklaven | (to) make sb. a slave |
| **descent** [dɪˈsent] | Herkunft, Abstammung | She is of Indian ~.<br>(F) la descente |
| **belief (in)** [bɪˈliːf] | Glaube (an) | verb: (to) **believe (in)** [bɪˈliːv] –<br>noun: **belief (in)** [bɪˈliːf] |
| (to) **apply (to)** [əˈplaɪ] | zutreffen, gelten (für) | He seems to think the rules don't ~ **to** him. |
| **property** [ˈprɒpəti] | Eigentum, Besitz | The things you own are your ~.<br>(F) la propriété |
| (to) **influence** [ˈɪnfluəns] | beeinflussen | Even today, the Beatles still ~ musicians all over the world.   (F) influencer<br>verb: (to) **influence** – noun: **influence** |
| **throughout ...** [θruːˈaʊt] | der/die/das ganze ... (hindurch); überall in ... | I didn't go away last summer. I stayed at home ~ the school holidays.<br>How often people should fly is being discussed ~ all of Europe. |

# Dictionary

Das **Dictionary** besteht aus **zwei alphabetischen Wörterlisten**:
**English – German** (S. 194–228) und **German – English** (S. 229–262)

Im **English – German Dictionary** kannst du nachschlagen, wenn du wissen möchtest, was ein englisches Wort bedeutet, wie man es ausspricht oder wie es geschrieben wird.

Im **Dictionary** werden folgende **Abkürzungen und Symbole** verwendet:

*pl* = *plural*   •   sth. = something   •   sb. = somebody   •   jn. = jemanden   •   jm. = jemandem
*infml* = *informal* (umgangssprachlich)   •   *fml* = *formal* (formell, förmlich)
AE = American English   •   BE = British English
° Mit diesem Kringel sind Wörter markiert, die nicht zum Lernwortschatz gehören.

Die **Fundstellenangaben** zeigen, wo ein Wort zum ersten Mal vorkommt:
I = erster Band (Jahrgangsstufe 5)   •   II = zweiter Band (Jahrgangsstufe 6)   •   III = dritter Band (Jahrgangsstufe 7)   •
IV 1 (26) = vierter Band (Jahrgangsstufe 8), Unit 1, Seite 26

**Tipps zur Arbeit mit einem Wörterbuch** findest du im Skills File auf Seite 134.

## A

**a** [ə] ein, eine I   **a 1960s band** eine Band aus den 60er Jahren (des 20. Jahrhunderts) II   **a bit** ein bisschen, etwas I   **a few** ein paar, einige II   **a lot** viel I   **… a day/week/year** … pro Tag/Woche/Jahr I
**abandon** [ə'bændən] zurücklassen, verlassen, im Stich lassen IV 1 (26)
**abbreviation** [ə,bri:vi'eɪʃn] Abkürzung II
**able** ['eɪbl]: **be able to do sth.** etwas tun können; fähig sein / in der Lage sein, etwas zu tun II
**about** [ə'baʊt]:
1. **about yourself** über dich selbst I   **It's about a seagull.** Es geht um eine Möwe. / Es handelt von einer Möwe. I   **the best thing about …** das Beste an … III   **What about …?** Wie wäre es mit …? II   **What about you?** Und du? / Und was ist mit dir? Und ihr? / Und was ist mit euch? I   **What is the story about?** Wovon handelt die Geschichte? / Worum geht es in der Geschichte? I
2. ungefähr I   **about 300 people** ungefähr 300 Leute I
3. **be about to do sth.** im Begriff sein, etwas zu tun IV 2 (52)
**above** [ə'bʌv] über, oberhalb (von); oben, darüber II
**abroad** [ə'brɔ:d] im/ins Ausland IV 1 (17)
**absolute** ['æbsəlu:t] absolut IV 1 (20)
**absolutely** ['æbsəlu:tli] absolut, vollkommen, total IV 1 (20)
**absurd** [əb'sɜ:d] absurd IV 1 (15)
**abuse** [ə'bju:s] Missbrauch IV 3 (97)
**abuse (sb./sth)** [ə'bju:z] (jn./etwas) missbrauchen IV 3 (97)
**accent** ['æksənt] Akzent III
°**accept** [ək'sept] akzeptieren, annehmen
**access (to)** ['ækses] Zugang, Zutritt (zu) I

**accident** ['æksɪdənt] Unfall; Zufall III
   **by accident** zufällig III
**according to …** [ə'kɔ:dɪŋ] … zufolge; laut … II
**account** [ə'kaʊnt] Account, Konto III
°**achieve** [ə'tʃi:v] erreichen, erzielen, schaffen
**acoustics (pl)** [ə'ku:stɪks] Akustik IV 1 (10)
°**acre** ['eɪkə] Flächenmaß *(ca. 4 000 m²)*
**across** [ə'krɒs]: **across from each other** einander gegenüber IV 3 (86)   **across the street** (quer) über die Straße II   °**across the country** überall im Land, im ganzen Land
**act** [ækt]:
1. schauspielern II   **act sth. out** etwas vorspielen I
°2. handeln; sich verhalten
**act** [ækt]:
1. Tat, Akt, Handlung IV 1 (12)
°2. Gesetz
**action** ['ækʃn] Action; Handlung, Tat I
**active** ['æktɪv] aktiv IV 1 (18)
**activist** ['æktɪvɪst] Aktivist/in IV 2 (65)
**activity** [æk'tɪvəti], *pl* **activities** Aktivität I   **free-time activity** Freizeitaktivität I
**actor** ['æktə] Schauspieler/in I
**actual** ['æktʃuəl] tatsächliche(r, s), wirkliche(r, s) III
**actually** ['æktʃuəli] eigentlich; übrigens; tatsächlich III
**ad** [æd] *(kurz für:* **advertisement***)* Werbespot, Werbung; Anzeige, Inserat III
**add (to)** [æd] hinzufügen, ergänzen, addieren (zu) I
**adder** ['ædə] Kreuzotter II
**address** [ə'dres]:
1. Adresse, Anschrift I
2. **address sb.** jn. ansprechen, anreden IV 3 (96)   **address sth. to sb.** etwas an jn. richten IV 3 (96)
**adjective** ['ædʒɪktɪv] Adjektiv II
**admire** [əd'maɪə] bewundern IV 1 (35)

**adopted** [ə'dɒptɪd] adoptiert, Adoptiv- II
**adult** ['ædʌlt] Erwachsene(r) II
**advance** [əd'vɑ:ns]: **in advance** im Voraus IV 1 (21)
**advantage** [əd'vɑ:ntɪdʒ] Vorteil IV 1 (8/9)
**adventure** [əd'ventʃə] Abenteuer II
**adverb** ['ædvɜ:b] Adverb III
**advert** ['ædvɜ:t] *(kurz für:* **advertisement***)* Werbespot, Werbung; Anzeige, Inserat III
**advertise** ['ædvətaɪz] Werbung machen (für); inserieren III
**advertisement** [əd'vɜ:tɪsmənt] *(kurz auch:* **ad, advert***)* Werbespot, Werbung, Anzeige, Inserat III
**advertising** ['ædvətaɪzɪŋ] Werbung, Reklame III
**affect** [ə'fekt] beeinflussen, betreffen, sich auswirken auf IV 2 (57)
**afraid** [ə'freɪd]: **be afraid (of sth./sb.)** Angst haben (vor etwas/jm.) III
°**Afro-Caribbean** [,æfrəʊ kærɪ'bi:ən] Afro-karibisch; Afrokaribe/Afrokaribin
**after** ['ɑ:ftə]:
1. nach I   **after that** danach I
2. nachdem II
3. **run after sb.** hinter jm. herrennen I
**afternoon** [,ɑ:ftə'nu:n] Nachmittag I   **in the afternoon** nachmittags, am Nachmittag I   **on Monday afternoon** am Montagnachmittag I
**again** [ə'gen] wieder; noch einmal I   **again and again** immer wieder II   °**once again** noch einmal, wieder einmal
**against** [ə'genst] gegen I
**age** [eɪdʒ]:
1. Alter I   **… is your age** … ist so alt wie du II
2. Zeitalter III
**It's been ages …** Es ist ewig her … III
**That was ages ago.** Das ist ewig her. III
**ago** [ə'gəʊ]: **two days ago** vor zwei Tagen II

# English – German

**agree** [əˈgriː]: **agree on sth.** sich auf etwas einigen I **agree with sb.** jm. zustimmen I
**agreement** [əˈgriːmənt] Einigung; Zustimmung; Vereinbarung, Absprache IV 2 (42)
°**agricultural** [ˌægrɪˈkʌltʃərəl] landwirtschaftlich, Agrar-
**air** [eə] Luft II
**airport** [ˈeəpɔːt] Flughafen II
**aisle** [aɪl] Gang II
**album** [ˈælbəm] Album II
**alive** [əˈlaɪv]: **be alive** leben, am Leben sein III
**all** [ɔːl] alles; alle I **all alone** ganz allein II **all around her** überall um sie herum III **all day** den ganzen Tag (lang) I **all in all** alles in allem III **all of Plymouth** ganz Plymouth, das ganze Plymouth I **all over the country / the city / the world** im ganzen Land / in der ganzen Stadt / auf der ganzen Welt II **All the best** Mit besten Grüßen, Alles Gute (*Briefschluss*) IV 1 (21) **all the time** die ganze Zeit II **be all ears** (*infml*) ganz Ohr sein (*gespannt zuhören*) IV 1 (22) **of all time** aller Zeiten III
**all right** [ɔːl ˈraɪt] okay; in Ordnung I
**alligator** [ˈælɪgeɪtə] Alligator III
**allow** [əˈlaʊ] erlauben, zulassen II **be allowed to do sth.** etwas tun dürfen I
**allowance** [əˈlaʊəns] (AE) Taschengeld IV 3 (88)
**almost** [ˈɔːlməʊst] fast, beinahe I
**alone** [əˈləʊn] allein II **all alone** ganz allein II
**along** [əˈlɒŋ]:
1. **along the street** die Straße entlang I
2. **come along** mit-, herkommen I
°**sing along** mitsingen
°**alongside** [əˌlɒŋˈsaɪd] neben; längs
**aloud** [əˈlaʊd]: **read aloud** laut (vor)lesen I
**already** [ɔːlˈredi] schon, bereits I
**also** [ˈɔːlsəʊ] auch I
°**alternative** [ɔːlˈtɜːnətɪv]:
1. alternativ
2. Alternative
**although** [ɔːlˈðəʊ] obwohl II
**altitude** [ˈæltɪtjuːd] Höhe III
**altogether** [ˌɔːltəˈgeðə] insgesamt, alles in allem II
**always** [ˈɔːlweɪz] immer I
**am** [əm, em]: **4 am** 4 Uhr morgens I
**amazing** [əˈmeɪzɪŋ] erstaunlich, unglaublich III
**amount** [əˈmaʊnt] Menge; Betrag (*Geld*) IV 2 (62)
**amphitheatre** [ˈæmfɪθɪətə] Amphitheater IV 3 (81)
**an** [æn, ən] ein, eine I **... an hour ...** pro Stunde I
**ancestor** [ˈænsestə] Vorfahr/in III
°**ancestral land** [ænˈsestrəl] Land der Vorfahren
**ancestry** [ˈænsestri] Abstammung IV 2 (54)

**and** [ænd], [ənd] und I **both ... and ...** sowohl ... als auch ... III
**angel** [ˈeɪndʒl] Engel III
**angry** [ˈæŋgri] wütend I **angry with sb.** böse/wütend auf jn. II
**animal** [ˈænɪml] Tier I **state animal** Wappentier II
**anniversary** [ˌænɪˈvɜːsəri] Jahrestag IV 1 (16)
**announcement** [əˈnaʊnsmənt] Durchsage, Ansage III
**anonymous** [əˈnɒnɪməs] anonym IV 1 (35)
**another** [əˈnʌðə]:
1. ein(e) andere(r, s) I
2. noch ein(e) I
**one another** sich (gegenseitig), einander III
**answer** [ˈɑːnsə]:
1. antworten; beantworten I **answer the phone** ans Telefon gehen II
2. Antwort I
**ant** [ænt] Ameise I
°**antelope** [ˈæntɪləʊp], *pl* **antelope** *or* **antelopes** Antilope
**anthem** [ˈænθəm] Hymne II
**anticipation** [ænˌtɪsɪˈpeɪʃn] Vorfreude, Erwartung; Voraussahnung IV 3 (95)
**any** [ˈeni]:
1. **Are there any ...?** Gibt es (irgendwelche) ...? I **not ... any more** nicht mehr I **There aren't any ...** Es gibt/sind keine ... I °**(at) any time** zu jeder Zeit, jederzeit
°2. jegliche/r/s, jede/r beliebige
**anybody** [ˈenibɒdi] (irgend)jemand I **not ... anybody** niemand I
**anyone** [ˈeniwʌn] (irgend)jemand I **not ... anyone** niemand I
**anything** [ˈeniθɪŋ] (irgend)etwas I **not ... anything** nichts I
**anyway** [ˈeniweɪ] sowieso IV 2 (47) **Anyway, ...** Jedenfalls ... / Wie dem auch sei ... / Aber egal ... II **And anyway, ...** Und überhaupt, ... III
**anywhere** [ˈeniweə] überall(hin) IV 1 (20)
**apart** [əˈpɑːt] auseinander; getrennt III
**apartment** [əˈpɑːtmənt] Wohnung II
**apostrophe** [əˈpɒstrəfi] Apostroph, Auslassungszeichen I
**app** [æp] App IV 1 (12)
**appear** [əˈpɪə] erscheinen, auftauchen II
**apply (to)** [əˈplaɪ] zutreffen, gelten (für) IV 3 (97)
**appointment** [əˈpɔɪntmənt] Verabredung, Termin II
**approach** [əˈprəʊtʃ] sich nähern, herannahen II
**April** [ˈeɪprəl] April I
**aquarium** [əˈkweəriəm] Aquarium; Aquarienhaus I
°**Arab Spring** [ˌærəb ˈsprɪŋ] Arabischer Frühling
**architect** [ˈɑːkɪtekt] Architekt/in III
**archive** [ˈɑːkaɪv] Archiv IV 1 (10)
**Arctic** [ˈɑːktɪk] arktisch, Polar-; die Arktis IV 2 (48)

**are** [ɑː] bist; sind; seid I **The DVDs are ...** Die DVDs kosten ... I
**area** [ˈeəriə] Bereich; Gebiet, Gegend I
**aren't** [ɑːnt]: **you aren't ...** (= you are not) du bist nicht ...; du bist kein/e ...; ihr seid nicht ...; ihr seid kein/e ... I
**argue** [ˈɑːgjuː] streiten; sich streiten III
**argument** [ˈɑːgjumənt]:
1. Argument I
2. Streit, Auseinandersetzung III
**arm** [ɑːm] Arm II
**armchair** [ˈɑːmtʃeə] Sessel I
**army** [ˈɑːmi] Armee IV 3 (84)
**aroma** [əˈrəʊmə] Duft, Aroma IV 1 (17)
**around** [əˈraʊnd]:
1. **around ... um ... herum** **all around her** überall um sie herum III
2. **around the library** in der Bücherei umher, durch die Bücherei I
3. **walk/run/... around** herum-, umherrennen/-gehen II
**arrange** [əˈreɪndʒ] anordnen I
**arrest** [əˈrest] verhaften, festnehmen III
**arrival** [əˈraɪvl] Ankunft II
**arrive** [əˈraɪv] ankommen, eintreffen I
**arrow** [ˈærəʊ] Pfeil IV 3 (90)
**art** [ɑːt] Kunst I **work of art** Kunstwerk III
**article** [ˈɑːtɪkl] Artikel I
**artist** [ˈɑːtɪst] Künstler/in III
**artwork** [ˈɑːtwɜːk] Kunstwerk III
**as** [æz]:
1. als, während II
2. da, weil III
3. **(not) as big as** (nicht) so groß wie II **just as big** genauso groß III
4. **as a child** als Kind II
5. **as if** als ob III
6. **as soon as** sobald, sowie III
7. **as well** auch, ebenso II
**ash** [æʃ] Asche III **ashes** (*pl*) Asche (*sterbliche Überreste*) III
**ask** [ɑːsk] fragen I **ask a question** eine Frage stellen I **ask for sth.** um etwas bitten II **ask sb. the way** jn. nach dem Weg fragen II **ask sb. to do sth.** jemanden bitten, etwas zu tun I
**asleep** [əˈsliːp]: **be asleep** schlafen II
°**aspect** [ˈæspekt] Aspekt
**assemble** [əˈsembl] zusammenkommen; (sich) versammeln; zusammenbauen, montieren IV 3 (90)
**assignment** [əˈsaɪnmənt] (AE) Aufgabe, Arbeitsauftrag (*in der Schule oder daheim zu erledigen*) III
**assistant** [əˈsɪstənt] Verkäufer/in II
**astronaut** [ˈæstrənɔːt] Astronaut/in III
**at** [æt], [ət]:
1. (*in Ortsangaben*) an, bei, in I **at 14 Dean Street** in der Dean Street 14 I **at Grandma's** bei Oma II **at home** zu Hause, daheim I **at school** in der Schule I **at the top (of)** oben, am oberen Ende (von)
2. (*in Zeitangaben*) um, an I **at first** zuerst, anfangs, am Anfang II **at lunch-**

# Dictionary

**time** mittags ı **at night** nachts, in der Nacht ı **at one time** zur selben Zeit, gleichzeitig ııı **at the moment** gerade, im Moment ı **at the weekend** am Wochenende ı
3. **at last** endlich, schließlich ı **at least** zumindest, wenigstens ıı
**ate** [et], [eɪt] *siehe* **eat**
**Atlantic** [ətˈlæntɪk]: **the Atlantic (Ocean)** der Atlantik, der Atlantische Ozean ıı
**atmosphere** [ˈætməsfɪə] Atmosphäre; Stimmung ıı
**attached** [əˈtætʃt]: **be attached to sth.** an etwas hängen *(befestigt sein)*; an etwas angehängt/beigeheftet sein ııı
**attack** [əˈtæk]:
1. angreifen ıı
2. Angriff ıı
°**attend** [əˈtend] besuchen, gehen zu
°**attention** [əˈtenʃn]: **pay attention (to)** achten (auf), aufpassen (auf)
**attic** [ˈætɪk] Dachboden ı **in the attic** auf dem Dachboden ı
°**attitude (to/towards)** [ˈætɪtjuːd] Einstellung, (Geistes-)Haltung (zu/gegenüber)
**attract** [əˈtrækt] anziehen, anlocken ıv 1 (17)
**attraction** [əˈtrækʃn] Attraktion; Anziehungspunkt ııı
**audience** [ˈɔːdiəns] Publikum, Zuschauer/innen, Zuhörer/innen ıı
**audio** [ˈɔːdiəʊ] Audio-, Ton- ıv 1 (10)
**audition** [ɔːˈdɪʃn] Vorsprechen, Vorsingen, Vorspielen ıı
**August** [ˈɔːgəst] August ı
**aunt** [ɑːnt] Tante ı
°**aurora borealis** [ɔːˌrɔːrə bɔːriˈeɪlɪs] Nordlicht, nördliches Polarlicht
**author** [ˈɔːθə] Autor/in ı
**autumn** [ˈɔːtəm] Herbst ı
**available** [əˈveɪləbl] erhältlich, verfügbar; erreichbar *(am Telefon)* ııı
**avenue** [ˈævənjuː] Allee, Boulevard ııı
**average** [ˈævərɪdʒ] durchschnittlich; Durchschnitt ııı **on average** im Durchschnitt, durchschnittlich ııı
°**avoid** [əˈvɔɪd] (ver)meiden
**awake** [əˈweɪk] wach ıv 2 (58)
**award** [əˈwɔːd]:
1. Preis *(Auszeichnung)* ıv 2 (49)
2. **award sb. sth.** (*or* **award sth. to sb.**) jm. etwas zuerkennen, zusprechen, verleihen ıv 2 (49)
°**aware** [əˈweə]: **be aware of sth.** etwas wissen, sich einer Sache bewusst sein
**away** [əˈweɪ] weg, fort ı
**awesome** [ˈɔːsəm] *(bes. AE, infml)* klasse, großartig ııı
**awful** [ˈɔːfl] schrecklich, fürchterlich ıı

# B

**baby** [ˈbeɪbi] Baby ıv 2 (40) **baby seal** Robbenjunges; Heuler ı
**back** [bæk]:
1. zurück ı **back in Ottawa** zu Hause in Ottawa ıv 1 (11)
2. Rücken ı **back to back** Rücken an Rücken ıv 3 (86) **from the back of the bus** aus dem hinteren Teil des Busses ı
**back sth. up** [ˌbæk ˈʌp] etwas belegen; etwas untermauern, etwas bekräftigen ıv 2 (45)
**background** [ˈbækgraʊnd] Hintergrund ı **background file** Hintergrundinformation(en) ı
**backpack** [ˈbækpæk] Rucksack ııı
**backwards** [ˈbækwədz] rückwärts, nach hinten ıv 1 (26)
**bacon** [ˈbeɪkən] Schinkenspeck ıı
**bad** [bæd] schlecht, schlimm ı
**badlands** (*pl*) [ˈbædlændz] Ödland ıv 3 (66/67)
**bag** [bæg] Tasche, Beutel, Tüte ı **school bag** Schultasche ı
**bake** [beɪk] backen ıv 2 (40)
**bake sale** [ˈbeɪk seɪl] Kuchenbasar ıv 2 (40)
**baker** [ˈbeɪkə] Bäcker/in ıv 1 (20)
**baker's shop** [ˈbeɪkəz ʃɒp] Bäckerei ıv 1 (20)
**bakery** [ˈbeɪkəri] Bäckerei ıv 1 (20)
**balcony** [ˈbælkəni] Balkon ııı
**ball** [bɔːl] Ball ı
**balloon** [bəˈluːn] (Luft-)Ballon ıı
**band** [bænd]:
1. Band, Musikgruppe ı
°2. Gruppe, Schar (von Menschen)
**bang** [bæŋ]:
1. Knall ı
2. **bang (on) sth.** auf etwas schlagen ıv 2 (58)
**bank** [bæŋk]:
1. Bank (Geldinstitut) ııı
2. Flussufer ııı
**bar** [bɑː] Riegel *(Schokolade, Müsli)*; Tafel *(Schokolade)* ııı
**bar chart** [ˈbɑː tʃɑːt] Balkendiagramm ıv 2 (38/39)
**barbecue** [ˈbɑːbɪkjuː] Grill; Grillfest/-party ıı
**barely** [ˈbeəli] kaum ıv 3 (86)
**bark** [bɑːk] bellen ı
**barman** [ˈbɑːmən], *pl* **barmen** Barkeeper ııı
**barn** [bɑːn] Scheune, Stadel ıı
**barrel** [ˈbærəl] Fass ıv 1 (35)
**baseball** [ˈbeɪsbɔːl] Baseball ıı
°**based on** [beɪst] basierend auf
**basket** [ˈbɑːskɪt] Korb ı
**basketball** [ˈbɑːskɪtbɔːl] Basketball ı
**bath** [bɑːθ] Bad ıı
°**bathing suit** [ˈbeɪðɪŋ suːt] Badeanzug
**bathroom** [ˈbɑːθruːm] Badezimmer, Bad ı
**battery** [ˈbætəri] Batterie, Akku ııı

**battle** [ˈbætl] Schlacht; Kampf ıı
**Bavaria** [bəˈveəriə] Bayern ı
**bay** [beɪ] Bucht ıv 3 (86)
**bcc (to) (blind carbon copy)** [ˌblaɪnd ˌkɑːbən ˈkɒpi] Blindkopie (an) *(in E-Mails)* ıv 1 (21)
**BCE (before the Common Era)** [bɪˌfɔː ðə ˌkɒmən ˈɪərə] vor Christus (= vor der Christlichen Zeitrechnung) ıv 1 (17)
**be** [bi], **was/were, been** sein ı
**beach** [biːtʃ] Strand ı
°**bead** [biːd] Perle *(aus Holz, Glas etc.)*
°**beadwork** [ˈbiːdwɜːk] Perlarbeit
**bean** [biːn] Bohne ııı
**bear** [beə] Bär ı
**beard** [bɪəd] Bart ıı
**beat** [biːt], **beat, beaten** schlagen; besiegen ıı
**beaten** [ˈbiːtn] *siehe* **beat**
**beautiful** [ˈbjuːtɪfl] schön ı
**beaver** [ˈbiːvə] Biber ıv 2 (40) **eager beaver** jd., der eifrig und fleißig ist ıv 2 (40)
**became** [bɪˈkeɪm] *siehe* **become**
**because** [bɪˈkɒz] weil ı
**because of** [bɪˈkɒz əv] wegen ıv 1 (11)
**become** [bɪˈkʌm], **became, become** werden ı
**bed** [bed] Bett ı
**bed & breakfast** [ˌbed ən ˈbrekfəst] Frühstückspension; Zimmer mit Frühstück ııı
**bedroom** [ˈbedruːm] Schlafzimmer ı
**beef** [biːf] Rindfleisch ıı **roast beef** Rinderbraten ıı
**been** [biːn] *siehe* **be Have you ever been to …?** Bist du jemals in … gewesen? ıı
**beep** [biːp] piepen ıı
**before** [bɪˈfɔː]:
1. bevor ı
2. vor ı **before school/lessons** vor der Schule *(vor Schulbeginn)* / vorm Unterricht ı
3. (vorher) schon mal ıı **before long** schon bald ııı **not/never before** (vorher) noch nie ıı
**began** [bɪˈgæn] *siehe* **begin**
**begin** [bɪˈgɪn], **began, begun** beginnen, anfangen ı
**beginner** [bɪˈgɪnə] Anfänger/in ııı
**beginning** [bɪˈgɪnɪŋ] Anfang, Beginn ııı
**begun** [bɪˈgʌn] *siehe* **begin**
**behave** [bɪˈheɪv] sich verhalten, sich benehmen ııı
°**behaviour** [bɪˈheɪvjə] Verhalten; Benehmen
**behind** [bɪˈhaɪnd] hinter ı **from behind** von hinten ıı
**belief (in)** [bɪˈliːf] Glaube (an) ıv 3 (97)
**believe (in)** [bɪˈliːv] glauben (an) ıı
**bell** [bel] Klingel, Glocke ı
**belong to sb.** [bɪˈlɒŋ] jm. gehören; zu jm. gehören ııı

# English – German

**below** [bɪˈləʊ] unter, unterhalb (von); unten, darunter III
**belt** [belt] Gürtel; Band *(zum Transport)* IV 3 (90)
**bend down** [bend ˈdaʊn], **bent, bent** sich hinunterbeugen, sich bücken III **bend over** sich bücken, sich vorbeugen IV 1 (28)
**bent** [bent] *siehe* **bend**
**besides** [bɪˈsaɪdz] außerdem III
**best** [best] beste(r, s) I **All the best** Mit besten Grüßen / Alles Gute *(Briefschluss)* IV 1 (21) **the best ...** der/die/das beste ..., die besten ... I **the best thing about ...** das Beste an ... III
**bet** [bet], **bet, bet** wetten III
**better** [ˈbetə] besser I **better than ever** besser als je zuvor II **I'd better ... (= I had better ...)** Ich sollte lieber ... III
**between** [bɪˈtwiːn] zwischen I
**big** [bɪɡ] groß I **big wheel** Riesenrad I
**bike** [baɪk] Fahrrad I **ride a bike** Rad fahren I
**bilingual** [baɪˈlɪŋɡwəl] zweisprachig III
**bill** [bɪl] Rechnung IV 1 (24)
°**billion** [ˈbɪljən] Milliarde
**bird** [bɜːd] Vogel I
**birth** [bɜːθ] Geburt I
**birthday** [ˈbɜːθdeɪ] Geburtstag I **My birthday is in May.** Ich habe im Mai Geburtstag. I **My birthday is on 5th May.** Ich habe am 5. Mai Geburtstag. I **When's your birthday?** Wann hast du Geburtstag? I
**birthplace** [ˈbɜːθpleɪs] Geburtsort II
**biscuit** [ˈbɪskɪt] Plätzchen, Keks I
°**bison** [ˈbaɪsn], *pl* **bison** Bison
**bit** [bɪt]:
1. *siehe* **bite**
2. Stück(chen), Teil III
**a bit** ein bisschen, etwas I
**bite** [baɪt]:
1. Biss, Bissen III
2. **bite, bit, bitten** beißen I
**bitten** [ˈbɪtn] *siehe* **bite**
**bitter** [ˈbɪtə] erbittert; verbittert; bitter IV 3 (75)
**black** [blæk] schwarz I
°**blank** [blæŋk] freie Stelle, Leerstelle *(in einem Text)*
**blanket** [ˈblæŋkɪt] Decke *(zum Zudecken)* I
**blew** [bluː] *siehe* **blow**
**blister** [ˈblɪstə] Blase *(z.B. auf der Haut)* IV 2 (47)
**block** [blɒk]:
1. (Häuser-, Wohn-)Block III
2. blockieren, sperren III
**blog** [blɒɡ] Blog II
**blond** [blɒnd] *(bei Frauen oft:* **blonde**) blond I
**blood** [blʌd] Blut II
**bloodline** [ˈblʌdlaɪn] Stammbaum IV 3 (85)
**bloom** [bluːm] blühen III
**blow** [bləʊ], **blew, blown: blow sb. away** *(AE, infml)* jn. total umhauen IV 3 (81) **blow sth. out** etwas auspusten, ausblasen II **blow sth. up** etwas in die Luft sprengen IV 1 (35) **blow the horn** hupen III **blow the whistle** pfeifen *(auf der Trillerpfeife)* III
**blown** [bləʊn] *siehe* **blow**
**blubber** [ˈblʌbə] Tran *(aus dem Speck von Walen, Robben oder Fischen gewonnenes Öl)* IV 2 (41)
**blue** [bluː] blau I
**blueberry** [ˈbluːbəri] Blaubeere, Heidelbeere I
**board** [bɔːd] (Wand-)Tafel I
**board game** [ˈbɔːd ɡeɪm] Brettspiel III
**boarding pass** [ˈbɔːdɪŋ pɑːs] Bordkarte II
**boarding school** [ˈbɔːdɪŋ skuːl] Internat II
**boat** [bəʊt] Boot, Schiff I
**body** [ˈbɒdi]:
1. Körper I **part of the body** Körperteil II
2. Leiche III
3. Hauptteil *(eines Textes)* III
**bonfire** [ˈbɒnfaɪə] (großes Freuden-)Feuer IV 1 (34)
**book** [bʊk] Buch I
**bookmark** [ˈbʊkmɑːk]:
1. Lesezeichen IV 2 (44)
2. markieren; zu den Lesezeichen hinzufügen *(Computer)* IV 2 (44)
**bookshop** [ˈbʊkʃɒp] Buchladen, Buchhandlung I
**boot** [buːt]:
1. Stiefel II
2. Kofferraum *(Auto)* IV 3 (68)
**border** [ˈbɔːdə] Grenze III
°**boreal** [ˈbɔːriəl] boreal *(Nord-, Nordwind-)*
**bored** [bɔːd]: **be/feel bored** gelangweilt sein, sich langweilen II
**boring** [ˈbɔːrɪŋ] langweilig I
**born** [bɔːn]: **be born** geboren sein/werden II
**borough** [ˈbʌrə], [ˈbɜːrəʊ] (Stadt-)Bezirk III
**borrow** [ˈbɒrəʊ] (aus)leihen, sich borgen IV 3 (74)
**both** [bəʊθ] beide II **both ... and ...** sowohl ... als auch ... III
**bottle** [ˈbɒtl] Flasche I
**bottom** [ˈbɒtəm]: **at the bottom (of)** unten, am unteren Ende (von) II
**bought** [bɔːt] *siehe* **buy**
**bouldering** [ˈbəʊldərɪŋ] Bouldern *(Klettern in Absprunghöhe, ohne Seil)* II
**bounce** [baʊns] aufspringen (lassen), hüpfen (lassen), prellen *(Ball)* IV 2 (58)
**boundary** [ˈbaʊndri] Grenze IV 3 (69)
**boundary line** [ˈbaʊndri laɪn] Trennlinie IV 3 (69)
**bow** [baʊ] sich verbeugen, sich verneigen II
**bowl** [bəʊl] Schüssel II
**box** [bɒks] Kasten, Kiste, Kästchen I
**Boxing Day** [ˈbɒksɪŋ deɪ] 2. Weihnachtstag *(26. Dezember)* I

**boy** [bɔɪ] Junge, Bub I
**boycott** [ˈbɔɪkɒt]:
1. Boykott IV 3 (87)
2. boykottieren IV 3 (87)
**boyfriend** [ˈbɔɪfrend] (fester) Freund III
°**bracket** [ˈbrækɪt] Klammer
°**brainstorm** [ˈbreɪnstɔːm] Ideen *(ungeordnet)* sammeln
**brand** [brænd] Marke, Markenname *(bei Produkten)* IV 1 (17)
**brass band** [ˌbrɑːs ˈbænd] (Blech-)Blaskapelle III
**bread** [bred] Brot I
**break** [breɪk] Pause I
**break** [breɪk], **broke, broken:**
1. zerbrechen, kaputt machen I
2. brechen, kaputt gehen I
**breakfast** [ˈbrekfəst] Frühstück I **bed & breakfast** Frühstückspension; Zimmer mit Frühstück III **have breakfast** frühstücken I
**breath** [breθ] Atem, Atemzug II **..., he said under his breath.** ..., sagte er flüsternd / murmelte er. III
**breathe (in/out)** [briːð] (ein-/aus-)atmen IV 2 (58)
**bred** [bred] *siehe* **breed**
**breed** [briːd], **bred, bred** brüten, Junge bekommen; hervorrufen IV 2 (62)
**breeding ground** [ˈbriːdɪŋ ɡraʊnd] Brutplatz; Brutstätte IV 2 (62)
**breeze** [briːz] Brise I
**brick** [brɪk] Ziegelstein; Ziegel- IV 1 (25)
**bridge** [brɪdʒ] Brücke I
**bright** [braɪt] strahlend, leuchtend, hell I °**a bright spark** ein heller Kopf
**brilliant** [ˈbrɪliənt] großartig, genial, glänzend II
**bring** [brɪŋ], **brought, brought** (mit-, her)bringen I **bring in (hay)** (Heu) einbringen I
**British** [ˈbrɪtɪʃ] britisch I
**brochure** [ˈbrəʊʃə] Broschüre, Prospekt III
**broke** [brəʊk] *siehe* **break**
**broken** [ˈbrəʊkən]:
1. *siehe* **break**
2. zerbrochen, kaputt; gebrochen II
**brother** [ˈbrʌðə] Bruder I
**brought** [brɔːt] *siehe* **bring**
**brown** [braʊn] braun I
**buck** [bʌk] *(infml für:* **dollar**) Dollar III
**bucket** [ˈbʌkɪt] Eimer I
**buddy** [ˈbʌdi] *(infml)* Freund/in, Kumpel IV 3 (68)
**buffalo** [ˈbʌfələʊ], *pl* **buffalo** *or* **buffaloes** Büffel; Bison IV 3 (84)
**build** [bɪld], **built, built** bauen II
**builder** [ˈbɪldə] Bauarbeiter/in; Bauunternehmer/in IV 2 (58)
**building** [ˈbɪldɪŋ] Gebäude II
**built** [bɪlt] *siehe* **build**
°**bullet point** [ˈbʊlɪt pɔɪnt] Aufzählungszeichen *(Punkt)*
**bumblebee** [ˈbʌmblbiː] Hummel IV 3 (70)
°**bundle** [ˈbʌndl] Bündel, Knäuel
**buoy** [bɔɪ], [ˈbuːi] Boje III

# Dictionary

**burger** ['bɜːgə] Hamburger II
**burial** ['berɪəl] Beerdigung, Begräbnis IV 3 (75)
**burial site** ['berɪəl saɪt] Begräbnisstätte IV 3 (75)
**burn** [bɜːn] brennen; verbrennen IV 1 (18)
**burst** [bɜːst]**, burst, burst** platzen III
**bury** ['beri] begraben, beerdigen III
**bus** [bʌs] Bus I **go by bus** mit dem Bus fahren I
**busy** ['bɪzi] belebt, geschäftig, hektisch III **be busy** beschäftigt sein; viel zu tun haben I
**but** [bʌt], [bət] aber I
**butterfly** ['bʌtəflaɪ] Schmetterling I
**buy** [baɪ]**, bought, bough**t kaufen I
**by** [baɪ]:
1. **by ...** von ... II
2. **by the sea** am Meer I
3. **go by car/bus/...** mit dem Auto/Bus/... fahren I
4. **by 8 am** bis (spätestens) 8 Uhr morgens IV 2 (47) **by the time** als; wenn IV 1 (29)
**by accident** zufällig III **by mistake** aus Versehen III **by the way** übrigens III
**one by one** einer nach dem anderen II
**Bye.** [baɪ] (auch: **Bye-bye.**) Servus. / Auf Wiedersehen. I
**byline** ['baɪlaɪn] Zeile mit Angabe des Verfassers/der Verfasserin eines Zeitungsartikels IV 1 (17)

## C

**café** ['kæfeɪ] Café I
**cage** [keɪdʒ] Käfig I
**cake** [keɪk] Kuchen I
**calendar** ['kælɪndə] Kalender III
**call** [kɔːl]:
1. anrufen; rufen; nennen I **call out the names** die Namen aufrufen II
2. Anruf; Telefongespräch I
**called** [kɔːld]: **be called** heißen, genannt werden I
**caller** ['kɔːlə] Anrufer/in II
**calm** [kɑːm] ruhig III
**came** [keɪm] siehe **come**
**camera** ['kæmərə] Fotoapparat, Kamera I **video camera** Videokamera I
°**camera person** ['kæmərə pɜːrsn], pl **camera people** Kameramann/-frau
**cameraman** ['kæmrəmæn], pl **cameramen** Kameramann I
**camper** ['kæmpə] Camper/in IV 2 (61)
**campfire** ['kæmpfaɪə] Lagerfeuer IV 2 (49)
**camping** ['kæmpɪŋ] Camping, Zelten I **go camping** zelten/campen gehen II
**campsite** ['kæmpsaɪt] Zeltplatz I
**can** [kæn], [kən]:
1. können I **we can't ..., we cannot ...** wir können nicht ... I
2. dürfen I
**can** [kæn] Dose III

**candle** ['kændl] Kerze I
**canteen** [kæn'tiːn] Kantine, (Schul-)Mensa I
**cap** [kæp] Mütze, Kappe II
**capable (of)** ['keɪpəbl] fähig (zu), imstande (zu) IV 2 (65)
**capital** ['kæpɪtl] Hauptstadt I
**capital letter** [,kæpɪtl 'letə] Großbuchstabe I
°**capitol** ['kæpɪtl]: **state capitol** Staatskapitol
**captain** ['kæptɪn] Kapitän/in I
**caption** ['kæpʃn] Bildunterschrift I
**car** [kɑː] Auto I **go by car** mit dem Auto fahren I
**car park** ['kɑː pɑːk] Parkplatz (Gelände zum Abstellen von mehreren Autos) IV 3 (68)
**caravan** ['kærəvæn] Wohnwagen II
**card (to)** [kɑːd] Karte (an) I
**care** [keə]: **care about sth.** etwas wichtig nehmen III **I don't care about money.** Geld ist mir egal. III **I really care about animals.** Tiere liegen mir sehr am Herzen. / Tiere sind mir sehr wichtig. III **People don't care.** Es ist den Leuten egal. III **Who cares?** Na und? / Wen interessiert das? III °**care for sb.** sich kümmern um jn; jm. beistehen; sorgen für jn.
**careful** ['keəfl] vorsichtig I
**carefully** ['keəfəli] aufmerksam; sorgfältig III
°**caribou** ['kærɪbuː], pl **caribou** Karibu
**carnival** ['kɑːnɪvl] Karneval, Fasching III
**carpenter** ['kɑːpəntə] Tischler/in, Zimmerer/Zimmerin III
**carrot** ['kærət] Möhre, Karotte III
**carry** ['kæri] tragen III
**carry-on bag** ['kæri ɒn] Handgepäckstück, (kleine) Reisetasche II
**cart** [kɑːt] Karren I
**carve** [kɑːv] meißeln, schnitzen; (in Stein) hauen IV 3 (66/67)
**case** [keɪs]:
1. Kiste (Getränke); Behälter, Kasten, Gehäuse IV 2 (40) **glass case** Vitrine IV 2 (40)
2. Fall IV 1 (20) **in case ... falls ...**; für den Fall, dass ... IV 1 (20) **in (the) case of** im Falle von IV 1 (20)
**cash** [kæʃ] Bargeld; (infml auch:) Geld IV 3 (70) **pay cash** bar bezahlen IV 3 (70)
**cash desk** ['kæʃ desk] Kasse (in Geschäften) I
**cast** [kɑːst] Besetzung; Mitwirkende (Theaterstück, Film) II
**castle** ['kɑːsl] Burg, Schloss I
**cat** [kæt] Katze I
**catch** [kætʃ]**, caught, caught** fangen I **Catch you later.** (infml) Bis später dann! IV 1 (11)
**cathedral** [kə'θiːdrəl] Kathedrale, Dom I
**Catholic** ['kæθlɪk] Katholik/in; katholisch I
**caught** [kɔːt] siehe **catch** °**be/get caught (in)** festhängen (in)

**cave** [keɪv] Höhle II
**cc (to) (carbon copy)** [,kɑːbən 'kɒpi] Nachrichtlich; Kopie (an) (in E-Mails) IV 1 (21)
**CE (Common Era)** [,kɒmən 'ɪərə] Christliche Zeitrechnung IV 1 (17)
**celebrate** ['selɪbreɪt] feiern II
**celebration** [,selɪ'breɪʃn] Feier II
**celebrity** [sə'lebrəti] Prominente/r, Promi IV 1 (21)
**cell phone** ['sel fəʊn] (AE) Mobiltelefon, Handy I
**cellar** ['selə] Keller IV 1 (16)
**Celtic** ['keltɪk] keltisch III
**cemetery** ['semətri], ['semətəri] Friedhof III
**cent** [sent] Cent III
**centimetre (cm)** ['sentɪmiːtə] Zentimeter III
**central** ['sentrəl] zentral, Zentral-, Mittel- I
**centre** ['sentə] Zentrum; Mitte I **shopping centre** Einkaufszentrum I
**century** ['sentʃəri] Jahrhundert I
**ceremony** ['serəməni] Feier, Zeremonie IV 2 (49)
**certain** ['sɜːtn] sichere(r, s); gewisse(r, s), bestimmte(r, s) IV 1 (27)
**certainly** ['sɜːtnli] sicher(lich), auf jeden Fall, freilich II
**chain** [tʃeɪn] Kette I
**chair** [tʃeə] Stuhl I
**challenge** ['tʃælɪndʒ]:
1. Herausforderung III
2. **challenge sb. (to sth.)** jn. herausfordern (zu etwas) III
**champion** ['tʃæmpiən] Meister/in, Champion II
°**championship** ['tʃæmpiənʃɪp] Meisterschaft
**chance** [tʃɑːns] Gelegenheit, Möglichkeit, Chance II
**change** [tʃeɪndʒ]:
1. (ver)ändern; sich (ver)ändern II **change one's mind** seine Meinung ändern, es sich anders überlegen IV 3 (80)
2. umsteigen II
3. wechseln III **change money** Geld wechseln, umtauschen III
**change** [tʃeɪndʒ]:
1. Wechselgeld II
°2. Veränderung, Wechsel
**channel** ['tʃænl] Kanal; Sender IV 1 (10)
**chaos** ['keɪɒs] Chaos I
**character** ['kærəktə] Figur, Person (in Roman, Film, Theaterstück usw.) I
**charge** ['tʃɑːdʒ] (auf)laden III
**charity** ['tʃærəti] Wohlfahrtsorganisation; Wohltätigkeit, wohltätige Zwecke II
**chart** [tʃɑːt] Diagramm; Tabelle IV 2 (38/39)
**chat** [tʃæt]:
1. chatten; plaudern III
2. Chat; Unterhaltung (Gespräch) IV 1 (11)
**cheap** [tʃiːp] billig, preiswert I
**check** [tʃek]:
1. Überprüfung, Kontrolle I

# English – German

**2.** (über)prüfen, kontrollieren I
**check sth. in** etwas einchecken, aufgeben *(Gepäck)* II **check sth. out** *(infml)* sich etwas anschauen, anhören; etwas ausprobieren III
**check-in desk** [ˈtʃek ɪn desk] Abflugschalter, Abfertigungsschalter II
**check-up** [ˈtʃek ʌp] Check-up *(medizinische Vorsorgeuntersuchung)* IV 3 (93)
**checklist** [ˈtʃeklɪst] Checkliste II
**cheer** [tʃɪə] jubeln I **cheer sb. up** jn. aufheitern IV 3 (80) **Cheer up!** Kopf hoch! / Lass den Kopf nicht hängen! IV 3 (80)
**cheese** [tʃiːz] Käse I
**chemist** [ˈkemɪst] Apotheker/in II **at the chemist's** in der Apotheke, beim Apotheker II
**chess** [tʃes] Schach I
**chest** [tʃest] Brust, Brustkorb II
**chew** [tʃuː] kauen IV 2 (61) **chew sth. up** etwas zerkauen IV 2 (61)
**chicken** [ˈtʃɪkɪn] Huhn; (Brat-)Hähnchen III
**child** [tʃaɪld], *pl* **children** Kind I
**childhood** [ˈtʃaɪldhʊd] Kindheit IV 1 (17)
**children** [ˈtʃɪldrən] plural of **child**
**chill** [tʃɪl] Kühle, Kälte IV 3 (80)
**chips** *(pl)* [tʃɪps] Pommes frites II
**chocolate** [ˈtʃɒklət]:
**1.** Schokolade I
**2.** Praline II
°**choice** [tʃɔɪs] (Aus-)Wahl I
**choir** [ˈkwaɪə] Chor II
**choose** [tʃuːz], **chose, chosen** aussuchen, (aus)wählen; sich aussuchen I
**chorus** [ˈkɔːrəs] Refrain II
**chose** [tʃəʊz] siehe **choose**
**chosen** [ˈtʃəʊzn] siehe **choose**
**Christianity** [ˌkrɪstiˈænəti] Christentum IV 3 (86)
**Christmas** [ˈkrɪsməs] Weihnachten I **Merry Christmas!** Frohe Weihnachten! I
**Christmas Day** [ˌkrɪsməs ˈdeɪ] **1.** Weihnachtstag *(25. Dezember)* I
**Christmas Eve** [ˌkrɪsməs ˈiːv] Heiligabend I
**Christmas pudding** [ˌkrɪsməs ˈpʊdɪŋ] kein Pudding, sondern ein Nachtisch aus Butter, Zucker, Mehl, Rosinen, Nüssen, Eiern, Gewürzen, der traditionell zu Weihnachten gegessen wird I
**chubby** [ˈtʃʌbi] pummelig, mollig II
**church** [tʃɜːtʃ] Kirche I
**cinema** [ˈsɪnəmə] Kino I
**circa (c.)** [ˈsɜːkə] zirka (ca.) IV 1 (8/9)
**circle** [ˈsɜːkl] Kreis II
**circular** [ˈsɜːkjələ] rund IV 3 (93)
**citizen** [ˈsɪtɪzn] Staatsbürger/in IV 2 (65)
**citizenship** [ˈsɪtɪzənʃɪp] Staatsbürgerschaft IV 2 (65)
**city** [ˈsɪti] Stadt, Großstadt I
**civil rights** *(pl)* [ˌsɪvl ˈraɪts] Bürgerrechte IV 3 (96)
**claim** [kleɪm]:
**1.** angeben, behaupten IV 1 (17)

**2.** Behauptung IV 1 (17)
°**3.** beanspruchen, fordern
**clan** [klæn] Clan, Sippe IV 3 (90)
**clap** [klæp] (Beifall) klatschen I **Clap your hands.** Klatscht in die Hände. I
°**clarification** [ˌklærəfɪˈkeɪʃn] Klärung, Klarstellung, Erläuterung
°**clash** [klæʃ] Zusammenstoß, Auseinandersetzung, Konflikt
**class** [klɑːs] (Schul-)Klasse I
**class trip** [ˈklɑːs trɪp] Klassenausflug IV 1 (8/9)
**classmate** [ˈklɑːsmeɪt] Mitschüler/in, Klassenkamerad/in I
**classroom** [ˈklɑːsruːm] Klassenzimmer I
**clean** [kliːn]:
**1.** sauber machen, putzen I
**2.** sauber II
**clear** [klɪə]:
**1.** klar, deutlich II
**2.** räumen; abräumen II
**clear the land of the people** die Menschen vom Land vertreiben IV 3 (86)
**clever** [ˈklevə] klug, schlau I
**click** [klɪk] klicken III
**cliff** [klɪf] Klippe II
**climate** [ˈklaɪmət] Klima IV 2 (61)
**climb** [klaɪm]:
**1.** klettern; hinaufklettern (auf) I **climb a tree/a tower** auf einen Baum / einen Turm klettern I
**2.** Aufstieg, Anstieg III
**clock** [klɒk] (Wand-, Stand-, Turm-)Uhr I
**close** [kləʊz] schließen, zumachen II
**close (to)** [kləʊs] nah, dicht (bei, an) I
**close-up** [ˈkləʊs ʌp] Nahaufnahme *(Film)* IV 1 (15)
**closed** [kləʊzd] geschlossen I
**closely** [ˈkləʊsli]: **look closely** genau/näher hinschauen IV 2 (61)
**closet** [ˈklɒzɪt] *(bes. AE)* Wandschrank *(oft begehbar)* III
**clothes** *(pl)* [kləʊðz] Kleidung, Kleidungsstücke I
**clothing** *(no pl)* [ˈkləʊðɪŋ] Kleidung IV 3 (70) **piece of clothing** Kleidungsstück IV 3 (70)
**cloud** [klaʊd] Wolke II
**cloudless** [ˈklaʊdləs] wolkenlos IV 3 (81)
**cloudy** [ˈklaʊdi] bewölkt II
**clown** [klaʊn] Clown II
**club** [klʌb] Klub, Verein I **join a club** in einen Klub eintreten; sich einem Klub anschließen I
**clue** [kluː] (Lösungs-)Hinweis; Anhaltspunkt III
**clueless** [ˈkluːləs] ratlos; ahnungslos, unbedarft IV 3 (80)
**co-educational** [ˌkəʊ edʒuˈkeɪʃnəl] *(kurz auch:* **coed***)* koedukativ, gemischt *(mit beiden Geschlechtern, z.B. Schulen)* IV 2 (40)
**coach** [kəʊtʃ]:
**1.** Trainer/in IV 2 (40)
**2. coach sb.** jn. trainieren, jm. Unterricht geben IV 2 (63)

**coal** [kəʊl] Kohle III
**coal mine** [ˈkəʊl maɪn] Kohlebergwerk III
**coast** [kəʊst] Küste I
**coat** [kəʊt] Mantel II
**cocoa** [ˈkəʊkəʊ] Kakao II
**coed** [ˌkəʊ ˈed] siehe **co-educational**
**coffee** [ˈkɒfi] Kaffee I
°**coffers** *(pl)* [ˈkɒfəz] (Staats-)Schatulle, (Staats-)Säckel
**coin** [kɔɪn] Münze I
**cola** [ˈkəʊlə] Cola I
**cold** [kəʊld]:
**1.** kalt I **be cold** frieren I
**2. have a cold** eine Erkältung haben, erkältet sein II
**collapse** [kəˈlæps] einstürzen; zusammenbrechen III
**collect** [kəˈlekt] sammeln I
**college** [ˈkɒlɪdʒ] Hochschule IV 3 (74)
**collocation** [ˌkɒləˈkeɪʃn] Kollokation *(Wörter, die oft zusammen vorkommen)* IV 2 (61)
**colloquial** [kəˈləʊkwiəl] umgangssprachlich IV 2 (41)
**colon** [ˈkəʊlən] Doppelpunkt II
**colonial** [kəˈləʊniəl] kolonial, Kolonial- IV 3 (96)
**colonist** [ˈkɒlənɪst] Kolonist/in, Siedler/in IV 3 (96)
°**colonizer** [ˈkɒlənaɪzə] Kolonisator/in
**colony** [ˈkɒləni] Kolonie II
**colour** [ˈkʌlə] Farbe I **What colour …?** Welche Farbe …? I
**coloured** [ˈkʌləd] farbig, bunt III
**colourful** [ˈkʌləfl] farbenfroh, farbenprächtig, bunt III
**column** [ˈkɒləm] Säule III
**combination** [ˌkɒmbɪˈneɪʃn] Kombination, Verbindung IV 2 (64)
**combine** [kəmˈbaɪn] verbinden, kombinieren IV 2 (64)
**come** [kʌm]**, came, come:**
**1.** kommen I **come across sb./sth.** auf jn./etwas stoßen, jn./etwas (zufällig) treffen III **come along** mitkommen, herkommen I **come down with sth.** etwas bekommen *(Krankheit)*, an etwas erkranken III **come in** hereinkommen I **Come on, Dad.** Na los, Dad! / Komm, Dad! I **come over (to)** herüberkommen (zu/nach), vorbeikommen (bei) III **come up** auftauchen; vorkommen, erwähnt werden IV 3 (80) **come up with sth.** etwas haben, auf etwas kommen *(Idee, Vorschlag)* III
**2. come true** wahr werden IV 2 (46) **a dream come true** ein wahr gewordener Traum IV 2 (46)
**comedy** [ˈkɒmədi] Komödie II
**comfortable** [ˈkʌmftəbl] bequem II
°**comfortless** [ˈkʌmftləs] trostlos; ungemütlich, unbehaglich
**comma** [ˈkɒmə] Komma II
**commemorate sb./sth.** [kəˈmeməreɪt] jemandes/einer Sache gedenken IV 1 (22)

# Dictionary

**comment** [ˈkɒment]:
1. Bemerkung, Kommentar III
2. **comment (on sth.)** sich äußern (zu etwas), (etwas) kommentieren III

**common** [ˈkɒmən]:
1. häufig; weit verbreitet III
2. **have sth. in common** etwas gemeinsam haben, etwas miteinander gemein haben IV 3 (90)
°3. gemeinsam

**Commonwealth** [ˈkɒmənwelθ] Gemeinschaft der Länder des ehemaligen Britischen Weltreichs IV 1 (11)

°**communicate (with sb.)** [kəˈmjuːnɪkeɪt] (mit jm.) kommunizieren; sich (mit jm.) verständigen

**communication** [kəˌmjuːnɪˈkeɪʃn] Kommunikation, Verständigung III **Information and Communications Technology** Informations- und Kommunikationstechnologie I

**community** [kəˈmjuːnəti] Gemeinschaft, Gemeinde IV 2 (41)

**company** [ˈkʌmpəni] Firma, Gesellschaft III

**compare** [kəmˈpeə] vergleichen III **compared to …** verglichen mit … III

**comparison** [kəmˈpærɪsn] Vergleich IV 2 (45) **make comparisons** Vergleiche anstellen IV 2 (45)

**compass** [ˈkʌmpəs] Kompass IV 3 (91)

**compassion (for)** [kəmˈpæʃn] Mitleid (mit); Mitgefühl; Barmherzigkeit IV 2 (65)

**compete (with)** [kəmˈpiːt] (in Wettbewerben) antreten (gegen); konkurrieren (mit) IV 2 (40)

**competition** [ˌkɒmpəˈtɪʃn] Wettbewerb II

**competitive** [kəmˈpetətɪv] leistungsorientiert, ehrgeizig; wettbewerbsorientiert IV 2 (45)

**competitor** [kəmˈpetɪtə] Wettbewerbsteilnehmer/in; Konkurrent/in, Konkurrenz IV 2 (61)

**complain** [kəmˈpleɪn] sich beschweren, sich beklagen III

**complaint** [kəmˈpleɪnt] Beschwerde IV 3 (96) **make a complaint (about sth.)** eine Beschwerde vorbringen (über etwas), etwas beanstanden IV 3 (96)

**complete** [kəmˈpliːt]:
1. vervollständigen IV 1 (35)
2. vollständig, komplett IV 1 (35)

**computer** [kəmˈpjuːtə] Computer I

**concentrate (on sth.)** [ˈkɒnsntreɪt] sich konzentrieren (auf etwas) III

**concert** [ˈkɒnsət] Konzert I

**conclusion** [kənˈkluːʒn] Schluss(folgerung) III

**condemn** [kənˈdem] verurteilen, verdammen IV 2 (64)

**confederacy** [kənˈfedərəsi] Bund, Bündnis, Konföderation IV 3 (91)

°**confederation** [kənˌfedəˈreɪʃn] Bund, Konföderation

**confident** [ˈkɒnfɪdənt] (selbst)sicher; zuversichtlich IV 3 (74)

**conflict** [ˈkɒnflɪkt] Konflikt, Auseinandersetzung, Streit IV 3 (75)

**confront sb. (with)** [kənˈfrʌnt] jn. konfrontieren (mit) IV 3 (66/67)

**confrontation** [ˌkɒnfrʌnˈteɪʃn] Konfrontation, Auseinandersetzung IV 3 (66/67)

**confuse** [kənˈfjuːz] verwirren; verwechseln IV 3 (80)

**Congratulations (on sth.)!** [kənˌgrætʃʊˈleɪʃnz] Herzlichen Glückwunsch (zu etwas)! IV 1 (25)

**congress** [ˈkɒŋgres] Kongress IV 3 (87)

°**coniferous** [kəˈnɪfərəs] Nadel-

°**connected** [kəˈnektɪd]: **be connected** verbunden sein III

°**connection** [kəˈnekʃn] Verbindung; Anschluss

°**conquistador** [kɒnˈkwɪstədɔː], pl **conquistadores** Konquistador (spanischer Eroberer)

°**conquistadores** [kɒnˌkwɪstəˈdɔːreɪz] plural of **conquistador**

**consent** [kənˈsent]:
1. einwilligen, zustimmen IV 3 (96)
2. Einwilligung, Zustimmung; Genehmigung IV 3 (96)

**consequence** [ˈkɒnsɪkwəns] Folge, Konsequenz III

°**consider sth.** [kənˈsɪdə] über etwas nachdenken, sich etwas überlegen; etwas erwägen

°**consist of** [kənˈsɪst_əv] bestehen aus

**consonant** [ˈkɒnsənənt] Konsonant, Mitlaut I

**conspirator** [kənˈspɪrətə] Verschwörer/in IV 1 (34)

**constitution** [ˌkɒnstɪˈtjuːʃn] Verfassung IV 3 (96)

**consult** [kənˈsʌlt]: **consult sb.** jn. fragen, konsultieren IV 1 (11) **consult with sb.** (AE) sich mit jm. beraten IV 1 (11)

**contact** [ˈkɒntækt]:
1. Kontakt IV 1 (12) **make eye contact** Blickkontakt herstellen III
2. **contact sb.** Kontakt aufnehmen mit jm., sich in Verbindung setzen mit jm. IV 1 (12)

**contact details** (pl) [ˈkɒntækt ˌdiːteɪlz] Kontaktdaten IV 1 (21)

**contemporary** [kənˈtemprəri] modern, zeitgenössisch IV 2 (65)

**content** [ˈkɒntent] Inhalt III

°**contest** [ˈkɒntest] Wettbewerb

**context** [ˈkɒntekst] (Text-, Satz-)Zusammenhang, Kontext II

°**continent** [ˈkɒntɪnənt] Kontinent

**continental** [ˌkɒntɪˈnentl] kontinental IV 3 (87)

°**continually** [kənˈtɪnjuəli] ständig, dauernd

**continue** [kənˈtɪnjuː] sich fortsetzen, weitergehen III **continue sth.** etwas fortsetzen III

**contrast** [kənˈtrɑːst] gegenüberstellen, vergleichen IV 2 (53)

**contrast** [ˈkɒntrɑːst] Kontrast, Gegensatz IV 2 (53)

**control** [kənˈtrəʊl]:
1. Kontrolle IV 3 (69)
2. kontrollieren, regulieren IV 3 (69)

**conversation** [ˌkɒnvəˈseɪʃn] Gespräch, Unterhaltung II

**cook** [kʊk] kochen; zubereiten III

**cookie** [ˈkʊki] (AE) Keks, Plätzchen II

**cool** [kuːl]:
1. cool II
2. kühl II

**coordinator** [kəʊˈɔːdɪneɪtə] Koordinator/in III

**copy** [ˈkɒpi]:
1. kopieren, abschreiben I
2. Kopie; Exemplar II

**core** [kɔː] Kern; Basis IV 2 (65) **… are core to …** … bilden den Kern von …, … sind zentral für … IV 2 (65)

**corn** (no pl) [kɔːn] (AE) Mais II

**corner** [ˈkɔːnə] Ecke I **on the corner of Church Road and London Road** Church Road, Ecke London Road II

**corner shop** [ˈkɔːnə ʃɒp] Laden an der Ecke; Tante-Emma-Laden I

**cornflakes** [ˈkɔːnfleɪks] Cornflakes I

**corral** [kəˈrɑːl] Gehege; (Vieh-)Pferch IV 3 (74)

**correct** [kəˈrekt]:
1. richtig, korrekt II
2. korrigieren, verbessern II

°**correction** [kəˈrekʃn] Berichtigung, Korrektur

**corridor** [ˈkɒrɪdɔː] Gang, Korridor III

°**cos (= because)** [kəz] (infml) weil

**cost** [kɒst], **cost, cost** kosten II

**costume** [ˈkɒstjuːm] Kostüm, Verkleidung II

**cottage** [ˈkɒtɪdʒ] Häuschen, Cottage II

**cotton** [ˈkɒtn] Baumwolle III

**cough** [kɒf]: **have a cough** Husten haben II

**could** [kʊd]:
1. he could … er konnte … I **we couldn't …** wir konnten nicht … I
2. **it could** es könnte II

**council** [ˈkaʊnsl] Ausschuss; Rat (Stadtrat, Gemeinderat u.Ä.) III

**count (to …)** [kaʊnt] zählen (bis) I

**counter** [ˈkaʊntə] Theke; Ladentisch IV 3 (68)

**country** [ˈkʌntri] Land I

**countryside** [ˈkʌntrisaɪd] Landschaft, ländliche Gegend II

**county** [ˈkaʊnti] Grafschaft (in Großbritannien) I

**couple** [ˈkʌpl]: **a couple** ein Paar; ein paar III

**course** [kɔːs] Kurs, Lehrgang I

**courtyard** [ˈkɔːtjɑːd] Hof, Innenhof; Vorplatz II

**cousin** [ˈkʌzn] Cousin, Cousine I

**cover** [ˈkʌvə]:
1. bedecken, zudecken III **cover sth. up** etwas abdecken, zudecken IV 1 (16)

# English – German

2. behandeln, abdecken, ansprechen *(Thema; Fragen)* III
**cow** [kaʊ] Kuh II
**cowboy** [ˈkaʊbɔɪ] Cowboy IV 3 (77)
**coyote** [kaɪˈəʊti] Kojote IV 2 (58)
**crab** [kræb] Krebs I
**cracker** [ˈkrækə] Knallbonbon I
**crash** [kræʃ]:
1. crashen II
2. abstürzen *(Flugzeug; Computer)* III
3. Krachen; Unfall, Zusammenstoß IV 3 (88)

**crate** [kreɪt] Kiste; Kasten *(für Getränke)* IV 3 (87)
**crazy** [ˈkreɪzi] verrückt III
**cream** [kriːm] Sahne I **ice cream** (Speise-)Eis I
**create** [kriˈeɪt] schaffen, erschaffen, kreieren III
**creation** [kriˈeɪʃn] Schaffung; Kreation, Werk IV 3 (81)
**creative** [kriˈeɪtɪv] kreativ IV 3 (81)
**credits** *(pl)* [ˈkredɪts] Credits *(Vor- oder Nachspann, z.B. eines Films)* IV 1 (15)
**creep** [kriːp], **crept, crept** schleichen; kriechen IV 1 (27)
**crept** [krept] *siehe* **creep**
**crib sheet** [ˈkrɪb ʃiːt] *(infml)* Spickzettel, Merkzettel II
**cricket** [ˈkrɪkɪt] Kricket I
**criticize sb. (for)** [ˈkrɪtɪsaɪz] jn. kritisieren *(wegen)* IV 3 (81)
°**crop** [krɒp] Feldfrucht, Anbaupflanze; Ernte
**cross** [krɒs] überqueren, kreuzen; sich kreuzen II
**cross-country** [ˌkrɒs ˈkʌntri] Skilanglauf; Querfeldeinrennen IV 2 (46)
°**crossing** [ˈkrɒsɪŋ] Überquerung; Überfahrt; Kreuzung
**crowd** [kraʊd] (Menschen-)Menge II
**crowded** [ˈkraʊdɪd] voller Menschen; überfüllt II
**crown** [kraʊn] Krone II
**crude** [kruːd] roh, grob IV 3 (75)
**crude oil** [ˌkruːd ˈɔɪl] Rohöl IV 3 (75)
**crush** [krʌʃ] (zer)quetschen; (aus)pressen IV 3 (95)
**cry** [kraɪ]:
1. schreien; weinen II
2. Schrei, Ruf IV 1 (26)

**cultural** [ˈkʌltʃərəl] kulturell IV 1 (10)
**culture** [ˈkʌltʃə] Kultur II
**cup** [kʌp] Tasse I **a cup of tea** eine Tasse Tee I
**cupboard** [ˈkʌbəd] Schrank I
**curds** *(pl)* [kɜːdz] Quark IV 2 (41)
**curious** [ˈkjʊəriəs] wissbegierig, neugierig III
**currency** [ˈkʌrənsi] Währung III
**curry** [ˈkʌri] Curry(gericht) I
**customs** *(pl)* [ˈkʌstəmz] Bräuche, Gebräuche, Sitten IV 3 (86)
**cut** [kʌt], **cut, cut** schneiden II
**Cut!** Schnitt! *(beim Filmen)* III
°**cuz** [kʌz] *infml für* **cousin**

**cyberbullying** [ˈsaɪbəbʊliɪŋ] Cyber-Mobbing *(Verleumdung/Diffamierung in sozialen Medien)* III

# D

**dad** [dæd] Papa, Vati I
**daily** [ˈdeɪli] täglich III
**dam** [dæm] Damm, Staudamm IV 2 (58)
**dance** [dɑːns]:
1. tanzen I
2. Tanz II

**dance floor** [ˈdɑːns flɔː] Tanzfläche II
**dancer** [ˈdɑːnsə] Tänzer/in II
**danger** [ˈdeɪndʒə] Gefahr II
**dangerous** [ˈdeɪndʒərəs] gefährlich I
**dark** [dɑːk]:
1. dunkel I
2. Dunkelheit III

**darkness** [ˈdɑːknəs] Dunkelheit, Finsternis III
**date** [deɪt]:
1. Datum III
2. Verabredung, Date III
3. **date from** stammen aus *(zeitlich)* III

**daughter** [ˈdɔːtə] Tochter II
**day** [deɪ] Tag I **day of the week** Wochentag I **all day** den ganzen Tag (lang) I
**daylight** [ˈdeɪlaɪt] Tageslicht IV 1 (22)
**dead** [ded] tot I
**dear** [dɪə] liebe(r, s) I **Dear Sir or Madam** Sehr geehrte Damen und Herren II **Oh dear!** Oje! II
**death** [deθ] Tod III
**December** [dɪˈsembə] Dezember I
**decide** [dɪˈsaɪd] beschließen, sich entscheiden I
°**deciduous** [dɪˈsɪdʒuəs] Laub- *(jedes Jahr die Blätter verlierend)*
**decision** [dɪˈsɪʒn] Entscheidung III
**deck** [dek] Deck *(eines Schiffes)* I
**declaration** [ˌdekləˈreɪʃn] Erklärung, Verkündung II **the Declaration of Independence** die Unabhängigkeitserklärung *(der Vereinigten Staaten im Jahr 1776)* II
**declare** [dɪˈkleə] verkünden, erklären IV 3 (69)
**deep** [diːp] tief II
**deer** [dɪə], *pl* **deer** Reh, Hirsch III
**defeat** [dɪˈfiːt] besiegen, schlagen III
**defend sb./sth. (against sb./sth.)** [dɪˈfend] jn./etwas verteidigen *(gegen jn./etwas)* II
°**definition** [defɪˈnɪʃn] Definition
**delete** [dɪˈliːt] löschen; streichen III
**delicious** [dɪˈlɪʃəs] köstlich, lecker II
°**delish** [dɪˈlɪʃ] *(infml, kurz für:* **delicious***)* köstlich, lecker
**deliver** [dɪˈlɪvə] (aus)liefern IV 2 (62)
**demand** [dɪˈmɑːnd]:
1. fordern, verlangen IV 3 (96)
2. Forderung, Anforderung IV 3 (96)

**on demand** auf Abruf, nach Bedarf III

**democracy** [dɪˈmɒkrəsi] Demokratie IV 2 (65)
**democratic** [ˌdeməˈkrætɪk] demokratisch IV 2 (65)
**demonstration** [ˌdemənˈstreɪʃn] Demonstration, Vorführung II
**den** [den] Bau, Höhle *(z.B. von Raubtier)* IV 2 (58)
**dentist** [ˈdentɪst] Zahnarzt/-ärztin II
°**department** [dɪˈpɑːtmənt] Amt, Ministerium; Abteilung
**depend on sth.** [dɪˈpend] von etwas abhängen; auf etwas angewiesen sein III
**descent** [dɪˈsent] Herkunft, Abstammung IV 3 (97)
**describe sth. (to sb.)** [dɪˈskraɪb] (jm.) etwas beschreiben II
**description** [dɪˈskrɪpʃn] Beschreibung IV 2 (44)
**descriptive** [dɪˈskrɪptɪv] beschreibend IV 2 (41)
**desert** [ˈdezət] Wüste IV 3 (93)
**design** [dɪˈzaɪn]:
1. Design; Gestaltung III
2. entwerfen, konstruieren, entwickeln IV 1 (19)

**design and technology** [dɪˌzaɪn ənd tekˈnɒlədʒi] Design und Technik I
**desk** [desk] Schreibtisch I
**despite** [dɪˈspaɪt] trotz IV 3 (75)
**dessert** [dɪˈzɜːt] Nachtisch, Nachspeise I
**destination** [ˌdestɪˈneɪʃn] Reiseziel, Fahrtziel; Bestimmungsort IV 1 (10)
°**destiny** [ˈdestəni] Schicksal; Vorsehung
**destroy** [dɪˈstrɔɪ] zerstören II
**destruction** [dɪˈstrʌkʃn] Zerstörung, Vernichtung IV 2 (64)
**detail** [ˈdiːteɪl] Detail, Einzelheit III
**detective** [dɪˈtektɪv] Detektiv/in IV 2 (59)
°**detox** [ˈdiːtɒks] *(infml)* Entzug, Entgiftung(sbehandlung)
**develop** [dɪˈveləp] (sich) entwickeln IV 2 (47)
**development** [dɪˈveləpmənt] Entwicklung IV 2 (47)
°**diagram** [ˈdaɪəgræm] Diagramm
**dialect** [ˈdaɪəlekt] Dialekt IV 1 (17)
**dialogue** [ˈdaɪəlɒg] Dialog II
**diary** [ˈdaɪəri] Tagebuch; Kalender I
°**keep a diary** (ein) Tagebuch führen
**dictionary** [ˈdɪkʃənri] alphabetisches Wörterverzeichnis, Wörterbuch I
**did** [dɪd] *siehe* **do**
**He didn't run.** Er rannte nicht. I
**die** [daɪ] sterben I **die out** aussterben III
**difference** [ˈdɪfrəns] Unterschied II
**different** [ˈdɪfrənt] verschieden; anders I
**difficult** [ˈdɪfɪkəlt] schwierig, schwer III
°**difficulty** [ˈdɪfɪkəlti] Schwierigkeit(en)
**dig** [dɪg], **dug, dug** graben IV 3 (75)
**digital** [ˈdɪdʒɪtl] digital III
**dining room** [ˈdaɪnɪŋ ruːm] Esszimmer I
**dinner** [ˈdɪnə] Abendessen, Abendbrot I
**have dinner** zu Abend essen I
**dinosaur** [ˈdaɪnəsɔː] Dinosaurier I

# Dictionary

**diplomatic** [ˌdɪpləˈmætɪk] diplomatisch, Diplomaten- IV 1 (11)
**direct** [dəˈrekt] direkt II **direct train** durchgehender Zug II
**direction** [dəˈrekʃn] Richtung IV 1 (26)
**director** [dəˈrektə]:
1. Leiter/in III
2. Regisseur/in II
**dirt** [dɜːt] Dreck II
**dirty** [ˈdɜːti] schmutzig II
**disadvantage** [ˌdɪsədˈvɑːntɪdʒ] Nachteil IV 1 (8/9)
°**disagree** [ˌdɪsəˈɡriː] nicht zustimmen, widersprechen
**disappear** [ˌdɪsəˈpɪə] verschwinden II
**disappoint sb.** [ˌdɪsəˈpɔɪnt] jn. enttäuschen IV 3 (80)
**disappointed** [ˌdɪsəˈpɔɪntɪd] enttäuscht IV 3 (80)
**disappointing** [ˌdɪsəˈpɔɪntɪŋ] enttäuschend IV 3 (80)
**disco** [ˈdɪskəʊ] Disko I
**discover** [dɪˈskʌvə] entdecken IV 1 (20)
**discovery** [dɪˈskʌvəri] Entdeckung IV 1 (20)
°**discuss** [dɪˈskʌs] diskutieren (über)
**discussion** [dɪˈskʌʃn] Diskussion III
**disease** [dɪˈziːz] (ansteckende) Krankheit III
**disguise** [dɪsˈɡaɪz] (sich) verkleiden; (sich) tarnen IV 3 (87)
**disgusting** [dɪsˈɡʌstɪŋ] ekelhaft, widerlich III
**dish** [dɪʃ] Gericht (Mahlzeit); Schüssel, Schale IV 3 (95)
**dishes** (pl) [ˈdɪʃɪz]: **wash the dishes** das Geschirr abwaschen, spülen II
**dislike** [dɪsˈlaɪk] nicht mögen, nicht leiden können III
°**displace** [dɪsˈpleɪs] verdrängen, vertreiben
**dissatisfied** [dɪsˈsætɪsfaɪd] unzufrieden IV 3 (75)
**distance** [ˈdɪstəns] Distanz, Entfernung; Strecke IV 1 (27) **keep your distance (from)** Abstand halten (zu/von) IV 1 (27)
°**distinct** [dɪˈstɪŋkt] verschieden, unterschiedlich; deutlich
**district** [ˈdɪstrɪkt] Bezirk, Gebiet, (Stadt-)Viertel IV 1 (20)
**ditch** [dɪtʃ] Graben III
**diverse** [daɪˈvɜːs] unterschiedlich, vielfältig IV 1 (17)
**diversity** [daɪˈvɜːsəti] Vielfalt IV 1 (17)
°**divide (up) (into)** [dɪˈvaɪd] auf-/einteilen (in)
**divorce** [dɪˈvɔːs] Scheidung III
**divorced** [dɪˈvɔːst] geschieden I
**dizzy** [ˈdɪzi] schwindlig III
**do** [duː], **did, done** machen, tun I **do sport** Sport treiben I **Don't go.** Geh nicht. I **he doesn't have time** er hat keine Zeit I
**dock** [dɒk] Hafen, Dock III
**doctor** [ˈdɒktə] Arzt/Ärztin, Doktor II

**document** [ˈdɒkjumənt] Dokument; Text(datei) IV 3 (96)
**documentary** [ˌdɒkjuˈmentri] Dokumentarfilm III
**dog** [dɒɡ] Hund I **walk the dog** mit dem Hund rausgehen, den Hund ausführen III
**doll** [dɒl] Puppe III
**dollar** [ˈdɒlə] Dollar ($) III
**dome** [dəʊm] Kuppel II
**done** [dʌn] siehe **do**
**donut** [ˈdəʊnʌt] (AE) Donut (ringförmiges Gebäck aus Hefeteig) IV 2 (47)
**door** [dɔː] Tür I
**doorbell** [ˈdɔːbel] Türklingel, Türglocke II
**doorway** [ˈdɔːweɪ] Eingang III
**dosh** [dɒʃ] Knete (infml für Geld) IV 3 (70)
**double** [ˈdʌbl] Doppel- I
**dough** [dəʊ] Teig (Hefeteig) IV 3 (83)
**down** [daʊn] hinunter, herunter; nach unten I **down there** da/dort unten; nach da/dort unten II **up and down** auf und ab; rauf und runter I
**downhill** [ˌdaʊnˈhɪl] bergab III
**download sth.** [ˌdaʊnˈləʊd] etwas herunterladen III
**downstairs** [ˌdaʊnˈsteəz] unten; nach unten (im Haus) I
**downstream** [ˌdaʊnˈstriːm] flussabwärts III
**downtown** [ˈdaʊntaʊn]: **in downtown Albuquerque** (AE) im Zentrum von Albuquerque II
**dozen** [ˈdʌzn], pl **dozen** Dutzend IV 2 (46)
**draft** [drɑːft] Entwurf II
**drama** [ˈdrɑːmə] Schauspiel; darstellende Kunst II
**drank** [dræŋk] siehe **drink**
**draw** [drɔː], **drew, drawn** zeichnen I
**draw** [drɔː] (bes. BE) Unentschieden III
**drawing** [ˈdrɔːɪŋ] Zeichnung I
**drawn** [drɔːn] siehe **draw**
**dream** [driːm] Traum I **a dream come true** ein wahr gewordener Traum IV 2 (46)
**dress** [dres]:
1. Kleid I
2. sich kleiden, sich anziehen IV 2 (52) **dress up** sich verkleiden; sich schick anziehen II **get dressed** sich anziehen IV 2 (52)
**drew** [druː] siehe **draw**
**drink** [drɪŋk]:
1. Getränk I
2. **drink, drank, drunk** trinken I
**drive** [draɪv], **drove, driven**:
1. (mit dem Auto) fahren I
2. treiben; antreiben IV 1 (17)
°**drive-in** [ˈdraɪv ɪn] Drive-In(-Restaurant); Autokino
**driven** [ˈdrɪvn] siehe **drive**
**driver's license** [ˈdraɪvəz laɪsns] (AE) Führerschein IV 3 (72)
**driving licence** [ˈdraɪvɪŋ laɪsns] Führerschein IV 3 (71)
°**droop** [druːp] herabhängen

**drop** [drɒp]:
1. fallen III
2. **drop sth.** etwas fallen lassen II
**drove** [drəʊv] siehe **drive**
**drum** [drʌm] Trommel I **drums** (pl) Schlagzeug I **play the drums** Schlagzeug spielen I
**drummer** [ˈdrʌmə] Trommler/in; Schlagzeuger/in III
**drunk** [drʌŋk] siehe **drink**
**dry** [draɪ] trocken III
**dude** [djuːd] (bes. AE, Slang) Typ, Kerl III
**dug** [dʌɡ] siehe **dig**
**during** [ˈdjʊərɪŋ] während III
**dust** [dʌst] Staub III
**dusty** [ˈdʌsti] staubig IV 3 (66/67)
**DVD** [ˌdiːviːˈdiː] DVD I

# E

**each** [iːtʃ] jeder, jede, jedes (einzelne) II **each other** sich (gegenseitig), einander III **They're £2.75 each.** Sie kosten je 2 Pfund 75. (2,75 pro Stück) I
**eager** [ˈiːɡə] eifrig; begeistert IV 2 (40) **eager beaver** jd., der eifrig und fleißig ist IV 2 (40) **be eager to do sth.** etwas unbedingt tun wollen IV 2 (40)
**eagle** [ˈiːɡl] Adler IV 3 (90)
**ear** [ɪə] Ohr I **be all ears** (infml) ganz Ohr sein (gespannt zuhören) IV 1 (22)
**early** [ˈɜːli] früh I **He's in his early thirties.** Er ist Anfang dreißig. IV 3 (84)
**earn** [ɜːn] verdienen (Geld) IV 3 (70)
**earphones** (pl) [ˈɪəfəʊnz] Ohrhörer, Kopfhörer II
**earring** [ˈɪərɪŋ] Ohrring III
**earth** [ɜːθ]: **(the) earth** (oft auch: **Earth**) (die) Erde (der Planet) II **on earth** auf der Erde II
**east** [iːst] Osten; nach Osten; östlich III
**eastbound** [ˈiːstbaʊnd] Richtung Osten III
**Easter** [ˈiːstə] Ostern I
**eastern** [ˈiːstən] östlich, Ost- III
°**eastward(s)** [ˈiːstwəd] ostwärts, nach/gen Osten
**easy** [ˈiːzi] leicht, einfach I
**eat** [iːt], **ate, eaten** essen I
**eaten** [ˈiːtn] siehe **eat**
**economic** [ˌiːkəˈnɒmɪk] wirtschaftlich, Wirtschafts- IV 3 (96)
°**economics** [ˌiːkəˈnɒmɪks] Wirtschaftslehre
**edge** [edʒ] Rand, Kante III
**edit** [ˈedɪt] bearbeiten; schneiden (Film, Video) I
**editor** [ˈedɪtə] Redakteur/in; Herausgeber/in III
**educate sb.** [ˈedʒukeɪt] jn. ausbilden, unterrichten, erziehen IV 3 (71)
**education** [ˌedʒuˈkeɪʃn] (Schul-, Aus-)Bildung; Erziehung III
°**educational** [ˌedʒuˈkeɪʃnl] Erziehungs-, Bildungs-

# English – German

**educator** [ˈedʒukeɪtə] Pädagoge/Pädagogin IV 2 (65)
°**effect** [ɪˈfekt] (Aus-)Wirkung, Einfluss, Effekt
°**effective** [ɪˈfektɪv] effektiv, wirksam
**e.g.** [ˌiːˈdʒiː] (from Latin: exempli gratia) z.B. (zum Beispiel) II
**egg** [eg] Ei I
**eight** [eɪt] acht I
**either** [ˈaɪðə], [ˈiːðə]: **either … or …** entweder … oder … III  **not … either** auch nicht I
**elder** [ˈeldə] Älteste(r) (z.B. eines Stammes) IV 2 (41)
**elect sb. (to be) sth.** [ɪˈlekt] jn. zu etwas wählen IV 3 (93)
**election** [ɪˈlekʃn] Wahl (Abstimmung) IV 3 (93)
°**electronic** [ɪˌlekˈtrɒnɪk] elektronisch
**element** [ˈelɪmənt] Element III
**elephant** [ˈelɪfənt] Elefant I
**elevator** [ˈelɪveɪtə] (bes. AE) Fahrstuhl, Aufzug, Lift II
**eleven** [ɪˈlevn] elf I
**else** [els]: **everyone else** alle anderen; sonst jeder IV 1 (11)
**email** [ˈiːmeɪl]:
1. E-Mail I
2. **email (sb. sth.)** (jm. etwas) mailen IV 1 (12)
**embarrassing** [ɪmˈbærəsɪŋ] peinlich III
**embassy** [ˈembəsi] Botschaft (diplomatische Vertretung) IV 1 (17)
**emerge (from …)** [ɪˈmɜːdʒ] herauskommen, hervortreten, auftauchen (aus …) IV 1 (22)
**emigrant** [ˈemɪgrənt] Auswanderer, Auswanderin IV 1 (17)
**emigrate** [ˈemɪgreɪt] auswandern, emigrieren III
**emigration** [ˌemɪˈgreɪʃn] Auswanderung IV 1 (17)
**emphasis** [ˈemfəsɪs] Betonung, Hervorhebung III
°**emphasize** [ˈemfəsaɪz] betonen, hervorheben
**empire** [ˈempaɪə] Reich, Imperium III
**employ sb.** [ɪmˈplɔɪ] jn. anstellen, beschäftigen IV 1 (32)
**empty** [ˈempti]:
1. leer III
2. leeren IV 3 (86)
**encore** [ˈɒŋkɔː] Zugabe II
°**encounter** [ɪnˈkaʊntə] Begegnung
**encourage** [ɪnˈkʌrɪdʒ] ermutigen, ermuntern IV 2 (47)
**end** [end]:
1. Ende, Schluss I
2. enden; beenden III
**ending** [ˈendɪŋ]:
1. Endung I
2. Ende, (Ab-)Schluss II
**enemy** [ˈenəmi] Feind/in III
**energy** [ˈenədʒi] Energie, Kraft III

**engine** [ˈendʒɪn] Motor, Maschine IV 3 (66/67)  **search engine** Suchmaschine IV 3 (66/67)
**English** [ˈɪŋglɪʃ] Englisch; englisch I  **in English** auf Englisch I
°**English-speaking** [ˈɪŋglɪʃ spiːkɪŋ] englischsprachig
**enjoy** [ɪnˈdʒɔɪ] genießen III  **enjoy yourself** sich amüsieren, Spaß haben III
**enough** [ɪˈnʌf] genug I
**enslave sb.** [ɪnˈsleɪv] jn. versklaven IV 3 (97)
**enter** [ˈentə]:
1. betreten, hineingehen in; eintreten II
2. **enter a password** ein Passwort eingeben III
**entertainer** [ˌentəˈteɪnə] Unterhaltungskünstler/in, Entertainer/in IV 2 (65)
°**entire** [ɪnˈtaɪə] gesamte(r, s), ganze(r, s)
**entrance** [ˈentrəns] Eingang III
**entry** [ˈentri]:
1. Eintrag, Eintragung (im Tagebuch, Wörterbuch) II
2. Eintritt, Zutritt III
**environment** [ɪnˈvaɪrənmənt] Umwelt; Umfeld, Umgebung IV 2 (58)
**environmental** [ɪnˌvaɪrənˈmentl] Umwelt- IV 2 (58)
**epidemic** [ˌepɪˈdemɪk]:
1. Epidemie IV 3 (84)
2. epidemisch IV 3 (84)
**equal** [ˈiːkwəl] gleich, gleichgestellt IV 3 (97)
**equality** [iˈkwɒləti] Gleichheit, Gleichberechtigung IV 3 (97)
**equally** [iːkwəli] gleichermaßen, genauso III
**equipment** (no pl) [ɪˈkwɪpmənt] Ausrüstung II
**era** [ˈɪərə] Ära, Epoche IV 1 (8/9)
**escalator** [ˈeskəleɪtə] Rolltreppe IV 1 (19)
**escape** [ɪˈskeɪp]:
1. Flucht III
2. fliehen III
**especially** [ɪˈspeʃli] besonders, vor allem II
**establish** [ɪˈstæblɪʃ] etablieren, gründen, aufbauen, einrichten IV 3 (84)
**etc. (et cetera)** [etˈsetərə] usw. (und so weiter) I
**EU** [ˌiːˈjuː] EU (Europäische Union) III
**euro (€)** [ˈjʊərəʊ] Euro III
**Europe** [ˈjʊərəp] Europa III
**European Union** [ˌjʊərəpiːən ˈjuːniən] Europäische Union I
°**evaluate** [ɪˈvæljueɪt] bewerten, einschätzen; auswerten
**even** [ˈiːvn] sogar II  **not even** (noch) nicht einmal II
**even if** [ˈiːvn ɪf] selbst wenn II
**even though** [ˌiːvn ˈðəʊ] selbst wenn, obwohl (betont) IV 3 (80)
**evening** [ˈiːvnɪŋ] Abend I  **in the evening** abends, am Abend I
**event** [ɪˈvent] Ereignis II

**ever** [ˈevə] jemals II  **better than ever** besser als je zuvor II  **Have you ever been to …?** Bist du jemals in … gewesen? II  **ever since** seitdem, seither IV 1 (17)  °**ever more people** fortwährend/immer mehr Menschen
°**evergreen** [ˈevəgriːn] immergrün (Pflanzen)
**every** [ˈevri] jede(r, s) I
**everybody** [ˈevribɒdi] jeder; alle I
**everyday** [ˈevrideɪ] Alltags- I
**everyone** [ˈevriwʌn] jeder; alle I
**everything** [ˈevriθɪŋ] alles I
**everywhere** [ˈevriweə] überall II
**evidence (no pl)** [ˈevɪdəns] Nachweis(e), Beweis(e) IV 2 (45)
**evil** [ˈiːvl]:
1. (das) Böse; (das) Übel IV 3 (90)
2. bösartig, übel, schlecht IV 3 (90)
**exact** [ɪgˈzækt] genau III
**exactly** [ɪgˈzæktli] genau III
**example** [ɪgˈzɑːmpl] Beispiel II  **for example** zum Beispiel II
**excellent** [ˈeksələnt] ausgezeichnet, hervorragend I
**except** [ɪkˈsept] außer, bis auf II
**exception** [ɪkˈsepʃn] Ausnahme IV 2 (43)
**exceptional** [ɪkˈsepʃənl] außergewöhnlich IV 2 (43)
**exchange** [ɪksˈtʃeɪndʒ]:
1. Austausch; Austausch- III
°2. austauschen
**excited** [ɪkˈsaɪtɪd] aufgeregt, gespannt I
**exciting** [ɪkˈsaɪtɪŋ] aufregend, spannend I
**exclamation mark** [ˌekskləˈmeɪʃn mɑːk] Ausrufezeichen II
**Excuse me, …** [ɪkˈskjuːz miː] Entschuldigung, … / Entschuldigen Sie, … (Darf ich mal stören?) II
**execute** [ˈeksɪkjuːt] hinrichten IV 1 (35)
**execution** [ˌeksɪˈkjuːʃn] Hinrichtung IV 1 (35)
**exercise** [ˈeksəsaɪz] Aufgabe, Übung I
**exercise book** [ˈeksəsaɪz bʊk] Schulheft, Übungsheft I
**exhibition** [ˌeksɪˈbɪʃn] Ausstellung; Messe IV 1 (16)
**exist** [ɪgˈzɪst] existieren IV 1 (17)
**exit** [ˈeksɪt] Ausgang; Ausfahrt IV 2 (42)
°**expanse** [ɪkˈspæns] Fläche, Weite
°**expansion** [ɪkˈspænʃn] Expansion
**expect sth.** [ɪkˈspekt] etwas erwarten III
**expedition** [ˌekspəˈdɪʃn] Expedition IV 2 (46)
**expensive** [ɪkˈspensɪv] teuer I
**experience** [ɪkˈspɪəriəns]:
1. erfahren, erleben III
2. (no pl) Erfahrung(en) III
**expert** [ˈekspɜːt] Experte/Expertin III
**explain sth. to sb.** [ɪkˈspleɪn] jm. etwas erklären, erläutern I
**explode** [ɪkˈspləʊd] explodieren III
**explore** [ɪkˈsplɔː] erkunden, erforschen III
°**explorer** [ɪkˈsplɔːrə] Forschungsreisende(r), Entdecker/in

# Dictionary

**explosive** [ɪkˈspləʊsɪv]:
1. explosiv IV 1 (34)
2. Sprengstoff; Sprengsatz IV 1 (34)

**export** [ˈekspɔːt] Export, Ausfuhr III

°**exposure** [ɪkˈspəʊʒə] Unterkühlung; Ausgesetztsein

**express** [ɪkˈspres] ausdrücken, zum Ausdruck bringen IV 1 (13)

**expression** [ɪkˈspreʃn] Ausdruck IV 1 (13)

°**extend** [ɪkˈstend] sich erstrecken; sich ausdehnen; ausdehnen

°**exterior** [ɪkˈstɪəriə] Äußere(s), Außenansicht, Außenseite

°**extract** [ˈekstrækt] Auszug *(aus einem Buch, Film)*

**extreme** [ɪkˈstriːm]:
1. extrem IV 3 (81)
2. Extrem IV 3 (81)

**eye** [aɪ] Auge I | **make eye contact** Blickkontakt herstellen III

## F

**fabulous** [ˈfæbjələs] sagenhaft, fabelhaft IV 1 (20)

**face** [feɪs] Gesicht I | **face to face** von Angesicht zu Angesicht IV 1 (12)

°**faced** [feɪst]: **be faced with** konfrontiert werden mit

**fact** [fækt] Tatsache, Fakt III | **in fact** eigentlich, in Wirklichkeit III

**factor** [ˈfæktə] Faktor III

**factory** [ˈfæktri] Fabrik II

**fail** [feɪl] scheitern; (es) nicht schaffen IV 1 (17)

**failure** [ˈfeɪljə] Misserfolg, Fehlschlag IV 1 (17)

**fair** [feə] fair, gerecht I

°**faith** [feɪθ] Vertrauen, Glaube(n)

**fall** [fɔːl] (AE) Herbst I

**fall** [fɔːl], **fell, fallen** fallen, stürzen; hinfallen I | **fall asleep** einschlafen I | **fall off a bike** vom Fahrrad (herunter)fallen III

**fallen** [ˈfɔːlən] *siehe* **fall**

**false** [fɔːls] falsch III

**familiar (to sb. / with sth.)** [fəˈmɪliə] (jm. / mit etwas) vertraut IV 2 (52)

**family** [ˈfæməli] Familie I | **a family of four** eine vierköpfige Familie III | **the Blackwell family** (die) Familie Blackwell I

°**family line** [ˈfæməli laɪn] Familienzweig

**family tree** [ˌfæməli ˈtriː] (Familien-)Stammbaum I

**famine** [ˈfæmɪn] Hungersnot I

**famous (for)** [ˈfeɪməs] berühmt (für, wegen) I

**fan** [fæn] Fan, Anhänger I

**fantastic** [fænˈtæstɪk] fantastisch I

**far** [fɑː] weit (entfernt) I | **so far** bis jetzt; bis hierher III

**farm** [fɑːm]:
1. Bauernhof, Farm I

°2. *(Land)* bewirtschaften; Landwirtschaft betreiben

**farmer** [ˈfɑːmə] Bauer/Bäuerin, Landwirt/in I

**farming** [ˈfɑːmɪŋ] Landwirtschaft IV 3 (75)

°**farmland** [ˈfɑːmlænd] Ackerland

°**farthest** [ˈfɑːðɪst] am weitesten (entfernt)

**fascist** [ˈfæʃɪst]:
1. Faschist/in IV 1 (34)
2. faschistisch IV 1 (34)

**fashion** [ˈfæʃn] Mode II

**fast** [fɑːst] schnell I | **be fast** vorgehen *(Uhr)* III

**fat** [fæt] dick, fett I

**father** [ˈfɑːðə] Vater I

**fault** [fɔːlt] Schuld, Fehler III

**favourite** [ˈfeɪvərɪt] Lieblings- I | **my favourite day** mein Lieblingstag I

**fear** [fɪə]:
1. fürchten, befürchten IV 3 (94)
2. **fear (of)** Angst (vor) IV 3 (94)

°**feather** [ˈfeðə] Feder *(eines Vogels)*

**feature** [ˈfiːtʃə] Merkmal, Eigenschaft IV 1 (15)

**February** [ˈfebruəri] Februar I

**fed** [fed] *siehe* **feed**

**feed** [fiːd] Feed *(abonnierbare elektronische Nachricht im Internet)* IV 1 (12)

**feed** [fiːd], **fed, fed** füttern I | **feeding time** Fütterungszeit I

**feedback** *(no pl)* [ˈfiːdbæk] Rückmeldung, Feedback III

**feel** [fiːl], **felt, felt**:
1. fühlen; sich fühlen I | **I don't feel well.** Mir geht's nicht gut. / Ich fühle mich nicht gut. II | **I feel sick.** Mir ist schlecht. II
2. sich anfühlen III

**feeling** [ˈfiːlɪŋ] Gefühl I

**feet** [fiːt] plural of **foot**

**fell** [fel] *siehe* **fall**

**fellow** [ˈfeləʊ]:
1. Mit- IV 2 (46)
°2. *(infml)* Kerl, Mann

**felt** [felt] *siehe* **feel**

**felt pen** [ˌfelt ˈpen] Filzstift I

**fence** [fens] Zaun II

**ferry** [ˈferi] Fähre I

**festival** [ˈfestɪvl] Fest, Festival II

**few** [fjuː] wenige IV 2 (59) | **a few** ein paar, einige II

**fiction** [ˈfɪkʃn] Belletristik, Prosa(literatur); Märchen, Fiktion IV 3 (95)

**field** [fiːld] Feld, Acker, Weide II

**fierce** [fɪəs] heftig, wild III

**fifth** [fɪfθ] Fünftel IV 3 (84)

**fight** [faɪt]:
1. Kampf, Schlägerei IV 2 (53)
2. **fight, fought, fought** kämpfen I | **fight sb.** jn. bekämpfen II

**fighter** [ˈfaɪtə] Kämpfer/in II

**figure** [ˈfɪgə]:
1. Zahl, Ziffer III
2. Figur, Gestalt III

**file** [faɪl]: **background file** Hintergrundinformation(en) I | **grammar file** Zusammenfassung der Grammatik jeder Unit I | **skills file** Übersicht über Lern- und Arbeitstechniken I

**fill** [fɪl] füllen III

**film** [fɪlm]:
1. filmen I
2. Film I

°**film-maker** [ˈfɪlm meɪkə] Filmemacher/in

**final** [ˈfaɪnl]:
1. Finale, Endspiel I
2. letzte(r, s) IV 2 (49)

**finally** [ˈfaɪnəli] endlich, schließlich III

°**finance** [ˈfaɪnæns] Geld, Kapital; Finanz-

**financial** [faɪˈnænʃl] finanziell IV 1 (31)

**find** [faɪnd], **found, found** finden I | **find sth. out** etwas herausfinden II

**fine** [faɪn] gut, in Ordnung, prima II | **Fine, thanks.** Gut, danke. I | **That's fine.** Es ist gut so. II

**fine** [faɪn]:
1. Geldstrafe IV 2 (47)
2. **fine sb.** jn. zu einer Geldstrafe verurteilen IV 2 (47)

**finger** [ˈfɪŋgə] Finger II

**finish** [ˈfɪnɪʃ] enden I | **finish sth.** etwas beenden; mit etwas fertig werden/sein I | **We're finished.** Wir sind fertig. I

**fire** [ˈfaɪə]:
1. Feuer I
2. (ab)schießen, (ab)feuern IV 1 (15)

**fireplace** [ˈfaɪəpleɪs] Kamin II

**firework** [ˈfaɪəwɜːk] Feuerwerkskörper II

**fireworks** *(pl)* Feuerwerk II

**firm** [fɜːm] fest, sicher; verbindlich IV 3 (81)

**first** [fɜːst] zuerst, als Erstes I | **First, ...** Erstens, ... I | **at first** zuerst, anfangs, am Anfang II | **in the first place** erstens, in erster Linie; überhaupt IV 2 (45) | **the first day** der erste Tag

**Firstly, ...** [ˈfɜːstli] Erstens ... IV 2 (45)

**fish** [fɪʃ]:
1. *pl* **fish** Fisch I
2. **fish sth. out** etwas herausfischen III

°**fishbowl discussion** [ˈfɪʃbəʊl dɪskʌʃn] Innen-/Außenkreis-Diskussion

**fishing village** [ˈfɪʃɪŋ vɪlɪdʒ] Fischerdorf II

**fit** [fɪt] fit, in Form II

**fit** [fɪt]:
1. Übereinstimmung; Passform, Sitz IV 2 (65) | **... are a natural fit.** ... passen von Natur aus gut zusammen IV 2 (65)
°2. passen (zu)

**five** [faɪv] fünf I

**fixed** [fɪkst] fest, festgelegt II

**fizzy drink** [ˌfɪzi ˈdrɪŋk] kohlensäurehaltiges Erfrischungsgetränk IV 3 (70)

**flag** [flæg] Fahne, Flagge I

**flash** [flæʃ] Lichtblitz II | **a flash of lightning** ein Blitz II

**flash fiction** [ˈflæʃ fɪkʃn] Flash Fiction *(literarische Gattung: Kurzgeschichten mit bis ca. 1000 Wörtern)* IV 2 (58)

# English – German

**flashlight** ['flæʃlaɪt] (AE) Taschenlampe III
**flat** [flæt] Wohnung I
**flat** [flæt] flach; eben IV 3 (83)
°**flatland(s)** ['flætlænd] Tiefland
**flavour** ['fleɪvə]:
1. (AE: **flavor**) Geschmack, Geschmacksrichtung II
2. **flavour sth. with sth.** etwas mit etwas aromatisieren, würzen IV 3 (93)
**fled** [fled] siehe **flee**
**flee (from)** [fliː], **fled, fled** flüchten (aus), fliehen (vor) IV 1 (17)
**flew** [fluː] siehe **fly**
**flight** [flaɪt] Flug IV 1 (32)
**float** [fləʊt] schwimmen, (auf der Wasseroberfläche) treiben IV 1 (29)
**floodlight(s)** ['flʌdlaɪt] Flutlicht IV 3 (81)
**floor** [flɔː]:
1. Fußboden I
2. Stock(werk) I
**flow** [fləʊ]:
1. fließen, strömen IV 1 (16)
2. Fluss, Strom IV 1 (16)
**flower** ['flaʊə] Blume; Blüte II
**flown** [fləʊn] siehe **fly**
**fly** [flaɪ], **flew, flown** fliegen II
**focus** ['fəʊkəs]:
1. Mittelpunkt, Hauptpunkt, Schwerpunkt IV 2 (63)
2. **focus on sth.** sich auf etwas konzentrieren IV 2 (63)
**fold** [fəʊld] falten III
**folk** [fəʊk] (pl, infml) Leute III
**follow** ['fɒləʊ] folgen I  **Follow me.** Folge mir. / Folgt mir. I
**follower** ['fɒləʊə] Follower (Anhänger/in, Fan) IV 1 (12)
**food** [fuːd] Essen; Lebensmittel; Futter I
°**foosball** ['fuːzbɔːl] (AE) Tischfußball
**foot** [fʊt], pl **feet** Fuß (auch Längenmaß: 30,5 cm) II  **go on foot** (zu Fuß) gehen III  **on foot** zu Fuß III
**football** ['fʊtbɔːl] Fußball I
**footprint** ['fʊtprɪnt] Fußabdruck II
°**footsore** ['fʊtsɔː] mit wunden Füßen
**footstep** ['fʊtstep] Schritt (Geräusch); Fußabdruck IV 3 (66/67)
**for** [fɔː], [fə] für I  **for a while** eine Weile, eine Zeit lang III  **for example** zum Beispiel II  **for free** kostenlos, umsonst II  **for hours/weeks/...** seit Stunden/Wochen/... III  **for miles** meilenweit I  **for the first time** zum ersten Mal III  **go for a walk** einen Spaziergang machen, spazieren gehen I  **How's that for acoustics?** Ist das nicht eine tolle Akustik? / Das nennt man tolle Akustik! IV 1 (10)  **What's for homework?** Was haben wir als Hausaufgabe auf? I  **What's for lunch?** Was gibt es zum Mittagessen? I
**forbade** [fə'bæd] siehe **forbid**
**forbid** [fə'bɪd], **forbade, forbidden** verbieten, untersagen IV 3 (75)
**forbidden** [fə'bɪdn] siehe **forbid**
**force sb. to do sth.** [fɔːs] jn. zwingen, etwas zu tun IV 3 (69)  **They were forced further west / from their land.** Sie wurden weiter nach Westen / von ihrem Land vertrieben. IV 3 (69)
**forearm** ['fɔːrɑːm] Unterarm III
**foreground** ['fɔːgraʊnd] Vordergrund I
**foreign** ['fɒrən] ausländisch, fremd IV (17)
**foreign language** [fɒrən 'læŋgwɪdʒ] Fremdsprache IV 1 (17)
**foreigner** ['fɒrənə] Ausländer/in; Fremde/r IV 1 (17)
**forest** ['fɒrɪst] Wald II
**forever** [fər'evə] (BE auch: **for ever**) (für) immer; ewig II
**forgave** [fə'geɪv] siehe **forgive**
**forget** [fə'get], **forgot, forgotten** vergessen I
**forgive** [fə'gɪv], **forgave, forgiven** verzeihen IV 3 (93)
**forgiven** [fə'gɪvn] siehe **forgive**
**forgot** [fə'gɒt] siehe **forget**
**forgotten** [fə'gɒtn] siehe **forget**
**fork** [fɔːk] Gabel II
**form** [fɔːm]:
1. bilden, formen III
2. **form (of)** Form (von) I
**formal** ['fɔːml] formell, förmlich IV 1 (20)
**former** ['fɔːmə] ehemalige(r, s), frühere(r, s) I
**fort** [fɔːt] Fort (Befestigungsanlage) IV 1 (32)
°**fortune** ['fɔːtʃuːn] Glück; Vermögen
**forward(s)** ['fɔːwəd], ['fɔːwədz] nach vorne; vorwärts IV 3 (94)  **look forward to sth.** sich auf etwas freuen II
°**fossil fuel** ['fɒsl fjuːəl] fossiler Brennstoff
**fought** [fɔːt] siehe **fight**
**foul** [faʊl] Foul(spiel) IV 2 (53)
**found** [faʊnd]:
1. siehe **find**
2. gründen III
**foundation** [faʊn'deɪʃn] Gründung; Fundament, Grundlage IV 3 (96)
**fountain** ['faʊntən] (Spring-)Brunnen IV 3 (68)
**four** [fɔː] vier I
**fourth** [fɔːθ] (AE) Viertel IV 3 (84)
**fox** [fɒks] Fuchs IV 2 (58)
**frame** [freɪm] Rahmen; Gestell, Fahrgestell IV 1 (15)
**freak** [friːk] Freak, Fan IV 1 (16)
**free** [friː]:
1. frei I
2. kostenlos II  **for free** kostenlos, umsonst III
**free time** [friː 'taɪm] Freizeit, freie Zeit I
**free-time activity** [ˌfriː taɪm æk'tɪvəti] Freizeitaktivität I
**freedom** ['friːdəm] Freiheit IV 2 (65)
**freeze** [friːz], **froze, frozen** (ge)frieren; erstarren IV 1 (26)  **freeze over** vereisen, zufrieren, überfrieren IV 3 (94)
**French** [frentʃ] Französisch I

**French fries** (pl) [ˌfrentʃ 'fraɪz] (AE) Pommes frites I
**frequent** ['friːkwənt] häufig IV 1 (26)
**fresh** [freʃ] frisch II
**Friday** ['fraɪdeɪ], ['fraɪdi] Freitag I
**friend** [frend] Freund/in I
**friendly** ['frendli] freundlich I
**fries** (pl) [fraɪz] (AE) (kurz für: **French fries**) Pommes frites I
**fright** [fraɪt]: **in fright** ängstlich, erschrocken III
**frightened** ['fraɪtnd] verängstigt IV 1 (28)  **be frightened of sth.** Angst haben vor etwas IV 1 (28)
**fringe** [frɪndʒ] Fransen; Pony(fransen) IV 2 (65)
**frisbee** ['frɪzbi] Frisbee II
°**frites** (pl) [friːts] (kurz für: **Pommes frites**) Pommes frites
**frog** [frɒg] Frosch I
**from** [frɒm], [frəm] aus, von I  **from ... to ...** von ... bis ... I  **from behind** von hinten II  **from the back of the bus** aus dem hinteren Teil des Busses II  **I'm from Plymouth.** Ich bin aus Plymouth. / Ich komme aus Plymouth. I
**front** [frʌnt] Vorderseite I  **in front of** vor (räumlich) I  **to the front** nach vorn I
**frosting** ['frɒstɪŋ] Zuckerguss IV 2 (41)
**frown** [fraʊn]:
1. die Stirn runzeln II
2. Stirnrunzeln IV 1 (22)
**froze** [frəʊz] siehe **freeze**
**frozen** ['frəʊzn]:
1. siehe **freeze**
2. tiefgekühlt; gefroren III
**fruit** [fruːt] Obst, Früchte; Frucht I
**fruit salad** [ˌfruːt 'sæləd] Obstsalat I
**frustrate** [frʌ'streɪt] frustrieren IV 2 (47)
**fry** [fraɪ] braten (in der Pfanne) IV 2 (41)
°**frybread** ['fraɪbred] Brotteig, gebraten oder in Öl frittiert
**full (of)** [fʊl] voll (von, mit) I
**full moon** [ˌfʊl 'muːn] Vollmond I
**full sentence** [ˌfʊl 'sentəns] ganzer Satz II
**full stop** [ˌfʊl 'stɒp] Punkt (Satzzeichen) II
**fully** ['fʊli] völlig, vollkommen IV 3 (81)
**fun** [fʌn] Spaß I  **have fun** Spaß haben, sich amüsieren I  **make fun of sb./sth.** sich über jn./etwas lustig machen III  **That sounds fun.** Das klingt nach Spaß. I  **That's fun.** Das macht Spaß. I  **Was it fun?** Hat es Spaß gemacht? I
**fun park** ['fʌn pɑːk] Vergnügungspark I
**funny** ['fʌni] witzig, komisch I
**fur** [fɜː] Fell IV 2 (59)
**furniture** (no pl) ['fɜːnɪtʃə] Möbel III
**further** ['fɜːðə] weiter II
**furthest** ['fɜːðɪst] am weitesten II
**future** ['fjuːtʃə] Zukunft; zukünftige(r, s) II

# Dictionary

## G

**gallery** [ˈgæləri] Galerie III
**gallop** [ˈgæləp]:
 1. Galopp IV 3 (66/67)
 2. galoppieren IV 3 (66/67)
**game** [geɪm]:
 1. Spiel I
 °2. Wild *(Tiere, Fleisch)*
**gang** [gæŋ] Gang (Bande) IV 1 (33)
°**gap** [gæp] Lücke
**garage** [ˈgærɑːʒ], [ˈgærɪdʒ] Garage I
**garbage** [ˈgɑːbɪdʒ] *(AE)* Müll, Abfall III
**garden** [ˈgɑːdn] Garten I
**gardener** [ˈgɑːdnə] Gärtner/in III
**gardening** [ˈgɑːdnɪŋ] Gärtnern, Gartenarbeit I
**gas** [gæs]:
 1. Gas IV 2 (62)
 2. *(AE)* Benzin III
**gas station** [ˈgæs steɪʃn] *(AE)* Tankstelle III
**gate** [geɪt] Tor, Pforte, Gatter II
**gave** [geɪv] *siehe* **give**
**gaze** [geɪz] blicken, starren III
**gear** [gɪə] Ausrüstung IV 2 (46)
**gel** [dʒel] Gel II
**general** [ˈdʒenrəl] allgemein IV 3 (93) **in general** im Allgemeinen, generell IV 3 (93)
**generally** [ˈdʒenrəli] generell, allgemein I
**generation** [ˌdʒenəˈreɪʃn] Generation I
°**genocide** [ˈdʒenəsaɪd] Völkermord
°**geographical** [ˌdʒiːəˈgræfɪkl] geographisch
**geography** [dʒiˈɒgrəfi] Geografie I
**German** [ˈdʒɜːmən] Deutsch; deutsch I **in German** auf Deutsch I
**get** [get], **got, got**:
 1. bekommen I **get sb. to do sth.** jn. dazu bringen, etwas zu tun IV 3 (90) **get the hang of sth.** *(infml)* den Dreh raushaben/rausbekommen (bei etwas); etwas kapieren III **get the vote** das Stimmrecht erhalten IV 2 (65) **get to do sth.** etwas tun können/dürfen; die Möglichkeit haben/bekommen, etwas zu tun IV 3 (70)
 2. **get sth.** (sich) etwas besorgen, (sich) etwas holen I
 3. gelangen, (hin)kommen I **get in touch (with sb.)** (mit jm.) Kontakt aufnehmen; sich (mit jm.) in Verbindung setzen II **get in(to) a car/taxi** in ein Auto/Taxi einsteigen II **get into trouble** in Schwierigkeiten geraten, Ärger kriegen III **get lost** sich verlaufen, sich verirren III **get off (the bus/boat)** (aus dem Bus/Boot) aussteigen I **get on** vorankommen, zurechtkommen II **get on (the bus/boat)** (in den Bus / das Boot) einsteigen I **get out of a car/taxi** aus einem Auto/Taxi aussteigen II **get up** aufstehen I
 4. **get angry/cold/…** wütend/ kalt/… werden I **get paid** bezahlt werden III
**get ready (for)** sich fertig machen (für); sich vorbereiten (auf) II
 5. **get sth.** etwas verstehen, mitbekommen I **Did you get it?** *(infml)* Hast du es verstanden? / Hast du es mitbekommen? I
**ghost** [gəʊst] Geist, Gespenst I
**giant** [ˈdʒaɪənt]:
 1. Riese III
 2. riesige(r, s) IV 3 (81)
**gift** [gɪft] Geschenk; Gabe; Talent IV 3 (86)
**giraffe** [dʒəˈrɑːf] Giraffe I
**girl** [gɜːl] Mädchen I
**girlfriend** [ˈgɜːlfrend] (feste) Freundin III
**give** [gɪv], **gave, given** geben I **give a presentation** ein Referat halten IV 3 (66/67) **give a talk (about)** einen Vortrag / eine Rede halten (über) I **give sb. a hug** jn. umarmen I **give sb. a lift** jn. mitnehmen II **give up** aufgeben III
**given** [ˈgɪvn] *siehe* **give**
**glad** [glæd] froh, dankbar III
**glass** [glɑːs] Glas II **a glass of …** ein Glas … II
**glass case** [ˌglɑːs ˈkeɪs] Vitrine IV 2 (40)
**glasses** *(pl)* [ˈglɑːsɪz] (eine) Brille II
**global** [ˈgləʊbl] global, weltweit IV 2 (62)
**global warming** [ˌgləʊbl ˈwɔːmɪŋ] Erderwärmung IV 2 (62)
**glove** [glʌv] Handschuh I **a pair of gloves** ein Paar Handschuhe II
**glue** [gluː] Klebstoff I
**glue stick** [ˈgluː stɪk] Klebestift I
**glum** [glʌm] niedergeschlagen, bedrückt, mürrisch IV 3 (80)
**go** [gəʊ], **went, gone**:
 1. gehen; fahren I **go by** vergehen, vorübergehen *(Zeit)* III **go by car/bus/…** mit dem Auto/Bus/… fahren I **go down** untergehen *(Sonne)* I **go for a walk** einen Spaziergang machen, spazieren gehen I **go in** hineingehen II **go on** im Gang sein; andauern III **go on (with)** weiterreden, fortfahren (mit); weitermachen (mit) I **go sailing** segeln; segeln gehen I **go shopping** einkaufen gehen I **go to war** in den Krieg ziehen IV 3 (96) **go together** zusammenpassen, zueinander passen; zu etwas passen; zu etwas gehören II **go with sth.** zu etwas passen; zu etwas gehören II **go wrong** schiefgehen III **Here we go.** Los geht's. / Jetzt geht's los. I °**go (somewhere)** (irgendwo) hingehören
 2. werden II **go hard/bad/mad** hart/schlecht/verrückt werden II **go red** rot werden, erröten II
 3. **Have a go.** Versuch's mal. I
**goal** [gəʊl]:
 1. Tor *(Sport)* II
 2. Ziel *(Absicht, Lebensziel)* II
**goat** [gəʊt] Ziege I
**god, God** [gɒd] Gott III
**going to** [ˈgəʊɪŋ tʊ]: **He is going to visit his dad.** Er hat vor, seinen Vater zu besuchen. / Er wird seinen Vater besuchen. I
**gold** [gəʊld]:
 1. Gold I
 2. golden, Gold- II
**golden** [ˈgəʊldn] golden, aus Gold IV 3 (77)
**gone** [gɒn] *siehe* **go** **be gone** weg sein, nicht (mehr) da sein III
**good** [gʊd]:
 1. gut I **Good luck!** Viel Glück! I **Good morning.** Guten Morgen. I **be good at kung fu** gut sein in Kung-Fu I **smell good** gut riechen II
 2. brav I
**good-looking** [ˌgʊd ˈlʊkɪŋ] gutaussehend II
**Goodbye.** [ˌgʊdˈbaɪ] Auf Wiedersehen. I
**Goodnight.** [ˌgʊdˈnaɪt] Gute Nacht! IV 1 (12)
**goods** *(pl)* [gʊdz] Waren, Güter I
**got** [gɒt] *siehe* **get** **have got** haben I
**govern** [ˈgʌvən] regieren III
**government** [ˈgʌvənmənt] Regierung II
**governor** [ˈgʌvənə] Gouverneur/in III
**grab** [græb] schnappen, packen III
**grade** [greɪd]:
 1. Klasse, Jahrgang(sstufe) IV 2 (43)
 2. (Schul-)Note, Zensur IV 2 (43) **passing grade** Note/Zensur, mit der man bestanden hat IV 2 (47)
**graffiti** [grəˈfiːti] Graffiti IV 3 (81)
°**grain** [greɪn] Getreide; Korn
**gram** [græm] Gramm II
**grammar** [ˈgræmə] Grammatik I
**grammar file** [ˈgræmə faɪl] Zusammenfassung der Grammatik jeder Unit I
**grandfather** [ˈgrænfɑːðə] Großvater I
**grandma** [ˈgrænmɑː] Oma I
**grandmother** [ˈgrænmʌðə] Großmutter I
**grandpa** [ˈgrænpɑː] Opa I
**grandparents** *(pl)* [ˈgrænpeərənts] Großeltern I
**granite** [ˈgrænɪt] Granit IV 3 (81)
**graphic** [ˈgræfɪk] grafisch; anschaulich IV 1 (34)
°**graphic designer** [ˌgræfɪk dɪˈzaɪnə] Grafiker/in, Grafikdesigner/in
**graphic novel** [ˌgræfɪk ˈnɒvl] Bildroman, Comicroman IV 1 (34)
**graphics** *(pl)* [ˈgræfɪks] Grafiken III
**grass** [grɑːs] Gras; Rasen I
°**grassland** [ˈgrɑːslænd] Grasland, Steppe(ngebiet)
**grateful** [ˈgreɪtfl] dankbar IV 1 (21)
**grave** [greɪv] Grab II
**gravel** [ˈgrævl] Kies, Schotter III
**gravestone** [ˈgreɪvstəʊn] Grabstein III
**gravy** [ˈgreɪvi] Bratensoße IV 2 (41)
**great** [greɪt] großartig I
**Great Britain (GB)** [ˌgreɪt ˈbrɪtn] Großbritannien I
**great-grandfather** [ˌgreɪt ˈgrænfɑːðə] Urgroßvater III

**great-grandmother** [ˌgreɪt ˈgrænmʌðə] Urgroßmutter III
**greatly** [ˈgreɪtli] stark, erheblich IV 3 (84)
**green** [griːn] grün I
**greenhouse gas** [ˌgriːnhaʊs ˈgæs] Treibhausgas IV 2 (62)
**greeting** [ˈgriːtɪŋ] Gruß(formel), Begrüßung IV 1 (12)
**grew** [gruː] *siehe* **grow**
**grey** [greɪ] grau I
**grid** [grɪd] Gitter; Raster; Rechteckschema III
**grin** [grɪn]:
1. grinsen III
2. (ein/das) Grinsen IV 3 (68)

**grind** [graɪnd], **ground, ground** (zer-)mahlen IV 1 (16)
**grizzly (bear)** [ˌgrɪzli ˈbeə] Grizzlybär IV 2 (62)
**groan** [grəʊn]:
1. stöhnen III
2. Stöhnen II

**ground** [graʊnd]:
1. **ground sb.** jm. Hausarrest/Ausgehverbot erteilen III
2. *siehe* **grind**

**ground** [graʊnd] (Erd-)Boden II **rugby ground** Rugby-Platz/-Spielfeld III
**group (of)** [gruːp] Gruppe I
**grow** [grəʊ], grew, grown:
1. anbauen, anpflanzen I
2. wachsen I **grow up** erwachsen werden; aufwachsen I
3. **grow darker/old/...** (allmählich) dunkler/alt/... werden III

**growl** [graʊl] knurren III
**grown** [grəʊn] *siehe* **grow**
**guard** [gɑːd]:
1. Wachposten, Wache II
2. bewachen III

**guess** [ges]:
1. raten, erraten I **Guess what, Dad ...** Stell dir vor, Dad .../Weißt du was, Dad ... I
2. **I guess ...** Ich nehme an, ... / Ich denke, ... III
°3. Vermutung II

**guest** [gest] Gast III
**guide** [gaɪd]:
1. Fremdenführer/in; Reiseleiter/in II
2. führen, begleiten III

°**guidebook** [ˈgaɪdbʊk] Reiseführer *(Buch)*
**guideline** [ˈgaɪdlaɪn] Richtlinie IV 2 (46)
**guinea pig** [ˈgɪni pɪg] Meerschweinchen I
**guitar** [gɪˈtɑː] Gitarre I **play the guitar** Gitarre spielen I
**gun** [gʌn] Schusswaffe IV 2 (58)
**gunpowder** [ˈgʌnpaʊdə] Schießpulver IV 1 (34)
**guy** [gaɪ]:
1. Typ, Kerl II **guys** (*pl*) Leute II
2. Guy-Fawkes-Puppe IV 1 (34)

**gym** [dʒɪm] Turnhalle I
**gymnastics** [dʒɪmˈnæstɪks] Gymnastik, Turnen I

# H

**habit** [ˈhæbɪt] (An-)Gewohnheit III
**habitat** [ˈhæbɪtæt] Lebensraum IV 2 (61)
**hack** [hæk] hacken *(Computer)* IV 1 (34)
**hacker** [ˈhækə] Hacker/in *(Computer)* IV 1 (35)
**hacktivist** [ˈhæktɪvɪst] Hacktivist/in *(politisch engagierte/r Häcker/in)* IV 1 (35)
**had** [hæd] *siehe* **have I'd better ... (= I had better ...)** Ich sollte lieber ... III
**hair** [heə] Haar, Haare I
**hairdresser** [ˈheədresə] Friseur/in III
**half** [hɑːf]:
1. halbe(r, s) I **half an hour** eine halbe Stunde III **half past ten** halb elf (10.30 / 22.30) I
2. *pl* **halves** Hälfte; Halbzeit I **an hour and a half** eineinhalb Stunden, anderthalb Stunden I

**hall** [hɔːl] Halle, Saal IV 2 (46) **school hall** Aula IV 2 (46)
**halves** [hɑːvz] *plural of* **half**
**hamburger** [ˈhæmbɜːgə] Hamburger II
**hammer** [ˈhæmə]:
1. Hammer III
2. hämmern III

**hamster** [ˈhæmstə] Hamster I
**hand** [hænd]:
1. Hand I **on the one hand** einerseits IV 1 (26) **on the other hand** andererseits IV 1 (26)
2. **hand sb. sth.** jm. etwas geben, reichen III **hand sth. in** etwas abgeben; etwas einreichen II

**handout** [ˈhændaʊt] Handout, Handzettel III
**handshake** [ˈhændʃeɪk] Handschlag, Händedruck III
**handsome** [ˈhænsəm] attraktiv, gut aussehend III
**hang** [hæŋ]:
1. **get the hang of sth.** den Dreh raushaben/rausbekommen (bei etwas); etwas kapieren III
2. **hang, hung, hung** hängen II **hang out** *(infml)* abhängen, rumhängen III

**happen (to)** [ˈhæpən] geschehen, passieren (mit) I
**happiness** [ˈhæpɪnəs] Glück, Zufriedenheit IV 3 (97)
**happy** [ˈhæpi] glücklich, froh I
**harbour** [ˈhɑːbə] Hafen I
**hard** [hɑːd]:
1. schwer, schwierig; hart I
2. **try hard** sich anstrengen; sich (große) Mühe geben III

**hardly** [ˈhɑːdli] kaum IV 3 (81)
**harm** [hɑːm]:
1. *(no pl)* Schaden, Schäden, Verletzung IV 3 (93) **do harm (to) sb. / do sb. harm** jm. Schaden zufügen IV 3 (93)
2. **harm sb.** jm. schaden, jn. schädigen, verletzen IV 3 (93)

**harmless** [ˈhɑːmləs] harmlos III

**harmonica** [hɑːˈmɒnɪkə] Mundharmonika III
°**harsh** [hɑːʃ] hart, streng
**harvest** [ˈhɑːvɪst]:
1. Ernte III
°2. ernten

**has** [hæz]: **he/she has** er/sie hat I
**hat** [hæt] Hut I **paper hat** Papierhut I
**hate** [heɪt]:
1. Hass IV 2 (65)
2. hassen IV 2 (65)

°**haul** [hɔːl] Strecke, Weg
**haunt** [hɔːnt] Lieblingsort IV 1 (17)
**have** [hæv], [həv], **had, had** haben I **have a cold** eine Erkältung haben, erkältet sein II **Have a go.** Versuch's mal. I **have a look (at sth.)** nachschauen; einen Blick auf etwas werfen III **have a shower** (sich) duschen II **have breakfast** frühstücken I **have dinner** zu Abend essen I **have fun** Spaß haben, sich amüsieren I **have got** haben I **have lunch** zu Mittag essen I **have to do** tun müssen I **Have you ever been to ...?** Bist du jemals in ... gewesen? II **I'll have a tea/burger** Ich nehme einen Tee/Hamburger ... *(beim Essen, im Restaurant)* II
°**hawk** [hɔːk] Habicht
**hay** [heɪ] Heu II
**he** [hiː] er I
**head** [hed]:
1. Kopf I
2. Oberhaupt, Leiter/in III
3. *(with prep / with adv)* Richtung ... gehen, fahren; sich nach ... aufmachen; zusteuern auf ... IV 3 (70) **head for sth.** auf etwas zusteuern/zugehen/zufahren III **head out** aufbrechen, sich auf den Wegmachen IV 2 (46)

**head teacher** [ˌhed ˈtiːtʃə] Schulleiter/in III
**headache** [ˈhedeɪk]: **have a headache** Kopfschmerzen haben II
**heading** [ˈhedɪŋ] Überschrift III
**headline** [ˈhedlaɪn] Überschrift; Schlagzeile IV 1 (17)
**headphones** (*pl*) [ˈhedfəʊnz] Kopfhörer IV 1 (10)
**headword** [ˈhedwɜːd] Stichwort *(im Wörterbuch)* III
**heal** [hiːl] heilen IV 3 (90)
**health** [helθ] Gesundheit IV 2 (43)
**health care** [ˈhelθ keə] Gesundheitsfürsorge, medizinische Versorgung IV 2 (65)
**health service** [ˈhelθ sɜːvɪs] Gesundheitswesen III
**healthy** [ˈhelθi] gesund IV 2 (43)
**hear** [hɪə], **heard, heard** hören I
**heard** [hɜːd] *siehe* **hear**
**heart** [hɑːt] Herz II
°**heartland** [ˈhɑːtlænd] Zentrum *(Herz eines Landes)*
**heartless** [ˈhɑːtləs] herzlos IV 3 (81)

# Dictionary

**heat** [hiːt]:
1. erwärmen, erhitzen IV 1 (27)
2. Hitze, Wärme IV 1 (27)

°**heating** [ˈhiːtɪŋ] Heizung
**heaven** [ˈhevn] Himmel *(im religiösen Sinn)* III
**heavy** [ˈhevi] schwer *(von Gewicht)* II **heavy rain** starker Regen, heftiger Regen II
°**hectare** [ˈhekteə] Hektar (10000 m²)
**held** [held] *siehe* **hold**
**helicopter** [ˈhelɪkɒptə] Helikopter, Hubschrauber III
**Hello.** [həˈləʊ] Hallo. / Grüß Gott. I **Say hello to … for me.** Grüß … von mir. II
**help** [help]:
1. helfen I **help yourself** sich bedienen, zugreifen III
2. Hilfe I

**helper** [ˈhelpə] Helfer/in II
**helpful** [ˈhelpfl] hilfsbereit; hilfreich, nützlich IV 3 (75)
**her** [hɜː], [hə]:
1. ihr, ihre I **her best friend** ihr bester Freund / ihre beste Freundin I
2. sie; ihr I

**herd** [hɜːd] Herde, Rudel IV 3 (84)
**here** [hɪə] hier; hierher I **Here we go.** Los geht's. / Jetzt geht's los. I **Here you are.** Bitte sehr. / Hier bitte. II **near here** (hier) in der Nähe II **over here** hier herüber; hier drüben II **round here** hier in der Gegend III **up here** hier oben; nach hier oben II
°**heritage** [ˈherɪtɪdʒ] (Kultur-, Natur-) Erbe
**hero** [ˈhɪərəʊ], *pl* **heroes** Held/in III
**hers** [hɜːz] ihrer, ihre, ihrs *(zu „she")* II
**herself** [hɜːˈself] sie/sich selbst/selber *(zu „she")* III
**hesitate** [ˈhezɪteɪt] zögern IV 1 (29)
**Hi.** [haɪ] Hallo. IV 1 (12)
**hid** [hɪd] *siehe* **hide**
**hidden** [ˈhɪdn] *siehe* **hide**
**hide** [haɪd], **hid, hidden** (sich) verstecken I
**hide-and-seek** [ˌhaɪd‿ən ˈsiːk] Versteckspiel IV 1 (33)
**high** [haɪ] hoch I
**high commission** [ˌhaɪ kəˈmɪʃn] Diplomatische Vertretung eines Commonwealth-Landes in einem anderen Commonwealth-Land IV 1 (11)
°**high-quality** [ˌhaɪ ˈkwɒləti] von hoher Qualität, hochwertig
°**high-rise** [ˈhaɪ raɪz] Hochhaus
**high school** [ˈhaɪ skuːl] *(AE)* Schule für 14- bis 18-Jährige III
**highlight** [ˈhaɪlaɪt] hervorheben, markieren *(mit Textmarker)* II
**highway** [ˈhaɪweɪ] *(AE)* Fernstraße *(in den USA; oft mit vier oder mehr Spuren)* IV 3 (68)
**hike** [haɪk] wandern IV 3 (77)
**hill** [hɪl] Hügel I
**hilly** [ˈhɪli] hügelig IV 2 (47)
**him** [hɪm] ihn; ihm I

**himself** [hɪmˈself] er/ihn/ihm/sich selbst/selber III
**hip** [hɪp] Hüfte III
**hire** [ˈhaɪə] *(Person)* einstellen; mieten, leihen IV 3 (70)
**his** [hɪz]:
1. **his friend** sein/e Freund/in I
2. seiner, seine, seins II

**hiss** [hɪs] zischen II
**historic** [hɪˈstɒrɪk] historisch *(geschichtlich bedeutsam)* II
**historical** [hɪˈstɒrɪkl] historisch, geschichtlich IV 3 (91)
**history** [ˈhɪstri] Geschichte I **natural history** Naturkunde I
**hit** [hɪt], hit, hit:
1. schlagen II
2. prallen, stoßen gegen I
3. treffen II

**hobby** [ˈhɒbi] Hobby I
**hockey** [ˈhɒki] Hockey I
**hold** [həʊld]:
1. Griff III
2. **hold, held, held** halten I; *(Veranstaltung)* abhalten IV 1 (18) **Hold on a minute.** *(oft auch kurz:* **Hold on.)** Bleib / Bleiben Sie am Apparat. *(am Telefon)* II **hold onto sth.** sich an etwas festhalten III

**hole** [həʊl] Loch II
**holiday** [ˈhɒlədeɪ]:
1. Urlaub I **holidays** *(pl)* Ferien I **be on holiday** im Urlaub sein I **go on holiday** in Urlaub fahren I
2. Feiertag III

**home** [həʊm] Heim, Zuhause I **at home** zu Hause, daheim I **be home to sth.** Heimat sein für etwas; etwas beheimaten III **come home** nach Hause kommen I **go home** nach Hause gehen I
°**homeland** [ˈhəʊmlænd] Heimat(land)
°**homestead** [ˈhəʊmsted] Land, das den Siedlern in Nordamerika im 19. Jahrhundert kostenlos zur Verfügung gestellt wurde
**hometown** [ˌhəʊmˈtaʊn] Heimatstadt I
**homework** [ˈhəʊmwɜːk] Hausaufgabe(n) I **Do your homework.** Mach deine Hausaufgaben. I **What's for homework?** Was haben wir als Hausaufgabe auf? I
**honey** [ˈhʌni] Honig; *(infml, als Anrede:)* Schatz, Schätzchen I
**honk** [hɒŋk] hupen IV 3 (68)
**honour** [ˈɒnə] Ehre II
**hook** [hʊk] Haken III
**hop** [hɒp] hüpfen II
**hope** [həʊp] hoffen I
**horn** [hɔːn]:
1. Hupe III **blow the horn** hupen II
2. Horn IV 1 (15)

**horse** [hɔːs] Pferd I
°**horseback** [ˈhɔːsbæk]: **on horseback** zu Pferd, auf dem Pferd
**hospital** [ˈhɒspɪtl] Krankenhaus II
**host** [həʊst] Gastgeber/in; Moderator/in III

**host family** [ˈhəʊst fæməli] Gastfamilie I
**host parents** *(pl)* [ˈhəʊst peərənts] Gasteltern IV 1 (23)
**hostel** [ˈhɒstl] Herberge, Wohnheim III
**hot** [hɒt] heiß I
**hotbed** [ˈhɒtbed] Nährboden IV 3 (87)
**hotel** [həʊˈtel] Hotel II
**hotline** [ˈhɒtlaɪn] Hotline IV 2 (58)
**hour** [ˈaʊə] Stunde I **… an hour** … pro Stunde I **an hour and a half** eineinhalb Stunden, anderthalb Stunden III **half an hour** eine halbe Stunde III
**house** [haʊs] Haus I
**how** [haʊ] wie I **How are you?** Wie geht's? / Wie geht es dir/euch? I **How do you know …?** Woher weißt/kennst du …? III **How do you like it?** Wie findest du es (sie/ihn)? / Wie gefällt es (sie/er) dir? I **How many …?** Wie viele …? I **How much …?** Wie viel …? I **How much is/are …?** Was kostet/kosten …? I **How old are you?** Wie alt bist du? I **how to do sth.** wie man etwas macht / machen kann / machen soll I **How's things?** *(infml)* Wie geht's? IV 1 (12)
**howl** [haʊl] heulen IV 2 (58)
**hub** [hʌb] Mittelpunkt, (Verkehrs-)Knotenpunkt IV 1 (32)
**hug** [hʌg]:
1. **hug sb.** jn. umarmen II
2. **give sb. a hug** jn. umarmen II

**huge** [hjuːdʒ] riesig, sehr groß III
°**hugger** [ˈhʌgə] jd., der jn./etwas umarmt
°**Huguenots** *(pl)* [ˈhjuːgənəʊ] Hugenotten
**hum** [hʌm] summen; brummen III
**human** [ˈhjuːmən]:
1. Mensch III
2. menschlich III

**humorous** [ˈhjuːmərəs] humorvoll, witzig IV 1 (15)
**humour** [ˈhjuːmə]: **sense of humour** (Sinn für) Humor III
**hundred** [ˈhʌndrəd]: **a/one hundred** einhundert I
**hung** [hʌŋ] *siehe* **hang**
**hungry** [ˈhʌŋgri] **be hungry** hungrig sein, Hunger haben I
**hunt** [hʌnt]:
1. jagen III **hunt sb./sth. down** auf jn./etwas Jagd machen III
2. Jagd III

**hunter** [ˈhʌntə] Jäger/in IV 2 (58)
**hurricane** [ˈhʌrɪkən], [ˈhʌrɪkeɪn] Hurrikan, Orkan II
**hurry** [ˈhʌri] eilen; sich beeilen II **hurry up** sich beeilen I
**hurt** [hɜːt], **hurt, hurt**:
1. schmerzen, wehtun I
2. verletzen I

**be hurt** verletzt sein I **get hurt** sich verletzen IV 2 (53)
**husband** [ˈhʌzbənd] Ehemann III
**hyphen** [ˈhaɪfən] Bindestrich II

# I

**I** [aɪ] ich I **I'm (= I am)** Ich bin I
**ice** [aɪs] Eis II
**ice cream** [ˌaɪs ˈkriːm] (Speise-)Eis I
**ice rink** [ˈaɪs rɪŋk] Eisbahn IV 2 (38/39)
**ice skating** [ˈaɪs skeɪtɪŋ] Schlittschuhlaufen II
**iced tea** [ˌaɪst ˈtiː] Eistee II
**ICT** [ˌaɪ siː ˈtiː] Informations- und Kommunikationstechnologie I
**ID card** [ˌaɪ ˈdiː kɑːd] Personalausweis III
**idea** [aɪˈdɪə] Idee; Vorstellung I **No idea.** (infml) Keine Ahnung. IV 1 (11)
**ideal** [aɪˈdɪəl] ideal IV 2 (47)
°**identify** [aɪˈdentɪfaɪ] erkennen, (sich) identifizieren **identify oneself (as)** sich zu erkennen geben (als)
**identity** [aɪˈdentəti] Identität IV 1 (35)
**idiom** [ˈɪdiəm] Redewendung IV 1 (25)
**if** [ɪf]:
1. wenn, falls I **if-clause** Nebensatz mit *if* III
2. ob III **as if** als ob III
**igloo** [ˈɪɡluː] Iglu IV 2 (41)
**ill** [ɪl] krank II
**illness** [ˈɪlnəs] Krankheit III
**illuminate** [ɪˈluːmɪneɪt] erleuchten, beleuchten III
**illustration** [ˌɪləˈstreɪʃn] Abbildung, Illustration IV 1 (17)
**image** [ˈɪmɪdʒ] Bild, Abbild; Vorstellung III
°**imagination** [ɪˌmædʒɪˈneɪʃn] Fantasie, Vorstellungskraft
**imagine sth.** [ɪˈmædʒɪn] sich etwas vorstellen I
°**imitate** [ˈɪmɪteɪt] imitieren
**immediately** [ɪˈmiːdiətli] sofort III
**immigrant** [ˈɪmɪɡrənt] Einwanderer/Einwanderin IV 1 (17)
**immigrate** [ˈɪmɪɡreɪt] einwandern IV 1 (17)
**immigration** [ˌɪmɪˈɡreɪʃn] Einwanderung IV 1 (17)
°**impact** [ˈɪmpækt] Einfluss, Auswirkung
**impatient** [ɪmˈpeɪʃnt] ungeduldig III
**impolite** [ˌɪmpəˈlaɪt] unhöflich III
**important** [ɪmˈpɔːtnt] wichtig I
**impossible** [ɪmˈpɒsəbl] unmöglich II
**impression** [ɪmˈpreʃn] Eindruck III
**improve** [ɪmˈpruːv] verbessern; sich verbessern III
**improvement** [ɪmˈpruːvmənt] Verbesserung III
**in** [ɪn] in I **in 1580** im Jahr 1580 I **in England** in England I **in fact** eigentlich, in Wirklichkeit III **in fright** ängstlich, erschrocken III **in front of** vor (räumlich) I **in German/English** auf Deutsch/Englisch I **in my opinion** meiner Meinung nach III **in some/many ways** in mancher/vielerlei Hinsicht III **in the attic** auf dem Dachboden I **in the first place** erstens, in erster Linie; überhaupt IV 2 (45) **in the middle** in der Mitte I **in the morning/afternoon/evening** am Morgen / am Nachmittag / am Abend I **in the photo/picture** auf dem Foto/Bild I **in the world** auf der Welt I **in this way** auf diese Weise III **in time** rechtzeitig I **be in** zu Hause sein II **be in trouble** in Schwierigkeiten sein; Ärger kriegen I **come in** hereinkommen I
**inch** [ɪntʃ] Zoll (Längenmaß; 2,54 cm) III
°**include** [ɪnˈkluːd] (mit) einschließen
**included** [ɪnˈkluːdɪd] inbegriffen II
**including** [ɪnˈkluːdɪŋ] einschließlich; darunter (auch) III
°**increase (by)** [ɪnˈkriːs] steigern, (sich) erhöhen; steigen, zunehmen (um)
**incredible** [ɪnˈkredəbl] unglaublich III
**independence** [ˌɪndɪˈpendəns] Unabhängigkeit II **the Declaration of Independence** die Unabhängigkeitserklärung (der Vereinigten Staaten im Jahr 1776) II
**independent** [ˌɪndɪˈpendənt] unabhängig III
**Indian** [ˈɪndiən]:
1. Inder/in; indisch II
2. Indianer/in III
**indigenous (to)** [ɪnˈdɪdʒənəs] einheimisch (in) IV 2 (54) **indigenous people** Einheimische, Ureinwohner/innen IV 2 (54)
**individual** [ˌɪndɪˈvɪdʒuəl]:
1. Einzelne/r, Individuum; Person IV 2 (65)
2. individuell, Individual- IV 2 (65)
**indoor** [ˈɪndɔː] Innen-; Hallen- III
**industry** [ˈɪndəstri] Industrie III
**infect** [ɪnˈfekt] infizieren; verseuchen IV 3 (84)
**infection** [ɪnˈfekʃn] Infektion IV 3 (84)
**infer sth. (from sth.)** [ɪnˈfɜː] (fml) etwas (aus etwas) folgern IV 2 (59)
**infinitive** [ɪnˈfɪnətɪv] Infinitiv II
**influence** [ˈɪnfluəns]:
1. Einfluss III
2. beeinflussen IV 3 (97)
**informal** [ɪnˈfɔːml] informell, locker IV 2 (20)
**information (about)** (no pl) [ˌɪnfəˈmeɪʃn] Information(en) (über) I **Information and Communications Technology** Informations- und Kommunikationstechnologie I
**informational** [ˌɪnfəˈmeɪʃənl] Informations- IV 2 (41)
**inhabit (a region)** [ɪnˈhæbɪt] (eine Region) bewohnen IV 2 (61)
**inhabitant** [ɪnˈhæbɪtənt] Einwohner/in, Bewohner/in IV 1 (17)
°**inherent** [ɪnˈhɪərənt] angeboren, innewohnend
°**inherently** [ɪnˈhɪərəntli] von Natur aus
°**inner** [ˈɪnə] innere(r, s)
°**inner tube** [ˌɪnə ˈtjuːb] Schlauch (in einem Reifen)
**insect** [ˈɪnsekt] Insekt IV 2 (58)
**inside** [ˌɪnˈsaɪd]:
1. drinnen; nach drinnen I
2. **inside the dome** in der Kuppel, innerhalb der Kuppel IV 1 (10)
3. **the inside** die Innenseite; das Innere III
**inspire** [ɪnˈspaɪə] inspirieren IV 2 (46)
**instead** [ɪnˈsted] stattdessen II **instead of** anstelle von, statt III
**instrument** [ˈɪnstrəmənt] Instrument I
**insult** [ˈɪnsʌlt]:
1. Beleidigung IV 3 (80)
2. **insult sb.** jn. beleidigen IV 3 (80)
**insulted** beleidigt II
°**intact** [ɪnˈtækt] intakt
°**integrate** [ˈɪntɪɡreɪt] (sich) integrieren
**intelligent** [ɪnˈtelɪdʒənt] intelligent IV 2 (65)
**intentional** [ɪnˈtenʃənl] absichtlich, vorsätzlich IV 3 (84)
**interact** [ˌɪntərˈækt] (miteinander) interagieren, kommunizieren IV 2 (47)
°**interest sb.** [ˈɪntrəst] jn. interessieren
**interested** [ˈɪntrəstɪd]: **be interested (in)** interessiert sein (an), sich interessieren (für) I
**interesting** [ˈɪntrəstɪŋ] interessant I
°**interior** [ɪnˈtɪəriə] Innere(s), Innenansicht, Innenseite
**international** [ˌɪntəˈnæʃnəl] international I
**internet** [ˈɪntənet] Internet I **on the internet** im Internet I
**interpret** [ɪnˈtɜːprɪt] interpretieren; dolmetschen (gesprochenen Text mündlich wiedergeben) IV 2 (58)
**interpretation** [ɪnˌtɜːprɪˈteɪʃn] Interpretation; (das) Dolmetschen IV 2 (58)
**interpreter** [ɪnˈtɜːprɪtə] Dolmetscher/in IV 2 (58)
**interrupt** [ˌɪntəˈrʌpt] unterbrechen II
**interview** [ˈɪntəvjuː]:
1. Interview II
2. befragen, interviewen IV 2 (58)
°**interviewer** [ˈɪntəvjuːə] Interviewer/in
**into** [ˈɪntu]: **into the kitchen** in die Küche (hinein) I **be into sth.** (infml) etwas mögen, auf etwas stehen III
**intonation** [ˌɪntəˈneɪʃn] Intonation, Satzmelodie I
**introduce sth./sb. (to sb.)** [ˌɪntrəˈdjuːs] etwas/jn. (jm.) vorstellen II
**introduction** [ˌɪntrəˈdʌkʃn] Einleitung, Einführung III
**Inuit** [ˈɪnjuɪt] Inuit (kanadische Ureinwohner/innen) IV 2 (41)
**Inuktitut** [ɪˈnʊktɪtʊt] Inuktitut (Sprache der Inuit) IV 2 (41)
**invade (a country)** [ɪnˈveɪd] (in ein Land) einmarschieren II
**invent** [ɪnˈvent] erfinden IV 1 (35)
**invention** [ɪnˈvenʃn] Erfindung IV 1 (35)
**invitation (to)** [ˌɪnvɪˈteɪʃn] Einladung (zu, nach) I
**invite sb. (to)** [ɪnˈvaɪt]:
1. jn. einladen (zu) II
2. jn. auffordern (zu) III
**irregular** [ɪˈreɡjələ] unregelmäßig II

# Dictionary

**is** [ɪz]: **Is that you?** Bist du's? / Bist du das? ı **The camera is …** Die Kamera kostet … ı
**island** [ˈaɪlənd] Insel ı
**isn't** [ˈɪznt]: **he/she/it isn't …** (= he/she/it is not) er/sie/es ist nicht …; er/sie/es ist kein/e … ı
°**issue** [ˈɪʃuː] (Streit-)Frage, Problem, Thema
**it** [ɪt] er, sie, es *(Dinge/Tiere)* ı **it's …** (= it is) er/sie/es ist … ı
°**itinerary** [aɪˈtɪnərəri] Reiseroute, Reiseplan
**its name** [ɪts] sein Name / ihr Name ı
**itself** [ɪtˈself] es/sich selbst/selber ııı

## J

**jacket** [ˈdʒækɪt] Jacke, Jackett ıı
**jam** [dʒæm] Marmelade ı
**January** [ˈdʒænjuəri] Januar ı
**jeans** *(pl)* [dʒiːnz] Jeans ı
**jeep** [dʒiːp] Jeep ııı
**jerk** [dʒɜːk] *(infml)* Trottel, Depp ııı
**jersey** [ˈdʒɜːzi] Trikot ııı
**Jew** [dʒuː] Jude/Jüdin ıv 1 (17)
**jewellery** *(no pl)* [ˈdʒuːəlri] (*AE:* **jewelry**) Schmuck ııı
**jewels** *(pl)* [ˈdʒuːəlz] Juwelen ıı
**Jewish** [ˈdʒuːɪʃ] jüdisch ıv 1 (17)
**jigsaw** [ˈdʒɪgsɔː] Puzzle ıı
**job** [dʒɒb]:
1. Job, (Arbeits-)Stelle ı
2. Aufgabe ıı
**jogging** [ˈdʒɒgɪŋ] (das) Joggen ıv 3 (70)
**join** [dʒɔɪn]:
1. **join a club** in einen Klub eintreten; sich einem Klub anschließen ı **join in** mitmachen ıı
2. **join sth.** etwas verbinden ııı
**joke** [dʒəʊk]:
1. Witz ı
2. Witze machen, scherzen ıv 2 (52) **joke around** herumscherzen ıv 2 (52) **You're joking! / You must be joking!** Du machst wohl Witze! / Das kann doch nicht dein Ernst sein! ıv 2 (52)
**journey** [ˈdʒɜːni] Reise, Fahrt ıı
**judo** [ˈdʒuːdəʊ] Judo ı
**juggle sth.** [ˈdʒʌgl] mit etwas jonglieren ıı
**juggler** [ˈdʒʌglə] Jongleur/in ıı
**juice** [dʒuːs] Saft ıı
**July** [dʒuˈlaɪ] Juli ı
**jump** [dʒʌmp]:
1. Sprung ı
2. springen ı **jump up** hochspringen ıı
**junction** [ˈdʒʌŋkʃn] (Straßen-)Kreuzung ııı
**June** [dʒuːn] Juni ı
**junior** [ˈdʒuːniə] Junioren- ı **junior team** Jugendmannschaft, Juniorenmannschaft ı
**just** [dʒʌst]:
1. (einfach) nur, bloß ı
2. gerade (eben), soeben ıı **just after …** gleich nachdem / kurz nachdem … ı **just then** genau in dem Moment; gerade dann ıı
3. **just as boring/exciting** genauso langweilig/aufregend ııı **just like …** genau wie … ıı
°**justify** [ˈdʒʌstɪfaɪ] rechtfertigen, begründen

## K

**kayak** [ˈkaɪæk] Kajak ııı
**kayaking** [ˈkaɪækɪŋ] Kajakfahren ııı
**keen** [kiːn]: **be keen on doing sth.** wild darauf sein, etwas zu tun ııı **be keen on sth.** wild auf etwas sein ııı
**keep** [kiːp], **kept, kept:**
1. halten ıı
2. behalten ııı
3. aufbewahren ııı
**keep back** fernbleiben, zurückbleiben ıv 2 (61) **keep (on) doing sth.** etwas immer wieder / immer weiter tun; etwas ständig tun ııı **keep sth. away from** etwas fernhalten von ııı **keep sth. out of** etwas heraushalten aus ııı **keep sth. up** etwas aufrechterhalten, fortsetzen; weitermachen mit etwas ıv 3 (68) **keep sth. warm/fresh** etwas warm/frisch halten ııı **keep up (with sb.)** (mit jm.) Schritt halten ıv 2 (40) **keep your distance (from)** Abstand halten (zu/von) ıv 1 (27) °**keep a diary** (ein) Tagebuch führen
**kept** [kept] *siehe* **keep**
**key** [kiː] Schlüssel ıı
**key point** [ˈkiː pɔɪnt] Kernpunkt, Hauptpunkt ıı
**keyword** [ˈkiːwɜːd] Schlüsselwort ı
**kick** [kɪk] treten ıı
**kid** [kɪd] *(infml)* Kind; Jugendliche(r) ı
**kill** [kɪl] töten ıı
**kilo** [ˈkiːləʊ] *siehe* **kilogram**
**kilogram (kilo, kg)** [ˈkɪləgræm] Kilo(gramm) (kg) ı
**kilometre** [ˈkɪləmiːtə], [kɪˈlɒmɪtə] Kilometer ıı
**kind** [kaɪnd]:
1. freundlich, nett ıı
2. *(n)* **a kind of …** eine Art (von) … ı
3. *(adv)* **kind of scary** *(infml)* irgendwie unheimlich, ganz schön unheimlich ıı
**king** [kɪŋ] König ıı
**kingdom** [ˈkɪŋdəm] Königreich ııı
**kiss** [kɪs] küssen; sich küssen ıı
**kit** [kɪt] Ausrüstung ı
**kitchen** [ˈkɪtʃɪn] Küche ı
**knee** [niː] Knie ıı
**kneel** [niːl], **knelt, knelt** knien ıı
**knelt** [nelt] *siehe* **kneel**
**knew** [njuː] *siehe* **know**
**knife** [naɪf], *pl* **knives** Messer ıı
**knight** [naɪt] Ritter ıı
**knives** [naɪvz] *plural of* **knife**

**know** [nəʊ], **knew, known** wissen; kennen ı **know about sth.** sich mit etwas auskennen; über etwas Bescheid wissen ı **…, you know.** …, weißt du. / …, wissen Sie. ı **How do you know …?** Woher weißt/kennst du …? ııı **I don't know.** Ich weiß (es) nicht. ı
**known** [nəʊn] *siehe* **know** **well known** bekannt ı
**kung fu** [ˌkʌŋ ˈfuː] Kung Fu ı

## L

**label** [ˈleɪbl]:
1. beschriften; etikettieren ıı
2. Beschriftung; Schild, Etikett ıı
**lack** [læk]:
1. **lack (of)** Mangel (an) ıv 2 (47) **for lack of** aus Mangel an ıv 2 (47)
2. **sb. lacks sth.** jm. fehlt es an etwas ıv 2 (47)
**Ladies and gentlemen** [ˌleɪdɪz ən ˈdʒentlmən] Meine Damen und Herren / Sehr geehrte Damen und Herren ııı
**laid** [leɪd] *siehe* **lay**
**lain** [leɪn] *siehe* **lie**
**lake** [leɪk] (Binnen-)See ı
**lamb** [læm] Lamm ıı
**lamp** [læmp] Lampe ı
**land** [lænd]:
1. Land ı
2. landen; an Land gehen ıı
**landing** [ˈlændɪŋ] Landungssteg ııı
°**landscape** [ˈlændskeɪp] Landschaft; Landschaftsbild
**language** [ˈlæŋgwɪdʒ] Sprache ı
**laptop** [ˈlæptɒp] Laptop *(tragbarer PC)* ııı
**large** [lɑːdʒ] groß ı
**last** [lɑːst]:
1. letzte(r, s) ı **last weekend/Friday** letztes Wochenende / letzten Freitag ı **last year's musical** das Musical vom letzten Jahr ıı
2. zuletzt, das letzte Mal ııı
3. **at last** endlich, schließlich ı
**last (for)** [lɑːst] (an)dauern; halten *(von Bestand sein)* ıv 1 (22)
**late** [leɪt] spät ı **He's in his late thirties.** Er ist Ende dreißig. ıv 3 (84) **stay up late** lang aufbleiben ıı **You're late.** Du bist spät dran. / Du bist zu spät. ı
**later** [ˈleɪtə] später ı **Catch you later.** *(infml)* Bis später dann! ıv 1 (11) **See you later.** Bis bald. / Bis nachher. ı
**Latin** [ˈlætɪn] lateinisch; Latein ıv 1 (26)
**laugh** [lɑːf] lachen ı **laugh at sb./sth.** über jn./etwas lachen; jn. auslachen ııı
**law** [lɔː] Gesetz ııı
**lawn** [lɔːn] Rasen ııı
**lay** [leɪ] *siehe* **lie**
**lay** [leɪ], **laid, laid** legen ııı **lay sth. down** etwas festsetzen, festlegen ıv 3 (96) °**lay by** rasten, Halt machen
**layout** [ˈleɪaʊt] Layout, Gestaltung ıı
**lead** [liːd], **led, led** führen, leiten ııı

# English – German

**leader** ['liːdə] Leiter/in III
**lean** [liːn] sich lehnen; sich beugen III
**learn** [lɜːn] lernen I
**least** [liːst]: **at least** zumindest, wenigstens II
**leather** ['leðə] Leder III
**leave** [liːv], **left, left:**
1. (ab)fahren; (weg)gehen I
2. verlassen; zurücklassen I
3. lassen II
**leave a message** eine Nachricht hinterlassen II **leave sth.** etwas übrig lassen II
**leave sth. out** etwas weglassen, auslassen II
**led** [led] siehe **lead**
**left** [left] siehe **leave** **be left** übrig sein III
**left** [left] linke(r, s); (nach) links I **on the left** links / auf der linken Seite I
**turn left** (nach) links abbiegen II
**leg** [leg] Bein I **pull sb.'s leg** (infml) jn. auf den Arm nehmen (veräppeln) IV 1 (25)
**legend** ['ledʒənd] Legende, Sage II
**legendary** ['ledʒəndri] legendär, berühmt III
**leisure centre** ['leʒə sentə] Freizeitpark, Freizeitzentrum II
**length** [leŋθ] Länge; Dauer III
**lens** [lenz] (Kamera-)Objektiv, Linse (Optik) IV 2 (47) °**under a new lens** aus einem neuen Blickwinkel
**less (than)** [les] weniger (als) III
**lesson** ['lesn] (Unterrichts-)Stunde I **before lessons** vorm Unterricht I
**let** [let], **let, let** lassen I **Let me show you ...** Lass mich dir ... zeigen. I **Let's ...** Lass(t) uns ... I
**letter** ['letə]:
1. Brief I
2. Buchstabe I
°**level** ['levl] Grad, Stufe; Niveau, Ebene
**liberty** ['libəti] Freiheit III
**library** ['laibrəri] Bibliothek, Bücherei I
**licence** ['laisns] Genehmigung, Lizenz IV 2 (49)
**licence plate** ['laisns pleit] (AE) Nummernschild, Autokennzeichen IV 2 (64)
**lie** [lai], **lay, lain** liegen II **lie down** sich hinlegen III
**life** [laif], pl **lives** Leben I **way of life** Lebensweise IV 3 (90)
**life jacket** ['laif dʒækit] Schwimmweste I
**lifestyle** ['laifstail] Lebensstil IV 3 (84)
**lift** [lift]:
1. (BE) Fahrstuhl, Aufzug, Lift I
2. Mitfahrgelegenheit II **give sb. a lift** jn. mitnehmen II
**lift sth.** [lift] etwas heben, hochheben, anheben III **lift sth. up** etwas hochheben IV 1 (26)
**light** [lait]:
1. Licht I
2. **light brown/blue/...** hellbraun/-blau/... III
3. **light, lit, lit** anzünden II **light** up aufleuchten III **light sth. up** etwas erhellen (aufleuchten lassen) II
**lightning** (no pl) ['laitniŋ] Blitz(e) II **a flash of lightning** ein Blitz II
**like** [laik] mögen, gernhaben I **I like ...** Ich mag ... I **I like swimming/sailing/...** Ich schwimme/segele/... gern. I **I'd like ...** (= I would like ...) Ich hätte gern ... / Ich möchte ... I **I'd like to go** Ich möchte gehen / Ich würde gern gehen I **I'd like you to ...** Ich möchte, dass du ... II **What would you like to eat?** Was möchtest du essen? I
**like** [laik]:
1. **like boys** wie Buben I **like that** so (auf diese Weise) I **like this** so (auf diese Weise) I **just like ...** genau wie ... II **What was it like?** Wie war es? II **What's she like?** Wie ist sie? / Wie ist sie so? I
2. (conjunction; infml) als ob III
3. **She was like: "Stop ..."** (infml) Und sie so: „Stopp ..." III
**likely** ['laikli]: **be likely to do sth.** wahrscheinlich etwas tun (werden) IV 2 (63)
**likes and dislikes** (pl) [,laiks ən 'dislaiks] Vorlieben und Abneigungen I
**line** [lain]:
1. Zeile I
2. Leine, (Angel-)Schnur III
3. (U-Bahn-)Linie II
4. Reihe II
5. (AE) Schlange (wartender Menschen) II
**be/stand/wait in line** (AE) Schlange stehen, sich anstellen II
°**6. (family) line** (Familien-)Zweig
**link** [liŋk] verbinden, verknüpfen I
**linking word** ['liŋkiŋ wɜːd] Bindewort III
**lion** ['laiən] Löwe I
**lip** [lip] Lippe II
**list** [list]:
1. Liste I
2. auflisten IV 3 (96)
**listen** ['lisn] zuhören, horchen I **listen to sb.** jm. zuhören I **listen to sth.** sich etwas anhören I
**listener** ['lisənə] Zuhörer/in I
**lit** [lit] siehe **light**
°**literal** ['litərəl] wörtlich, buchstäblich
**literature** ['litrətʃə] Literatur II
**litter bin** ['litə bin] Abfalleimer I
**little** [litl] klein II **a little** ein bisschen, ein wenig, etwas II
**live** [liv] leben; wohnen I
**lively** ['laivli] lebendig, lebhaft IV 1 (20)
**lives** [laivz] plural of **life**
**living room** ['liviŋ ruːm] Wohnzimmer I
**loads of ...** [ləudz] (infml) eine Menge (von) ... IV 1 (20)
**lobster** ['lɒbstə] Hummer II
**local** ['ləukl] örtlich, Lokal-; am/vom Ort III
**located** [ləu'keitid]: **be located (in ...)** (in ...) liegen, sich (in ...) befinden IV 2 (62)
**location** [ləu'keiʃn] Ort, Platz, Lage; Drehort (z.B. von Filmen) IV 2 (62)
**lock** [lɒk]:
1. abschließen (z.B. Tür) IV 2 (64)
2. Schloss (z.B. Türschloss) IV 2 (64)
**locker** ['lɒkə] Schließfach, Spind III
**log in/out** [lɒg] sich ein-/ausloggen III
**logbook** ['lɒgbuk] Fahrtenbuch II
°**LOL (laugh-out-loud)** [,el ˌəʊ ˈel] laut lachen(d) (Internet)
**lonely** ['ləunli] einsam I
**long** [lɒŋ] lang I **no longer / not any longer** nicht mehr, nicht länger IV 2 (56)
**long shot** ['lɒŋ ʃɒt] Totale (Film) IV 1 (15)
°**longhouse** ['lɒŋhaus] Langhaus (bei den amerik. Ureinwohner/innen)
**look** [luk]:
1. schauen I **look after sb.** auf jn. aufpassen; sich um jn. kümmern II **look around (the farm)** sich (auf der Farm) umsehen I **look at** anschauen, ansehen I **look for sth.** etwas suchen I **look forward to sth.** sich auf etwas freuen II **look happy/angry/...** glücklich/wütend/... aussehen I **look into sth.** etwas untersuchen, prüfen III **look sth. up** etwas nachschlagen III **look up** hochsehen, aufschauen II
2. **have a look (at sth.)** nachschauen; einen Blick auf etwas werfen II
**lorry** ['lɒri] (BE) Lastwagen, LKW III
**lose** [luːz], **lost, lost** verlieren II
**lost** [lɒst] siehe **lose**
**lot** [lɒt]: **lots of ... / a lot of ...** viel ..., viele ... I **a lot** viel I **That helped us a lot.** Das hat uns sehr geholfen. I
**loud** [laud] laut I **in a loud voice** mit lauter Stimme II
**loudspeaker** [,laud'spiːkə] Lautsprecher; Megaphon II
**Love, ...** [lʌv] Alles Liebe, ... / Liebe Grüße, ... (Briefschluss) I
**love** [lʌv] lieben, sehr mögen I **I'd love to ...** Ich würde sehr gern ... I
**lovely** ['lʌvli] schön, hübsch, herrlich II
**low** [ləu] niedrig, tief IV 3 (94)
**luck** [lʌk]: **Good luck!** Viel Glück! I
**luckily** ['lʌkili] glücklicherweise III
**lucky** ['lʌki]: **be lucky** Glück haben I **Lucky you.** Du Glückspilz. II
°**lumberjack** ['lʌmbədʒæk] Holzfäller/in
**lunch** [lʌntʃ] Mittagessen I **have lunch** zu Mittag essen I **What's for lunch?** Was gibt es zum Mittagessen? I
**lunchtime** ['lʌntʃtaim] Mittagszeit I **at lunchtime** mittags I
**luxurious** [lʌg'ʒuəriəs] luxuriös III

# M

**machine** [mə'ʃiːn] Maschine, Gerät III
**mad** [mæd]:
1. verrückt I
2. **mad (at sb. / about sth.)** (AE, infml) wütend (auf jn./wegen etwas) IV 3 (86)

# Dictionary

**madam** ['mædəm]: **Dear Sir or Madam** Sehr geehrte Damen und Herren II
**made** [meɪd] *siehe* **make** **be made of sth.** aus etwas (gemacht) sein II **be made up of** sich zusammensetzen aus; gebildet sein/werden aus IV 2 (46) °**be made to do sth.** gezwungen werden, etwas zu tun; etwas tun müssen
**magazine** [ˌmægə'ziːn] Zeitschrift I
**magic** ['mædʒɪk] magisch, Zauber- II
**magical** ['mædʒɪkl] zauberhaft, wundervoll; magisch III
**magnificent** [mæg'nɪfɪsnt] prächtig IV 1 (10)
**mail** [meɪl] E-Mail II
**main** [meɪn] Haupt- II
**main clause** ['meɪn klɔːz] Hauptsatz II
**mainly** ['meɪnli] hauptsächlich, vorwiegend IV 3 (69)
**majority** [mə'dʒɒrəti] Mehrheit, Mehrzahl III
**make** [meɪk], **made, made** machen; herstellen I **make (money)** (Geld) verdienen IV 3 (70) **make a wish** sich etwas wünschen I **make eye contact** Blickkontakt herstellen III **make friends** Freunde finden I **make fun of sb./sth.** sich über jn./etwas lustig machen III **make it** es schaffen, Erfolg haben IV 2 (47) **make sb. sth.** jn. zu etwas machen II **make sth. up** sich etwas ausdenken III **make sure that …** sich vergewissern, dass …; darauf achten, dass …; dafür sorgen, dass … II **make the finals** es (bis) zum Finale schaffen IV 2 (47) **I couldn't make your party.** Ich habe es nicht geschafft, zu eurer Party zu kommen. IV 2 (47) °**make sb. do sth.** jn. dazu bringen, etwas zu tun
**make-up** ['meɪk_ʌp] Makeup II
**malaria** [mə'leəriə] Malaria II
**mall** [mɔːl] (großes) Einkaufszentrum I
**man** [mæn], *pl* **men** Mann I
**man-made** [ˌmæn 'meɪd] künstlich, Kunst- III
**manage sth.** ['mænɪdʒ] etwas schaffen; etwas zustande bringen III
**manager** ['mænɪdʒə] Geschäftsführer/in, Manager/in IV 3 (70)
°**maniac** ['meɪniæk] Fanatiker/in; Irre(r), Wahnsinnige(r)
°**manifest** ['mænɪfest] offensichtlich, offenkundig
**manufacturing (industry)** [ˌmænju'fæktʃərɪŋ] Fertigungsindustrie, verarbeitende Industrie III
**many** ['meni] viele I **How many …?** Wie viele …? I
**map** [mæp] Landkarte; Stadtplan I **on the map** auf der Landkarte; auf dem Stadtplan I
**maple** ['meɪpl] Ahorn IV 2 (64)
**maple syrup** [ˌmeɪpl 'sɪrəp] Ahornsirup IV 2 (64)
**marathon** ['mærəθən] Marathon II
**March** [mɑːtʃ] März I

°**march** [mɑːtʃ] Marsch
**mark** [mɑːk]:
1. (Schul-)Note, Zensur IV 2 (43)
2. markieren II **mark sth. up** etwas markieren, kennzeichnen II
**market** ['mɑːkɪt] Markt I
**marmalade** ['mɑːməleɪd] Marmelade (aus Zitrusfrüchten) I
**marmot** ['mɑːmət] Murmeltier IV 2 (62)
**married (to)** ['mærɪd] verheiratet (mit) I
**marry** ['mæri] heiraten III
°**marshmallow** [ˌmɑːʃ'mæləʊ] Marshmallow (weiche Süßigkeit, ähnlich wie Mäusespeck)
**mask** [mɑːk] Maske II
**mass destruction** [ˌmæs dɪ'strʌkʃn] Massenvernichtung IV 2 (64)
**master** ['mɑːstə] Meister/in
**match** [mætʃ] Spiel, Wettkampf, Match I
**match** [mætʃ] (passend) zusammenfügen III °**match with/to** zuordnen
**material** [mə'tɪəriəl] Material, Stoff III
**mathematics** [ˌmæθə'mætɪks] Mathematik IV 2 (47)
**maths** [mæθs] Mathematik I
°**matrilineal** [ˌmætrɪ'lɪniəl] matrilineal (in der Erbfolge der mütterlichen Linie folgend)
**matter** ['mætə]: **What's the matter?** Was ist denn? / Was ist los? I
**May** [meɪ] Mai I
**may** [meɪ] dürfen II **May I have a word with you?** Kann ich dich/Sie kurz sprechen? II **they may be at home** sie sind vielleicht daheim III
**maybe** ['meɪbi] vielleicht I
**mayor** [meə] Bürgermeister/in II
**me** [miː] mich; mir I **Me too.** Ich auch. I **It's me.** Ich bin's. I
**meal** [miːl] Mahlzeit, Essen III
**mean** [miːn], **meant, meant**:
1. meinen, sagen wollen II
2. bedeuten II
**meaning** ['miːnɪŋ] Bedeutung II
**meant** [ment] *siehe* **mean**
**meat** [miːt] Fleisch I
**medal** ['medl] Medaille I
**media** (pl) ['miːdiə] Medien III **social media** (pl) soziale Medien III
**mediation** [ˌmiːdi'eɪʃn] Sprachmittlung, Mediation I
**medicine** ['medsn], ['medɪsn] Medizin; Arznei II
**medium** ['miːdiəm] mittelgroß; mittel- III
**meet** [miːt], **met, met**:
1. treffen, kennenlernen I **Meet your classmates.** Triff deine Mitschüler/innen. / Lerne deine Mitschüler/innen kennen. I **Nice to meet you.** Freut mich, dich/euch/Sie kennenzulernen. I
2. sich treffen I
°**meeting** ['miːtɪŋ] Treffen; Zusammenkunft
**melt** [melt] schmelzen II
**member** ['membə] Mitglied IV 1 (11)
**meme** [miːm] (Internet-)Mem III

**memorial** [mə'mɔːriəl] Denkmal; Gedenk- III
**memory** ['meməri] Erinnerung II
**men** [men] *plural of* **man**
**Merry Christmas!** [ˌmeri 'krɪsməs] Frohe Weihnachten! I
**mesmerizing** ['mezməraɪzɪŋ] fesselnd, hypnotisierend II
**message** ['mesɪdʒ]:
1. Nachricht II **leave a message** eine Nachricht hinterlassen II
2. Botschaft, Aussage III
3. **message (sb.)** (jm.) eine (elektronische) Nachricht schicken/übermitteln IV 1 (12)
**messenger** ['mesɪndʒə] Kurier/in, Bote/Botin IV 1 (12)
**messenger service** ['mesɪndʒə sɜːvɪs] Messenger (Dienst zur Nachrichtenübermittlung im Internet) IV 1 (12)
**met** [met] *siehe* **meet**
**metal** ['metl] Metall; Metall- III
°**Métis** [meɪ'tiː] Métis (Nachfahren europäischer Einwanderer/-innen in Kanada)
**metre** ['miːtə] Meter I
**mid-** [mɪd]: **He's in his mid-thirties.** Er ist Mitte dreißig. IV 3 (84) **the mid-1800s** Mitte des 19. Jahrhunderts IV 3 (84)
**middle** ['mɪdl] Mitte I **in the middle** in der Mitte I
**middle school** ['mɪdl skuːl] (AE) Mittelschule (für 11- bis 14-Jährige) IV 2 (41)
**midnight** ['mɪdnaɪt] Mitternacht I
**Midwest** [mɪd'west] Mittlerer Westen (der USA) IV 3 (66/67)
**might** [maɪt]: **it might be …** es könnte … sein; vielleicht ist es … II
°**migrate** [maɪ'greɪt] (aus-/ab-)wandern, ziehen
°**migration** [maɪ'greɪʃn] Migration, Zu-/Aus-/Abwanderung
°**migratory** ['maɪgrətri] Zug- (wandernd)
°**migratory bird** [ˌmaɪgrətri 'bɜːd] Zugvogel
**mile** [maɪl] Meile (ca. 1,6 km) I **for miles** meilenweit I
**military** ['mɪlətri]:
1. militärisch IV 3 (96)
2. Militär IV 3 (96)
**milk** [mɪlk] Milch I
**mill** [mɪl] Mühle IV 1 (16)
°**mill about** [ˌmɪl ə'baʊt] herumlaufen
**million** ['mɪljən] Million I
**mind** [maɪnd]:
1. aufpassen auf, achten auf IV 1 (25)
2. etwas dagegen haben III **Do you mind …?** Stört es Sie, …? / Haben Sie etwas dagegen, …? III **if you don't mind** wenn Sie nichts dagegen haben III
**mind** [maɪnd] Verstand, Sinn, Geist IV 3 (80) **change one's mind** seine Meinung ändern, es sich anders überlegen IV 3 (80)
**mind map** ['maɪnd mæp] Mindmap I
**mine** [maɪn] meiner, meine, meins II

# English – German

**mine** [maɪn]:
1. Bergwerk, Mine III **coal mine** Kohlebergwerk III
2. abbauen *(Bodenschätze)* III
3. Mine *(Militär)* III

**minibus** ['mɪnibʌs] Kleinbus I
**minister** ['mɪnɪstə] Minister/in IV 2 (49)
**minority** [maɪ'nɒrəti] Minderheit III
**minute** ['mɪnɪt] Minute I **a two-minute talk** ein zweiminütiger Vortrag II **Hold on a minute.** (*oft auch kurz:* **Hold on.**) Bleib / Bleiben Sie am Apparat. *(am Telefon)* II **Just a minute.** Einen Moment. / Moment mal. IV 3 (80) **Wait a minute.** Warte einen Moment. / Moment mal. I
**mirror** ['mɪrə] Spiegel II
**miss** [mɪs]:
1. vermissen III
2. verpassen II

**Miss Bell** [mɪs] Frau Bell *(übliche Anrede von Lehrerinnen)* I
**missing** ['mɪsɪŋ]: **be missing** fehlen II **the missing words** die fehlenden Wörter I
**mist** [mɪst] (leichter) Nebel, Dunst(schleier) II
**mistake** [mɪ'steɪk] Fehler II **by mistake** aus Versehen III
**mix** [mɪks] Mischung II
**mixed bag** [ˌmɪkst 'bæg] *etwa:* bunte Mischung II
**mixture** ['mɪkstʃə] Mischung IV 1 (17)
**mobile (phone)** [ˌməʊbaɪl 'fəʊn] Mobiltelefon, Handy I
**model** ['mɒdl] Modell III
°**moderator** ['mɒdəreɪtə] Moderator/in *(bei Debatten)*; Vermittler/in
**modern** ['mɒdən] modern III
**mom** [mɒm], [mɑːm] *(AE)* Mutti, Mama IV 1 (11)
**moment** ['məʊmənt] Moment I **at the moment** gerade, im Moment I
**monarch** ['mɒnək] Monarch/in III
**Monday** ['mʌndeɪ], ['mʌndi] Montag I **on Monday** am Montag I
**money** ['mʌni] Geld I
**monkey** ['mʌŋki] Affe I
**monster** ['mɒnstə] Monster I
**month** [mʌnθ] Monat I
**monthly** ['mʌnθli] monatlich III
**monument (to)** ['mɒnjumənt] Monument, Denkmal (für / zum Gedenken an) IV 1 (22)
**mood** [muːd] Stimmung, Laune IV 3 (68)
**moon** [muːn] Mond I **full moon** Vollmond II
**moonlight** ['muːnlaɪt] Mondlicht III
**moor** [mɔː] Hochmoor II
°**moose** [muːs], *pl* **moose** Elch
**mop** [mɒp]:
1. wischen (Fußboden) III
2. Wischmopp III

**more** [mɔː] mehr I **more beautiful (than)** schöner (als) II **not … any more** nicht mehr II **one more photo** noch ein Foto; ein weiteres Foto II
**morning** ['mɔːnɪŋ] Morgen, Vormittag I **Good morning.** Guten Morgen. I **in the morning** morgens, vormittags, am Morgen/Vormittag I **tomorrow morning** morgen früh I
**most** [məʊst]: **most people / most of them** die meisten Menschen / die meisten von ihnen II **(the) most beautiful** der/die/das schönste …; am schönsten II
**mostly** ['məʊstli] größtenteils, hauptsächlich; meistens IV 2 (41)
**mother** ['mʌðə] Mutter I
°**motivation** [ˌməʊtɪ'veɪʃn] Motivation
**motor** ['məʊtə] Motor III
**motorbike** ['məʊtəbaɪk] Motorrad IV 3 (70)
**motorcycle** ['məʊtəsaɪkl] Motorrad IV 3 (70)
**mountain** ['maʊntən] Berg I
**mountain-biking** ['maʊntən baɪkɪŋ] Mountainbiken III
**mouth** [maʊθ] Mund; Maul I
**move** [muːv]:
1. bewegen; sich bewegen I
2. **move (to)** umziehen (nach) II **move in** einziehen II **move into a house** in ein Haus (ein)ziehen II
3. Zug (bei Brettspielen) II

**movement** ['muːvmənt] Bewegung III
**movie** ['muːvi] *(bes. AE)* Film II
**movie theater** ['muːvi θɪətə] *(AE)* Kino IV 3 (88)
**MP3 player** [ˌem piː 'θriː pleɪə] MP3-Player I
**Mr Schwarz** ['mɪstə] Herr Schwarz I
**Mrs Schwarz** ['mɪsɪz] Frau Schwarz I
**much** [mʌtʃ] viel I **How much …?** Wie viel …? I **How much is/are …?** Was kostet/kosten …? I
**mud** [mʌd] Schlamm, Matsch II
**mug** [mʌɡ]: **a mug (of)** ein Becher II
**multicultural** [ˌmʌltiˈkʌltʃərəl] multikulturell IV 1 (17)
**multiculturalism** [ˌmʌltiˈkʌltʃərəlɪzm] Multikulturismus, kulturelle Vielfalt IV 1 (17)
**multilingual** [ˌmʌltiˈlɪŋɡwəl] mehrsprachig IV 2 (56)
**multilingualism** [ˌmʌltiˈlɪŋɡwəlɪzm] Mehrsprachigkeit IV 2 (56)
°**multiple** ['mʌltɪpl] mehrere, zahlreiche
**mum** [mʌm] Mama, Mutti I
**mural** ['mjʊərəl] Wandgemälde IV 1 (16)
**museum** [mjuˈziːəm] Museum I
**music** ['mjuːzɪk] Musik I
**musical** ['mjuːzɪkl] Musical II
**musician** [mjuˈzɪʃn] Musiker/in III
°**musk ox** ['mʌsk ˌɒks], *pl* **musk oxen** Moschusochse
**must** [mʌst] müssen I **you mustn't do it** du darfst es nicht tun I
°**mutual** ['mjuːtʃuəl] gegenseitige(r, s)
**my** [maɪ] mein, meine, mein I **My birthday is in May.** Ich habe im Mai Geburtstag. I **my name is …** ich heiße … I
**myself** [maɪ'self] ich/mich/mir selbst/selber III
**mythical** ['mɪθɪkl] mythisch; fiktiv IV 1 (17)
°**mythical beast** [ˌmɪθɪkl 'biːst] Fabelwesen

## N

**name** [neɪm]:
1. Name I **my name is …** ich heiße … I **What's your name?** Wie heißt du? / Wie heißt ihr? I
2. (be)nennen IV 1 (18)

**narration** [nəˈreɪʃn] Erzählung, Schilderung III
**narrator** [nəˈreɪtə] Erzähler/in; Sprecher/in IV
**narrow** ['nærəʊ]:
1. schmal, eng II
2. (sich) verengen IV 3 (86) **narrow sth. down (to sth.)** etwas eingrenzen; etwas (auf etwas) reduzieren IV 3 (86)

°**narwhal** ['nɑːwəl] Narwal
**nation** ['neɪʃn] Nation, Volk III
**national** ['næʃnəl] national, National- I
**national park** [ˌnæʃnəl 'pɑːk] Nationalpark IV 2 (49)
**nationalist** ['næʃnəlɪst] Nationalist/in; nationalistisch IV 1 (17)
**nationality** [ˌnæʃəˈnæləti] Staatsangehörigkeit, Nationalität IV 3 (71)
**native** ['neɪtɪv] Mutter- II **Native American** amerikanischer Ureinwohner/amerikanische Ureinwohnerin III **native language** Muttersprache III **native speaker** Muttersprachler/in III °**native to** einheimisch in
**natural** ['nætʃrəl] natürlich II **natural history** Naturkunde I **natural world** (Welt der) Natur II
**nature** ['neɪtʃə] (die) Natur IV 3 (97)
**navy** ['neɪvi] Marine I
**near** [nɪə] in der Nähe von, nahe (bei) I **near here** (hier) in der Nähe I
**nearby** ['nɪəbaɪ]: **a nearby town** eine nahegelegene Stadt II
**nearly** ['nɪəli] fast, beinahe III
**necessary** ['nesəsəri] notwendig, nötig III
**neck** [nek] Hals II
**need** [niːd]:
1. brauchen, benötigen I **need to do sth.** etwas tun müssen II **you needn't do it** du musst es nicht tun, du brauchst es nicht zu tun I
°2. Bedarf, Bedürfnis, Notwendigkeit

**needle** ['niːdl] Nadel IV 3 (90)
**negative** ['negətɪv] negativ IV 2 (64)
**neighbour** ['neɪbə] (*AE:* **neighbor**) Nachbar/in II
**neighbourhood** ['neɪbəhʊd] (*AE:* **neighborhood**) Viertel, Gegend, Umgebung; Nachbarschaft IV 1 (20)

# Dictionary

**neither** [ˈnaɪðə], [niːðə]: **Me neither.** Ich auch nicht. III
**nephew** [ˈnefjuː], [ˈnevjuː] Neffe III
**nervous** [ˈnɜːvəs] nervös, aufgeregt I
**netball** [ˈnetbɔːl] Korbball II
°**network** [ˈnetwɜːk] Netz(werk)
**never** [ˈnevə] nie, niemals I
**new** [njuː] neu I
**New Year's Eve** [ˌnjuː jɪəzˈiːv] Silvester II
**news** (no pl) [njuːz]:
1. Nachrichten I
2. Neuigkeiten II
**newspaper** [ˈnjuːspeɪpə] Zeitung III
**next** [nekst]:
1. als Nächstes III
2. nächste(r, s)  **next year's musical** das Musical vom nächsten Jahr II
**next to** [ˈnekst tʊ] neben I
**nice** [naɪs] nett, schön I  **Nice to meet you.** Freut mich, dich/euch/Sie kennenzulernen. I
**nickname** [ˈnɪkneɪm] Spitzname IV 1 (22)
**niece** [niːs] Nichte III
**night** [naɪt] Nacht I  **at night** nachts, in der Nacht I
°**nightfall** [ˈnaɪtfɔːl] Einbruch der Dunkelheit
**nine** [naɪn] neun I
**nineteen forties** [ˌnaɪntiːnˈfɔːtiz]: **in the 1940s** in den 40er-Jahren (des 20. Jahrhunderts) IV 1 (10)
**no** [nəʊ]:
1. nein I
2. kein(e) I  **No way!** auf keinen Fall! / Kommt nicht in Frage! III  **No worries.** (infml) Kein Problem! / Gern geschehen! III
**no one** [ˈnəʊ wʌn] niemand I
**noble** [ˈnəʊbl] stattlich, prächtig; edel; adlig IV 3 (95)
**nobody** [ˈnəʊbədi] niemand I
**nod** [nɒd] nicken II
**noise** [nɔɪz] Geräusch, Lärm I
**noisy** [ˈnɔɪzi] laut, lärmend, voller Lärm I
**nomadic** [nəʊˈmædɪk] nomadisch, Nomaden- IV 3 (75)
°**nominalized adjective** [ˈnɒmɪnəlaɪzd] substantiviertes Adjektiv
**none (of …)** [nʌn] keine(r, s) (von …) III
**normal** [ˈnɔːml] normal IV 1 (24)
**north** [nɔːθ]:
1. (nach) Norden; Nord- I
2. nördlich III
**north-east** [ˌnɔːθˈiːst] Nordosten; nach Nordosten; nordöstlich III
**north-eastern** [ˌnɔːθˈiːstən] nordöstlich, Nordost- IV 3 (95)
**north-west** [ˌnɔːθˈwest] Nordwesten; nach Nordwesten; nordwestlich III
**northbound** [ˈnɔːθbaʊnd] Richtung Norden III
**northern** [ˈnɔːðən] nördlich, Nord- II
**nose** [nəʊz] Nase I
**nostalgic** [nɒˈstældʒɪk] nostalgisch IV 1 (17)

**not** [nɒt] nicht I  **not … yet** noch nicht I  **not even** (noch) nicht einmal II  **not till three** erst um drei, nicht vor drei II
**note** [nəʊt]:
1. Note (Musik) III
2. Notiz, Mitteilung I  **make notes (on sth.)** (sich) Notizen machen (über/zu etwas) (zur Vorbereitung) II  **take notes** (sich) Notizen machen (beim Lesen oder Zuhören) II
3. **note sth. down** (sich) etwas notieren; etwas aufschreiben IV 2 (59)
**nothing** [ˈnʌθɪŋ] (gar) nichts I
**notice** [ˈnəʊtɪs] (be)merken III
**noun** [naʊn] Nomen III
**novel** [ˈnɒvl] Roman III
**novelist** [ˈnɒvəlɪst] Romanautor/in IV 2 (65)
**November** [nəʊˈvembə] November I
**now** [naʊ] nun, jetzt I  **now that …** jetzt, wo … / nun, da … III
**nowhere** [ˈnəʊweə] nirgendwo; nirgendwohin
**nuclear** [ˈnjuːklɪə] Kern-, Atom-, Nuklear- IV 1 (34)
**nuclear power** [ˌnjuːklɪəˈpaʊə] Atomenergie, Kernenergie IV 1 (34)
**number** [ˈnʌmbə]:
1. Zahl, Nummer, Ziffer I
2. Anzahl IV 2 (62)
**number plate** [ˈnʌmbə pleɪt] Nummernschild, Autokennzeichen IV 2 (64)

# O

**o** [əʊ] Null (in Telefonnummern) I
**o'clock** [əˈklɒk]: **ten o'clock** 10 Uhr / 22 Uhr I
**object** [ˈɒbdʒɪkt] Objekt, Gegenstand III
**observation deck** [ˌɒbzəˈveɪʃn dek] Aussichtsplattform I
°**occupation** [ˌɒkjuˈpeɪʃn] Besetzung; Besatzungszeit
°**occupy** [ˈɒkjupaɪ]:
1. einnehmen; besetzen
2. bewohnen
**ocean** [ˈəʊʃn] Ozean I
**October** [ɒkˈtəʊbə] Oktober I
**of** [ɒv], [əv] von I  **of all time** aller Zeiten II
**of course** [əv ˈkɔːs] natürlich, selbstverständlich I
**off** [ɒf] von … herunter III  **Off you go now.** Ab mit euch jetzt! / Los mit euch jetzt! III  **be off** ausgeschaltet sein, aus sein (Radio, Licht usw.) III  **fall off a bike** vom Fahrrad (herunter)fallen III  **run off** wegrennen III  **take sth. off** etwas ausziehen III
**offend sb.** [əˈfend] jn. beleidigen; jn. stören IV 3 (81)
**offensive** [əˈfensɪv] beleidigend, anstößig IV 3 (81)
**offer** [ˈɒfə] anbieten II
**office** [ˈɒfɪs] Büro III

**official** [əˈfɪʃl]:
1. amtlich, Amts- I
2. Beamte(r), Beamtin III
**official language** Amtssprache IV 2 (56)
**often** [ˈɒfn], [ˈɒftən] oft I
**oh** [əʊ]: Oh, it's you. Ach, du bist es. I  **Oh dear!** Oje! II
**oil** [ɔɪl] Öl II
**old** [əʊld] alt I  **How old are you?** Wie alt bist du? I
°**old-fashioned** [ˌəʊld ˈfæʃnd] altmodisch
°**Olympic** [əˈlɪmpɪk] olympisch
**on** [ɒn]:
1. auf I  **on average** im Durchschnitt, durchschnittlich III  **on demand** auf Abruf, nach Bedarf II  **on earth** auf der Erde II  **on Monday** am Montag I  **on Monday afternoon** am Montagnachmittag I  **on my/your/their/… own** allein II  **on the corner of Church Road and London Road** Church Road, Ecke London Road II  **on the internet** im Internet I  **on the left/right** links/rechts; auf der linken/rechten Seite I  **on the map** auf der Landkarte; auf dem Stadtplan I  **on the phone** am Telefon II
**on the plane** im Flugzeug II  **on the radio** im Radio II  **on top of each other** übereinander, aufeinander II  **on TV** im Fernsehen II  **go on a boat trip** einen Bootsausflug machen I
2. **be on** eingeschaltet sein, an sein (Radio, Licht usw.); laufen, übertragen werden (Programm, Sendung) III
3. weiter- II  **straight on** geradeaus weiter II  **walk/sail on** weitergehen/ weitersegeln II
**once** [wʌns]:
1. einmal I
2. einst, (früher) einmal II
°**once again** [ˌwʌns əˈgen] noch einmal, wieder einmal
**one** [wʌn]:
1. eins I  **one by one** einer nach dem anderen II  **one more photo** noch ein Foto; ein weiteres Foto II  **one night/day** eines Nachts/Tages II
2. **one another** sich (gegenseitig), einander III
3. **a white one** ein weißer / eine weiße / ein weißes II  **this one** diese(r, s) II  **two black ones** zwei schwarze II  **Which one?** Welche(r, s)? II
**onion** [ˈʌnjən] Zwiebel III
**online** [ˌɒnˈlaɪn] online II
**only** [ˈəʊnli]:
1. nur, bloß I
2. erst I
3. **the only …** der/die/das einzige …; die einzigen … II
**onto** [ˈɒntʊ] auf (… hinauf) I  **hold onto** sich festhalten an III
**open** [ˈəʊpən]:
1. öffnen, aufmachen I
2. offen, geöffnet I

# English – German

**opening** ['əʊpənɪŋ] Öffnung III
**opening times** (pl) ['əʊpənɪŋ taɪmz] Öffnungszeiten III
**opinion** [ə'pɪnjən] Meinung III | **in my opinion** meiner Meinung nach III
**opinion piece** [ə'pɪnjən piːs] Stellungnahme IV 1 (17)
**opportunity** [ˌɒpə'tjuːnəti] Gelegenheit, Möglichkeit, Chance IV 3 (95)
**opposite** ['ɒpəzɪt]:
1. Gegenteil I
2. gegenüber (von) II
3. gegenüberliegende(r, s); entgegengesetzte(r, s) IV 1 (10)
**option** ['ɒpʃn] Wahl(möglichkeit), Option IV 2 (43)
**optional** ['ɒpʃənl] wahlweise, freiwillig IV 2 (43)
**or** [ɔː] oder I | **either ... or ...** entweder ... oder ... III
**oral** ['ɔːrəl] mündlich IV 3 (90)
**orange** ['ɒrɪndʒ]:
1. Orange, Apfelsine II
2. orange(farben) I
°**orator** ['ɒrətə] Redner/in
**orca** ['ɔːkə] Orca (Killerwal) IV 2 (62)
**order** ['ɔːdə]:
1. ordnen, anordnen IV 2 (45)
2. Reihenfolge I | **word order** Wortstellung I | °**in order to** um ... zu
**order** ['ɔːdə]:
1. bestellen I
2. Bestellung IV 2 (41)
**organization** [ˌɔːgənaɪ'zeɪʃn] Organisation IV 1 (11)
**organize** ['ɔːgənaɪz] organisieren; ordnen I
**organizer** ['ɔːgənaɪzə] Organisator/in IV 2 (46)
**origin** ['ɒrɪdʒɪn] Ursprung, Herkunft IV 1 (10)
**original** [ə'rɪdʒənl] Original-; ursprüngliche(r, s) II
**other** ['ʌðə] andere(r, s) I | **each other** sich (gegenseitig), einander II | °**the other way (a)round** umgekehrt
**our** ['aʊə] unser/e I
**ours** ['aʊəz] unserer, unsere, unseres II
**ourselves** [ɑː'selvz], [aʊə'selvz] wir/uns selbst/selber III
**out** [aʊt] heraus, hinaus, nach draußen II | **out and about** unterwegs II | **out of ...** aus ... (heraus/hinaus) II | **be out** nicht zu Hause sein, nicht da sein II
**outbreak** ['aʊtbreɪk] Ausbruch (z.B. Krankheit, Regenschauer) IV 3 (86)
**outcome** ['aʊtkʌm] Ausgang (einer Geschichte); Ergebnis, Resultat IV 2 (53)
**outdoor** ['aʊtdɔː] Außen-, im Freien II
**outdoors** [ˌaʊt'dɔːz] im Freien, draußen IV 3 (77)
°**outline** ['aʊtlaɪn] Entwurf, Übersicht
**outside** [ˌaʊt'saɪd]:
1. draußen; nach draußen I
2. **outside of** außerhalb (von) IV 3 (68)
**outside Rosie's Diner** vor Rosie's Diner;

außerhalb von Rosie's Diner II
3. **the outside** die Außenseite, das Äußere III
**oval** ['əʊvl] oval III
**over** ['əʊvə]:
1. über I | **over 20 people/years** über/mehr als 20 Leute/Jahre I | **over here** hier herüber; hier drüben II | **over there** da drüben, dort drüben II | **over to ...** hinüber zu/nach ... I | **all over the country / the city / the world** im ganzen Land / in der ganzen Stadt / auf der ganzen Welt II | **run over (to)** hinüberrennen (zu/nach) II
2. **be over** vorbei sein, zu Ende sein I
°**overland** ['əʊvəlænd] über Land, auf dem Landweg
**overlook** [ˌəʊvə'lʊk] überblicken; übersehen IV 1 (10)
**overthrew** [ˌəʊvə'θruː] siehe **overthrow**
**overthrow** [ˌəʊvə'θrəʊ], **overthrew, overthrown** stürzen (Regierung, Staatsoberhaupt usw.) III
**overthrown** [ˌəʊvə'θrəʊn] siehe **overthrow**
**own** [əʊn]:
1. besitzen II
2. **my own film/room/...** mein eigener Film / mein eigenes Zimmer / ... II | **of one's own** eigene(r, s) IV 3 (77)
3. **on my/your/their/... own** allein II
**owner** ['əʊnə] Besitzer/in III

# P

**p** [piː] Abkürzung für „pence", „penny" I
°**Pacific Ocean** [pəˌsɪfɪk 'əʊʃn] Pazifischer Ozean, Pazifik
**pack** [pæk] packen; einpacken II
**packet** ['pækɪt] Packung, Päckchen II
**page** [peɪdʒ] Seite I | **What page are we on?** Auf welcher Seite sind wir? I
**paid** [peɪd] siehe **pay** | **get paid** bezahlt werden III
**pain** [peɪn] Schmerz(en) IV 1 (26)
**paint** [peɪnt] (an)streichen; (an)malen II
**painted** ['peɪntɪd] bemalt, angemalt II
**painter** ['peɪntə] Maler/in III
**painting** ['peɪntɪŋ] Gemälde, Bild III
**pair** [peə]: **a pair (of)** ein Paar I | **a pair of trousers** eine Hose I
**palace** ['pæləs] Palast, Schloss III
**palm tree** ['pɑːm triː] Palme III
**pancake** ['pænkeɪk] Pfannkuchen, Eierkuchen II
°**panel discussion** ['pænl dɪˌskʌʃn] Podiumsdiskussion
°**panellist** ['pænəlɪst] Diskussionsteilnehmer/in; Mitglied eines Gremiums
**panic** ['pænɪk] in Panik geraten III
**pants** (pl) [pænts] (AE) Hose III
**paper** ['peɪpə] Papier; Zeitung I
**paper hat** ['peɪpə hæt] Papierhut I
**parade** [pə'reɪd] Parade, Umzug II

**paragraph** ['pærəgrɑːf] Absatz (in einem Text) I
**paraphrase** ['pærəfreɪz]:
1. umschreiben, mit anderen Worten sagen III
2. Umschreibung III
**parents** (pl) ['peərənts] Eltern I
**park** [pɑːk]:
1. Park I | **fun park** Vergnügungspark I
2. parken III
**parka** ['pɑːkə] Parka IV 2 (38/39)
**parking lot** ['pɑːkɪŋ lɒt] (AE) Parkplatz (Gelände zum Abstellen von mehreren Autos) IV 3 (68)
**parking space** ['pɑːkɪŋ speɪs] Parkplatz (Parklücke) IV 3 (68)
**parliament** ['pɑːləmənt] Parlament I
**part** [pɑːt]:
1. Teil II | **part of speech** Wortart III | **part of the body** Körperteil II | **take part (in)** teilnehmen (an) III
2. **part with sth.** sich von etwas trennen IV 1 (34)
**partner** ['pɑːtnə] Partner/in I
**party** ['pɑːti] Party I
**pass** [pɑːs]:
1. vergehen, vorübergehen (Zeit) III
2. **pass sth. around** etwas herumgeben, herumreichen II | **pass sth. on (to sb.)** (jm.) etwas weitergeben, weitersagen, weiterleiten IV 3 (90)
3. **pass sth./sb.** an etwas/jm. vorbeigehen/vorbeifahren II
4. **pass (a test / an exam)** (einen Test / eine Prüfung) bestehen, schaffen IV 2 (47)
**passing grade** Note/Zensur, mit der man bestanden hat IV 2 (47)
°5. **pass a law** ein Gesetz verabschieden
**passenger** ['pæsɪndʒə] Passagier/in; Fahrgast II
**passive** ['pæsɪv] passiv IV 1 (18)
**passport** ['pɑːspɔːt] (Reise-)Pass II
**password** ['pɑːswɜːd] Passwort II
**past** [pɑːst]:
1. Vergangenheit I
2. vorbei (an), vorüber (an) II
3. **half past ten** halb elf (10.30 / 22.30) I | **quarter past ten** Viertel nach zehn (10.15 / 22.15) I
**pat** [pæt]:
1. Klaps, (ein/das) Tätscheln III
2. tätscheln III
**path** [pɑːθ] Pfad, Weg II
**patient** ['peɪʃnt] geduldig III
**patriotism** ['peɪtriətɪzəm] Patriotismus IV 3 (81)
**pattern** ['pætn] Muster III
**pause** [pɔːz] innehalten, pausieren; eine Pause einlegen III
**pavement** ['peɪvmənt] Gehweg, Bürgersteig II
**paw** [pɔː] Pfote IV 2 (58)
**pay (for sth.)** [peɪ], **paid, paid** (etwas) bezahlen II

# Dictionary

**PE** [ˌpiː ˈiː] Sportunterricht, Turnen I
**peace** [piːs] Friede, Frieden III
**peaceful** [ˈpiːsfl] friedlich II
**peacemaker** [ˈpiːsmeɪkə] Friedensstifter/in IV 3 (90)
**peak** [piːk] Gipfel II
**pebble** [ˈpebl] Kieselstein III
**pedestrian** [pəˈdestrɪən] Fußgänger/in III
**pedestrian zone** [pəˈdestrɪən zəʊn] Fußgängerzone II
°**peer** [pɪə] Gleichaltrige/r, Ebenbürtige/r, jemand aus derselben sozialen Gruppe
**pen** [pen] Kugelschreiber, Stift, Füller I
**penalty** [ˈpenəlti] Strafe IV 2 (52)
**penalty box** [ˈpenəlti bɒks] Strafbank (Eishockey) IV 2 (52)
**pence (p)** [pens] Pence (plural of **penny**) I
**pencil** [ˈpensl] Bleistift I
**pencil case** [ˈpensl keɪs] Federmäppchen I
**penny** [ˈpeni] Penny I
**people** [ˈpiːpl]:
1. Leute, Menschen I
2. pl **peoples** Volk IV 1 (17)
**pepper** [ˈpepə] Pfeffer I
**per** [pə], [pɜː]: **per cent (%)** Prozent I
**per day/hour** pro Tag/Stunde III
**perfect** [ˈpɜːfɪkt] perfekt, ideal I
**perform** [pəˈfɔːm] auftreten (Künstler/in) III
**performance** [pəˈfɔːməns] Aufführung, Vorstellung, Auftritt III
°**period** [ˈpɪərɪəd] Zeit(raum), Zeitspanne
°**permafrost** [ˈpɜːməfrɒst] Permafrost(boden)
°**permission** [pəˈmɪʃn] Erlaubnis
**persecution** [ˌpɜːsɪˈkjuːʃn] Verfolgung IV 1 (17)
**perseverance** [ˌpɜːsɪˈvɪərəns] Ausdauer, Beharrlichkeit IV 2 (47)
**person** [ˈpɜːsn] Person I
**personal** [ˈpɜːsənl] persönlich IV 2 (41)
**perspective** [pəˈspektɪv] Perspektive IV 2 (58)
**pet** [pet] Haustier I
**petrol** [ˈpetrəl] Benzin III
**petrol station** [ˈpetrəl steɪʃn] Tankstelle III
°**pheasant** [ˈfeznt], pl **pheasant** or **pheasants** Fasan
**phone** [fəʊn]:
1. Telefon I **answer the phone** ans Telefon gehen II **mobile phone** Mobiltelefon, Handy I **on the phone** am Telefon II
2. **phone sb.** jn. anrufen I
**phone call** [ˈfəʊn kɔːl] Anruf; Telefongespräch I
**photo** [ˈfəʊtəʊ] Foto I **in the photo** auf dem Foto I **take photos** fotografieren, Fotos machen I
**phrase** [freɪz] Ausdruck, (Rede-)Wendung I
°**physical** [ˈfɪzɪkl] körperlich, physisch

**Physical Education** [ˌfɪzɪkl ˌedʒuˈkeɪʃn] Sportunterricht, Turnen I
°**physics** [ˈfɪzɪks] Physik
**piano** [piˈænəʊ] Klavier, Piano I **play the piano** Klavier spielen I
°**pic** (infml for **picture**) [pɪk] Bild
**pick up** [ˌpɪk ˈʌp]: **pick sb. up** jn. abholen II **pick sth. up** etwas aufheben (vom Boden), etwas hochheben II
**pickup (truck)** [ˈpɪkʌp] Pritschenwagen IV 3 (68)
**picnic** [ˈpɪknɪk] Picknick I
**picture** [ˈpɪktʃə] Bild I **in the picture** auf dem Bild I
**pie** [ˈpaɪ] Obstkuchen; Pastete II
**pie chart** [ˈpaɪ tʃɑːt] Tortendiagramm IV 2 (38/39)
**piece** [piːs] Stück III **a piece of …** ein Stück … III
**pig** [pɪɡ] Schwein I
**pigeon** [ˈpɪdʒɪn] (Stadt-)Taube III
**pike** [paɪk] Spieß IV 1 (35)
**pile** [paɪl] Stapel, Haufen III
**pilgrim** [ˈpɪlɡrɪm] Pilger/in III
**pine (tree)** [paɪn] Kiefer (Baum) IV 3 (90)
**pink** [pɪŋk] pink, rosa I
°**pioneer** [ˌpaɪəˈnɪə] Pionier/in, Vorreiter/in
**pipe** [paɪp] (Tabaks-)Pfeife III
**pipeline** [ˈpaɪplaɪn] Pipeline IV 2 (62)
**pirate** [ˈpaɪrət] Pirat/in II
**pity** [ˈpɪti]: **It was a pity that …** Es war schade, dass … I
**pizza** [ˈpiːtsə] Pizza I
**place** [pleɪs] Ort, Platz, Stelle I **in the first place** erstens, in erster Linie; überhaupt IV 2 (45) **take place** stattfinden; spielen, sich abspielen (Geschichte, Handlung) I
°**placemat** [ˈpleɪsmæt] Platzdeckchen
**plains** (pl) [pleɪnz] Ebene IV 3 (84)
**plan** [plæn]:
1. Plan I
2. planen II
**plane** [pleɪn] Flugzeug II
**planet** [ˈplænɪt] Planet I
**plant** [plɑːnt]:
1. Pflanze II
2. pflanzen II
**plaster** [ˈplɑːstə] (Heft-)Pflaster II
**plastic** [ˈplæstɪk] Plastik, Kunststoff II
**plate** [pleɪt] Teller I **a plate of …** ein Teller … I
**platform** [ˈplætfɔːm] Bahnsteig, Gleis II
**play** [pleɪ]:
1. spielen I **play sb.** gegen jn. spielen III **play the piano/guitar/drums** Klavier/Gitarre/Schlagzeug spielen I
2. abspielen (CD, DVD) I
3. Theaterstück I
**player** [ˈpleɪə] Spieler/in I **MP3 player** MP3-Player I
**playlist** [ˈpleɪlɪst] Playlist (Abspielliste) IV 2 (41)
**please** [pliːz] bitte I

**plot** [plɒt]:
1. sich verschwören IV 1 (34)
2. Verschwörung IV 1 (34)
**plotter** [ˈplɒtə] Verschwörer/in IV 1 (35)
**pm** [ˌpiː ˈem]: **4 pm** 4 Uhr nachmittags / 16 Uhr II
**pocket** [ˈpɒkɪt] Tasche (Manteltasche, Hosentasche usw.) II
**pocket money** [ˈpɒkɪt mʌni] Taschengeld IV 3 (88)
**poem** [ˈpəʊɪm] Gedicht II
**pogrom** [ˈpɒɡrəm] Pogrom IV 1 (17)
**point** [pɔɪnt]:
1. Punkt I **point of view** Standpunkt III **from my point of view** aus meiner Sicht III °**to the point** auf den Punkt
2. 3.5 (three point five) 3,5 (drei Komma fünf) II
°3. Spitze (z.B. eines Speers)
**point** [pɔɪnt]: **point sth. at sb.** etwas auf jn. richten I **point sth. out (to sb.)** (jn.) auf etwas hinweisen II **point to sth.** auf etwas zeigen, deuten I
**polar** [ˈpəʊlə] polar IV 2 (38/39)
**polar bear** [ˈpəʊlə beə] Eisbär IV 2 (38/39)
°**pole** [pəʊl] Pol
**police** (pl) [pəˈliːs] Polizei I
**police department** [pəˈliːs dɪˌpɑːtmənt] Polizei(behörde) IV 2 (64)
**police officer** [pəˈliːs ˌɒfɪsə] Polizist/in I
**police station** [pəˈliːs steɪʃn] Polizeiwache/-revier II
**policeman** [pəˈliːsmən] Polizist I
**policy** [ˈpɒləsi] Politik, Richtlinie(n), Bestimmung(en) IV 1 (17)
**Polish** [ˈpəʊlɪʃ] Polnisch; polnisch I
**polite** [pəˈlaɪt] höflich II
°**political** [pəˈlɪtɪkl] politisch
**politics** [ˈpɒlətɪks] Politik III
**pollute** [pəˈluːt] (die Umwelt) verschmutzen IV 2 (54)
**pollution** [pəˈluːʃn] (Umwelt-)Verschmutzung IV 2 (54)
**pony** [ˈpəʊni] Pony II
**pool** [puːl] Schwimmbad, -becken I
**poor** [pɔː], [pʊə] arm I
°**pop** [pɒp] Limonade
**pop (music)** [pɒp] Pop(musik) II
**popcorn** [ˈpɒpkɔːn] Popcorn IV 3 (88)
**pope** [pəʊp] Papst III
**popular (with)** [ˈpɒpjələ] populär, beliebt (bei) I
**populate** [ˈpɒpjuleɪt] bevölkern, besiedeln IV 3 (94)
**population** [ˌpɒpjuˈleɪʃn] Bevölkerung, Einwohner(zahl) III
**porch** [pɔːtʃ] Veranda (AE); Vorbau, Vordach (BE) III
**port** [pɔːt] Hafenstadt I
°**portray** [pɔːˈtreɪ] porträtieren, darstellen
**position** [pəˈzɪʃn] Position, Standort, Platz; (Arbeits-)Stelle IV 3 (82)
**positive** [ˈpɒzətɪv] positiv IV 2 (64)
°**possess** [pəˈzes] besitzen
°**possibility** [ˌpɒsəˈbɪləti] Möglichkeit
**possible** [ˈpɒsəbl] möglich II

# English – German

**post** [pəʊst]:
1. Posting *(auf Blog)*, Blog-Eintrag III
2. **post sth.** etwas posten III

**post office** [ˈpəʊst ˌɒfɪs] Postamt II
**postcard** [ˈpəʊstkɑːd] Postkarte I
**poster** [ˈpəʊstə] Poster I   **study poster** Lernposter II
**pot** [pɒt] Gefäß; Topf III
**potato** [pəˈteɪtəʊ], *pl* **potatoes** Kartoffel I   **roast potatoes** *(pl)* Bratkartoffeln *(im Backofen in Fett gebackene Kartoffeln)* I
**pound (£)** [paʊnd] Pfund *(britische Währung)* I
**pour** [pɔː] gießen II
**poutine** [puːˈtiːn] Poutine *(Pommes frites mit Käse in Bratensoße)* IV 2 (41)
**poverty** [ˈpɒvəti] Armut IV 3 (86)
**powder** [ˈpaʊdə] Pulver IV 3 (95)
**power** [ˈpaʊə] Macht; Kraft, Stärke; Energie, Strom III
**powerful** [ˈpaʊəfl] mächtig, kräftig, stark III
°**powwow** [ˈpaʊwaʊ] Versammlung *(amerik. Ureinwohner/innen)*, Kriegsrat
**practical** [ˈpræktɪkl] praktisch III
**practice** [ˈpræktɪs]:
1. Übung I
2. *(AE)* praktizieren; üben, trainieren IV 3 (74)
°3. Praxis, Vorgehensweise

**practise** [ˈpræktɪs] üben, trainieren I
**prairie** [ˈpreəri] Prärie IV 3 (66/67)
**prediction** [prɪˈdɪkʃn] Vorhersage, Voraussage III
°**preparation** [ˌprepəˈreɪʃn] Vorbereitung; Zubereitung
**prepare (for)** [prɪˈpeə] sich vorbereiten (auf) I   **prepare sth.** etwas vorbereiten I
**prescription** [prɪˈskrɪpʃn] *(ärztliches)* Rezept II
**present** [ˈpreznt]:
1. Geschenk I
2. Gegenwart II

**present sth. (to sb.)** [prɪˈzent] *(jm.)* etwas präsentieren, vorstellen II
**presentation** [ˌprezn̩ˈteɪʃn] Präsentation, Vorstellung II   **give a presentation** ein Referat halten IV 3 (66/67)
**president** [ˈprezɪdənt] Präsident/in II
**press** [pres] drücken III
**pressure** [ˈpreʃə] Druck III
**pretend** [prɪˈtend] so tun, als ob III
**pretty** [ˈprɪti]:
1. hübsch II
2. **pretty old/expensive/…** ziemlich alt/teuer/… IV 1 (11)

**prevent** [prɪˈvent] verhindern, vorbeugen IV 2 (49)   **prevent sb. from doing sth.** jn. daran hindern, etwas zu tun IV 2 (49)
**prevention** [prɪˈvenʃn] Vermeidung, Vorbeugung IV 2 (49)
**price** [praɪs] *(Kauf-)*Preis I
**pride** [praɪd]:
1. Stolz IV 2 (65)
2. **pride oneself on sth.** stolz sein auf etwas IV 2 (65)

°**primarily** [praɪˈmerəli] vor allem, hauptsächlich, vorrangig
**primary school** [ˈpraɪməri skuːl] Grundschule IV 2 (41)
**prime minister** [ˌpraɪm ˈmɪnɪstə] Premierminister/in II
**prince** [prɪns] Prinz II
**princess** [ˌprɪnˈses] Prinzessin II
**principal** [ˈprɪnsəpl] *(AE)* Schulleiter/in IV 2 (47)
**priority** [praɪˈɒrəti] Priorität IV 3 (83)
**prison** [ˈprɪzn] Gefängnis I
**prisoner** [ˈprɪznə] Gefangene(r) III
**prize** [praɪz] Preis, Gewinn II
**probable** *(adj)* [ˈprɒbəbl] wahrscheinlich III
**probably** *(adv)* [ˈprɒbəbli] wahrscheinlich II
**problem** [ˈprɒbləm] Problem I
°**process** [ˈprəʊses] Prozess; Verfahren, Ablauf
**proclamation** [ˌprɒkləˈmeɪʃn] Proklamation, Ankündigung, Bekanntmachung IV 3 (69)
**produce** [prəˈdjuːs] produzieren, herstellen IV 2 (58)
**producer** [prəˈdjuːsə] Produzent/in IV 2 (58)
**product** [ˈprɒdʌkt] Produkt IV 2 (58)
**production** [prəˈdʌkʃn] Produktion IV 2 (58)
°**professional** [prəˈfeʃənl] professionell, Profi-
**professor** [prəˈfesə] Professor/in IV 2 (58)
**profile** [ˈprəʊfaɪl] Profil; Beschreibung, Porträt I
**program** [ˈprəʊɡræm]:
1. *(Computer-)*Programm IV 3 (76)
2. *(AE)* Programm; *(Fernseh-/Radio-)*Sendung IV 3 (76)
3. programmieren IV 3 (76)

**programme** [ˈprəʊɡræm] Programm, *(Radio-, Fernseh-)*Sendung I
**project** [ˈprɒdʒekt] Projekt II
**promise** [ˈprɒmɪs]:
1. versprechen I
2. (ein) Versprechen II

**promote sth.** [prəˈməʊt] etwas fördern; für etwas werben III
°**prompt** [prɒmpt] Stichwort, Vorgabe
°**pronounce** [prəˈnaʊns] aussprechen
**pronunciation** [prəˌnʌnsiˈeɪʃn] Aussprache I
**property** [ˈprɒpəti] Eigentum, Besitz IV 3 (97)
**protect sb./sth. (from sb./sth.)** [prəˈtekt] jn./etwas (be)schützen (vor jm./etwas) IV 1 (16)
**protection** [prəˈtekʃn] Schutz IV 2 (47)
**protective** [prəˈtektɪv] schützend, beschützend, Schutz- IV 1 (27)
**protest** [ˈprəʊtest]:
1. Protest III
2. protestieren III

**Protestant** [ˈprɒtɪstənt] Protestant/in; protestantisch III

**proud (of)** [praʊd] stolz (auf) III
**prove** [pruːv] nachweisen, beweisen IV 1 (26)
**province** [ˈprɒvɪns] Provinz IV 1 (17)
**pub** [pʌb] Kneipe, Lokal III
**public** [ˈpʌblɪk] öffentliche(r, s) III
°**puck** [pʌk] Puck
**pull** [pʊl] ziehen I   **pull sb.'s leg** *(infml)* jn. auf den Arm nehmen *(veräppeln)* IV 1 (25)   **pull sth. out** etwas herausziehen II
**pullover** [ˈpʊləʊvə] Pullover II
**punctuation** [ˌpʌŋktʃuˈeɪʃn] Zeichensetzung II
**punishment** [ˈpʌnɪʃmənt] Bestrafung, Strafe III
**puppet** [ˈpʌpɪt] Marionette, Handpuppe II
**purple** [ˈpɜːpl] violett, lila I
**purpose** [ˈpɜːpəs] Absicht, Sinn, Zweck, Ziel IV 3 (93)   **on purpose** mit Absicht IV 3 (93)
**pursuit (of)** [pəˈsjuːt] Streben (nach); Jagd (auf) IV 3 (97)
**push** [pʊʃ] drücken, schieben, stoßen I
**put** [pʊt], **put, put** legen, stellen, *(etwas wohin)* tun I   **put out a fire** ein Feuer löschen IV 2 (49)   **put sth. down** etwas hinlegen III   **put sth. on** etwas anziehen *(Kleidung)*; etwas aufsetzen *(Hut, Helm)* II   **put sth. together** etwas zusammenstellen, zusammensetzen IV 2 (38/39)   **put sth. up** etwas aufstellen, aufbauen *(Zelt)* IV 2 (47)
**puzzle** [ˈpʌzl] Rätsel II

# Q

**qualify** [ˈkwɒlɪfaɪ] (sich) qualifizieren IV 3 (68)
**quarter** [ˈkwɔːtə]:
1. *(Stadt-)*Viertel III
2. **quarter past ten** Viertel nach zehn (10.15 / 22.15) I   **quarter to eleven** Viertel vor elf (10.45 / 22.45) I

**queen** [kwiːn] Königin I
**question** [ˈkwestʃən] Frage I
**question mark** [ˈkwestʃən mɑːk] Fragezeichen II
**questionnaire** [ˌkwestʃəˈneə] Fragebogen II
**queue** [kjuː]:
1. Schlange stehen, sich anstellen II
2. Schlange, Reihe *(wartender Menschen)* II

**quick** [kwɪk] schnell II
**quiet** [ˈkwaɪət] ruhig, still, leise I
**quite** [kwaɪt] ziemlich II
**quiver** [ˈkwɪvə] zittern IV 2 (58)
**quiz** [kwɪz] Quiz, Ratespiel I
**quote** [kwəʊt] Zitat IV 2 (65)

# Dictionary

## R

**rabbit** ['ræbɪt] Kaninchen I
**race** [reɪs]:
1. Rennen I
2. rasen III
**race** [reɪs] Rasse IV 1 (17)
**racial** ['reɪʃl] ethnisch, rassisch; Rassen- IV 1 (17)
**radio** ['reɪdiəʊ] Radio II **on the radio** im Radio II
**raft** [rɑːft] Schlauchboot *(wildwassertauglich)*; Floß III
**rafting** [ˌwaɪtwɔːtə 'rɑːftɪŋ]: **whitewater rafting** Wildwasserfahren *(im Schlauchboot)* III
**railing** ['reɪlɪŋ] Geländer III
**railroad** ['reɪlrəʊd] *(AE)* Eisenbahn III
**railway** ['reɪlweɪ] *(BE)* Eisenbahn III
**rain** [reɪn]:
1. regnen II
2. Regen II
**rainbow** ['reɪnbəʊ] Regenbogen III
**raincoat** ['reɪnkəʊt] Regenmantel II
**rainforest** ['reɪnfɒrɪst] Regenwald II
**rainy** ['reɪni] regnerisch II
**raise money (for)** [reɪz] Geld sammeln (für) II
**rally** ['ræli] Rallye II
**ran** [ræn] *siehe* **run**
°**ranch** [rɑːntʃ] Ranch *(Viehfarm)*
**rang** [ræŋ] *siehe* **ring**
°**ranking** ['ræŋkɪŋ] Einstufung, Rangfolge
°**rapid** ['ræpɪd] rapide, rasch, schnell
**rat** [ræt] Ratte I
**rather than** ['rɑːðə ðən] statt, anstatt III
**rattlesnake** ['rætlsneɪk] Klapperschlange III
**raven** ['reɪvn] Rabe III
°**re-read** [ˌriːˈriːd], **re-read, re-read** noch einmal lesen
**reach** [riːtʃ] erreichen III **reach (for)** greifen (nach) III **reach over** die Hand ausstrecken III **reach out a hand (to sb.)** die Hand ausstrecken (nach jm.) IV 1 (28)
**react (to)** [riˈækt] reagieren (auf) III
**reaction (to)** [riˈækʃn] Reaktion (auf) IV 1 (15)
**read** [riːd], **read, read** lesen I **read aloud** laut (vor)lesen I
**reader** ['riːdə] Leser/in II
**ready** ['redi] bereit, fertig I **get ready (for)** sich fertig machen (für); sich vorbereiten (auf) II
**real** ['riːəl] echt, wirklich II
**realistic** *(adj)* [ˌriːəˈlɪstɪk] realistisch IV 1 (15)
**realistically** *(adv)* [ˌriːəˈlɪstɪkli] realistisch IV 1 (15)
**reality** [riˈæləti] Realität, Wirklichkeit IV 2 (45)
**realize sth.** ['riːəlaɪz] etwas erkennen; sich einer Sache bewusst werden III

**really** ['rɪəli] echt, wirklich I **I really care about animals.** Tiere liegen mir sehr am Herzen. / Tiere sind mir sehr wichtig. III
**reason** ['riːzn] Grund, Begründung I
**rebel** ['rebəl] Rebell/in IV 1 (34)
**rebellion** [rɪˈbeljən] Rebellion, Aufstand IV 1 (35)
**rebuild** [ˌriːˈbɪld], **rebuilt, rebuilt** wiederaufbauen IV
**recall sth.** [rɪˈkɔːl] sich an etwas erinnern IV 2 (47)
**receive** [rɪˈsiːv] erhalten, empfangen IV 2 (63)
**recent** *(adj)* ['riːsnt] aktuell, jüngst; kürzlich geschehen/erfolgt IV 2 (46)
**recently** *(adv)* ['riːsntli] in letzter Zeit; vor Kurzem IV 1 (17)
**recipe** ['resəpi] (Koch-)Rezept II
°**recognize** ['rekəgnaɪz] erkennen; wiedererkennen
**recommend sth. (to sb.)** [ˌrekəˈmend] (jm.) etwas empfehlen IV 2 (55)
**recommendation** [ˌrekəmənˈdeɪʃn] Empfehlung IV 2 (55)
**recorder** [rɪˈkɔːdə] Blockflöte II
**recreate sth.** [ˌriːkriˈeɪt] etwas nachbilden, nachmachen IV 2 (46)
**red** [red] rot I **go red** rot werden, erröten II
**referee** [ˌrefəˈriː] Schiedsrichter/in IV 2 (52)
°**reflection** [rɪˈflekʃn] *(BE auch:* reflexion*)* Nachdenken, Überlegung; Spiegelbild, Reflexion
**refuse** [rɪˈfjuːz] sich weigern, ablehnen IV 3 (90) **refuse to do sth.** sich weigern, etwas zu tun / es ablehnen, etwas zu tun IV 3 (90)
**region** ['riːdʒən] Region II
**regret** [rɪˈgret]:
1. bedauern, bereuen IV 1 (22)
2. (das) Bedauern IV 1 (22)
**regular** ['regjələ] regelmäßig II
**reins** *(pl)* [reɪnz] Zügel III
°**related** [rɪˈleɪtɪd] verwandt **related to** verbunden mit
°**relation** [rɪˈleɪʃn] Beziehung, Verhältnis
**relationship** [rɪˈleɪʃnʃɪp] Beziehung, Verhältnis III
**relax** [rɪˈlæks] sich entspannen, sich ausruhen II
**relaxed** [rɪˈlækst] entspannt III
°**reliability** [rɪˌlaɪəˈbɪləti] Zuverlässigkeit, Verlässlichkeit
°**reliable** [rɪˈlaɪəbl] verlässlich, zuverlässig
**religion** [rɪˈlɪdʒən] Religion I
**remain** [rɪˈmeɪn] (ver)bleiben II
**remember sth.** [rɪˈmembə]:
1. sich an etwas erinnern I
2. an etwas denken *(etwas nicht vergessen)* II
3. sich etwas merken II
**remind sb.** [rɪˈmaɪnd] jn. erinnern III
**remote control** [rɪˌməʊt kənˈtrəʊl] *(kurz auch:* **remote***)* Fernbedienung III

°**removal** [rɪˈmuːvl] Entfernung *(Beseitigung)*
**remove** [rɪˈmuːv] entfernen, beseitigen; ausziehen *(Kleidung)* IV 3 (90)
**rename sth.** [ˌriːˈneɪm] etwas umbenennen, umtaufen IV 2 (46)
**repeat** [rɪˈpiːt] wiederholen II
**repeatedly** [rɪˈpiːtɪdli] wiederholt IV 1 (27)
**reply** [rɪˈplaɪ]:
1. **reply (to)** antworten (auf); erwidern, entgegnen III
°2. Antwort
**report** [rɪˈpɔːt]:
1. Bericht, Reportage II
2. berichten III
**represent** [ˌreprɪˈzent] vertreten, repräsentieren IV 3 (96)
**representation** [ˌreprɪzenˈteɪʃn] (Interessens-)Vertretung, Darstellung, Repräsentanz IV 3 (87)
**representative** [ˌreprɪˈzentətɪv] Repräsentant/in, Abgeordnete(r) IV 3 (96)
**republic** [rɪˈpʌblɪk] Republik III
**request** [rɪˈkwest] Wunsch, Bitte; Anfrage IV 3 (88)
**rescue** ['reskjuː]:
1. Rettung; Rettungs- I
2. retten II
**research** [rɪˈsɜːtʃ]:
1. erforschen, untersuchen, recherchieren IV 3 (91)
2. *(no pl)* Recherche, Forschung(en) III
°**researcher** [rɪˈsɜːtʃə] Forscher/in
**reservation** [ˌrezəˈveɪʃn] Reservat, Reservation II
**reserve** [rɪˈzɜːv]:
1. Schutzgebiet III **dark sky reserve** Lichtschutzgebiet III
2. Reservat IV 2 (64)
**reserve sth.** [rɪˈzɜːv] etwas reservieren, buchen III
**resident** ['rezɪdənt] Anwohner/in, Bewohner/in IV 2 (65)
°**residential school** [rezɪˌdenʃl 'skuːl] Internat
°**resist** [rɪˈzɪst] sich widersetzen (gegen), sich wehren (gegen)
**resistance** [rɪˈzɪstəns] Widerstand IV 1 (35)
**resort** [rɪˈzɔːt] Ferienanlage; Ferienort IV 2 (55)
**respect** [rɪˈspekt]:
1. Respekt IV 2 (47)
2. respektieren, achten IV 2 (47)
°**respond (to)** [rɪˈspɒnd] reagieren, antworten (auf)
**responsible** [rɪˈspɒnsəbl] verantwortlich II
**rest** [rest]:
1. ruhen, sich ausruhen III
2. Rest III
**restaurant** ['restrɒnt] Restaurant I
**restless** ['restləs] unruhig, rastlos IV 3 (93)

## English – German

°**restoration** [ˌrestəˈreɪʃn] Restaurierung *(auch: Wiederherstellung der britischen Monarchie im Jahre 1660)*
**result** [rɪˈzʌlt] Ergebnis, Resultat II
°**retell** [ˌriːˈtel]**, retold, retold** nacherzählen
°**retold** [ˌriːˈtəʊld] *siehe* **retell**
**return** [rɪˈtɜːn]:
1. zurückkehren, zurückkommen IV 3 (80)
2. Rückkehr II
3. *(kurz für:* **return ticket***)* (Hin- und) Rückfahrkarte II
**return ticket** [rɪˌtɜːn ˈtɪkɪt] (Hin- und) Rückfahrkarte II
**review** [rɪˈvjuː] Rezension, Besprechung, Kritik III
**revise** [rɪˈvaɪz] überarbeiten; *(Lernstoff)* wiederholen III
**revision** [rɪˈvɪʒn] Wiederholung *(des Lernstoffs)* II
**revolution** [ˌrevəˈluːʃn] Revolution IV 3 (87)
**revolutionary** [ˌrevəˈluːʃənəri]:
1. revolutionär IV 3 (96)
2. Revolutionär/in IV 3 (96)
°**rewrite** [ˌriːˈraɪt] neu schreiben, umschreiben
°**rez** [rez] *(kurz für:* **reservation**) Reservat, Reservation
**rhyme** [raɪm] Reim; Vers I
**rhythm** [ˈrɪðəm] Rhythmus III
**rich** [rɪtʃ] reich I
**ridden** [ˈrɪdn] *siehe* **ride**
**ride** [raɪd]:
1. Fahrt I  **give sb. a ride** jn. (im Auto) mitnehmen IV 3 (80)
2. Ritt, Ausritt III
**ride** [raɪd]**, rode, ridden:**
1. reiten II
2. fahren I  **ride a bike** Rad fahren I
**riding** [ˈraɪdɪŋ] Reiten I
**right** [raɪt]:
1. richtig I  **…, right?** …, nicht wahr? II  **all right** okay; in Ordnung I  **sb. is right** jemand hat Recht I  **That's right.** Das stimmt. I
2. Recht IV 2 (65)  **civil rights** *(pl)* Bürgerrechte IV 3 (96)
3. **right after you** gleich nach dir II  **right behind you** direkt hinter dir, genau hinter dir II  **right now** jetzt gerade II
4. rechts I  **on the right** rechts / auf der rechten Seite I  **turn right** (nach) rechts abbiegen II
**ring** [rɪŋ] Ring II
**ring** [rɪŋ]**, rang, rung** klingeln, läuten II
**rink** [rɪŋk] *(kurz für:* **ice rink, skating rink**) Eisbahn; Rollschuhbahn IV 2 (38/39)
**rise up** [ˌraɪz ˈʌp]**, rose, risen** aufragen, emporragen *(Berge, Säulen, Türme, …)* III
**risen** [ˈrɪzn] *siehe* **rise**
**risk** [rɪsk] Risiko III  **take a risk** ein Risiko eingehen III
**river** [ˈrɪvə] Fluss I

**road** [rəʊd] Straße I  **at 8 Beach Road** in der Beach Road (Nummer) 8 I  **in Beach Road** in der Beach Road I
**roar** [rɔː] brüllen; tosen, dröhnen III
**roast beef** [ˌrəʊst ˈbiːf] Rinderbraten I
**roast potatoes** *(pl)* [ˌrəʊst pəˈteɪtəʊz] Bratkartoffeln *(im Backofen in Fett gebackene Kartoffeln)* I
°**robe** [rəʊb] Robe *(Gewand)*
**rock** [rɒk]:
1. Fels, Felsen I
2. schaukeln, schwanken III
3. **rock (music)** Rock(musik) II
**rocky** [ˈrɒki] felsig, steinig II
**rode** [rəʊd] *siehe* **ride**
**rodeo** [ˈrəʊdiəʊ] Rodeo IV 3 (66/67)
**role** [rəʊl] Rolle *(in einem Theaterstück, Film)* II
**role-play** [ˈrəʊl pleɪ] Rollenspiel IV 1 (23)
**roll** [rəʊl]:
1. rollen I
2. Rolle IV 3 (68)
**roller coaster** [ˈrəʊlə kəʊstə] Achterbahn III
**Roman** [ˈrəʊmən] Römer/in; römisch II
**roof** [ruːf] Dach II
**room** [ruːm] Raum, Zimmer I
**root** [ruːt] Wurzel IV 3 (90)
**rope** [rəʊp] Seil III
**rose** [rəʊz] *siehe* **rise**
**rose** [rəʊz] Rose II
**rough** [rʌf] rau; grob; hart III
**round** [raʊnd]:
1. rund III
2. round … um (… herum); in (… umher) IV 1 (11)  **round here** hier in der Gegend III
**roundabout** [ˈraʊndəbaʊt] Kreisverkehr II
**route** [ruːt] Strecke, Route III
**routine** [ruːˈtiːn] Routine III
**royal** [ˈrɔɪəl] königlich II
**rubber** [ˈrʌbə] Radiergummi I
**rubbish** [ˈrʌbɪʃ] Müll, Abfall I
**rucksack** [ˈrʌksæk] *(BE)* Rucksack I
**rude** [ruːd] unhöflich; unverschämt III
**rugby** [ˈrʌɡbi] Rugby III
**rugby ground** [ˈrʌɡbi ɡraʊnd] Rugby-Platz/-Spielfeld III
**ruin** [ˈruːɪn] Ruine II
**rule** [ruːl]:
1. Regel, Vorschrift II
2. Herrschaft IV 3 (97)
3. **rule sth.** etwas beherrschen, über etwas herrschen III
**ruler** [ˈruːlə] Lineal I
**run** [rʌn]**, ran, run:**
1. rennen, laufen I  **run after sb.** hinter jm. herrennen I  **run off** wegrennen III
2. verlaufen *(Straße; Grenze)* III
**rung** [rʌŋ] *siehe* **ring**
**runner** [ˈrʌnə] Läufer/in II
**running water** [ˌrʌnɪŋ ˈwɔːtə] fließend(es) Wasser II
**rush** [rʌʃ] eilen, stürzen III

**rusty** [ˈrʌsti] rostig; verrostet III

## S

**sacred (to)** [ˈseɪkrɪd] heilig (für) IV 3 (75)
**sad** [sæd] traurig I
**safari** [səˈfɑːri] Safari I
**safe** [seɪf] sicher, in Sicherheit II
**said** [sed] *siehe* **say**
**sail** [seɪl] segeln I
**sailing** [ˈseɪlɪŋ]: **go sailing** segeln; segeln gehen I
**sailing boat** [ˈseɪlɪŋ bəʊt] Segelboot I
**salad** [ˈsæləd] Salat *(als Gericht oder Beilage)* I  **fruit salad** Obstsalat I
**sales** *(pl)* [seɪlz] Umsatz, Absatz; Verkäufe II
**salmon** [ˈsæmən]*, pl* **salmon** Lachs IV 3 (95)
**salt** [sɔːlt] Salz III
**samba** [ˈsæmbə] Samba I
**same** [seɪm]: **the same (as)** der-/die-/dasselbe (wie) I
**sand** [sænd] Sand I
**sandals** *(pl)* [ˈsændlz] Sandalen IV 3 (93)
**sandwich** [ˈsænwɪtʃ], [ˈsænwɪdʒ] Sandwich, *(zusammengeklapptes)* belegtes Brot I
**sang** [sæŋ] *siehe* **sing**
**sat** [sæt] *siehe* **sit**
**satisfied** [ˈsætɪsfaɪd] zufrieden(gestellt) IV 3 (75)
**satisfy sb.** [ˈsætɪsfaɪ] jn. zufriedenstellen, jn. befriedigen IV 3 (75)
**Saturday** [ˈsætədeɪ], [ˈsætədi] Samstag I
**save** [seɪv]:
1. retten I
2. **save (up)** *(z.B. Geld)* sparen IV 3 (70)
**saw** [sɔː] *siehe* **see**
**say** [seɪ]**, said, said** sagen I  **Say hello to … for me.** Grüß … von mir. II  **It says here: …** Hier steht: … / Es heißt hier: … I
°**scaffolding** [ˈskæfəldɪŋ] (Bau-)Gerüst
**scan sth. (for sth.)** [skæn] etwas (nach etwas) absuchen III  **scan a text** einen Text schnell nach bestimmten Wörtern/ Informationen absuchen II
**scare sb.** [skeə] jn. erschrecken; jm. Angst machen II
**scared** [skeəd] verängstigt II
**scary** [ˈskeəri] unheimlich, gruselig I
**scene** [siːn] Szene I
**school** [skuːl] Schule I  **at school** in der Schule I  **before school** vor der Schule (vor Schulbeginn) I  **boarding school** Internat II  **high school** *(USA)* Schule für 14- bis 18-Jährige III
**school bag** [ˈskuːl bæɡ] Schultasche I
**school hall** [ˌskuːl ˈhɔːl] Aula IV 2 (46)
**school subject** [ˌskuːl ˈsʌbdʒɪkt] Schulfach I
**science** [ˈsaɪəns] Naturwissenschaft I

# Dictionary

**scientist** ['saɪəntɪst] Naturwissenschaftler/in III
**scone** [skɒn] *kleines rundes Milchbrötchen, leicht süß, oft mit Rosinen* I
**score** [skɔː]:
1. ein Tor schießen, einen Treffer erzielen I
2. Spiel-/Punktestand; *(im Spiel/Sport erzielter)* Punkt IV 2 (52) **What's the score?** Wie steht es? *(z.B. beim Fußballspiel)* IV 2 (52)
**scream** [skriːm] schreien II
**screen** [skriːn] Bildschirm II
**sculpture** ['skʌlptʃə] Skulptur IV 3 (81)
**sea** [siː] Meer I
**sea level** ['siː levl] Meeresspiegel II
**seafood** ['siːfuːd] Meeresfrüchte I
**seagull** ['siːgʌl] Möwe I
**seal** [siːl] Robbe I
**search** [sɜːtʃ]:
1. Suche IV 1 (26)
2. **search for sth.** (nach) etwas suchen IV 1 (26)
**search engine** ['sɜːtʃ ˌendʒɪn] Suchmaschine IV 3 (66/67)
°**season** ['siːzn] Saison; Jahreszeit
**seat** [siːt] Sitz, Platz I **take a seat** Platz nehmen III
**second** ['sekənd]:
1. zweite(r, s) I **Second, ...** Zweitens, ... I
2. Sekunde II
**Secondly, ...** ['sekəndli] Zweitens ... IV 2 (45)
**section** ['sekʃn] Abschnitt, Teilstück III
°**secure sth.** [sɪ'kjʊə] (sich etwas) sichern, sicherstellen
°**sedentary** ['sedntri] sesshaft; sitzend
**see** [siː], **saw, seen** sehen; besuchen I **see (a doctor)** (einen Arzt/eine Ärztin) aufsuchen II **See you later.** Bis bald. / Bis nachher. I **..., you see.** ..., weißt du. I **I see.** Aha! / Verstehe. II
**seed** [siːd] Samen III
°**seek** [siːk], **sought, sought** suchen (nach); anstreben
**seem (to be/do)** [siːm] (zu sein/zu tun) scheinen III
**seen** [siːn] *siehe* **see**
°**select** [sɪ'lekt] (aus)wählen
°**self-** [self] selbst-, Selbst-
°**self-governing** [ˌself 'gʌvənɪŋ] autonom, selbstverwaltet
**sell** [sel], **sold, sold** verkaufen I
°**semester** [sɪ'mestə] Semester
**semi-** ['semi] halb-; Halb- III
**semicircular** [ˌsemi'sɜːkjələ] halbrund IV 3 (93)
**send** [send], **sent, sent** schicken, senden I
**sense (of)** [sens] Sinn (für) III **sense of humour** (Sinn für) Humor III
°**sensible** ['sensəbl] vernünftig
**sent** [sent] *siehe* **send**
**sentence** ['sentəns] Satz I **full sentence** ganzer Satz II

**separate** ['sepəreɪt] trennen IV 1 (26)
**separate** ['seprət] getrennt, separat IV 2 (54)
**September** [sep'tembə] September I
°**sequence** ['siːkwəns] *(richtige)* Reihenfolge, Abfolge
**series** ['sɪəriːz], *pl* **series** Serie; (Sende-)Reihe IV 2 (58)
**serious** ['sɪəriəs] ernst; ernsthaft III
**serve** [sɜːv] servieren *(Essen, Getränke)*; bedienen *(Kundschaft)*; dienen IV 2 (41)
**service** ['sɜːvɪs]:
1. Dienst(leistung) IV 2 (41) **health service** Gesundheitswesen III **social services** *(pl)* Sozialwesen, soziale Dienste III
2. Gottesdienst III
**set** [set] Satz, Set II
**set** [set], **set, set**:
1. legen, stellen, setzen IV 2 (46) **set out** aufbrechen, sich auf den Weg machen IV 2 (46) **set sth. up** etwas aufstellen, aufbauen, errichten; etwas einrichten III **set the stage (for)** den Weg bereiten (für) IV 3 (87)
2. untergehen (Sonne) II
°**setting** ['setɪŋ]:
1. Schauplatz *(z.B. Film/Geschichte)*
2. Einstellung *(Gerät, Suchmaschine)*
3. Umgebung, Rahmen, Umfeld
**settle** ['setl]:
1. sich niederlassen, sich ansiedeln II
°2. besiedeln
**settlement** ['setlmənt] (Be-)Siedlung IV 3 (69)
**settler** ['setlə] Siedler/in II
**seven** ['sevn] sieben I
**several** ['sevrəl] mehrere, verschiedene II
**shadow** ['ʃædəʊ] Schatten II
**shake** [ʃeɪk], **shook, shaken** schütteln II
**shaken** ['ʃeɪkən] *siehe* **shake**
**Shall I ...?** [ʃæl] Soll ich ...? III
**shape** [ʃeɪp]:
1. Form, Gestalt II
°2. **shape sth.** etwas formen °**the shaping of ...** das Formen/die Formung des/der/von ...
**share sth.** [ʃeə] (sich) etwas teilen IV 1 (12)
**shark** [ʃɑːk] Hai I
**sharp** [ʃɑːp] scharf III
**sharpener** ['ʃɑːpnə] (An-)Spitzer I
**she** [ʃiː] sie I
**sheep** [ʃiːp], *pl* **sheep** Schaf II
°**sheet** [ʃiːt] Blatt (Papier)
**shelf** [ʃelf], *pl* **shelves** Regal I
**shelter** ['ʃeltə] Unterkunft III
**shelves** [ʃelvz] *plural of* **shelf**
**shine** [ʃaɪn], **shone, shone** leuchten; scheinen *(Sonne)* II
**shiny** ['ʃaɪni] glänzend IV 2 (52)
**ship** [ʃɪp] Schiff I
**shirt** [ʃɜːt] Hemd II
**shocked** [ʃɒkt] schockiert, entsetzt II

**shoe** [ʃuː] Schuh I
**shone** [ʃɒn] *siehe* **shine**
**shook** [ʃʊk] *siehe* **shake**
**shoot** [ʃuːt], **shot, shot** schießen; erschießen III
**shop** [ʃɒp]:
1. Laden I **corner shop** Laden an der Ecke; Tante-Emma-Laden I
2. einkaufen I
**shop assistant** ['ʃɒp əˌsɪstənt] Verkäufer/in I
**shopper** ['ʃɒpə] (Ein-)Käufer/in II
**shopping** ['ʃɒpɪŋ] Einkaufen I **do the/some shopping** (die) Einkäufe erledigen, einkaufen II **go shopping** einkaufen gehen I
**shopping centre** ['ʃɒpɪŋ sentə] Einkaufszentrum I
**shopping mall** ['ʃɒpɪŋ mɔːl] *(großes)* Einkaufszentrum I
**shore** [ʃɔː] Ufer *(eines Sees)*, Strand II
**short** [ʃɔːt] kurz I
**shorts** *(pl)* [ʃɔːts] Shorts, kurze Hose I
**shot** [ʃɒt]:
1. *siehe* **shoot**
2. Schuss; Geschoss, Schrot IV 3 (95)
3. Aufnahme, Foto; *(Film)* Einstellung, Szene III
**should** [ʃʊd], [ʃəd]: **I should ...** Ich sollte ... II
**shoulder** ['ʃəʊldə] Schulter II
**shout** [ʃaʊt] schreien, rufen I
**show** [ʃəʊ]:
1. Show II
2. **show, showed, shown** zeigen I **show off** angeben, prahlen IV 3 (70)
°**show-and-tell** [ˌʃəʊ ən 'tel] etwa: Anschauungsunterricht *(Schüler/innen bringen Dinge mit u. erzählen etwas darüber)*
**shower** ['ʃaʊə] Dusche II **have/take a shower** (sich) duschen II
**shown** [ʃəʊn] *siehe* **show**
**shrub** [ʃrʌb] Strauch, Busch III
**shut, shut, shut** [ʃʌt]: **shut sb. up** jn. einsperren IV 3 (95) **shut sth. down** etwas schließen IV 3 (87)
°**shy** [ʃaɪ] schüchtern, scheu
**sick** [sɪk] krank I **I feel sick.** Mir ist schlecht. II **I'm going to be sick.** Ich muss mich übergeben. II
**sickness** ['sɪknəs] Krankheit; Übelkeit II **travel sickness** Reisekrankheit II
**side** [saɪd] Seite II
**sidewalk** ['saɪdwɔːk] *(AE)* Gehweg, Bürgersteig II
**sigh** [saɪ] seufzen III
**sight** [saɪt] Anblick III **sights** *(pl)* Sehenswürdigkeiten I
**sign** [saɪn]:
1. Schild; Zeichen I **no sign of ...** keine Spur von ... III
2. **sign (sth.)** (etwas) unterschreiben IV 2 (46) **sign up (for)** sich anmelden (für) IV 2 (46)
**signal** ['sɪgnəl] Signal, Zeichen II

**silence** [ˈsaɪləns]:
1. Stille; Schweigen IV 3 (66/67)
2. zum Schweigen bringen IV 3 (66/67)

**silent** [ˈsaɪlənt] lautlos, leise; schweigend III

**silky** [ˈsɪlki] seidig I

**silly** [ˈsɪli]:
1. albern; blöd I
2. Dummerchen I

**similar (to sth./sb.)** [ˈsɪmələ] (etwas/jm.) ähnlich I

**similarity** [ˌsɪməˈlærəti] Ähnlichkeit, Gemeinsamkeit IV 2 (47)

**simple** [ˈsɪmpl] einfach, unkompliziert III

**since** [sɪns]:
1. seit III **since 10 o'clock/last week/…** seit 10 Uhr/letzter Woche/… III
2. seitdem, inzwischen IV 1 (17) **(ever) since** seitdem, seither IV 1 (17)

**sincerely** [sɪnˈsɪəli]: **Yours sincerely** Mit freundlichen Grüßen (Briefschluss) IV 1 (21)

**sing** [sɪŋ], **sang, sung** singen I °**sing along** mitsingen

**singer** [ˈsɪŋə] Sänger/in II

**single** [ˈsɪŋgl]:
1. ledig, alleinstehend I
2. (kurz für: **single ticket**) Einzelfahrschein; einfache Fahrkarte II
°3. einzelne(r, s)

**Sir** [sɜː]:
1. Sir (britischer Adelstitel) IV 1 (10)
2. **Dear Sir/Madam** Sehr geehrte Damen und Herren II

**siren** [ˈsaɪrən] Sirene III

**sister** [ˈsɪstə] Schwester I

**sit** [sɪt], **sat, sat** sitzen; sich setzen I **sit down** sich hinsetzen I **sit sb. down** jn. bitten, sich hinzusetzen IV 2 (47) **sit up** sich aufsetzen III

**site** [saɪt] Ort, Platz, Stelle, Stätte IV 1 (20)

**situation** [ˌsɪtʃuˈeɪʃn] Situation III

**six** [sɪks] sechs I

**sixth** [sɪksθ] Sechstel IV 3 (84)

**size** [saɪz] Größe I **What size tea would you like?** Wie groß soll der/dein Tee sein? II

**sizzle** [ˈsɪzl] brutzeln, zischen III

**skate** [skeɪt] Schlittschuh laufen, eislaufen IV 2 (52)

**skates** (pl) [ˈskeɪtsfɪ] Inlineskates I

**skating** [ˈskeɪtɪŋ]:
1. Inlineskaten, Rollschuhlaufen I
2. (kurz für: **ice skating**) Schlittschuhlaufen II

**skating rink** [ˈskeɪtɪŋ rɪŋk] Rollschuhbahn IV 2 (38/39)

**ski** [skiː]:
1. Ski; Ski- IV 2 (46)
2. Ski laufen, Ski fahren IV 2 (46)

**skier** [ˈskiːə] Skiläufer/in IV 2 (46)

**skilful** [ˈskɪlfl] (AE auch: **skillful**) geschickt, gut IV 3 (83)

**skill** [skɪl] Fertigkeit II **study skills** Lern- und Arbeitstechniken I

**skills file** [ˈskɪlz faɪl] Übersicht über Lern- und Arbeitstechniken I

**skim a text** [skɪm] einen Text überfliegen (um den Inhalt grob zu erfassen) III

**skin** [skɪn] Haut; Fell IV 2 (41)

**skinny** [ˈskɪni] mager, dünn, dürr III

**skirt** [skɜːt] Rock II

**skull** [skʌl] Schädel I

**sky** [skaɪ] Himmel II

**skyline** [ˈskaɪlaɪn] Skyline; Horizont III

**skyscraper** [ˈskaɪskreɪpə] Wolkenkratzer III

°**slang** [slæŋ] Slang (Umgangssprache)

**slap** [slæp]:
1. Schlag IV 3 (68)
2. knallen, schlagen (auf); klatschen (z.B. Regen) IV 3 (68) **slap sb.'s face** jm. eine Ohrfeige verpassen (ins Gesicht schlagen) IV 3 (68)

**sled** [sled]:
1. Schlitten IV 2 (46)
2. Schlitten fahren, rodeln IV 2 (46)

**sledge** [sledʒ]:
1. Schlitten IV 2 (46)
2. Schlitten fahren, rodeln IV 2 (46)

**sleep** [sliːp]:
1. Schlaf III
2. **sleep, slept, slept** schlafen III

**sleepover** [ˈsliːpəʊvə] Pyjama-Party, Schlafparty I

**sleepy** [ˈsliːpi] schläfrig II

**slept** [slept] siehe **sleep**

**slid** [slɪd] siehe **slide**

**slide** [slaɪd]:
1. Dia; Folie (Präsentationssoftware) IV 3 (68)
2. **slide, slid, slid** gleiten, rutschen; schieben, gleiten lassen IV 2 (52)

**slippery** [ˈslɪpəri] rutschig, glatt III

**slither** [ˈslɪðə] gleiten; schlittern III

**slow** [sləʊ] langsam I **be slow** nachgehen (Uhr) III

**small** [smɔːl] klein I

**small talk** [ˈsmɔːl tɔːk] Smalltalk (spontan geführtes Gespräch) III

**smallpox** [ˈsmɔːlpɒks] Pocken (Erkrankung) IV 3 (84)

**smell** [smel]:
1. riechen I **smell good** gut riechen II **smell sth.** an etwas riechen I
2. Geruch III

**smelly** [ˈsmeli] stinkend IV 2 (47) **be smelly** stinken IV 2 (47)

**smile** [smaɪl]:
1. (ein/das) Lächeln I
2. lächeln I **smile at sb.** jn. anlächeln I

**smiley** [ˈsmaɪli] Smiley I

**smoke** [sməʊk]:
1. Rauch III
2. rauchen III

**smooth** [smuːð] glatt, eben, ruhig IV 3 (66/67)

**smuggle** [ˈsmʌgl] schmuggeln I

**smuggler** [ˈsmʌglə] Schmuggler/in I

**smuggling** [ˈsmʌglɪŋ] der Schmuggel, das Schmuggeln I

**snack** [snæk] Snack, Imbiss I

**snake** [sneɪk] Schlange II

**sneakers** (pl) [ˈsniːkəz] (AE) Sportschuhe IV 3 (70)

**sneeze** [sniːz] niesen I

**sniff** [snɪf] schnüffeln, schnuppern; schniefen IV 2 (58)

**snow** [snəʊ] Schnee II

**snowball** [ˈsnəʊbɔːl] Schneeball IV 2 (52)

**so** [səʊ]:
1. also; deshalb, daher I
2. **so cool/nice** so cool/nett I **so far** bis jetzt; bis hierher II **so that …** (oft auch kurz: **so …**) sodass …, damit … II
3. **So?** Und? / Na und? I **So what?** Na und? IV 3 (68)
4. **I think so.** Ich glaube ja. IV 1 (23) **I don't think so.** Das glaube/denke ich nicht. IV 1 (23) **If so, …** Wenn ja, … / Wenn das der Fall ist, … IV 1 (23)

**soaking wet** [ˌsəʊkɪŋ ˈwet] völlig durchnässt, klitschnass IV 3 (95)

**soccer** [ˈsɒkə] Fußball I

**social** [ˈsəʊʃl] sozial IV 2 (54)

**social media** (pl) [ˌsəʊʃl ˈmiːdiə] soziale Medien III

**social services** (pl) [ˌsəʊʃl ˈsɜːvɪsɪz] Sozialwesen, soziale Dienste III

**society** [səˈsaɪəti] (die) Gesellschaft IV 2 (64)

**sock** [sɒk] Socke II

**soda** [ˈsəʊdə] (AE) (auch: **soda pop**) Limonade IV 3 (70)

**sofa** [ˈsəʊfə] Sofa I

**soft** [sɒft] weich I **in a soft voice** sanft; mit leiser Stimme II

°**solar** [ˈsəʊlə] Sonnen-, Solar-

**sold** [səʊld] siehe **sell**

**soldier** [ˈsəʊldʒə] Soldat/in II

**solo** [ˈsəʊləʊ] Solo- I

**solution (to)** [səˈluːʃn] Lösung (für) (Problem, Aufgabe) IV 2 (45)

**solve** [sɒlv] lösen (Rätsel, Problem), lüften (Geheimnis) IV 2 (45)

**some** [sʌm], [səm] einige, ein paar; etwas I

**somebody** [ˈsʌmbədi] jemand I

**somehow** [ˈsʌmhaʊ] irgendwie IV 1 (35)

**someone** [ˈsʌmwʌn] jemand I

**something** [ˈsʌmθɪŋ] etwas I

**sometimes** [ˈsʌmtaɪmz] manchmal I

**somewhere** [ˈsʌmweə] irgendwo, irgendwohin II

**son** [sʌn] Sohn II

**song** [sɒŋ] Lied I

**soon** [suːn] bald I **as soon as** sobald, sowie III

°**sophisticated** [səˈfɪstɪkeɪtɪd] hoch entwickelt, anspruchsvoll

**sorcerer** [ˈsɔːsərə] Zauberer, Hexenmeister IV 3 (84)

# Dictionary

**sore** [sɔː] wund ΙΙ **have a sore throat** Halsschmerzen haben ΙΙ
**sorrow** [ˈsɒrəʊ] Kummer, Leid IV 3 (90)
**sorry** [ˈsɒri]: (I'm) sorry. Tut mir leid. / Entschuldigung. I **I'm sorry about …** Es tut mir leid wegen … I
°**sought** [sɔːt] siehe **seek**
**sound** [saʊnd]:
 1. Laut I
 2. Geräusch; Klang I
 3. klingen, sich (gut usw.) anhören I
**soup** [suːp] Suppe I
**source** [sɔːs] Quelle (auch: Textquelle) IV 3 (84)
**south** [saʊθ] Süden; nach Süden; südlich III
**south-east** [ˌsaʊθ ˈiːst] Südosten; nach Südosten; südöstlich III
**south-west** [ˌsaʊθ ˈwest] Südwesten; nach Südwesten; südwestlich III
**southbound** [ˈsaʊθbaʊnd] Richtung Süden I
**southern** [ˈsʌðən] südlich, Süd- III
**souvenir** [ˌsuːvəˈnɪə] Andenken, Souvenir II
**space** [speɪs] Weltraum; Platz, Raum II
**spaghetti** [spəˈgeti] Spaghetti I
**Spanish** [ˈspænɪʃ] Spanisch; spanisch I
°**spark** [spɑːk] Funke **a bright spark** ein heller Kopf
**sparkle** [ˈspɑːkl] funkeln, glitzern, glänzen IV 2 (58)
**speak** [spiːk], **spoke, spoken** sprechen, reden I **speak to sb.** mit jm. sprechen II
**speaker** [ˈspiːkə] Sprecher/in, Redner/in I
°**spear** [spɪə] Speer, Lanze
**special** [ˈspeʃl] besondere(r, s) I
°**species** [ˈspiːʃiːz], pl **species** Art (Biologie) I
°**specific** [spəˈsɪfɪk] bestimmte(r, s), spezielle(r, s) I
**speculate** [ˈspekjʊleɪt] spekulieren, Vermutungen anstellen III
**sped** [sped] siehe **speed**
**speech** [spiːtʃ] (offizielle) Rede II **part of speech** Wortart III
°**speech bubble** [ˈspiːtʃ bʌbl] Sprechblase
**speed** [spiːd]:
 1. Geschwindigkeit III
 2. **speed up, sped, sped** beschleunigen; schneller werden/machen IV 2 (68)
**spell** [spel] buchstabieren I
**spelling** [ˈspelɪŋ] Rechtschreibung; Schreibweise II
**spend, spent, spent** [spend]: **spend money (on)** Geld ausgeben (für) III **spend time (on)** Zeit verbringen (mit) III
**spent** [spent] siehe **spend**
**spin around** [ˌspɪn əˈraʊnd], **spun, spun** sich (im Kreis) drehen; herumwirbeln III
**spiral** [ˈspaɪərəl] spiralförmig IV 1 (22)

**spirit** [ˈspɪrɪt] Geist, Seele; Stimmung; Einstellung IV 2 (40) **lift sb.'s spirits** jn. aufmuntern IV 2 (40)
**splash sb.** [splæʃ] jn. nass spritzen III
**split** [splɪt], **split, split** aufteilen; (sich) trennen; spalten IV 2 (57)
**split screen** [ˌsplɪt ˈskriːn] geteilter Bildschirm; Bildschirm(auf)teilung IV 2 (57)
**spoke** [spəʊk] siehe **speak**
**spoken** [ˈspəʊkən] siehe **speak**
**spoon** [spuːn] Löffel I
**sport** [spɔːt] Sport; Sportart I **do sport** Sport treiben I
**sportscast** [ˈspɔːtskɑːst] (AE) Sportsendung IV 2 (38/39)
°**sportsperson** [ˈspɔːtspɜːsn], pl **sportspeople** Sportler/in
**spot** [spɒt] Fleck, Punkt I **on the spot** an Ort und Stelle, sogleich IV 3 (70)
**spray** [spreɪ] (be)sprühen, sprayen IV 3 (81)
**spread** [spred], **spread, spread** (sich) ausbreiten, verbreiten III
**spring** [sprɪŋ] Frühling I
°**springtime** [ˈsprɪŋtaɪm] Frühling(szeit)
**spun** [spʌn] siehe **spin**
**square** [skweə]:
 1. Feld (auf Brettspiel) III
 2. Kästchen (auf Papier) III
 3. Platz (in der Stadt) II
 4. Quadrat III
 5. quadratisch III
 **square kilometre (sq km)** Quadratkilometer (km²) III
**squash** [skwɒʃ] Kürbis III
**squeeze** [skwiːz] drücken, pressen; (sich) zwängen, (sich) quetschen IV 3 (74)
**St = Saint** [seɪnt] St (= Sankt) IV 1 (10)
**stadium** [ˈsteɪdiəm] Stadion IV 2 (52)
**stage** [steɪdʒ] Bühne II **set the stage (for)** den Weg bereiten (für) IV 3 (87)
**staircase** [ˈsteəkeɪs] Treppe; Treppenhaus IV 1 (22)
**stairs** (pl) [steəz] Treppe; Treppenstufen II
**stall** [stɔːl] (Markt-)Stand II
**stamp** [stæmp] Stempel II
**stand** [stænd], **stood, stood**:
 1. stehen; sich (hin)stellen II **stand up** aufstehen I
 2. **I can't stand …** Ich kann … nicht ausstehen/ertragen. IV 3 (76)
**standard** [ˈstændəd] Standard; Standard- I
**stank** [stæŋk] siehe **stink**
**star** [stɑː]:
 1. (Film-, Pop-)Star I
 2. Stern III
**stare (at sb./sth.)** [steə] (jn./etwas an)starren III
**start** [stɑːt] anfangen, beginnen I
°**starvation** [stɑːˈveɪʃn] Hunger(tod), (das) Verhungern
**starve** [stɑːv] hungern III **be starving** einen Riesenhunger haben III
**state** [steɪt] Staat I

**state** [steɪt] darlegen, erklären IV 2 (45)
**state animal** [ˌsteɪt ˈænɪml] Wappentier II
°**state capitol** [ˌsteɪt ˈkæpɪtl] Staatskapitol (Parlamentsgebäude)
°**State Opening of Parliament** [ˌsteɪt ˈəʊpənɪŋ əv ˈpɑːləmənt] (in GB) offizielle Parlamentseröffnung (durch den Monarchen/die Monarchin)
**statement** [ˈsteɪtmənt] Aussage(satz); Feststellung, Behauptung IV 2 (45)
**station** [ˈsteɪʃn] Bahnhof I
**statistical** [stəˈtɪstɪkl] statistisch IV 2 (45)
**statistics** (pl) [stəˈtɪstɪks] Statistik(en) IV 2 (45)
**statue** [ˈstætʃuː] Statue III
**status** [ˈsteɪtəs] Status IV 2 (59)
**stay** [steɪ] bleiben I **stay (at/with)** (vorübergehend) wohnen, übernachten (in/bei) II **stay up late** lang aufbleiben II **stay in touch (with sb.)** (mit jm.) Kontakt halten; (mit jm.) in Verbindung bleiben II
**steak** [steɪk] Steak IV 3 (77)
**steal** [stiːl], **stole, stolen** stehlen, rauben IV 1 (26)
**steam** [stiːm] Dampf III
**steam train** [ˈstiːm treɪn] Zug mit Dampflok III
**steel** [stiːl] Stahl III
**steep** [stiːp] steil III
**steer** [stɪə] steuern, lenken I
**steering wheel** [ˈstɪərɪŋ wiːl] Lenkrad II
**step** [step]:
 1. Schritt I
 2. Stufe III
**stereotype** [ˈsteriətaɪp] Stereotyp, Klischee(vorstellung) IV 2 (41)
**stereotypical** [ˌsteriəˈtɪpɪkl] stereotyp, klischeehaft IV 2 (41)
**stick** [stɪk] Stock III **glue stick** Klebestift I
**stick, stuck, stuck** [stɪk]: **stick sth. into sth.** etwas in etwas stechen, stecken II
**sticky** [ˈstɪki] klebrig II
**still** [stɪl]:
 1. (immer) noch I
 2. trotzdem, dennoch II
 3. still, ruhig III
 °4. Standbild
**stilts** (pl) [stɪlts] Stelzen III
**stink** [stɪŋk], **stank, stunk** stinken IV 1 (29)
**stole** [stəʊl] siehe **steal**
**stolen** [ˈstəʊlən] siehe **steal**
**stomach** [ˈstʌmək] Magen II
**stone** [stəʊn] Stein II
**stood** [stʊd] siehe **stand**
**stop** [stɒp]:
 1. Halt; Station, Haltestelle II
 2. anhalten, stoppen I
 3. aufhören II **Stop it!** (infml) Hör auf (damit)! / Lass das! II
°**storage** [ˈstɔːrɪdʒ] Aufbewahrung, Lagerung, Speicherung

**store** [stɔː]:
1. aufbewahren, lagern; speichern IV 3 (70)
2. (AE) Laden, Geschäft II

**storey** [ˈstɔːri], *pl* **storeys** Stock, Stockwerk, Etage III

**storm** [stɔːm] Sturm, Unwetter, Gewitter II

**story** [ˈstɔːri], *pl* **stories**:
1. Geschichte, Erzählung I
2. (AE) Stock, Stockwerk, Etage III

**storyteller** [ˈstɔːritelə] (Geschichten-)Erzähler/in IV 3 (90)

°**straggle** [ˈstrægl] kriechen; zurückbleiben

**straight** [streɪt]:
1. gerade II
2. direkt, geradewegs III  **straight on** geradeaus weiter II

**strange** [streɪndʒ] seltsam, komisch I

**strawberry** [ˈstrɔːbəri] Erdbeere II

**stream** [striːm]:
1. Bach II
2. strömen III
3. streamen III

**street** [striːt] Straße I  **at 14 Dean Street** in der Dean Street 14 I  **in Dean Street** in der Dean Street I

**street artist** [ˈstriːt ˌɑːtɪst] Straßenkünstler/in II

**strength** [streŋθ] Stärke, Kraft IV 3 (81)

**stress** [stres]:
1. Betonung I
2. betonen IV 3 (82)

°**stretch** [stretʃ] sich erstrecken

**strict** [strɪkt] streng III

**strike** [straɪk], **struck, struck** schießen (Ball, Puck); schlagen; treffen IV 2 (52)

**string** [strɪŋ] Saite III

°**strip down** [ˌstrɪp ˈdaʊn] sich ausziehen

**strong** [strɒŋ] stark, kräftig II

**strongly** [ˈstrɒŋli] heftig, entschieden, voll und ganz IV 3 (81)

**struck** [strʌk] *siehe* **strike**

**structure** [ˈstrʌktʃə] Struktur, Gliederung III

**stuck** [stʌk] *siehe* **stick**

**student** [ˈstjuːdənt] Schüler/in; Student/in I

**studio** [ˈstjuːdiəʊ] Studio I

**study** [ˈstʌdi] studieren; untersuchen, beobachten; lernen II

**study poster** [ˈstʌdi pəʊstə] Lernposter II

**study skills** [ˈstʌdi skɪlz] Lern- und Arbeitstechniken I

**stuff** [stʌf] (*infml*) Zeug, Kram III

**stumble** [ˈstʌmbl] stolpern; torkeln IV 1 (26)

**stunk** [stʌŋk] *siehe* **stink**

**stupid** [ˈstjuːpɪd] dumm, blöd III

**style** [staɪl] Stil II

**sub-clause** [ˈsʌb klɔːz] Nebensatz I

**sub-heading** [ˈsʌb hedɪŋ] Zwischenüberschrift; Kapitelüberschrift III

**subject** [ˈsʌbdʒɪkt]:
1. Schulfach I
2. Thema; (*in E-Mails*) Betreff IV 1 (21)

**subscribe to sth.** [səbˈskraɪb] etwas abonnieren IV 1 (12)

**subtitle** [ˈsʌbtaɪtl] Untertitel I

**suburb** [ˈsʌbɜːb] Vorstadt, Vorort IV 3 (77)

**subway** [ˈsʌbweɪ] (AE) U-Bahn II

**success** [səkˈses] Erfolg IV 3 (82)

**successful** [səkˈsesfl] erfolgreich II

**such** [sʌtʃ]: such a … so ein/e …; solch ein/e …  **such as** wie zum Beispiel IV 2 (62)

**suck** [sʌk]: **That sucks!** (*infml*) Das ist echt übel! III

**suddenly** [ˈsʌdnli] plötzlich, auf einmal I

**suffer (from)** [ˈsʌfə] leiden (an); erleiden IV 2 (47)

°**suffering** [ˈsʌfərɪŋ] (das) Leid, Leiden

**sugar** [ˈʃʊɡə] Zucker IV 3 (69)

**suggest sth.** [səˈdʒest] auf etwas hinweisen, hindeuten IV 2 (59)  **suggest sth. (to sb.)** (jm.) etwas vorschlagen III

**suggestion** [səˈdʒestʃən] Vorschlag III

**sum sth. up** [ˌsʌm ˈʌp] etwas zusammenfassen III

°**summary** [ˈsʌməri] Zusammenfassung

**summer** [ˈsʌmə] Sommer I

**summit** [ˈsʌmɪt] Gipfel III

**sun** [sʌn] Sonne I

**Sunday** [ˈsʌndeɪ], [ˈsʌndi] Sonntag I

**sung** [sʌŋ] *siehe* **sing**

**sunglasses** (*pl*) [ˈsʌnɡlɑːsɪz] (eine) Sonnenbrille II

**sunny** [ˈsʌni] sonnig II

**sunrise** [ˈsʌnraɪz] Sonnenaufgang IV 3 (70)

**sunset** [ˈsʌnset] Sonnenuntergang IV 3 (70)

**supermarket** [ˈsuːpəmɑːkɪt] Supermarkt II

**supply** [səˈplaɪ]:
1. Versorgung, Lieferung; Vorrat IV 3 (75)
2. liefern, bereitstellen, zur Verfügung stellen IV 3 (75)

**support** [səˈpɔːt]:
1. Unterstützung IV 1 (27)
2. unterstützen IV 1 (27)

**sure** [ʃʊə], [ʃɔː] sicher I  **make sure that …** sich vergewissern, dass …; darauf achten, dass …; dafür sorgen, dass …

**surf** [sɜːf] surfen II

**surface** [ˈsɜːfɪs] Oberfläche III

**surfing** [ˈsɜːfɪŋ] Surfen, Wellenreiten II

**surprise** [səˈpraɪz]:
1. Überraschung I
2. überraschen IV 3 (81)

**surprised** [səˈpraɪzd] überrascht I

**surprisingly** [səˈpraɪzɪŋli] überraschenderweise IV 3 (81)

°**surround** [səˈraʊnd] umgeben

**survey** [ˈsɜːveɪ] Umfrage, Studie III

°**survival** [səˈvaɪvl] Überleben

**survive** [səˈvaɪv] überleben III

**swallow** [ˈswɒləʊ] (ver)schlucken IV 1 (28)

**swam** [swæm] *siehe* **swim**

**swamp** [swɒmp] Sumpf, Marschland III

°**swap** [swɒp] tauschen

**sweat** [swet]:
1. Schweiß IV 1 (28)
2. schwitzen IV 1 (28)

**sweet** [swiːt] süß II

**sweets** (*pl*) [swiːts] Süßigkeiten II

**swim** [swɪm], **swam, swum** schwimmen I

**swimmer** [ˈswɪmə] Schwimmer/in I

**swimming pool** [ˈswɪmɪŋ puːl] Schwimmbad, Schwimmbecken I

**switch** [swɪtʃ]:
1. Schalter III
°2. wechseln, (ver)tauschen

**sword** [sɔːd] Schwert I

**swum** [swʌm] *siehe* **swim**

**syllable** [ˈsɪləbl] Silbe I

**symbol** [ˈsɪmbl] Symbol I

**syrup** [ˈsɪrəp] Sirup IV 2 (64)

°**system** [ˈsɪstəm] System

# T

**table** [ˈteɪbl]:
1. Tisch I
2. Tabelle I

**table tennis** Tischtennis II

**tablet** [ˈtæblət] (*bes. BE*) Tablette II

**take** [teɪk], **took, taken**:
1. (*Zeit*) brauchen; dauern I
2. nehmen, mitnehmen; (weg-, hin)bringen I  **take (a test / an exam / a course)** (einen Test / eine Prüfung / einen Kurs) machen IV 2 (47)  **take a risk** ein Risiko eingehen III  **take a seat** Platz nehmen III  **take a shower** (sich) duschen II  **take a walk** (*bes. AE*) spazieren gehen, einen Spaziergang machen III  **take notes** (sich) Notizen machen (*beim Lesen oder Zuhören*) II  **take part in sth.** an etwas teilnehmen II

**take photos** fotografieren, Fotos machen I  **take place** stattfinden; spielen, sich abspielen (*Geschichte, Handlung*) I  **take sth. down** etwas wegreißen, abbauen (*z.B. Zaun, Zelt*) IV 2 (58)  **take sth. off** etwas ausziehen (*Kleidung*); etwas absetzen (*Hut, Helm*) II  **take sth. out** etwas herausnehmen II  °**take turns** sich abwechseln

**takeaway** [ˈteɪkəweɪ]:
1. Restaurant/Imbissgeschäft, das auch Essen zum Mitnehmen verkauft II
2. Essen zum Mitnehmen II

**taken** [ˈteɪkən] *siehe* **take**

**takeout** [ˈteɪkaʊt] (AE) Essen zum Mitnehmen II

**talent** [ˈtælənt] Talent, Begabung II

**talented** [ˈtæləntɪd] begabt, talentiert II

# Dictionary

**talk** [tɔːk]:
1. **talk (to)** reden (mit), sich unterhalten (mit) I
2. Vortrag, Referat, Rede I **give a talk (about)** einen Vortrag / eine Rede halten (über) I **small talk** Smalltalk *(spontan geführtes Gespräch)* III

**tall** [tɔːl] groß *(Person)*; hoch *(Gebäude, Baum)* I

**tap** [tæp]:
1. tippen, (vorsichtig) klopfen II
2. (leichtes) Klopfen III

**task** [tɑːsk] Aufgabe I

**taste** [teɪst] schmecken I **taste sth.** etwas kosten *(probieren)*; etwas schmecken II

**tasty** [ˈteɪsti] lecker II

**taught** [tɔːt] siehe **teach**

**tax** [tæks] (die) Steuer IV 3 (81)

**taxation** [tækˈseɪʃn] Besteuerung, Steuern IV 3 (87)

**taxi** [ˈtæksi] Taxi II

**taxpayer** [ˈtækspeɪə] Steuerzahler/in IV 3 (81)

**tea** [tiː]:
1. Tee I **iced tea** Eistee I
2. leichte Nachmittags- oder Abendmahlzeit II

**teach** [tiːtʃ], **taught, taught** unterrichten, lehren III **teach sb. to do sth.** jm. beibringen / jn. lehren, etwas zu tun III

**teacher** [ˈtiːtʃə] Lehrer/in I

**team** [tiːm] Team, Mannschaft I

**tear** [tɪə] Träne II

**tear, tore, torn** [teə]: **tear sth. down** etwas abreißen III

**teaspoon** [ˈtiːspuːn] Teelöffel II

**teen** [tiːn] Teenager/in II

**teenager** [ˈtiːneɪdʒə] Teenager IV 2 (46)

°**teepee** [ˈtiːpiː] Tipi *(Indianerzelt)*

**teeth** [tiːθ] plural of **tooth**

**telephone** [ˈtelɪfəʊn] Telefon I

**telephone box** [ˈtelɪfəʊn bɒks] Telefonzelle III

**tell, told, told** [tel]: **tell (about)** erzählen (von); berichten (über) I **tell sb. (not) to do sth.** jn. auffordern, etwas (nicht) zu tun; jm. sagen, dass er/sie etwas (nicht) tun soll III **tell sb. the way (to …)** jm. den Weg (nach …) beschreiben II

°**temperate** [ˈtempərət] gemäßigt; maßvoll

**temperature** [ˈtemprətʃə] Temperatur, Fieber II **have a temperature** Fieber haben II

**ten** [ten] zehn I

°**tend (to) sb./sth.** [tend] sich kümmern um jn./etwas, jn./etwas pflegen

**tennis** [ˈtenɪs] Tennis I **table tennis** Tischtennis II

**tense** [tens] *(grammatische)* Zeit, Tempus II

**tension** [ˈtenʃn] Spannung; Verspannung(en) IV 2 (52)

**tent** [tent] Zelt II

**term** [tɜːm] Trimester II
**terrain** [təˈreɪn] Terrain, Gelände IV 2 (46)
**terrible** [ˈterəbl] schrecklich, furchtbar II
**territory** [ˈterətri] Gebiet, Territorium IV 2 (46)
**terrorist** [ˈterərɪst] terroristische(r, s); Terrorist/in III

**test** [test]:
1. Test I
2. testen, prüfen III

**text** [tekst]:
1. Text I
2. SMS II
3. **text sb.** jm. eine SMS schicken I

**text message** [ˈtekst mesɪdʒ] SMS II

°**textbook** [ˈtekstbʊk] Schulbuch, Lehrbuch

**than** [ðæn], [ðən]: **bigger than** größer als II

**thank** [θæŋk]: **thank sb.** jm. danken IV 2 (40) **Thank you.** Danke. I

**thankful** [ˈθæŋkfl] dankbar IV 2 (41)

**thanks** [θæŋks] danke I **thanks to Maya** dank Maya II

**that** [ðæt]:
1. das (dort) I **that group** die Gruppe (dort), jene Gruppe I **that's why** deshalb, darum I **after that** danach I **Is that you?** Bist du's? / Bist du das? I **like that** so (auf diese Weise) I
2. dass I **it shows that …** es zeigt, dass … I **It was through storytellers that they learned …** Durch Geschichtenerzähler/innen lernten sie … IV 3 (90) **Now that …** Jetzt, wo … / Nun, da … III **so that …** sodass …, damit … II
3. der, die, das; die *(Relativpronomen)* II

**the** [ðə]:
1. der, die, das; die I
2. **the more …, the more …** je mehr …, desto mehr … IV 1 (17)

**theatre** [ˈθɪətə] Theater I

**their** [ðeə] ihr/e *(zu „they")* I

**theirs** [ðeəz] ihrer, ihre, ihrs II

**them** [ðem], [ðəm] sie; ihnen I

**theme** [θiːm] Thema II

**themselves** [ðəmˈselvz] sie/sich selbst/selber *(zu „they")* III

**then** [ðen] dann I **just then** genau in dem Moment; gerade dann II

**there** [ðeə] da, dort; dahin, dorthin I **There are …** Es sind … / Es gibt … I **There's … (= There is …)** Es ist … / Es gibt … I **Are there any …?** Gibt es (irgendwelche) …? I **over there** da drüben, dort drüben I

**thermometer** [θəˈmɒmɪtə] Thermometer II

**these** [ðiːz] diese (hier) II

**they** [ðeɪ] sie (Plural) I **they're … (= they are)** sie sind … I

**thick** [θɪk] dick II

**thief** [θiːf], pl **thieves** Dieb/in II

**thieves** [θiːvz] plural of **thief**

**thing** [θɪŋ] Sache, Ding I

**think, thought, thought** [θɪŋk] denken, glauben I **think (about)** nachdenken (über) I **think of sth.** sich etwas ausdenken; an etwas denken I

**third** [θɜːd]:
1. dritte(r, s) I **Third, …** Drittens, … I
2. Drittel IV 3 (84)

**Thirdly, …** [ˈθɜːdli] Drittens … IV 2 (45)

**thirsty** [ˈθɜːsti]: **be thirsty** durstig sein, Durst haben II

**this** [ðɪs] dies; diese(r, s) I **this afternoon/evening/…** heute Nachmittag/Abend/… I **This is …** Dies ist … / Das ist … I **this one** diese(r, s) I **this time** dieses Mal II **this year's musical** das diesjährige Musical II **like this** so (auf diese Weise) I

**thorough** [ˈθʌrə] gründlich; sorgfältig IV 3 (81)

**thoroughly** [ˈθʌrəli] völlig, total IV 3 (81)

**those** [ðəʊz] die … dort; jene I

**though** [ðəʊ] obwohl IV 3 (80) **even though** selbst wenn, obwohl *(betont)* IV 3 (80)

**thought** [θɔːt]:
1. Gedanke III
2. siehe **think** **be thought of as …** angesehen werden als … IV 2 (64)

**thousand** [ˈθaʊznd] Tausend, tausend II

**threat** [θret] (Be-)Drohung IV 3 (75)

**threaten** [ˈθretn] (be)drohen IV 3 (75)

**three** [θriː] drei I

**threw** [θruː] siehe **throw**

**throat** [θrəʊt] Hals, Kehle II **have a sore throat** Halsschmerzen haben II

**through** [θruː] durch I

**throughout …** [θruːˈaʊt] der/die/das ganze … (hindurch); überall in … IV 3 (97)

**throw** [θrəʊ], **threw, thrown** werfen I

**thrown** [θrəʊn] siehe **throw**

**thunder** [ˈθʌndə] Donner II

**Thursday** [ˈθɜːzdeɪ], [ˈθɜːzdi] Donnerstag I

**ticket** [ˈtɪkɪt]:
1. Eintrittskarte I
2. Fahrkarte I **return ticket** (Hin- und) Rückfahrkarte II **single ticket** Einzelfahrschein; einfache Fahrkarte II
3. Strafzettel IV 2 (64)

**ticket office** [ˈtɪkɪt ˌɒfɪs] Fahrkartenschalter; Kasse *(für den Verkauf von Eintrittskarten)* III

**tight** [taɪt] fest, eng; knapp, eng anliegend *(Kleidung)* IV 3 (74)

**tighten** [ˈtaɪtn] spannen, festziehen, nachziehen III

**till** [tɪl] bis I **not till three** erst um drei, nicht vor drei II

**time** [taɪm]:
1. Zeit; Uhrzeit I **all the time** die ganze Zeit II **be in time for the bus** den Bus erreichen; rechtzeitig zum Bus kommen III **feeding time** Fütterungszeit I **of all time** aller Zeiten II **on**

# English – German

**time** pünktlich IV 2 (47)   **opening times** *(pl)* Öffnungszeiten III   **What time is it?** Wie spät ist es? I
2. Mal I   **at a time** gleichzeitig, auf einmal; jeweils IV 2 (47)   **at one time** zur selben Zeit, gleichzeitig III   **for the first time** zum ersten Mal III   **one at a time** einzeln, nacheinander IV 2 (47)   **this time** dieses Mal II
**timeline** ['taɪmlaɪn] Zeitstrahl, Zeitleiste II
**timer** ['taɪmə] Zeitmesser III
**timetable** ['taɪmteɪbl]:
1. Stundenplan I
2. Fahrplan III
**tin** [tɪn] Dose II
**tiny** ['taɪni] winzig III
**tip** [tɪp] Tipp I
°**tire** ['taɪə] (AE) Reifen
**tired** ['taɪəd] müde I
**titanium** [tɪ'teɪniəm] Titan *(Metall)* IV (15)
**title** ['taɪtl] Titel, Überschrift I
**to** [tu], [tə]:
1. zu, nach I
2. um zu II
3. **Nice to meet you.** Freut mich, dich/euch/Sie kennenzulernen. I
4. **count to …** zählen bis … I   **from … to …** von … bis … I
5. **quarter to eleven** Viertel vor elf (10.45 / 22.45) I
**toast** [təʊst] Toast III
**toboggan** [tə'bɒgən] Schlitten IV 2 (64)
**today** [tə'deɪ] heute I
**toe** [təʊ] Zeh II
**together** [tə'geðə] zusammen I   **go together** zusammenpassen, zueinander passen III
**toilet** ['tɔɪlət] Toilette I
**told** [təʊld] *siehe* **tell**
**tolerance (of/for)** ['tɒlərəns] Toleranz (für/gegenüber) IV 1 (17)
**tolerant (of/towards)** ['tɒlərənt] tolerant (gegenüber) IV 1 (17)
**tomato** [tə'mɑːtəʊ], *pl* **tomatoes** Tomate I
**tomorrow** [tə'mɒrəʊ] morgen II   **tomorrow morning** morgen früh II
**tongue** [tʌŋ] Zunge II
**tongue-twister** ['tʌŋ twɪstə] Zungenbrecher II
**tonight** [tə'naɪt] heute Nacht, heute Abend II
**tonne** [tʌn] Tonne (= 1.000 kg) IV 2 (62)
**too** [tuː]:
1. auch I   **Me too.** Ich auch. I
2. **too late/cold/big/…** zu spät/kalt/groß/… I
**took** [tʊk] *siehe* **take**
**tooth** [tuːθ], *pl* **teeth** Zahn II
**toothache** ['tuːθeɪk]: **have a toothache** Zahnschmerzen haben II
**top** [tɒp]:
1. Spitze, oberes Ende I   **at the top (of)** oben, am oberen Ende (von) II

**on top of each other** übereinander, aufeinander III
2. Spitzen- I
3. Top, Oberteil I
**top hat** [ˌtɒp 'hæt] Zylinder *(Hut)* IV 2 (59)
**topic** ['tɒpɪk] Thema, Themengebiet II
**topic sentence** [ˌtɒpɪk 'sentəns] Satz, der in das Thema eines Absatzes einführt II
**topping** ['tɒpɪŋ] Überzug, Belag; Soße IV 2 (48)   **with a cheese topping** mit Käse überbacken IV 2 (48)
**torch** [tɔːtʃ]:
1. Taschenlampe II
2. Fackel II
**tore** [tɔː] *siehe* **tear**
**torn** [tɔːn] *siehe* **tear**
**tortoise** ['tɔːtəs] (Land-)Schildkröte III
**torture** ['tɔːtʃə]:
1. Folter IV 1 (35)
2. foltern, quälen IV 1 (35)
**total** ['təʊtl]: **a total of …** eine Gesamtsumme von …; insgesamt III
**totally** ['təʊtəli] völlig, total III
**touch** [tʌtʃ]:
1. berühren, anfassen I
2. **get in touch (with sb.)** (mit jm.) Kontakt aufnehmen; sich (mit jm.) in Verbindung setzen II   **stay in touch (with sb.)** (mit jm.) Kontakt halten; (mit jm.) in Verbindung bleiben II
**tough** [tʌf] (knall)hart; zäh, robust IV 2 (46)
**tour (of)** [tʊər ˌəv] Rundgang, Rundfahrt, Reise (durch) I
**tour guide** ['tʊə gaɪd] Reiseführer/in IV 1 (22)
**tourist** ['tʊərɪst] Tourist/in I
**tourist (information) office** ['tʊərɪst ˌɒfɪs] Touristeninformation, Fremdenverkehrsbüro IV 1 (11)
**tourist (information) bureau** ['tʊərɪst ˌbjʊərəʊ] (AE) Touristeninformation, Fremdenverkehrsbüro IV 1 (11)
**touristy** ['tʊərɪsti] *(infml)* touristisch IV 1 (20)
**tournament** ['tʊənəmənt], ['tɔːnəmənt] Turnier IV 2 (38/39)
**towards** [tə'wɔːdz] auf … zu, in Richtung (von) III
**tower** ['taʊə] Turm I
**town** [taʊn] Stadt I
**toy** [tɔɪ] Spielzeug I
°**trace sth. back (to)** [ˌtreɪs 'bæk] etwas zurückverfolgen (bis)
**track** [træk] (Bahn-)Gleis III
**tractor** ['træktə] Traktor II
**trade** [treɪd]:
1. Handel III
2. handeln, Handel (be)treiben IV 3 (96)
**trader** ['treɪdə] Händler/in IV 2 (59)
**tradition** [trə'dɪʃn] Tradition I
**traditional** [trə'dɪʃənl] traditionell II
**traffic** ['træfɪk] Verkehr III

**traffic light(s)** ['træfɪk laɪt] (Verkehrs-) Ampel III
**trail** [treɪl] Weg, Pfad III
**train** [treɪn] Zug I   **direct train** durchgehender Zug I   **steam train** Zug mit Dampflok III
**train (sb.)** [treɪn] trainieren; jn. trainieren II
**trainer** ['treɪnə] Turnschuh I
**training** ['treɪnɪŋ] Training(sstunde) I
**trance** [trɑːns] Trance III
**transform** [træns'fɔːm] (sich) verwandeln; umwandeln IV 1 (17)
**translate** [træns'leɪt] übersetzen II
**translation** [træns'leɪʃn] Übersetzung III
**transparency** [træns'pærənsi] Folie III
**transport** ['trænspɔːt] Verkehrsmittel; Transport(wesen) III
**transport** [træn'spɔːt] transportieren, befördern IV 3 (70)
**trapped** [træpt]: **be trapped** gefangen sein, in der Falle sitzen IV 1 (27)
**travel** ['trævl] reisen I
**travel sickness** ['trævl sɪknəs] Reisekrankheit II
**traveller** ['trævələ] Reisende(r) I
°**treasure** ['treʒə] Schatz
**treat** [triːt]:
1. Hochgenuss, besonderes Vergnügen; *(besondere)* Leckerei IV 1 (17)
2. **treat sb. (to sth.)** jn. (zu etwas) einladen IV 1 (17)
°3. **treat sb./sth.** jn./etwas behandeln
**treaty** ['triːti] (Staats-)Vertrag, Abkommen IV 2 (64)
**tree** [triː] Baum I
°**treeless** ['triːləs] baumlos
**trek** [trek] Wanderung, Treck IV 2 (46)
**trend** [trend]:
1. im Trend liegen, angesagt sein IV 1 (12)
2. Trend IV 1 (12)
**trendy** ['trendi] modisch, „angesagt" IV 1 (16)
**triangular** [traɪ'æŋgjələ] dreieckig III
**tribe** [traɪb] (Volks-)Stamm I
**trick** [trɪk] Kunststück, Trick II
**trip** [trɪp] Ausflug; Reise I   **go on a boat trip** einen Bootsausflug machen I
**troop** [truːp] Truppe *(Militär)* IV 3 (69)
**trophy** ['trəʊfi] Pokal; Trophäe I
**tropical** ['trɒpɪkl] tropisch, Tropen- III
**trouble** ['trʌbl]: **be in trouble** in Schwierigkeiten sein; Ärger kriegen I   **get into trouble** in Schwierigkeiten geraten, Ärger kriegen III
**troubled** ['trʌbld] unruhig, mit Problemen belastet; beunruhigt; bekümmert, besorgt IV 3 (75)
**trousers** *(pl)* ['traʊzəz] Hose I
**truck** [trʌk] *(bes. AE)* Lastwagen, LKW III
**true** [truː] wahr I   **come true** wahr werden IV 2 (46)
**trumpet** ['trʌmpɪt] Trompete I

# Dictionary

**trunk** [trʌŋk] (AE) Kofferraum IV 3 (68)
**trust** [trʌst]:
1. Vertrauen IV 1 (27)
2. trauen, vertrauen IV 1 (27)

**truth** [truːθ] Wahrheit II
**try** [traɪ]:
1. Versuch III
2. (aus)probieren; versuchen I **try hard** sich anstrengen; sich (große) Mühe geben III **try out for sth.** (AE) sich bewerben um etwas (einen Platz, eine Rolle etc.) IV 3 (74) **try sth. on** etwas anprobieren III

**T-shirt** [ˈtiːʃɜːt] T-Shirt I
**tube** [tjuːb]:
°**1.** Schlauch; Tube; Rohr, Röhre
2. **the Tube** (no pl) die U-Bahn (in London) III

°**tubing** [ˈtjuːbɪŋ] Tubing (mit Reifen/Schlauch im Wasser treiben)
**tuck** [tʌk] stecken, klemmen IV 3 (68)
**Tuesday** [ˈtjuːzdeɪ], [ˈtjuːzdi] Dienstag I
**tulip** [ˈtjuːlɪp] Tulpe II
°**tundra** [ˈtʌndrə] Tundra
**tune** [tjuːn]:
1. Melodie III
2. stimmen (Instrument) III

**tunnel** [ˈtʌnl] Tunnel II
**turkey** [ˈtɜːki] Pute, Truthahn I
**turn** [ˌtɜːn_əˈraʊnd]:
1. **turn around** sich umdrehen I **turn left/right** (nach) links/rechts abbiegen II **turn sth. around** etwas wenden, umdrehen I **turn sth. off** etwas ausschalten II **turn sth. on** etwas einschalten I **turn sth. up/down** etwas lauter/leiser stellen III **turn to sb.** sich jm. zuwenden; sich an jn. wenden II
°**turn sth. up/down** etwas hochdrehen/-regeln / herunterdrehen/-regeln
2. **turn into sth.** sich in etwas verwandeln, zu etwas werden IV 2 (40) **turn red/brown/cold** rot/braun/kalt werden III **turn sb./sth. into sth.** jn./etwas in etwas verwandeln IV 2 (40)
3. **(It's) my turn.** Ich bin dran / an der Reihe. I °**take turns** sich abwechseln

**TV** [ˌtiːˈviː] Fernsehen, Fernsehgerät I **on TV** im Fernsehen III **watch TV** fernsehen I
**tweet** [twiːt] Tweet IV 1 (12)
**twelve** [twelv] zwölf I
**twice** [twaɪs] zweimal I
**twins** (pl) [twɪnz] Zwillinge I
**twitch** [twɪtʃ] zucken IV 2 (58)
**two** [tuː] zwei I
**type (of)** [taɪp] Typ, Art, Sorte (von) III
**typical (of)** [ˈtɪpɪkl] typisch (für) III
°**tyre** [ˈtaɪə] (BE) Reifen

# U

**umbrella** [ʌmˈbrelə] Schirm, Regenschirm I

**uncle** [ˈʌŋkl] Onkel I
**under** [ˈʌndə] unter I
**underground** [ˌʌndəˈɡraʊnd] unterirdisch, unter der Erde III
**underground** [ˈʌndəɡraʊnd]: **the underground** (BE) die U-Bahn II
**underline** [ˌʌndəˈlaɪn] unterstreichen II
**underlying** [ˌʌndəˈlaɪɪŋ] zugrunde liegend; darunter liegend II
**understand, understood, understood** [ˌʌndəˈstænd] verstehen I
°**understanding** [ˌʌndəˈstændɪŋ] Verständnis
**understood** [ˌʌndəˈstʊd] siehe **understand**
**uneducated** [ʌnˈedʒukeɪtɪd] ungebildet IV 3 (71)
**unfair** [ʌnˈfeə] unfair III
°**unfinished** [ʌnˈfɪnɪʃt] unvollendet
**unfriendly** [ʌnˈfrendli] unfreundlich I
**unhappy** [ʌnˈhæpi] unglücklich I
**unhealthy** [ʌnˈhelθi] ungesund IV 2 (43)
**unicorn** [ˈjuːnɪkɔːn] Einhorn IV 1 (15)
**uniform** [ˈjuːnɪfɔːm] (Schul-)Uniform I
**unify** [ˈjuːnɪfaɪ] (ver)einen, vereinigen IV 3 (90)
**union** [ˈjuːnɪən] Union; Vereinigung, Verband IV 3 (93)
**unique** [juˈniːk] einmalig, einzigartig IV 1 (17)
**unit** [ˈjuːnɪt] Kapitel, Lektion I
**united** [juˈnaɪtɪd] vereinigt I **United Kingdom (UK)** Vereinigtes Königreich I **United States** Vereinigte Staaten (von Amerika) III
°**unity** [ˈjuːnəti] Einheit
**university** [ˌjuːnɪˈvɜːsəti] Universität II
**unlike** [ˌʌnˈlaɪk] anders als, im Gegensatz zu IV 3 (82)
**unlock** [ʌnˈlɒk] aufschließen, entsperren IV 2 (64)
**unpack** [ˌʌnˈpæk] auspacken III
**unsubscribe (from) sth.** [ˌʌnsəbˈskraɪb] etwas abbestellen, kündigen; sich aus einer Mailingliste austragen lassen IV 1 (12)
**until** [ənˈtɪl] bis II **not until 1912** erst im Jahr 1912; nicht vor 1912 III
**unusual** [ʌnˈjuːʒʊəl] ungewöhnlich III
**up** [ʌp] hinauf, herauf; (nach) oben I **up and down** auf und ab; rauf und runter I **up here** hier oben; nach hier oben II **up to** bis (zu) II **What's up?** Was gibt's? / Was ist los? III °**it is up to sb. (to do sth.)** es ist jemandes Sache / es liegt an jm. (etwas zu tun)
**update sth.** [ˌʌpˈdeɪt] etwas aktualisieren, auf den neuesten Stand bringen III
**uphill** [ˌʌpˈhɪl] bergauf III
**upload sth.** [ˌʌpˈləʊd] etwas hochladen III
**upstairs** [ˌʌpˈsteəz] oben; nach oben I
**upstream** [ˌʌpˈstriːm] flussaufwärts III
**upwards** [ˈʌpwədz] nach oben IV 1 (25)
°**urban** [ˈɜːbən] städtisch, urban

**US (United States)** [ˌjuːˈes] Vereinigte Staaten (von Amerika) III
**us** [ʌs], [əs] uns I
**use** [juːz] benutzen, verwenden I
**used to** [ˈjuːst tə]: **the trail I used to take** der Weg, den ich (früher immer) genommen habe III
°**useful** [ˈjuːsfl] nützlich, hilfreich
**usual** [ˈjuːʒʊəl] gewöhnlich, üblich III
**usually** [ˈjuːʒʊəli] meistens, normalerweise, gewöhnlich I

# V

**vacate** [vəˈkeɪt] (fml) räumen (Zimmer, Gebäude) IV 2 (47)
**vacation** [vəˈkeɪʃn] (AE) Urlaub II
**valley** [ˈvæli] Tal II
**value** [ˈvæljuː] Wert IV 3 (87) **values** (pl) Werte, Wertvorstellungen IV 3 (87) **It's good value (for money).** Es ist sein Geld wert. / Es ist preiswert. IV 3 (87)
**van** [væn] Transporter, Lieferwagen III
**variety** [vəˈraɪəti] Variante, Sorte, Art IV 3 (70)
°**various** [ˈveəriəs] (mehrere) verschiedene
**vary** [ˈveəri] unterschiedlich sein, verschieden sein II
**vegetables** (pl) [ˈvedʒtəblz] Gemüse I
**vegetarian** [ˌvedʒəˈteəriən] Vegetarier/in; vegetarisch II
**vehicle** [ˈviːəkl] Fahrzeug IV 3 (70)
**vendetta** [venˈdetə] Blutrache; Hetzkampagne IV 1 (34)
**verb** [vɜːb] Verb III
**verse** [vɜːs] Vers, Strophe II
**version** [ˈvɜːʃn] Version IV 2 (46)
**very** [ˈveri] sehr I
**vet** [vet] Tierarzt/Tierärztin III
**vibe** [vaɪb] (infml) Ausstrahlung, Atmosphäre IV 1 (17)
**vibration** [vaɪˈbreɪʃn] Vibration III
**Victorian** [vɪkˈtɔːriən] viktorianisch; Viktorianer/in IV 1 (8/9)
**video** [ˈvɪdiəʊ] Video I
**video camera** [ˈvɪdiəʊ kæmərə] Videokamera I
**view** [vjuː]:
1. Ansicht, Meinung III **in my view** meiner Meinung nach III
2. **view (of)** Aussicht, Blick (auf) I

**vigorous** [ˈvɪɡərəs] energisch, kräftig III
**village** [ˈvɪlɪdʒ] Dorf I
**violence** [ˈvaɪələns] Gewalt, Gewalttätigkeit IV 3 (75)
**violent** [ˈvaɪələnt] gewalttätig; gewaltsam IV 3 (75)
**visa** [ˈviːzə] Visum III
°**visible** [ˈvɪzəbl] sichtbar
**visit** [ˈvɪzɪt]:
1. Besuch I
2. besuchen I

**visitor** [ˈvɪzɪtə] Besucher/in, Gast I
°**visual** [ˈvɪʒʊəl] visuell; optisch

# English – German

**vocabulary** [vəˈkæbjələri] Vokabelverzeichnis, Wörterverzeichnis I
**voice** [vɔɪs] Stimme I **in a loud voice** mit lauter Stimme II **in a soft voice** sanft; mit leiser Stimme II
**volunteer** [ˌvɒlənˈtɪə]:
1. freiwillig/ehrenamtlich arbeiten *(unbezahlt)* IV 1 (21)
2. Freiwillige(r), Ehrenamtliche(r) IV 1 (21) **volunteer work** freiwillige/ehrenamtliche Arbeit IV 1 (21)
**vote** [vəʊt]:
1. Stimme *(bei Wahlen)* IV 2 (65) **get the vote** das Stimmrecht erhalten IV 2 (65)
2. wählen, zur Wahl gehen; (ab)stimmen IV 2 (65) **vote for/against sb./sth.** für/gegen jn./etwas stimmen IV 2 (65)
**vowel** [ˈvaʊəl] Vokal, Selbstlaut I

# W

**wagon** [ˈwægən] Planwagen, (Pferde-)Fuhrwerk IV 3 (95)
**wagon train** [ˈwægən treɪn] Planwagenkolonne IV 3 (95)
**waist** [weɪst] Taille II
**wait (for)** [weɪt] warten (auf) I **Wait a minute.** Warte einen Moment. / Moment mal. I **I can't wait to see …** Ich kann es kaum erwarten, … zu sehen. II
**wake up** [ˌweɪk ˈʌp], **woke, woken** aufwachen I **wake sb. up** jn. (auf)wecken II
**walk** [wɔːk]:
1. Spaziergang I **go for a walk** einen Spaziergang machen, spazieren gehen I **take a walk** *(bes. AE)* spazieren gehen, einen Spaziergang machen I
2. (zu Fuß) gehen I **walk sb. somewhere** jn. irgendwohin begleiten/führen *(zu Fuß)* IV 3 (74) **walk the dog** mit dem Hund rausgehen, den Hund ausführen III
**walkie-talkie** [ˌwɔːki ˈtɔːki] Walkie-Talkie IV 1 (19)
**wall** [wɔːl] Mauer; Wand II
°**walrus** [ˈwɔːlrəs] Walross
**wander** [ˈwɒndə] herumlaufen; herumirren II
**want** [wɒnt]: **want sth.** etwas (haben) wollen I **want to do sth.** etwas tun wollen I **I want you to …** Ich möchte, dass du … II
**war** [wɔː] Krieg IV 1 (17) **First/Second World War** *or* **World War I / World War II** erster/zweiter Weltkrieg IV 1 (17) **go to war** in den Krieg ziehen IV 3 (96)
**warm** [wɔːm] warm I
°**warmth** [wɔːmθ] Wärme; Herzlichkeit
**warning** [ˈwɔːnɪŋ] Warnung III
°**warrior** [ˈwɒriə] Krieger/in
**was** [wɒz], [wəz] *siehe* **be**

**wash** [wɒʃ] waschen; wischen III **wash the dishes** *(pl)* das Geschirr abwaschen, spülen II
**waste** [weɪst] Müll, Abfall IV 2 (58)
**waste product** [ˈweɪst prɒdʌkt] Abfallprodukt IV 2 (58)
**watch** [wɒtʃ] Armbanduhr I
**watch (sth.)** [wɒtʃ] sich etwas anschauen; beobachten I **Watch out!** Pass auf! / Vorsicht! I **watch TV** fernsehen I
**watcher** [ˈwɒtʃə] Beobachter/in I
**water** [ˈwɔːtə] Wasser I
**water fountain** [ˈwɔːtə faʊntən] Trinkbrunnen IV 3 (68)
**waterfall** [ˈwɔːtəfɔːl] Wasserfall II
**wave** [weɪv] Welle II
**wave (at sb.)** [weɪv] (jm. zu)winken III
**way** [weɪ]:
1. Weg I **ask sb. the way** jn. nach dem Weg fragen II **on the way to …** auf dem Weg zu/nach … I **tell sb. the way (to …)** jm. den Weg (nach …) beschreiben II **that way** dort entlang; in die Richtung II **by the way** übrigens III
2. Art und Weise III **in some/many ways** in mancher/vielerlei Hinsicht III **in this way** auf diese Weise III **No way!** Auf keinen Fall! / Kommt nicht in Frage! II
3. **way before …** lange/weit vor … IV 3 (86) **he's way too good/clever** *(bes. AE)* er ist viel zu gut/clever III
**way of life** [ˌweɪ əv ˈlaɪf] Lebensweise IV 3 (90)
**we** [wiː] wir I
**weak** [wiːk] schwach IV (28)
°**wealth** [welθ] Wohlstand, Reichtum
**weapon** [ˈwepən] Waffe IV 2 (64)
**wear** [weə], **wore, worn** tragen *(Kleidung)* I
°**weary** [ˈwɪəri] müde, erschöpft, matt
**weather** [ˈweðə] Wetter II
**website** [ˈwebsaɪt] Website I
**wedding** [ˈwedɪŋ] Hochzeit, Trauung II
**Wednesday** [ˈwenzdeɪ], [ˈwenzdi] Mittwoch I
**week** [wiːk] Woche I
**weekend** [ˌwiːkˈend] Wochenende I **at the weekend** am Wochenende I
**weekly** [ˈwiːkli] wöchentlich III
**weigh** [weɪ] wiegen I
**weird** [wɪəd] seltsam, komisch III
**weirdo** [ˈwɪədəʊ] *(infml)* Spinner/in III
**welcome** [ˈwelkəm]:
1. **Welcome to Plymouth.** Willkommen in Plymouth. I
2. **You're welcome.** Bitte, gern geschehen. / Nichts zu danken. II
3. **welcome sb. (to)** jn. begrüßen (in), jn. willkommen heißen (in) IV 3 (75)
**welcoming** [ˈwelkəmɪŋ] (gast)freundlich IV 3 (75)
°**welfare** [ˈwelfeə] Wohl, Wohlergehen
**Well, …** [wel] Nun, … / Also, … / Na ja, … I

**well** [wel]:
1. gut *(Adv.)* II **well known** bekannt II **go well** gut laufen, gut gehen II
2. *(gesundheitlich)* gut, gesund I **I don't feel well.** Mir geht's nicht gut. / Ich fühle mich nicht gut. II
3. **as well** auch, ebenso III
**well** [wel] Quelle, Brunnen IV 1 (16)
**Welsh** [welʃ] Walisisch; walisisch I
**went** [went] *siehe* **go**
**were** [wɜː] *siehe* **be**
**west** [west] Westen; nach Westen; westlich III
**westbound** [ˈwestbaʊnd] Richtung Westen III
**western** [ˈwestən] westlich, West- III
°**westward(s)** [ˈwestwəd] westwärts, nach/gen Westen
**wet** [wet] nass I **soaking wet** völlig durchnässt, klitschnass IV 3 (95)
**whale** [weɪl] Wal I
**what?** [wɒt] was? I **So what?** Na und? IV 3 (68) **What about …?** Wie wäre es mit …? I **What about you?** Und du? / Und was ist mit dir? Und ihr? / Und was ist mit euch? I **What colour …?** Welche Farbe …? I **What is the story about?** Wovon handelt die Geschichte? / Worum geht es in der Geschichte? I **What page are we on?** Auf welcher Seite sind wir? I **What programmes …?** Welche Programme …? / Welche Art von Programmen …? I **What size tea would you like?** Wie groß soll der/dein Tee sein? II **What time is it?** Wie spät ist es? I **What was it like?** Wie war es? II **What's for homework?** Was haben wir als Hausaufgabe auf? I **What's for lunch?** Was gibt es zum Mittagessen? I **What's up?** Was gibt's? / Was ist los? II **What's your name?** Wie heißt du? / Wie heißt ihr? I
**whatever** [ˌwɒtˈevə] was (auch) immer III
**wheat** [wiːt] Weizen IV 1 (16)
**wheel** [wiːl] Rad II; *(kurz für:* **steering wheel)** Lenkrad II **big wheel** Riesenrad I
**when** [wen]:
1. als *(zeitlich)* I
2. wenn I
3. wann I **When's your birthday?** Wann hast du Geburtstag? I
**whenever** [ˌwenˈevə] wann (auch) immer IV 3 (68)
**where** [weə] wo / wohin I **Where are you from?** Woher kommst du? I
**whether** [ˈweðə] ob III
**which** [wɪtʃ]:
1. welche(r, s)? *(Fragewort)* I
2. der/die/das *(Relativpronomen)* I
3. **Which one?** Welche(r, s)? I
**while** [waɪl]:
1. während II

# Dictionary

**2. a while** eine Weile, einige Zeit III
**for a while** eine Weile, eine Zeit lang III
**whine** [waɪn] winseln; jammern IV 2 (58)
**whisper** ['wɪspə] flüstern II
**whistle** ['wɪsl]:
1. pfeifen II
2. (Triller-)Pfeife III
**white** [waɪt] weiß I
**whitewater** ['waɪtwɔːtə] Wildwasser III
**whitewater rafting** [ˌwaɪtwɔːtə 'rɑːftɪŋ] Wildwasserfahren *(im Schlauchboot)* III
**who** [huː]:
1. wer *(Fragewort)* I **Who likes Abby?** Wer mag Abby? I
2. wen; wem *(Fragewort)* II **Who does Abby like?** Wen mag Abby? II **Who did you tell?** Wem hast es erzählt? II
3. der, die, das; die *(Relativpronomen)* II
**whole** [həʊl] ganze(r, s), gesamte(r, s) I
**whose** [huːz]:
1. wessen I
2. deren, dessen *(Relativpronomen)* II **cities whose names ...** Städte, deren Namen ... II
**why** [waɪ] warum I **that's why** deshalb, darum I
°**wicket** ['wɪkɪt] Wicket *(Tor beim Cricket)*
**wide** [waɪd] breit II
°**widely** ['waɪdli] weit (verbreitet), in großem Umfang
**wife** [waɪf], *pl* **wives** Ehefrau III
**wild** [waɪld] wild I
°**wilderness** ['wɪldənəs] Wildnis
**wildlife** ['waɪldlaɪf] Tiere *(in freier Wildbahn)*, Tierwelt IV 2 (58)
**will** [wɪl]: **we'll miss the girls** (= we will miss the girls) wir werden die Mädchen verpassen II
**win** [wɪn], **won, won** gewinnen I
**wind** [wɪnd] Wind II
**windmill** ['wɪndmɪl] Windmühle IV 1 (16)
**window** ['wɪndəʊ] Fenster I
**windy** ['wɪndi] windig II
**wing** [wɪŋ] Flügel III
**winner** ['wɪnə] Gewinner/in, Sieger/in I
**winter** ['wɪntə] Winter I
**wireless** ['waɪələs] drahtlos, Funk- IV 1 (10)
**wise** [waɪz] weise II
**wish** [wɪʃ]:
1. wünschen II **I wish it was warmer.** Ich wünschte, es wäre wärmer. II
2. Wunsch I **make a wish** sich etwas wünschen I
**with** [wɪð]:
1. mit I
2. bei I
**without** [wɪ'ðaʊt] ohne I
**witness** ['wɪtnəs]:
1. Zeuge/Zeugin IV 2 (46)
2. **witness sth.** etwas (mit)erleben, Zeuge/Zeugin werden von etwas IV 2 (46)
**wives** [waɪvz] *plural of* **wife**
**wizard** ['wɪzəd] Zauberer IV 2 (61)
**woke** [wəʊk] *siehe* **wake (up)**

**woken** ['wəʊkən] *siehe* **wake (up)**
°**wolf** [wʊlf], *pl* **wolves** Wolf
**wolverine** ['wʊlvəriːn] Bärenmarder IV 2 (62)
°**wolves** [wʊlvz] *plural of* **wolf**
**woman** ['wʊmən], *pl* **women** Frau I
**women** ['wɪmɪn] *plural of* **woman**
**won** [wʌn] *siehe* **win**
**wonder** ['wʌndə]:
1. Wunder *(etwas Außergewöhnliches/Erstaunliches)* IV 3 (81)
2. sich fragen, gern wissen wollen III
**wonderful** ['wʌndəfəl] wunderbar II
**wood** [wʊd] Holz II
**wooden** ['wʊdn] hölzern; Holz- III
°**woodland** ['wʊdlənd] Waldgebiet
**word** [wɜːd] Wort I **May I have a word with you?** Kann ich dich/Sie kurz sprechen? I
**word order** [ˌwɜːd ˈɔːdə] Wortstellung I
**wordbank** ['wɜːdbæŋk] „Wortspeicher" I
°**wordle** [ˈwɜːdl] Anwendung, die beliebige Wörter/Texte zu Wortwolken umformt
°**wore** [wɔː] *siehe* **wear**
**work** [wɜːk]:
1. arbeiten I °**work sth. out** etwas herausfinden, etwas herausarbeiten
2. funktionieren II
3. Arbeit I
**work of art** [ˌwɜːk əv ˈɑːt] Kunstwerk III
**workbook** ['wɜːkbʊk] Arbeitsheft I
**worker** ['wɜːkə] Arbeiter/in II
**worksheet** ['wɜːkʃiːt] Arbeitsblatt II
**workshop** ['wɜːkʃɒp]:
1. Workshop, Lehrgang II
2. Werkstatt III
**world** [wɜːld] Welt I **in the world** auf der Welt I
**worn** [wɔːn] *siehe* **wear**
**worried** ['wʌrid] besorgt, beunruhigt I
**worry** ['wʌri]:
1. **worry (about)** sich Sorgen machen (wegen, um) II
2. **No worries.** *(infml)* Kein Problem! / Gern geschehen! III
**worse** [wɜːs] schlechter II
**worst** [wɜːst]: **the worst** der/die/das schlechteste ...; die schlechtesten ... II
**worth** [wɜːθ] wert III
**would** [wʊd]:
1. **I'd like ...** (= I would like ...) Ich hätte gern ... / Ich möchte ... I **it would be ...** es wäre ... II **What would you like?** Was hättest du gern?/ Was möchtest du? I **What would you like to eat?** Was möchtest du essen? I **You would have liked him.** Du hättest ihn gemocht. III
°**2. they would steal ...** sie stahlen (früher) immer/häufig ...
**write** [raɪt], **wrote, written** schreiben I
**write sth. down** etwas aufschreiben II
**writer** ['raɪtə] Schreiber/in; Schriftsteller/in III

**written** ['rɪtn] *siehe* **write**
**wrong** [rɒŋ] falsch, verkehrt I **go wrong** schiefgehen III **No, that's wrong.** Nein, das ist falsch. / Nein, das stimmt nicht. I **sb. is wrong** jemand irrt sich; jemand hat Unrecht II **What's wrong with Justin/you?** Was fehlt Justin/dir? / Was ist los mit Justin/dir? II
**wrote** [rəʊt] *siehe* **write**

## Y

**yacht** [jɒt] Jacht III
**year** [jɪə]:
1. Jahr I **this year's musical** das diesjährige Musical II
2. Jahrgang(sstufe) I
**yearly** ['jɪəli] jährlich III
**yell** [jel] schreien II
**yellow** ['jeləʊ] gelb I
**yes** [jes] ja I
**yesterday** ['jestədeɪ], ['jestədi] gestern I
**yet** [jet]:
1. (und) doch, dennoch IV 2 (47)
2. **Have you ... yet?** Hast du schon ...? II
3. **not ... yet** noch nicht I
**yoga** ['jəʊgə] Yoga I
**yoghurt** ['jɒgət] Joghurt I
**you** [juː]:
1. du; Sie; ihr I
2. dir; dich; euch; Ihnen I
3. man III
**young** [jʌŋ] jung I
**your** [jɔː], [jə] dein/e; euer/eure; Ihr/e I
**yours** [jɔːz] deiner, deine, deins; eurer, eure, eures II **Yours, Finn** Dein/Euer Finn *(Briefschluss)* IV 1 (21)
**yourself** [jɔːˈself], [jəˈself] dich/dir; (Sie) sich selbst/selber III
**yourselves** [jɔːˈselvz], [jəˈselvz] ihr/euch; (Sie) sich selbst/selber III
**youth** [juːθ] Jugend; Jugend- III
**youth hostel** ['juːθ hɒstl] Jugendherberge III
**yummy** ['jʌmi] *(infml)* lecker I

## Z

**zone** [zəʊn] Zone II **pedestrian zone** Fußgängerzone II
**zoo** [zuː] Zoo I

# Dictionary

## German – English

Das **German – English Dictionary** enthält den **Lernwortschatz** von **Access Bayern**, Bände **5 – 8**.
Es kann dir eine erste Hilfe sein, wenn du vergessen hast, wie etwas auf Englisch heißt.

Wenn du wissen möchtest, wo das entsprechende englische Wort zum ersten Mal in **Access Bayern** vorkommt, dann kannst du im **English – German Dictionary** (194 – 228) nachschlagen.

Im **German – English Dictionary** werden folgende **Abkürzungen** verwendet:

*pl* = plural • *sth.* = something • *sb.* = somebody • *jn.* = jemanden • *jm.* = jemandem
*infml* = informal (umgangssprachlich) • *fml* = formal (formell, förmlich)
*AE* = American English • *BE* = British English

## A

**ab: Ab mit euch jetzt!** Off you go now **auf und ab** up and down
**abbauen** *(z.B. Zaun, Zelt)* take down [ˌteɪk ˈdaʊn] **etwas abbauen** *(Bodenschätze)* mine sth. [maɪn]
**abbestellen** unsubscribe (from) [ˌʌnsəbˈskraɪb]
**abbiegen: (nach) links/rechts abbiegen** turn left/right
**Abbild** image [ˈɪmɪdʒ]
**Abbildung** illustration [ˌɪləˈstreɪʃn]
**abdecken** cover up [ˌkʌvərˈʌp]; *(Thema; Fragen)* cover [ˈkʌvə]
**Abend** evening [ˈiːvnɪŋ] **am Abend** in the evening **heute Abend** tonight [təˈnaɪt] **zu Abend essen** have dinner
**Abendbrot, -essen** dinner [ˈdɪnə]
**abends** in the evening [ˈiːvnɪŋ]
**Abenteuer** adventure [ədˈventʃə]
**aber** but [bʌt], [bət]
**abfahren** leave [liːv]
**Abfall** rubbish [ˈrʌbɪʃ] *(bes. BE)*; waste [weɪst]; garbage *(AE)* [ˈgɑːbɪdʒ]
**Abfalleimer** litter bin [ˈlɪtə bɪn]
**Abfallprodukt** waste product [ˈweɪst prɒdʌkt]
**Abfertigungsschalter** check-in desk [ˈtʃek ɪn desk]
**abfeuern** fire [faɪə]
**Abflugschalter** check-in desk [ˈtʃek ɪn desk]
**abgeben: etwas abgeben** *(einreichen)* hand sth. in
**Abgeordnete(r)** representative [ˌreprɪˈzentətɪv]
**abhalten** *(Veranstaltung)* hold [həʊld]
**abhängen: abhängen von** depend on [dɪˈpend]; *(rumhängen)* hang out *(infml)* [ˌhæŋˈaʊt]
**abholen: jn. abholen** pick sb. up [ˌpɪkˈʌp]
**Abkommen** treaty [ˈtriːti]
**Abkürzung** abbreviation [əˌbriːviˈeɪʃn]
**ablehnen** refuse **es ablehnen, etwas zu tun** refuse to do sth.
**Abneigung: Vorlieben und Abneigungen** likes and dislikes *(pl)* [ˌlaɪks ən ˈdɪslaɪks]
**abonnieren** subscribe to [səbˈskraɪb]
**abräumen** clear [klɪə]

**abreißen: etwas abreißen** tear sth. down [ˌteə ˈdaʊn]
**Abruf: auf Abruf** *(nach Bedarf)* on demand [dɪˈmɑːnd]
**Absatz** *(in einem Text)* paragraph [ˈpærəgrɑːf]; *(Umsatz, Verkäufe)* sales *(pl)* [seɪlz]
**abschießen** fire [faɪə]
**abschließen** *(z.B. Tür)* lock [lɒk]
**Abschluss** *(Ende)* ending [ˈendɪŋ]
**Abschnitt** *(Teilstück)* section [ˈsekʃn]
**abschreiben** copy [ˈkɒpi]
**absetzen: etwas absetzen** *(Hut, Helm)* take sth. off [ˌteɪk ˈɒf]
**Absicht** purpose [ˈpɜːpəs] **mit Absicht** on purpose
**absichtlich** intentional [ɪnˈtenʃənl]; on purpose [ɒn ˈpɜːpəs]
**absolut** absolute [ˈæbsəluːt]; *(adv)* absolutely [ˈæbsəluːtli]
**abspielen** *(CD, DVD)* play [pleɪ] **sich abspielen** *(Geschichte, Handlung)* take place [teɪk ˈpleɪs]
**Absprache** agreement [əˈgriːmənt]
**Abstammung** ancestry [ˈænsestri]; descent [dɪˈsent]
**Abstand halten (zu/von)** keep your distance (from) [ˌkiːp jə ˈdɪstəns]
**abstimmen** *(bei Wahlen)* vote [vəʊt]
**abstürzen** *(Flugzeug; Computer)* crash [kræʃ]
**absuchen: einen Text schnell nach bestimmten Wörtern/Informationen absuchen** scan a text [skæn] **etwas (nach etwas) absuchen** scan sth. (for sth.)
**absurd** absurd [əbˈsɜːd]
**abwaschen: das Geschirr abwaschen** wash the dishes *(pl)*
**Account** account [əˈkaʊnt]
**acht** eight [eɪt]
**achten** *(respektieren)* respect [rɪˈspekt] **achten auf** mind [maɪnd] **darauf achten, dass …** *(dafür sorgen, dass …)* make sure that …
**Achterbahn** roller coaster [ˈrəʊlə kəʊstə]
**Acker** field [fiːld]
**Action** action [ˈækʃn]
**addieren (zu)** add (to) [æd]
**Adjektiv** adjective [ˈædʒɪktɪv]
**Adler** eagle [ˈiːgl]
**adlig** noble [ˈnəʊbl]
**adoptiert, Adoptiv-** adopted [əˈdɒptɪd]

**Adresse** address [əˈdres]
**Adverb** adverb [ˈædvɜːb]
**Affe** monkey [ˈmʌŋki]
**Aha!** *(Verstehe.)* I see.
**ähnlich: (etwas/jm.) ähnlich** similar (to sth./sb.) [ˈsɪmələ]
**Ähnlichkeit** similarity [ˌsɪməˈlærəti]
**Ahnung: Keine Ahnung.** No idea. *(infml)* [ˌnəʊ aɪˈdɪə]
**ahnungslos** clueless [ˈkluːləs]
**Ahorn** maple [ˈmeɪpl]
**Ahornsirup** maple syrup [ˌmeɪpl ˈsɪrəp]
**Akku** battery [ˈbætəri]
**Akt** *(Tat)* act [ækt]
**aktiv** active [ˈæktɪv]
**Aktivist/in** activist [ˈæktɪvɪst]
**Aktivität** activity [ækˈtɪvəti]
**aktualisieren: etwas aktualisieren** update sth. [ˌʌpˈdeɪt]
**aktuell** recent [ˈriːsnt]
**Akustik** acoustics *(pl)* [əˈkuːstɪks]
**Akzent** accent [ˈæksənt]
**albern** silly [ˈsɪli]
**Album** album [ˈælbəm]
**alle** all [ɔːl]; *(jeder)* everybody [ˈevribɒdi]; everyone [ˈevriwʌn]
**aller Zeiten** of all time
**Allee** avenue [ˈævənjuː]
**allein** alone [əˈləʊn]; on my/your/their/… own **ganz allein** all alone
**alleinstehend** single [ˈsɪŋgl]
**alles** everything [ˈevriθɪŋ]; all [ɔːl] **alles in allem** all in all; altogether [ˌɔːltəˈgeðə] **Alles Liebe, …** *(Briefschluss)* Love, … [lʌv] **vor allem** especially [ɪˈspeʃli]
**allgemein** general [ˈdʒenrəl]; *(adv)* generally [ˈdʒenrəli] **im Allgemeinen** in general
**Alligator** alligator [ˈælɪgeɪtə]
**Alltags-** everyday [ˈevrideɪ]
**alphabetisches Wörterverzeichnis** dictionary [ˈdɪkʃənri]
**als** 1. *(zeitlich)* when [wen]; by the time; *(während)* as [æz] **als Erstes** first [fɜːst] **als Nächstes** next [nekst] 2. **als Kind** as a child 3. **größer als** bigger than [ðæn], [ðən] **schöner als** more beautiful than 4. **als ob** as if; like *(infml)* **so tun, als ob** pretend [prɪˈtend] 5. **sowohl … als auch …** both … and … [bəʊθ]

two hundred and twenty-nine 229

# Dictionary

**also** (deshalb, daher) so [səʊ]; **Also, …** Well, … [wel]
**alt** old [əʊld]
**Alter** age [eɪdʒ]
**Älteste(r)** (z.B. eines Stammes) elder [ˈeldə]
**am** 1. (in Ortsangaben) at [æt], [ət] **am Meer** by the sea [baɪ] **am Telefon** on the phone
2. (in Zeitangaben) **am Abend** in the evening [ˈiːvnɪŋ] **am Anfang** at first [ət ˈfɜːst] **am Montag/Dienstag/…** on Monday/Tuesday/… **am Morgen/Vormittag** in the morning **am Nachmittag** in the afternoon [ˌɑːftəˈnuːn] **am Samstagnachmittag** on Saturday afternoon **am Wochenende** at the weekend [ˌwiːkˈend]
3. **am schönsten** (the) most beautiful [məʊst] **am weitesten** furthest [ˈfɜːðɪst]
**Ameise** ant [ænt]
**amerikanische/r Ureinwohner/in** Native American [ˌneɪtɪv əˈmerɪkən]
**Ampel** traffic light(s) [ˈtræfɪk laɪt]
**Amphitheater** amphitheatre [ˈæmfɪθɪətə]
**amtlich, Amts-** official [əˈfɪʃl]
**Amtssprache** official language [əˌfɪʃl ˈlæŋgwɪdʒ]
**amüsieren: sich amüsieren** enjoy yourself [ɪnˈdʒɔɪ]; have fun [fʌn]
**an** 1. (in Ortsangaben) at [æt], [ət]
2. **an sein** (eingeschaltet) be on
**anbauen** (anpflanzen) grow [grəʊ]
**anbieten** offer [ˈɒfə]
**Anblick** sight [saɪt]
**andauern** last (for) [lɑːst]; (im Gang sein) go on
**Andenken** souvenir [ˌsuːvəˈnɪə]
**andere(r, s)** other [ˈʌðə] **alle anderen** everyone else [els] **ein(e) andere(r, s)** another [əˈnʌðə] **einer nach dem anderen** one by one
**Andererseits …** On the other hand …
**ändern; sich ändern** change [tʃeɪndʒ]
**anders** (verschieden) different [ˈdɪfrənt] **anders als** unlike [ˌʌnˈlaɪk] **es sich anders überlegen** change one's mind [maɪnd]
**anderthalb Stunden** an hour and a half
**Anfang** beginning [bɪˈgɪnɪŋ] **am Anfang** at first [ət ˈfɜːst] **Er ist Anfang dreißig.** He's in his early thirties. [ˈɜːli]
**anfangen** begin [bɪˈgɪn]; start [stɑːt]
**Anfänger/in** beginner [bɪˈgɪnə]
**anfangs** at first [ət ˈfɜːst]
**anfassen** touch [tʌtʃ]
**Anforderung** demand [dɪˈmɑːnd]
**Anfrage** request [rɪˈkwest]
**anfühlen: sich anfühlen** feel [fiːl]
**angeben** (behaupten) claim [kleɪm]; (prahlen) show off [ʃəʊ ˈɒf]
**angehängt: an etwas angehängt sein** be attached to sth. [əˈtætʃt]

**Angelschnur** line [laɪn]
**angemalt** painted [ˈpeɪntɪd]
**angesagt** (modisch) trendy [ˈtrendi]
**angesehen werden als …** be thought of as … [θɔːt]
**Angesicht: von Angesicht zu Angesicht** face to face [ˌfeɪs tə ˈfeɪs]
**angewiesen sein auf** depend on [dɪˈpend]
**Angewohnheit** habit [ˈhæbɪt]
**angreifen** attack [əˈtæk]
**Angriff** attack [əˈtæk]
**Angst (vor)** fear (of) [fɪə] **Angst haben (vor)** be afraid (of) [əˈfreɪd]; be frightened (of) [ˈfraɪtnd] **jm. Angst machen** scare sb. [skeə]
**ängstlich** (erschrocken) in fright [fraɪt]
**anhalten** stop [stɒp]
**Anhaltspunkt** (Lösungshinweis) clue [kluː]
**Anhänger** (Fan) fan [fæn]
**anheben** lift [lɪft]
**anhören: sich etwas anhören** listen to sth. [ˈlɪsn]; (probeweise) check sth. out (infml) [ˌtʃek ˈaʊt] **sich gut anhören** (gut klingen) sound good [saʊnd]
**ankommen** arrive [əˈraɪv]
**Ankündigung** (Proklamation) proclamation [ˌprɒkləˈmeɪʃn]
**Ankunft** arrival [əˈraɪvl]
**anlächeln: jn. anlächeln** smile at sb. [smaɪl]
**anlocken** attract [əˈtrækt]
**anmalen** paint [peɪnt]
**anmelden: sich anmelden (für)** sign up (for) [ˌsaɪn ˈʌp]
**annehmen: Ich nehme an, …** I guess … [ges]
**anonym** anonymous [əˈnɒnɪməs]
**anordnen** order [ˈɔːdə]; (in eine bestimmte Ordnung bringen) arrange [əˈreɪndʒ]
**anpflanzen** grow [grəʊ]
**anprobieren** try on [ˌtraɪ ˈɒn]
**anreden: jn. anreden** address sb. [əˈdres]
**Anruf** (phone) call [ˈfəʊn kɔːl]
**anrufen** call [kɔːl]; phone [fəʊn]
**Anrufer/in** caller [ˈkɔːlə]
**Ansage** announcement [əˈnaʊnsmənt]
**anschauen: etwas anschauen** look at sth. [lʊk] **sich etwas anschauen** watch sth. [wɒtʃ]; (probeweise) check sth. out (infml) [ˌtʃek ˈaʊt]
**anschaulich** graphic [ˈgræfɪk]
**anschließen: sich einem Klub anschließen** join a club [dʒɔɪn]
**Anschrift** address [əˈdres]
**ansehen: etwas ansehen** look at sth. [lʊk]; (beobachten) watch sth. [wɒtʃ]
**Ansicht** view [vjuː]
**ansiedeln: sich ansiedeln** settle [ˈsetl]
**Anspitzer** sharpener [ˈʃɑːpnə]
**ansprechen** (Thema; Fragen) cover [ˈkʌvə] **jn. ansprechen** address sb. [əˈdres]

**anstarren: jn./etwas anstarren** stare at sb./sth. [steə]
**anstatt** rather than [ˈrɑːðə ðən]
**anstelle von** instead of [ɪnˈsted ˌəv]
**anstellen: jn. anstellen** (jm. Arbeit geben) employ sb. [ɪmˈplɔɪ] **sich anstellen** (Schlange stehen) queue (BE) [kjuː]; be/stand/wait in line (AE)
**Anstieg** climb [klaɪm]
**anstößig** offensive [əˈfensɪv]
**anstreichen** paint [peɪnt]
**anstrengen: sich anstrengen** try hard [ˌtraɪ ˈhɑːd]
**antreiben** drive [draɪv]
**antreten (gegen)** (in Wettbewerben) compete (with) [kəmˈpiːt]
**Antwort** answer [ˈɑːnsə]
**antworten** answer [ˈɑːnsə] **antworten (auf)** reply (to) [rɪˈplaɪ]
**Anwohner/in** resident [ˈrezɪdənt]
**Anzahl** number [ˈnʌmbə]
**Anzeige** (Inserat) advertisement (kurz auch: ad, advert) [ədˈvɜːtɪsmənt], [æd], [ˈædvɜːt]
**anziehen** attract [əˈtrækt] **etwas anziehen** (Kleidung) put sth. on [ˌpʊt ˈɒn]
**sich anziehen** (Kleidung anziehen) dress; get dressed **sich schick anziehen** dress up [ˌdres ˈʌp]
**Anziehungspunkt** attraction [əˈtrækʃn]
**anzünden** light [laɪt]
**Apfelsine** orange [ˈɒrɪndʒ]
**Apostroph** apostrophe [əˈpɒstrəfi]
**Apotheke** chemist [ˈkemɪst] **in der Apotheke** at the chemist's
**Apotheker/in** chemist [ˈkemɪst] **beim Apotheker** at the chemist's
**App** app [æp]
**Apparat: Bleib / Bleiben Sie am Apparat.** (am Telefon) Hold on (a minute). [ˌhəʊld ˈɒn]
**April** April [ˈeɪprəl]
**Aquarium, Aquariumhaus** aquarium [əˈkweəriəm]
**Ära** era [ˈɪərə]
**Arbeit** work [wɜːk]
**arbeiten** work [wɜːk]
**Arbeiter/in** worker [ˈwɜːkə]
**Arbeitsauftrag** (in der Schule oder daheim zu erledigen) assignment (AE) [əˈsaɪnmənt]
**Arbeitsblatt** worksheet [ˈwɜːkʃiːt]
**Arbeitsheft** workbook [ˈwɜːkbʊk]
**Arbeitsstelle** job [dʒɒb]
**Architekt/in** architect [ˈɑːkɪtekt]
**Archiv** archive [ˈɑːkaɪv]
**Ärger kriegen** be in trouble [ˈtrʌbl]; get into trouble
**Argument** argument [ˈɑːgjumənt]
**Arktis; arktisch** Arctic [ˈɑːktɪk]
**Arm** arm [ɑːm] **jn. auf den Arm nehmen** (veräppeln) pull sb.'s leg (infml) [pʊl]
**arm** poor [pɔː], [pʊə]
**Armbanduhr** watch [wɒtʃ]

# German – English

**Armee** army [ˈɑːmi]
**Armut** poverty [ˈpɒvəti]
**Aroma** aroma [əˈrəʊmə]
**aromatisieren: etwas aromatisieren mit** flavour sth. with [ˈfleɪvə]
**Art** (Variante) variety [vəˈraɪəti] **eine Art (von)** a kind of [kaɪnd]; a type of [taɪp] **Art und Weise** way [weɪ]
**Artikel** article [ˈɑːtɪkl]
**Arznei** medicine [ˈmedsn], [ˈmedɪsn]
**Arzt/Ärztin** doctor [ˈdɒktə]
**Asche** ash [æʃ]; (sterbliche Überreste) ashes (pl) [ˈæʃɪz]
**Astronaut/in** astronaut [ˈæstrənɔːt]
**Atem** breath [breθ]
**Atemzug** breath [breθ]
**Atlantik: der Atlantik, der Atlantische Ozean** the Atlantic (Ocean) [ətˈlæntɪk]
**atmen** breathe [briːð]
**Atmosphäre** atmosphere [ˈætməsfɪə]; vibe (infml) [vaɪb]
**Atom-** nuclear [ˈnjuːkliə]
**Atomenergie** nuclear power [ˌnjuːkliə ˈpaʊə]
**Attraktion** attraction [əˈtrækʃn]
**attraktiv** handsome [ˈhænsəm]
**auch** also [ˈɔːlsəʊ]; too [tuː]; as well [əz ˈwel] **auch nicht** not … either [ˈaɪðə], [ˈiːðə] **Ich auch. Me too. sowohl … als auch …** both … and … [bəʊθ]
**Audio-** audio [ˈɔːdiəʊ]
**auf** on [ɒn] **auf das Boot (hinauf)** onto the boat [ˈɒntʊ] **auf dem Bild** in the picture **auf dem Dachboden** in the attic **auf dem Foto** in the photo **auf dem Weg zu/nach …** on the way to … [weɪ] **auf den Bahnhof/auf Mr Bell zu** towards the station/towards Mr Bell [təˈwɔːdz] **auf der Erde** on earth [ɜːθ] **auf der Landkarte / dem Stadtplan** on the map **auf der Welt** in the world **auf Deutsch/Englisch** in German/English **auf einmal** (plötzlich) suddenly [ˈsʌdnli]; (gleichzeitig) at a time **auf etwas zeigen/deuten** point to sth. [pɔɪnt] **auf jn. aufpassen** look after sb. **Auf keinen Fall!** No way! [nəʊ ˈweɪ] **auf und ab** up and down [ˌʌp ən ˈdaʊn] **Auf welcher Seite sind wir?** What page are we on? **Auf Wiedersehen.** Goodbye. [ˌɡʊdˈbaɪ]
**aufbauen** establish [ɪˈstæblɪʃ]; set up [ˌset ˈʌp]; (Zelt) put up [ˌpʊt ˈʌp]
**aufbewahren** keep [kiːp]; store [stɔː]
**aufbleiben: lang aufbleiben** stay up late
**aufbrechen** (sich auf den Weg machen) head out [ˌhed ˈaʊt]; set out [ˌset ˈaʊt]
**aufeinander** on top of each other
**auffordern: jn. auffordern, etwas (nicht) zu tun** tell sb. (not) to do sth. [tel] **jn. auffordern (zu)** (zu etwas einladen) invite sb. (to) [ɪnˈvaɪt]
**Aufführung** performance [pəˈfɔːməns]
**Aufgabe** job [dʒɒb]; task [tɑːsk]; exercise [ˈeksəsaɪz]; (in der Schule oder daheim zu erledigen) assignment (AE) [əˈsaɪnmənt]
**aufgeben** give up **etwas aufgeben** (Gepäck) check sth. in [ˌtʃek ˈɪn]
**aufgeregt** (gespannt) excited [ɪkˈsaɪtɪd]; (nervös) nervous [ˈnɜːvəs]
**aufheben: etwas aufheben** (vom Boden) pick sth. up [ˌpɪk ˈʌp]
**aufheitern: jn. aufheitern** cheer sb. up [ˌtʃɪər ˈʌp]
**aufhören** stop [stɒp] **Hör auf (damit)! Stop it!** (infml)
**aufladen** (Akku) charge [ˈtʃɑːdʒ]
**aufleuchten** light up [ˌlaɪt ˈʌp]
**auflisten** list [lɪst]
**aufmachen** open [ˈəʊpən] **sich nach … aufmachen** head to …/for … [hed]
**aufmerksam** (adv) carefully [ˈkeəfəli]
**aufmuntern: jn. aufmuntern** lift sb.'s spirits [ˈspɪrɪts]
**Aufnahme** (Foto) shot [ʃɒt]
**aufpassen: auf etwas aufpassen** (auf etwas achten; vorsichtig sein) mind sth. [maɪnd] **auf jn. aufpassen** look after sb.
**aufragen** (Berge, Säulen, Türme, …) rise up [ˌraɪz ˈʌp]
**aufrechterhalten** keep up [ˌkiːp ˈʌp]
**aufregend** exciting [ɪkˈsaɪtɪŋ]
**aufrufen: die Namen aufrufen** call out the names
**aufschauen** (hochsehen) look up [lʊkˈʌp]
**aufschließen** unlock [ʌnˈlɒk]
**aufschreiben: etwas aufschreiben** note sth. down [ˌnəʊt ˈdaʊn]; write sth. down
**aufsetzen: sich aufsetzen** sit up **etwas aufsetzen** (Hut, Helm) put sth. on [ˌpʊt ˈɒn]
**aufspringen (lassen)** bounce [baʊns]
**Aufstand** (Rebellion) rebellion [rɪˈbeljən]
**aufstehen** get up [ˌɡet ˈʌp]; stand up [ˌstænd ˈʌp]
**aufstellen** put up [ˌpʊt ˈʌp]; set up [ˌset ˈʌp]
**Aufstieg** (am Berg) climb [klaɪm]
**aufsuchen** (Arzt/Ärztin) see [siː]
**auftauchen** (erscheinen) appear [əˈpɪə], come up [ˌkʌm ˈʌp] **auftauchen aus …** emerge from … [ɪˈmɜːdʒ]
**aufteilen** split [splɪt]
**auftreten** (Künstler/in) perform [pəˈfɔːm]
**Auftritt** performance [pəˈfɔːməns]
**aufwachen** wake up [ˌweɪk ˈʌp]
**aufwachsen** grow up [ˌɡrəʊ ˈʌp]
**aufwecken: jn. aufwecken** wake sb. up [ˌweɪk ˈʌp]
**Aufzug** elevator (bes. AE) [ˈelɪveɪtə]; lift (BE) [lɪft]
**Auge** eye [aɪ]
**August** August [ˈɔːɡəst]
**Aula** school hall [ˌskuːl ˈhɔːl]
**aus** 1. from [frɒm], [frəm] **aus dem hinteren Teil des Busses** from the back of the bus **Ich bin aus … / Ich komme aus …** I'm from … **eine Band aus den 60er Jahren** a 1960s band
2. **aus … heraus** out of … [ˌaʊt əv]
4. **aus etwas** (gemacht) **sein** be made of sth. [meɪd]
5. **aus sein** (ausgeschaltet) be off [ɒf]
**ausatmen** breathe out [briːð ˈaʊt]
**Ausbildung** education [ˌedʒuˈkeɪʃn]
**ausblasen: etwas ausblasen** blow sth. out [bləʊ ˈaʊt]
**ausbreiten; sich ausbreiten** spread [spred]
**Ausbruch** (z.B. Krankheit, Regenschauer) outbreak [ˈaʊtbreɪk]
**Ausdauer** perseverance [ˌpɜːsɪˈvɪərəns]
**ausdenken: sich etwas ausdenken** (erfinden) make sth. up; (sich vorstellen) think of sth.
**Ausdruck** expression [ɪkˈspreʃn]; (Redewendung) phrase [freɪz] **zum Ausdruck bringen** express [ɪkˈspres]
**ausdrücken** express [ɪkˈspres]
**auseinander** apart [əˈpɑːt]
**Auseinandersetzung** argument [ˈɑːɡjumənt]; conflict [ˈkɒnflɪkt]; confrontation [ˌkɒnfrʌnˈteɪʃn]
**Ausfahrt** exit [ˈeksɪt]
**Ausflug** trip [trɪp]
**Ausfuhr** export [ˈekspɔːt]
**ausführen: den Hund ausführen** walk the dog
**Ausgang** exit [ˈeksɪt]; (einer Geschichte) outcome [ˈaʊtkʌm]
**ausgeben: Geld ausgeben (für)** spend money (on) [spend]
**Ausgehverbot: jm. Ausgehverbot erteilen** ground sb. [ɡraʊnd]
**ausgezeichnet** excellent [ˈeksələnt]
**auskennen: sich mit etwas auskennen** know about sth.
**auslachen: jn. auslachen** laugh at sb. [lɑːf]
**Ausland: im/ins Ausland** abroad [əˈbrɔːd]
**Ausländer/in** foreigner [ˈfɒrənə]
**ausländisch** foreign [ˈfɒrən]
**auslassen: etwas auslassen** (weglassen) leave sth. out
**Auslassungszeichen** apostrophe [əˈpɒstrəfi]
**ausleihen: sich etwas (aus)leihen** borrow sth. [ˈbɒrəʊ]
**ausliefern** deliver [dɪˈlɪvə]
**ausloggen: sich ausloggen** log out [ˌlɒɡ ˈaʊt]
**Ausnahme** exception [ɪkˈsepʃn]
**auspacken** unpack [ˌʌnˈpæk]
**auspressen** crush [krʌʃ]

# Dictionary

**ausprobieren** try [traɪ]  **etwas ausprobieren** (sich etwas probeweise anschauen/anhören) check sth. out (infml) [ˌtʃək_'aʊt]
**auspusten: etwas auspusten** blow sth. out [bləʊ]
**Ausritt** ride [raɪd]
**Ausrufezeichen** exclamation mark [ˌekskləˈmeɪʃn mɑːk]
**ausruhen: sich ausruhen** relax [rɪˈlæks];  rest [rest]
**Ausrüstung** equipment (no pl) [ɪˈkwɪpmənt];  gear [gɪə];  kit [kɪt]
**Aussage** (Aussagesatz) statement ['steɪtmənt];  (Botschaft) message ['mesɪdʒ]
**ausschalten: etwas ausschalten** turn sth. off [ˌtɜːn_ˈɒf]
**Ausschuss** (Rat) council ['kaʊnsl]
**aussehen: glücklich/wütend/… aussehen** look happy/angry/…  **gut aussehend** handsome ['hænsəm]
**Außen-** (im Freien) outdoor ['aʊtdɔː]
**Außenseite** the outside [ˌaʊtˈsaɪd]
**außer** (bis auf) except [ɪkˈsept]
**außerdem** besides [bɪˈsaɪdz]
**außergewöhnlich** (Adj) exceptional [ɪkˈsepʃənl]
**außerhalb (von)** outside of [aʊtˈsaɪd]  **außerhalb von Rosie's Diner** outside Rosie's Diner
**äußern: sich äußern (zu etwas)** comment (on sth.) ['kɒment]
**Aussicht (auf)** view (of) [vjuː]
**Aussichtsplattform** observation deck [ˌɒbzəˈveɪʃn dek]
**Aussprache** pronunciation [prəˌnʌnsiˈeɪʃn]
**ausstehen: Ich kann … nicht ausstehen.** I can't stand … [stænd]
**aussteigen: aus dem Bus/Boot aussteigen** get off the bus/boat  **aus einem Auto/Taxi aussteigen** get out of a car/taxi
**Ausstellung** exhibition [ˌeksɪˈbɪʃn]
**aussterben** die out [ˌdaɪ_ˈaʊt]
**Ausstrahlung** vibe (infml) [vaɪb]
**ausstrecken: die Hand ausstrecken** reach over [ˌriːtʃ_ˈəʊvə]  **die Hand nach jm. ausstrecken** reach out a hand to sb. [ˌriːtʃ_ˈaʊt]
**aussuchen: (sich) etwas aussuchen** choose sth. [tʃuːz]
**Austausch; Austausch-** exchange [ɪksˈtʃeɪndʒ]
**austragen: sich aus einer Mailingliste austragen lassen** unsubscribe [ˌʌnsəbˈskraɪb]
**auswählen** choose [tʃuːz]
**Auswanderer/Auswanderin** emigrant ['emɪgrənt]
**auswandern** emigrate ['emɪgreɪt]
**Auswanderung** emigration [ˌemɪˈgreɪʃn]
**auswirken: sich auswirken auf** affect [əˈfekt]

**ausziehen: etwas ausziehen** (Kleidung) take sth. off [ˌteɪk_ˈɒf];  remove sth. [rɪˈmuːv]
**Auto** car [kɑː]  **mit dem Auto fahren** go by car
**Autokennzeichen** number plate ['nʌmbə pleɪt];  licence plate (AE) ['laɪsns pleɪt]
**Autor/in** author ['ɔːθə]

# B

**Baby** baby ['beɪbi]
**Bach** stream [striːm]
**backen** bake [beɪk]
**Bäcker/in** baker ['beɪkə]
**Bäckerei** bakery ['beɪkəri];  baker's shop ['beɪkəz ʃɒp]
**Bad** bath [bɑːθ];  bathroom ['bɑːθruːm]
**Badezimmer** bathroom ['bɑːθruːm]
**Bahnhof** station ['steɪʃn]
**Bahnsteig** platform ['plætfɔːm]
**bald** soon [suːn]  **Bis bald.** See you (later).  **schon bald** before long [bɪˌfɔː ˈlɒŋ]
**Balkendiagramm** bar chart ['bɑː tʃɑːt]
**Balkon** balcony ['bælkəni]
**Ball** ball [bɔːl]
**Ballon** (Luftballon) balloon [bəˈluːn]
**Band** (Musikgruppe) band [bænd];  (zum Transport) belt [belt]
**Bank** (Geldinstitut) bank [bæŋk]
**Bär** bear [beə]
**bar bezahlen** pay cash [peɪ ˈkæʃ]
**Bärenmarder** wolverine ['wʊlvəriːn]
**Bargeld** cash [kæʃ]
**Barkeeper** barman, pl barmen ['bɑːmən]
**Barmherzigkeit** compassion [kəmˈpæʃn]
**Bart** beard [bɪəd]
**Baseball** baseball ['beɪsbɔːl]
**Basis** (Kern) core [kɔː]
**Basketball** basketball ['bɑːskɪtbɔːl]
**Batterie** battery ['bætəri]
**Bau** (eines Raubtiers) den [den]
**Bauarbeiter/in** builder ['bɪldə]
**bauen** build [bɪld]
**Bauer/Bäuerin** farmer ['fɑːmə]
**Bauernhof** farm [fɑːm]
**Baum** tree [triː]
**Baumwolle** cotton ['kɒtn]
**Bauunternehmer/in** builder ['bɪldə]
**Bayern** Bavaria [bəˈveəriə]
**Beamte(r), Beamtin** official [əˈfɪʃl]
**beanstanden** make a complaint about [kəmˈpleɪnt]
**beantworten** answer ['ɑːnsə]
**bearbeiten** edit ['edɪt]
**Becher** mug [mʌg]
**Bedarf: nach Bedarf** on demand [dɪˈmɑːnd]
**bedauern** regret [rɪˈgret]
**Bedauern** regret [rɪˈgret]
**bedecken** cover ['kʌvə]
**bedeuten** mean [miːn]
**Bedeutung** meaning ['miːnɪŋ]

**bedienen** (Kundschaft) serve [sɜːv]  **sich bedienen** help yourself
**bedrohen** threaten ['θretn]
**Bedrohung** threat [θret]
**bedrückt** glum [glʌm]
**beeilen: sich beeilen** hurry (up) [ˌhʌri_ˈʌp]
**beeinflussen** influence ['ɪnfluəns];  affect [əˈfekt]
**beenden** end [end];  finish [ˈfɪnɪʃ]
**beerdigen** bury ['beri]
**Beerdigung** burial ['beriəl]
**befinden: sich befinden (in …)** be located (in …) [ləʊˈkeɪtɪd]
**befördern** transport [trænˈspɔːt]
**befragen** interview ['ɪntəvjuː]
**befriedigen** (zufriedenstellen) satisfy ['sætɪsfaɪ]
**befürchten** fear [fɪə]
**begabt** talented ['tæləntɪd]
**Begabung** talent ['tælənt]
**begeistert** eager ['iːgə]
**Beginn** beginning [bɪˈgɪnɪŋ]
**beginnen** begin [bɪˈgɪn];  start [stɑːt]
**begleiten: jn. irgendwohin begleiten** (zu Fuß) walk sb. somewhere [wɔːk]
**begraben** bury ['beri]
**Begräbnis** burial ['beriəl]
**Begräbnisstätte** burial site ['beriəl saɪt]
**Begriff: im Begriff sein, etwas zu tun** be about to do sth. [əˈbaʊt]
**Begründung** reason [ˈriːzn]
**begrüßen: jn. begrüßen (in)** welcome sb. (to) ['welkəm]
**Begrüßung** greeting ['griːtɪŋ]
**behalten** keep [kiːp]
**Behälter** case [keɪs]
**behandeln** (Thema; Fragen) cover ['kʌvə]
**Beharrlichkeit** perseverance [ˌpɜːsɪˈvɪərəns]
**behaupten** claim [kleɪm]
**Behauptung** claim [kleɪm];  statement ['steɪtmənt]
**beheimaten: etwas beheimaten** be home to sth.
**beherrschen** (herrschen über) rule [ruːl]
**bei** (in Ortsangaben) at [æt], [ət]  **bei Oma** at Grandma's  **bei jm. sein** be with sb.
**beibringen: jm. beibringen, etwas zu tun** teach sb. to do sth.
**beide** both [bəʊθ]
**Beifall klatschen** clap [klæp]
**beigeheftet: an etwas beigeheftet sein** be attached to sth. [əˈtætʃt]
**Bein** leg [leg]
**beinahe** almost [ˈɔːlməʊst];  nearly ['nɪəli]
**Beispiel** example [ɪgˈzɑːmpl]  **wie zum Beispiel** such as ['sʌtʃ_əz]  **zum Beispiel** e.g. [ˌiːˈdʒiː];  for example
**beißen** bite [baɪt]
**bekämpfen: jn. bekämpfen** fight sb. [faɪt]
**bekannt** well known

**Bekanntmachung** proclamation [ˌprɒkləˈmeɪʃn]
**beklagen: sich beklagen** complain [kəmˈpleɪn]
**bekommen** get [gɛt]; *(Krankheit)* come down with
**bekümmert** troubled [ˈtrʌbld]
**Belag** *(Überzug, Soße)* topping [ˈtɒpɪŋ]
**belastet: mit Problemen belastet** troubled [ˈtrʌbld]
**belebt** busy [ˈbɪzi]
**belegen** *(Meinung/Argument untermauern)* back up [ˌbækˈʌp]
**beleidigen: jn. beleidigen** insult sb. [ɪnˈsʌlt]; offend sb. [əˈfɛnd]
**beleidigend** offensive [əˈfɛnsɪv]
**beleidigt** insulted [ɪnˈsʌltɪd]
**Beleidigung** insult [ˈɪnsʌlt]
**beleuchten** illuminate [ɪˈluːmɪneɪt]
**beliebt (bei)** popular (with) [ˈpɒpjələ]
**bellen** bark [bɑːk]
**Belletristik** fiction [ˈfɪkʃn]
**bemalt** painted [ˈpeɪntɪd]
**bemerken** notice [ˈnəʊtɪs]
**Bemerkung** comment [ˈkɒmɛnt]
**benehmen: sich benehmen** behave [bɪˈheɪv]
**benennen** name [neɪm]
**benötigen** need [niːd]
**benutzen** use [juːz]
**Benzin** gas *(AE)* [gæs]; petrol [ˈpɛtrəl]
**beobachten** watch [wɒtʃ]; *(untersuchen, studieren)* study [ˈstʌdi]
**Beobachter/in** watcher [ˈwɒtʃə]
**bequem** comfortable [ˈkʌmftəbl]
**beraten: sich mit jm. beraten** consult with sb. *(AE)* [kənˈsʌlt]
**Bereich** *(Gebiet)* area [ˈeəriə]
**bereit** ready [ˈrɛdi]
**bereiten: den Weg bereiten (für)** set the stage (for) [ˌsɛt ðə ˈsteɪdʒ]
**bereits** already [ɔːlˈrɛdi]
**bereitstellen** supply [səˈplaɪ]
**bereuen** regret [rɪˈgrɛt]
**Berg** mountain [ˈmaʊntən]
**bergab** downhill [ˌdaʊnˈhɪl]
**bergauf** uphill [ˌʌpˈhɪl]
**Bergwerk** mine [maɪn]
**Bericht** report [rɪˈpɔːt]
**berichten** report [rɪˈpɔːt] **berichten (über)** tell (about) [tɛl]
**beruhigen: sich beruhigen** quiet down [ˌkwaɪət ˈdaʊn]
**berühmt (für, wegen)** famous (for) [ˈfeɪməs]; *(legendär)* legendary [ˈlɛdʒəndri]
**berühren** touch [tʌtʃ]
**beschäftigen: jn. beschäftigen** *(jm. Arbeit geben)* employ sb. [ɪmˈplɔɪ]
**beschäftigt sein** be busy [ˈbɪzi]
**Bescheid: über etwas Bescheid wissen** know about sth.
**beschleunigen** speed up [ˌspiːdˈʌp]
**beschließen** decide [dɪˈsaɪd]
**beschreiben: (jm.) etwas beschreiben** describe sth. (to sb.) [dɪˈskraɪb]

**jm. den Weg (nach …) beschreiben** tell sb. the way (to …) [tɛl]
**beschreibend** descriptive [dɪˈskrɪptɪv]
**Beschreibung** description [dɪˈskrɪpʃn]; profile [ˈprəʊfaɪl]
**beschriften** label [ˈleɪbl]
**Beschriftung** label [ˈleɪbl]
**beschützen: jn./etwas beschützen (vor jm./etwas)** protect sb./sth. (from sb./sth.) [prəˈtɛkt]
**beschützend** protective [prəˈtɛktɪv]
**Beschwerde** complaint [kəmˈpleɪnt] **eine Beschwerde vorbringen (über etwas)** make a complaint (about sth.)
**beschweren: sich beschweren** complain [kəmˈpleɪn]
**beseitigen** remove [rɪˈmuːv]
**Besetzung** *(Theaterstück, Film)* cast [kɑːst]
**besiedeln** populate [ˈpɒpjuleɪt]
**Besiedlung** settlement [ˈsɛtlmənt]
**besiegen** beat [biːt]; defeat [dɪˈfiːt]
**Besitz** property [ˈprɒpəti]
**besitzen** own [əʊn]
**Besitzer/in** owner [ˈəʊnə]
**besondere(r, s)** special [ˈspɛʃl]
**besonders** especially [ɪˈspɛʃli]
**besorgen: (sich) etwas besorgen** get sth. [gɛt]
**besorgt** troubled [ˈtrʌbld]; worried [ˈwʌrid]
**Besprechung** review [rɪˈvjuː]
**besprühen** spray [spreɪ]
**besser** better [ˈbɛtə] **besser als je zuvor** better than ever [ˈɛvə]
**beste(r, s)** best [bɛst] **das Beste an …** the best thing about … **ihr bester Freund / ihre beste Freundin** her best friend
**bestehen: einen Test / eine Prüfung bestehen** pass (a test / an exam) [pɑːs]
**bestellen** order [ˈɔːdə]
**Bestellung** order [ˈɔːdə]
**Besteuerung** taxation [tækˈseɪʃn]
**bestimmte(r, s)** certain [ˈsɜːtn]
**Bestimmung(en)** policy [ˈpɒləsi]
**Bestimmungsort** destination [ˌdɛstɪˈneɪʃn]
**Bestrafung** punishment [ˈpʌnɪʃmənt]
**Besuch** visit [ˈvɪzɪt]
**besuchen** visit [ˈvɪzɪt]; see [siː]
**Besucher/in** visitor [ˈvɪzɪtə]
**betonen** stress [strɛs]
**Betonung** stress [strɛs]; *(Hervorhebung)* emphasis [ˈɛmfəsɪs]
**Betrag** *(Geld)* amount [əˈmaʊnt]
**Betreff** *(in E-Mails)* subject [ˈsʌbdʒɪkt]
**betreffen** *(sich auswirken auf)* affect [əˈfɛkt]
**betreten** enter [ˈɛntə]
**Bett** bed [bɛd]
**beugen: sich beugen** lean [liːn]
**beunruhigt** troubled [ˈtrʌbld]; worried [ˈwʌrid]
**Beutel** bag [bæg]
**bevölkern** populate [ˈpɒpjuleɪt]

**Bevölkerung** population [ˌpɒpjuˈleɪʃn]
**bevor** before [bɪˈfɔː]
**bewachen** guard [gɑːd]
**bewegen; sich bewegen** move [muːv]
**Bewegung** movement [ˈmuːvmənt]
**Beweis(e)** evidence [ˈɛvɪdəns]
**beweisen** prove [pruːv]
**bewerben: sich bewerben um etwas** *(einen Platz, eine Rolle etc.)* try out for sth. *(AE)* [ˌtraɪˈaʊt]
**bewohnen: (eine Region) bewohnen** inhabit (a region) [ɪnˈhæbɪt]
**Bewohner/in** inhabitant [ɪnˈhæbɪtənt]; resident [ˈrɛzɪdənt]
**bewölkt** cloudy [ˈklaʊdi]
**bewundern** admire [ədˈmaɪə]
**bewusst: sich einer Sache bewusst werden** realize sth. [ˈriːəlaɪz]
**bezahlen** pay **etwas bezahlen** pay for sth. **bezahlt werden** get paid [peɪd]
**Beziehung** relationship [rɪˈleɪʃnʃɪp]
**Bezirk** district [ˈdɪstrɪkt]; borough [ˈbʌrə], [ˈbɜːrəʊ]
**Biber** beaver [ˈbiːvə]
**Bibliothek** library [ˈlaɪbrəri]
**Bild** picture [ˈpɪktʃə]; *(Gemälde)* painting [ˈpeɪntɪŋ] **auf dem Bild** in the picture
**bilden** form [fɔːm] **gebildet sein/werden aus** be made up of [ˌmeɪdˈʌp]
**Bildroman** graphic novel [ˌgræfɪk ˈnɒvl]
**Bildschirm** screen [skriːn] **geteilter Bildschirm** split screen [ˌsplɪt ˈskriːn]
**Bildschirm(auf)teilung** split screen [ˌsplɪt ˈskriːn]
**Bildung** *(Schulbildung, Ausbildung)* education [ˌɛdʒuˈkeɪʃn]
**Bildunterschrift** caption [ˈkæpʃn]
**billig** cheap [tʃiːp]
**Bindestrich** hyphen [ˈhaɪfən]
**Bindewort** linking word [ˈlɪŋkɪŋ wɜːd]
**bis** till [tɪl]; until [ənˈtɪl] **bis auf** *(außer)* except [ɪkˈsɛpt] **Bis bald. / Bis nachher.** See you (later). **bis jetzt / bis hierher** so far **Bis später dann!** Catch you later. *(infml)* **bis (spätestens) 8 Uhr morgens** by 8 am **bis (zu)** up to **von … bis** from … to
**Bison** buffalo, *pl* buffalo *or* buffaloes [ˈbʌfələʊ]
**Biss** bite [baɪt]
**bisschen: ein bisschen** a bit [əˈbɪt]; a little
**Bissen** bite [baɪt]
**Bitte** request [rɪˈkwɛst]
**bitte** 1. *(in Fragen und Aufforderungen)* please [pliːz]
2. **Bitte sehr. / Hier bitte.** Here you are.
3. **Bitte, gern geschehen.** *(Nichts zu danken.)* You're welcome. [ˈwɛlkəm]
**bitten: jemanden bitten, etwas zu tun** ask sb. to do sth. **um etwas bitten** ask for sth.
**bitter** bitter [ˈbɪtə]

# Dictionary

**Blase** (z.B. auf der Haut) blister ['blɪstə]
**Blaskapelle** brass band [ˌbrɑːs 'bænd]
**blau** blue [bluː]
**Blaubeere** blueberry ['bluːbəri]
**bleiben** stay [steɪ]; remain [rɪ'meɪn]
 **Bleib / Bleiben Sie am Apparat.** (am Telefon) Hold on (a minute). [ˌhəʊld_'ɒn]
**Bleistift** pencil ['pensl]
**Blick (auf)** (Aussicht) view (of) [vjuː]
 **einen Blick auf etwas werfen** have a look (at sth.)
**blicken** gaze [geɪz]
**Blickkontakt herstellen** make eye contact ['kɒntækt]
**Blindkopie** (in E-Mails) bcc (= blind carbon copy) [ˌblaɪnd kɑːbən 'kɒpi]
**Blitz(e)** lightning (no pl) ['laɪtnɪŋ] **ein Blitz** a flash of lightning
**Block** (Häuser-, Wohnblock) block [blɒk]
**Blockflöte** recorder [rɪ'kɔːdə]
**blockieren** block [blɒk]
**blöd** (albern) silly ['sɪli]; (dumm) stupid ['stjuːpɪd]
**Blog** blog [blɒg]
**Blog-Eintrag** post [pəʊst]
**blond** blond (bei Frauen oft: blonde) [blɒnd]
**bloß** just [dʒʌst]; only ['əʊnli]
**blühen** bloom [bluːm]
**Blume** flower ['flaʊə]
**Blut** blood [blʌd]
**Blüte** flower ['flaʊə]
**Blutrache** vendetta [ven'detə]
**Boden** (Erdboden) ground [graʊnd]
**Bohne** bean [biːn]
**Boje** buoy [bɔɪ], ['buːi]
**Boot** boat [bəʊt]
**Bootsausflug: einen Bootsausflug machen** go on a boat trip ['bəʊt trɪp]
**Bordkarte** boarding pass ['bɔːdɪŋ pɑːs]
**borgen: sich etwas borgen** borrow sth. ['bɒrəʊ]
**bösartig** evil ['iːvl]
**böse** evil ['iːvl] **(das) Böse** evil **böse auf jn.** angry with sb. ['æŋgri]
**Bote/Botin** messenger ['mesɪndʒə]
**Botschaft** (Aussage) message ['mesɪdʒ]; (diplomatische Vertretung) embassy ['embəsi]
**Boulevard** avenue ['ævənjuː]
**Boykott** boycott ['bɔɪkɒt]
**boykottieren** boycott ['bɔɪkɒt]
**braten** (in der Pfanne) fry [fraɪ]
**Bratensoße** gravy ['greɪvi]
**Brathähnchen** chicken ['tʃɪkɪn]
**Bratkartoffeln** (im Backofen in Fett gebackene Kartoffeln) roast potatoes (pl) [ˌrəʊst pə'teɪtəʊz]
**Bräuche** customs (pl) ['kʌstəmz]
**brauchen** need [niːd]; (Zeit) take [teɪk] **du brauchst es nicht zu tun** you needn't do it ['niːdnt]
**braun** brown [braʊn]
**brav** good [gʊd]
**brechen** (kaputt gehen) break [breɪk]

**breit** wide [waɪd]
**brennen** burn [bɜːn]
**Brettspiel** board game ['bɔːd geɪm]
**Brief** letter ['letə]
**Brille: (eine) Brille** glasses (pl) ['glɑːsɪz]
**bringen** (mit-, herbringen) bring [brɪŋ]; (weg-, hinbringen) take [teɪk] **etwas zustande bringen** (etwas schaffen) manage sth. ['mænɪdʒ] **jn. dazu bringen, etwas zu tun** get sb. to do sth.
**Brise** breeze [briːz]
**britisch** British ['brɪtɪʃ]
**Broschüre** brochure ['brəʊʃə]
**Brot** bread [bred] **belegtes Brot** (zusammengeklappt) sandwich ['sænwɪtʃ], ['sænwɪdʒ]
**Brücke** bridge [brɪdʒ]
**Bruder** brother ['brʌðə]
**brüllen** roar [rɔː]
**brummen** hum [hʌm]
**Brunnen** fountain ['faʊntən]; well [wel]
**Brust(korb)** chest [tʃest]
**brüten** breed [briːd]
**Brutplatz** breeding ground ['briːdɪŋ graʊnd]
**Brutstätte** breeding ground ['briːdɪŋ graʊnd]
**brutzeln** sizzle ['sɪzl]
**Bub** boy [bɔɪ]
**Buch** book [bʊk]
**buchen** reserve [rɪ'zɜːv]
**Bücherei** library ['laɪbrəri]
**Buchhandlung** bookshop ['bʊkʃɒp]
**Buchladen** bookshop ['bʊkʃɒp]
**Buchstabe** letter ['letə]
**buchstabieren** spell [spel]
**Bucht** bay [beɪ]
**bücken: sich bücken** bend down; bend over [bend]
**Büffel** buffalo, pl buffalo or buffaloes ['bʌfələʊ]
**Bühne** stage [steɪdʒ]
**Bund** (Bündnis) confederacy [kən'fedərəsi]
**Bündnis** confederacy [kən'fedərəsi]
**bunt** coloured ['kʌləd]; colourful ['kʌləfl]
**Burg** castle [kɑːsl]
**Bürgermeister/in** mayor [meə]
**Bürgerrechte** civil rights (pl) [ˌsɪvl 'raɪts]
**Bürgersteig** pavement ['peɪvmənt]; sidewalk (AE) ['saɪdwɔːk]
**Büro** office ['ɒfɪs]
**Bus** bus [bʌs] **mit dem Bus fahren** go by bus
**Busch** shrub [ʃrʌb]

# C

**Café** café ['kæfeɪ]
**campen gehen** go camping
**Camper/in** camper ['kæmpə]
**Camping** camping ['kæmpɪŋ]

**Cent** cent [sent]
**Champion** champion ['tʃæmpiən]
**Chance** chance [tʃɑːns]; opportunity [ˌɒpə'tjuːnəti]
**Chaos** chaos ['keɪɒs]
**Chat** chat [tʃæt]
**chatten** chat [tʃæt]
**Check-up** (medizinische Vorsorgeuntersuchung) check-up ['tʃek_ʌp]
**Checkliste** checklist ['tʃeklɪst]
**Chor** choir ['kwaɪə]
**Christentum** Christianity [ˌkrɪsti'ænəti]
**Christliche Zeitrechnung** CE (= Common Era) [ˌkɒmən_'ɪərə] **vor der Christlichen Zeitrechnung** BCE (= before the Common Era)
**Christus: vor Christus** (= vor der Christlichen Zeitrechnung) BCE (= before the Common Era)
**Clan** clan [klæn]
**Clown** clown [klaʊn]
**Cola** cola ['kəʊlə]
**Comicroman** graphic novel [ˌgræfɪk 'nɒvl]
**Computer** computer [kəm'pjuːtə]
**cool** cool [kuːl]
**Cornflakes** cornflakes ['kɔːnfleɪks]
**Cottage** cottage ['kɒtɪdʒ]
**Cousin, Cousine** cousin ['kʌzn]
**Cowboy** cowboy ['kaʊbɔɪ]
**crashen** crash [kræʃ]
**Curry(gericht)** curry ['kʌri]
**Cyber-Mobbing** (Verleumdung o. Diffamierung in sozialen Medien) cyberbullying ['saɪbəbʊliɪŋ]

# D

**da** 1. (weil) as [æz], [əz]
 2. (dort) there [ðeə] **da drüben** over there
 3. **nicht da sein** be out **nicht (mehr) da sein** be gone [gɒn]
**Dach** roof [ruːf]
**Dachboden** attic ['ætɪk] **auf dem Dachboden** in the attic
**dagegen: etwas dagegen haben** mind [maɪnd] **wenn Sie nichts dagegen haben** if you don't mind **Haben Sie etwas dagegen, …?** Do you mind …?
**daheim** at home
**daher** (deshalb) so [səʊ]
**dahin** there [ðeə]
**Damen: Meine Damen und Herren** Ladies and gentlemen [ˌleɪdiz_ən 'dʒentlmən] **Sehr geehrte Damen und Herren** Dear Sir or Madam [sɜː], ['mædəm]
**damit …** so that … (oft auch kurz: so …)
**Damm** dam [dæm]
**Dampf** steam [stiːm]
**danach** after that
**dank Maya** thanks to Maya

# German – English

**dankbar** grateful ['greɪtfl]; thankful ['θæŋkfl]; *(froh)* glad [glæd]
**Danke.** Thank you. ['θæŋk juː]; Thanks. [θæŋks]
**danken: jm. danken** thank sb. [θæŋk] **Nichts zu danken.** *(Bitte, gern geschehen.)* You're welcome. ['welkəm]
**dann** then [ðen] **gerade dann** just then
**darlegen** state [steɪt]
**darstellende Kunst** drama ['drɑːmə]
**Darstellung** representation [ˌreprɪzen'teɪʃn]
**darüber** *(oberhalb)* above [ə'bʌv]
**darum** that's why
**darunter** *(unterhalb)* below [bɪ'ləʊ] **darunter (auch)** *(einschließlich)* including [ɪn'kluːdɪŋ] **darunter liegend** underlying [ˌʌndə'laɪɪŋ]
**das** 1. *(Artikel)* the [ðə]
2. **das (dort)** that [ðæt]
3. *(Relativpronomen)* that [ðæt], [ðət]; which [wɪtʃ]; *(bei Personen)* who [huː]
**dass: es zeigt, dass ...** it shows that ... [ðæt], [ðət] **Ich möchte, dass du ...** I want you to ...
**dasselbe (wie)** the same (as) [seɪm]
**Date** date [deɪt]
**Datum** date [deɪt]
**Dauer** length [leŋθ]
**dauern** last (for) [lɑːst]; take [teɪk]
**Deck** *(eines Schiffes)* deck [dek]
**Decke** *(zum Zudecken)* blanket ['blæŋkɪt]
**dein/e** your [jɔː], [jə] **Dein Finn** *(Briefschluss)* Yours, Finn [jɔːz]
**deiner, deine, deins** yours [jɔːz]
**Demokratie** democracy [dɪ'mɒkrəsi]
**demokratisch** democratic [ˌdemə'krætɪk]
**Demonstration** demonstration [ˌdemən'streɪʃn]
**denken** think [θɪŋk] **an etwas denken** think of sth.; *(etwas nicht vergessen)* remember sth. [rɪ'membə] **Das denke ich nicht.** I don't think so.
**Denkmal** memorial [mə'mɔːriəl] **Denkmal (für/zum Gedenken an)** monument (to) ['mɒnjumənt]
**denn: Was ist denn?** What's the matter? ['mætə]
**dennoch** still [stɪl]; yet [jet]
**Depp** jerk *(infml)* [dʒɜːk]
**der** 1. *(Artikel)* the [ðə]
2. *(Relativpronomen)* that [ðæt], [ðət]; which [wɪtʃ]; *(bei Personen)* who [huː]
**deren** *(Relativpronomen)*: **Städte, deren Namen ...** cities whose names ...
**derselbe (wie)** the same (as) [seɪm]
**deshalb** so [səʊ]; that's why
**Design** design [dɪ'zaɪn] **Design und Technik** design and technology [dɪˌzaɪn ənd tek'nɒlədʒi]
**dessen** *(Relativpronomen)*: **ein Junge/Mädchen, dessen Name ...** a boy/girl whose name ... [huːz]

**desto: je mehr ..., desto mehr ...** the more ..., the more ... [ðə]
**Detail** detail ['diːteɪl]
**Detektiv/in** detective [dɪ'tektɪv]
**deuten auf** point to [pɔɪnt]
**deutlich** clear [klɪə]
**Deutsch; deutsch** German ['dʒɜːmən]
**Dezember** December [dɪ'sembə]
**Dia** slide [slaɪd]
**Diagramm** chart [tʃɑːt]
**Dialekt** dialect ['daɪəlekt]
**Dialog** dialogue ['daɪəlɒg]
**dich** you [juː]; yourself [jɔː'self], [jə'self]
**dicht (bei, an)** close (to) [kləʊs]
**dick** thick [θɪk]; fat [fæt]
**die** 1. *(Artikel)* the [ðə]
2. *(Relativpronomen)* that [ðæt], [ðət]; which [wɪtʃ]; *(bei Personen)* who [huː]
**Dieb/in** thief, *pl* thieves [θiːf]
**dienen** serve [sɜːv]
**Dienst(leistung)** service ['sɜːvɪs] **soziale Dienste** social services *(pl)* [ˌsəʊʃl 'sɜːvɪsɪz]
**Dienstag** Tuesday ['tjuːzdeɪ], ['tjuːzdi]
**dies (hier)** this [ðɪs] **Dies ist ...** This is ... **Dies sind ...** These are ...
**diese(r, s)** this **dieser Ort / dieses Fach** this place/subject **diese Orte/Fächer** these places/subjects
**Diese(r, s) (hier).** This one.
**dieselbe(n) (wie)** the same (as) [seɪm]
**diesjährig: das diesjährige Musical** this year's musical
**digital** digital ['dɪdʒɪtl]
**Ding** thing [θɪŋ]
**Dinosaurier** dinosaur ['daɪnəsɔː]
**diplomatisch, Diplomaten-** diplomatic [ˌdɪplə'mætɪk]
**dir** you [juː]; yourself [jɔː'self], [jə'self]
**direkt** direct [də'rekt]; straight [streɪt] **direkt hinter dir** right behind you
**Disko** disco ['dɪskəʊ]
**Diskussion** discussion [dɪ'skʌʃn]
**Distanz** distance ['dɪstəns]
**doch: und doch** *(dennoch)* yet [jet]
**Dock** dock [dɒk]
**Doktor** doctor ['dɒktə]
**Dokument** document ['dɒkjumənt]
**Dokumentarfilm** documentary [ˌdɒkju'mentri]
**Dollar ($)** dollar; *(infml)* buck [bʌk]
**dolmetschen** *(gesprochenen Text mündlich wiedergeben)* interpret [ɪn'tɜːprɪt]
**Dolmetschen** interpretation [ɪnˌtɜːprɪ'teɪʃn]
**Dolmetscher/in** interpreter [ɪn'tɜːprɪtə]
**Dom** cathedral [kə'θiːdrəl]
**Donner** thunder ['θʌndə]
**Donnerstag** Thursday ['θɜːzdeɪ], ['θɜːzdi]
**Donut** *(ringförmiges Gebäck aus Hefeteig)* donut *(AE)* ['dəʊnʌt]
**Doppel-** double ['dʌbl]
**Doppelpunkt** colon ['kəʊlən]
**Dorf** village ['vɪlɪdʒ]

**dort** there [ðeə] **dort drüben** over there **dort entlang** that way **die Gruppe dort** *(jene Gruppe)* that group [ðæt], [ðət]
**dorthin** there [ðeə]
**Dose** can [kæn]; *(Lebensmittel)* tin [tɪn]
**drahtlos** wireless ['waɪələs]
**dran: Ich bin dran.** (It's) my turn. [tɜːn]
**draußen** outdoors [ˌaʊt'dɔːz]; outside [ˌaʊt'saɪd] **nach draußen** out; outside
**Dreck** dirt [dɜːt]
**Dreh: den Dreh raushaben/rausbekommen (bei)** get the hang (of) *(infml)* [hæŋ]
**drehen: sich (im Kreis) drehen** spin around [ˌspɪn_ə'raʊnd]
**Drehort** *(Film)* location [ləʊ'keɪʃn]
**drei** three [θriː]
**dreieckig** triangular [traɪ'æŋgjələ]
**drinnen; nach drinnen** inside [ˌɪn'saɪd]
**dritte(r, s)** third [θɜːd]
**Drittel** third [θɜːd]
**Drittens ...** Third ... [θɜːd]; Thirdly, ...
**drohen** threaten ['θretn]
**dröhnen** roar [rɔː]
**Drohung** threat [θret]
**drüben: da drüben, dort drüben** over there **hier drüben** over here
**Druck** pressure ['preʃə]
**drücken** press [pres]; squeeze [skwiːz]; *(schieben, stoßen)* push [pʊʃ]
**du** you [juː]
**Duft** aroma [ə'rəʊmə]
**dumm** stupid ['stjuːpɪd]
**Dummerchen** silly ['sɪli]
**dunkel** dark [dɑːk]
**Dunkelheit** dark; darkness ['dɑːknəs]
**dünn** skinny ['skɪni]
**Dunst(schleier)** mist [mɪst]
**durch** through [θruː]
**durchgehender Zug** direct train
**durchnässt: völlig durchnässt** soaking wet [ˌsəʊkɪŋ 'wet]
**Durchsage** announcement [ə'naʊnsmənt]
**Durchschnitt** average ['ævərɪdʒ] **im Durchschnitt** on average
**durchschnittlich** average ['ævərɪdʒ]; on average
**dürfen** can [kæn]; may [meɪ]; be allowed to [ə'laʊd] **du darfst es nicht tun** you mustn't do it ['mʌsnt] **etwas tun dürfen** be allowed to do sth; get to do sth.
**dürr** skinny ['skɪni]
**Durst haben** be thirsty ['θɜːsti]
**durstig sein** be thirsty ['θɜːsti]
**Dusche** shower ['ʃaʊə]
**duschen; sich duschen** have/take a shower
**Dutzend** dozen, *pl* dozen ['dʌzn]
**DVD** DVD [ˌdiːviː'diː]

# Dictionary

## E

**E-Mail** email [ˈiːmeɪl]; mail [meɪl]
**eben** flat [flæt]; smooth [smuːð]
**Ebene** plains (pl) [pleɪnz]
**ebenso** as well [əz ˈwel]
**echt** real [ˈriːəl]; really [ˈrɪəli]  **Das ist echt übel!** That sucks! (infml) [sʌks]
**Ecke** corner [ˈkɔːnə]  **Church Road, Ecke London Road** on the corner of Church Road and London Road  **Laden an der Ecke** corner shop [ˈkɔːnə ʃɒp]
**edel** noble [ˈnəʊbl]
**egal: Es ist den Leuten egal.** People don't care. [keə]  **Geld ist mir egal.** I don't care about money.
**Ehefrau** wife, pl wives [waɪf]
**ehemalige(r, s)** former [ˈfɔːmə]
**Ehemann** husband [ˈhʌzbənd]
**Ehre** honour [ˈɒnə]
**ehrenamtlich: ehrenamtlich arbeiten** (unbezahlt) volunteer [vɒlənˈtɪə]  **ehrenamtliche Arbeit** volunteer work
**Ehrenamtliche(r)** volunteer [ˌvɒlənˈtɪə]
**ehrgeizig** competitive [kəmˈpetətɪv]
**Ei** egg [eg]
**Eierkuchen** pancake [ˈpænkeɪk]
**eifrig** eager [ˈiːgə]
**eigene(r, s)** of one's own  **mein eigenes Zimmer** my own room
**Eigenschaft** feature [ˈfiːtʃə]
**eigentlich** actually [ˈæktʃʊəli]; (in Wirklichkeit) in fact [ɪn ˈfækt]
**Eigentum** property [ˈprɒpəti]
**eilen** hurry [ˈhʌri]; rush [rʌʃ]
**Eimer** bucket [ˈbʌkɪt]
**ein(e):** (Artikel) a, an [ə], [ən]  **ein(e) andere(r, s)** another [əˈnʌðə]  **noch ein(e)** another [əˈnʌðə]  **einer nach dem anderen** one by one  **eines Nachts/Tages** one night/day
**einander** (sich gegenseitig) each other [iːtʃ ˈʌðə]; one another
**einatmen** breathe in [briːð ˈɪn]
**einbringen** (Heu) bring in
**einchecken: etwas einchecken** (Gepäck) check sth. in [ˌtʃek ˈɪn]
**Eindruck** impression [ɪmˈpreʃn]
**eineinhalb Stunden** an hour and a half
**Einerseits ...** On the one hand ...
**einfach** easy [ˈiːzi]; (unkompliziert) simple [ˈsɪmpl]  **einfache Fahrkarte** single (kurz für: single ticket) [ˈsɪŋgl]  **einfach nur** (bloß) just [dʒʌst]
**Einfluss** influence [ˈɪnfluəns]
**Einführung** introduction [ˌɪntrəˈdʌkʃn]
**Eingang** doorway [ˈdɔːweɪ]; entrance [ˈentrəns]
**eingeben: ein Passwort eingeben** enter a password [ˈentə]
**eingehen: ein Risiko eingehen** take a risk
**eingeschaltet sein** (Radio, Licht usw.) be on
**eingrenzen** narrow. down [ˌnærəʊ ˈdaʊn]

**einheimisch (in)** indigenous (to) [ɪnˈdɪdʒənəs]  **Einheimische** indigenous people
**Einhorn** unicorn [ˈjuːnɪkɔːn]
**einhundert** a/one hundred [ˈhʌndrəd]
**einige** a few [ə ˈfjuː]; some [sʌm], [səm]
**einigen: sich auf etwas einigen** agree on sth. [əˈgriː]
**Einigung** agreement [əˈgriːmənt]
**einkaufen** shop [ʃɒp]  **einkaufen gehen** go shopping [ˈʃɒpɪŋ]
**Einkaufszentrum** shopping centre [ˈʃɒpɪŋ sentə]; (sehr groß) (shopping) mall [mɔːl]
**einladen: jn. einladen (zu)** invite sb. (to) [ɪnˈvaɪt]
**Einladung (zu, nach)** invitation (to) [ˌɪnvɪˈteɪʃn]
**Einleitung** introduction [ˌɪntrəˈdʌkʃn]
**einloggen: sich einloggen** log in [ˌlɒg ˈɪn]
**einmal** once [wʌns]  **auf einmal** (plötzlich) suddenly [ˈsʌdnli]  **früher einmal** once  **(noch) nicht einmal** not even
**einmalig** unique [juˈniːk]
**einmarschieren** (in ein Land) invade (a country) [ɪnˈveɪd]
**einpacken** pack [pæk]
**einreichen: etwas einreichen** hand sth. in
**einrichten** establish [ɪˈstæblɪʃ]; set up [ˌset ˈʌp]
**eins** one [wʌn]
**einsam** lonely [ˈləʊnli]
**einschalten: etwas einschalten** turn sth. on [ˌtɜːn ˈɒn]
**einschlafen** fall asleep [ˌfɔːl əˈsliːp]
**einschließlich** including [ɪnˈkluːdɪŋ]
**einsperren: jn. einsperren** shut sb. up [ˌʃʌt ˈʌp]
**einst** once [wʌns]
**einsteigen: in ein Auto/Taxi einsteigen** get in(to) a car/taxi  **in einen Bus/ein Flugzeug/einen Zug einsteigen** get on a bus/plane/train
**einstellen** (Person) hire [haɪə]
**Einstellung** (Film, Szene) shot [ʃɒt]; (Geisteshaltung) spirit [ˈspɪrɪt]
**einstürzen** collapse [kəˈlæps]
**Eintrag(ung)** (im Tagebuch, Wörterbuch) entry [ˈentri]
**eintreffen** arrive [əˈraɪv]
**eintreten** (hineingehen) enter [ˈentə]  **in einen Klub eintreten** join a club [dʒɔɪn]
**Eintritt** entry [ˈentri]
**Eintrittskarte** ticket [ˈtɪkɪt]
**Einwanderer/Einwanderin** immigrant [ˈɪmɪgrənt]
**einwandern** immigrate [ˈɪmɪgreɪt]
**Einwanderung** immigration [ˌɪmɪˈgreɪʃn]
**einwilligen** consent [kənˈsent]
**Einwilligung** consent [kənˈsent]
**Einwohner(zahl)** population [ˌpɒpjuˈleɪʃn]

**Einwohner/in** inhabitant [ɪnˈhæbɪtənt]
**Einzelfahrschein** single (ticket) [ˈsɪŋgl]
**Einzelheit** detail [ˈdiːteɪl]
**einzeln** (einer nach dem anderen) one at a time [taɪm]
**Einzelne/r** individual [ˌɪndɪˈvɪdʒuəl]
**einziehen** move in  **in ein Haus einziehen** move into a house
**einzigartig** unique [juˈniːk]
**einzige: der/die/das einzige ...; die einzigen ...** the only ... [ˈəʊnli]
**Eis** ice; (Speiseeis) ice cream [ˌaɪs ˈkriːm]
**Eisbahn** rink (kurz für: ice rink) [rɪŋk]
**Eisbär** polar bear [ˈpəʊlə beə]
**Eisenbahn** railroad (AE) [ˈreɪlrəʊd]; railway (BE) [ˈreɪlweɪ]
**eislaufen** skate [skeɪt]
**Eistee** iced tea [ˌaɪst ˈtiː]
**ekelhaft** disgusting [dɪsˈgʌstɪŋ]
**Elefant** elephant [ˈelɪfənt]
**Element** element [ˈelɪmənt]
**elf** eleven [ɪˈlevn]
**Eltern** parents (pl) [ˈpeərənts]
**emigrieren** emigrate [ˈemɪgreɪt]
**empfangen** receive [rɪˈsiːv]
**empfehlen: (jm.) etwas empfehlen** recommend sth. (to sb.) [rekəˈmend]
**Empfehlung** recommendation [ˌrekəmənˈdeɪʃn]
**emporragen** (Berge, Säulen, Türme, ...) rise up [ˌraɪz ˈʌp]
**Ende** end [end]; ending [ˈendɪŋ]  **am oberen Ende (von)** at the top (of)  **am unteren Ende (von)** at the bottom (of) [ˈbɒtəm]  **Er ist Ende dreißig.** He's in his late thirties.  **zu Ende sein** be over [ˈəʊvə]
**enden** finish [ˈfɪnɪʃ]; end [end]
**endlich** at last [ət ˈlɑːst]; finally [ˈfaɪnəli]
**Endspiel** final [ˈfaɪnl]
**Endung** ending [ˈendɪŋ]
**Energie** energy [ˈenədʒi]; power [ˈpaʊə]
**energisch** vigorous [ˈvɪgərəs]
**eng** narrow [ˈnærəʊ]; (Beziehung, Team) tight [taɪt]  **eng anliegend** (Kleidung) tight [taɪt]
**Engel** angel [ˈeɪndʒl]
**Englisch; englisch** English [ˈɪŋglɪʃ]
**entdecken** discover [dɪˈskʌvə]
**Entdeckung** discovery [dɪˈskʌvəri]
**Entertainer/in** entertainer [ˌentəˈteɪnə]
**entfernen** (beseitigen) remove [rɪˈmuːv]
**entfernt: weit entfernt** far [fɑː]
**Entfernung** distance [ˈdɪstəns]
**entgegengesetzte(r, s)** opposite [ˈɒpəzɪt]
**entgegnen** reply (to) [rɪˈplaɪ]
**entlang: die Straße entlang** along the street [əˈlɒŋ]  **dort entlang** that way
**entscheiden: sich entscheiden** decide [dɪˈsaɪd]
**Entscheidung** decision [dɪˈsɪʒn]
**entschieden** (adv: voll und ganz) strongly [ˈstrɒŋli]

# German – English

**Entschuldigung.** (I'm) sorry. ['sɒri]
**Entschuldigung, … / Entschuldigen Sie, …** (Darf ich mal stören?) Excuse me, … [ɪk'skjuːz miː]
**entsetzt** shocked [ʃɒkt]
**entspannen: sich entspannen** relax [rɪ'læks]
**entspannt** relaxed [rɪ'lækst]
**entsperren** unlock [ʌn'lɒk]
**enttäuschen** disappoint [ˌdɪsə'pɔɪnt]
**enttäuschend** disappointing [ˌdɪsə'pɔɪntɪŋ]
**enttäuscht** disappointed [ˌdɪsə'pɔɪntɪd]
**entweder … oder …** either … or … ['aɪðə], ['iːðə]
**entwerfen** design [dɪ'zaɪn]
**entwickeln: sich entwickeln** develop [dɪ'veləp] **etwas entwickeln** design sth. [dɪ'zaɪn]
**Entwicklung** development [dɪ'veləpmənt]
**Entwurf** draft [drɑːft]
**Epidemie; epidemisch** epidemic [ˌepɪ'demɪk]
**Epoche** era ['ɪərə]
**er** he [hiː]; (Ding/Tier) it [ɪt]
**erbittert** bitter ['bɪtə]
**Erdbeere** strawberry ['strɔːbəri]
**Erdboden** ground [graʊnd]
**Erde** (der Planet) (the) earth (auch: Earth) [ɜːθ]
**Erderwärmung** global warming [ˌgləʊbl 'wɔːmɪŋ]
**Ereignis** event [ɪ'vent]
**erfahren** experience [ɪk'spɪəriəns]
**Erfahrung(en)** experience (no pl) [ɪk'spɪəriəns]
**erfinden** invent [ɪn'vent]
**Erfindung** invention [ɪn'venʃn]
**Erfolg** success [sək'ses] **Erfolg haben** make it ['meɪk ɪt]
**erfolgreich** successful [sək'sesfl]
**erforschen** explore [ɪk'splɔː]; research [rɪ'sɜːtʃ]
**Erfrischungsgetränk** (kohlensäurehaltig) fizzy drink [ˌfɪzi 'drɪŋk]
**ergänzen (zu)** add (to) [æd]
**Ergebnis** outcome ['aʊtkʌm]; result [rɪ'zʌlt]
**erhalten** get [get]; receive [rɪ'siːv] **das Stimmrecht erhalten** get the vote [vəʊt]
**erhältlich** available [ə'veɪləbl]
**erheblich** (adv) greatly ['greɪtli]
**erhellen: etwas erhellen** (aufleuchten lassen) light sth. up [ˌlaɪt 'ʌp]
**erhitzen** heat [hiːt]
**erinnern: jn. erinnern** remind sb. [rɪ'maɪnd] **sich an etwas erinnern** remember sth. [rɪ'membə]; recall sth. [rɪ'kɔːl]
**Erinnerung** memory ['meməri]
**erkältet sein** have a cold [kəʊld]
**Erkältung: eine Erkältung haben** have a cold [kəʊld]

**erkennen: etwas erkennen** (sich einer Sache bewusst werden) realize sth. ['rɪəlaɪz]
**erklären** explain [ɪk'spleɪn]; (verkünden) declare [dɪ'kleə]; (darlegen) state [steɪt] **jm. etwas erklären** explain sth. to sb. [ɪk'spleɪn]
**Erklärung** (Verkündung) declaration [ˌdeklə'reɪʃn]
**erkranken: an etwas erkranken** come down with sth.
**erkunden** explore [ɪk'splɔː]
**erlauben** allow [ə'laʊ]
**erläutern: jm. etwas erläutern** explain sth. to sb. [ɪk'spleɪn]
**erleben** experience [ɪk'spɪəriəns]; (Zeuge werden) witness ['wɪtnəs]
**erleiden** suffer (from) ['sʌfə]
**erleuchten** illuminate [ɪ'luːmɪneɪt]
**ermuntern** encourage [ɪn'kʌrɪdʒ]
**ermutigen** encourage [ɪn'kʌrɪdʒ]
**ernst(haft)** serious ['sɪəriəs]
**Ernte** harvest ['hɑːvɪst]
**erraten** guess [ges]
**erreichbar** (am Telefon) available [ə'veɪləbl]
**erreichen** reach [riːtʃ] **den Bus erreichen** (rechtzeitig) be in time for the bus
**errichten** set up [ˌset 'ʌp]
**erröten** go red
**erschaffen** create [kri'eɪt]
**erscheinen** appear [ə'pɪə]
**erschießen** shoot [ʃuːt]
**erschrecken: jn. erschrecken** scare sb. [skeə]
**erschrocken** in fright [fraɪt]
**erst** only ['əʊnli] **erst um drei** not till/until three [tɪl], [ən'tɪl]
**erstarren** freeze [friːz]
**erstaunlich** amazing [ə'meɪzɪŋ]
**erste(r, s)** first [fɜːst] **als Erstes** first **der erste Tag** the first day **in erster Linie** in the first place **zum ersten Mal** for the first time
**erstens** first, … [fɜːst]; firstly, …; (in erster Linie) in the first place
**erteilen: jm. Hausarrest/Ausgehverbot erteilen** ground sb. [graʊnd]
**ertragen: Ich kann … nicht ertragen.** I can't stand … [stænd]
**erwachsen werden** grow up [ˌgrəʊ 'ʌp]
**Erwachsene(r)** adult ['ædʌlt]
**erwähnt werden** come up [ˌkʌm 'ʌp]
**erwärmen** heat [hiːt]
**erwarten: etwas erwarten** expect sth. [ɪk'spekt] **Ich kann es kaum erwarten, … zu sehen.** I can't wait to see … [weɪt]
**Erwartung** (Vorausahnung) anticipation [ænˌtɪsɪ'peɪʃn]
**erwidern** reply (to) [rɪ'plaɪ]
**erzählen (von)** tell (about) [tel]
**Erzähler/in** narrator [nə'reɪtə]; (von Geschichten) storyteller ['stɔːrɪtelə]

**Erzählung** narration [nə'reɪʃn]; story ['stɔːri]
**erziehen** educate ['edʒukeɪt]
**Erziehung** education [ˌedʒu'keɪʃn]
**erzielen: einen Treffer erzielen** score [skɔː]
**es** it [ɪt] **es ist … /es gibt …** there's … (= there is …) **es sind … / es gibt …** there are … **es wäre …** it would be … [wʊd] **Ach, du bist es.** Oh, it's you. **Bist du's?** Is that you?
**Essen** (Lebensmittel) food [fuːd]; (Mahlzeit) meal [miːl]; (zum Mitnehmen) takeaway ['teɪkəweɪ]; takeout (AE) ['teɪkaʊt]
**essen** eat [iːt] **zu Abend/Mittag essen** have dinner/lunch
**Esszimmer** dining room ['daɪnɪŋ ruːm]
**etablieren** establish [ɪ'stæblɪʃ]
**Etage** storey, pl storeys (BE), story, pl stories (AE) ['stɔːri]
**ethnisch** racial ['reɪʃl]
**Etikett** label ['leɪbl]
**etikettieren** label ['leɪbl]
**Etui** case [keɪs]
**etwas** something ['sʌmθɪŋ]; (ein bisschen) a bit [ə 'bɪt]; a little [ə 'lɪtl]; some [sʌm], [səm]; (in Fragen: (irgend)etwas) anything ['eniθɪŋ]
**euch** you [juː]; yourselves [jɔː'selvz], [jə'selvz]
**euer/eure** your [jɔː], [jə] **Euer Finn** (Briefschluss) Yours, Finn [jɔːz]
**eurer, eure, eures** yours [jɔːz]
**Euro** euro (€), pl euros ['jʊərəʊ]
**Europa** Europe ['jʊərəp]
**europäisch: die Europäische Union** the EU (the European Union) [ˌjʊərəpiːən 'juːniən]
**ewig** for ever, forever [fər 'evə] **Es ist ewig her.** It's been ages. / That was ages ago. ['eɪdʒɪz]
**Exemplar** copy ['kɒpi]
**existieren** exist [ɪg'zɪst]
**Expedition** expedition [ˌekspə'dɪʃn]
**Experte/Expertin** expert ['ekspɜːt]
**explodieren** explode [ɪk'spləʊd]
**explosiv** explosive [ɪk'spləʊsɪv]
**Export** export ['ekspɔːt]
**extrem; Extrem** extreme [ɪk'striːm]

# F

**fabelhaft** fabulous ['fæbjələs]
**Fabrik** factory ['fæktri]
**Fackel** torch [tɔːtʃ]
**fähig (zu)** capable (of) ['keɪpəbl] **fähig sein, etwas zu tun** be able to do sth.
**Fahne** flag [flæg]
**Fähre** ferry ['feri]

# Dictionary

**fahren** go [gəʊ]; *(ein Auto)* drive [draɪv]
  **mit dem Auto/Bus fahren** go by car/bus  **Rad fahren** ride a bike
**Fahrgast** passenger ['pæsɪndʒə]
**Fahrgestell** frame [freɪm]
**Fahrkarte** ticket ['tɪkɪt]
**Fahrkartenschalter** ticket office ['tɪkɪt ˌɒfɪs]
**Fahrplan** timetable ['taɪmteɪbl]
**Fahrrad** bike [baɪk]
**Fahrstuhl** elevator *(bes. AE)* ['elɪveɪtə]; lift *(BE)* [lɪft]
**Fahrt** ride [raɪd]; *(Reise)* journey ['dʒɜːni]
**Fahrtenbuch** logbook ['lɒgbʊk]
**Fahrtziel** destination [ˌdestɪ'neɪʃn]
**Fahrzeug** vehicle ['viːəkl]
**fair** fair [feə]
**Fakt** fact [fækt]
**Faktor** factor ['fæktə]
**Fall: auf jeden Fall** certainly ['sɜːtnli]  **Auf keinen Fall!** No way! [ˌnəʊ 'weɪ]  **für den Fall, dass …** in case … [keɪs]  **im Falle von …** in (the) case of …  **Wenn das der Fall ist, …** If so, …
**Falle: in der Falle sitzen** be trapped [træpt]
**fallen** fall [fɔːl]; drop [drɒp]  **etwas fallen lassen** drop sth.  **vom Fahrrad fallen** fall off a bike
**falls** if [ɪf]; in case [keɪs]
**falsch** false [fɔːls]; wrong [rɒŋ]  **Nein, das ist falsch.** No, that's wrong.
**falten** fold [fəʊld]
**Familie** family ['fæməli]  **(die) Familie Blackwell** the Blackwell family  **eine vierköpfige Familie** a family of four
**Fan** fan [fæn]
**fangen** catch [kætʃ]
**fantastisch** fantastic [fæn'tæstɪk]
**Farbe** colour ['kʌlə]
**farbenfroh** colourful ['kʌləfl]
**farbenprächtig** colourful ['kʌləfl]
**farbig** coloured ['kʌləd]
**Farm** farm [fɑːm]
**Fasching** carnival ['kɑːnɪvl]
**Faschist/in** fascist ['fæʃɪst]
**faschistisch** fascist ['fæʃɪst]
**Fass** barrel ['bærəl]
**fast** almost ['ɔːlməʊst]; nearly ['nɪəli]
**Februar** February ['februəri]
**Federmäppchen** pencil case ['pensl keɪs]
**Feed** *(abonnierbare elektronische Nachricht im Internet)* feed [fiːd]
**Feedback** feedback *(no pl)* ['fiːdbæk]
**fehlen** be missing ['mɪsɪŋ]  **die fehlenden Wörter** the missing words  **jm. fehlt es an etwas** sb. lacks sth. [læks]  **Was fehlt dir?** What's wrong with you?
**Fehler** mistake [mɪ'steɪk]; *(Schuld)* fault [fɔːlt]
**Fehlschlag** failure ['feɪljə]
**Feier** celebration [ˌselɪ'breɪʃn]; ceremony ['serəməni]
**feiern** celebrate ['selɪbreɪt]

**Feiertag** holiday ['hɒlədeɪ]
**Feind/in** enemy ['enəmi]
**Feld** field [fiːld]; *(auf Brettspiel)* square [skweə]
**Fell** fur [fɜː]; skin [skɪn]
**Fels** rock [rɒk]
**Felsen** rock [rɒk]
**felsig** rocky ['rɒki]
**Fenster** window ['wɪndəʊ]
**Ferien** holidays *(pl)* ['hɒlədeɪz]
**Ferienanlage** resort [rɪ'zɔːt]
**Ferienort** resort [rɪ'zɔːt]
**Fernbedienung** remote control *(kurz auch:* remote) [rɪˌməʊt kən'trəʊl]
**fernbleiben** keep back [ˌkiːp 'bæk]
**fernhalten: etwas fernhalten von** keep sth. away from
**Fernsehen** TV [ˌtiː'viː]  **im Fernsehen** on TV
**fernsehen** watch TV [ˌwɒtʃ tiː'viː]
**Fernsehgerät** TV [ˌtiː'viː]
**Fernstraße** highway *(AE)* ['haɪweɪ]
**fertig: Wir sind fertig.** We're finished. ['fɪnɪʃt]; *(bereit)* We're ready.  **mit etwas fertig werden** finish sth. ['fɪnɪʃ]  **sich fertig machen (für)** get ready (for)
**Fertigkeit** skill [skɪl]
**Fertigungsindustrie** manufacturing (industry) [ˌmænju'fæktʃərɪŋ]
**fesselnd** mesmerizing ['mezməraɪzɪŋ]
**Fest** festival ['festɪvl]
**fest** firm [fɜːm]; *(festgelegt)* fixed [fɪkst]; *(nicht locker)* tight [taɪt]
**festhalten: sich an etwas festhalten** hold onto sth. [həʊld]
**Festival** festival ['festɪvl]
**festlegen** *(z.B. Regeln)* lay down [ˌleɪ 'daʊn]; set [set]
**festnehmen** arrest [ə'rest]
**Feststellung** statement ['steɪtmənt]
**festziehen** tighten ['taɪtn]
**fett** fat [fæt]
**Feuer** fire ['faɪə]; *(großes Freudenfeuer)* bonfire ['bɒnfaɪə]
**feuern** fire ['faɪə]
**Feuerwerk** fireworks *(pl)* ['faɪəwɜːks]
**Feuerwerkskörper** firework ['faɪəwɜːk]
**Fieber** temperature ['temprətʃə]  **Fieber haben** have a temperature
**Figur** figure ['fɪgə]; *(in Roman, Film, Theaterstück usw.)* character ['kærəktə]
**Fiktion** fiction ['fɪkʃn]
**fiktiv** *(mythisch)* mythical ['mɪθɪkl]
**Film** film [fɪlm]; movie *(bes. AE)* ['muːvi]
**filmen** film [fɪlm]
**Filzstift** felt pen [ˌfelt 'pen]
**Finale** final ['faɪnl]
**finanziell** financial [faɪ'nænʃl]
**finden** find [faɪnd]  **Freunde finden** make friends  **Wie findest du …?** How do you like …?
**Finger** finger ['fɪŋgə]
**Finsternis** darkness ['dɑːknəs]
**Firma** company ['kʌmpəni]

**Fisch** fish, *pl* fish [fɪʃ]
**Fischerdorf** fishing village ['fɪʃɪŋ vɪlɪdʒ]
**fit** fit [fɪt]
**flach** flat [flæt]
**Flagge** flag [flæg]
**Flasche** bottle ['bɒtl]
**Fleck** spot [spɒt]
**Fleisch** meat [miːt]
**fleißig: jd., der eifrig und fleißig ist** eager beaver [ˌiːgə 'biːvə]
**fliegen** fly [flaɪ]
**fliehen (aus, vor)** escape (from) [ɪ'skeɪp]; flee (from) [fliː]
**fließen** flow [fləʊ]
**fließend(es) Wasser** running water [ˌrʌnɪŋ 'wɔːtə]
**Floß** raft [rɑːft]
**Flucht** escape [ɪ'skeɪp]
**flüchten (aus)** flee (from) [fliː]
**Flug** flight [flaɪt]
**Flügel** wing [wɪŋ]
**Flughafen** airport ['eəpɔːt]
**Flugzeug** plane [pleɪn]
**Fluss** river ['rɪvə]; *(das Fließen)* flow [fləʊ]
**flussabwärts** downstream [ˌdaʊn'striːm]
**flussaufwärts** upstream [ˌʌp'striːm]
**Flussufer** bank [bæŋk]
**flüstern** whisper ['wɪspə]  **…, sagte er flüsternd.** …, he said under his breath. [breθ]
**Flutlicht** floodlight(s) ['flʌdlaɪt]
**Folge** consequence ['kɒnsɪkwəns]
**folgen** follow ['fɒləʊ]  **Folge mir. / Folgt mir.** Follow me. ['fɒləʊ miː]
**folgern: etwas (aus etwas) folgern** infer sth. (from sth.) *(fml)* [ɪn'fɜː]
**Folie** transparency [træns'pærənsi]; *(Präsentationssoftware)* slide [slaɪd]
**Folter** torture ['tɔːtʃə]
**foltern** torture ['tɔːtʃə]
**fordern** demand [dɪ'mɑːnd]
**fördern** *(werben für)* promote [prə'məʊt]
**Forderung** demand [dɪ'mɑːnd]
**Form** form [fɔːm]; *(Gestalt)* shape [ʃeɪp]  **in Form** fit [fɪt]
**formell** formal ['fɔːml]
**formen** form [fɔːm]
**förmlich** *(formell)* formal ['fɔːml]
**Forschung(en)** research *(no pl)* ['riːsɜːtʃ]
**Fort** *(Befestigungsanlage)* fort [fɔːt]
**fort** away [ə'weɪ]
**fortfahren** go on [ˌgəʊ 'ɒn]
**fortsetzen; sich fortsetzen** continue [kən'tɪnjuː]
**Foto** photo ['fəʊtəʊ]; shot [ʃɒt]  **auf dem Foto** in the photo  **Fotos machen** take photos
**Fotoapparat** camera ['kæmərə]
**fotografieren** take photos
**Foul(spiel)** foul [faʊl]
**Frage** question ['kwestʃən]  **eine Frage stellen** ask a question

# German – English

[ɑːsk]   **Kommt nicht in Frage!** No way! [ˌnəʊ ˈweɪ]
**Fragebogen** questionnaire [ˌkwestʃəˈneə]
**fragen** ask [ɑːsk]   **jn. fragen** ask sb.; consult sb. [kənˈsʌlt]   **jn. nach dem Weg fragen** ask sb. the way   **sich fragen** (gern wissen wollen) wonder [ˈwʌndə]
**Fragezeichen** question mark [ˈkwestʃən mɑːk]
**Fransen** fringe [frɪndʒ]
**Französisch** French [frentʃ]
**Frau** woman, pl women [ˈwʊmən], [ˈwɪmɪn]   **Frau Schwarz** Mrs Schwarz [ˈmɪsɪz]
**Freak** freak [friːk]
**frei** free [friː]   **freie Zeit** free time   **im Freien** outdoor [ˈaʊtdɔː]; outdoors [ˌaʊtˈdɔːz]
**Freiheit** freedom [ˈfriːdəm]; liberty [ˈlɪbəti]
**freilich** certainly [ˈsɜːtnli]
**Freitag** Friday [ˈfraɪdeɪ], [ˈfraɪdi]
**freiwillig** optional [ˈɒpʃənl]   **freiwillig arbeiten** (unbezahlt) volunteer [ˌvɒlənˈtɪə]   **freiwillige Arbeit** volunteer work
**Freiwillige(r)** volunteer [ˌvɒlənˈtɪə]
**Freizeit** free time
**Freizeitaktivität** free-time activity [ˌfriːtaɪm ækˈtɪvəti]
**Freizeitpark, -zentrum** leisure centre [ˈleʒə sentə]
**fremd** foreign [ˈfɒrən]
**Fremde/r** foreigner [ˈfɒrənə]
**Fremdenführer/in** guide [gaɪd]
**Fremdenverkehrsbüro** tourist (information) bureau (AE) [ˈtʊərɪst ˌbjʊərəʊ]; tourist (information) office [ˈtʊərɪst ˌɒfɪs]
**Fremdsprache** foreign language [fɒrən ˈlæŋgwɪdʒ]
**freuen: sich auf etwas freuen** look forward to sth. [ˈfɔːwəd]   **Freut mich, dich/euch/Sie kennenzulernen.** Nice to meet you.
**Freund/in** friend [frend]; buddy (infml) [ˈbʌdi]; (feste Freundin/fester Freund) girlfriend/boyfriend   **Freunde finden** make friends
**freundlich** friendly [ˈfrendli]; kind [kaɪnd]; (gastfreundlich) welcoming [ˈwelkəmɪŋ]   **Mit freundlichen Grüßen** (Briefschluss) Yours sincerely [ˌjɔːz sɪnˈsɪəli]
**Friede(n)** peace [piːs]
**Friedensstifter/in** peacemaker [ˈpiːsmeɪkə]
**Friedhof** cemetery [ˈsemətri], [ˈsemətəri]
**friedlich** peaceful [ˈpiːsfl]
**frieren** be cold; (gefrieren) freeze [friːz]
**Frisbee** frisbee [ˈfrɪzbi]
**frisch** fresh [freʃ]
**Friseur/in** hairdresser [ˈheədresə]

**froh** glad [glæd]; happy [ˈhæpi]
**Frosch** frog [frɒg]
**Frucht; Früchte** fruit [fruːt]
**früh** early [ˈɜːli]
**früher: früher einmal** once [wʌns]   **was ich (früher immer) gemacht habe** what I used to do [ˈjuːst tə]
**frühere(r, s)** former [ˈfɔːmə]
**Frühling** spring [sprɪŋ]
**Frühstück** breakfast [ˈbrekfəst]
**frühstücken** have breakfast [ˈbrekfəst]
**Frühstückspension** bed & breakfast
**frustrieren** frustrate [frʌˈstreɪt]
**Fuchs** fox [fɒks]
**fühlen; sich fühlen** feel [fiːl]
**führen** lead [liːd]; guide [gaɪd]   **jn. irgendwohin führen** (zu Fuß) walk sb. somewhere [wɔːk]
**Führerschein** driver's license (AE) [ˈdraɪvəz laɪsns]; driving licence [ˈdraɪvɪŋ laɪsns]
**Fuhrwerk** (mit Pferd/en) wagon [ˈwægən]
**füllen** fill [fɪl]
**Füller** pen [pen]
**Fundament** foundation [faʊnˈdeɪʃn]
**fünf** five [faɪv]
**Fünftel** fifth [fɪfθ]
**Funk-** (drahtlos) wireless [ˈwaɪələs]
**funkeln** sparkle [ˈspɑːkl]
**funktionieren** work [wɜːk]
**für** for [fɔː], [fə]   **für immer** for ever, forever [fərˈevə]
**furchtbar** terrible [ˈterəbl]
**fürchten** fear [fɪə]
**fürchterlich** awful [ˈɔːfl]
**Fuß** (auch Längenmaß, ca. 30,5 cm) foot, pl feet [fʊt], [fiːt]   **zu Fuß** on foot   **zu Fuß gehen** walk [wɔːk]
**Fußabdruck** footprint [ˈfʊtprɪnt]; footstep [ˈfʊtstep]
**Fußball** football [ˈfʊtbɔːl]; soccer [ˈsɒkə]
**Fußboden** floor [flɔː]
**Fußgänger/in** pedestrian [pəˈdestriən]
**Fußgängerzone** pedestrian zone [pəˈdestriən zəʊn]
**Futter** food [fuːd]
**füttern** feed [fiːd]
**Fütterungszeit** feeding time

# G

**Gabe** gift [gɪft]
**Gabel** fork [fɔːk]
**Galerie** gallery [ˈgæləri]
**Galopp** gallop [ˈgæləp]
**galoppieren** gallop [ˈgæləp]
**Gang** 1. aisle [aɪl]; corridor [ˈkɒrɪdɔː]   2. (Bande) gang [gæŋ]   3. **im Gang sein** go on
**ganz: ganz Plymouth** all of Plymouth   **voll und ganz** strongly [ˈstrɒŋli]
**ganze(r, s)** whole [həʊl]   **der/die/das ganze … (hindurch)** throughout …

[θruːˈaʊt]   **die ganze Zeit** all the time   **ganzer Satz** full sentence   **im ganzen Land / in der ganzen Stadt / auf der ganzen Welt** all over the country / the city / the world
**gar nichts** nothing [ˈnʌθɪŋ]
**Garage** garage [ˈgærɑːʒ], [ˈgærɪdʒ]
**Garten** garden [ˈgɑːdn]
**Gartenarbeit** gardening [ˈgɑːdnɪŋ]
**Gärtner/in** gardener [ˈgɑːdnə]
**Gärtnern** gardening [ˈgɑːdnɪŋ]
**Gas** gas [gæs]
**Gast** guest [gest]; (Besucher/in) visitor [ˈvɪzɪtə]
**Gasteltern** host parents (pl) [ˈhəʊst peərənts]
**Gastfamilie** host family [ˈhəʊst fæməli]
**gastfreundlich** welcoming [ˈwelkəmɪŋ]
**Gatter** gate [geɪt]
**Gebäude** building [ˈbɪldɪŋ]
**geben** give [gɪv]   **jm. etwas geben** (überreichen) hand sb. sth. [hænd]   **Es gibt …** There's …; There are …   **Gibt es (irgendwelche) …?** Are there any …? [ˈeni]   **Was gibt es zum Mittagessen?** What's for lunch?
**Gebiet** area [ˈeəriə]; territory [ˈterətri]
**geboren sein/werden** be born [bɔːn]
**Gebräuche** customs (pl) [ˈkʌstəmz]
**gebrochen** broken [ˈbrəʊkən]
**Geburt** birth [bɜːθ]
**Geburtsort** birthplace [ˈbɜːθpleɪs]
**Geburtstag** birthday [ˈbɜːθdeɪ]   **Ich habe am 5. Mai Geburtstag.** My birthday is on 5th May.   **Ich habe im Mai Geburtstag.** My birthday is in May.   **Wann hast du Geburtstag?** When's your birthday?
**Gedanke** thought [θɔːt]
**Gedenk-** memorial [məˈmɔːriəl]
**gedenken: jemandes/einer Sache gedenken** commemorate sb./sth. [kəˈmeməreɪt]
**Gedicht** poem [ˈpəʊɪm]
**geduldig** patient [ˈpeɪʃnt]
**geehrte: Sehr geehrte Damen und Herren** Ladies and gentlemen [ˌleɪdiz ən ˈdʒentlmən]; (Brief) Dear Sir or Madam [sɜː], [ˈmædəm]
**Gefahr** danger [ˈdeɪndʒə]
**gefährlich** dangerous [ˈdeɪndʒərəs]
**gefallen: Wie gefällt es (sie/er) dir?** How do you like it?
**gefangen sein** (festsitzen, in der Falle sitzen) be trapped [træpt]
**Gefangene(r)** prisoner [ˈprɪznə]
**Gefängnis** prison [ˈprɪzn]
**Gefäß** pot [pɒt]
**gefrieren** freeze [friːz]
**gefroren** frozen [ˈfrəʊzn]
**Gefühl** feeling [ˈfiːlɪŋ]
**gegen** against [əˈgenst]   **gegen jn. spielen** play sb. [pleɪ]

# Dictionary

**Gegend** area [ˈeəriə] **hier in der Gegend** round here [ˌraʊnd ˈhɪə] **ländliche Gegend** countryside [ˈkʌntrisaɪd]
**Gegensatz** (Kontrast) contrast [ˈkɒntrɑːst] **im Gegensatz zu** unlike [ˌʌnˈlaɪk]
**gegenseitig: sich gegenseitig** each other [iːtʃ ˈʌðə]; one another
**Gegenstand** object [ˈɒbdʒɪkt]
**Gegenteil** opposite [ˈɒpəzɪt]
**gegenüber (von)** opposite [ˈɒpəzɪt] **einander gegenüber** across from each other [əˈkrɒs]
**gegenüberliegende(r, s)** opposite [ˈɒpəzɪt]
**gegenüberstellen** contrast [kənˈtrɑːst]
**Gegenwart** present [ˈpreznt]
**Gehäuse** case [keɪs]
**Gehege** corral [kəˈrɑːl]
**gehen** 1. go [gəʊ]; (zu Fuß gehen) walk [wɔːk]; (weggehen) leave [liːv] **an Land gehen** land [lænd] **ans Telefon gehen** answer the phone **einkaufen gehen** go shopping [ˈʃɒpɪŋ] **gut gehen** (gut laufen, klappen) go well [wel] **Los geht's. / Jetzt geht's los.** Here we go. [ˌhɪə wi ˈgəʊ] **nach Hause gehen** go home **segeln gehen** go sailing [ˈseɪlɪŋ] **spazieren gehen** go for a walk **zur Wahl gehen** vote [vəʊt]
2. **Wie geht's? / Wie geht es dir/ euch?** How are you? [haʊ ˈɑː juː]; How's things? (infml) **Mir geht's nicht gut.** I don't feel well.
3. **Worum geht es in der Geschichte?** What is the story about? [əˈbaʊt] **Es geht um eine Möwe.** It's about a seagull.
**gehören: (zu) jm. gehören** belong to sb. [bɪˈlɒŋ] **zu etwas gehören** (zu etwas passen) go with sth.
**Gehweg** pavement [ˈpeɪvmənt]; sidewalk (AE) [ˈsaɪdwɔːk]
**Geist** (Gespenst) ghost [gəʊst]; (Seele) spirit [ˈspɪrɪt]; (Verstand, Sinn) mind [maɪnd]
**Gel** gel [dʒel]
**Gelände** (Terrain) terrain [təˈreɪn]
**Geländer** railing [ˈreɪlɪŋ]
**gelangen** (hinkommen) get [get]
**gelb** yellow [ˈjeləʊ]
**Geld** money [ˈmʌni]; (infml) cash **Geld ausgeben (für)** spend money (on) [spend] **Geld sammeln (für)** raise money (for) [reɪz] **Geld wechseln/ umtauschen** change [tʃeɪndʒ] **Es ist sein Geld wert.** It's good value (for money). [ˈvæljuː]
**Geldstrafe** fine [faɪn] **jn. zu einer Geldstrafe verurteilen** fine sb.
**Gelegenheit** chance [tʃɑːns]; opportunity [ˌɒpəˈtjuːnəti]
**gelten (für)** apply (to) [əˈplaɪ]
**Gemälde** painting [ˈpeɪntɪŋ]

**gemein: etwas miteinander gemein haben** have sth. in common [ɪn ˈkɒmən]
**Gemeinde** community [kəˈmjuːnəti]
**gemeinsam: etwas gemeinsam haben** have sth. in common [ɪn ˈkɒmən]
**Gemeinsamkeit** (Ähnlichkeit) similarity [ˌsɪməˈlærəti]
**Gemeinschaft** community [kəˈmjuːnəti]
**gemischt** (mit beiden Geschlechtern, z.B. Schulen) coed (= co-educational) [ˌkəʊˈed], [ˌkəʊ edʒuˈkeɪʃənl]
**Gemüse** vegetables (pl) [ˈvedʒtəblz]
**genannt werden** (heißen) be called [kɔːld]
**genau** 1. (adj) exact [ɪgˈzækt]
2. (adv) exactly [ɪgˈzæktli] **genau hinschauen** look closely [ˈkləʊsli]
**genau in dem Moment** just then
**genau wie …** just like … [ˈdʒʌst laɪk]
**genau hinter dir** right behind you
**genauso** equally [ˈiːkwəli] **genauso groß** just as big [ˈdʒʌst əz]
**Genehmigung** consent [kənˈsent]; licence [ˈlaɪsns]
**Generation** generation [ˌdʒenəˈreɪʃn]
**generell** (adv) generally [ˈdʒenrəli]; in general [ɪn ˈdʒenrəl]
**genial** brilliant [ˈbrɪliənt]
**genießen** enjoy [ɪnˈdʒɔɪ]
**genug** enough [ɪˈnʌf]
**geöffnet** open [ˈəʊpən]
**Geografie** geography [dʒiˈɒgrəfi]
**gerade** at the moment [ˈməʊmənt]; right now [raɪt naʊ]; (geradewegs) straight [streɪt] **gerade eben** just [dʒʌst]
**gerade dann** just then
**geradeaus weiter** straight on [streɪt ˈɒn]
**geradewegs** straight [streɪt]
**Gerät** machine [məˈʃiːn]
**geraten: in Panik geraten** panic [ˈpænɪk] **in Schwierigkeiten geraten** get into trouble
**Geräusch** sound [saʊnd]; (Lärm) noise [nɔɪz]
**gerecht** fair [feə]
**Gericht** (Mahlzeit) dish [dɪʃ]
**gern(e): Ich schwimme gern.** I like swimming. **Bitte, gern geschehen.** You're welcome. [ˈwelkəm]; No worries. (infml) [ˈwʌriz] **gern wissen wollen** wonder [ˈwʌndə] **Ich hätte gern …** I'd like … (= I would like …) **Was hättest du gern?** What would you like? [wʊd] **Ich würde sehr gern …** I'd love to … [lʌv]
**gernhaben** like [laɪk]
**Geruch** smell [smel]
**gesamte(r, s)** whole [həʊl]
**Gesamtsumme: eine Gesamtsumme von …** a total of … [ˈtəʊtl]
**Geschäft** store (AE) [stɔː]
**geschäftig** busy [ˈbɪzi]
**Geschäftsführer/in** manager [ˈmænɪdʒə]

**geschehen (mit)** happen (to) [ˈhæpən]
**Geschenk** present [ˈpreznt]; gift [gɪft]
**Geschichte** (Erzählung) story [ˈstɔːri]; (vergangene Zeiten) history [ˈhɪstri]
**Geschichtenerzähler/in** storyteller [ˈstɔːritelə]
**geschickt** skilful (AE auch: skillful) [ˈskɪlfl]
**geschieden** divorced [dɪˈvɔːst]
**Geschirr: das Geschirr abwaschen** wash the dishes (pl)
**geschlossen** closed [kləʊzd]
**Geschmack, Geschmacksrichtung** flavor (AE), flavour (BE) [ˈfleɪvə]
**Geschoss** (aus Waffe) shot [ʃɒt]
**Geschwindigkeit** speed [spiːd]
**Gesellschaft** company [ˈkʌmpəni]; society [səˈsaɪəti]
**Gesetz** law [lɔː]
**Gesicht** face [feɪs]
**gespannt** excited [ɪkˈsaɪtɪd]
**Gespenst** ghost [gəʊst]
**Gespräch** conversation [ˌkɒnvəˈseɪʃn]
**Gestalt** (Figur) figure [ˈfɪgə]; (Form) shape [ʃeɪp]
**Gestaltung** design [dɪˈzaɪn]; layout [ˈleɪaʊt]
**Gestell** frame [freɪm]
**gestern** yesterday [ˈjestədeɪ], [ˈjestədi]
**gesund** healthy [ˈhelθi]; well [wel]
**Gesundheit** health [helθ]
**Gesundheitsfürsorge** health care [ˈhelθ keə]
**Gesundheitswesen** health service [ˈhelθ sɜːvɪs]
**Getränk** drink [drɪŋk]
**getrennt** apart [əˈpɑːt]; separate [ˈseprət]
**Gewalt** violence [ˈvaɪələns]
**gewaltsam** violent [ˈvaɪələnt]
**gewalttätig** violent [ˈvaɪələnt]
**Gewalttätigkeit** violence [ˈvaɪələns]
**Gewinn** prize [praɪz]
**gewinnen** win [wɪn]
**Gewinner/in** winner [ˈwɪnə]
**gewisse(r, s)** certain [ˈsɜːtn]
**Gewitter** storm [stɔːm]
**Gewohnheit** habit [ˈhæbɪt]
**gewöhnlich** usual [ˈjuːʒuəl]; (normalerweise) usually [ˈjuːʒuəli]
**gießen** pour [pɔː]
**Gipfel** peak [piːk]; summit [ˈsʌmɪt]
**Giraffe** giraffe [dʒəˈrɑːf]
**Gitarre** guitar [gɪˈtɑː] **Gitarre spielen** play the guitar
**Gitter** grid [grɪd]
**glänzen** sparkle [ˈspɑːkl]
**glänzend** shiny [ˈʃaɪni]; brilliant [ˈbrɪliənt]
**Glas** glass [glɑːs]
**glatt** smooth [smuːð]; (rutschig) slippery [ˈslɪpəri]
**Glaube (an)** belief (in) [bɪˈliːf]
**glauben (an)** believe (in) [bɪˈliːv]; (denken) think [θɪŋk] **Das glaube ich**

# German – English

**nicht.** I don't think so. **Ich glaube ja.** I think so.
**gleich** 1. *(gleichberechtigt)* equal ['i:kwəl]
2. **gleich nachdem …** just after …
**gleich nach dir** right after you
**Gleichberechtigung** equality [ɪ'kwɒləti]
**gleichermaßen** equally [i:kwəli]
**gleichgestellt** equal ['i:kwəl]
**Gleichheit** equality [ɪ'kwɒləti]
**gleichzeitig** at one time; at a time
**Gleis** track [træk]; *(Bahnsteig)* platform ['plætfɔ:m]
**gleiten** slither ['slɪðə]; slide [slaɪd]
**Gliederung** structure ['strʌktʃə]
**glitzern** sparkle ['spa:kl]
**global** global ['gləʊbl]
**Glocke** bell [bel]
**Glück** luck [lʌk]; *(Zufriedenheit)* happiness ['hæpinəs] **Viel Glück!** Good luck! [lʌk] **Glück haben** be lucky ['lʌki]
**glücklich** happy ['hæpi]
**glücklicherweise** luckily ['lʌkɪli]
**Glückspilz: Du Glückspilz.** Lucky you.
**Gold; Gold-** gold [gəʊld]
**golden** *(aus Gold)* golden ['gəʊldən]
**Gott** god, God [gɒd]
**Gottesdienst** service ['sɜ:vɪs]
**Gouverneur/in** governor ['gʌvənə]
**Grab** grave [greɪv]
**Graben** ditch [dɪtʃ]
**graben** dig [dɪg]
**Grabstein** gravestone ['greɪvstəʊn]
**Graffiti** graffiti [grə'fi:ti]
**Grafiken** graphics *(pl)* ['græfɪks]
**grafisch** graphic ['græfɪk]
**Grafschaft** *(in Großbritannien)* county ['kaʊnti]
**Gramm** gram [græm]
**Grammatik** grammar ['græmə]
**Granit** granite ['grænɪt]
**Gras** grass [grɑ:s]
**grau** grey [greɪ]
**greifen (nach)** reach (for) [ri:tʃ]
**Grenze** border ['bɔ:də]; boundary ['baʊndri]
**Griff** hold [həʊld]
**Grill** barbecue ['ba:bɪkju:]
**Grillfest/-party** barbecue ['ba:bɪkju:]
**grinsen** grin [grɪn]
**Grinsen** grin [grɪn]
**Grizzlybär** grizzly (bear) [,grɪzli 'beə]
**grob** crude [kru:d]; rough [rʌf]
**groß** big [bɪg]; large [lɑ:dʒ]; *(Person)* tall [tɔ:l] **sehr groß** huge [hju:dʒ] **Wie groß soll der/dein Tee sein?** What size tea would you like?
**großartig** great; brilliant ['brɪliənt]; awesome *(bes. AE, infml)* ['ɔ:səm]
**Großbritannien** Great Britain (GB) [,greɪt 'brɪtn]
**Großbuchstabe** capital letter [,kæpɪtl 'letə]
**Größe** size [saɪz]

**Großeltern** grandparents *(pl)* ['grænpeərənts]
**Großmutter** grandmother ['grænmʌðə]
**Großstadt** city ['sɪti]
**größtenteils** mostly ['məʊstli]
**Großvater** grandfather ['grænfɑ:ðə]
**grün** green [gri:n]
**Grund** reason ['ri:zn]
**gründen** found [faʊnd]; establish [ɪ'stæblɪʃ]
**Grundlage** foundation [faʊn'deɪʃn]
**gründlich** thorough ['θʌrə]
**Grundschule** primary school ['praɪməri sku:l]
**Gründung** foundation [faʊn'deɪʃn]
**Gruppe** group (of) [gru:p]
**gruselig** scary ['skeəri]
**Gruß(formel)** greeting ['gri:tɪŋ]
**Grüße: Liebe Grüße, …** *(Briefschluss)* Love, … **Mit besten Grüßen** All the best **Mit freundlichen Grüßen** Yours sincerely [,jɔ:z sɪn'sɪəli]
**grüßen: Grüß Gott.** Hello. **Grüß … von mir.** Say hello to … for me.
**Gürtel** belt [belt]
**gut** good [gʊd]; *(gesundheitlich)* well; *(prima, in Ordnung)* fine [faɪn]; *(geschickt)* skilful (AE auch: skillful) ['skɪlfl] **gut sein in etwas** be good at sth. **Gut, danke.** Fine, thanks. **gut laufen, gut gehen** *(klappen)* go well **Mir geht's nicht gut. / Ich fühle mich nicht gut.** I don't feel well. **Alles Gute** *(Briefschluss)* All the best
**gutaussehend** good-looking [,gʊd 'lʊkɪŋ]; handsome ['hænsəm]
**Güter** goods *(pl)* [gʊdz]
**Guy-Fawkes-Puppe** guy [gaɪ]
**Gymnastik** gymnastics [dʒɪm'næstɪks]

# H

**Haar, Haare** hair [heə]
**haben** have [hæv], [həv]; have got **Durst haben** be thirsty ['θɜ:sti] **Glück haben** be lucky ['lʌki] **Hunger haben** be hungry ['hʌŋgri] **Recht/Unrecht haben** be right/wrong **viel zu tun haben** be busy ['bɪzi]
**hacken** *(Computer)* hack [hæk]
**Hacker/in** *(Computer)* hacker ['hækə]
**Hafen** harbour ['hɑ:bə]; dock [dɒk]
**Hafenstadt** port [pɔ:t]
**Hähnchen** chicken ['tʃɪkɪn]
**Hai** shark [ʃɑ:k]
**Haken** hook [hʊk]
**halb: halb elf (10.30 / 22.30)** half past ten ['hɑ:f pɑ:st] **eine halbe Stunde** half an hour
**halb-; Halb-** semi- ['semi] **halbrund** semicircular [,semi'sɜ:kjələ]
**Halbzeit** half, *pl* halves [hɑ:f], [hɑ:vz]
**Hälfte** half, *pl* halves [hɑ:f], [hɑ:vz]
**Halle** hall [hɔ:l]

**Hallen-** indoor ['ɪndɔ:]
**Hallo.** Hi. [haɪ]; Hello. [hə'ləʊ]
**Hals** neck [nek]; *(Kehle)* throat [θrəʊt]
**Halsschmerzen haben** have a sore throat [sɔ: 'θrəʊt]
**Halt** stop [stɒp]
**halten** hold [həʊld]; keep [ki:p]; *(von Bestand sein)* last [lɑ:st] **etwas warm/frisch halten** keep sth. warm/fresh **einen Vortrag / eine Rede halten (über)** give a talk (about) **ein Referat halten** give a presentation
**Haltestelle** stop [stɒp]
**Hamburger** burger ['bɜ:gə]; hamburger ['hæmbɜ:gə]
**Hammer** hammer ['hæmə]
**hämmern** hammer ['hæmə]
**Hamster** hamster ['hæmstə]
**Hand** hand [hænd]
**Händedruck** handshake ['hændʃeɪk]
**Handel** trade [treɪd]
**handeln** 1. *(Handel treiben)* trade [treɪd]
2. **Wovon handelt die Geschichte?** What is the story about? **Es handelt von einer Möwe.** It's about a seagull.
**Handgepäckstück** carry-on bag ['kæri_ɒn]
**Händler/in** trader ['treɪdə]
**Handlung** act [ækt]; action ['ækʃn]
**Handout** handout ['hændaʊt]
**Handpuppe** puppet ['pʌpɪt]
**Handschlag** handshake ['hændʃeɪk]
**Handschuh** glove [glʌv]
**Handy** mobile (phone) [,məʊbaɪl 'fəʊn]; cell phone (AE) ['sel fəʊn]
**Handzettel** handout ['hændaʊt]
**hängen** hang [hæŋ] **an etwas hängen** *(befestigt sein)* be attached to sth. [ə'tætʃt]
**harmlos** harmless ['hɑ:mləs]
**hart** hard [hɑ:d]; *(knallhart)* tough [tʌf]; *(rau)* rough [rʌf]
**Hass** hate [heɪt]
**hassen** hate [heɪt]
**hätte: Du hättest ihn gemocht.** You would have liked him. [wʊd]
**hauen** *(in Stein)* carve [kɑ:v]
**Haufen** pile [paɪl]
**häufig** frequent ['fri:kwənt]; common ['kɒmən]
**Haupt-** main [meɪn]
**Hauptpunkt** focus ['fəʊkəs]; key point ['ki: pɔɪnt]
**hauptsächlich** *(adv)* mainly ['meɪnli]; mostly ['məʊstli]
**Hauptsatz** main clause ['meɪn klɔ:z]
**Hauptstadt** capital ['kæpɪtl]
**Hauptteil** *(eines Textes)* body ['bɒdi]
**Haus** house [haʊs] **zu Hause** at home **zu Hause in …** *(daheim)* back in … **nach Hause gehen/kommen** go/come home **nicht zu Haus(e) sein** be out
**Hausarrest: jm. Hausarrest erteilen** ground sb. [graʊnd]

# Dictionary

**Hausaufgabe(n)** homework ['haʊmwɜːk]
  **Was haben wir als Hausaufgabe auf?** What's for homework?
**Häuschen** cottage ['kɒtɪdʒ]
**Haustier** pet [pet]
**Haut** skin [skɪn]
**heben** lift [lɪft]
**heftig** fierce [fɪəs]; strongly ['strɒŋli]
  **heftiger Regen** heavy rain ['hevi]
**Heidelbeere** blueberry ['bluːbəri]
**heilen** heal [hiːl]
**heilig (für)** sacred (to) ['seɪkrɪd]
**Heiligabend** Christmas Eve [ˌkrɪsməs ˈiːv]
**Heim** (*Zuhause*) home [həʊm]
**Heimat sein für etwas** be home to sth.
**Heimatstadt** hometown [ˌhəʊmˈtaʊn]
**heiraten** marry ['mæri]
**heiß** hot [hɒt]
**heißen** be called [kɔːld] **ich heiße …** my name is …
**hektisch** (*belebt, geschäftig*) busy ['bɪzi]
**Held/in** hero, *pl* heroes ['hɪərəʊ]
**helfen** help [help]
**Helfer/in** helper ['helpə]
**Helikopter** helicopter ['helɪkɒptə]
**hell** bright [braɪt]
**hellbraun/-blau** light brown/blue [laɪt]
**Hemd** shirt [ʃɜːt]
**herannahen** approach [əˈprəʊtʃ]
**herauf** up [ʌp]
**heraus** out [aʊt] **aus … heraus** out of … ['aʊt_əv]
**herausfinden: etwas herausfinden** find sth. out
**herausfischen: etwas herausfischen** fish sth. out
**herausfordern: jn. herausfordern (zu etwas)** challenge sb. (to sth.) ['tʃælɪndʒ]
**Herausforderung** challenge ['tʃælɪndʒ]
**Herausgeber/in** editor ['edɪtə]
**heraushalten: etwas heraushalten aus** keep sth. out of
**herauskommen (aus …)** emerge (from …) [ɪˈmɜːdʒ]
**herausnehmen: etwas herausnehmen** take sth. out [teɪk]
**herausziehen: etwas herausziehen** pull sth. out
**Herberge** hostel ['hɒstl]
**herbringen** bring [brɪŋ]
**Herbst** autumn ['ɔːtəm]; fall (*AE*) [fɔːl]
**Herde** herd [hɜːd]
**hereinkommen** come in
**Herkunft** descent [dɪˈsent]; origin ['ɒrɪdʒɪn]
**Herr Schwarz** Mr Schwarz ['mɪstə]
**Herren: Meine Damen und Herren / Sehr geehrte Damen und Herren** Ladies and gentlemen [ˌleɪdɪz_ən ˈdʒentlmən]; (*Brief*) Dear Sir or Madam [sɜː], ['mædəm]
**herrennen: hinter jm. herrennen** run after sb. [ˌrʌn_ˈɑːftə]

**herrlich** lovely ['lʌvli]
**Herrschaft** rule [ruːl]
**herrschen: über etwas herrschen** rule sth. [ruːl]
**herstellen** make [meɪk]; produce [prəˈdjuːs]
**herüber: hier herüber** over here
**herüberkommen (zu/nach)** come over (to)
**herum: um … herum** around … [əˈraʊnd] **um den See herum** around the lake **überall um sie herum** all around her
**herum-: etwas herumgeben/-reichen** pass sth. around [ˌpɑːs_əˈraʊnd]
**herumlaufen/-irren** wander ['wɒndə]
**herumrennen/-gehen** walk/run/… around **herumwirbeln** (*sich im Kreis drehen*) spin around [ˌspɪn_əˈraʊnd]
**herunter** down [daʊn]
**herunter-: etwas herunterladen** download sth. [ˌdaʊnˈləʊd] **vom Fahrrad herunterfallen** fall off a bike
**hervorheben** (*mit Textmarker*) highlight ['haɪlaɪt]
**Hervorhebung** emphasis ['emfəsɪs]
**hervorragend** excellent ['eksələnt]
**hervorrufen** breed [briːd]
**hervortreten (aus …)** emerge (from …) [ɪˈmɜːdʒ]
**Herz** heart [hɑːt] **Tiere liegen mir sehr am Herzen.** I really care about animals. [keə]
**Herzlichen Glückwunsch (zu etwas)!** Congratulations (on sth.)! [kənˌgrætʃʊˈleɪʃnz]
**herzlos** heartless ['hɑːtləs]
**Hetzkampagne** vendetta [venˈdetə]
**Heu** hay [heɪ]
**heulen** howl [haʊl]
**Heuler** (*Robbenjunges*) baby seal ['beɪbi siːl]
**heute** today [təˈdeɪ] **heute Nachmittag/Abend/…** this afternoon/evening/… **heute Nacht, heute Abend** tonight [təˈnaɪt]
**Hexenmeister** sorcerer ['sɔːsərə]
**hier** here [hɪə] **hier herüber; hier drüben** over here **hier in der Gegend** round here [ˌraʊnd ˈhɪə] **hier in der Nähe** near here **Hier steht: … / Es heißt hier: …** It says here: … (**nach**) **hier oben** up here
**hierher** here [hɪə] **bis hierher** so far
**Hilfe** help [help]
**hilfreich** helpful ['helpfl]
**hilfsbereit** helpful ['helpfl]
**Himmel** sky [skaɪ]; (*im religiösen Sinn*) heaven ['hevn]
**hinauf** up [ʌp] **auf … hinauf** onto ['ɒntʊ] **auf das Boot hinauf** onto the boat
**hinaufklettern (auf)** climb [klaɪm]
**hinaus** out [aʊt] **aus … hinaus** out of … ['aʊt_əv]

**hinbringen** take [teɪk]
**hindern: jn. daran hindern, etwas zu tun** prevent sb. from doing sth. [prɪˈvent]
**hindeuten auf** suggest [səˈdʒest]
**hinein: in die Küche hinein** into the kitchen ['ɪntʊ]
**hineingehen** go in; enter ['entə]
**hinfallen** fall [fɔːl]
**hinkommen** (*gelangen*) get [get]
**hinlegen: etwas hinlegen** put sth. down **sich hinlegen** lie down [ˌlaɪ ˈdaʊn]
**hinrichten** execute ['eksɪkjuːt]
**Hinrichtung** execution [ˌeksɪˈkjuːʃn]
**hinsetzen: sich hinsetzen** sit down [ˌsɪt ˈdaʊn] **jn. bitten, sich hinzusetzen** sit sb. down
**Hinsicht: in mancher/vielerlei Hinsicht** in some/many ways
**hinstellen: sich hinstellen** stand [stænd]
**hinten: nach hinten** backwards ['bækwədz] **von hinten** from behind
**hinter** behind [bɪˈhaɪnd] **hinter jm. herrennen** run after sb. [ˌrʌn_ˈɑːftə]
**hintere(r, s): aus dem hinteren Teil des Busses** from the back of the bus
**Hintergrund** background ['bækgraʊnd]
**Hintergrundinformation(en)** background file
**hinterlassen: eine Nachricht hinterlassen** leave a message
**hinüber zu/nach …** over to … ['əʊvə]
**hinüberrennen (zu/nach)** run over (to)
**hinunter** down [daʊn]
**hinunterbeugen: sich hinunterbeugen** bend down [bend]
**Hinweis** (*Lösungshinweis*) clue [kluː]
**hinweisen: (jn.) auf etwas hinweisen** point sth. out (to sb.) [ˌpɔɪnt_ˈaʊt] **es weißt darauf hin, dass …** (*hindeuten*) it suggests that … [səˈdʒest]
**hinzufügen (zu)** add (to) [æd]
**Hirsch** deer [dɪə]
**historisch** historical [hɪˈstɒrɪkl]; (*geschichtlich bedeutsam*) historic [hɪˈstɒrɪk]
**Hitze** heat [hiːt]
**Hobby** hobby ['hɒbi]
**hoch** high [haɪ]; (*Gebäude, Baum*) tall [tɔːl]
**Hochgenuss** treat ['triːt]
**hochheben** lift [lɪft]; lift up [ˌlɪft_ˈʌp]; pick up [ˌpɪk_ˈʌp]
**hochladen: etwas hochladen** upload sth. [ˌʌpˈləʊd]
**Hochmoor** moor [mɔː]
**Hochschule** college ['kɒlɪdʒ]
**hochsehen** look up [lʊkˈʌp]
**hochspringen** jump up [dʒʌmp ʌp]
**Hochzeit** wedding ['wedɪŋ]
**Hockey** hockey ['hɒki]
**Hof** courtyard ['kɔːtjɑːd]

**hoffen** hope [həʊp]
**höflich** polite [pəˈlaɪt]
**Höhe** altitude [ˈæltɪtjuːd]
**Höhle** cave [keɪv]; (eines Raubtiers) den [den]
**holen: (sich) etwas holen** get sth. [get]
**Holz** wood [wʊd]
**hölzern** wooden [ˈwʊdn]
**Honig** honey [ˈhʌni]
**horchen** listen [ˈlɪsn]
**hören** hear [hɪə]
**Horizont** skyline [ˈskaɪlaɪn]
**Horn** horn [hɔːn]
**Hose** trousers (pl) [ˈtraʊzəz]; pants (pl, AE) [pænts]
**Hotel** hotel [həʊˈtel]
**Hotline** hotline [ˈhɒtlaɪn]
**hübsch** pretty [ˈprɪti]; lovely [ˈlʌvli]
**Hubschrauber** helicopter [ˈhelɪkɒptə]
**Hüfte** hip [hɪp]
**Hügel** hill [hɪl]
**hügelig** hilly [ˈhɪli]
**Huhn** chicken [ˈtʃɪkɪn]
**Hummel** bumblebee [ˈbʌmblbiː]
**Hummer** lobster [ˈlɒbstə]
**Humor** (Sinn für Humor) sense of humour [ˌsens əv ˈhjuːmə]
**humorvoll** humorous [ˈhjuːmərəs]
**Hund** dog [dɒg] **mit dem Hund rausgehen, den Hund ausführen** walk the dog
**Hunger haben** be hungry [ˈhʌŋgri]
**Hungersnot** famine [ˈfæmɪn]
**hungrig sein** be hungry [ˈhʌŋgri]
**Hupe** horn [hɔːn]
**hupen** blow the horn [hɔːn]; honk [hɒŋk]
**hüpfen** hop [hɒp]
**hüpfen (lassen)** bounce [baʊns]
**Hurrikan** hurricane [ˈhʌrɪkən], [ˈhʌrɪkeɪn]
**Husten haben** have a cough [kɒf]
**Hut** hat [hæt]
**Hymne** anthem [ˈænθəm]
**hypnotisierend** mesmerizing [ˈmezməraɪzɪŋ]

# I

**ich** I [aɪ] **Ich auch.** Me too. **Ich auch nicht.** Me neither. [ˈnaɪðəl, ˈniːðə] **Ich bin's.** It's me. [miː] **ich selbst** myself [maɪˈself]
**ideal** ideal [aɪˈdɪəl]; perfect [ˈpɜːfɪkt]
**Idee** idea [aɪˈdɪə]
**Identität** identity [aɪˈdentəti]
**Iglu** igloo [ˈɪgluː]
**ihm** him [hɪm]
**ihn** him [hɪm]
**Ihnen** (höfliche Anrede) you [juː]
**ihnen** them [ðem], [ðəm]
**Ihr, Ihre** (vor Nomen, besitzanzeigend; zur höflichen Anrede „you") your [jɔː], [jə]
**ihr** (Plural von „you") you [juː]

**ihr, ihre** (vor Nomen, besitzanzeigend)
1. (zu „she") her [hɜː], [hə]
2. (zu „it", bei Dingen und Tieren) its
3. (zu „they") their [ðeə]
**ihrer, ihre, ihrs** 1. (zu „she") hers [hɜːz]
2. (zu „they") theirs [ðeəz]
**Illustration** illustration [ˌɪləˈstreɪʃn]
**im: im Fernsehen** on TV **im Flugzeug** on the plane **im Gang sein** go on **im Internet** on the internet **im Jahr 1580** in 1580 **im Radio** on the radio [ˈreɪdiəʊ]
**Image** image [ˈɪmɪdʒ]
**Imbiss** snack [snæk]
**immer** always [ˈɔːlweɪz] **immer noch** still **immer wieder** again and again **etwas immer wieder tun** keep (on) doing sth. **(für) immer** for ever, forever [fərˈevə] **wann (auch) immer** whenever [ˌwenˈevə] **was (auch) immer** whatever [ˌwɒtˈevə]
**Imperium** empire [ˈempaɪə]
**imstande (zu)** capable (of) [ˈkeɪpəbl]
**in** in [ɪn] **in (... umher)** round ... [raʊnd] **in den 40er-Jahren (des 20. Jahrhunderts)** in the 1940s **in den Krieg ziehen** go to war **in der Beach Road** in Beach Road **in der Beach Road 8** at 8 Beach Road **in der Dean Street** in Dean Street **in der Dean Street 14** at 14 Dean Street **in der Kuppel** (im Innern) inside **in der Mitte** in the middle **in der Schule** at school **in die Küche (hinein)** into the kitchen **in ein Haus (ein)ziehen** move into a house **in England** in England **in Ordnung** all right; fine **in Richtung Bahnhof** towards the station **in Schwierigkeiten sein** be in trouble
**inbegriffen** included [ɪnˈkluːdɪd]
**Inder/in** Indian [ˈɪndiən]
**Indianer/in** Indian [ˈɪndiən]
**indisch** Indian [ˈɪndiən]
**individuell, Individual-** individual [ˌɪndɪˈvɪdʒuəl]
**Individuum** individual [ˌɪndɪˈvɪdʒuəl]
**Industrie** industry [ˈɪndəstri] **verarbeitende Industrie** manufacturing (industry) [ˌmænjuˈfæktʃərɪŋ]
**Infektion** infection [ɪnˈfekʃn]
**Infinitiv** infinitive [ɪnˈfɪnətɪv]
**infizieren** infect [ɪnˈfekt]
**Information(en) (über)** information (about) (no pl) [ˌɪnfəˈmeɪʃn]
**Informations-** informational [ˌɪnfəˈmeɪʃənl]
**Informations- und Kommunikationstechnologie** ICT [ˌaɪ siː ˈtiː]; Information and Communications Technology [ˌɪnfəˌmeɪʃn ənd kəmjuːnɪˈkeɪʃnz teknɒlədʒi]
**informell** informal [ɪnˈfɔːml]
**Inhalt** content [ˈkɒntent]

**Inlineskaten** skating [ˈskeɪtɪŋ]
**Inlineskates** skates (pl) [skeɪtsfiː]
**innehalten** pause [pɔːz]
**Innen-** indoor [ˈɪndɔː]
**Innenhof** courtyard [ˈkɔːtjɑːd]
**Innenseite: die Innenseite** the inside [ˌɪnˈsaɪd]
**Innere: das Innere** the inside [ˌɪnˈsaɪd]
**innerhalb (von)** inside [ˌɪnˈsaɪd]
**Insekt** insect [ˈɪnsekt]
**Insel** island [ˈaɪlənd]
**Inserat** advertisement (kurz auch: ad, advert) [ədˈvɜːtɪsmənt], [æd], [ˈædvɜːt]
**inserieren** advertise [ˈædvətaɪz]
**insgesamt** (alles in allem) altogether [ˌɔːltəˈgeðə]; (Gesamtsumme von) a total of [ˈtəʊtl]
**inspirieren** inspire [ɪnˈspaɪə]
**Instrument** instrument [ˈɪnstrəmənt]
**intelligent** intelligent [ɪnˈtelɪdʒənt]
**interagieren; miteinander interagieren** interact [ˌɪntərˈækt]
**interessant** interesting [ˈɪntrəstɪŋ]
**interessiert (an)** interested (in) [ˈɪntrəstɪd]
**Internat** boarding school [ˈbɔːdɪŋ skuːl]
**international** international [ˌɪntəˈnæʃnəl]
**Internet** internet [ˈɪntənet]
**Interpretation** interpretation [ɪnˌtɜːprɪˈteɪʃn]
**interpretieren** interpret [ɪnˈtɜːprɪt]
**Interview** interview [ˈɪntəvjuː]
**interviewen** interview [ˈɪntəvjuː]
**Intonation** intonation [ˌɪntəˈneɪʃn]
**Inuit** (kanadische Ureinwohner/innen) Inuit [ˈɪnjuɪt]
**Inuktitut** (Sprache der Inuit) Inuktitut [ɪˈnʊktɪtʊt]
**inzwischen** since [sɪns]
**irgendetwas** anything [ˈeniθɪŋ]
**irgendjemand** anybody [ˈenibɒdi]; anyone [ˈeniwʌn]
**irgendwelche: Gibt es irgendwelche ...?** Are there any ...? [ˈeni]
**irgendwie** somehow [ˈsʌmhaʊ] **irgendwie unheimlich/gruselig** kind of scary [kaɪnd]
**irgendwo(hin)** somewhere [ˈsʌmweə]
**irren: sich irren** be wrong [rɒŋ]

# J

**ja** yes [jes] **Wenn ja, ...** If so, ... [səʊ]
**Jacht** yacht [jɒt]
**Jacke, Jackett** jacket [ˈdʒækɪt]
**Jagd** hunt [hʌnt] **Jagd (auf)** pursuit (of) [pəˈsjuːt] **auf jn./etwas Jagd machen** hunt sb./sth. down
**jagen** hunt [hʌnt]
**Jäger/in** hunter [ˈhʌntə]
**Jahr** year [jɪə] **eine Band aus den 60er Jahren** a 1960s band
**Jahrestag** anniversary [ˌænɪˈvɜːsəri]

# Dictionary

**Jahrgang(sstufe)** year [jɪə]; grade (AE) [greɪd]
**Jahrhundert** century ['sentʃəri]
**jährlich** yearly ['jɪəli]
**jammern** whine [waɪn]
**Januar** January ['dʒænjuəri]
**je: Sie kosten je 2 Pfund 75.** (2,75 pro Stück) They're £ 2.75 each. [iːtʃ] **besser als je zuvor** better than ever **je mehr ..., desto mehr ...** the more ..., the more ...
**Jeans** jeans (pl) [dʒiːnz]
**jede(r, s)** (jede(r, s) einzelne) each [iːtʃ] **jeder Tag** every day ['evri]
**Jedenfalls ...** Anyway, ... ['eniweɪ]
**jeder** (alle) everybody ['evrɪbɒdi]; everyone ['evriwʌn]
**Jeep** jeep [dʒiːp]
**jemals** ever ['evə] **Bist du jemals in ... gewesen?** Have you ever been to ...? [biːn]
**jemand** somebody ['sʌmbədi]; someone ['sʌmwʌn] **(irgend)jemand** anybody ['enibɒdi]; anyone ['eniwʌn]
**jene(r, s): jene Gruppe** that group [ðæt], [ðət], **jene Gruppen** those groups [ðəʊz]
**jetzt** now [naʊ] **Jetzt, wo ...** Now that ... **jetzt gerade** right now [raɪt 'naʊ] **bis jetzt** so far
**jeweils** (gleichzeitig, auf einmal) at a time [taɪm]
**Job** job [dʒɒb]
**Jogging** jogging ['dʒɒgɪŋ]
**Joghurt** yoghurt ['jɒgət]
**Jongleur/in** juggler ['dʒʌglə]
**jonglieren: mit etwas jonglieren** juggle sth. ['dʒʌgl]
**jubeln** cheer [tʃɪə]
**Jude/Jüdin** Jew [dʒuː]
**jüdisch** Jewish ['dʒuːɪʃ]
**Judo** judo ['dʒuːdəʊ]
**Jugend; Jugend-** youth [juːθ]
**Jugendherberge** youth hostel ['juːθ hɒstl]
**Jugendliche(r)** kid (infml) [kɪd]
**Jugendmannschaft** junior team ['dʒuːniə tiːm]
**Juli** July [dʒuˈlaɪ]
**jung** young [jʌŋ]
**Junge** boy [bɔɪ]
**Junge bekommen** breed [briːd]
**jüngst** recent ['riːsnt]
**Juni** June [dʒuːn]
**Junior/in; Junioren-** junior ['dʒuːniə]
**Juniorenmannschaft** junior team ['dʒuːniə tiːm]
**Juwelen** jewels (pl) ['dʒuːəlz]

# K

**Kaffee** coffee ['kɒfi]
**Käfig** cage [keɪdʒ]
**Kajak** kayak ['kaɪæk]
**Kajakfahren** kayaking ['kaɪækɪŋ]

**Kakao** cocoa ['kəʊkəʊ]
**Kalender** calendar ['kælɪndə]; diary ['daɪəri]
**kalt** cold [kəʊld]
**Kälte** chill [tʃɪl]
**Kamera** camera ['kæmərə]
**Kameramann** cameraman, pl cameramen ['kæmrəmæn]
**Kamin** fireplace ['faɪəpleɪs]
**Kampf** (Schlacht) battle ['bætl]; (Schlägerei) fight [faɪt]
**kämpfen** fight [faɪt] **gegen jn. kämpfen** fight sb. [faɪt]
**Kämpfer/in** fighter ['faɪtə]
**Kanal** channel ['tʃænl]
**Kaninchen** rabbit ['ræbɪt]
**Kante** edge [edʒ]
**Kantine** canteen [kæn'tiːn]
**kapieren** get the hang of [hæŋ]
**Kapitän/in** captain ['kæptɪn]
**Kapitel** unit ['juːnɪt]
**Kapitelüberschrift** sub-heading ['sʌb hedɪŋ]
**Kappe** cap [kæp]
**kaputt** broken ['brəʊkən] **kaputt gehen** break [breɪk] **etwas kaputt machen** break sth.
**Karneval** carnival ['kɑːnɪvl]
**Karotte** carrot ['kærət]
**Karren** cart [kɑːt]
**Karte (an)** card (to) [kɑːd]
**Kartoffel** potato, pl potatoes [pə'teɪtəʊ]
**Käse** cheese [tʃiːz]
**Kasse** (in Geschäften) cash desk ['kæʃ desk]; (für den Verkauf von Eintrittskarten) ticket office ['tɪkɪt ˌɒfɪs]
**Kästchen** box [bɒks]; (auf Papier) square [skweə]
**Kasten** box [bɒks]; case [keɪs]; (für Getränke) crate [kreɪt]
**Kathedrale** cathedral [kə'θiːdrəl]
**Katholik/in; katholisch** Catholic ['kæθlɪk]
**Katze** cat [kæt]
**kauen** chew [tʃuː]
**kaufen** buy [baɪ]
**Käufer/in** shopper ['ʃɒpə]
**Kaufpreis** price [praɪs]
**kaum** barely ['beəli]; hardly ['hɑːdli] **Ich kann es kaum erwarten, ... zu sehen.** I can't wait to see ... [weɪt]
**Kehle** throat [θrəʊt]
**kein(e)** no [nəʊ] **keine(r, s) (von ...)** none (of ...) [nʌn] **Auf keinen Fall!** No way! [ˌnəʊ 'weɪ] **Kein Problem!** No worries. (infml) ['wʌriz] **er hat keine Zeit** he doesn't have time **Es gibt/sind keine ...** There aren't any ... ['eni] **Ich mag kein Grün.** I don't like green. [dəʊnt]
**Keks** biscuit ['bɪskɪt]; cookie (AE) ['kʊki]
**Keller** cellar ['selə]
**keltisch** Celtic ['keltɪk]
**kennen** know [nəʊ] **Woher kennst du ...?** How do you know ...?

**kennenlernen** meet [miːt] **Freut mich, dich/euch/Sie kennenzulernen.** Nice to meet you.
**kennzeichnen: etwas kennzeichnen** (markieren) mark sth. up [ˌmɑːk'ʌp]
**Kerl** guy [gaɪ]; dude (bes. AE, Slang) [djuːd]
**Kern** core [kɔː] **... bilden den Kern von ...** ... are core to ...
**Kern-** nuclear ['njuːkliə]
**Kernenergie** nuclear power [ˌnjuːkliə 'paʊə]
**Kernpunkt** key point ['kiː pɔɪnt]
**Kerze** candle ['kændl]
**Kette** chain [tʃeɪn]
**Kiefer** (Baum) pine (tree) [paɪn]
**Kies** gravel ['grævl]
**Kieselstein** pebble ['pebl]
**Kilo(gramm) (kg)** kilogram (= kilo, kg) ['kɪləgræm]
**Kilometer** kilometre ['kɪləmiːtə], [kɪ'lɒmɪtə]
**Kind** child, pl children [tʃaɪld], ['tʃɪldrən]; kid (infml) [kɪd]
**Kindheit** childhood ['tʃaɪldhʊd]
**Kino** cinema ['sɪnəmə]; movie theater (AE) ['muːvi θɪətə]
**Kirche** church [tʃɜːtʃ]
**Kiste** box [bɒks]; case [keɪs]; (für Getränke) crate [kreɪt]
**Klang** sound [saʊnd]
**Klapperschlange** rattlesnake ['rætlsneɪk]
**Klaps** (Tätscheln) pat [pæt]
**klar** clear [klɪə]
**Klasse** (Schulklasse) class [klɑːs]; grade (AE) [greɪd]
**klasse** awesome (bes. AE, infml) ['ɔːsəm]
**Klassenausflug** class trip ['klɑːs trɪp]
**Klassenkamerad/in** classmate ['klɑːsmeɪt]
**Klassenzimmer** classroom ['klɑːsruːm]
**klatschen** (Beifall) clap [klæp]; (z.B. Regen) slap [slæp] **Klatscht in die Hände.** Clap your hands.
**Klavier** piano [pɪ'ænəʊ] **Klavier spielen** play the piano
**Klebestift** glue stick ['gluː stɪk]
**klebrig** sticky ['stɪki]
**Klebstoff** glue [gluː]
**Kleid** dress [dres]
**kleiden: sich kleiden** dress [dres]
**Kleidung** clothes (pl) [kləʊðz]; clothing (no pl) ['kləʊðɪŋ]
**Kleidungsstück** piece of clothing ['kləʊðɪŋ] **Kleidungsstücke** clothes (pl) [kləʊðz]
**klein** little ['lɪtl]; small [smɔːl]
**Kleinbus** minibus ['mɪnɪbʌs]
**klemmen** tuck [tʌk]
**klettern** climb [klaɪm] **auf einen Baum / einen Turm klettern** climb a tree/a tower
**klicken** click [klɪk]
**Klima** climate ['klaɪmət]

# German – English

**Klingel** bell [bel]
**klingeln** ring [rɪŋ]
**klingen** sound [saʊnd] **Das klingt nach Spaß.** That sounds fun.
**Klippe** cliff [klɪf]
**Klischee(vorstellung)** stereotype ['steriətaɪp]
**klischeehaft** stereotypical [ˌsteriə'tɪpɪkl]
**klitschnass** soaking wet [ˌsəʊkɪŋ 'wet]
**klopfen** *(leicht, vorsichtig)* tap [tæp]
**Klopfen** *(leicht, vorsichtig)* tap [tæp]
**Klub** club [klʌb] **in einen Klub eintreten; sich einem Klub anschließen** join a club [dʒɔɪn]
**klug** clever ['klevə]
**Knall** bang [bæŋ]
**Knallbonbon** cracker ['krækə]
**knallen** slap [slæp]
**knapp** *(Kleidung: eng)* tight [taɪt]
**Kneipe** pub [pʌb]
**Knete** *(infml für Geld)* dosh *(infml)* [dɒʃ]
**Knie** knee [niː]
**knien** kneel [niːl]
**knurren** growl [graʊl]
**kochen** cook [kʊk]
**Kochrezept** recipe ['resəpi]
**koedukativ** *(mit beiden Geschlechtern, z.B. Schulen)* coed (= co-educational) [ˌkəʊ_'ed], [ˌkəʊ_edʒu'keɪʃənl]
**Kofferraum** boot [buːt]; trunk *(AE)* [trʌŋk]
**Kohle** coal [kəʊl]
**Kohlebergwerk** coal mine ['kəʊl maɪn]
**Kojote** coyote [kaɪ'əʊti]
**Kollokation** *(Wörter, die oft zusammen vorkommen)* collocation [ˌkɒlə'keɪʃn]
**kolonial, Kolonial-** colonial [kə'ləʊniəl]
**Kolonie** colony ['kɒləni]
**Kolonist/in** colonist ['kɒlənɪst]
**Kombination** combination [ˌkɒmbɪ'neɪʃn]
**kombinieren** combine [kəm'baɪn]
**komisch** funny ['fʌni]; *(seltsam)* strange [streɪndʒ]; weird [wɪəd]
**Komma** comma ['kɒmə] **3,5 (drei Komma fünf)** 3.5 (three point five) [pɔɪnt]
**kommen** come [kʌm]; *(hinkommen, gelangen)* get [get] **Komm, Dad!** *(Na los!)* Come on, Dad. **nach Hause kommen** come home **auf etwas kommen** *(Idee, Vorschlag)* come up with sth. **Ich komme aus Plymouth.** I'm from Plymouth. **Woher kommst du?** Where are you from? [weə]
**Kommentar** comment ['kɒment]
**kommentieren** comment on ['kɒment]
**Kommunikation** communication [kəˌmjuːnɪ'keɪʃn]
**kommunizieren** interact [ɪntər'ækt]
**Komödie** comedy ['kɒmədi]
**Kompass** compass ['kʌmpəs]
**komplett** complete [kəm'pliːt]
**Konflikt** conflict ['kɒnflɪkt]
**Konföderation** confederacy [kən'fedərəsi]
**Konfrontation** confrontation [ˌkɒnfrʌn'teɪʃn]
**konfrontieren: jn. konfrontieren (mit)** confront sb. (with) [kən'frʌnt]
**Kongress** congress ['kɒŋgres]
**König** king [kɪŋ]
**Königin** queen [kwiːn]
**königlich** royal ['rɔɪəl]
**Königreich** kingdom ['kɪŋdəm] **das Vereinigte Königreich** the United Kingdom (UK) [juˌnaɪtɪd 'kɪŋdəm], [ˌjuː 'keɪ]
**Konkurrent/in** competitor [kəm'petɪtə]
**Konkurrenz** competitor [kəm'petɪtə]
**konkurrieren (mit)** compete (with) [kəm'piːt]
**können** can [kæn], [kən] **nicht können** can't [kɑːnt]; cannot ['kænɒt] **etwas tun können** be able to do sth. ['eɪbl]; *(die Möglichkeit haben/bekommen, etwas zu tun)* get to do sth. ['get tə] **Kann ich dich/Sie kurz sprechen?** May I have a word with you?
**konnte(n)** could [kʊd] **konnte(n) nicht** couldn't ['kʊdnt] **könnte(n) could** [kʊd] **Was könnte besser sein?** What could be better? **es könnte sein** it could/might be
**Konsequenz** consequence ['kɒnsɪkwəns]
**Konsonant** consonant ['kɒnsənənt]
**konstruieren** design [dɪ'zaɪn]
**konsultieren: jn. konsultieren** consult sb. [kən'sʌlt]
**Kontakt** contact ['kɒntækt] **Kontakt aufnehmen mit jm.** contact sb.; get in touch with sb. [tʌtʃ] **(mit jm.) Kontakt halten** stay in touch (with sb.)
**Kontaktdaten** contact details *(pl)* ['kɒntækt ˌdiːteɪlz]
**Kontext** context ['kɒntekst]
**kontinental** continental [ˌkɒntɪ'nentl]
**Konto** account [ə'kaʊnt]
**Kontrast** contrast ['kɒntrɑːst]
**Kontrolle** control [kən'trəʊl]; check [tʃek]
**kontrollieren** check [tʃek]; control [kən'trəʊl]
**konzentrieren: sich auf etwas konzentrieren** focus on sth. ['fəʊkəs_ɒn]; concentrate on sth. ['kɒnsntreɪt]
**Konzert** concert ['kɒnsət]
**Koordinator/in** coordinator [kəʊ'ɔːdɪneɪtə]
**Kopf** head [hed] **Kopf hoch! / Lass den Kopf nicht hängen!** Cheer up! [ˌtʃɪər_'ʌp]
**Kopfhörer** headphones *(pl)* ['hedfəʊnz]; earphones *(pl)* ['ɪəfəʊnz]
**Kopfschmerzen haben** have a headache ['hedeɪk]
**Kopie** copy ['kɒpi] **Kopie (an)** *(in E-Mails)* cc (= carbon copy) [ˌkɑːbən 'kɒpi]
**kopieren** copy ['kɒpi]
**Korb** basket ['bɑːskɪt]
**Korbball** netball ['netbɔːl]
**Körper** body ['bɒdi]
**Körperteil** part of the body ['bɒdi]
**korrekt** correct [kə'rekt]
**Korridor** corridor ['kɒrɪdɔː]
**korrigieren** correct [kə'rekt]
**kosten 1.** cost [kɒst] **Die DVDs kosten …** The DVDs are … **Die Kamera kostet …** The camera is … **Was kostet/kosten…?** How much is/are …?
**2. etwas kosten** *(probieren)* taste sth. [teɪst]
**kostenlos** free [friː]; for free
**köstlich** delicious [dɪ'lɪʃəs]
**Kostüm** costume ['kɒstjuːm]
**Krachen** crash [kræʃ]
**Kraft** power ['paʊə]; strength [streŋθ]; *(Energie)* energy ['enədʒi]
**kräftig** strong [strɒŋ]; vigorous ['vɪgərəs]; *(mächtig)* powerful ['paʊəfl]; *(energisch)* vigorous
**Kram** stuff *(infml)* [stʌf]
**krank** ill [ɪl]; sick [sɪk]
**Krankenhaus** hospital ['hɒspɪtl]
**Krankheit** illness ['ɪlnəs]; sickness ['sɪknəs]; *(ansteckend)* disease [dɪ'ziːz]
**Kreation** creation [kri'eɪʃn]
**kreativ** creative [kri'eɪtɪv]
**Krebs** *(Tier)* crab [kræb]
**kreieren** create [kri'eɪt]
**Kreis** circle ['sɜːkl]
**Kreisverkehr** roundabout ['raʊndəbaʊt]
**kreuzen; sich kreuzen** cross [krɒs]
**Kreuzotter** adder ['ædə]
**Kreuzung** junction ['dʒʌŋkʃn]
**Kricket** cricket ['krɪkɪt]
**kriechen** creep [kriːp]
**Krieg** war [wɔː] **in den Krieg ziehen** go to war
**Kritik** review [rɪ'vjuː]
**kritisieren: jn. kritisieren (wegen)** criticize sb. (for) ['krɪtɪsaɪz]
**Krone** crown [kraʊn]
**Küche** kitchen ['kɪtʃɪn]
**Kuchen** cake [keɪk]
**Kuchenbasar** bake sale ['beɪk seɪl]
**Kugelschreiber** pen [pen]
**Kuh** cow [kaʊ]
**kühl** cool [kuːl]
**Kühle** chill [tʃɪl]
**Kultur** culture ['kʌltʃə]
**kulturell** cultural ['kʌltʃərəl]
**Kummer** sorrow ['sɒrəʊ]
**kümmern: sich um jn. kümmern** look after sb.
**Kumpel** buddy *(infml)* ['bʌdi]
**kündigen** *(Abonnement, Mailingliste)* unsubscribe (from) [ˌʌnsəb'skraɪb]
**Kung Fu** kung fu [ˌkʌŋ 'fuː]

# Dictionary

**Kunst** art [ɑːt]  **Kunst-** (*künstlich*) man-made [ˌmæn ˈmeɪd]  **darstellende Kunst** drama [ˈdrɑːmə]
**Künstler/in** artist [ˈɑːtɪst]
**künstlich** man-made [ˌmæn ˈmeɪd]
**Kunststoff** plastic [ˈplæstɪk]
**Kunststück** trick [trɪk]
**Kunstwerk** artwork [ˈɑːtwɜːk]; work of art [ˌwɜːk_əv_ˈɑːt]
**Kuppel** dome [dəʊm]
**Kürbis** squash [skwɒʃ]
**Kurier/in** messenger [ˈmesɪndʒə]
**Kurs** course [kɔːs]
**kurz** short [ʃɔːt]  **kurze Hose** shorts (*pl*)  **kurz nachdem ...** just after ...  **vor Kurzem** recently [ˈriːsntli]
**kürzlich geschehen/erfolgt** recent [ˈriːsnt]
**küssen; sich küssen** kiss [kɪs]
**Küste** coast [kəʊst]

# L

**lächeln** smile [smaɪl]
**Lächeln** smile [smaɪl]
**lachen** laugh [lɑːf]  **über jn./etwas lachen** laugh at sb./sth.
**Lachs** salmon, *pl* salmon [ˈsæmən]
**Laden** shop [ʃɒp], store (*AE*) [stɔː]  **Laden an der Ecke, Tante-Emma-Laden** corner shop [ˈkɔːnə ʃɒp]
**laden** (*Akku*) charge [ˈtʃɑːdʒ]
**Ladentisch** counter [ˈkaʊntə]
**Lage** (*Ort, Platz*) location [ləʊˈkeɪʃn]  **in der Lage sein, etwas zu tun** be able to do sth. [ˈeɪbl]
**Lagerfeuer** campfire [ˈkæmpfaɪə]
**lagern** store [stɔː]
**Lamm** lamb [læm]
**Lampe** lamp [læmp]
**Land** land [lænd]; country [ˈkʌntri]  **an Land gehen** land
**landen** land [lænd]
**Landkarte** map [mæp]
**ländliche Gegend** countryside [ˈkʌntrisaɪd]
**Landschaft** countryside [ˈkʌntrisaɪd]
**Landungssteg** landing [ˈlændɪŋ]
**Landwirt/in** farmer [ˈfɑːmə]
**Landwirtschaft** farming [ˈfɑːmɪŋ]
**lang(e)** long [lɒŋ]  **lang(e) aufbleiben** stay up late  **lange vor** way before  **nicht länger** no longer; not ... any longer
**Länge** length [leŋθ]
**langsam** slow [sləʊ]
**langweilen: sich langweilen** be/feel bored [bɔːd]
**langweilig** boring [ˈbɔːrɪŋ]
**Lärm** noise [nɔɪz]
**lärmend** noisy [ˈnɔɪzi]
**lassen** leave [liːv]; let [let]  **etwas fallen lassen** drop sth. [drɒp]  **etwas übrig lassen** leave sth.  **Lass das! Stop it!** (*infml*)

**Lastwagen** lorry (*BE*) [ˈlɒri]; truck (*bes. AE*) [trʌk]
**lateinisch; Latein** Latin [ˈlætɪn]
**laufen** run [rʌn]; (*Programm, Sendung*) be on
**Läufer/in** runner [ˈrʌnə]
**Laune** mood [muːd]
**Laut** sound [saʊnd]
**laut** 1. loud [laʊd]; (*lärmend*) noisy [ˈnɔɪzi]  **laut (vor)lesen** read aloud [əˈlaʊd]  **etwas lauter stellen** turn sth. up [tɜːn]  **mit lauter Stimme** in a loud voice
2. **laut ...** (*... zufolge*) according to ... [əˈkɔːdɪŋ]
**läuten** ring [rɪŋ]
**lautlos** silent [ˈsaɪlənt]
**Lautsprecher** loudspeaker [ˌlaʊdˈspiːkə]
**Layout** layout [ˈleɪaʊt]
**Leben** life, *pl* lives [laɪf]  **am Leben sein** be alive [əˈlaɪv]
**leben** live [lɪv]; (*am Leben sein*) be alive [əˈlaɪv]
**lebendig** (*lebhaft*) lively [ˈlaɪvli]
**Lebensmittel** food [fuːd]
**Lebensraum** habitat [ˈhæbɪtæt]
**Lebensstil** lifestyle [ˈlaɪfstaɪl]
**Lebensweise** way of life [ˌweɪ_əv ˈlaɪf]
**lebhaft** lively [ˈlaɪvli]
**lecker** delicious [dɪˈlɪʃəs], tasty [ˈteɪsti]; yummy (*infml*) [ˈjʌmi]
**Leckerei** treat [triːt]
**Leder** leather [ˈleðə]
**ledig** single [ˈsɪŋgl]
**leer** empty [ˈempti]
**leeren** empty [ˈempti]
**legen** lay [leɪ]; put [pʊt]; set [set]
**legendär** legendary [ˈledʒəndri]
**Legende** legend [ˈledʒənd]
**lehnen: sich lehnen** lean [liːn]
**lehren** teach [tiːtʃ]  **jn. lehren, etwas zu tun** teach sb. to do sth.
**Lehrer/in** teacher [ˈtiːtʃə]
**Lehrgang** course [kɔːs]; workshop [ˈwɜːkʃɒp]
**Leiche** body [ˈbɒdi]
**leicht** easy [ˈiːzi]
**Leid** sorrow [ˈsɒrəʊ]
**leid: Tut mir leid.** (I'm) sorry. [ˈsɒri]  **Es tut mir leid wegen ...** I'm sorry about ...
**leiden (an)** suffer (from) [ˈsʌfə]  **nicht leiden können** dislike [dɪsˈlaɪk]
**leihen** hire [ˈhaɪə]  **sich etwas (aus-)leihen** borrow sth. [ˈbɒrəʊ]
**Leine** line [laɪn]
**leise** quiet [ˈkwaɪət]; (*lautlos*) silent [ˈsaɪlənt]  **etwas leiser stellen** turn sth. down [tɜːn]  **mit leiser Stimme** in a soft voice
**leistungsorientiert** competitive [kəmˈpetətɪv]
**leiten** lead [liːd]
**Leiter/in** director [dəˈrektə]; leader [ˈliːdə]; (*Oberhaupt*) head [hed]
**Lektion** unit [ˈjuːnɪt]

**lenken** steer [stɪə]
**Lenkrad** (steering) wheel [ˈstɪərɪŋ wiːl]
**Lern- und Arbeitstechniken** study skills [ˈstʌdi skɪlz]
**lernen** learn [lɜːn]; study [ˈstʌdi]
**Lernposter** study poster [ˈstʌdi pəʊstə]
**lesen** read [riːd]  **laut (vor)lesen** read aloud [əˈlaʊd]
**Leser/in** reader [ˈriːdə]
**Lesezeichen** (*Computer*) bookmark [ˈbʊkmɑːk]  **zu den Lesezeichen hinzufügen** bookmark
**letzte(r, s)** final [ˈfaɪnl]  **das letzte Mal** last [lɑːst]  **in letzter Zeit** recently [ˈriːsntli]  **letzten Freitag / letztes Wochenende** last Friday/weekend
**leuchten** shine [ʃaɪn]
**leuchtend** bright [braɪt]
**Leute** people [ˈpiːpl]; guys (*pl*) [gaɪz]; folk (*pl, infml*) [fəʊk]
**Licht** light [laɪt]
**Lichtblitz** flash [flæʃ]
**Lichtschutzgebiet** dark sky reserve [rɪˈzɜːv]
**Liebe: Alles Liebe, ... / Liebe Grüße, ...** (*Briefschluss*) Love, ... [lʌv]
**liebe(r, s)** dear [dɪə]
**lieben** love [lʌv]
**lieber: Ich sollte lieber ...** I'd better ... (= I had better ...)
**Lieblings-** favourite [ˈfeɪvərɪt]
**Lieblingsort** haunt [hɔːnt]
**Lied** song [sɒŋ]
**liefern** deliver [dɪˈlɪvə]; supply [səˈplaɪ]
**Lieferung** supply [səˈplaɪ]
**Lieferwagen** van [væn]
**liegen** lie [laɪ]  **in ... liegen** be located in ... [ləʊˈkeɪtɪd]  **Tiere liegen mir sehr am Herzen.** I really care about animals. [keə]
**Lift** elevator (*bes. AE*) [ˈelɪveɪtə]; lift (*BE*) [lɪft]
**lila** purple [ˈpɜːpl]
**Limonade** soda (*auch:* soda pop) (*AE*) [ˈsəʊdə]
**Lineal** ruler [ˈruːlə]
**Linie** (*U-Bahn-Linie*) line [laɪn]
**linke(r, s)** left [left]
**links** left [left]; (*auf der linken Seite*) on the left  **nach links** left  **(nach) links abbiegen** turn left
**Linse** (*Optik*) lens [lenz]
**Lippe** lip [lɪp]
**Liste** list [lɪst]
**Literatur** literature [ˈlɪtrətʃə]
**Lizenz** licence [ˈlaɪsns]
**LKW** lorry (*BE*) [ˈlɒri]; truck (*bes. AE*) [trʌk]
**Loch** hole [həʊl]
**locker** (*informell*) informal [ɪnˈfɔːml]
**Löffel** spoon [spuːn]
**Lokal-** (*am/vom Ort*) local [ˈləʊkl]
**Lokal** (*Kneipe*) pub [pʌb]
**los: Los geht's. / Jetzt geht's los.** Here we go.  **Los mit euch**

# German – English

**jetzt!** Off you go now. **Was ist los?** What's the matter?; What's up? **Was ist los mit dir?** What's wrong with you?
**löschen** delete [dɪˈliːt] **ein Feuer löschen** put out a fire [ˌpʊt ˈaʊt]
**lösen** (Rätsel, Problem) solve [sɒlv]
**Lösung (für)** (Problem, Aufgabe) solution (to) [səˈluːʃn]
**Lösungshinweis** clue [kluː]
**Löwe** lion [ˈlaɪən]
**Luft** air [eə] **etwas in die Luft sprengen** blow sth. up [ˌbləʊ ˈʌp]
**Luftballon** balloon [bəˈluːn]
**lüften** (Geheimnis) solve [sɒlv]
**lustig** funny **sich über jn./etwas lustig machen** make fun of sb./sth.
**luxuriös** luxurious [lʌgˈʒʊəriəs]

# M

**machen** (herstellen) make [meɪk]; (tun) do [duː] **einen Test / eine Prüfung / einen Kurs machen** take a test / an exam / a course **aus etwas gemacht sein** be made of sth. **Das macht Spaß.** That's fun. **Fotos machen** take photos **jn. zu etwas machen** make sb. sth. **sich fertig machen (für)** get ready (for) **sich über jn./etwas lustig machen** make fun of sb./sth. **wie man etwas macht / machen kann / machen soll** how to do sth.
**Macht** power [ˈpaʊə]
**mächtig** powerful [ˈpaʊəfl]
**Mädchen** girl [gɜːl]
**Magen** stomach [ˈstʌmək]
**mager** skinny [ˈskɪni]
**magisch** magic [ˈmædʒɪk]; magical [ˈmædʒɪkl]
**mahlen** grind [graɪnd]
**Mahlzeit** meal [miːl]
**Mai** May [meɪ]
**mailen: (jm.) etwas mailen** email (sb.) sth. [ˈiːmeɪl]
**Mais** corn (no pl) (AE) [kɔːn]
**Makeup** make-up [ˈmeɪkˌʌp]
**Mal** time [taɪm] **dieses Mal** this time **zum ersten Mal** for the first time
**mal: (vorher) schon mal** before [bɪˈfɔː]
**Malaria** malaria [məˈleəriə]
**malen** paint [peɪnt]
**Maler/in** painter [ˈpeɪntə]
**Mama** mum [mʌm]; mom (AE) [mɒm]
**man** you
**Manager/in** manager [ˈmænɪdʒə]
**manchmal** sometimes [ˈsʌmtaɪmz]
**Mangel (an)** lack (of) [læk] **aus Mangel an** for lack of
**Mann** man, pl men [mæn]
**Mannschaft** team [tiːm]
**Mantel** coat [kəʊt]
**Marathon** marathon [ˈmærəθən]
**Marine** navy [ˈneɪvi]
**Marionette** puppet [ˈpʌpɪt]
**Marke** (Markenname) brand [brænd]
**markieren** mark (up) [ˌmɑːkˈʌp]; bookmark [ˈbʊkmɑːk]; (mit Textmarker) highlight [ˈhaɪlaɪt]
**Markt** market [ˈmɑːkɪt]
**Marktstand** stall [stɔːl]
**Marmelade** jam [dʒæm]; (aus Zitrusfrüchten) marmalade [ˈmɑːməleɪd]
**Marschland** swamp [swɒmp]
**März** March [mɑːtʃ]
**Maschine** engine [ˈendʒɪn]; machine [məˈʃiːn]
**Maske** mask [mɑːk]
**Massenvernichtung** mass destruction [ˌmæs dɪˈstrʌkʃn]
**Match** match [mætʃ]
**Material** material [məˈtɪəriəl]
**Mathematik** mathematics [ˌmæθəˈmætɪks]; maths [mæθs]
**Matsch** mud [mʌd]
**Mauer** wall [wɔːl]
**Maul** mouth [maʊθ]
**Medaille** medal [ˈmedl]
**Mediation** mediation [ˌmiːdiˈeɪʃn]
**Medien** media (pl) [ˈmiːdiə] **soziale Medien** social media (pl) [ˌsəʊʃl ˈmiːdiə]
**Medizin** medicine [ˈmedsn], [ˈmedɪsn]
**medizinische Versorgung** health care [ˈhelθ keə]
**Meer** sea [siː] **am Meer** by the sea
**Meeresfrüchte** seafood [ˈsiːfuːd]
**Meeresspiegel** sea level [ˈsiː levl]
**Meerschweinchen** guinea pig [ˈgɪni pɪg]
**Megaphon** loudspeaker [ˌlaʊdˈspiːkə]
**mehr** more [mɔː] **nicht mehr** no longer, not any longer
**mehrere** several [ˈsevrəl]
**Mehrheit** majority [məˈdʒɒrəti]
**mehrsprachig** multilingual [ˌmʌltiˈlɪŋgwəl]
**Mehrsprachigkeit** multilingualism [ˌmʌltiˈlɪŋgwəlɪzm]
**Mehrzahl** majority [məˈdʒɒrəti]
**Meile** mile [maɪl]
**meilenweit** for miles [maɪlz]
**mein(e)** my [maɪ] **Meine Damen und Herren** Ladies and gentlemen [ˌleɪdiz ən ˈdʒentlmən]
**meinen** (sagen wollen) mean [miːn]
**meiner, meine, meins** mine [maɪn]
**Meinung** opinion [əˈpɪnjən]; view [vjuː] **meiner Meinung nach** in my view/opinion **seine Meinung ändern** change one's mind [maɪnd]
**meißeln** carve [kɑːv]
**meisten: die meisten Menschen / die meisten von ihnen** most people / most of them [məʊst]
**meistens** mostly; usually [ˈjuːʒuəli]
**Meister/in** master [ˈmɑːstə]; (Sport) champion [ˈtʃæmpiən]
**Melodie** tune [tjuːn]
**Menge** amount [əˈmaʊnt]; (Menschenmenge) crowd [kraʊd] **eine Menge**
... a lot of ...; lots of ...; loads of ... (infml)
**Mensa** (Kantine) canteen [kænˈtiːn]
**Mensch** human [ˈhjuːmən]
**Menschen** people [ˈpiːpl]
**Menschenmenge** crowd [kraʊd]
**menschlich** human [ˈhjuːmən]
**merken** (bemerken) notice [ˈnəʊtɪs] **sich etwas merken** remember sth. [rɪˈmembə]
**Merkmal** feature [ˈfiːtʃə]
**Merkzettel** crib sheet (infml) [ˈkrɪb ʃiːt]
**Messe** exhibition [ˌeksɪˈbɪʃn]
**Messer** knife, pl knives [naɪf], [naɪvz]
**Metall; Metall-** metal [ˈmetl]
**Meter** metre [ˈmiːtə]
**mich** me [miː] **mich selbst** myself [maɪˈself]
**mieten** hire [haɪə]
**Milch** milk [mɪlk]
**militärisch; Militär** military [ˈmɪlətri]
**Million** million [ˈmɪljən]
**Minderheit** minority [maɪˈnɒrəti]
**Mindmap** mind map [ˈmaɪnd mæp]
**Mine** (Bergwerk; Militär) mine [maɪn]
**Minister/in** minister [ˈmɪnɪstə]
**Minute** minute [ˈmɪnɪt] **ein zweiminütiger Vortrag** a two-minute talk
**mir** me [miː] **mir selbst** myself [maɪˈself] **Mir ist schlecht.** I feel sick. [sɪk]
**Mischung** mix [mɪks]; mixture [ˈmɪkstʃə]
**Missbrauch** abuse [əˈbjuːs]
**missbrauchen** abuse [əˈbjuːz]
**Misserfolg** failure [ˈfeɪljə]
**Mit-** fellow [ˈfeləʊ]
**mit** with [wɪð] **mit dem Bus/Auto fahren** go by bus/car **mit jm. sprechen** speak to sb. **mit lauter Stimme** in a loud voice
**mitbekommen: etwas mitbekommen** (verstehen) get sth. **Hast du es mitbekommen?** Did you get it? (infml)
**mitbringen** bring [brɪŋ]
**miterleben** witness [ˈwɪtnəs]
**Mitfahrgelegenheit** lift [lɪft] **jn. um eine Mitfahrgelegenheit bitten** ask sb. for a ride/a lift [raɪd]
**Mitgefühl** compassion [kəmˈpæʃn]
**Mitglied** member [ˈmembə]
**mitkommen** come along [ˌkʌm əˈlɒŋ]
**Mitlaut** consonant [ˈkɒnsənənt]
**Mitleid (mit)** compassion (for) [kəmˈpæʃn]
**mitmachen** join in [dʒɔɪn]
**mitnehmen** take [teɪk] **jn. mitnehmen** (im Auto) give sb. a ride/a lift
**Mitschüler/in** classmate [ˈklɑːsmeɪt]
**Mittag: zu Mittag essen** have lunch
**Mittagessen** lunch [lʌntʃ] **Was gibt es zum Mittagessen?** What's for lunch?
**mittags** at lunchtime
**Mittagszeit** lunchtime [ˈlʌntʃtaɪm]

# Dictionary

**Mitte** middle [ˈmɪdl]; *(Zentrum)* centre [ˈsentə] **in der Mitte** in the middle **Mitte des 19. Jahrhunderts** the mid-1800s **Er ist Mitte dreißig.** He's in his mid-thirties.
**Mitteilung** *(Notiz)* note [nəʊt]
**Mittel-** central [ˈsentrəl]
**mittel-; mittelgroß** medium [ˈmiːdiəm]
**Mittelpunkt** focus [ˈfəʊkəs]
**Mittelschule** *(für 11- bis 14-Jährige)* middle school *(AE)* [ˈmɪdl skuːl]
**Mitternacht** midnight [ˈmɪdnaɪt]
**Mittlerer Westen (der USA)** Midwest [mɪdˈwest]
**Mittwoch** Wednesday [ˈwenzdeɪ], [ˈwenzdi]
**Mitwirkende** *(Theaterstück, Film)* cast [kɑːst]
**Möbel** furniture *(no pl)* [ˈfɜːnɪtʃə]
**Mobiltelefon** mobile (phone) [ˌməʊbaɪl ˈfəʊn]; cell phone *(AE)* [ˈsel fəʊn]
**möchte: Ich möchte …** I'd like … (= I would like …) [ˌaɪd ˈlaɪk] **Ich möchte, dass du …** I want you to …; I'd like you to … **Ich möchte gehen** I'd like to go **Was möchtest du?** What would you like? **Was möchtest du essen?** What would you like to eat?
**Mode** fashion [ˈfæʃn]
**Modell** model [ˈmɒdl]
**Moderator/in** host [həʊst]
**modern** modern [ˈmɒdən]; *(zeitgenössisch)* contemporary [kənˈtemprəri]
**modisch** trendy [ˈtrendi]
**mögen** like [laɪk]; *(auf etwas stehen)* be into sth. *(infml)* **nicht mögen** dislike [dɪsˈlaɪk] **sehr mögen** love [lʌv]
**möglich** possible [ˈpɒsəbl]
**Möglichkeit** chance [tʃɑːns]; opportunity [ˌɒpəˈtjuːnəti] **die Möglichkeit haben/bekommen, etwas zu tun** get to do sth. [ˈget tə]
**Möhre** carrot [ˈkærət]
**mollig** chubby [ˈtʃʌbi]
**Moment** moment [ˈməʊmənt] **Einen Moment. / Moment mal.** Wait a minute. / Just a minute. [ˈmɪnɪt] **genau in dem Moment** just then **im Moment** at the moment
**Monarch/in** monarch [ˈmɒnək]
**Monat** month [mʌnθ]
**monatlich** monthly [ˈmʌnθli]
**Mond** moon [muːn]
**Mondlicht** moonlight [ˈmuːnlaɪt]
**Monster** monster [ˈmɒnstə]
**Montag** Monday [ˈmʌndeɪ], [ˈmʌndi]
**montieren** assemble [əˈsembl]
**Monument** monument [ˈmɒnjumənt]
**Morgen** morning [ˈmɔːnɪŋ]
**morgen** tomorrow [təˈmɒrəʊ] **morgen früh** tomorrow morning
**morgens** in the morning **4 Uhr morgens** 4 am [ˌeɪ ˈem]
**Motor** motor [ˈməʊtə]; engine [ˈendʒɪn]
**Motorrad** motorbike [ˈməʊtəbaɪk]; motorcycle [ˈməʊtəsaɪkl]

**Mountainbiken** mountain-biking [ˈmaʊntən baɪkɪŋ]
**Möwe** seagull [ˈsiːɡʌl]
**MP3-Player** MP3 player [ˌem piː ˈθriː pleɪə]
**müde** tired [ˈtaɪəd]
**Mühe: sich (große) Mühe geben** try hard [ˌtraɪ ˈhɑːd]
**Mühle** mill [mɪl]
**Müll** rubbish [ˈrʌbɪʃ]; waste [weɪst]; garbage *(AE)* [ˈɡɑːbɪdʒ]
**multikulturell** multicultural [ˌmʌltiˈkʌltʃərəl]
**Multikulturismus** multiculturalism [ˌmʌltiˈkʌltʃərəlɪzm]
**Mund** mouth [maʊθ]
**Mundharmonika** harmonica [hɑːˈmɒnɪkə]
**mündlich** oral [ˈɔːrəl]
**Münze** coin [kɔɪn]
**murmeln: …, murmelte er. …**, he said under his breath. [breθ]
**Murmeltier** marmot [ˈmɑːmət]
**mürrisch** glum [ɡlʌm]
**Museum** museum [mjuˈziːəm]
**Musical** musical [ˈmjuːzɪkl]
**Musik** music [ˈmjuːzɪk]
**Musiker/in** musician [mjuˈzɪʃn]
**Musikgruppe** band [bænd]
**müssen: etwas tun müssen** must do sth. [mʌst]; need to do sth. [niːd]; have to do sth. **du musst es nicht tun** you needn't do it [ˈniːdnt]
**Muster** pattern [ˈpætn]
**Mutter** mother [ˈmʌðə]
**Mutter-** native [ˈneɪtɪv]
**Muttersprache** native language [ˌneɪtɪv ˈlæŋɡwɪdʒ]
**Muttersprachler/in** native speaker [ˌneɪtɪv ˈspiːkə]
**Mutti** mum [mʌm]; mom *(AE)* [mɒm]
**Mütze** cap [kæp]
**mythisch** mythical [ˈmɪθɪkl]

# N

**Na: Na ja, …** Well, … **Na los, Dad!** Come on, Dad. **Na und?** So what?; So?; Who cares? [keə]
**nach** 1. *(örtlich)* to [tu], [tə] **nach draußen** outside [ˌaʊtˈsaɪd] **nach drinnen** inside [ˌɪnˈsaɪd] **nach Hause** home **nach oben** up [ʌp]; *(im Haus)* upstairs [ˌʌpˈsteəz] **nach unten** down [daʊn]; *(im Haus)* downstairs [ˌdaʊnˈsteəz] **nach vorn** to the front 2. *(zeitlich)* after [ˈɑːftə] **einer nach dem anderen** one by one **Viertel nach zehn (10.15 / 22.15)** quarter past ten [ˈkwɔːtə pɑːst]
**Nachbar/in** neighbour [ˈneɪbə]
**Nachbarschaft** neighbourhood [ˈneɪbəhʊd]
**nachbilden** recreate [ˌriːkriˈeɪt]

**nachdem** after [ˈɑːftə] **gleich nachdem …** just after …
**nachdenken (über)** think (about) [θɪŋk]
**nacheinander** *(einzeln, einer nach dem anderen)* one at a time [taɪm]
**nachgehen** *(Uhr)* be slow [sləʊ]
**nachmachen** recreate [ˌriːkriˈeɪt]
**Nachmittag** afternoon [ˌɑːftəˈnuːn] **am Nachmittag** in the afternoon
**nachmittags** in the afternoon [ˌɑːftəˈnuːn] **4 Uhr nachmittags** 4 pm [ˌpiː ˈem]
**Nachricht** message [ˈmesɪdʒ] **Nachrichten** news *(no pl)* [njuːz] **eine Nachricht hinterlassen** leave a message **jm. eine** *(elektronische)* **Nachricht schicken/übermitteln** message sb.
**nachrichtlich** *(in E-Mails)* cc (= carbon copy) [ˌkɑːbən ˈkɒpi]
**nachschauen** *(einen Blick werfen)* have a look
**nachschlagen: etwas nachschlagen** look sth. up
**Nachspeise** dessert [dɪˈzɜːt]
**nächste(r, s)** next [nekst] **das nächste Bild** the next picture **als Nächstes** next
**Nacht** night [naɪt] **eines Nachts** one night **Gute Nacht!** Goodnight. [ˌɡʊdˈnaɪt] **heute Nacht** tonight [təˈnaɪt] **in der Nacht** at night
**Nachteil** disadvantage [ˌdɪsədˈvɑːntɪdʒ]
**Nachtisch** dessert [dɪˈzɜːt]
**nachts** at night [ət ˈnaɪt]
**Nachweis(e)** evidence [ˈevɪdəns]
**nachweisen** prove [pruːv]
**nachziehen** *(spannen, festziehen)* tighten [ˈtaɪtn]
**Nadel** needle [ˈniːdl]
**Nahaufnahme** *(Film)* close-up [ˈkləʊsˌʌp]
**nahe (bei)** close (to) [kləʊs]; near [nɪə]
**Nähe: in der Nähe von** near [nɪə] **hier in der Nähe** near here
**nahegelegene(r, s)** nearby [ˈnɪəbaɪ]
**näher hinschauen** look closely [ˈkləʊsli]
**nähern: sich nähern** approach [əˈprəʊtʃ]
**Nährboden** hotbed [ˈhɒtbed]
**Name** name [neɪm]
**Nase** nose [nəʊz]
**nass** wet [wet] **jn. nass spritzen** splash sb. [splæʃ]
**Nation** nation [ˈneɪʃn]
**national, National-** national [ˈnæʃnəl]
**Nationalist/in** nationalist [ˈnæʃnəlɪst]
**nationalistisch** nationalist [ˈnæʃnəlɪst]
**Nationalität** nationality [ˌnæʃəˈnæləti]
**Nationalpark** national park [ˌnæʃnəl ˈpɑːk]
**Natur** nature [ˈneɪtʃə] **(Welt der) Natur** natural world [ˌnætʃrəl ˈwɜːld]
**Naturkunde** natural history [ˌnætʃrəl ˈhɪstri]

# German – English

**natürlich** natural ['nætʃrəl]; *(selbstverständlich)* of course [əv 'kɔːs]
**Naturwissenschaft** science ['saɪəns]
**Naturwissenschaftler/in** scientist ['saɪəntɪst]
**Nebel** *(leichter)* mist [mɪst]
**neben** next to ['nekst tʊ]
**Nebensatz** sub-clause ['sʌb klɔːz] **Nebensatz mit if** if-clause
**Neffe** nephew ['nefjuː], ['nevjuː]
**negativ** negative ['negətɪv]
**nehmen** take [teɪk] **etwas wichtig nehmen** care about sth. [keə] **Ich nehme einen Tee/Hamburger ...** *(beim Essen, im Restaurant)* I'll have a tea/burger/... **Platz nehmen** take a seat
**nein** no [nəʊ]
**nennen** call [kɔːl]; name [neɪm] **genannt werden** *(heißen)* be calle
**nervös** nervous ['nɜːvəs]
**nett** kind [kaɪnd]; nice [naɪs]
**neu** new [njuː] **etwas auf den neuesten Stand bringen** update sth. [ˌʌp'deɪt]
**neugierig** curious ['kjʊərɪəs]
**Neuigkeiten** news *(no pl)* [njuːz]
**neun** nine [naɪn]
**nicht** not [nɒt] **nicht mehr** no longer; not ... any longer; not ... any more **nicht mögen/nicht leiden können** dislike [dɪs'laɪk] **nicht vor drei** not till/until three **..., nicht wahr?** ..., right? **auch nicht** not ... either ['aɪðə], ['iːðə] **Geh nicht.** Don't go. **Ich mag Grün nicht.** I don't like green. **Ich weiß (es) nicht.** I don't know. **(noch) nicht einmal** not even **noch nicht** not ... yet
**Nichte** niece [niːs]
**nichts** nothing ['nʌθɪŋ]; not ... anything **Nichts zu danken.** You're welcome. ['welkəm]
**nicken** nod [nɒd]
**nie** never ['nevə] **(vorher) noch nie** not/never before [bɪ'fɔː]
**niedergeschlagen** glum [glʌm]
**niederlassen: sich niederlassen** settle ['setl]
**niedrig** low [ləʊ]
**niemals** never ['nevə]
**niemand** not ... anybody ['enɪbɒdɪ]; not ... anyone ['enɪwʌn]; no one ['nəʊ wʌn]; nobody ['nəʊbədɪ]
**niesen** sneeze [sniːz]
**nirgendwo(hin)** nowhere ['nəʊweə]
**noch** *(immer noch)* still [stɪl] **noch ein(e)** another [ə'nʌðə] **noch ein Foto** one more photo **noch einmal** again [ə'gen] **noch nicht** not ... yet **noch nicht einmal** not even **(vorher) noch nie** not/never before
**nomadisch, Nomaden-** nomadic [nəʊ'mædɪk]
**Nomen** noun [naʊn]
**Nord-** north [nɔːθ]; northern ['nɔːðən]

**Norden** north [nɔːθ] **Richtung Norden** northbound ['nɔːθbaʊnd]
**nördlich** north [nɔːθ]; northern ['nɔːðən]
**Nordost-** north-eastern [ˌnɔːθ_'iːstən]
**Nordosten, nach Nordosten** north-east
**nordöstlich** north-east [ˌnɔːθ_'iːst]; north-eastern [ˌnɔːθ_'iːstən]
**Nordwesten, nach Nordwesten** north-west
**nordwestlich** north-west [ˌnɔːθ 'west]
**normal** normal ['nɔːml]
**normalerweise** usually ['juːʒʊəlɪ]
**nostalgisch** nostalgic [nɒ'stældʒɪk]
**Note** *(Musik)* note [nəʊt]; *(Schulnote)* grade [greɪd]; mark [mɑːk]
**notieren: (sich) etwas notieren** note sth. down [ˌnəʊt 'daʊn]
**nötig** necessary ['nesəsərɪ]
**Notiz** note [nəʊt] **(sich) Notizen machen** *(beim Lesen oder Zuhören)* take notes; *(zur Vorbereitung)* make notes
**notwendig** necessary ['nesəsərɪ]
**November** November [nəʊ'vembə]
**Nuklear-** nuclear ['njuːklɪə]
**Null** *(in Telefonnummern)* o [əʊ]
**Nummer** number ['nʌmbə]
**Nummernschild** number plate ['nʌmbə pleɪt]; licence plate *(AE)* ['laɪsns pleɪt]
**nun** now [naʊ] **Nun, ...** Well, ... **Nun, da ...** Now that ...
**nur** only ['əʊnlɪ]; *(einfach nur)* just [dʒʌst]
**nützlich** helpful ['helpfl]

# O

**ob** if [ɪf]; whether ['weðə] **als ob** as if; like *(infml)* **so tun, als ob** pretend [prɪ'tend]
**oben** above [ə'bʌv]; at the top (of); up; upstairs [ˌʌp'steəz] **nach oben** up; upwards ['ʌpwədz]; *(im Haus)* upstairs **(nach) hier oben** up here **oberes Ende** top
**Oberfläche** surface ['sɜːfɪs]
**oberhalb (von)** above [ə'bʌv]
**Oberhaupt** head [hed]
**Oberteil** *(Top)* top [tɒp]
**Objekt** object ['ɒbdʒɪkt]
**Objektiv** *(Kamera)* lens [lenz]
**Obst** fruit [fruːt]
**Obstkuchen** pie [paɪ]
**Obstsalat** fruit salad [ˌfruːt 'sæləd]
**obwohl** although [ɔːl'ðəʊ]; though [ðəʊ]; *(betont)* even though [ˌiːvn 'ðəʊ]
**oder** or [ɔː] **entweder ... oder ...** either ... or ... ['aɪðə], ['iːðə]
**Ödland** badlands *(pl)* ['bædlændz]
**offen** open ['əʊpən]
**öffentliche(r, s)** public ['pʌblɪk]
**öffnen** open ['əʊpən]
**Öffnung** opening ['əʊpənɪŋ]

**Öffnungszeiten** opening times *(pl)* ['əʊpənɪŋ taɪmz]
**oft** often ['ɒfn], ['ɒftən]
**ohne** without [wɪ'ðaʊt]
**Ohr** ear [ɪə] **ganz Ohr sein** *(gespannt zuhören)* be all ears *(infml)* [ˌɔːl_'ɪəz]
**Ohrfeige: jm. eine Ohrfeige verpassen** *(ins Gesicht schlagen)* slap sb.'s face [slæp]
**Ohrhörer** earphones *(pl)* ['ɪəfəʊnz]
**Ohrring** earring ['ɪərɪŋ]
**Oje!** Oh dear! [əʊ]
**okay** all right [ɔːl 'raɪt]
**Oktober** October [ɒk'təʊbə]
**Öl** oil [ɔɪl]
**Oma** grandma ['grænmɑː]
**Onkel** uncle ['ʌŋkl]
**online** online [ˌɒn'laɪn]
**Opa** grandpa ['grænpɑː]
**Option** option ['ɒpʃn]
**Orange** orange ['ɒrɪndʒ]
**orange(farben)** orange ['ɒrɪndʒ]
**Orca** *(Killerwal)* orca ['ɔːkə]
**ordnen** order ['ɔːdə]; *(organisieren)* organize ['ɔːgənaɪz]
**Ordnung: in Ordnung** (OK) all right [ɔːl 'raɪt]; *(prima)* fine [faɪn]
**Organisation** organization [ˌɔːgənaɪ'zeɪʃn]
**Organisator/in** organizer ['ɔːgənaɪzə]
**organisieren** organize ['ɔːgənaɪz]
**Original-** original [ə'rɪdʒənl]
**Orkan** hurricane ['hʌrɪkən], ['hʌrɪkeɪn]
**Ort** place [pleɪs]; location [ləʊ'keɪʃn]; site [saɪt] **am/vom Ort** local ['ləʊkl] **an Ort und Stelle** *(sogleich)* on the spot [spɒt]
**örtlich** *(Lokal-)* local ['ləʊkl]
**Ost-** eastern ['iːstən]
**Osten, nach Osten** east [iːst] **Richtung Osten** eastbound ['iːstbaʊnd]
**Ostern** Easter ['iːstə]
**östlich** east [iːst]; eastern ['iːstən]
**oval** oval ['əʊvl]
**Ozean** ocean ['əʊʃn]

# P

**Paar** pair [peə]; *(Liebespaar)* couple ['kʌpl] **ein Paar Handschuhe** a pair of gloves
**paar: ein paar** a couple of ['kʌpl]; a few [ə 'fjuː]; some [sʌm], [səm]
**Päckchen** packet ['pækɪt]
**packen** pack [pæk]; *(schnappen)* grab [græb]
**Packung** packet ['pækɪt]
**Pädagoge/Pädagogin** educator ['edʒukeɪtə]
**Palast** palace ['pæləs]
**Palme** palm tree ['pɑːm triː]
**Panik: in Panik geraten** panic ['pænɪk]
**Papa** dad [dæd]
**Papier** paper ['peɪpə]
**Papierhut** paper hat ['peɪpə hæt]

# Dictionary

**Papst** pope [pəʊp]
**Parade** parade [pəˈreɪd]
**Park** park [pɑːk]
**Parka** parka [ˈpɑːkə]
**parken** park [pɑːk]
**Parkplatz** *(Parklücke)* parking space [ˈpɑːkɪŋ speɪs]; *(Gelände zum Abstellen von mehreren Autos)* car park [ˈkɑːpɑːk]; parking lot *(AE)* [ˈpɑːkɪŋ lɒt]
**Parlament** parliament [ˈpɑːləmənt]
**Partner/in** partner [ˈpɑːtnə]
**Party** party [ˈpɑːti]
**Pass** *(Reisepass)* passport [ˈpɑːspɔːt]
**Pass auf!** *(Vorsicht!)* Watch out! [ˌwɒtʃ ˈaʊt]
**Passagier/in** passenger [ˈpæsɪndʒə]
**passen: zueinander passen** go together **zu etwas passen** go with sth.
**Passform** fit [fɪt]
**passieren: passieren (mit)** happen (to) [ˈhæpən]
**passiv** passive [ˈpæsɪv]
**Passwort** password [ˈpɑːswɜːd] **ein Passwort eingeben** enter a password
**Pastete** pie [ˈpaɪ]
**Patriotismus** patriotism [ˈpeɪtrɪətɪzəm]
**Pause** break [breɪk] **eine Pause einlegen** pause [pɔːz]
**pausieren** pause [pɔːz]
**peinlich** embarrassing [ɪmˈbærəsɪŋ]
**Pence** pence (p) *(plural of penny)* [pens]
**Penny** penny [ˈpeni]
**perfekt** perfect [ˈpɜːfɪkt]
**Person** person [ˈpɜːsn]; *(Individuum)* individual [ɪndɪˈvɪdʒuəl]; *(in Roman, Film, Theaterstück usw.)* character [ˈkærəktə]
**Personalausweis** ID card [ˌaɪ ˈdiː kɑːd]
**persönlich** personal [ˈpɜːsənl]
**Perspektive** perspective [pəˈspektɪv]
**Pfad** path [pɑːθ]; trail [treɪl]
**Pfannkuchen** pancake [ˈpænkeɪk]
**Pfeffer** pepper [ˈpepə]
**Pfeife** *(Tabakspfeife)* pipe [paɪp]; *(Trillerpfeife)* whistle [ˈwɪsl]
**pfeifen** whistle [ˈwɪsl]; *(auf der Trillerpfeife)* blow the whistle [bləʊ]
**Pfeil** arrow [ˈærəʊ]
**Pferch** *(Vieh)* corral [kəˈrɑːl]
**Pferd** horse [hɔːs]
**Pferdefuhrwerk** wagon [ˈwægən]
**Pflanze** plant [plɑːnt]
**pflanzen** plant [plɑːnt]
**Pflaster** *(Heftpflaster)* plaster [ˈplɑːstə]
**Pforte** gate [ɡeɪt]
**Pfote** paw [pɔː]
**Pfund** *(britische Währung)* pound (£) [paʊnd]
**Piano** piano [piˈænəʊ]
**Picknick** picnic [ˈpɪknɪk]
**piepen** beep [biːp]
**Pilger/in** pilgrim [ˈpɪlɡrɪm]
**pink** pink [pɪŋk]
**Pipeline** pipeline [ˈpaɪplaɪn]
**Pirat/in** pirate [ˈpaɪrət]
**Pizza** pizza [ˈpiːtsə]
**Plan** plan [plæn]

**planen** plan [plæn]
**Planet** planet [ˈplænɪt]
**Planwagen** wagon [ˈwæɡən]
**Planwagenkolonne** wagon train [ˈwæɡən treɪn]
**Plastik** plastic [ˈplæstɪk]
**Platz** place [pleɪs]; site [saɪt]; location [ləʊˈkeɪʃn]; *(in der Stadt)* square [skweə]; *(Raum)* space [speɪs]; *(Sitz)* seat [siːt] **Platz nehmen** take a seat
**Plätzchen** biscuit [ˈbɪskɪt]; cookie *(AE)* [ˈkʊki]
**platzen** burst [bɜːst]
**plaudern** chat [tʃæt]
**plötzlich** suddenly [ˈsʌdnli]
**Pocken** *(Erkrankung)* smallpox [ˈsmɔːlpɒks]
**Pogrom** pogrom [ˈpɒɡrəm]
**Pokal** trophy [ˈtrəʊfi]
**Polar-** Arctic
**polar** polar [ˈpəʊlə]
**Politik** politics [ˈpɒlətɪks]; policy [ˈpɒləsi]
**Polizei** police *(pl)* [pəˈliːs]
**Polizei(behörde)** police department [pəˈliːs dɪˌpɑːtmənt]
**Polizeiwache/-revier** police station [pəˈliːs steɪʃn]
**Polizist** policeman [pəˈliːsmən]
**Polizist/in** police officer [pəˈliːs ˌɒfɪsə]
**Polnisch; polnisch** Polish [ˈpəʊlɪʃ]
**Pommes frites** chips *(pl)* [tʃɪps]; French fries *(pl, AE)* [fraɪz]
**Pony** pony [ˈpəʊni]
**Pony(fransen)** fringe [frɪndʒ]
**Pop(musik)** pop (music) [pɒp]
**Popcorn** popcorn [ˈpɒpkɔːn]
**populär** popular (with) [ˈpɒpjələ]
**Porträt** profile [ˈprəʊfaɪl]
**Position** position [pəˈzɪʃn]
**positiv** positive [ˈpɒzətɪv]
**Postamt** post office [ˈpəʊst ˌɒfɪs]
**posten: etwas posten** post sth. [pəʊst]
**Poster** poster [ˈpəʊstə]
**Posting** *(auf Blog)* post [pəʊst]
**Postkarte** postcard [ˈpəʊstkɑːd]
**Poutine** *(Pommes frites mit Käse in Bratensoße)* poutine [puːˈtiːn]
**prächtig** magnificent [mæɡˈnɪfɪsnt]; noble [ˈnəʊbl]
**prahlen (mit)** show off [ʃəʊ ˈɒf]
**praktisch** practical [ˈpræktɪkl]
**praktizieren** practice *(AE)* [ˈpræktɪs]
**Praline** chocolate [ˈtʃɒklət]
**prallen: gegen etwas prallen** hit [hɪt]
**Prärie** prairie [ˈpreəri]
**Präsentation** presentation [ˌpreznˈteɪʃn]
**präsentieren: (jm.) etwas präsentieren** *(vorstellen)* present sth. (to sb.) [prɪˈzent]
**Präsident/in** president [ˈprezɪdənt]
**Preis** *(Auszeichnung)* award [əˈwɔːd]; *(Gewinn)* prize [praɪz]; *(Kaufpreis)* price [praɪs]

**preiswert** cheap [tʃiːp] **Es ist preiswert.** It's good value (for money). [ˈvæljuː]
**prellen** *(Ball)* bounce [baʊns]
**Premierminister/in** prime minister [ˌpraɪm ˈmɪnɪstə]
**pressen** squeeze [skwiːz]
**prima** fine [faɪn]
**Prinz** prince [prɪns]
**Prinzessin** princess [ˌprɪnˈses]
**Priorität** priority [praɪˈɒrəti]
**Pritschenwagen** pickup (truck) [ˈpɪkʌp]
**pro: … pro Tag/Stunde** … per day/hour [pə], [pɜː]; … a day/hour
**probieren** try [traɪ]
**Problem** problem [ˈprɒbləm] **Kein Problem!** No worries. *(infml)* [ˈwʌriz]
**mit Problemen belastet** troubled [ˈtrʌbld]
**Produkt** product [ˈprɒdʌkt]
**Produktion** production [prəˈdʌkʃn]
**Produzent/in** producer [prəˈdjuːsə]
**produzieren** produce [prəˈdjuːs]
**Professor/in** professor [prəˈfesə]
**Profil** profile [ˈprəʊfaɪl]
**Programm** programme [ˈprəʊɡræm]; program *(AE)*; *(Computer)* program
**programmieren** program [ˈprəʊɡræm]
**Projekt** project [ˈprɒdʒekt]
**Proklamation** proclamation [ˌprɒkləˈmeɪʃn]
**Promi** celebrity [səˈlebrəti]
**Prominente/r** celebrity [səˈlebrəti]
**Prosa(literatur)** fiction [ˈfɪkʃn]
**Prospekt** brochure [ˈbrəʊʃə]
**Protest** protest [ˈprəʊtest]
**Protestant/in; protestantisch** Protestant [ˈprɒtɪstənt]
**protestieren** protest [prəˈtest]
**Provinz** province [ˈprɒvɪns]
**Prozent** per cent (%) [pə ˈsent]
**prüfen** *(testen)* test [test]; *(überprüfen)* check [tʃek]; *(untersuchen)* look into
**Publikum** audience [ˈɔːdiəns]
**Pullover** pullover [ˈpʊləʊvə]
**Pulver** powder [ˈpaʊdə]
**pummelig** chubby [ˈtʃʌbi]
**Punkt** point [pɔɪnt]; *(Fleck)* spot [spɒt]; *(im Spiel/Sport erzielt)* score [skɔː]; *(Satzzeichen)* full stop
**Punktestand** score [skɔː]
**pünktlich** on time [ɒn ˈtaɪm]
**Puppe** doll [dɒl]
**Pute** turkey [ˈtɜːki]
**putzen** clean [kliːn]
**Puzzle** jigsaw [ˈdʒɪɡsɔː]
**Pyjama-Party** sleepover [ˈsliːpəʊvə]

# Q

**Quadrat** square [skweə]
**quadratisch** square [skweə]
**Quadratkilometer (km²)** square kilometre (sq km) [ˌskweə ˈkɪləmiːtə]

## German – English

**quälen** torture ['tɔːtʃə]
**qualifizieren; sich qualifizieren** qualify ['kwɒlɪfaɪ]
**Quark** curds (pl) [kɜːdz]
**Quelle** well [wel]; (Textquelle) source [sɔːs]
**quer über die Straße** across the street [əˈkrɒs]
**Querfeldeinrennen** cross-country [ˌkrɒs ˈkʌntri]
**quetschen** crush [krʌʃ] **(sich) quetschen** squeeze [skwiːz]
**Quiz** quiz [kwɪz]

## R

**Rabe** raven [ˈreɪvn]
**Rad** wheel [wiːl]; (Fahrrad) bike [baɪk] **Rad fahren** ride a bike [ˌraɪd_ə ˈbaɪk]
**Radiergummi** rubber [ˈrʌbə]
**Radio** radio [ˈreɪdiəʊ] **im Radio** on the radio
**Rahmen** frame [freɪm]
**Rallye** rally [ˈræli]
**Rand** edge [edʒ]
**Rasen** lawn [lɔːn]; grass [ɡrɑːs]
**rasen** race [reɪs]
**Rasse** race [reɪs]
**rassisch; Rassen-** racial [ˈreɪʃl]
**Raster** grid [ɡrɪd]
**rastlos** restless [ˈrestləs]
**Rat** (Stadtrat, Gemeinderat u.Ä.) council [ˈkaʊnsl]
**raten** guess [ɡes]
**Ratespiel** quiz [kwɪz]
**ratlos** clueless [ˈkluːləs]
**Rätsel** puzzle [ˈpʌzl]
**Ratte** rat [ræt]
**rau** rough [rʌf]
**rauben** steal [stiːl]
**Rauch** smoke [sməʊk]
**rauchen** smoke [sməʊk]
**rauf und runter** up and down [ˌʌp_ən ˈdaʊn]
**Raum** (Platz; Weltraum) space [speɪs]; (Zimmer) room [ruːm]
**räumen** (abräumen, wegräumen) clear [klɪə]; (Zimmer, Gebäude) vacate (fml) [vəˈkeɪt]
**rausgehen: mit dem Hund rausgehen** walk the dog
**reagieren (auf)** react (to) [riˈækt]
**Reaktion (auf)** reaction (to) [riˈækʃn]
**realistisch** (adj) realistic [ˌriːəˈlɪstɪk]; (adv) realistically [ˌriːəˈlɪstɪkli]
**Realität** reality [riˈæləti]
**Rebell/in** rebel [ˈrebəl]
**Rebellion** rebellion [rɪˈbeljən]
**Recherche** research (no pl) [ˈriːsɜːtʃ]
**recherchieren** research [rɪˈsɜːtʃ]
**Rechnung** bill [bɪl]
**Recht** right [raɪts] **Recht haben** be right
**Rechteckschema** grid [ɡrɪd]

**rechts** right [raɪt]; (auf der rechten Seite) on the right **nach rechts** right **(nach) rechts abbiegen** turn right
**Rechtschreibung** spelling [ˈspelɪŋ]
**rechtzeitig zum Bus kommen** be in time for the bus
**Redakteur/in** editor [ˈedɪtə]
**Rede** talk [tɔːk]; (offizielle) speech [spiːtʃ] **eine Rede halten (über)** give a talk (about)
**reden** speak [spiːk] **reden (mit)** talk (to) [tɔːk]
**Redewendung** idiom [ˈɪdiəm]; phrase [freɪz]
**Redner/in** speaker [ˈspiːkə]
**reduzieren (auf)** narrow down (to)
**Referat** talk [tɔːk] **ein Referat halten** give a presentation [ˌprezn̩ˈteɪʃn]
**Refrain** chorus [ˈkɔːrəs]
**Regal** shelf, pl shelves [ʃelf]
**Regel** rule [ruːl]
**regelmäßig** regular [ˈreɡjələ]
**Regen** rain [reɪn] **starker/heftiger Regen** heavy rain [ˈhevi]
**Regenbogen** rainbow [ˈreɪnbəʊ]
**Regenmantel** raincoat [ˈreɪnkəʊt]
**Regenschirm** umbrella [ʌmˈbrelə]
**Regenwald** rainforest [ˈreɪnfɒrɪst]
**regieren** govern [ˈɡʌvən]
**Regierung** government [ˈɡʌvənmənt]
**Region** region [ˈriːdʒən]
**Regisseur/in** director [dəˈrektə]
**regnen** rain [reɪn]
**regnerisch** rainy [ˈreɪni]
**regulieren** control [kənˈtrəʊl]
**Reh** deer [dɪə]
**Reich** empire [ˈempaɪə]
**reich** rich [rɪtʃ]
**reichen: jm. etwas reichen** hand sb. sth. [hænd]
**Reihe** line [laɪn]; (wartender Menschen) queue [kjuː]; (Fernsehserie) series, pl series [ˈsɪəriːz] **Ich bin an der Reihe.** (It's) my turn. [tɜːn]
**Reihenfolge** order [ˈɔːdə]
**Reim** rhyme [raɪm]
**Reise** journey [ˈdʒɜːni]; trip [trɪp] **Reise (durch)** tour (of) [ˈtʊər_əv]
**Reiseführer/in** tour guide [ˈtʊə ɡaɪd]
**Reisekrankheit** travel sickness [ˈtrævl sɪknəs]
**Reiseleiter/in** guide [ɡaɪd]
**reisen** travel [ˈtrævl]
**Reisende(r)** traveller [ˈtrævələ]
**Reisepass** passport [ˈpɑːspɔːt]
**Reiseziel** destination [ˌdestɪˈneɪʃn]
**Reiten** riding [ˈraɪdɪŋ]
**reiten** ride [raɪd]
**Reklame** advertising [ˈædvətaɪzɪŋ]
**Religion** religion [rɪˈlɪdʒən]
**Rennen** race [reɪs]
**rennen** run [rʌn]
**Reportage** report [rɪˈpɔːt]
**Repräsentant/in** representative [ˌreprɪˈzentətɪv]
**repräsentieren** represent [ˌreprɪˈzent]

**Republik** republic [rɪˈpʌblɪk]
**Reservat, Reservation** reservation [ˌrezəˈveɪʃn]; reserve [rɪˈzɜːv]
**Reserve** reserve [rɪˈzɜːv]
**reservieren** reserve [rɪˈzɜːv]
**Respekt** respect [rɪˈspekt]
**respektieren** respect [rɪˈspekt]
**Rest** rest [rest]
**Restaurant** restaurant [ˈrestrɒnt]
**Resultat** outcome [ˈaʊtkʌm]; result [rɪˈzʌlt]
**retten** rescue [ˈreskjuː]; save [seɪv]
**Rettung; Rettungs-** rescue [ˈreskjuː]
**Revolution** revolution [ˌrevəˈluːʃn]
**revolutionär** revolutionary [ˌrevəˈluːʃənəri]
**Revolutionär/in** revolutionary [ˌrevəˈluːʃənəri]
**Rezension** review [rɪˈvjuː]
**Rezept** (Kochrezept) recipe [ˈresəpi]; (ärztlich) prescription [prɪˈskrɪpʃn]
**Rhythmus** rhythm [ˈrɪðəm]
**richten: etwas an jn. richten** address sth. to sb. [əˈdres] **etwas auf jn. richten** point sth. at sb. [pɔɪnt]
**richtig** right [raɪt]; correct [kəˈrekt]
**Richtlinie** guideline [ˈɡaɪdlaɪn]; (in der Politik) policy [ˈpɒləsi]
**Richtung** direction [dəˈrekʃn] **Richtung … gehen/fahren** head to …/for … [hed] **Richtung Norden** northbound [ˈnɔːθbaʊnd] **Richtung Osten** eastbound [ˈiːstbaʊnd] **Richtung Süden** southbound [ˈsaʊθbaʊnd] **Richtung Westen** westbound [ˈwestbaʊnd] **in die Richtung** that way **in Richtung Bahnhof/Mr Bell** towards the station/Mr Bell [təˈwɔːdz]
**riechen** smell [smel] **an etwas riechen** smell sth. **gut riechen** smell good
**Riegel** (Schokolade, Müsli) bar [bɑː]
**Riese** giant [ˈdʒaɪənt]
**Riesenhunger: einen Riesenhunger haben** be starving [ˈstɑːvɪŋ]
**Riesenrad** big wheel [bɪɡ ˈwiːl]
**riesige(r, s)** giant [ˈdʒaɪənt]; huge [hjuːdʒ]
**Rinderbraten** roast beef [ˌrəʊst ˈbiːf]
**Rindfleisch** beef [biːf]
**Ring** ring [rɪŋ]
**Risiko** risk [rɪsk] **ein Risiko eingehen** take a risk
**Ritt** ride [raɪd]
**Ritter** knight [naɪt]
**Robbe** seal [siːl]
**Robbenjunge** baby seal [ˈbeɪbi siːl]
**robust** tough [tʌf]
**Rock** skirt [skɜːt]
**Rock(musik)** rock (music) [rɒk]
**rodeln** sledge (BE) [sledʒ]; sled (AE) [sled]
**Rodeo** rodeo [ˈrəʊdiəʊ]
**roh** crude [kruːd]
**Rohöl** crude oil [ˌkruːd_ˈɔɪl]

# Dictionary

**Rolle** roll [rəʊl]; *(in einem Theaterstück, Film)* role
**rollen** roll [rəʊl]
**Rollenspiel** role-play ['rəʊl pleɪ]
**Rollschuhbahn** rink *(kurz für:* skating rink) [rɪŋk]
**Rollschuhlaufen** skating ['skeɪtɪŋ]
**Rolltreppe** escalator ['eskəleɪtə]
**Roman** novel ['nɒvl]
**Romanautor/in** novelist ['nɒvəlɪst]
**Römer/in** Roman ['rəʊmən]
**römisch** Roman ['rəʊmən]
**rosa** pink [pɪŋk]
**Rose** rose [rəʊz]
**rostig** rusty ['rʌsti]
**rot** red [red]  **rot/braun/kalt/… werden** turn red/brown/cold/… [tɜːn]  **rot werden** (erröten) go red
**Route** route [ruːt]
**Routine** routine [ruːˈtiːn]
**Rücken** back [bæk]  **Rücken an Rücken** back to back
**Rückfahrkarte** return (ticket) [rɪˈtɜːn]
**Rückkehr** return [rɪˈtɜːn]
**Rückmeldung** feedback *(no pl)* ['fiːdbæk]
**Rucksack** backpack ['bækpæk]; rucksack ['rʌksæk]
**rückwärts** backwards ['bækwədz]
**Rudel** herd [hɜːd]
**Ruf** (Schrei) cry [kraɪ]
**rufen** call [kɔːl]; shout [ʃaʊt]
**Rugby** rugby ['rʌgbi]
**Rugby-Platz/Rugby-Spielfeld** rugby ground ['rʌgbi graʊnd]
**ruhen** rest [rest]
**ruhig** smooth [smuːð]; still; *(Meer)* calm [kɑːm]; *(leise)* quiet ['kwaɪət]
**Ruine** ruin ['ruːɪn]
**rumhängen** hang out *(infml)* [ˌhæŋ ˈaʊt]
**rund** circular ['sɜːkjələ]; round [raʊnd]
**Rundfahrt, -gang (durch)** tour (of) ['tʊər əv]
**runter: rauf und runter** up and down [ˌʌp ən ˈdaʊn]
**runzeln: die Stirn runzeln** frown [fraʊn]
**rutschen** slide [slaɪd]
**rutschig** slippery ['slɪpəri]

## S

**Saal** hall [hɔːl]
**Sache** thing [θɪŋ]
**Safari** safari [səˈfɑːri]
**Saft** juice [djuːs]
**Sage** legend ['ledʒənd]
**sagen** say [seɪ]  **sagen wollen** (meinen) mean [miːn]  **jm. sagen, dass er/sie etwas (nicht) tun soll** tell sb. (not) to do sth.
**sagenhaft** fabulous ['fæbjələs]
**Sahne** cream [kriːm]
**Saite** string [strɪŋ]

**Salat** *(als Gericht oder Beilage)* salad ['sæləd]
**Salz** salt [sɔːlt]
**Samba** samba ['sæmbə]
**Samen** seed [siːd]
**sammeln** collect [kəˈlekt]  **Geld sammeln (für)** raise money (for) [reɪz]
**Samstag** Saturday ['sætədeɪ], ['sætədi]
**Sand** sand [sænd]
**Sandalen** sandals *(pl)* ['sændlz]
**Sandwich** sandwich ['sænwɪtʃ], ['sænwɪdʒ]
**sanft** *(mit leiser Stimme)* in a soft voice
**Sänger/in** singer ['sɪŋə]
**Sankt (St)** Saint (St) [seɪnt]
**Satz** sentence ['sentəns]; set [set]
**Satzmelodie** intonation [ˌɪntəˈneɪʃn]
**sauber** clean [kliːn]  **sauber machen** clean
**Säule** column ['kɒləm]
**Schach** chess [tʃes]
**schade: Es war schade, dass …** It was a pity that … ['pɪti]
**Schädel** skull [skʌl]
**schaden** harm [hɑːm]
**Schaden; Schäden** harm *(no pl)* [hɑːm]  **jm. Schaden zufügen** do harm (to) sb. / do sb. harm
**schädigen** harm [hɑːm]
**Schaf** sheep, *pl* sheep [ʃiːp]
**schaffen** create [kriˈeɪt]  **es/etwas schaffen** make it/sth.; manage sth. ['mænɪdʒ]
**Schaffung** creation [kriˈeɪʃn]
**Schale** dish [dɪʃ]
**Schalter** switch [swɪtʃ]
**scharf** sharp [ʃɑːp]
**Schatten** shadow ['ʃædəʊ]
**Schatz; Schätzchen** *(infml, als Anrede)* honey ['hʌni]
**schauen** look [lʊk]
**schaukeln** *(schwanken)* rock [rɒk]
**Schauspiel** drama ['drɑːmə]
**Schauspieler/in** actor ['æktə]
**schauspielern** act [ækt]
**Scheidung** divorce [dɪˈvɔːs]
**scheinen** 1. *(Sonne)* shine [ʃaɪn]  2. **zu sein/zu tun scheinen** seem to be/to do [siːm]
**scheitern** fail [feɪl]
**scherzen** joke [dʒəʊk]
**scheu** shy [ʃaɪ]
**Scheune** barn [bɑːn]
**schick: sich schick anziehen** dress up [ˌdres ˈʌp]
**schicken: einem Freund / einer Freundin eine SMS schicken** text a friend [tekst]  **jm. etwas schicken** send sth. to sb. [send]
**schieben** push [pʊʃ]; slide [slaɪd]
**Schiedsrichter/in** referee [ˌrefəˈriː]
**schiefgehen** go wrong
**schießen** shoot [ʃuːt]; *(feuern)* fire [faɪə]; *(Ball, Puck)* strike [straɪk]  **ein Tor schießen** score [skɔː]
**Schießpulver** gunpowder ['gʌnpaʊdə]

**Schiff** ship [ʃɪp]
**Schild** sign [saɪn]; *(Etikett)* label ['leɪbl]
**Schilderung** narration [nəˈreɪʃn]
**Schildkröte** *(Landschildkröte)* tortoise ['tɔːtəs]
**Schinkenspeck** bacon ['beɪkən]
**Schirm** umbrella [ʌmˈbrelə]
**Schlacht** battle ['bætl]
**Schlaf** sleep [sliːp]
**schlafen** be asleep [əˈsliːp]; sleep [sliːp]
**Schlafparty** sleepover ['sliːpəʊvə]
**schläfrig** sleepy ['sliːpi]
**Schlafzimmer** bedroom ['bedruːm]
**Schlag** slap [slæp]
**schlagen** hit [hɪt]; strike [straɪk]; *(besiegen)* beat [biːt]; defeat [dɪˈfiːt]
**schlagen (auf)** bang (on) [bæŋ]
**Schlägerei** fight [faɪt]
**Schlagzeile** headline ['hedlaɪn]
**Schlagzeug** drums *(pl)* [drʌmz]  **Schlagzeug spielen** play the drums
**Schlagzeuger/in** drummer ['drʌmə]
**Schlamm** mud [mʌd]
**Schlange** 1. *(Tier)* snake [sneɪk]  2. *(wartender Menschen)* queue (BE) [kjuː]; line (AE) [laɪn]  **Schlange stehen** queue; be/stand/wait in line (AE)
**schlau** clever ['klevə]
**Schlauchboot** *(wildwassertauglich)* raft [rɑːft]
**schlecht** bad [bæd]; *(böse, bösartig)* evil ['iːvl]  **schlechter** worse [wɜːs]  **der/die/das schlechteste …; am schlechtesten …** the worst [wɜːst]  **Mir ist schlecht.** I feel sick. [sɪk]
**schleichen** creep [kriːp]
**schließen** close [kləʊz]; shut down [ˌʃʌt ˈdaʊn]
**Schließfach** locker ['lɒkə]
**schließlich** at last; finally ['faɪnəli]
**schlimm** bad [bæd]
**Schlitten** sledge (BE) [sledʒ]; sled (AE) [sled]; toboggan [təˈbɒgən]  **Schlitten fahren** sledge (BE) [sledʒ]; sled (AE) [sled]
**schlittern** slither ['slɪðə]
**Schlittschuh laufen** skate [skeɪt]
**Schlittschuhlaufen** ice skating ['aɪs skeɪtɪŋ]
**Schloss** *(Burg)* castle ['kɑːsl]; *(Palast)* palace ['pæləs]; *(Türschloss)* lock [lɒk]
**schlucken** swallow ['swɒləʊ]
**Schluss** end [end]; ending ['endɪŋ]
**Schlüssel** key [kiː]
**Schlüsselwort** keyword ['kiːwɜːd]
**Schlussfolgerung** conclusion [kənˈkluːʒn]
**schmal** narrow ['nærəʊ]
**schmecken** taste [teɪst]
**schmelzen** melt [melt]
**Schmerz(en)** pain [peɪn]
**schmerzen** hurt [hɜːt]
**Schmetterling** butterfly ['bʌtəflaɪ]
**Schmuck** jewellery (BE) / jewelry (AE) *(no pl)* ['dʒuːəlri]

# German – English

**Schmuggel; das Schmuggeln** smuggling ['smʌglɪŋ]
**schmuggeln** smuggle ['smʌgl]
**Schmuggler/in** smuggler ['smʌglə]
**schmutzig** dirty ['dɜːti]
**schnappen** (*packen*) grab [græb]
**Schnee** snow [snəʊ]
**Schneeball** snowball ['snəʊbɔːl]
**schneiden** cut [kʌt]; (*Film, Video bearbeiten*) edit ['edɪt]
**schnell** fast [fɑːst]; quick [kwɪk] **schneller werden/machen** speed up [ˌspiːd_'ʌp]
**schniefen** sniff [snɪf]
**Schnitt!** (*beim Filmen*) Cut!
**schnitzen** carve [kɑːv]
**schnüffeln** sniff [snɪf]
**schnuppern** sniff [snɪf]
**Schnur** (*Angelschnur*) line [laɪn]
**schockiert** shocked [ʃɒkt]
**Schokolade** chocolate ['tʃɒklət]
**schon** already [ɔːl'redi] **schon bald** before long [bɪˌfɔː_'lɒŋ] **Hast du schon …?** Have you … yet? **(vorher) schon mal** before [bɪ'fɔː]
**schön** beautiful ['bjuːtɪfl]; (*hübsch*) lovely ['lʌvli]; (*nett*) nice [naɪs] **ganz schön teuer/…** kind of expensive/… (*infml*) [kaɪnd]
**Schotter** gravel ['grævl]
**Schrank** cupboard ['kʌbəd]
**schrecklich** awful ['ɔːfl]; terrible ['terəbl]
**Schrei** cry [kraɪ]
**schreiben** write [raɪt]
**Schreiber/in** writer ['raɪtə]
**Schreibtisch** desk [desk]
**Schreibweise** spelling ['spelɪŋ]
**schreien** scream [skriːm]; yell [jel]; shout [ʃaʊt]; (*weinen*) cry [kraɪ]
**Schriftsteller/in** writer ['raɪtə]
**Schritt** step [step]; (*Geräusch*) footstep ['fʊtstep] **(mit jm.) Schritt halten** keep up (with sb.) [ˌkiːp_'ʌp]
**Schrot** shot [ʃɒt]
**schüchtern** shy [ʃaɪ]
**Schuh** shoe [ʃuː]
**Schuld** fault [fɔːlt]
**Schule** school [skuːl] **in der Schule** at school
**Schüler/in** student ['stjuːdənt]
**Schulfach** (*school*) subject ['sʌbdʒɪkt]
**Schulheft** (*Übungsheft*) exercise book ['eksəsaɪz bʊk]
**Schulklasse** class [klɑːs]
**Schulleiter/in** head teacher [ˌhed 'tiːtʃə]; principal (*AE*) ['prɪnsəpl]
**Schulnote** grade [greɪd]; mark [mɑːk]
**Schultasche** school bag ['skuːl bæg]
**Schulter** shoulder ['ʃəʊldə]
**Schuluniform** uniform ['juːnɪfɔːm]
**Schuss** shot [ʃɒt]
**Schüssel** bowl [bəʊl]; dish [dɪʃ]
**Schusswaffe** gun [gʌn]
**schütteln** shake [ʃeɪk]
**Schutz** protection [prə'tekʃn]

**Schutz-** protective [prə'tektɪv]
**schützen: jn./etwas schützen (vor jm./etwas)** protect sb./sth. (from sb./sth.) [prə'tekt]
**Schutzgebiet** reserve [rɪ'zɜːv]
**schwach** weak [wiːk]
**schwanken** rock [rɒk]
**schwarz** black [blæk]
**Schweigen** silence ['saɪləns] **jn. zum Schweigen bringen** silence sb.
**schweigend** silent ['saɪlənt]
**Schwein** pig [pɪg]
**Schweiß** sweat [swet]
**schwer** (*schwierig*) difficult ['dɪfɪkəlt]; hard [hɑːd]; (*von Gewicht*) heavy ['hevi]
**Schwerpunkt** focus ['fəʊkəs]
**Schwert** sword [sɔːd]
**Schwester** sister ['sɪstə]
**schwierig** difficult ['dɪfɪkəlt]; hard [hɑːd]
**Schwierigkeiten: in Schwierigkeiten geraten** get into trouble **in Schwierigkeiten sein** be in trouble ['trʌbl]
**Schwimmbad, -becken** (swimming) pool [puːl]
**schwimmen** swim [swɪm]; (*auf der Wasseroberfläche*) float [fləʊt]
**Schwimmer/in** swimmer ['swɪmə]
**Schwimmweste** life jacket ['laɪf dʒækɪt]
**schwindlig** dizzy ['dɪzi]
**schwitzen** sweat [swet]
**sechs** six [sɪks]
**Sechstel** sixth [sɪksθ]
**See** (*Binnensee*) lake [leɪk]; (*die See, das Meer*) sea [siː]
**Seele** (*Geist*) spirit ['spɪrɪt]
**Segelboot** sailing boat ['seɪlɪŋ bəʊt]
**segeln** sail [seɪl] **segeln gehen** go sailing ['seɪlɪŋ]
**sehen** see [siː]
**Sehenswürdigkeiten** sights (*pl*) [saɪts]
**sehr** very ['veri] **Das hat uns sehr geholfen.** That helped us a lot.
**seidig** silky ['sɪlki]
**Seil** rope [rəʊp]
**sein** be [bi]
**sein(e): seine Schwester** his sister [hɪz] **sein Name** (*bei Dingen und Tieren*) its name [ɪts]
**seiner, seine, seins** his [hɪz]; (*bei Dingen und Tieren*) its [ɪts]
**seit** (*mit Zeitpunkt*) since [sɪns] **seit 10 Uhr/letzter Woche** since 10 o'clock/last week; (*mit Zeitraum*) for **seit Stunden/Wochen** for hours/weeks
**seitdem** since [sɪns]; ever since [ˌevə 'sɪns]
**Seite** 1. side [saɪd] **auf der linken Seite** on the left
2. (*Buchseite*) page [peɪdʒ] **Auf welcher Seite sind wir?** What page are we on?
**seither** since [sɪns]; ever since [ˌevə 'sɪns]
**Sekunde** second ['sekənd]

**selber, selbst** myself [maɪ'self]; yourself [jə'self]; himself [hɪm'self]; herself [hɜː'self]; itself [ɪt'self]; ourselves [ɑː'selvz], [aʊə'selvz]; yourselves [jɔː'selvz], [jə'selvz]; themselves [ðəm'selvz]
**selbst wenn** even if ['iːvn_ɪf]
**Selbstlaut** vowel ['vaʊəl]
**selbstsicher** confident ['kɒnfɪdənt]
**selbstverständlich** of course [əv 'kɔːs]
**seltsam** strange [streɪndʒ]; weird [wɪəd]
**senden: jm. etwas senden** send sth. to sb. [send]
**Sender** channel ['tʃænl]
**Sendereihe** series, *pl* series ['sɪəriːz]
**Sendung** (*Fernsehen, Radio*) program (*AE*) ['prəʊgræm]; programme
**separat** separate ['seprət]
**September** September [sep'tembə]
**Serie** series, *pl* series ['sɪəriːz]
**servieren** (*Essen, Getränke*) serve [sɜːv]
**Servus.** Bye. (*auch:* Bye-bye.) [baɪ]
**Sessel** armchair ['ɑːmtʃeə]
**Set** set [set]
**setzen: sich setzen** sit (down) [sɪt]
**seufzen** sigh [saɪ]
**Shorts** shorts (*pl*) [ʃɔːts]
**Show** show [ʃəʊ]
**sich** himself [hɪm'self]; herself [hɜː'self]; itself [ɪt'self]; (*zu „Sie"*) yourself [jɔː'self]; yourselves [jɔː'selvz]; (*3. Person Plural*) themselves [ðəm'selvz]
**sicher** (*in Sicherheit*) safe [seɪf]; (*selbstsicher*) confident ['kɒnfɪdənt]; (*gewiss*) sure [ʃʊə], [ʃɔː] **sicher(lich)** (*adv*) certainly ['sɜːtnli]
**sichere(r, s)** certain ['sɜːtn]
**Sicherheit: in Sicherheit** safe [seɪf]
**Sicht: aus meiner Sicht** from my point of view [ˌpɔɪnt_əv 'vjuː]
**Sie** you [juː]
**sie** she [ʃiː] **frag sie** ask her [hɜː]; (*Ding/Tier*) it; (*Plural*) they [ðeɪ] **frag sie** (*Plural*) ask them [ðem], [ðəm]
**sieben** seven ['sevn]
**Siedler/in** settler ['setlə]; colonist ['kɒlənɪst]
**Siedlung** settlement ['setlmənt]
**Sieger/in** winner ['wɪnə]
**Signal** signal ['sɪgnəl]
**Silbe** syllable ['sɪləbl]
**Silvester** New Year's Eve [ˌnjuː jɪəz_'iːv]
**singen** sing [sɪŋ]
**Sinn** (*Verstand, Geist*) mind [maɪnd]; (*Zweck*) purpose ['pɜːpəs] **Sinn (für)** sense (of) [sens] **Sinn für Humor** sense of humour
**Sippe** clan [klæn]
**Sir** (*britischer Adelstitel*) Sir [sɜː]
**Sirene** siren ['saɪrən]
**Sirup** syrup ['sɪrəp]
**Sitten** customs (*pl*) [ˈkʌstəmz]
**Situation** situation [ˌsɪtʃu'eɪʃn]
**Sitz** seat [siːt]; (*Passform*) fit [fɪt]
**sitzen** sit [sɪt]

# Dictionary

**Ski** ski [skiː]  **Ski laufen/fahren** ski
**Skilanglauf** cross-country [ˌkrɒs ˈkʌntri]
**Skiläufer/in** skier [ˈskiːə]
**Skulptur** sculpture [ˈskʌlptʃə]
**Skyline** skyline [ˈskaɪlaɪn]
**Smalltalk** (spontan geführtes Gespräch) small talk [ˈsmɔːl tɔːk]
**Smiley** smiley [ˈsmaɪli]
**SMS** text [tekst]; text message [ˈtekst mesɪdʒ]  **einem Freund / einer Freundin eine SMS schicken** text a friend
**Snack** snack [snæk]
**so**  1. (auf diese Weise) like that; like this  **so tun, als ob** pretend [prɪˈtend]  **Und sie so: „Stopp …"** She was like: "Stop …" (infml)
2. **so ein/e …** such a … [sʌtʃ]
3. **so cool/nett** so cool/nice  **(nicht) so groß wie** (not) as big as
**sobald** as soon as [əz ˈsuːn‿əz]
**Socke** sock [sɒk]
**sodass …** so that … (oft auch kurz: so …)
**soeben** just [dʒʌst]
**Sofa** sofa [ˈsəʊfə]
**sofort** immediately [ɪˈmiːdiətli]
**sogar** even [ˈiːvn]
**sogleich** on the spot [spɒt]
**Sohn** son [sʌn]
**solch ein/e …** such a … [sʌtʃ]
**Soldat/in** soldier [ˈsəʊldʒə]
**sollen: Soll ich …?** Shall I …? [ʃæl]  **Ich sollte …** I should … [ʃʊd], [ʃəd]  **Ich sollte lieber …** I'd better … (= I had better …)  **jm. sagen, dass er/sie etwas (nicht) tun soll** tell sb. (not) to do sth.
**Solo-** solo [ˈsəʊləʊ]
**Sommer** summer [ˈsʌmə]
**Sonne** sun [sʌn]
**Sonnenaufgang** sunrise [ˈsʌnraɪz]
**Sonnenbrille** sunglasses (pl) [ˈsʌnɡlɑːsɪz]
**Sonnenuntergang** sunset [ˈsʌnset]
**sonnig** sunny [ˈsʌni]
**Sonntag** Sunday [ˈsʌndeɪ], [ˈsʌndi]
**sonst: sonst jeder** everyone else [els]
**sorgen: dafür sorgen, dass …** make sure that …
**Sorgen: sich Sorgen machen (wegen, um)** worry (about) [ˈwʌri]
**sorgfältig** thorough [ˈθʌrə]; (adv) carefully [ˈkeəfəli]
**Sorte** (Variante) variety [vəˈraɪəti]; (Typ, Art) type (of) [taɪp]
**Soße** topping [ˈtɒpɪŋ]
**Souvenir** souvenir [ˌsuːvəˈnɪə]
**sowie** (sobald) as soon as [əz ˈsuːn‿əz]
**sowieso** anyway [ˈeniweɪ]
**sowohl … als auch …** both … and … [bəʊθ]
**sozial** social [ˈsəʊʃl]  **soziale Dienste** social services (pl) [ˌsəʊʃl ˈsɜːvɪsɪz]
**soziale Medien** social media (pl) [ˌsəʊʃl ˈmiːdiə]
**Sozialwesen** social services (pl) [ˌsəʊʃl ˈsɜːvɪsɪz]

**Spaghetti** spaghetti [spəˈɡeti]
**spalten** split [splɪt]
**Spanisch; spanisch** Spanish [ˈspænɪʃ]
**spannen** (festziehen) tighten [ˈtaɪtn]
**spannend** exciting [ɪkˈsaɪtɪŋ]
**Spannung** tension [ˈtenʃn]
**sparen** (z.B. Geld) save (up) [seɪv]
**Spaß** fun [fʌn]  **Spaß haben** have fun  **Das klingt nach Spaß.** That sounds fun.  **Das macht Spaß.** That's fun.  **Hat es Spaß gemacht?** Was it fun?
**spät** late [leɪt]  **Du bist spät dran. / Du bist zu spät.** You're late.  **Wie spät ist es?** What time is it?
**später** later [ˈleɪtə]  **Bis später dann!** Catch you later. (infml) [ˌkætʃ ju ˈleɪtə]
**spazieren gehen** go for a walk [wɔːk]; take a walk (bes. AE)
**Spaziergang** walk [wɔːk]  **einen Spaziergang machen** go for a walk; take a walk (bes. AE)
**speichern** store [stɔː]
**Speiseeis** ice cream [ˌaɪs ˈkriːm]
**spekulieren** speculate [ˈspekjuleɪt]
**sperren** block [blɒk]
**Spickzettel** crib sheet (infml) [ˈkrɪb ʃiːt]
**Spiegel** mirror [ˈmɪrə]
**Spiel** game [ɡeɪm]; (Wettkampf, Match) match [mætʃ]
**spielen** play [pleɪ]; (Geschichte, Handlung) take place [teɪk ˈpleɪs]  **gegen jn. spielen** (Sport) play sb.  **Klavier/Gitarre/Schlagzeug spielen** play the piano/guitar/drums
**Spieler/in** player [ˈpleɪə]
**Spielstand** score [skɔː]
**Spielzeug** toy [tɔɪ]
**Spieß** pike [paɪk]
**Spind** locker [ˈlɒkə]
**Spinner/in** weirdo (infml) [ˈwɪədəʊ]
**spiralförmig** spiral [ˈspaɪrəl]
**Spitze; Spitzen-** (oberes Ende) top [tɒp]
**Spitzer** (Anspitzer) sharpener [ˈʃɑːpnə]
**Spitzname** nickname [ˈnɪkneɪm]
**Sport(art)** sport [spɔːt]  **Sport treiben** do sport
**Sportschuhe** sneakers (AE, pl) [ˈsniːkəz]
**Sportsendung** sportscast (AE) [ˈspɔːtskɑːst]
**Sportunterricht** PE (Physical Education) [ˌpiː ˈiː]
**Sprache** language [ˈlæŋɡwɪdʒ]
**Sprachmittlung** mediation [ˌmiːdiˈeɪʃn]
**sprayen** spray [spreɪ]
**sprechen (mit jm.)** speak (to sb.) [spiːk]
**Sprecher/in** narrator [nəˈreɪtə]; speaker [ˈspiːkə]
**sprengen: etwas in die Luft sprengen** blow sth. up [ˌbləʊ ˈʌp]
**Sprengsatz** explosive [ɪkˈspləʊsɪv]
**Sprengstoff** explosive [ɪkˈspləʊsɪv]
**Springbrunnen** water fountain [ˈwɔːtə faʊntən]
**springen** jump [dʒʌmp]
**spritzen: jn. nass spritzen** splash sb. [splæʃ]

**sprühen** spray [spreɪ]
**Sprung** jump [dʒʌmp]
**spülen** wash the dishes (pl)
**Spur: keine Spur von …** no sign of … [saɪn]
**St (= Sankt)** St = Saint [seɪnt]
**Staat** state [steɪt]
**Staatsangehörigkeit** nationality [ˌnæʃəˈnæləti]
**Staatsbürger/in** citizen [ˈsɪtɪzn]
**Staatsbürgerschaft** citizenship [ˈsɪtɪzənʃɪp]
**Staatsvertrag** treaty [ˈtriːti]
**Stadel** barn [bɑːn]
**Stadion** stadium [ˈsteɪdiəm]
**Stadt** town [taʊn]; (Großstadt) city [ˈsɪti]
**Stadtbezirk** borough [ˈbʌrə], [ˈbɜːrəʊ]
**Stadtplan** map [mæp]
**Stadtviertel** quarter [ˈkwɔːtə]
**Stahl** steel [stiːl]
**Stamm** (Volksstamm) tribe [traɪb]
**Stammbaum** bloodline [ˈblʌdlaɪn]; (gezeichnet) family tree
**stammen aus** (zeitlich) date from [deɪt]
**Stand** (Marktstand) stall [stɔːl]  **etwas auf den neuesten Stand bringen** update sth. [ˌʌpˈdeɪt]
**Standard; Standard-** standard [ˈstændəd]
**ständig: etwas ständig tun** keep (on) doing sth. [kiːp]
**Standort** position [pəˈzɪʃn]
**Standpunkt** point of view [ˌpɔɪnt‿əv ˈvjuː]
**Standuhr** clock [klɒk]
**Stapel** pile [paɪl]
**stark** powerful [ˈpaʊəfl]; strong [strɒŋ]; (adv: erheblich) greatly [ˈɡreɪtli]  **starker Regen** heavy rain [ˈhevi]
**Stärke** power [ˈpaʊə]; strength [streŋθ]
**starren** gaze [ɡeɪz]; stare [steə]
**Station** (Haltestelle) stop [stɒp]
**Statistik(en)** statistics (pl) [stəˈtɪstɪks]
**statistisch** statistical [stəˈtɪstɪkl]
**statt** instead of [ɪnˈsted‿əv]; rather than [ˈrɑːðə ðən]
**stattdessen** instead [ɪnˈsted]
**Stätte** site [saɪt]
**stattfinden** take place [teɪk ˈpleɪs]
**stattlich** noble [ˈnəʊbl]
**Statue** statue [ˈstætʃuː]
**Status** status [ˈsteɪtəs]
**Staub** dust [dʌst]
**staubig** dusty [ˈdʌsti]
**Staudamm** dam [dæm]
**Steak** steak [steɪk]
**stechen: etwas in etwas stechen** stick sth. into sth. [stɪk]
**stecken** tuck [tʌk]  **etwas in etwas stecken** stick sth. into sth. [stɪk]
**stehen** stand [stænd]  **auf etwas stehen** (etwas mögen) be into sth. (infml)  **Hier steht: …** It says here: …  **Wie steht es?** (z.B. beim Fußballspiel) What's the score? [skɔː]
**stehlen** steal [stiːl]

# German – English

**steil** steep [stiːp]
**Stein** stone [stəʊn]
**steinig** rocky ['rɒki]
**Stelle** place [pleɪs]; site [saɪt]; (Arbeitsstelle) job [dʒɒb] **an Ort und Stelle** (sogleich) on the spot [spɒt]
**stellen** put [pʊt]; set [set] **eine Frage stellen** ask a question **etwas lauter/leiser stellen** turn sth. up/down [tɜːn] **sich (hin)stellen** stand [stænd]
**Stellungnahme** opinion piece [əˈpɪnjən piːs]
**Stelzen** stilts (pl) [stɪlts]
**Stempel** stamp [stæmp]
**sterben** die [daɪ]
**Stereotyp** stereotype ['steriətaɪp]
**stereotyp** stereotypical [ˌsteriəˈtɪpɪkl]
**Stern** star [stɑː]
**Steuer** (finanziell) tax [tæks] **Steuern** (Besteuerung) taxation [tækˈseɪʃn]
**steuern** steer [stɪə]
**Steuerzahler/in** taxpayer [ˈtækspeɪə]
**Stich: im Stich lassen** abandon [əˈbændən]
**Stichwort** (im Wörterbuch) headword [ˈhedwɜːd]
**Stiefel** boot [buːt]
**Stift** pen [pen]
**Stil** style [staɪl]
**still** quiet [ˈkwaɪət]; still [stɪl]
**Stille** silence [ˈsaɪləns]
**Stimme** voice [vɔɪs]; (bei Wahlen) vote [vəʊt] **mit lauter/leiser Stimme** in a loud/soft voice
**stimmen** (Instrument) tune [tjuːn]; (abstimmen) vote [vəʊt] **für/gegen jn./etwas stimmen** vote for/against sb./sth. **Ja, das stimmt.** Yes, that's right. **Nein, das stimmt nicht.** No, that's wrong.
**Stimmrecht** vote [vəʊt] **das Stimmrecht erhalten** get the vote
**Stimmung** atmosphere [ˈætməsfɪə]; mood [muːd]; spirit [ˈspɪrɪt]
**stinken** be smelly [ˈsmeli]; stink [stɪŋk]
**stinkend** smelly [ˈsmeli]
**Stirn: die Stirn runzeln** frown [fraʊn]
**Stirnrunzeln** frown [fraʊn]
**Stock** stick [stɪk]; (Etage) floor [flɔː]; (Stockwerk) storey, pl storeys (BE), story, pl stories (AE) [ˈstɔːri]
**Stoff** material [məˈtɪəriəl]
**stöhnen** groan [grəʊn]
**Stöhnen** groan [grəʊn]
**stolpern** stumble [ˈstʌmbl]
**Stolz** pride [praɪd]
**stolz (auf)** proud (of) [praʊd] **stolz auf etwas sein** pride oneself on sth. [praɪd]
**stoppen** stop [stɒp]
**stören: jn. stören** (jm. missfallen) offend sb. [əˈfend] **Stört es Sie, …?** Do you mind …?
**stoßen** push [pʊʃ] **auf jn./etwas stoßen** (zufällig treffen) come across sb./sth. **gegen etwas stoßen** hit [hɪt]

**Strafbank** (Eishockey) penalty box [ˈpenəlti bɒks]
**Strafe** penalty [ˈpenəlti]; punishment [ˈpʌnɪʃmənt]
**Strafzettel** ticket [ˈtɪkɪt]
**strahlend** bright [braɪt]
**Strand** beach [biːtʃ]; (Ufer eines Sees) shore [ʃɔː]
**Straße** street [striːt]; road [rəʊd]
**Straßenkreuzung** junction [ˈdʒʌŋkʃn]
**Straßenkünstler/in** street artist [ˌstriːt ˈɑːtɪst]
**Strauch** shrub [ʃrʌb]
**streamen** stream [striːm]
**Streben (nach)** pursuit (of) [pəˈsjuːt]
**Strecke** route [ruːt]; (Distanz) distance [ˈdɪstəns]
**streichen** (anstreichen) paint [peɪnt]; (löschen, tilgen) delete [dɪˈliːt]
**Streit** argument [ˈɑːgjumənt]; conflict [ˈkɒnflɪkt]
**streiten; sich streiten** argue [ˈɑːgjuː]
**streng** strict [strɪkt]
**Strom** (das Fließen) flow [fləʊ]; (elektrisch) power [ˈpaʊə]
**strömen** flow [fləʊ]; stream [striːm]
**Strophe** verse [vɜːs]
**Struktur** structure [ˈstrʌktʃə]
**Stück: ein Stück …** a piece of … [piːs]
**Stückchen** bit [bɪt]
**Student/in** student [ˈstjuːdənt]
**Studie** (Umfrage) survey [ˈsɜːveɪ]
**studieren** study [ˈstʌdi]
**Studio** studio [ˈstjuːdiəʊ]
**Stufe** step [step]
**Stuhl** chair [tʃeə]
**Stunde** hour [ˈaʊə]; (Unterrichtsstunde) lesson [ˈlesn] **eine halbe Stunde** half an hour
**Stundenplan** timetable [ˈtaɪmteɪbl]
**Sturm** storm [stɔːm]
**stürzen** fall [fɔːl]; rush [rʌʃ]; (Regierung, Staatsoberhaupt usw.) overthrow [ˌəʊvəˈθrəʊ]
**Suche** search [sɜːtʃ]
**suchen: etwas suchen** look for sth. **(nach) etwas suchen** search for sth. [sɜːtʃ]
**Suchmaschine** search engine [ˈsɜːtʃ ˌendʒɪn]
**Süd-** southern [ˈsʌðən]
**Süden, nach Süden** south [saʊθ] **Richtung Süden** southbound [ˈsaʊθbaʊnd]
**südlich** south [saʊθ]; southern [ˈsʌðən]
**Südosten, nach Südosten** south-east [ˌsaʊθˈiːst]
**südöstlich** south-east [ˌsaʊθˈiːst]
**Südwesten, nach Südwesten** south-west [ˌsaʊθˈwest]
**südwestlich** south-west [ˌsaʊθˈwest]
**summen** hum [hʌm]
**Sumpf** swamp [swɒmp]
**Supermarkt** supermarket [ˈsuːpəmɑːkɪt]
**Suppe** soup [suːp]
**Surfen** surfing [ˈsɜːfɪŋ]

**surfen** surf [sɜːf]
**süß** sweet [swiːt]
**Süßigkeiten** sweets (pl) [swiːts]
**Symbol** symbol [ˈsɪmbl]
**Szene** scene [siːn]; (Film) shot [ʃɒt]

# T

**T-Shirt** T-shirt [ˈtiː ʃɜːt]
**Tabelle** table [ˈteɪbl]; chart [tʃɑːt]
**Tablette** tablet (bes. BE) [ˈtæblət]
**Tafel** (Schokolade) bar [bɑː]; (Schultafel) board [bɔːd]
**Tag** day [deɪ] **den ganzen Tag (lang)** all day **eines Tages** one day
**Tagebuch** diary [ˈdaɪəri]
**Tageslicht** daylight [ˈdeɪlaɪt]
**täglich** daily [ˈdeɪli]
**Taille** waist [weɪst]
**Tal** valley [ˈvæli]
**Talent** gift [gɪft]; talent [ˈtælənt]
**talentiert** talented [ˈtæləntɪd]
**Tankstelle** gas station (AE) [ˈgæs steɪʃn]; petrol station [ˈpetrəl steɪʃn]
**Tante** aunt [ɑːnt]
**Tante-Emma-Laden** corner shop
**Tanz** dance [dɑːns]
**tanzen** dance [dɑːns]
**Tänzer/in** dancer [ˈdɑːnsə]
**Tanzfläche** dance floor [ˈdɑːns flɔː]
**tarnen** disguise [dɪsˈgaɪz]
**Tasche** bag [bæg]; (Manteltasche, Hosentasche usw.) pocket [ˈpɒkɪt]
**Taschengeld** allowance (AE) [əˈlaʊəns]; pocket money [ˈpɒkɪt mʌni]
**Taschenlampe** torch (BE) [tɔːtʃ]; flashlight (AE) [ˈflæʃlaɪt]
**Tasse** cup [kʌp] **eine Tasse Tee** a cup of tea
**Tat** (Handlung) act [ækt]; action [ˈækʃn]
**Tatsache** fact [fækt]
**tatsächlich** (adv) actually [ˈæktʃuəli]
**tatsächliche(r, s)** actual [ˈæktʃuəl]
**tätscheln; Tätscheln** pat [pæt]
**Taube** (Stadttaube) pigeon [ˈpɪdʒɪn]
**Tausend, tausend** thousand [ˈθaʊznd]
**Taxi** taxi [ˈtæksi]
**Team** team [tiːm]
**Technik: Design und Technik** design and technology [dɪˌzaɪn ənd tekˈnɒlədʒi]
**Tee** tea [tiː] **eine Tasse Tee** a cup of tea
**Teelöffel** teaspoon [ˈtiːspuːn]
**Teenager** teenager [ˈtiːneɪdʒə]
**Teenager/in** teen [tiːn]
**Teig** (Hefeteig) dough [dəʊ]
**Teil** part [pɑːt]; bit [bɪt]
**teilen: (sich) etwas teilen** share sth. [ʃeə] **geteilter Bildschirm** split screen [ˌsplɪt ˈskriːn]
**teilnehmen (an)** take part (in)
**Teilstück** section [ˈsekʃn]
**Telefon** phone [fəʊn]; telephone [ˈtelɪfəʊn] **ans Telefon gehen** answer the phone

# Dictionary

**Telefongespräch** (phone) call [ˈfəʊn kɔːl]
**Telefonzelle** telephone box [ˈtelɪfəʊn bɒks]
**Teller** plate [pleɪt]   **ein Teller ...** a plate of ...
**Temperatur** temperature [ˈtemprətʃə]
**Tempus** (grammatisch) tense [tens]
**Tennis** tennis [ˈtenɪs]
**Termin** (Verabredung) appointment [əˈpɔɪntmənt]
**Terrain** terrain [təˈreɪn]
**Territorium** territory [ˈterətri]
**Terrorist/in** terrorist [ˈterərɪst]
**terroristische(r, s)** terrorist [ˈterərɪst]
**Test** test [test]
**testen** test [test]
**teuer** expensive [ɪkˈspensɪv]
**Text** text [tekst]
**Text(datei)** document [ˈdɒkjumənt]
**Textquelle** source [sɔːs]
**Textzusammenhang** context [ˈkɒntekst]
**Theater** theatre [ˈθɪətə]
**Theaterstück** play [pleɪ]
**Theke** counter [ˈkaʊntə]
**Thema** theme [θiːm]; topic [ˈtɒpɪk]; subject [ˈsʌbdʒɪkt]
**Thermometer** thermometer [θəˈmɒmɪtə]
**tief** deep [diːp]; low [ləʊ]
**tiefgekühlt** frozen [ˈfrəʊzn]
**Tier** animal [ˈænɪml]   **Tiere** (in freier Wildbahn) wildlife [ˈwaɪldlaɪf]
**Tierarzt/Tierärztin** vet [vet]
**Tierwelt** wildlife [ˈwaɪldlaɪf]
**Tipp** tip [tɪp]
**tippen** (vorsichtig klopfen) tap [tæp]
**Tisch** table [ˈteɪbl]
**Tischler/in** carpenter [ˈkɑːpəntə]
**Tischtennis** table tennis
**Titan** (Metall) titanium [tɪˈteɪnɪəm]
**Titel** title [ˈtaɪtl]
**Tochter** daughter [ˈdɔːtə]
**Tod** death [deθ]
**Toilette** toilet [ˈtɔɪlət]
**tolerant (gegenüber)** tolerant (of/towards) [ˈtɒlərənt]
**Toleranz (für/gegenüber)** tolerance (of/for) [ˈtɒlərəns]
**Tomate** tomato, pl tomatoes [təˈmɑːtəʊ]
**Ton-** audio [ˈɔːdiəʊ]
**Tonne (= 1.000 kg)** tonne [tʌn]
**Top** (Oberteil) top [tɒp]
**Topf** pot [pɒt]
**Tor** gate [geɪt]; (Sport) goal [gəʊl]   **ein Tor schießen** score (a goal) [skɔː]
**torkeln** stumble [ˈstʌmbl]
**Tortendiagramm** pie chart [ˈpaɪ tʃɑːt]
**tosen** roar [rɔː]
**tot** dead [ded]
**total** (adv) absolutely [ˈæbsəluːtli]; thoroughly [ˈθʌrəli]; totally [ˈtəʊtəli]
**Totale** (Film) long shot [ˈlɒŋ ʃɒt]
**töten** kill [kɪl]
**Tourist/in** tourist [ˈtʊərɪst]
**Touristeninformation** tourist (information) bureau (AE) [ˈtʊərɪst ˌbjʊərəʊ]; tourist (information) office [ˈtʊərɪst ˌɒfɪs]

**touristisch** touristy (infml) [ˈtʊərɪsti]
**Tradition** tradition [trəˈdɪʃn]
**traditionell** traditional [trəˈdɪʃənl]
**tragen** carry [ˈkæri]; (Kleidung) wear [weə]
**Trainer/in** coach [kəʊtʃ]
**trainieren** practise (BE) [ˈpræktɪs]; practice (AE); train [treɪn]   **jn. trainieren** coach sb. [kəʊtʃ]; train sb.
**Training(sstunde)** training [ˈtreɪnɪŋ]
**Traktor** tractor [ˈtræktə]
**Tran** (Öl aus dem Speck von Walen, Robben oder Fischen) blubber [ˈblʌbə]
**Trance** trance [trɑːns]
**Träne** tear [tɪə]
**Transport(wesen)** transport [ˈtrænspɔːt]
**Transporter** (Lieferwagen) van [væn]
**transportieren** transport [trænˈspɔːt]
**trauen** trust [trʌst]
**Traum** dream [driːm]
**traurig** sad [sæd]
**Trauung** wedding [ˈwedɪŋ]
**Treck** trek [trek]
**treffen** meet [miːt]   **sich treffen** meet   **etwas treffen** hit sth.; strike sth.   **jn./etwas zufällig treffen** come across sb./sth.
**Treffer: einen Treffer erzielen** score [skɔː]
**treiben** (antreiben) drive [draɪv]; (auf der Wasseroberfläche) float [fləʊt]   **Sport treiben** do sport
**Treibhausgas** greenhouse gas [ˌgriːnhaʊs ˈgæs]
**Trend** trend [trend]
**trennen** separate [ˈsepəreɪt]   **(sich) trennen** split [splɪt]   **sich von etwas trennen** part with sth. [ˈpɑːt wɪð]
**Trennlinie** boundary line [ˈbaʊndri laɪn]
**Treppe** stairs (pl) [steəz]
**Treppe(nhaus)** staircase [ˈsteəkeɪs]
**Treppenstufen** stairs (pl) [steəz]
**treten** kick [kɪk]
**Trick** trick [trɪk]
**Trikot** jersey [ˈdʒɜːzi]
**Trimester** term [tɜːm]
**Trinkbrunnen** water fountain [ˈwɔːtə faʊntən]
**trinken** drink [drɪŋk]
**trocken** dry [draɪ]
**Trommel** drum [drʌm]
**Trommler/in** drummer [ˈdrʌmə]
**Trompete** trumpet [ˈtrʌmpɪt]
**Trophäe** trophy [ˈtrəʊfi]
**tropisch, Tropen-** tropical [ˈtrɒpɪkl]
**Trottel** jerk (infml) [dʒɜːk]
**trotz** despite [dɪˈspaɪt]
**trotzdem** still [stɪl]
**Truppe** (Militär) troop [truːp]
**Truthahn** turkey [ˈtɜːki]
**Tulpe** tulip [ˈtjuːlɪp]
**tun** do [duː]; (etwas wohin tun) put   **so tun, als ob** pretend [prɪˈtend]   **Tut mir leid.** (I'm) sorry. [ˈsɒri]   **viel zu tun haben** be busy [ˈbɪzi]
**Tunnel** tunnel [ˈtʌnl]

**Tür** door [dɔː]
**Türklingel, -glocke** doorbell [ˈdɔːbel]
**Turm** tower [ˈtaʊə]
**Turmuhr** clock [klɒk]
**Turnen** gymnastics [dʒɪmˈnæstɪks]; (Sportunterricht) PE (Physical Education) [ˌpiːˈiː]
**Turnhalle** gym [dʒɪm]
**Turnier** tournament [ˈtʊənəmənt], [ˈtɔːnəmənt]
**Turnschuh** trainer [ˈtreɪnə]
**Tüte** bag [bæg]
**Tweet** tweet [twiːt]
**Typ** (Art, Sorte) type (of) [taɪp]; (Kerl) dude (bes. AE, Slang) [djuːd]; guy [gaɪ]
**typisch (für)** typical (of) [ˈtɪpɪkl]

# U

**U-Bahn** subway (AE) [ˈsʌbweɪ]; the underground (BE) [ˈʌndəgraʊnd]; (in London) the Tube (no pl) [tjuːb]
**Übel** evil [ˈiːvl]
**übel** (z.B. Geruch) evil [ˈiːvl]   **Das ist echt übel!** That sucks! (infml) [sʌks]   **Mir ist übel.** I feel sick. [sɪk]
**Übelkeit** sickness [ˈsɪknəs]
**üben** practise (BE) [ˈpræktɪs]; practice (AE)
**über** 1. (räumlich) over [ˈəʊvə]; (oberhalb) above [əˈbʌv]   **(quer) über die Straße** across the street [əˈkrɒs] 2. (mehr als) over   **über 20 Leute/Jahre/...** over 20 people/years/... 3. **über mich/dich/dich selbst/Miss Bell** about me/you/yourself/Miss Bell [əˈbaʊt]
**überall** everywhere [ˈevriweə]; anywhere [ˈeniweə]   **überall in ...** throughout ... [θruːˈaʊt]   **überall um sie herum** all around her
**überarbeiten** revise [rɪˈvaɪz]
**überbacken: mit Käse überbacken** with a cheese topping [ˈtɒpɪŋ]
**überblicken** overlook [ˌəʊvəˈlʊk]
**übereinander** on top of each other
**Übereinstimmung** fit [fɪt]
**überfliegen: einen Text überfliegen** (um den Inhalt grob zu erfassen) skim a text [skɪm]
**überfrieren** freeze over [ˌfriːz ˈəʊvə]
**überfüllt** crowded [ˈkraʊdɪd]
**übergeben: Ich muss mich übergeben.** I'm going to be sick. [sɪk]
**überhaupt** in the first place   **Und überhaupt, ...** And anyway, ... [ˈeniweɪ]
**überleben** survive [səˈvaɪv]
**überlegen: es sich anders überlegen** change one's mind [maɪnd]
**übernachten (in/bei)** stay (at/with) [steɪ]
**überprüfen** check [tʃek]
**Überprüfung** check [tʃek]
**überqueren** cross [krɒs]

# German – English

**überraschen** surprise [səˈpraɪz]
**überraschenderweise** surprisingly [səˈpraɪzɪŋli]
**überrascht** surprised [səˈpraɪzd]
**Überraschung** surprise [səˈpraɪz]
**Überschrift** heading [ˈhedɪŋ]; headline [ˈhedlaɪn]; title [ˈtaɪtl]
**übersehen** overlook [ˌəʊvəˈlʊk]
**übersetzen** translate [trænsˈleɪt]
**Übersetzung** translation [trænsˈleɪʃn]
**Überzug** *(Belag, Soße)* topping [ˈtɒpɪŋ]
**üblich** usual [ˈjuːʒʊəl]
**übrig: übrig sein** be left [left]   **etwas übrig lassen** leave sth.
**übrigens** by the way [ˌbaɪ ðə ˈweɪ]; actually [ˈæktʃʊəli]
**Übung** practice [ˈpræktɪs]; exercise [ˈeksəsaɪz]
**Übungsheft** exercise book [ˈeksəsaɪz bʊk]
**Ufer** *(eines Sees)* shore [ʃɔː]
**Uhr** *(Armbanduhr)* watch [wɒtʃ]; *(Wand-, Stand-, Turmuhr)* clock [klɒk]   **4 Uhr morgens** 4 am [ˌeɪˈem]   **4 Uhr nachmittags / 16 Uhr** 4 pm [ˌpiːˈem]   **10 Uhr / 22 Uhr** ten o'clock [əˈklɒk]   **um 1 Uhr/13 Uhr** at 1 o'clock
**Uhrzeit** time [taɪm]
**um**   1. *(räumlich)* **um den See (herum)** (a)round the lake   2. *(in Zeitangaben)* at [æt], [ət]   **um 1 Uhr/13 Uhr** at 1 o'clock   3. **um etwas bitten** ask for sth.   4. **um zu** to [tu]
**umarmen: jn. umarmen** give sb. a hug [hʌg]; hug sb.
**umbenennen** rename [ˌriːˈneɪm]
**umdrehen, sich umdrehen** turn around [ˌtɜːn əˈraʊnd]
**Umfeld** environment [ɪnˈvaɪrənmənt]
**Umfrage** survey [ˈsɜːveɪ]
**umgangssprachlich** colloquial [kəˈləʊkwɪəl]
**Umgebung** environment [ɪnˈvaɪrənmənt]; *(Viertel, Gegend)* neighbourhood [ˈneɪbəhʊd]
**umhauen: jn. total umhauen** blow sb. away *(AE, infml)* [ˌbləʊ əˈweɪ]
**umher: in der Bücherei / auf dem Strand umher** around the library/the beach [əˈraʊnd]
**umherrennen/-gehen/…** walk/run/… around
**Umsatz** sales *(pl)* [seɪlz]
**umschreiben** paraphrase [ˈpærəfreɪz]
**Umschreibung** paraphrase [ˈpærəfreɪz]
**umsehen: sich (auf der Farm) umsehen** look around (the farm)
**umsonst** *(kostenlos)* for free
**umsteigen** change [tʃeɪndʒ]
**umtaufen** rename [ˌriːˈneɪm]
**umtauschen** *(Geld)* change [tʃeɪndʒ]
**umwandeln** transform [trænsˈfɔːm]
**Umwelt** environment [ɪnˈvaɪrənmənt]
**Umwelt-** environmental [ɪnˌvaɪrənˈmentl]
**Umweltverschmutzung** pollution [pəˈluːʃn]
**umziehen (nach)** move (to) [muːv]
**Umzug** *(Parade)* parade [pəˈreɪd]
**unabhängig** independent [ˌɪndɪˈpendənt]
**Unabhängigkeit** independence [ˌɪndɪˈpendəns]
**Unabhängigkeitserklärung: die Unabhängigkeitserklärung** *(der Vereinigten Staaten im Jahr 1776)* the Declaration of Independence
**unbedarft** *(ahnungslos)* clueless [ˈkluːləs]
**unbedingt: etwas unbedingt tun wollen** be eager to do sth. [ˈiːgə]
**und** and [ænd], [ənd]   **Und du? / Und was ist mit dir?** What about you?   **Und überhaupt, …** And anyway, … [ˈeniweɪ]   **Na und?** So what?; So?; *(Wen interessiert das?)* Who cares? [keə]
**Unentschieden** draw *(bes. BE)* [drɔː]
**unfair** unfair [ʌnˈfeə]
**Unfall** accident [ˈæksɪdənt]; crash [kræʃ]
**unfreundlich** unfriendly [ʌnˈfrendli]
**ungebildet** uneducated [ʌnˈedʒukeɪtɪd]
**ungeduldig** impatient [ɪmˈpeɪʃnt]
**ungefähr** about [əˈbaʊt]
**ungesund** unhealthy [ʌnˈhelθi]
**ungewöhnlich** unusual [ʌnˈjuːʒʊəl]
**unglaublich** incredible [ɪnˈkredəbl]; *(erstaunlich)* amazing [əˈmeɪzɪŋ]
**unglücklich** unhappy [ʌnˈhæpi]
**unheimlich** scary [ˈskeəri]
**unhöflich** impolite [ˌɪmpəˈlaɪt]; *(unverschämt)* rude [ruːd]
**Uniform** uniform [ˈjuːnɪfɔːm]
**Union** union [ˈjuːnɪən]
**Universität** university [ˌjuːnɪˈvɜːsəti]
**unkompliziert** simple [ˈsɪmpl]
**unmöglich** impossible [ɪmˈpɒsəbl]
**Unrecht haben** be wrong [rɒŋ]
**unregelmäßig** irregular [ɪˈregjələ]
**unruhig** restless [ˈrestləs]; troubled [ˈtrʌbld]
**uns** us [ʌs], [əs]; ourselves [ɑːˈselvz], [aʊəˈselvz]
**unser(e) …** our … [aʊə]
**unserer, unsere, unseres** ours [ˈaʊəz]
**unten** *(am unteren Ende)* at the bottom (of) [ˈbɒtəm]; *(unterhalb)* below [bɪˈləʊ]   **nach unten** down [daʊn]; *(im Haus)* downstairs [ˌdaʊnˈsteəz]   **(nach) da/dort unten** down there
**unter** under [ˈʌndə]; below [bɪˈləʊ]   **unter der Erde** underground [ˌʌndəˈgraʊnd]
**Unterarm** forearm [ˈfɔːrɑːm]
**unterbrechen** interrupt [ˌɪntəˈrʌpt]
**untergehen** *(Sonne)* go down [ˌgəʊˈdaʊn]; set [set]
**unterhalb (von)** below [bɪˈləʊ]
**unterhalten: sich unterhalten (mit)** talk (to) [tɔːk]
**Unterhaltung** *(Gespräch)* chat [tʃæt]; conversation [ˌkɒnvəˈseɪʃn]
**Unterhaltungskünstler/in** entertainer [ˌentəˈteɪnə]
**unterirdisch** underground [ˌʌndəˈgraʊnd]
**Unterkunft** shelter [ˈʃeltə]
**untermauern** back up [ˌbækˈʌp]
**Unterricht: jm. Unterricht geben** coach sb. [kəʊtʃ]
**unterrichten** teach [tiːtʃ]
**untersagen** forbid [fəˈbɪd]
**Unterschied** difference [ˈdɪfrəns]
**unterschiedlich** diverse [daɪˈvɜːs]   **unterschiedlich sein** vary [ˈveəri]
**unterschreiben** sign [saɪn]
**unterstreichen** underline [ˌʌndəˈlaɪn]
**unterstützen** support [səˈpɔːt]
**Unterstützung** support [səˈpɔːt]
**untersuchen** research [rɪˈsɜːtʃ]; study [ˈstʌdi]   **etwas untersuchen** *(prüfen)* look into sth.
**Untertitel** subtitle [ˈsʌbtaɪtl]
**unterwegs** out and about
**unverschämt** rude [ruːd]
**Unwetter** storm [stɔːm]
**unzufrieden** dissatisfied [dɪsˈsætɪsfaɪd]
**Ureinwohner/innen** indigenous people [ɪnˈdɪdʒənəs]
**Urgroßmutter** great-grandmother
**Urgroßvater** great-grandfather
**Urlaub** holiday [ˈhɒlədeɪ]; vacation *(AE)* [vəˈkeɪʃn]   **im Urlaub sein** be on holiday   **in Urlaub fahren** go on holiday
**Ursprung** origin [ˈɒrɪdʒɪn]
**ursprünglich** *(adv)* in the first place
**ursprüngliche(r, s)** original [əˈrɪdʒənl]
**usw. (und so weiter)** etc. (et cetera) [etˈsetərə]

# V

**Variante** variety [vəˈraɪəti]
**Vater** father [ˈfɑːðə]
**Vati** dad [dæd]
**Vegetarier/in** vegetarian [ˌvedʒəˈteərɪən]
**vegetarisch** vegetarian [ˌvedʒəˈteərɪən]
**Verabredung** date [deɪt]; *(Termin)* appointment [əˈpɔɪntmənt]
**Veranda** porch *(AE)* [pɔːtʃ]
**verändern; sich verändern** change [tʃeɪndʒ]
**verängstigt** scared [skeəd]; frightened [ˈfraɪtnd]
**verantwortlich** responsible [rɪˈspɒnsəbl]
**verarbeitende Industrie** manufacturing (industry) [ˌmænjuˈfæktʃərɪŋ]
**Verb** verb [vɜːb]
**Verband** *(Vereinigung)* union [ˈjuːnɪən]
**verbessern** *(korrigieren)* correct [kəˈrekt]; *(besser werden/machen)* improve [ɪmˈpruːv]   **sich verbessern** improve
**Verbesserung** improvement [ɪmˈpruːvmənt]
**verbeugen: sich verbeugen** bow [baʊ]
**verbieten** forbid [fəˈbɪd]
**verbinden** link [lɪŋk]; *(kombinieren)* combine [kəmˈbaɪn]   **etwas verbinden** join sth. [dʒɔɪn]

# Dictionary

**verbindlich** firm [fɜːm]
**Verbindung** (Kombination) combination [ˌkɒmbɪˈneɪʃn] **in Verbindung bleiben** stay in touch **sich in Verbindung setzen mit jm.** contact sb. [ˈkɒntækt]; get in touch with sb. [tʌtʃ]
**verbittert** bitter [ˈbɪtə]
**verbleiben** remain [rɪˈmeɪn]
**verbreiten** spread [spred]
**verbreitet: weit verbreitet** common [ˈkɒmən]
**verbrennen** burn [bɜːn]
**verbringen: Zeit verbringen (mit)** spend time (on) [spend]
**verbunden sein** be connected [kəˈnektɪd]
**verdammen** condemn [kənˈdem]
**verdienen: Geld verdienen** make money; (durch Arbeit) earn money [ɜːn]
**Verein** club [klʌb]
**Vereinbarung** agreement [əˈgriːmənt]
**vereinigen** unify [ˈjuːnɪfaɪ]
**vereinigt** united [juːˈnaɪtɪd] **das Vereinigte Königreich** the United Kingdom (UK) [juːˌnaɪtɪd ˈkɪŋdəm], [ˌjuːˈkeɪ]
**Vereinigte Staaten (von Amerika)** US (United States) [ˌjuːˈes]
**Vereinigung** (Verband) union [ˈjuːniən]
**vereisen** freeze over [ˌfriːz ˈəʊvə]
**verengen; sich verengen** narrow [ˈnærəʊ]
**Verfassung** constitution [ˌkɒnstɪˈtjuːʃn]
**Verfolgung** persecution [ˌpɜːsɪˈkjuːʃn]
**verfügbar** available [əˈveɪləbl]
**Verfügung: zur Verfügung stellen** supply [səˈplaɪ]
**Vergangenheit** past [pɑːst]
**vergehen** (Zeit) go by; pass [pɑːs]
**vergessen** forget [fəˈget]
**vergewissern: sich vergewissern, dass …** make sure that …
**Vergleich** comparison [kəmˈpærɪsn] **Vergleiche anstellen** make comparisons
**vergleichen** compare [kəmˈpeə]; contrast [kənˈtrɑːst] **verglichen mit …** compared to … [kəmˈpeəd]
**Vergnügungspark** fun park [ˈfʌn pɑːk]
**verhaften** arrest [əˈrest]
**verhalten: sich verhalten** behave [bɪˈheɪv]
**Verhältnis** relationship [rɪˈleɪʃnʃɪp]
**verheiratet (mit)** married (to) [ˈmærɪd]
**verhindern** prevent [prɪˈvent]
**verirren: sich verirren** get lost [lɒst]
**Verkäufe** sales (pl) [seɪlz]
**verkaufen** sell [sel]
**Verkäufer/in** assistant [əˈsɪstənt]; shop assistant [ˈʃɒp əˌsɪstənt]
**Verkehr** traffic [ˈtræfɪk]
**Verkehrsampel** traffic light(s) [ˈtræfɪk laɪt]
**Verkehrsknotenpunkt** hub [hʌb]
**Verkehrsmittel** transport [ˈtrænspɔːt]
**verkehrt** wrong [rɒŋ]
**verkleiden: (sich) verkleiden** disguise [dɪsˈgaɪz] **sich verkleiden als** dress up as [ˌdresˈʌp]

**Verkleidung** costume [ˈkɒstjuːm]
**verknüpfen** link [lɪŋk]
**verkünden** declare [dɪˈkleə]
**Verkündung** declaration [ˌdekləˈreɪʃn]
**verlangen** demand [dɪˈmɑːnd]
**verlassen** abandon [əˈbændən]; leave [left]
**verlaufen** (Straße; Grenze) run [rʌn] **sich verlaufen** get lost [lɒst]
**verleihen: jm. etwas verleihen** award sb. sth.; award sth. to sb. [əˈwɔːd]
**verletzen** harm [hɑːm]; hurt [hɜːt] **sich verletzen** get hurt **verletzt sein** be hurt
**verlieren** lose [luːz]
**Vermeidung** prevention [prɪˈvenʃn]
**vermissen** miss [mɪs]
**Vermutungen anstellen** speculate [ˈspekjuleɪt]
**verneigen: sich verneigen** bow [baʊ]
**Vernichtung** destruction [dɪˈstrʌkʃn]
**verpassen** miss [mɪs]
**verrostet** rusty [ˈrʌsti]
**verrückt** crazy [ˈkreɪzi]; mad [mæd]
**Vers** rhyme [raɪm]; (Strophe) verse [vɜːs]
**versammeln; sich versammeln** assemble [əˈsembl]
**verschieden** different [ˈdɪfrənt] **verschieden sein** vary [ˈveəri]
**verschiedene** (mehrere) several [ˈsevrəl]
**verschlucken** swallow [ˈswɒləʊ]
**verschmutzen** (Umwelt) pollute [pəˈluːt]
**Verschmutzung** (Umwelt) pollution [pəˈluːʃn]
**verschwinden** disappear [ˌdɪsəˈpɪə]
**verschwören: sich verschwören** plot [plɒt]
**Verschwörer/in** conspirator [kənˈspɪrətə]; plotter [ˈplɒtə]
**Verschwörung** plot [plɒt]
**Versehen: aus Versehen** by mistake
**verseuchen** infect [ɪnˈfekt]
**Version** version [ˈvɜːʃn]
**versklaven** enslave [ɪnˈsleɪv]
**Versorgung** supply [səˈplaɪ]
**Verspannung(en)** tension [ˈtenʃn]
**versprechen** promise [ˈprɒmɪs]
**Versprechen** promise [ˈprɒmɪs]
**Verstand** mind [maɪnd]
**Verständigung** communication [kəˌmjuːnɪˈkeɪʃn]
**verstecken; sich verstecken** hide [haɪd]
**Versteckspiel** hide-and-seek [ˌhaɪd ən ˈsiːk]
**verstehen** understand [ˌʌndəˈstænd]; (mitbekommen, kapieren) get sth. (infml) **Hast du es verstanden?** Did you get it? **Verstehe.** I see.
**Versuch** try [traɪ]
**versuchen** try [traɪ] **Versuch's mal.** Have a go.
**verteidigen: jn./etwas verteidigen (gegen jn./etwas)** defend sb./sth. (against sb./sth.) [dɪˈfend]
**Vertrag** (Staatsvertrag) treaty [ˈtriːti]
**vertrauen** trust [trʌst]

**Vertrauen** trust [trʌst]
**vertraut: (jm. / mit etwas) vertraut** familiar (to sb. / with sth.) [fəˈmɪliə]
**vertreiben: die Menschen vom Land vertreiben** clear the land of the people [klɪə] **Sie wurden weiter nach Westen / von ihrem Land vertrieben.** They were forced further west / from their land. [fɔːs]
**vertreten** represent [ˌreprɪˈzent]
**Vertretung** (Interessensvertretung) representation [ˌreprɪzenˈteɪʃn]
**verurteilen** condemn [kənˈdem] **jn. zu einer Geldstrafe verurteilen** fine sb. [faɪn]
**vervollständigen** complete [kəmˈpliːt]
**verwandeln: (sich) verwandeln** transform [trænsˈfɔːm] **jn./etwas in etwas verwandeln** turn sb./sth. into sth. [tɜːn] **sich in etwas verwandeln** turn into sth.
**verwechseln** confuse [kənˈfjuːz]
**verwenden** use [juːz]
**verwirren** confuse [kənˈfjuːz]
**verzeihen** forgive [fəˈgɪv]
**Vibration** vibration [vaɪˈbreɪʃn]
**Video** video [ˈvɪdiəʊ]
**Videokamera** video camera [ˈvɪdiəʊ ˌkæmərə]
**viel** much [mʌtʃ]; a lot (of) [lɒt]; lots of [ˈlɒtsˌəv] **viel zu tun haben** be busy [ˈbɪzi] **er ist viel zu gut/clever** he's way too good/clever (bes. AE)
**viele** many [ˈmeni]; a lot of; lots of
**Vielfalt** diversity [daɪˈvɜːsəti] **kulturelle Vielfalt** multiculturalism [ˌmʌltiˈkʌltʃərəlɪzm]
**vielfältig** diverse [daɪˈvɜːs]
**vielleicht** maybe [ˈmeɪbi] **vielleicht ist es …** it could/might be … [maɪt] **sie sind vielleicht daheim** they may be at home
**vier** four [fɔː]
**Viertel** (Stadtviertel) quarter [ˈkwɔːtə]; district [ˈdɪstrɪkt]; (Nachbarschaft) neighbourhood [ˈneɪbəhʊd] **ein Viertel** (Bruchzahl) a quarter; a fourth (AE) [fɔːθ]
**Viertel vor elf (10.45 / 22.45)** quarter to eleven [ˈkwɔːtə tʊ] **Viertel nach zehn (10.15 / 22.15)** quarter past ten
**viktorianisch; Viktorianer/in** Victorian [vɪkˈtɔːriən]
**violett** purple [ˈpɜːpl]
**Visum** visa [ˈviːzə]
**Vogel** bird [bɜːd]
**Vokabelverzeichnis** vocabulary [vəˈkæbjələri]
**Vokal** vowel [ˈvaʊəl]
**Volk** people, pl peoples [ˈpiːpl]; nation [ˈneɪʃn]
**Volksstamm** tribe [traɪb]
**voll (von, mit)** full (of) [fʊl] **voll und ganz** strongly [ˈstrɒŋli] **voller Menschen** crowded [ˈkraʊdɪd]

# German – English

**völlig** (adv) fully ['fʊli]; thoroughly ['θʌrəli]; totally ['təʊtəli]; absolutely ['æbsəluːtli]
**vollkommen** (adv) fully ['fʊli]; thoroughly ['θʌrəli]; totally ['təʊtəli]; absolutely ['æbsəluːtli]
**Vollmond** full moon [,fʊl 'muːn]
**vollständig** complete [kəm'pliːt]
**von** [ɒv], [əv]; from [frɒm], [frəm] **von … herunter** off [ɒf] **von hinten** from behind **ein Lied von …** a song by … [baɪ] **von … bis …** from … to …
**vor** 1. (räumlich) in front of [ɪn 'frɒnt ˌəv]; (außerhalb) outside [ˌaʊt'saɪd]
2. (zeitlich) before [bɪ'fɔː] **vor der Schule** (vor Schulbeginn) before school **vorm Unterricht** before lessons **vor zwei Tagen** two days ago [ə'gəʊ] **nicht vor drei** not till/until three **Viertel vor elf (10.45 / 22.45)** quarter to eleven ['kwɔːtə]
3. **vor allem** (insbesondere) especially [ɪ'speʃli]
**vorankommen** get on [ˌget'ɒn]
**Voraus: im Voraus** in advance [ɪn ˌəd'vɑːns]
**Vorausahnung** anticipation [ænˌtɪsɪ'peɪʃn]
**Voraussage** prediction [prɪ'dɪkʃn]
**Vorbau** porch (BE) [pɔːtʃ]
**vorbei** (zu Ende) over ['əʊvə] **vorbei an** past [pɑːst]
**vorbeifahren/-gehen an etwas/jm.** pass sth./sb. [pɑːs]
**vorbeikommen (bei)** come over (to)
**vorbereiten: etwas vorbereiten** prepare sth. [prɪ'peə] **sich vorbereiten (auf)** get ready (for) ['redi]; prepare (for)
**vorbeugen** (verhindern) prevent [prɪ'vent] **sich vorbeugen** (sich bücken) bend over [ˌbend ˌ'əʊvə]
**Vorbeugung** prevention [prɪ'venʃn]
**Vordach** porch (BE) [pɔːtʃ]
**Vordergrund** foreground ['fɔːgraʊnd]
**Vorderseite** front [frʌnt]
**Vorfahr/in** ancestor ['ænsestə]
**Vorfreude** anticipation [ænˌtɪsɪ'peɪʃn]
**Vorführung** demonstration [ˌdemən'streɪʃn]
**vorgehen** (Uhr) be fast
**vorhaben: Er hat vor, seinen Vater zu besuchen.** He is going to visit his dad.
**vorher: vorher noch nie** not/never before [bɪ'fɔː] **vorher schon mal** before
**Vorhersage** prediction [prɪ'dɪkʃn]
**vorkommen** (erwähnt werden) come up [ˌkʌm ˌ'ʌp]
**vorlesen: laut vorlesen** read aloud [ə'laʊd]
**Vorlieben und Abneigungen** likes and dislikes (pl) [ˌlaɪks ən 'dɪslaɪks]
**Vormittag** morning ['mɔːnɪŋ]

**vorn(e): nach vorne** forward(s) ['fɔːwəd], ['fɔːwədz]; to the front
**Vorort** suburb ['sʌbɜːb]
**Vorplatz** courtyard ['kɔːtjɑːd]
**Vorrat** supply [sə'plaɪ]
**vorsätzlich** intentional [ɪn'tenʃənl]
**Vorschlag** suggestion [sə'dʒestʃən]
**vorschlagen: (jm.) etwas vorschlagen** suggest sth. (to sb.) [sə'dʒest]
**Vorschrift** rule [ruːl]
**Vorsicht!** (Pass auf!) Watch out! [ˌwɒtʃ ˌ'aʊt]
**vorsichtig** careful ['keəfl]
**Vorsingen/-spielen/-sprechen** (Theater) audition [ɔː'dɪʃn]
**vorspielen: etwas vorspielen** act sth. out [ˌækt ˌ'aʊt]
**Vorstadt** suburb ['sʌbɜːb]
**vorstellen: (jm.) etwas/jn. vorstellen** introduce sth./sb. (to sb.) [ˌɪntrə'djuːs]; (präsentieren) present sth. (to sb.) [prɪ'zent] **sich etwas vorstellen** imagine sth. [ɪ'mædʒɪn] **Stell dir vor, Dad …** Guess what, Dad …
**Vorstellung** (Aufführung) performance [pə'fɔːməns]; (Bild, Abbild) image ['ɪmɪdʒ]; (Idee) idea [aɪ'dɪə]; (Präsentation) presentation [ˌprezn'teɪʃn]
**Vorteil** advantage [əd'vɑːntɪdʒ]
**Vortrag** talk [tɔːk] **einen Vortrag halten (über)** give a talk (about)
**vorüber (an)** past [pɑːst]
**vorübergehen** (Zeit) go by; pass [pɑːs]
**vorwärts** forward(s) ['fɔːwəd], ['fɔːwədz]
**vorwiegend** (adv) mainly ['meɪnli]

# W

**wach** awake [ə'weɪk]
**Wache** guard [gɑːd]
**Wachposten** guard [gɑːd]
**wachsen** grow [grəʊ]
**Waffe** weapon ['wepən]
**Wahl** (Abstimmung) election [ɪ'lekʃn] **zur Wahl gehen** vote [vəʊt]
**wählen** (sich aussuchen) choose [tʃuːz]; (zur Wahl gehen) vote [vəʊt] **jn. zu etwas wählen** elect sb. (to be) sth. [ɪ'lekt]
**Wahlmöglichkeit** (Option) option ['ɒpʃn]
**wahlweise** optional ['ɒpʃənl]
**wahr** true [truː] **wahr werden** come true **…, nicht wahr?** …, right? [raɪt]
**während** 1. during ['djʊərɪŋ] **während des Spiels** during the match
2. while [waɪl] **während wir spielten** while we were playing
3. (als) as [æz]
**Wahrheit** truth [truːθ]
**wahrscheinlich** (adj) probable ['prɒbəbl]; (adv) probably ['prɒbəbli] **wahrscheinlich etwas tun (werden)** be likely to do sth. ['laɪkli]
**Währung** currency ['kʌrənsi]
**Wal** whale [weɪl]

**Wald** forest ['fɒrɪst]
**Walisisch; walisisch** Welsh [welʃ]
**Walkie-Talkie** walkie-talkie [ˌwɔːki 'tɔːki]
**Wand** wall [wɔːl]
**wandern** hike [haɪk]
**Wanderung** trek [trek]
**Wandgemälde** mural ['mjʊərəl]
**Wandschrank** (oft begehbar) closet (bes. AE) ['klɒzɪt]
**Wanduhr** clock [klɒk]
**wann** when [wen] **Wann hast du Geburtstag?** When's your birthday? **wann (auch) immer** whenever [ˌwen'evə]
**Wappentier** state animal [ˌsteɪt ˌ'ænɪml]
**wäre: es wäre …** it would be … [wʊd] **Ich wünschte, es wäre wärmer.** I wish it was warmer. **Wie wäre es mit …?** What about …?
**Waren** goods (pl) [gʊdz]
**warm** warm [wɔːm]
**Wärme** heat [hiːt]
**Warnung** warning ['wɔːnɪŋ]
**warten (auf)** wait (for) [weɪt] **Warte einen Moment.** Wait a minute.
**warum?** why? [waɪ]
**was** what [wɒt] **was (auch) immer** whatever [ˌwɒt'evə] **Was gibt's? / Was ist los?** What's up? **Was gibt es zum Mittagessen?** What's for lunch? **Was haben wir als Hausaufgabe auf?** What's for homework? **Was hättest du gern? / Was möchtest du?** What would you like? **Was ist denn? / Was ist los?** What's the matter? **Was könnte besser sein?** What could be better? **Was kostet/kosten …?** How much is/are …? [haʊ 'mʌtʃ]
**waschen** wash [wɒʃ]
**Wasser** water ['wɔːtə] **fließend(es) Wasser** running water [ˌrʌnɪŋ 'wɔːtə]
**Wasserfall** waterfall ['wɔːtəfɔːl]
**Website** website ['websaɪt]
**Wechselgeld** change [tʃeɪndʒ]
**wechseln** change [tʃeɪndʒ]
**wecken: jn. (auf)wecken** wake sb. up [ˌweɪk ˌ'ʌp]
**Weg** way [weɪ]; (Pfad) path [pɑːθ]; trail [treɪl] **auf dem Weg zu/nach …** on the way to … **den Weg bereiten (für)** set the stage (for) [ˌset ðə ˈsteɪdʒ] **jm. den Weg (nach …) beschreiben** tell sb. the way (to …) [tel] **jn. nach dem Weg fragen** ask sb. the way **sich auf den Weg machen** head out [ˌhed ˌ'aʊt]; set out [ˌset ˌ'aʊt]
**weg** away [ə'weɪ] **weg sein** be gone [gɒn]
**wegbringen** take [teɪk]
**wegen** because of [bɪ'kɒz ˌəv] **berühmt wegen** famous for ['feɪməs] **Es tut mir leid wegen …** I'm sorry about …
**weggehen** leave [liːv]
**weglassen: etwas weglassen** leave sth. out [ˌliːv ˌ'aʊt]

# Dictionary

**wegreißen** (z.B. Zaun) take down [ˌteɪk ˈdaʊn]
**wegrennen** run off
**wehtun** hurt [hɜːt]
**weich** soft [sɒft]
**Weide** field [fiːld]
**weigern: sich weigern** refuse **sich weigern, etwas zu tun** refuse to do sth.
**Weihnachten** Christmas [ˈkrɪsməs] **Frohe Weihnachten!** Merry Christmas! [ˌmeri ˈkrɪsməs]
**Weihnachtstag: 1. Weihnachtstag** (25. Dezember) Christmas Day **2. Weihnachtstag** (26. Dezember) Boxing Day [ˈbɒksɪŋ deɪ]
**weil** because [bɪˈkɒz]; as [æz]
**Weile: eine Weile** a while; for a while [waɪl]
**weinen** cry [kraɪ]
**Weise: Art und Weise** way [weɪ] **auf diese Weise** in this way
**weise** wise [waɪz]
**weiß** white [waɪt]
**weit** (entfernt) far [fɑː] **weit verbreitet** common [ˈkɒmən] **weit vor ...** (zeitlich) way before ...
**weiter** further [ˈfɜːðə] **geradeaus weiter** straight on [streɪt ˈɒn]
**weitergeben: (jm.) etwas weitergeben** pass sth. on (to sb.) [ˌpɑːs ˈɒn]
**weitergehen** continue [kənˈtɪnjuː]; (weiterlaufen) walk on [ɒn]
**weiterleiten: (jm.) etwas weiterleiten** pass sth. on (to sb.) [ˌpɑːs ˈɒn]
**weitermachen** go on [ˌɡəʊ ˈɒn] **weitermachen mit etwas** keep sth. up [ˌkiːp ˈʌp]
**weiterreden** go on [ˌɡəʊ ˈɒn]
**weitersagen: (jm.) etwas weitersagen** pass sth. on (to sb.) [ˌpɑːs ˈɒn]
**Weizen** wheat [wiːt]
**welche(r, s)** which [wɪtʃ] **Auf welcher Seite sind wir?** What page are we on? **Welche Farbe ...?** What colour ...? **Welche Wörter ...?** (von diesen Wörtern) Which words ...? **Welche(r, s)?** Which one?
**Welle** wave [weɪv]
**Wellenreiten** surfing [ˈsɜːfɪŋ]
**Welt** world [wɜːld] **Welt der Natur** natural world [ˌnætʃrəl ˈwɜːld] **auf der Welt** in the world
**Weltkrieg: erster/zweiter Weltkrieg** First/Second World War; World War I / II [ˌwɜːld ˈwɔː]
**Weltraum** space [speɪs]
**weltweit** global [ˈɡləʊbl]
**wem** who **Wem hast es erzählt?** Who did you tell?
**wen** who **Wen kennt Sam?** Who does Sam know?
**wenden** (umdrehen) turn around **sich an jn. wenden** turn to sb. [tɜːn]
**Wendung** (Ausdruck) phrase [freɪz]
**wenig: ein wenig** a little
**wenige** few [fjuː]

**weniger (als)** less (than) [les]
**wenigstens** at least [ət ˈliːst]
**wenn 1.** when [wen]; by the time [ˌbaɪ ðə ˈtaɪm]
**2.** (falls) if [ɪf] **selbst wenn** even if [ˈiːvn ˌɪf]; even though [ˌiːvn ˈðəʊ]
**wer** who [huː]
**werben für etwas** promote sth. [prəˈməʊt]
**Werbung** (Reklame) advertising [ˈædvətaɪzɪŋ]; (Werbespot) advertisement [ədˈvɜːtɪsmənt] (kurz auch: ad [æd], advert [ˈædvɜːt]) **Werbung machen (für)** advertise [ˈædvətaɪz]
**werden 1.** become [bɪˈkʌm]; (allmählich) **dunkler/alt/... werden** grow darker/old/... **hart/schlecht/verrückt werden** go hard/bad/mad **rot/braun/kalt/... werden** turn red/brown/cold/... [tɜːn] **rot werden** (erröten) go red **wahr werden** come true **wütend/kalt/... werden** get angry/cold/... **zu etwas werden** turn into sth.
**2.** (Zukunft) **Er wird seinen Vater besuchen.** (vorhaben) He is going to visit his dad. **wir werden die Mädchen treffen** (Vorhersage, Vermutung) we'll meet the girls (= we will meet the girls)
**werfen** throw [θrəʊ] **einen Blick auf etwas werfen** have a look (at sth.)
**Werk** (Kreation) creation [kriˈeɪʃn]
**Werkstatt** workshop [ˈwɜːkʃɒp]
**Wert** value [ˈvæljuː]
**wert** worth [wɜːθ] **Es ist sein Geld wert.** It's good value (for money). [ˈvæljuː]
**Werte** values (pl) [ˈvæljuːz]
**Wertvorstellungen** values (pl) [ˈvæljuːz]
**wessen** whose [huːz]
**West-** western [ˈwestən]
**Westen, nach Westen** west Richtung Westen westbound [ˈwestbaʊnd]
**westlich** west [west]; western [ˈwestən]
**Wettbewerb** competition [ˌkɒmpəˈtɪʃn]
**wettbewerbsorientiert** competitive [kəmˈpetətɪv]
**Wettbewerbsteilnehmer/in** competitor [kəmˈpetɪtə]
**wetten** bet [bet]
**Wetter** weather [ˈweðə]
**Wettkampf** match [mætʃ]
**wichtig** important [ɪmˈpɔːtnt] **etwas wichtig nehmen** care about sth. [keə] **Tiere sind mir sehr wichtig.** I really care about animals.
**widerlich** disgusting [dɪsˈɡʌstɪŋ]
**Widerstand** resistance [rɪˈzɪstəns]
**wie 1. wie?** (Fragewort) how? [haʊ] **Wie alt bist du?** How old are you? **Wie findest du ...? / Wie gefällt dir ...?** How do you like ...? **Wie heißt du? / Wie heißt ihr?** What's your name? **Wie ist sie? / Wie ist sie so?** What's she like? **Wie spät ist es?** What time is it? **Wie viel ...?** How

much ...? **Wie viele ...?** How many ...? **Wie war es?** What was it like?
**2. wie Buben** like boys **wie zum Beispiel** such as [ˈsʌtʃ ˌəz] **genau wie ...** just like ... [ˈdʒʌst laɪk] **Wie dem auch sei ...** Anyway, ... [ˈeniweɪ]
**3. (nicht) so groß wie** (not) as big as **der-/die-/dasselbe wie** the same as [seɪm]
**wieder** again [əˈɡen] **immer wieder** again and again
**wiederaufbauen** rebuild [ˌriːˈbɪld]
**wiederholen** repeat [rɪˈpiːt]; (Lernstoff) revise [rɪˈvaɪz]
**wiederholt** (adv) repeatedly [rɪˈpiːtɪdli]
**Wiederholung** (des Lernstoffs) revision [rɪˈvɪʒn]
**Wiedersehen: Auf Wiedersehen.** Bye. (auch: Bye-bye.) [baɪ]
**wiegen** weigh [weɪ]
**wild** wild [waɪld]; fierce [fɪəs] **wild auf etwas sein** be keen on sth. [kiːn] **wild darauf sein, etwas zu tun** be keen on doing sth.
**Wildwasser** whitewater [ˈwaɪtwɔːtə]
**Wildwasserfahren** (im Schlauchboot) whitewater rafting [ˌwaɪtwɔːtə ˈrɑːftɪŋ]
**willkommen: jn. willkommen heißen (in)** welcome sb. (to) [ˈwelkəm] **Willkommen in Plymouth.** Welcome to Plymouth. [ˈwelkəm]
**Wind** wind [wɪnd]
**windig** windy [ˈwɪndi]
**Windmühle** windmill [ˈwɪndmɪl]
**winken** wave [weɪv]
**winseln** whine [waɪn]
**Winter** winter [ˈwɪntə]
**winzig** tiny [ˈtaɪni]
**wir** we [wiː]
**wirklich** actual [ˈæktʃuəl]; real [ˈriːəl]; really [ˈrɪəli]
**Wirklichkeit** reality [riˈælɪti] **in Wirklichkeit** (eigentlich) in fact [ɪn ˈfækt]
**wirtschaftlich, Wirtschafts-** economic [ˌiːkəˈnɒmɪk]
**wischen** wash [wɒʃ]; (Fußboden) mop [mɒp]
**Wischmopp** mop [mɒp]
**wissbegierig** curious [ˈkjʊəriəs]
**wissen** know [nəʊ] **Weißt du was, ...** Guess what, ... **..., weißt du. / ..., wissen Sie.** ..., you know., ..., you see. **gern wissen wollen** (sich fragen) wonder [ˈwʌndə] **Ich weiß (es) nicht.** I don't know. **über etwas Bescheid wissen** know about sth. **Woher weißt du ...?** How do you know ...?
**Witz** joke [dʒəʊk] **Witze machen** joke **Du machst wohl Witze!** (= Das kann doch nicht dein Ernst sein!) You're joking! / You must be joking!
**witzig** funny [ˈfʌni]; humorous [ˈhjuːmərəs]
**wo** where [weə]
**Woche** week [wiːk]

## German – English

**Wochenende** weekend [ˌwiːkˈend]   **am Wochenende** at the weekend
**Wochentag** day of the week
**wöchentlich** weekly [ˈwiːkli]
**Woher kommst du?** Where are you from?
**wohin** where [weə]
**Wohlfahrtsorganisation** charity [ˈtʃærəti]
**Wohltätigkeit** *(wohltätige Zwecke)* charity [ˈtʃærəti]
**wohnen** live [lɪv]; *(vorübergehend)* stay [steɪ]
**Wohnheim** hostel [ˈhɒstl]
**Wohnung** apartment [əˈpɑːtmənt]; flat [flæt]
**Wohnwagen** caravan [ˈkærəvæn]
**Wohnzimmer** living room [ˈlɪvɪŋ ruːm]
**Wolke** cloud [klaʊd]
**Wolkenkratzer** skyscraper [ˈskaɪskreɪpə]
**wolkenlos** cloudless [ˈklaʊdləs]
**wollen: etwas (haben) wollen** want sth. [wɒnt]   **etwas tun wollen** want to do sth.   **wollen, dass jemand etwas tut** want sb. to do sth.   **etwas unbedingt tun wollen** be eager to do sth. [ˈiːgə]
**Workshop** workshop [ˈwɜːkʃɒp]
**Wort** word [wɜːd]   **etwas mit anderen Worten sagen** paraphrase sth. [ˈpærəfreɪz]
**Wortart** part of speech [ˌpɑːt‿əv ˈspiːtʃ]
**Wörterbuch** dictionary [ˈdɪkʃənri]
**Wörterverzeichnis** vocabulary [vəˈkæbjələri]   **alphabetisches Wörterverzeichnis** dictionary [ˈdɪkʃənri]
**Wortspeicher** wordbank [ˈwɜːdbæŋk]
**Wortstellung** word order [ˈwɜːd‿ɔːdə]
**Wovon handelt die Geschichte?** What is the story about?
**wund** sore [sɔː]
**Wunder** *(etwas Außergewöhnliches/Erstaunliches)* wonder [ˈwʌndə]
**wunderbar** wonderful [ˈwʌndəfəl]
**wundervoll** *(zauberhaft)* magical [ˈmædʒɪkl]
**Wunsch** wish [wɪʃ]; request [rɪˈkwest]
**wünschen** wish [wɪʃ]   **Ich wünschte, es wäre wärmer.** I wish it was warmer.   **sich etwas wünschen** make a wish
**würde: Ich würde gern …** I'd like to …   **Ich würde sehr gern …** I'd love to … [lʌv]
**Wurzel** root [ruːt]
**würzen: etwas würzen mit** flavour sth. with [ˈfleɪvə]
**Wüste** desert [ˈdezət]
**wütend (auf jn.)** angry (with sb.) [ˈæŋɡri]; mad (at sb.) *(AE, infml)* [mæd]   **wütend wegen etwas** mad about sth. *(AE, infml)*

## Y

**Yoga** yoga [ˈjəʊɡə]

## Z

**zäh** tough [tʌf]
**Zahl** number [ˈnʌmbə]; *(Ziffer)* figure [ˈfɪɡə]
**zählen (bis)** count (to) [kaʊnt]
**Zahn** tooth, *pl* teeth [tuːθ]
**Zahnarzt/-ärztin** dentist [ˈdentɪst]
**Zahnschmerzen haben** have a toothache [ˈtuːθeɪk]
**Zauber-** magic [ˈmædʒɪk]
**Zauberer** wizard [ˈwɪzəd]; *(Hexenmeister)* sorcerer [ˈsɔːsərə]
**zauberhaft** magical [ˈmædʒɪkl]
**Zaun** fence [fens]
**z.B. (zum Beispiel)** e.g. (for example) [ˌiːˈdʒiː]
**Zeh** toe [təʊ]
**zehn** ten [ten]
**Zeichen** sign [saɪn]; *(Signal)* signal [ˈsɪɡnəl]
**Zeichensetzung** punctuation [ˌpʌŋktʃuˈeɪʃn]
**zeichnen** draw [drɔː]
**Zeichnung** drawing [ˈdrɔːɪŋ]
**zeigen** show [ʃəʊ]   **auf etwas zeigen** point to sth. [pɔɪnt]   **es zeigt, dass …** it shows that …
**Zeile** line [laɪn]
**Zeit** 1. time [taɪm]   **Zeit verbringen (mit)** spend time (on) [spend]   **aller Zeiten** of all time   **einige Zeit** a while [waɪl]   **in letzter Zeit** recently [ˈriːsntli]   **zur selben Zeit** at one time   2. *(grammatische Zeit, Tempus)* tense [tens]
**Zeitalter** age [eɪdʒ]
**zeitgenössisch** contemporary [kənˈtemprəri]
**Zeitleiste** timeline [ˈtaɪmlaɪn]
**Zeitmesser** timer [ˈtaɪmə]
**Zeitrechnung: Christliche Zeitrechnung** CE (= Common Era) [ˌkɒmən‿ˈɪərə]
**Zeitschrift** magazine [ˌmæɡəˈziːn]
**Zeitstrahl** timeline [ˈtaɪmlaɪn]
**Zeitung** newspaper [ˈnjuːspeɪpə]; paper [ˈpeɪpə]
**Zelt** tent [tent]
**Zelten** camping [ˈkæmpɪŋ]
**zelten gehen** go camping
**Zeltplatz** campsite [ˈkæmpsaɪt]
**Zensur** grade [ɡreɪd]; mark [mɑːk]
**Zentimeter** centimetre (cm) [ˈsentɪmiːtə]
**zentral; Zentral-** central [ˈsentrəl]   **… sind zentral für …** … are core to … [kɔː]
**Zentrum** centre [ˈsentə]; hub [hʌb]   **im Zentrum von Albuquerque** in downtown Albuquerque *(AE)* [ˈdaʊntaʊn]
**zerbrechen** break [breɪk]
**zerbrochen** broken [ˈbrəʊkən]
**Zeremonie** ceremony [ˈserəməni]
**zerkauen** chew up [ˌtʃuːˈʌp]
**zermahlen** grind [ɡraɪnd]
**zerquetschen** crush [krʌʃ]
**zerstören** destroy [dɪˈstrɔɪ]
**Zerstörung** destruction [dɪˈstrʌkʃn]
**Zeug** stuff *(infml)* [stʌf]
**Zeuge/Zeugin** witness [ˈwɪtnəs]   **Zeuge/Zeugin werden von etwas** witness sth. [ˈwɪtnəs]
**Ziege** goat [ɡəʊt]
**Ziegelstein; Ziegel-** brick [brɪk]
**ziehen** pull [pʊl]   **in ein Haus ziehen** move into a house
**Ziel** *(Absicht)* purpose [ˈpɜːpəs]; *(Lebensziel)* goal [ɡəʊl]
**ziemlich alt/teuer/…** quite old/expensive/… [kwaɪt]; pretty old/expensive/… [ˈprɪti]
**Ziffer** figure [ˈfɪɡə]; number [ˈnʌmbə]
**Zimmer** room [ruːm]   **Zimmer mit Frühstück** bed & breakfast
**Zimmerer/Zimmerin** carpenter [ˈkɑːpəntə]
**zirka (ca.)** circa (c.) [ˈsɜːkə]
**zischen** hiss [hɪs]; sizzle [ˈsɪzl]
**Zitat** quote [kwəʊt]
**zittern** quiver [ˈkwɪvə]
**zögern** hesitate [ˈhezɪteɪt]
**Zoll** *(Längenmaß)* inch [ɪntʃ]
**Zone** zone [zəʊn]
**Zoo** zoo [zuː]
**zu** 1. *(örtlich)* to [tuː], [tə]   **zu Hause** at home   **zu Hause sein** be in   **nicht zu Hause sein** be out   2. **zu spät/kalt/groß/…** too late/cold/big/… [tuː]   **er ist viel zu gut/clever** he's way too good/clever *(bes. AE)*   3. **um zu** to [tuː]
**zubereiten** cook [kʊk]
**zucken** twitch [twɪtʃ]
**Zucker** sugar [ˈʃʊɡə]
**Zuckerguss** frosting [ˈfrɒstɪŋ]
**zudecken** cover [ˈkʌvə]; cover up [ˌkʌvərˈʌp]
**zueinander passen** go together
**zuerkennen: jm. etwas zuerkennen** award sb. sth.; award sth. to sb. [əˈwɔːd]
**zuerst** first [fɜːst]; *(anfangs)* at first [ət ˈfɜːst]
**zufahren: auf etwas zufahren** head for sth. [hed]
**Zufall** accident [ˈæksɪdənt]
**zufällig** by accident
**zufolge** according to … [əˈkɔːdɪŋ]
**zufrieden(gestellt)** satisfied [ˈsætɪsfaɪd]
**Zufriedenheit** happiness [ˈhæpinəs]
**zufriedenstellen** satisfy [ˈsætɪsfaɪ]
**zufrieren** freeze over [ˌfriːz‿ˈəʊvə]
**Zug** train [treɪn]; *(bei Brettspielen)* move [muːv]   **durchgehender Zug** direct train
**Zugabe** encore [ˈɒŋkɔː]
**Zugang (zu)** access (to) [ˈækses]
**zugehen: auf etwas zugehen** head for sth. [hed]
**Zügel** reins *(pl)* [reɪnz]
**zugreifen** *(sich bedienen)* help yourself

# Dictionary

**zugrunde liegend** underlying [ˌʌndəˈlaɪɪŋ]
**Zuhause** home [həʊm]
**zuhören** listen [ˈlɪsn]   **Hör(t) mir zu.** Listen to me.
**Zuhörer/in** listener [ˈlɪsənə]   **Zuhörer/innen** (Publikum) audience [ˈɔːdiəns]
**Zukunft** future [ˈfjuːtʃə]
**zukünftige(r, s)** future [ˈfjuːtʃə]
**zulassen** allow [əˈlaʊ]
**zuletzt** (das letzte Mal) last [lɑːst]
**zum Beispiel** for example [fər_ɪgˈzɑːmpl]
**zumachen** close [kləʊz]
**zumindest** at least [ət ˈliːst]
**Zunge** tongue [tʌŋ]
**Zungenbrecher** tongue-twister [ˈtʌŋ twɪstə]
**zurechtkommen** get on [ˌgetˈɒn]
**zurück** back [bæk]
**zurückbleiben** keep back [ˌkiːp ˈbæk]
**zurückkehren** return [rɪˈtɜːn]
**zurückkommen** return [rɪˈtɜːn]
**zurücklassen** abandon [əˈbændən]; leave [left]
**zusammen** together [təˈgeðə]
**zusammenbauen** assemble [əˈsembl]
**zusammenbrechen** collapse [kəˈlæps]
**zusammenfassen: etwas zusammenfassen** sum sth. up [ˌsʌm_ˈʌp]

**zusammenfügen: zu etwas passen** match sth. [mætʃ]
**Zusammenhang** (Satz-, Textzusammenhang) context [ˈkɒntekst]
**zusammenkommen** (sich versammeln) assemble [əˈsembl]
**zusammenpassen** go together
   … **passen von Natur aus gut zusammen** … are a natural fit. [fɪt]
**zusammensetzen** put together [təˈgeðə]   **sich zusammensetzen aus** be made up of [ˌmeɪd_ˈʌp]
**zusammenstellen** put together [təˈgeðə]
**Zusammenstoß** crash [kræʃ]
**Zuschauer/innen** (Publikum) audience [ˈɔːdiəns]
**zuschlagen** strike [straɪk]
**zusprechen: jm. etwas zusprechen** award sb. sth.; award sth. to sb. [əˈwɔːd]
**zustande: etwas zustande bringen** manage sth. [ˈmænɪdʒ]
**zusteuern auf** head for [hed]
**zustimmen** consent [kənˈsent]   **jm. zustimmen** agree with sb. [əˈgriː]
**Zustimmung** agreement [əˈgriːmənt]; consent [kənˈsent]
**zutreffen (für)** apply (to) [əˈplaɪ]
**Zutritt** entry [ˈentri]   **Zutritt zu** access to [ˈækses]

**zuversichtlich** confident [ˈkɒnfɪdənt]
**zuvor: besser als je zuvor** better than ever [ˈevə]
**zuwenden: sich jm. zuwenden** turn to sb. [tɜːn]
**zuwinken: jm. zuwinken** wave at sb. [ˈweɪv_ət]
**zwängen; sich zwängen** squeeze [skwiːz]
**Zweck** purpose [ˈpɜːpəs]
**zwei** two [tuː]   **zwei schwarze** two black ones
**zweimal** twice [twaɪs]
**zweisprachig** bilingual [baɪˈlɪŋgwəl]
**zweite(r, s)** second [ˈsekənd]
**Zweitens …** Second … [ˈsekənd]; Secondly, …
**Zwiebel** onion [ˈʌnjən]
**Zwillinge** twins (pl) [twɪnz]
**zwingen: jn. zwingen, etwas zu tun** force sb. to do sth. [fɔːs]
**zwischen** between [bɪˈtwiːn]
**Zwischenüberschrift** sub-heading [ˈsʌb hedɪŋ]
**zwölf** twelve [twelv]
**Zylinder** (Hut) top hat [ˌtɒp ˈhæt]


# English sounds

| | | | | |
|---|---|---|---|---|
| [iː] | gr**ee**n, h**e**, s**ea** | [d] | **d**a**d**, win**d**ow, goo**d** | |
| [i] | happ**y**, monk**ey** | [t] | **t**en, le**tt**er, a**t** | |
| [ɪ] | b**i**g, **i**n, **e**xpensive | [g] | **g**ood, a**g**ain, ba**g** | |
| [e] | r**e**d, y**e**s, ag**ai**n, br**ea**kfast | [k] | **c**at, **k**it**ch**en, ba**ck** | |
| [æ] | c**a**t, **a**nimal, **a**pple, bl**a**ck | [m] | **m**u**m**, **m**an, re**m**e**m**ber | |
| [ɑː] | cl**a**ss, **a**sk, c**a**r, p**a**rk | [n] | **n**o, o**n**e, te**n** | |
| [ɒ] | s**o**ng, **o**n, d**o**g, wh**a**t | [ŋ] | so**ng**, you**ng**, u**n**cle, tha**n**ks | |
| [ɔː] | d**oo**r, **o**r, b**a**ll, f**ou**r, m**o**rning | [l] | he**ll**o, **l**ike, o**l**d, sma**ll** | |
| [uː] | bl**ue**, r**u**ler, t**oo**, tw**o**, y**ou** | [r] | **r**ed, **r**uler, f**r**iend, so**rr**y | |
| [ʊ] | b**oo**k, g**oo**d, p**u**llover | [w] | **w**e, **w**here, **o**ne | |
| [ʌ] | m**u**m, b**u**s, c**o**lour | [j] | **y**ou, **y**es, **u**niform | |
| [ɜː] | g**ir**l, **ear**ly, h**er**, w**or**k, T-sh**ir**t | [f] | **f**amily, a**f**ter, laug**h** | |
| [ə] | **a** partn**er**, **a**gain, t**o**day | [v] | ri**v**er, **v**ery, se**v**en, ha**v**e | |
| | | [s] | **s**ister, po**s**ter, ye**s** | |
| [eɪ] | n**a**me, **eigh**t, pl**ay**, gr**ea**t | [z] | plea**s**e, **z**oo, qui**z**, hi**s**, mu**s**ic | |
| [aɪ] | t**i**me, r**igh**t, m**y**, **I** | [ʃ] | **sh**op, sta**ti**on, Engli**sh** | |
| [ɔɪ] | b**oy**, t**oi**let, n**oi**se | [ʒ] | televi**si**on, u**su**ally | |
| [əʊ] | **o**ld, n**o**, r**oa**d, yell**ow** | [tʃ] | tea**ch**er, **ch**ild, wa**tch** | |
| [aʊ] | t**ow**n, n**ow**, h**ou**se | [dʒ] | **G**ermany, **j**ob, pro**j**ect, oran**ge** | |
| [ɪə] | h**ere**, **yea**r, **i**d**ea** | | | |
| [eə] | wh**ere**, p**air**, sh**are**, th**eir** | [θ] | **th**anks, **th**ree, ba**th**room | |
| [ʊə] | t**our** | [ð] | **th**e, **th**is, fa**th**er, wi**th** | |
| [b] | **b**oat, ta**b**le, ver**b** | [h] | **h**ere, w**h**o, be**h**ind | |
| [p] | **p**ool, **p**a**p**er, sho**p** | [x] | lo**ch** | |

> Am besten kannst du dir die Aussprache der einzelnen Lautzeichen einprägen, wenn du dir zu jedem Zeichen ein einfaches Wort merkst – das [iː] ist der **green**-Laut, das [eɪ] ist der **name**-Laut usw.

# Partner pages

## 9 Role play
← p. 14

c) Use your notes to act out a conversation at the tourist information office.

> **Tourist B**
> - You are a teenage tourist from an EU country but do not speak German.
> - You are here with your mother or father and have two days to look at the area.
> - You like all types of sport and want to find out what you could do here.
> - You're especially interested in skateboarding and cycling.
> - You're a vegetarian and love camping when the weather is fine.

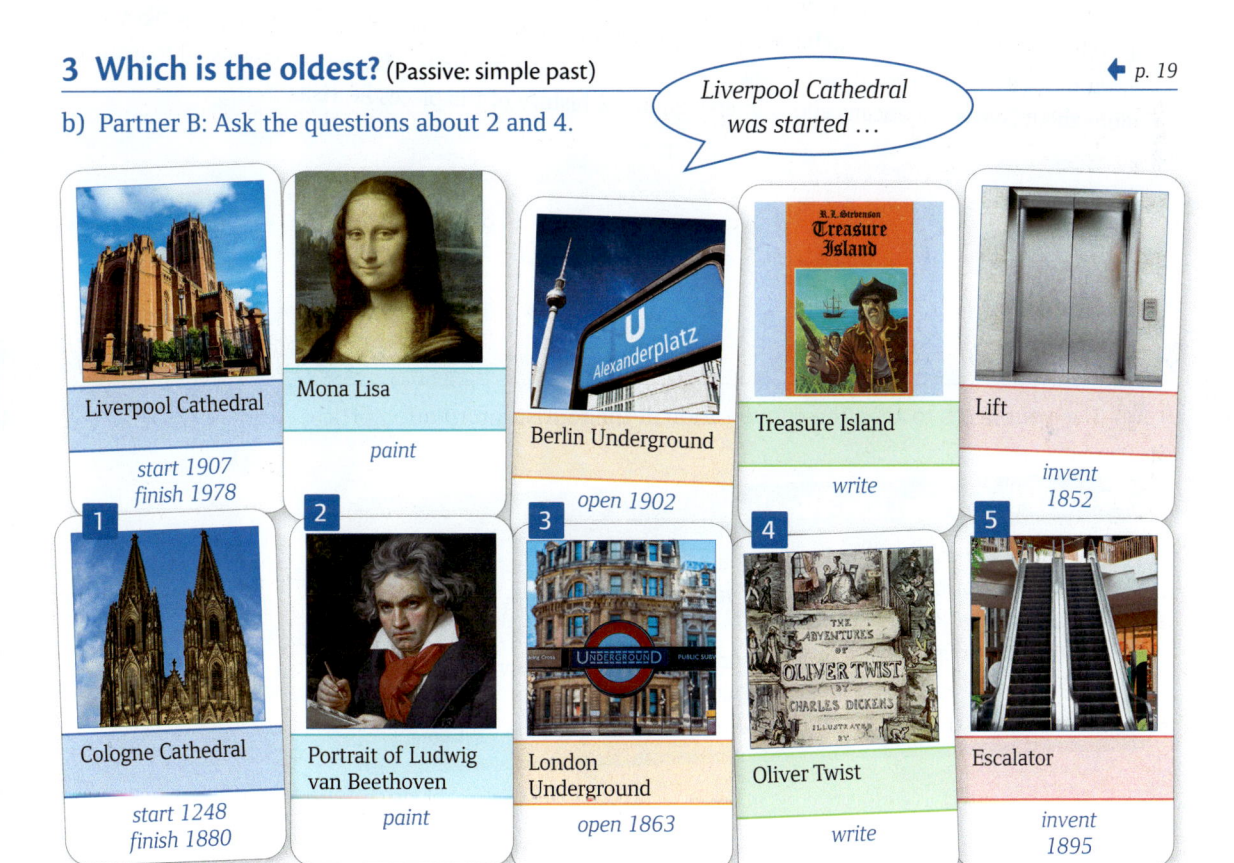

## 3 Which is the oldest? (Passive: simple past)
← p. 19

b) Partner B: Ask the questions about 2 and 4.

*Liverpool Cathedral was started …*

**Liverpool Cathedral** — start 1907 / finish 1978

**Mona Lisa** — paint

**Berlin Underground** — open 1902

**Treasure Island** — write

**Lift** — invent 1852

**1 Cologne Cathedral** — start 1248 / finish 1880

**2 Portrait of Ludwig van Beethoven** — paint

**3 London Underground** — open 1863

**4 Oliver Twist** — write

**5 Escalator** — invent 1895

two hundred and sixty-three  263

# Partner pages

## 5 THINKING ABOUT LANGUAGE Idioms
← p. 25

Explain to your partner in English what the German idioms mean.

> Ich drück' dir die Daumen.

> Schnee von gestern

## 4 A day out in Mobridge
← p. 77

Partner B:

### Max

Max is a quiet boy and likes watching events and people in everyday situations. He is shy, especially around big groups of people he doesn't know. He also loves being outdoors, hiking, swimming, fishing and climbing. Max enjoys watching movies and has started to make short films of his own. He likes all kinds of food and enjoys eating hamburgers, French fries and big steaks. He is very interested to learn more about Native Americans and is interested in the history of the places he visits.

## 9 Role play
← p. 14

c) Use your notes to act out a conversation at the tourist information office.

### Tourist Information Worker

- You work at the visitor centre in your area.
- You love the job and always want to do your best for the visitors who come to the centre.
- You know everything there is to know about your area and a few favourite things to do and see, which you always recommend to visitors.
- But you always try to make sure they have an interesting time in your area.

# List of names

## Place names
Aspen [ˈæspən]
the **Battery** [ˈbætri]
**Bavaria** [bəˈveəriə]
**Berlin** [bɜːˈlɪn]
**Beverly Hills** [ˌbevəli ˈhɪlz]
the **Black Hills** [ˌblæk ˈhɪlz]
**Bourbon Street** [ˈbɜːbən]
the **Bronx** [brɒŋks]
**Brooklyn** [ˈbrʊklɪn]
**Cape Horn** [ˌkeɪp ˈhɔːn]
**Chinatown** [ˈtʃaɪnətaʊn]
the **Colorado River** [ˌkɒləˈrɑːdəʊ]
**Coney Island** [ˌkəʊni ˈaɪlənd]
**Corral Canyon** [ˈkɒrəl]
**Death Valley** [ˌdeθ ˈvæli]
**Delhi** [ˈdeli]
**El Paso** [el ˈpæsəʊ]
**Ellis Island** [ˌelɪs ˈaɪlənd]
the **Empire State Building** [ˈempaɪə]
**Ferguson** [ˈfɜːɡəsən]
**Fifth Avenue** [ˈævənjuː]
**Guangdong** [ˌgwæŋˈdʊŋ]
**Harlem** [ˈhɑːləm]
**Hollywood** [ˈhɒliwʊd]
the **Hudson River** [ˈhʌdsn]
**Jersey City** [ˌdʒɜːzi ˈsɪti]
**La Jolla** [ləˈhɔɪə]
**Las Vegas** [læs ˈveɪɡəs]
**Los Angeles** [lɒs ˈændʒəliːz]
**Malibu** [ˈmælɪbuː]
**Manhattan** [ˌmænˈhætn]
**Mesa Verde** [ˌmeɪsə ˈvɜːd]
**Milwaukee** [mɪlˈwɔːki]
the **Mississippi River** [ˌmɪsɪˈsɪpi]
the **Missouri River** [mɪˈzʊəri]
**Mobridge** [ˈməʊbrɪdʒ]
**Moss Beach** [ˌmɒs ˈbiːtʃ]
**Mount Rushmore** [ˈrʌʃmɔː]
**New Orleans** [ˌnuː ˈɔːlənz], [ˌnjuː ˈɔːliənz]
**New York** [ˌnjuː ˈjɔːk]
the **Pacific** [pəˈsɪfɪk]
**Paha Sapa** [pɑːˌhɑːˈsɑːpɑː]
**Pala Alto** [ˌpæləʊ ˈæltəʊ]
**Pine Ridge** [ˌpaɪn ˈrɪdʒ]
**Pollock** [ˈpɒlək]
**Queens** [kwiːnz]
**Rapid City** [ˌræpɪd ˈsɪti]
**Redondo** [rɪˈdɒndə]
the **Rio Grande** [ˌriːəʊ ˈɡrænd]
**Sacramento** [ˌsækrəˈmentəʊ]
**San Francisco** [ˌsæn frənˈsɪskəʊ]
**Sangre de Cristo** [ˌsæŋɡri də ˈkrɪstəʊ]
**Santa Fe** [ˌsæntə ˈfeɪ]
**Sierra Nevada** [siˌerə nəˈvɑːdə]
**Silicon Valley** [ˌsɪlɪkən ˈvæli]
**Skid Row** [ˌskɪd ˈrəʊ]
**Slidell** [ˈslaɪdel]
**Stanford** [ˈstænfəd]
the **Starview Hotel** [ˈstɑːvjuː]
**Staten Island** [ˌstætn ˈaɪlənd]
**Taos** [taʊs]
**Tasmania** [tæzˈmeɪniə]
**Washington** [ˈwɒʃɪŋtn]
**Watertown** [ˈwɔːtətaʊn]
**Wounded Knee** [ˌwuːdɪd ˈniː]

## First names
**Ado** [ˈeɪdəʊ]
**Alex** [ˈælɪks], [ˈæleks]
**Alfred** [ˈælfrɪd]
**Allan** [ˈælən]
**Barack** [bəˈræk]
**Bobby** [ˈbɒbi]
**Brandon** [ˈbrændən]
**Brianna** [briˈænə]
**Cecile** [səˈsiːl]
**Claire** [kleə]
**Clementa** [kləˈmentə]
**Cody** [ˈkəʊdi]
**Connor** [ˈkɒnə]
**Craig** [kreɪɡ], [kreɡ]
**Darius** [ˈdæriəs]
**Darren** [ˈdærən]
**David** [ˈdeɪvɪd]
**D'Avila** [dəˈviːlə]
**Dodie** [ˈdəʊdi]
**Drew** [druː]
**Eliot** [ˈeliət]
**Eugene** [ˈjuːdʒiːn], [juːˈdʒiːn]
**Eva** [ˈiːvə]
**Gene** [dʒiːn]
**Hailey** [ˈheɪli]
**Jack** [dʒæk]
**James** [dʒeɪmz]
**Jana** [ˈdʒænə]
**Jasmine** [ˈdʒæzmɪn]
**Jason** [ˈdʒeɪsən]
**Jeff** [dʒef]
**Joann** [dʒəʊˈæn]
**Jodi** [ˈdʒəʊdi]
**Joey** [ˈdʒəʊi]
**Joseph** [ˈdʒəʊzeθ], [ˈdʒəʊseθ]
**Juan** [wɑːn]
**Judy** [ˈdʒuːdi]
**Julie** [ˈdʒuːli]
**Katrina** [kəˈtriːnə]
**Kaya** [ˈkaɪə], [keɪə]
**Keri** [ˈkeri]
**Laura** [ˈlɔːrə]
**Lennox** [ˈlenəks]
**Luis** [ˈluːɪs]
**Luther** [ˈluːθə]
**Marcos** [ˈmɑːkəʊs], [ˈmɑːkɒs]
**Margot** [ˈmɑːɡəʊ]
**Martha** [ˈmɑːθə]
**Mateo** [mæˈteɪəʊ]
**Michael** [ˈmaɪkl]
**Mitch** [mɪtʃ]
**Moog** [muːɡ]
**Nicole** [nɪˈkəʊl]
**Randall** [ˈrændl]
**Raul** [raʊl]
**René** [ˈreneɪ], [rəˈneɪ]
**Rosa** [ˈrəʊzə]
**Ruby** [ˈruːbi]
**Rudy** [ˈruːdi]
**Saanvi** [sɑːnˈviː]
**Sara** [ˈseərə], [ˈsɑːrə]
**Sarah** [ˈseərə]
**Taylor** [ˈteɪlə]
**Tyler** [ˈtaɪlə]
**Walter** [ˈwɒltə]
**Wei** [weɪ]
**Woody** [ˈwʊdi]
**Zoe** [ˈzəʊi]

## Family names
**Abrams** [ˈeɪbrəmz]
**Bruchac** [ˈbruːʃæk]
**Chao** [tʃaʊ]
**Dylan** [ˈdɪlən]
**Feldman** [ˈfeldmən]
**Goldfinch** [ˈɡəʊldfɪntʃ]
**Goldstein** [ˈɡəʊldstiːn], [ˈɡəʊldstaɪn]
**Guthrie** [ˈɡʌθri]
**Hitchcock** [ˈhɪtʃkɒk]
**Hubbard** [ˈhʌbəd]
**Jones** [dʒəʊnz]
**Jordan** [ˈdʒɔːdn]
**Kelada** [kəˈlɑːdə]
**Landrieu** [ˈlændruː]
**LaPlace** [ləˈplæs]
**Lombard** [ˈlɒmbɑːd]
**Marshall** [ˈmɑːʃl]
**McKenzie** [məˈkenzi]
**Maisel** [ˈmeɪzl]
**Moreno** [məˈreɪnəʊ]
**Myers** [ˈmaɪəz]
**Newton** [ˈnjuːtn]
**Obama** [əʊˈbɑːmə]
**O'Sullivan** [əʊˈsʌləvən]
**Pape** [peɪp]
**Parker** [ˈpɑːkə]
**Peters** [ˈpiːtəz]
**Pinckney** [ˈpɪŋkni]
**Red Hawk** [red ˈhɔːk]
**Robison** [ˈrɒbɪsən]
**Smith-Simmons** [ˌsmɪθˈsɪmənz]
**Stuyvesant** [ˈstaɪvəsənt]
**Washington** [ˈwɒʃɪŋtən]
**Watkins** [ˈwɒtkɪnz]
**Wilkins** [ˈwɪlkɪnz]
**Williams** [ˈwɪliəmz]
**Wright** [raɪt]
**Yang** [ˈjæŋ]

## Other names
**Apache** [əˈpætʃi]
**Arapaho** [əˈræpəhəʊ]
**Birdman** [ˈbɜːdmæn]
**Blackfoot** [ˈblækfʊt]
**Cherokee** [ˌtʃerəˈkiː]
**Cheyenne** [ʃaɪˈæn]
**Comanche** [kəˈmæntʃi]
**Cornbread** [ˈkɔːnbred]
**Iroquois** [ˈɪrəkwɔɪ]
**Jim Crow** [ˌdʒɪm ˈkrəʊ]
**Koluscap** [ˈkɒlʊskæp]
**Ku Klux Klan** [ˌkuː klʌks ˈklæn]
**Lakota** [ləˈkəʊtə]
**Maliseet** [ˈmæləˌsiːt]
**Mi'kmaq** [ˈmɪkmæk]
**Mohawk** [ˈməʊhɔːk]
**MOMA** [ˈməʊmə]
**Oglala Lakota** [əʊˌɡlɑːlə ləˈkəʊtə]
**Paiute** [ˌpaɪˈuːt]
**Pepito** [pəˈpiːtəʊ]
**Pepys** [piːps]
**Pheasant** [ˈfeznt]
**Pueblo** [ˈpwebləʊ]
**Scherr-Howe** [ˌʃeəˈhaʊ]
**Shoshone** [ʃəʊˈʃəʊni]
**Sioux** [suː]
**The Grateful Dead** [ˌɡreɪtfl ˈded]
**Tlingit** [ˈtlɪŋɡɪt]
**Yankee** [ˈjæŋki]

# Countries and continents

| Country/Continent | Adjective | Person | People |
|---|---|---|---|
| *Marco is from **Italy**.* | *Pizza is **Italian**.* | *Marco is **an Italian**.* | ***The Italians** invented pizza.* |
| **Africa** [ˈæfrɪkə] *Afrika* | African [ˈæfrɪkən] | an African | the Africans |
| **Albania** [ælˈbeɪniə] *Albanien* | Albanian [ælˈbeɪniən] | an Albanian | the Albanians |
| **Asia** [ˈeɪʒə, ˈeɪʃə] *Asien* | Asian [ˈeɪʃn, ˈeɪʒn] | an Asian | the Asians |
| **Australia** [ɒˈstreɪliə] *Australien* | Australian [ɒˈstreɪliən] | an Australian | the Australians |
| **Austria** [ˈɒstriə] *Österreich* | Austrian [ˈɒstriən] | an Austrian | the Austrians |
| **Belarus** [ˌbelˈruːs] *Weißrussland* | Belarusian [ˌbelˈruːsiən] | a Belarusian | the Belarusians |
| **Belgium** [ˈbeldʒəm] *Belgien* | Belgian [ˈbeldʒən] | a Belgian | the Belgians |
| **Bosnia and Herzegovina** [ˈbɒzniə ən ˌhɜːtsəgəˈviːnə] *Bosnien und Herzegowina* | Bosnian [ˈbɒzniən]; Herzegovinian [ˌhɜːtsəgəˈvɪniən] | a Bosnian; a Herzegovinian | the Bosnians; the Herzegovinians |
| **Canada** [ˈkænədə] *Kanada* | Canadian [kəˈneɪdiən] | a Canadian | the Canadians |
| **China** [ˈtʃaɪnə] *China* | Chinese [ˌtʃaɪˈniːz] | a Chinese | the Chinese |
| **Croatia** [krəʊˈeɪʃə] *Kroatien* | Croatian [krəʊˈeɪʃn] | a Croatian | the Croatians |
| the **Czech Republic** [ˌtʃek rɪˈpʌblɪk] *Tschechien, die Tschechische Republik* | Czech [tʃek] | a Czech | the Czechs |
| **Denmark** [ˈdenmɑːk] *Dänemark* | Danish [ˈdeɪnɪʃ] | a Dane [deɪn] | the Danes |
| **England** [ˈɪŋglənd] *England* | English [ˈɪŋglɪʃ] | an Englishman / an Englishwoman | the English |
| **Estonia** [eˈstəʊniə] *Estland* | Estonian [eˈstəʊniən] | an Estonian | the Estonians |
| **Europe** [ˈjʊərəp] *Europa* | European [ˌjʊərəˈpiːən] | a European | the Europeans |
| **Finland** [ˈfɪnlənd] *Finnland* | Finnish [ˈfɪnɪʃ] | a Finn [fɪn] | the Finns |
| **France** [frɑːns] *Frankreich* | French [frentʃ] | a Frenchman / a Frenchwoman | the French |
| **Germany** [ˈdʒɜːməni] *Deutschland* | German [ˈdʒɜːmən] | a German | the Germans |
| **(Great) Britain** [ˈbrɪtn] *Großbritannien* | British [ˈbrɪtɪʃ] | a Briton [ˈbrɪtn] | the British |
| **Greece** [griːs] *Griechenland* | Greek [griːk] | a Greek | the Greeks |
| **Hungary** [ˈhʌŋgəri] *Ungarn* | Hungarian [hʌŋˈgeəriən] | a Hungarian | the Hungarians |
| **Iceland** [ˈaɪslənd] *Island* | Icelandic [aɪsˈlændɪk] | an Icelander [ˈaɪsləndə] | the Icelanders |
| **India** [ˈɪndiə] *Indien* | Indian [ˈɪndiən] | an Indian | the Indians |
| **Ireland** [ˈaɪələnd] *Irland* | Irish [ˈaɪrɪʃ] | an Irishman / an Irishwoman | the Irish |
| **Italy** [ˈɪtəli] *Italien* | Italian [ɪˈtæliən] | an Italian | the Italians |
| **Jamaica** [dʒəˈmeɪkə] *Jamaika* | Jamaika [dʒəˈmeɪkən] | a Jamaican | the Jamaicans |
| **Kosovo** [ˈkɒsəvəʊ] *Kosovo* | Kosovan [ˈkɒsəvən] | a Kosovan | the Kosovans |
| **Latvia** [ˈlætviə] *Lettland* | Latvian [ˈlætviən] | a Latvian | the Latvians |
| **Lithuania** [ˌlɪθjuˈeɪniə] *Litauen* | Lithuanian [ˌlɪθjuˈeɪniə] | a Lithuanian | the Lithuanians |

# Countries and continents

| Country/Continent | Adjective | Person | People |
|---|---|---|---|
| *Marco is from Italy.* | *Pizza is Italian.* | *Marco is an Italian.* | *The Italians invented pizza.* |
| **Luxembourg** [ˈlʌksəmbɜːg] Luxemburg | Luxembourg | a Luxembourger [ˈlʌksəmbɜːgə] | the Luxembourgers |
| **Macedonia** [ˌmæsəˈdəʊniə] Mazedonien | Macedonian [ˌmæsəˈdəʊniən] | a Macedonian | the Macedonians |
| **Malta** [ˈmɔːltə] Malta | Maltese [mɔːlˈtiːz] | a Maltese | the Maltese |
| **Mexico** [ˈmeksɪkəʊ] Mexiko | Mexican [ˈmeksɪkən] | a Mexican | the Mexicans |
| **Moldova** [mɒlˈdəʊvə] Moldawien | Moldovan [mɒlˈdəʊvən] | a Moldovan | the Moldovans |
| **Montenegro** [ˌmɒntɪˈniːgrəʊ] Montenegro | Montenegrin [ˌmɒntɪˈniːgrɪn] | a Montenegrin | the Montenegrins |
| the **Netherlands** [ˈneðələndz] die Niederlande | Dutch [dʌtʃ] | a Dutchman / a Dutchwoman | the Dutch |
| **North America** [ˌnɔːθ_əˈmerɪkə] Nordamerika | North American [ˌnɔːθ_əˈmerɪkən] | a North American | the North Americans |
| **Northern Ireland** [ˌnɔːðən_ˈaɪələnd] Nordirland | Northern Irish [ˌnɔːðən_ˈaɪrɪʃ] | a Northern Irishman / a Northern Irishwoman | the Northern Irish |
| **Norway** [ˈnɔːweɪ] Norwegen | Norwegian [nɔːˈwiːdʒən] | a Norwegian | the Norwegians |
| **Poland** [ˈpəʊlənd] Polen | Polish [ˈpəʊlɪʃ] | a Pole [pəʊl] | the Poles |
| **Polynesia** [ˌpɒlɪˈniːziə], [ˌpɒlɪˈniːʒə] Polynesien | Polynesian [ˌpɒlɪˈniːziən], [ˌpɒlɪˈniːʒən] | a Polynesian | the Polynesians |
| **Portugal** [ˈpɔːtʃʊgl] Portugal | Portuguese [ˌpɔːtʃʊˈgiːz] | a Portuguese | the Portuguese |
| **Romania** [ruˈmeɪniə] Rumänien | Romanian [ruˈmeɪniən] | a Romanian | the Romanians |
| **Russia** [ˈrʌʃə] Russland | Russian [ˈrʌʃn] | a Russian | the Russians |
| **Scotland** [ˈskɒtlənd] Schottland | Scottish [ˈskɒtɪʃ] | a Scot [skɒt]; a Scotsman / a Scotswoman | the Scots, the Scottish |
| **Serbia** [ˈsɜːbiə] Serbien | Serbian [ˈsɜːbiən] | a Serbian | the Serbians |
| **Slovakia** [sləʊˈvækiə] die Slowakei | Slovak [ˈsləʊvæk] | a Slovak | the Slovaks |
| **Slovenia** [sləʊˈviːniə] Slowenien | Slovenian [sləʊˈviːniən] | a Slovenian | the Slovenians |
| **South America** [ˌsaʊθ_əˈmerɪkə] Südamerika | South American [ˌsaʊθ_əˈmerɪkən] | a South American | the South Americans |
| **Spain** [speɪn] Spanien | Spanish [ˈspænɪʃ] | a Spaniard [ˈspænɪəd] | the Spanish |
| **Sweden** [ˈswiːdn] Schweden | Swedish [ˈswiːdɪʃ] | a Swede [swiːd] | the Swedes |
| **Switzerland** [ˈswɪtsələnd] die Schweiz | Swiss [swɪs] | a Swiss | the Swiss |
| **Turkey** [ˈtɜːki] die Türkei | Turkish [ˈtɜːkɪʃ] | a Turk [tɜːk] | the Turks |
| **Ukraine** [juːˈkreɪn] die Ukraine | Ukrainian [juːˈkreɪniən] | a Ukrainian | the Ukrainians |
| the **United Kingdom** [juːˌnaɪtɪd ˈkɪŋdəm] das Vereinigte Königreich | British [ˈbrɪtɪʃ] | a Briton [ˈbrɪtn] | the British |
| the **United States of America** [juːˌnaɪtɪd ˌsteɪts_əv_əˈmerɪkə] die Vereinigten Staaten von Amerika | American [əˈmerɪkən] | an American | the Americans |
| **Vietnam** [ˌviːetˈnæm], [ˌviːetˈnɑːm] die Ukraine | Vietnamese [viːˌetnəˈmiːz] | a Vietnamese | the Vietnamese |
| **Wales** [weɪlz] Wales | Welsh [welʃ] | a Welshman/-woman | the Welsh |

# Irregular verbs

| infinitive | simple past | past participle | |
|---|---|---|---|
| (to) be | was; were | been | sein |
| (to) beat | beat | beaten | schlagen; besiegen |
| (to) become | became | become | werden |
| (to) begin | began | begun | beginnen, anfangen |
| (to) bend | bent | bent | sich bücken, sich beugen |
| (to) bite [aɪ] | bit [ɪ] | bitten [ɪ] | beißen |
| (to) blow sth. out | blew | blown | etwas auspusten, ausblasen |
| (to) break [eɪ] | broke | broken | brechen; zerbrechen |
| (to) bring | brought | brought | (mit-, her)bringen |
| (to) build | built | built | bauen |
| (to) burst into tears | burst | burst | in Tränen ausbrechen |
| (to) buy | bought | bought | kaufen |
| (to) catch | caught | caught | fangen |
| (to) choose [uː] | chose [əʊ] | chosen [əʊ] | aussuchen, (aus)wählen; sich aussuchen |
| (to) come | came | come | kommen |
| (to) cost | cost | cost | kosten |
| (to) cut | cut | cut | schneiden |
| (to) do | did | done [ʌ] | tun, machen |
| (to) draw | drew | drawn | zeichnen |
| (to) drive [aɪ] | drove [əʊ] | driven [ɪ] | (mit dem Auto) fahren |
| (to) drink | drank | drunk | trinken |
| (to) eat | ate [et, eɪt] | eaten | essen |
| (to) fall | fell | fallen | fallen, stürzen; hinfallen |
| (to) feed | fed | fed | füttern |
| (to) feel | felt | felt | fühlen; sich fühlen |
| (to) fight | fought | fought | (be)kämpfen |
| (to) find | found | found | finden |
| (to) fly | flew | flown | fliegen |
| (to) forget | forgot | forgotten | vergessen |
| (to) freeze | froze | frozen | (ge)frieren; zufrieren; einfrieren |
| (to) get | got | got | bekommen; holen; werden; gelangen |
| (to) give | gave | given | geben |
| (to) go | went | gone [ɒ] | gehen |
| (to) grow | grew | grown | wachsen; anbauen, anpflanzen |
| (to) hang | hung | hung | hängen |
| (to) have | had | had | haben |
| (to) hear [ɪə] | heard [ɜː] | heard [ɜː] | hören |
| (to) hide [aɪ] | hid [ɪ] | hidden [ɪ] | verstecken; sich verstecken |
| (to) hit | hit | hit | schlagen |
| (to) hold | held | held | halten |
| (to) hurt | hurt | hurt | schmerzen, wehtun; verletzen |
| (to) keep | kept | kept | behalten; aufheben, aufsparen; aufbewahren |

# Irregular verbs

| infinitive | simple past | past participle | |
|---|---|---|---|
| (to) **kneel** [niːl] | **knelt** [nelt] | **knelt** [nelt] | knien |
| (to) **know** [nəʊ] | **knew** [njuː] | **known** [nəʊn] | wissen; kennen |
| (to) **lead** [iː] | **led** | **led** | führen, leiten |
| (to) **leave** [iː] | **left** | **left** | (weg)gehen; abfahren; (zurück)lassen; verlassen |
| (to) **lend sb. sth.** | **lent** | **lent** | jm. etwas leihen |
| (to) **let** | **let** | **let** | lassen |
| (to) **lie** | **lay** | **lain** | liegen |
| (to) **light** [aɪ] | **lit** [ɪ] | **lit** [ɪ] | anzünden |
| (to) **lose** [uː] | **lost** [ɒ] | **lost** [ɒ] | verlieren |
| (to) **make** | **made** | **made** | machen; herstellen |
| (to) **mean** [iː] | **meant** [e] | **meant** [e] | bedeuten; meinen |
| (to) **meet** [iː] | **met** [e] | **met** | treffen; sich treffen; kennenlernen |
| (to) **pay** | **paid** | **paid** | bezahlen |
| (to) **put** | **put** | **put** | (etwas wohin) tun, legen, stellen |
| (to) **read** [iː] | **read** [e] | **read** [e] | lesen |
| (to) **ride** [aɪ] | **rode** | **ridden** [ɪ] | reiten; (Rad) fahren |
| (to) **ring** | **rang** | **rung** | klingeln, läuten |
| (to) **rise up** [aɪ] | **rose** | **risen** [ɪ] | aufragen, emporragen |
| (to) **run** | **ran** | **run** | rennen, laufen |
| (to) **say** [eɪ] | **said** [e] | **said** [e] | sagen |
| (to) **see** | **saw** | **seen** | sehen |
| (to) **sell** | **sold** | **sold** | verkaufen |
| (to) **send** | **sent** | **sent** | schicken, senden |
| (to) **set sth. up** | **set** | **set** | etwas errichten, aufbauen; etwas arrangieren |
| (to) **shake** | **shook** | **shaken** | schütteln |
| (to) **shine** | **shone** [BE: ɒ, AE: əʊ] | **shone** [ɒ, əʊ] | scheinen (Sonne) |
| (to) **shoot** [uː] | **shot** [ɒ] | **shot** [ɒ] | schießen; erschießen |
| (to) **sing** | **sang** | **sung** | singen |
| (to) **sit** | **sat** | **sat** | sitzen; sich setzen |
| (to) **sleep** | **slept** | **slept** | schlafen |
| (to) **speak** [iː] | **spoke** | **spoken** | sprechen |
| (to) **spend** | **spent** | **spent** | (Zeit) verbringen; (Geld) ausgeben |
| (to) **spin around** | **spun** | **spun** | sich (im Kreis) drehen; herumwirbeln |
| (to) **spread** [e] | **spread** [e] | **spread** [e] | ausbreiten, verbreiten; sich ausbreiten, verbreiten |
| (to) **stand** | **stood** | **stood** | stehen; sich (hin)stellen |
| (to) **steal** | **stole** | **stolen** | stehlen |
| (to) **stick** | **stuck** | **stuck** | stechen, stecken |
| (to) **swear** [eə] | **swore** | **sworn** | schwören |
| (to) **swim** | **swam** | **swum** | schwimmen |
| (to) **take** | **took** | **taken** | (mit)nehmen; (weg-, hin)bringen; dauern |
| (to) **teach** | **taught** | **taught** | unterrichten, lehren |
| (to) **tear down** [teə] | **tore** | **torn** | abreißen |

## Irregular verbs

| infinitive | simple past | past participle | |
|---|---|---|---|
| (to) tell | told | told | erzählen, berichten |
| (to) think | thought | thought | denken, glauben |
| (to) throw | threw | thrown | werfen |
| (to) tread [e] | trod | trodden | treten |
| (to) understand | understood | understood | verstehen |
| (to) wake up | woke up | woken up | aufwachen; (auf)wecken |
| (to) wear [eə] | wore [ɔː] | worn [ɔː] | tragen (Kleidung) |
| (to) win | won [ʌ] | won [ʌ] | gewinnen |
| (to) write | wrote | written | schreiben |

## Early finisher – Lösungen

### How much do you know about the Commonwealth?

1 a)   2 c)   3 b)   4 c)   5 b)   6 b)

### Canadian food?

1 B   2 C   3 A   4 D

### American city quiz

A 4 Washington
B 6 Los Angeles
C 5 Seattle
D 3 Memphis
E 1 Boston

**New York City (suggestions)**
- first visit by Europeans 1524
- first name Nouvelle Angoulême
- largest city in USA
- main street is Broadway
- famous for its logo

### A capital city

1           re **P** ly
2           Cal **I** fornia
3   Empire Stat **E** Building
4           hai **R**
5           d **R** ive
6           rod **E** o

### Good adjectives

a) 1 Sleepless   4 Homeless
   2 Eventful    5 Colourful
   3 rainless    6 Endless

b) 1 heartless   4 spotless   7 restful
   2 peaceful    5 noiseless  8 thoughtful
   3 endless     6 eventful   9 rainless

# Classroom English

## Zu Beginn und am Ende des Unterrichts

| | |
|---|---|
| Guten Morgen, Frau … | **Good morning, Mrs/Miss …** *(bis 12 Uhr)* |
| Guten Tag, Herr … | **Good afternoon, Mr …** *(ab 12 Uhr)* |
| Entschuldigung, dass ich zu spät komme. | **Sorry I'm late.** |
| Auf Wiedersehen! / Bis morgen. | **Goodbye. / See you tomorrow.** |

## Du brauchst Hilfe

| | |
|---|---|
| Können Sie/Kannst du mir bitte helfen? | **Can you help me, please?** |
| Auf welcher Seite sind wir, bitte? | **What page are we on, please?** |
| Was heißt … auf Englisch/Deutsch? | **What's … in English/German?** |
| Können Sie/Kannst du mir bitte … buchstabieren? | **Can you spell …, please?** |
| Können Sie es bitte an die Tafel schreiben? | **Can you write it on the board, please?** |

## Hausaufgaben und Übungen

| | |
|---|---|
| Tut mir leid, ich habe mein Schulheft nicht dabei. | **Sorry, I don't have my exercise book.** |
| Kann ich bitte vorlesen? | **Can I read, please?** |
| Ich verstehe diese Übung nicht. | **I don't understand this exercise.** |
| Ich kann Nummer 3 nicht lösen. | **I can't do number 3.** |
| Entschuldigung, ich bin noch nicht fertig. | **Sorry, I haven't finished.** |
| Ich habe … Ist das auch richtig? | **I have … Is that right too?** |
| Tut mir leid, das weiß ich nicht. | **Sorry, I don't know.** |
| Was haben wir (als Hausaufgabe) auf? | **What's for homework?** |

## Wenn es Probleme gibt

| | |
|---|---|
| Kann ich es auf Deutsch sagen? | **Can I say it in German?** |
| Können Sie/Kannst du bitte lauter sprechen? | **Can you speak louder, please?** |
| Können Sie/Kannst du das bitte noch mal sagen? | **Can you say that again, please?** |
| Kann ich bitte das Fenster öffnen/zumachen? | **Can I open/close the window, please?** |
| Kann ich bitte zur Toilette gehen? | **Can I go to the toilet, please?** |

## Partnerarbeit

| | |
|---|---|
| Kann ich mit Julian arbeiten? | **Can I work with Julian?** |
| Kann ich bitte dein Lineal/deinen Filzstift/… haben? | **Can I have your ruler/felt tip/…, please?** |
| Danke. / Vielen Dank. | **Thank you. / Thanks a lot.** |
| Du bist dran. | **It's your turn.** |

# Instructions

**Diese Arbeitsanweisungen findest du häufig im Schülerbuch.**

| | |
|---|---|
| Act out the song. | Spiele das Lied vor. |
| Add more words to the table. | Füge weitere Wörter zur Tabelle hinzu. |
| Ask/Answer the questions. | Stelle/Beantworte die Fragen. |
| Check/Compare with a partner. | Prüfe/Vergleiche mit einem Partner/einer Partnerin. |
| Choose the correct/right words. | Wähle die richtigen Wörter. |
| Copy the words from the box. | Schreibe die Wörter aus dem Kästchen ab. |
| Correct the sentences. | Verbessere/Korrigiere die Sätze. |
| Exchange your ideas with a partner. | Tausche deine Ideen mit deinem/deiner Partner/in aus. |
| Find this information. | Finde/Suche diese Informationen. |
| Find out about cities in Britain. | Informiere dich über Großstädte in Großbritannien. |
| Find quotes in the text. | Finde Zitate im Text. |
| Finish/Complete the table below. | Vervollständige die Tabelle unten. |
| Get more words from page 44. | Hole zusätzliche Wörter von Seite 44. |
| Give reasons. | Gib Gründe an. |
| Give your text to another pair. | Gebt euren Text einem anderen Paar. |
| Go on with new ideas. | Mache weiter mit neuen Ideen. |
| Hang the poster up in your classroom. | Hänge das Poster im Klassenzimmer auf. |
| Hold up the card. | Halte die Karte hoch. |
| Imagine you're Silky. | Stelle dir vor, du bist Silky. |
| Label your drawing. | Beschrifte deine Zeichnung. |
| Learn the rhyme. | Lerne den Reim/Vers auswendig. |
| Leave space for your answers. | Lasse Platz für deine Antworten. |
| Listen to Morph. | Höre Morph zu. |
| Look at page 10. | Siehe auf Seite 10 nach. / Siehe dir Seite 10 an. |
| Look at the picture. | Schaue dir das Bild an. |
| Look up the word if you don't understand it. | Schlage das Wort nach, wenn du es nicht verstehst. |
| Make appointments with three partners. | Verabrede dich mit drei Partnern/Partnerinnen. |
| Make groups of three. | Bildet Dreiergruppen. |
| Match the words to the pictures. | Ordne die Wörter den Bildern zu. |
| Practise the words. | Übe die Wörter. |
| Put all the verbs in the right place. | Setze alle Verben an der richtigen Stelle ein. |
| Put the card into your MyBook. | Lege die Karte in dein MyBook. |
| Put up your hand. | Melde dich. |
| Read the dialogue out loud to your group. | Lies deiner Gruppe den Dialog laut vor. |
| Rewrite the text. | Schreibe den Text neu. |
| Scan the text to find these words. | Überfliege den Text und versuche, diese Wörter zu finden. |
| Sing along with the chorus. | Singe den Refrain mit. |
| Start a profile for Sam. | Fange ein Profil für Sam an. |
| Swap your texts. | Tauscht eure Texte aus. |
| Swap cards with another team. | Tauscht Karten mit einem anderen Team. |
| Take turns. | Wechselt euch ab. |
| Talk to different partners about the photo. | Rede mit verschiedenen Partnern/Partnerinnen über das Foto. |
| Talk to your partner like this: … | Rede so mit deinem Partner/deiner Partnerin: … |
| Think of a sentence. | Denke dir einen Satz aus. |
| Use these words: … | Verwende diese Wörter: … |
| Walk around the classroom. | Gehe im Klassenzimmer herum. |
| Write down the letters in the right order. | Schreibe die Buchstaben in der richtigen Reihenfolge auf. |

# Quellenverzeichnis

## Titelbild

**Adobe Stock** (Collage: Boot: chrisdorney; Vereinigte Staaten Flagge: moonrun); **Mauritius Images** (Collage: Tower Bridge (geschlossen): Alamy/Sergio Nogueira).

## Illustrationen/Karten

**Tobias Dahmen**, Utrecht (S. 25/5a li., S. 25/5a re., S. 40/Mi., S. 40/ob. li., S. 41/Mi., S. 41/Junge, S. 41/Mädchen, S. 63, S. 76/un. Mi., S. 77, S. 95/ob., S. 110, S. 136, S. 139, S. 141, S. 143, S. 145, S. 148, S. 149); **Carlos Borrell Eiköter**, Berlin (S. 8/Mi. li., S. III); **Eric Gira** (S. 8/Mi., S. 30/ob., S. 37/un. li., S. 37/un. re., S. 50/Kanada, S. 56/ob., S. 78); **Gregor Mecklenburg** (S. 48/1, S. 48/2, S. 48/3, S. 48/4, S. 48/5, S. 48/6, S. 60); **M.B.Schulz**, Düsseldorf (S. 71/A, S. 71/B, S. 109/A, S. 109/B); **Michael Fleischmann**, Waldegg (S. 191/1. Bild v. ob.); **Sapna Richter** (S. 76/un. re., S. 128, S. 130, S. 132); **Thomas Klein** (S. II); **Cornelsen/Till Nachtmann** (S. 102/Karte, S. 102/ob. re., S. 103, S. 104, S. 105); **Cornelsen/Ungermeyer** (S. 13, S. 55, S. 134); Cornelsen/Zweiband (S. 92).

## Fotos

**Adobe Stock** (S. 38/F: linusstrandholm@gmail.com/Linus; S. 68/Schränke: lmel900; S. 98: karenfoleyphoto; S. 112/1: f11photo; S. 112/6: f11photo; S. 112/3: Henryk Sadura; S. 112/4: quasarphotos; S. 112/5: RG; S. 113: spiritofamerica; S. 126/un. re.: Miriam Dörr; S. 129: pressmaster); **akg-images** (S. 39/D: Horizons/Ton Koene; S. 39/B: Horizons; S. 50/Eisbär: Horizons; S. 61/ob. li.: Horizons; S. 84/B: North Wind Picture Archives; S. 96: Heritage Images/Fine Art Images); **bpk** (S. 69: DeA Picture Library/Biblioteca Ambrosiana; S. 84/A: Smithsonian American Art Museum/Art Resource); **Bridgeman Images** (S. 4/ob. re., S. 9/B: Look and Learn; S. 13/Mi.: National Gallery, London; S. 89: Granger; S. 93/2 un.: Julien Faure/Leextra; S. 97/ob. li.: Granger; S. 115/2 un.: A. Dagli Orti / De Agostini Picture Library; S. 115/4 ob.: Lebrecht Authors; S. 115/2 ob., S. 263/2 un.: A. Dagli Orti / De Agostini Picture Library; S. 263/4 ob.: Lebrecht Authors; S. 263/2 ob.); **imago images** (S. 38/E: Pacific Press Agency); **Imago Stock & People GmbH** (S. 16/4: ZUMA Press; S. 34/A: ZUMA Press; S. 35/D: United Archives; S. 65/g: UPI Photo; **interfoto e.k.** (S. 8/C: Mary Evans/Illustrated London News Ltd; S. 9/D: Austrian Archives; S. 84/C: Science & Society; S. 90/ob. re.: H. ARMSTRONG ROBERTS; S. 90/un. re.: Granger, NYC; S. 90/Mi. re.: Science & Society; S. 115/4 un.: Mary Evans; S. 263/4 un.: Mary Evans;); **Laurence Harger** (S. 80/ob. re.: Nürnberg); **mauritius images** (S. 4/un. li., S. 39/G: Alamy/Vlad Ghiea; S. 6/ob. re., S. 67/B: Alamy/Nancy G Western Photography, Nancy Greifenhagen; S. 10/ob. re., S. 31/C: Travel Collection; S. 10/ob. li.: Alamy/Marcus Davidson; S. 16/6: Alamy/Paul Gapper; S. 31/B: Alamy/Marcus Davidson; S. 35/C: Alamy/S Swenson; S. 51/un.: Science Faction;S. 67/F: Alamy/Jim Parkin; S. 81: Alamy/Bill Bachmann; S. 126: Alamy/Picture Partners); **Nigel Wilson Photography**, Bristol (S. 68/ Teenagerin Mitte und gezogene Person, S. 80/ob. re.); **Panther Media GmbH** (S. 17: Markus Mainka); **Shutterstock.com** (S. 4/ob. li.: pisaphotography; S. 5/un. li.: Dan Breckwoldt; S. 5/Mi.: Serban Bogdan; S. 6/ob. li.: critterbiz; S. 7: eurobanks; S. 8/A: Engel Ching; S. 10/un. re.: Alex Cimbal; S. 10/un. li.: Victor Moussa; S. 11/ob. li.: f11photo; S. 11/un. re.: FenlioQ; S. 11/ob. li.: mimagephotography; S. 11/Smileys: Ricardo Romero; S. 12; S. 14: Matt Gibson; S. 16/1 Frau mit Koffer: mimagephotography; S. 16/1 Hintergr.: Rocketclips, Inc.; S. 16/2: stockfour; S. 16/ 5: Willy Barton; S. 18: arboursabroad; S. 19/Ob. re.: DJ Cockburn; S. 19/Ob. li.: Patryk Kosmider; S. 22/ob. re.: Bikeworldtravel; S. 22/Mi.: pcruciatti; S. 24/li.: 2p2play; S. 24/re.: TristanBM; S. 25/ob. re.: Antonio Guillem; S. 30/un.: 470images; S. 31/D: FenlioQ; S. 33: Luis Molinero; S. 36/1: 4kclips; S. 36/2: Aleksa Georg; S. 36/3: Konstantin Shevtsov; S. 36/4: John-Alex; S. 36/5: Heiko Wittenborn; S. 37/ob.: Serban Bogdan; S. 38/A: Pi-Lens; S. 38/C; S. 40/ob. re.: 7505811966; S. 40/Lauren: Marian Weyo; S. 40/un. re.: Pi-Lens; S. 41/ob. re.: Marc Bruxelle; S. 42/3: F. JIMENEZ MECA; S. 42/ob.: stockfour; S. 46/li.: Marian Weyo; S. 46/1. Bild v. r.: Rawpixel.com; S. 49: Alex Farias; S. 50/Karibu: Heiko Wittenborn; S. 50/Biber: Jody Ann; S. 50/Präriehund: m_grageda; S. 50/Schwarzbär: Menno Schaefer; S. 51/ob.: Dan Breckwoldt; S. 52: MintImages; S. 55/ob.: Rawpixel.com; S. 55/un.: Wlad Go; S. 56/un.: WorldStock; S. 58/ob.: AndreAnita; S. 58/un.: DarZel; S. 59: Annette Shaff; S. 61/ob. re.: Audrey Guay Photography; S. 64: Jurie Maree; S. 65/d, S. 65/e, S. 65/f: Art Babych; S. 65/c: Evan El-Amin; S. 65/a: Kathy Hutchins; S. 65/b: Markus Wissmann; S. 65/h: s_bukley; S. 66/A: critterbiz; S. 66/C: Diane Garcia; S. 66/E: Leigh Trail; S. 67/D: photo.ua; S. 68/Teenagerin li., S. 68/Teenager im Hintergrund: Monkey Business Images; S. 70/li.: Africa Studio; S. 70/re.: Cookie Studio; S. 72: Bjoern Wylezich; S. 73/ob. li.: Chepe Nicoli; S. 73/un. li.: MARK D GIROUARD; S. 73/un. re.: Steve Oehlenschlager; S. 73/ob. re.: Suzanne Tucker; S. 74/ob. re.: Astor57; S. 74/un. re.: ChiccoDodiFC; S. 75: Diego G Diaz; S. 79: Everett Collection; S. 87/8: PANGI; S. 87/4: patrimonio designs ltd; S. 87/1; S. 87/3; S. 87/9: Dario Sabljak; S. 88: Viktor Birkus; S. 91/1. Bild v. ob.: Aitor Lamadrid Lopez; S. 91/2. Bild. v. ob.: Iakov Filimonov; S. 93/Flagge re.: Maximumvector; S. 93/Flagge li.: octopusaga; S. 93/2 ob.: William Perugini; S. 95/un.: Victorian Traditions; S. 97/Un. re.: eurobanks; S. 97/Hintergrund: Mike Flippo; S. 97/Ob. re.: Oleg Golovnev; S. 99/Flagge li.: Maximumvector; S. 99/Flagge re.: octopusaga; S. 100/1: Chris Jenner; S. 100/2: chrisdorney; S. 100/3: lunamarina; S. 101/5: andre quinou; S. 101/4: shawnwil23; S. 102: Marquess Kilian Beck; S. 102/ob. re.: Marquess Kilian Beck; S. 112/C: larik_malasha; S. 112/B: Leonard Whistler; S. 112/A: martiapunts; S. 112/D: Olga Dubravina; S. 112/2: Taiga; S. 115/3 un.: Mario Hagen; S. 115/1 ob.: Claudio Divizia; S. 115/5 ob.: Carsten Reisinger; S. 115/5 un.: Ekkachai; S. 115/3 ob.: PHOTOCREO Michal Bednarek; S. 115/1 un.: Taras Vyshnya; S. 117: sarahdesign; S. 118: AVAVA; S. 120, S. 124: Cornelsen/Bonnie Glänzer; S. 131: Creaktiva; S. 156: ValentinT; S. 157/Un. re. Hupe:

# Quellenverzeichnis

Fotos593; S. 157/un. re. Horn: robmoffat; S. 158/ob. re. Getreide: 5 second Studio; S. 158/Ob. re. Kaffeemühle: Happy cake Happy cafe; S. 158/ob. re. Windmühle: symbiot; S. 161: DeepMeaning; S. 162: ANTONIO TRUZZI; S. 163: macgyverhh; S. 166/un. re.: hjochen; S. 166/Mi. re.: Stepan Bormotov; S. 166/ob. re.: Vaternam; S. 167/Ob. re. Diagramme: Ico Maker; S. 167/Mi. re.: Jody Ann; S. 167/ob. re. Eisbahn: sayu; S. 168/un. re.: Moving Moment; S. 168/ob. re.: Piotr Piatrouski; S. 171: Susan Montgomery; S. 173: Dutourdumonde Photography; S. 175/un. re.: Sandra Standbridge; S. 175/ob. re.: Seregraff; S. 175/Mi. re.: Warren Metcalf; S. 176: Subidubi; S. 177/ob. re.: Astrid Gast; S. 177/un. re.: Mikhail Semenov; S. 177/ob. li.: Volodymyr Burdiak; S. 178: SandyKni; S. 180/ob. re.: CoolKengzz; S. 180/un. re.; S. 181: tawatchai.m; S. 182/ob. re.: Ant Cooper; S. 182/un. re.; S. 183: eddo; S. 185/Un. re.: Gts; S. 185/ob. re.: NotionPic; S. 186/un. re.: albund; S. 186/ob. re.: Morphart Creation; S. 187/ob. re.: Joseph Sohm; S. 187/un. re. Spülmaschine: Menzl Guenter; S. 187/Un. re. Rücken an Rücken: Voyagerix; S. 187/Un. re. Kinder: ZikG; S. 188/Mi. re.: Oleksandr_Delyk; S. 188/ob. re.: Ruth Lawton; S. 189: IvanDbajo; S. 190/ob. re.: canbedone; S. 190/un. re.: gowithstock; S. 191/3. Bild v. ob.: azure1; S. 191/2. Bild v. ob.: elmm; S. 191/4. Bild v. ob.: Slawomir Fajer; S. 263/3 un.: Mario Hagen; S. 263/1 ob.: Claudio Divizia; S. 263/5 ob.: Carsten Reisinger; S. 263/5 un.: Ekkachai; S. 263/3 ob.: PHOTOCREO Michal Bednarek; S. 263/1 un.: Taras Vyshnya.

## Filmstill

**Guillaume Blanchet, Qc., Can./ Interfilm Berlin Management GmbH** aus „The Man who lived on His Bike" (S. 57/ob. li., S. 57/ob. Mi., S. 57/ob. re.); **Cornelsen/Crooked Letter Films**, N.Y. (S. 127/un. re., S. 127/ob. re., S. 127/Mi. re.); **Ninian Doff, UK/Interfilm Berlin Management GmbH** aus „Cool Unicorn Bruv" (S. 15/ob. li., S. 15/ob. Mi., S. 15/ob. re); **Cornelsen/ koloro-Design, Julia Hintz** (S. 99/Mi. re) ; **Christopher Nataanii Cegielski/interfilm Berlin Management GmbH** aus „Bloodlines" : (S. 85/1. Bild v. ob., S. 85/2. Bild v. ob., S. 85/3. Bild v. ob., S. 85/1, S. 85/2, S. 85/3).

## Collage

**S. 68 Drew and Kaya in Hallway** ( Cornelsen/M.B.Schulz, Düsseldorf; Students walking along hallway: Shutterstock.com/Monkey Business Images; Mädchen an Spind: Shutterstock.com/Monkey Business Images; High School Locker: stock-adobe.com/lmel900; Kaya und Drew: Cornelsen/Nigel Wilson Photography, Bristol); **S. 80 Drew, Kaya and Bobby on Car Park** (Cornelsen/M.B.Schulz, Düsseldorf; Kaya, Drew and Bobby: Cornelsen/Nigel Wilson Photography, Bristol; Parking Lot: Cornelsen/Laurence Harger, Nürnberg).

## Text

**Belkofer-Krönhert, Sabine** (S. 53: Auszug v. „Curling und Eisstockschießen: So funktioniert's", AOK Rheinland/Hamburg & Sabine Belkofer-Krönhert, 04.12.2016); **David Fermer / Till Nachtmann** (S. 114-117: Auszug v. "The Adventures of Jack London", Book 3: Forty Mile", Cornelsen / David Fermer und Till Nachtman, ISBN 9783060358854, 2019); **Eyers, Jonathan** (S. 28-31: Auszug v. "The Thieves of Pudding Lane" by Jonathan Eyers, A & C Black, an imprint of Bloomsbury Publishing PLC, 2014); **MacKinnon**, Catou (S. 44: Auszug v. „Nunavik teens on 90-km trek across frozen tundra", Catou MacKinnon, CBC News Canada, 1.3540690; 18.04.2016).

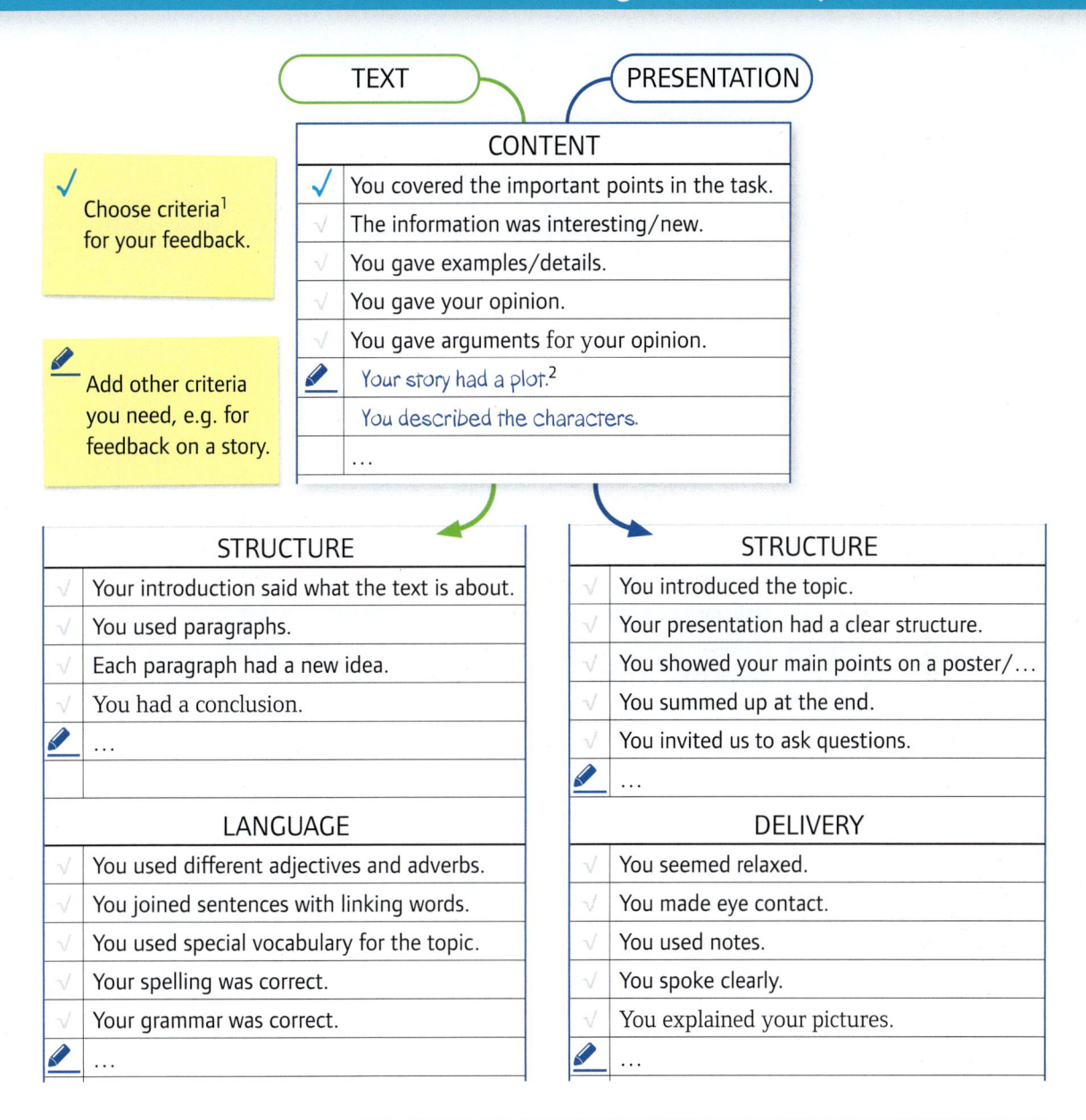

# Giving feedback to your classmates

(TEXT) (PRESENTATION)

### CONTENT

| | |
|---|---|
| ✓ | You covered the important points in the task. |
| √ | The information was interesting/new. |
| √ | You gave examples/details. |
| √ | You gave your opinion. |
| √ | You gave arguments for your opinion. |
| ✎ | *Your story had a plot.*[2] |
| | *You described the characters.* |
| | … |

✓ Choose criteria[1] for your feedback.

✎ Add other criteria you need, e.g. for feedback on a story.

### STRUCTURE

| | |
|---|---|
| √ | Your introduction said what the text is about. |
| √ | You used paragraphs. |
| √ | Each paragraph had a new idea. |
| √ | You had a conclusion. |
| ✎ | … |

### STRUCTURE

| | |
|---|---|
| √ | You introduced the topic. |
| √ | Your presentation had a clear structure. |
| √ | You showed your main points on a poster/… |
| √ | You summed up at the end. |
| √ | You invited us to ask questions. |
| ✎ | … |

### LANGUAGE

| | |
|---|---|
| √ | You used different adjectives and adverbs. |
| √ | You joined sentences with linking words. |
| √ | You used special vocabulary for the topic. |
| √ | Your spelling was correct. |
| √ | Your grammar was correct. |
| ✎ | … |

### DELIVERY

| | |
|---|---|
| √ | You seemed relaxed. |
| √ | You made eye contact. |
| √ | You used notes. |
| √ | You spoke clearly. |
| √ | You explained your pictures. |
| ✎ | … |

---

### TIPS

1. Use the criteria you chose to assess your classmate's work.

2. Give details when you say what a classmate did/didn't do well.
   Always start with something positive.

   | Where | What |
   |---|---|
   | In the first paragraph you | *wrote a good introduction ….* |
   | At the end of your presentation you | *didn't ask if we had questions /…* |

3. Suggest how the classmate could do better.
   You could try to *use more linking words like* **and** *or* **because** */ use more pictures / …*

---

[1] **criteria** *(pl)* [kraɪˈtɪərɪə] Kriterien  [2] **plot** [plɒt] Handlung

# Giving feedback to your classmates: Phrases

You can use emoticons (☺ ...) when you assess a classmate's work.

| CONTENT | 😀 | 🙂 | 😐 | ☹ |
|---|---|---|---|---|
| You covered the important points in the task. | ✓ | | | |
| The information was interesting/new/... | | | ✓ | |
| You gave examples/details/... | | | | |

The phrases below can help you when you give feedback and make suggestions.

### 😀

Your introduction / ideas / pictures / ... was / were brilliant! / clever! / interesting!

I really liked the way you structured your text. / summed up at the end. / explained your pictures ....

Here's an example of what I liked.

### 🙂

Your introduction / ideas / pictures / ... was / were quite good. / quite interesting. / mostly OK.

You structured your text / explained your pictures / summed up ... quite well.

Here's an example of what you did well. / could improve.

### 😐

Some of your ideas / examples / pictures / ... were quite good. / interesting. / all right.

Your introduction / grammar / ... was OK, but ...

You didn't (always) use linking words. / speak very clearly. / ...

I don't think you checked your text very carefully. / gave very good examples. / used enough adjectives. / ...

Maybe you could join up these sentences. / use captions under your pictures. / ...

### ☹

You forgot to / You didn't cover the important points. / use paragraphs. / introduce your subject. / sum up at the end. / ...

You almost never used linking words. / gave examples. / made eye contact with us. / ...

I don't think you did enough research. / spent much time on your text. / had a good conclusion. / ...

If I were you I would start a new paragraph here. / write the conclusion again. / ...